"Twelve weeks ago I couldn't turn on a Cisco router let alone program one to work. After using Todd Lammle's book not only can I program one, but I am on the verge of taking the test for CCNA. Lammle makes learning the Cisco router fun and easy."

Amazon Reader Review

"If you haven't heard by now, Todd Lammle is THE Networking Guru. Stick with his books for all your Cisco certification needs."

Amazon Reader Review

"You can tell Todd Lammle has been working with Cisco routers for a long time to get this kind of information in a book."

Amazon Reader Review

"Simply put Mr. Lammle is a legend. His first CCNA book was excellent and the [second edition] combined with the [*CCNA: Virtual Lab*] helped me to further understand the concepts needed to pass the CCNA exam ... I thank Mr. Lammle for helping me get certified"

Amazon Reader Review

"The best thing about Todd's book is that he explains in the languages you encounter in the CCNA exam. This will truly make you prepared for the exam."

Amazon Reader Review

"Todd Lammle is an expert in the Internetworking arena and knows his stuff. I've taken his CCNA class, and I am here to tell you he's definitely Cisco smart and knows TCP/IP extremely well. I will definitely be investing in every book he publishes concerning the Cisco certification, and I recommend Todd to anyone who is serious about obtaining the Cisco Certifications."

Amazon Reader Review

"Lammle gives the basics in an easy to understand and follow manner."

Amazon Reader Review

"Todd Lammle's approach to subnet masking was the work of a genius. He approaches all topics with that human touch that attempts to demystify routers and routing for ordinary souls."

Amazon Reader Review

"The way that Todd explains these concepts is superb."

Amazon Reader Review

"Lammle writes in a fashion that helps you retain the material without getting bored."

Amazon Reader Review

CCNA: Cisco Certified Network Associate
Study Guide, 4th Edition

Exam 640-801

OBJECTIVE	CHAPTER
Planning & Designing	
Design a simple LAN using Cisco Technology	3, 5
Design an IP addressing scheme to meet design requirements	3, 5
Select an appropriate routing protocol based on user requirements	5, 6
Design a simple internetwork using Cisco technology	3, 5, 6
Develop an access list to meet user specifications	10
Choose WAN services to meet customer requirements	11
Implementation & Operation	
Configure routing protocols given user requirements	5, 6
Configure IP addresses, subnet masks, and gateway addresses on routers and hosts	4, 5
Configure a router for additional administrative functionality	4, 5
Configure a switch with VLANS and inter-switch communication	8
Implement a LAN	4, 8
Customize a switch configuration to meet specified network requirements	8
Manage system image and device configuration files	9
Perform an initial configuration on a router	4, 5
Perform an initial configuration on a switch	4, 5
Implement access lists	10
Implement simple WAN protocols	11
Troubleshooting	
Utilize the OSI model as a guide for systematic network troubleshooting	9
Perform LAN and VLAN troubleshooting	3, 5, 8, 9
Troubleshoot routing protocols	5
Troubleshoot IP addressing and host configuration	3, 5, 9
Troubleshoot a device as part of a working network	3, 5, 9

SYBEX

OBJECTIVE	CHAPTER
Troubleshooting	
Troubleshoot an access list	10
Perform simple WAN troubleshooting	11
Technology	
Describe network communications using layered models	1
Describe the Spanning Tree process	7
Compare and contrast key characteristics of LAN environments	1
Evaluate the characteristics of routing protocols	5
Evaluate TCP/IP communication process and its associated protocols	2, 3, 5
Describe the components of network devices	1
Evaluate rules for packet control	1, 10
Evaluate key characteristics of WANs	11

 Exam objectives are subject to change at any time without prior notice and at Cisco's sole discretion. Please visit Cisco's web site (www.cisco.com/traincert) and click the Learning and Events link for the most current listing of exam objectives.

SYBEX

CCNA:
Cisco Certified
Network Associate
Study Guide
Fourth Edition

CCNA™:
Cisco® Certified
Network Associate
Study Guide
Fourth Edition

Todd Lammle

San Francisco • London

Associate Publisher: Neil Edde
Acquisitions Editor: Maureen Adams
Developmental Editor: Jeff Kellum
Production Editor: Elizabeth Campbell
Technical Editors: Toby Skandier, Craig Vazquez
Copyeditor: Suzanne Goraj
Compositor: Happenstance Type-O-Rama
Graphic Illustrator: Happenstance Type-O-Rama
CD Coordinator: Dan Mummert
CD Technician: Kevin Ly
Proofreaders: Emily Hsuan, Laurie O'Connell, Nancy Riddiough
Indexer: Lynnzee Elze
Book Designer: Bill Gibson
Cover Designer: Archer Design
Cover Photographer: Andrew Ward/Life File

SYBEX

To Our Valued Readers:

Thank you for looking to Sybex for your CCNA exam prep needs. Computer Reseller News recently ranked the CCNA #3 in its list of the "10 Hot Certifications for 2003," and it's no wonder. While the CCNA is positioned as a first-tier internetworking certification, Cisco has gone to great lengths to ensure that the exam accurately validates practical knowledge and skills that companies are seeking today.

Sybex is proud to have helped hundreds of thousands of CCNA candidates prepare for their exams over the years. It has always been Sybex's mission to teach individuals how to utilize technologies in the real world, not to simply feed them answers to test questions. Just as Cisco is committed to establishing measurable standards for certifying internetworking professionals, Sybex is committed to providing those professionals with the means of acquiring the skills and knowledge they need to meet those standards.

The author, editors, and technical reviewers have worked hard to ensure that this Study Guide is comprehensive, in-depth, and pedagogically sound. We're confident that this book, along with the collection of cutting-edge software study tools included on the CD, will meet and exceed the demanding standards of the certification marketplace and help you, the CCNA certification exam candidate, succeed in your endeavors.
Good luck in pursuit of your CCNA certification!

Neil Edde
Associate Publisher—Certification
Sybex, Inc.

Acknowledgments

For trying to keep my path straight and focused, I need to thank Neil Edde, Maureen Adams and Jeff Kellum. This is no easy task for you and I applaud your patience and dedication to our vision.

Elizabeth Campbell was instrumental in the success of this book. Without her hard work and dedication to a flawless book, as well as her ability to dance long after the music has stopped, this book would never have come together as quickly as it has. The quality of this book comes directly from the dazzling performance of Elizabeth. Thank you!

As Pygmalion always strove for the ideal of perfection, I have currently had the privilege to work with the modern-day version in the name of an amazing tech editor named Toby Skandier. A superb person with an uncanny eye for the details that matter, Toby has contributed immensely to make this book the quality product it is. And not to forget the Eye of Accuracy—none other than the infallible Michael Woznicki. This man is the reason personified that this entire book was totally put together in precisely the way it should be. Kudos and many thanks to both of these adroit professionals—cheers guys!

Thanks also to the CD team whose hard work has resulted in a power-packed CD test engine. Thanks also to the compositors at Happenstance Type-O-Rama that laid out the fine pages you are reading. Suzanne Goraj's trained eye weeded out any grammar and spelling problems; Thanks Suzanne! Thanks also go to Craig Vazquez who gave the book its final technical once-over, and gave us his thumbs-up!

Contents at a Glance

Table of Contents

Introduction

Welcome to the exciting world of Cisco certification! You have picked up this book because you want something better—namely, a better job with more satisfaction. Rest assured that you have made a good decision. Cisco certification can help you get your first networking job, or more money and a promotion if you are already in the field.

Cisco certification can also improve your understanding of the internetworking of more than just Cisco products: You will develop a complete understanding of networking and how different network topologies work together to form a network. This is beneficial to every networking job and is the reason Cisco certification is in such high demand, even at companies with few Cisco devices.

Cisco is the king of routing and switching, the Microsoft of the internetworking world. The Cisco certifications reach beyond the popular certifications, such as the MCSE and CNE, to provide you with an indispensable factor in understanding today's network—insight into the Cisco world of internetworking. By deciding that you want to become Cisco certified, you are saying that you want to be the best—the best at routing and the best at switching. This book will lead you in that direction.

Cisco—A Brief History

Many readers may already be familiar with Cisco and what they do. However, those of you who are new to the field, just coming in fresh from your MCSE, and those of you who maybe have 10 or more years in the field but wish to brush up on the new technology may appreciate a little background on Cisco.

In the early 1980s, Len and Sandy Bosack, a married couple who worked in different computer departments at Stanford University, were having trouble getting their individual systems to communicate (like many married people). So in their living room they created a gateway server that made it easier for their disparate computers in two different departments to communicate using the IP protocol. In 1984, they founded cisco Systems (notice the small *c*) with a small commercial gateway server product that changed networking forever. Some people think the name was intended to be San Francisco Systems but the paper got ripped on the way to the incorporation lawyers—who knows? In 1992, the company name was changed to Cisco Systems, Inc.

The first product the company marketed was called the Advanced Gateway Server (AGS). Then came the Mid-Range Gateway Server (MGS), the Compact Gateway Server (CGS), the Integrated Gateway Server (IGS), and the AGS+. Cisco calls these "the old alphabet soup products."

In 1993, Cisco came out with the amazing 4000 router and then created the even more amazing 7000, 2000, and 3000 series routers. These are still around and evolving (almost daily, it seems).

Cisco has since become an unrivaled worldwide leader in networking for the Internet. Its networking solutions can easily connect users who work from diverse devices on disparate networks. Cisco products make it simple for people to access and transfer information without regard to differences in time, place, or platform.

In the big picture, Cisco provides end-to-end networking solutions that customers can use to build an efficient, unified information infrastructure of their own or to connect to someone else's. This is an important piece in the Internet/networking–industry puzzle because a common architecture that delivers consistent network services to all users is now a functional imperative. Because Cisco Systems offers such a broad range of networking and Internet services and capabilities, users who need to regularly access their local network or the Internet can do so unhindered, making Cisco's wares indispensable.

Cisco answers this need with a wide range of hardware products that form information networks using the Cisco Internetwork Operating System (IOS) software. This software provides network services, paving the way for networked technical support and professional services to maintain and optimize all network operations.

Along with the Cisco IOS, one of the services Cisco created to help support the vast amount of hardware it has engineered is the Cisco Certified Internetwork Expert (CCIE) program, which was designed specifically to equip people to effectively manage the vast quantity of installed Cisco networks. The business plan is simple: If you want to sell more Cisco equipment and have more Cisco networks installed, ensure that the networks you install run properly.

Clearly, having a fabulous product line isn't all it takes to guarantee the huge success that Cisco enjoys—lots of companies with great products are now defunct. If you have complicated products designed to solve complicated problems, you need knowledgeable people who are fully capable of installing, managing, and troubleshooting them. That part isn't easy, so Cisco began the CCIE program to equip people to support these complicated networks. This program, known colloquially as the Doctorate of Networking, has also been very successful, primarily due to its extreme difficulty. Cisco continuously monitors the program, changing it as it sees fit, to make sure that it remains pertinent and accurately reflects the demands of today's internetworking business environments.

Building upon the highly successful CCIE program, Cisco Career Certifications permit you to become certified at various levels of technical proficiency, spanning the disciplines of network design and support. So, whether you're beginning a career, changing careers, securing your present position, or seeking to refine and promote your position, this is the book for you!

Cisco's Network Support Certifications

Initially, to secure the coveted CCIE, you took only one test and then you were faced with the (extremely difficult) lab, an all-or-nothing approach that made it tough to succeed. In response, Cisco created a series of new certifications to help you get the coveted CCIE, as well as aid prospective employers in measuring skill levels. With these new certifications, which make for a better approach to preparing for that almighty lab, Cisco opened doors that few were allowed through before. So, what are these stepping-stone certifications and how do they help you get your CCIE?

Cisco Certified Network Associate (CCNA)

The CCNA certification was the first in the new line of Cisco certifications, and was the precursor to all current Cisco certifications. Now, you can become a Cisco Certified Network Associate for the meager cost of this book, plus $125 for the test. And you don't have to stop there—you can choose to continue with your studies and achieve a higher certification, called the Cisco Certified

Network Professional (CCNP). Someone with a CCNP has all the skills and knowledge he or she needs to attempt the CCIE lab. However, because no textbook can take the place of practical experience, we'll discuss what else you need to be ready for the CCIE lab shortly.

Why Become a CCNA?

Cisco, not unlike Microsoft or Novell, has created the certification process to give administrators a set of skills and to equip prospective employers with a way to measure skills or match certain criteria. Becoming a CCNA can be the initial step of a successful journey toward a new, highly rewarding, and sustainable career.

The CCNA program was created to provide a solid introduction not only to the Cisco Internetwork Operating System (IOS) and Cisco hardware, but also to internetworking in general, making it helpful to you in areas that are not exclusively Cisco's. At this point in the certification process, it's not unrealistic to imagine that future network managers—even those without Cisco equipment—could easily require Cisco certifications for their job applicants.

If you make it through the CCNA and are still interested in Cisco and internetworking, you're headed down a path to certain success.

What Skills Do You Need to Become a CCNA?

To meet the CCNA certification skill level, you must be able to understand or do the following:

- Install, configure, and operate simple-routed LAN, routed WAN, and switched LAN and LANE networks.

- Understand and be able to configure IP, IGRP, serial interfaces, Frame Relay, IP RIP, VLANs, Ethernet, and access lists.

- Install and/or configure a network.

- Optimize WAN through Internet-access solutions that reduce bandwidth and WAN costs, using features such as filtering with access lists, bandwidth on demand (BOD), and dial-on-demand routing (DDR).

How Do You Become a CCNA?

The way to become a CCNA is to pass one little test (CCNA exam 640-801). Then—poof!—you're a CCNA. (Don't you wish it were that easy?) True, it's just one test, but you still have to possess enough knowledge to understand what the test writers are saying (and to read between the lines—trust me).

However, Cisco has announced a two-step process that you can take in order to become a CCNA that may be easier then taking one longer exam. These tests are:

- Exam 640-811: Interconnecting Cisco Networking Devices (ICND)

- Exam 640-821: Introduction to Cisco Networking Technologies (INTRO)

You spend more money if you take these two exams instead of the 640-801 exam, but it may be easier to break up the exam into two smaller exams. That's a personal choice. Understand that this book is designed to prepare you to pass the 640-801 exam, although it will likely help you pass both 640-811 and 640-821 as well.

I can't stress this enough—it's critical that you have some hands-on experience with Cisco routers. If you can get hold of some 2500 routers, you're set. But if you can't, we've worked hard to provide hundreds of configuration examples throughout this book to help network administrators (or people who want to become network administrators) learn what they need to know to pass the CCNA exam.

One way to get the hands-on router experience you'll need in the real world is to attend one of the seminars offered by GlobalNet Training Solutions, Inc., which is owned and run by myself. The seminars are 5 days and 11 days long and will teach you everything you need to become a CCNA (or even a CCNP and CCSP). Each student gets hands-on experience by configuring at least three routers and two switches. See www.globalnettraining.com for more information.

 For hands-on training with Todd Lammle, please see www.globalnettraining.com.

Cisco Certified Network Professional (CCNP)

So you're thinking, "Great, what do I do after I get my CCNA?" Well, if you want to become a CCIE in Routing and Switching (the most popular certification), understand that there's more than one path to that much-coveted CCIE certification. The first way is to continue studying and become a Cisco Certified Network Professional (CCNP), which means four more tests in addition to the CCNA certification.

The CCNP program will prepare you to understand and comprehensively tackle the internetworking issues of today and beyond—and it is not limited to the Cisco world. You will undergo an immense metamorphosis, vastly increasing your knowledge and skills through the process of obtaining these certifications.

While you don't need to be a CCNP or even a CCNA to take the CCIE lab, it's extremely helpful if you already have these certifications.

What Skills Do You Need to Become a CCNP?

Cisco demands a certain level of proficiency for its CCNP certification. In addition to mastering the skills required for the CCNA, you should be able to do the following:

- Install, configure, operate, and troubleshoot complex routed LAN, routed WAN, and switched LAN networks, along with dial-access services.

- Understand complex networks, such as IP, IGRP, IPX, async routing, AppleTalk, extended access lists, IP RIP, route redistribution, IPX RIP, route summarization, OSPF, VLSM, BGP, serial, IGRP, Frame Relay, ISDN, ISL, X.25, DDR, PSTN, PPP, VLANs, Ethernet, ATM LAN emulation, access lists, 802.10, FDDI, and transparent and translational bridging.

- Install and/or configure a network to increase bandwidth, attain quicker network response times, and improve reliability and quality of service.

- Maximize performance through campus LANs, routed WANs, and remote access.

- Improve network security.
- Create a global intranet.
- Provide access security to campus switches and routers.
- Provide increased switching and routing bandwidth—end-to-end resiliency services.
- Provide custom queuing and routed priority services.

How Do You Become a CCNP?

After becoming a CCNA, the four exams you must take to get your CCNP are as follows:

At the time of this printing Sybex is working on a full complement of CCNP Study Guides for the new exams. Look for them in the bookstores in late 2003. Visit www.sybex.com for more information.

Exam 642-801: Building Scalable Cisco Internetworks (BSCI) This exam continues to build on the fundamentals learned in the CCNA course. It focuses on large multiprotocol internetworks and how to manage them with access lists, queuing, tunneling, route distribution, route maps, BGP, EIGRP, OSPF, and route summarization.

Exam 642-811: Building Cisco Multilayer Switched Networks (BCMSN) This exam tests your knowledge of the Cisco Catalyst switches.

Exam 642-821: Building Cisco Remote Access Networks (BCRAN) This exam determines whether you really understand how to install, configure, monitor, and troubleshoot Cisco ISDN and dial-up-access products. You must understand PPP, ISDN, Frame Relay, and authentication.

Exam 642-831: Cisco Internet Troubleshooting (CIT) This exam tests you extensively on the Cisco troubleshooting skills needed for Ethernet and Token Ring LANs, IP, IPX, and AppleTalk networks, as well as ISDN, PPP, and Frame Relay networks.

www.routersim.com has a complete Cisco router simulator for all CCNP exams.

And if you hate tests, you can take fewer of them by signing up for the CCNA exam and the BCRAN and the CIT exams, and then taking just one more long exam called the Composite exam (642-891). Doing this also gives you your CCNP, but beware—it's a really long test that fuses all the material from the BSCI and BCMSN exams into one exam and costs $187.50. Good luck!

Remember that test objectives and tests can change at any time without notice. Always check the Cisco website for the most up-to-date information.

Cisco Certified Internetwork Expert (CCIE)

You've become a CCNP, and now your sights are fixed on getting your Cisco Certified Internetwork Expert (CCIE). What do you do next? Cisco recommends a *minimum* of two years of on-the-job experience for those seeking their CCIE. After jumping that hurdle, you then have to pass the written CCIE Qualification Exam before taking the actual lab.

How Do You Become a CCIE?

There are actually four CCIE certifications, and you must pass a written exam for each one of them before attempting the hands-on lab:

CCIE Service Provider   The CCIE Communications and Services track covers IP and IP routing, optical networking, DSL, dial, cable, wireless, WAN switching, content networking, and voice.

CCIE Routing and Switching   The CCIE Routing and Switching track covers IP and IP routing, non-IP desktop protocols such as IPX, and bridge- and switch-related technologies.

CCIE Security   The CCIE Security track covers IP and IP routing as well as specific expert security components and maintenance on large internetworks.

CCIE Voice   The CCIE Voice track covers the technologies and applications that make up a Cisco Enterprise VoIP solution.

Once you decide what CCIE track you are going to follow, here are the steps you should follow:

1. Attend the GlobalNet Training CCIE hands-on lab program described at www.globalnettraining.com. (Cisco doesn't actually recommend this step, but I do!)

2. Pass the qualification exam, administered by Prometric or Pearson VUE. (This costs $300 per exam, so hopefully you'll pass it the first time.)

3. Pass the one-day, hands-on lab at Cisco. This costs $1,250 per lab, and many people fail it two or more times. Some people never make it through—it's very difficult. Cisco has added and deleted testing sites, so it's best to check the Cisco website for the most current information and testing locations. Take into consideration that you might just need to add travel costs to that $1,250!

Cisco's Network Design Certifications

In addition to the network support certifications, Cisco has created another certification track for network designers. The two certifications within this track are the Cisco Certified Design Associate (CCDA) and Cisco Certified Design Professional (CCDP) certifications. If you're reaching for the CCIE stars, we highly recommend the CCNP and CCDP certifications before attempting the lab (or attempting to advance your career).

The certifications will give you the knowledge you need to design routed LAN, routed WAN, and switched LAN and ATM LANE networks.

Cisco Certified Design Associate (CCDA)

To become a CCDA, you must pass the Design exam (640-861). To pass this test, you must understand how to do the following:

-   Design simple routed LAN, routed WAN, and switched LAN and ATM LANE networks.

- Use Network-layer addressing.
- Filter with access lists.
- Use and propagate VLAN.
- Size networks.

 The *CCDA: Cisco Certified Design Associate Study Guide, 2nd Edition* (Sybex, 2003) is the most cost-effective way to study for and pass your CCDA exam.

Cisco Certified Design Professional (CCDP)

To get your CCDP, you first get your CCNA or CCDA certification. Then you must take the Designing Cisco Network Service Architectures (642-871) exam, in addition to the BSCI and BCMSN exams, which were discussed earlier.

CCDP certification skills include the following:

- Designing complex routed LAN, routed WAN, and switched LAN and ATM LANE networks
- Building upon the base level of the CCDA technical knowledge

CCDPs must also demonstrate proficiency in the following:

- Network-layer addressing in a hierarchical environment
- Traffic management with access lists
- Hierarchical network design
- VLAN use and propagation
- Performance considerations: required hardware and software; switching engines; memory, cost, and minimization

Cisco Certified Security Professional (CCSP)

Like the CCNP and CCDP, the CCSP was created to provide evidence of your technical worth in the area of security. The CCSP certification provides you with a way to demonstrate your skills in security by using Cisco gear, specifically IDS, PIX Firewall, and VPN Concentrators.

How Do You Become a CCSP?

You have to pass five exams to get your CCSP:

Exam 642-501: Securing Cisco IOS Networks (SECUR)   This exam is the first test in the series that provides a background in securing Cisco IOS networks. Not only is this exam part of the CCSP certification track, it is also part of the Cisco Firewall Specialist, Cisco VPN Specialist, and Cisco IDS Specialist certifications, which are discussed below. To pass this exam, you must understand how to plug the holes in a Cisco IOS network.

Exam 642-521: Cisco Secure PIX Firewall Advanced (CSPFA)   This is one of the exams associated with the Cisco Certified Security Professional and the Cisco Firewall Specialist certifications. To pass the CSPFA exam, you must be able to describe, configure, verify, and manage the PIX Firewall product family.

Exam 643-531: Cisco Secure Intrusion Detection System (CSIDS) This exam is needed to achieve your CCSP or the Cisco IDS Specialist certification. To pass the Cisco Security Intrusion Detection System exam, you must understand and have the skills needed to design, install, and configure a Cisco Intrusion Protection solution for small, medium, and enterprise networks.

Exam 642-511: Cisco Secure Virtual Networks (CSVPN) This is one of the exams associated with the CCSP and the Cisco VPN Specialist certifications. To pass this exam, you need to have the experience and ability to describe, configure, verify, and manage the Cisco PN 3000 Concentrator, Cisco VPN Software Client, and Cisco VPN 3002 Hardware Client feature set.

Exam 642-541: Cisco SAFE Implementation (CSI) The Cisco SAFE Implementation (CSI) exam is used only in the CCSP certification track. To pass the SAFE Implementation exam, you must be able to use and implement the principles and axioms presented in the SAFE Small, Mid-size and Remote (SMR) User White Paper, which can be found at www.cisco.com/go/safe. In addition to the white paper, you must be able to create a complete end-to-end solution using Cisco IOS routers, PIX Firewalls, VPN Concentrators, Cisco IDS Sensors, Cisco Host IDS, and the Cisco VPN Client.

The *CCSP: Securing Cisco IOS Networks Study Guide* (Sybex, 2003) will help you pass exam 642-501. In addition, Sybex plans to release titles on the other four CCSP exams in late 2003.

Cisco Security Specializations

There are quite a few new Cisco security specializations certifications offered.

Cisco security specializations certifications focus on the growing need for knowledgeable network professionals who can implement complete security solutions. All of these new Cisco specialist security certifications require a valid CCNA:

Cisco Firewall Specialist To achieve your Cisco Firewall Specialist certification, you must be able to secure a network access using Cisco IOS Software and Cisco PIX Firewall technologies. The two exams you must pass to achieve the Cisco Firewall Specialist certification are Securing Cisco IOS Networks (642-501) and Cisco Secure PIX Firewall Advanced (CSPFA 642-521).

Cisco IDS Specialist To achieve your IDS specialist certifications, you must be able to both operate and monitor Cisco IOS Software and IDS technologies to detect and respond to intrusion activities. The two exams you must pass to achieve the Cisco IDS Specialist certification are Securing Cisco IOS Networks (642-501) and Cisco Secure Intrusion Detection System (CSIDS 643-531).

Cisco VPN Specialist To achieve your VPN certification, you must have the knowledge to configure VPNs across shared public networks using Cisco IOS Software and Cisco VPN 3000 Series Concentrator technologies. The two exams you must pass to achieve the Cisco VPN Specialist certification are Securing Cisco IOS Networks (642-501) and Cisco Secure Virtual Networks (CSVPN 642-511).

In addition to these security specializations, there are a number of other specializations Cisco offers. Visit Cisco's site for a complete list of the tracks they offer.

What Does This Book Cover?

This book covers everything you need to know in order to become CCNA certified. However, taking the time to study and practice with routers or a router simulator is the real key to success.

Most of the Hands-on Labs in the book assume that you have Cisco routers to play with. If you don't you can purchase the CCNA Virtual Lab, Platinum Edition from Sybex, or the more robust Virtual Lab from www.routersim.com. Both products will assist you in completing all of the Hands-on Labs.

The information you will learn in this book, and need to know for the CCNA exam, is listed in the following bullet points:

- Chapter 1 introduces you to internetworking. You will learn the basics of the Open Systems Interconnection (OSI) model the way Cisco wants you to learn it. Ethernet networking and standards are discussed in detail in this chapter as well. There are written labs and plenty of review questions to help you. Do not skip the labs in this chapter!

- Chapter 2 provides you with the background necessary for success on the exam as well as in the real world by discussing TCP/IP. This in-depth chapter covers the very beginnings of the Internet Protocol stack and then goes all the way to IP addressing and understanding the difference between a network address and broadcast address.

- Chapter 3 introduces you to subnetting. You will be able to subnet a network in your head after reading this chapter. In addition, you'll learn about Variable Length Subnet Masks (VLSMs) and how to design a network using VLSM. Plenty of help is found in this chapter if you do not skip the Written Lab and Review Questions.

- Chapter 4 introduces you to the Cisco Internetwork Operating System (IOS) and command-line interface (CLI). In this chapter you will learn how to turn on a router and configure the basics of the IOS, including setting passwords, banners, and more. IP configuration will be discussed and a Hands-on Lab will help you gain a firm grasp of the concepts taught in the chapter. Before you go through the Hands-on Labs, be sure to complete the Written Labs and Review Questions.

- Chapter 5 teaches you about IP routing. This is a fun chapter, because you will begin to build your network, add IP addresses, and route data between routers. You will also learn about static, default, and dynamic routing using RIP and IGRP. Written and Hands-on Labs will help you understand IP routing to the fullest.

- Chapter 6 dives into the more complex dynamic routing with Enhanced IGRP and OSPF routing. The Written Labs, Hands-on Labs, and Review Questions will help you master these routing protocols.

- Chapter 7 gives you a background on layer 2 switching and how switches perform address learning and make forwarding and filtering decisions. Network loops and how to avoid them with the Spanning Tree Protocol (STP) will be discussed, as well as the different LAN switch types used by Cisco switches. Go through the Written Labs and Review Questions as well as the Hands-on Labs to learn how to configure basic layer 2 switching on an internetwork.

- Chapter 8 covers virtual LANs and how you can use them in your internetwork. This chapter also covers the nitty-gritty of VLANs and the different concepts and protocols used with VLANs. The Written Lab and Review Questions will reinforce the VLAN material.

- Chapter 9 provides you with the management skills needed to run a Cisco IOS network. Backing up and restoring the IOS, as well as router configuration, is covered, as are the troubleshooting tools necessary to keep a network up and running. Before performing the Hands-on Labs in this chapter, complete the Written Labs and Review Questions.

- Chapter 10 covers access lists, which are created on routers to filter the network. IP standard, extended, and named access lists are covered in detail. Written and Hands-on Labs, along with Review Questions, will help you study for the access-list portion of the CCNA exam.

- Chapter 11 concentrates on Cisco wide area network (WAN) protocols. This chapter covers HDLC, PPP, Frame Relay, and ISDN in depth. You must be proficient in all these protocols to be successful on the CCNA exam. Do not skip the Written Lab, Review Questions, or Hands-on Labs found in this chapter.

- Appendix A lists all the Cisco IOS commands used in this book. It is a great reference if you need to look up what a certain command does and is used for.

- The Glossary is a handy resource for Cisco terms. This is a great tool for understanding some of the more obscure terms used in this book.

How to Use This Book

If you want a solid foundation for the serious effort of preparing for the Cisco Certified Network Associate (CCNA) exam, then look no further. I have spent hundreds of hours putting together this book with the sole intention of helping you to pass the CCNA exam and learn how to configure Cisco routers and switches.

This book is loaded with valuable information, and you will get the most out of your studying time if you understand how I put the book together.

To best benefit from this book, I recommend the following study method:

1. Take the assessment test immediately following this introduction. (The answers are at the end of the test.) It's OK if you don't know any of the answers; that is why you bought this book! Carefully read over the explanations for any question you get wrong and note which chapters the material comes from. This information should help you plan your study strategy.

2. Study each chapter carefully, making sure that you fully understand the information and the test objectives listed at the beginning of each chapter. Pay extra-close attention to any chapter where you missed questions in the assessment test.

3. Complete each Written Lab at the end of each chapter. Do *not* skip this written exercise, as it directly relates to the CCNA exam and what you must glean from the chapter you just read. Do not just skim this lab! Make sure you understand completely the reason for each answer.

4. Complete all Hands-on Labs in the chapter, referring to the text of the chapter so that you understand the reason for each step you take. If you do not have Cisco equipment available, be sure to study the examples carefully, or check out the Sybex CCNA Virtual Lab, Platinum Edition for router simulator software that provides drag-and-drop networking configurations. This will help you gain hands-on experience configuring Cisco routers and switches.

I also provide a more robust version of the Virtual Lab at www.routersim.com.

5. Answer all of the Review Questions related to that chapter. (The answers appear at the end of the chapter.) Note the questions that confuse you and study those sections of the book again. Do not just skim these questions! Make sure you understand completely the reason for each answer.

6. Try your hand at the practice exams that are included on the companion CD. The questions in these exams appear only on the CD. This will give you a complete overview of the type of questions you can expect to see on the real CCNA exam. Check out www.routersim.com for more Cisco exam prep questions.

7. Also on the companion CD is a software simulation program called CertSim that will help you prepare for the new simulation questions on the CCNA 640-801 exam. This will really help you understand the feel of the actual CCNA exam simulation questions, so don't skip this valuable study tool.

8. Test yourself using all the flashcards on the CD. There are brand new and updated flashcard programs on the CD to help you prepare for the CCNA exam. These are a great study tool!

The electronic flashcards can be used on your Windows computer, Pocket PC, or on your Palm device.

9. Make sure you read the "Exam Essentials," "Key Terms," and "Commands Used in This Chapter" sections at the end of the chapters. Appendix A lists all the commands used in the book, including an explanation for each command. The Glossary defines all of the Key Terms as well as other terms that a CCNA should know.

To learn every bit of the material covered in this book, you'll have to apply yourself regularly, and with discipline. Try to set aside the same time period every day to study, and select a comfortable and quiet place to do so. If you work hard, you will be surprised at how quickly you learn this material.

If you follow the steps listed above, and really study and practice the Review Questions, CD exams, electronic flashcards, and Written and Hands-on Labs, it would be hard to fail the CCNA exam.

What's on the CD?

We worked hard to provide some really great tools to help you with your certification process. All of the following tools should be loaded on your workstation when studying for the test.

The Sybex Test Preparation Software

The test preparation software prepares you to pass the CCNA exam. In this test engine, you will find all the review and assessment questions from the book, plus four additional bonus exams that appear exclusively on the CD.

Please visit the Cisco training and certification website at http://www.cisco.com/en/US/learning/le3/learning_career_certifications_and_learning_paths_home.html for the latest exam information.

RouterSim's CertSim

In addition to multiple-choice and drag-and-drop questions, Cisco has included some questions on the CCNA exam that simulate working on routers and switches in a network environment. In response, we have included a simulation question program called CertSim on our test engine. We designed our program to help further your hands-on networking skills and better prepare you for when you are faced with a simulation question at the testing center.

The new RouterSim CertSim product simulates the new CCNA exam with multiple-choice, drag-and-drop, and simulation questions. This is a valuable study tool, so do not skip this product when studying for your CCNA exam!

Electronic Flashcards for PC, Pocket PC, and Palm Devices

To prepare for the exam, you can read this book, study the Review Questions at the end of each chapter, and work through the practice exams included in the book and on the companion CD. But wait, there's more! You can also test yourself with the flashcards included on the CD. If you can get through these difficult questions and understand the answers, you'll know you're ready for the CCNA exam.

The flashcards include over 200 questions specifically written to hit you hard and make sure you are ready for the exam. Between the review questions, practice exams, CertSim program, and flashcards, you'll be more than prepared for the exam.

CCNA: Cisco Certified Network Associate Study Guide in PDF

Sybex offers the *CCNA: Cisco Certified Network Associate Study Guide* in PDF on the CD so you can read the book on your PC or laptop. This will be helpful to readers who travel and don't want to carry a book, as well as to readers who prefer to read from their computer. (Acrobat Reader 5 is also included on the CD.)

Where Do You Take the Exams?

You may take the CCNA exam at any of the more than 800 Prometric Authorized Testing Centers around the world (`www.2test.com`), or call 800-204-EXAM (3926). You can also register and take the exams at a Pearson VUE authorized center as well (`www.vue.com`) or call (877) 404-EXAM (3926).

To register for a Cisco Certified Network Associate exam:

1. Determine the number of the exam you want to take. (The CCNA exam number is 640-801.)

2. Register with the nearest Prometric Registration Center or Pearson VUE testing center. At this point, you will be asked to pay in advance for the exam. At the time of this writing, the exams are $125 each and must be taken within one year of payment. You can schedule exams up to six weeks in advance or as late as the same day you want to take it—but if you fail a Cisco exam, you must wait 72 hours before you will be allowed to retake the exam. If something comes up and you need to cancel or reschedule your exam appointment, contact Prometric or Pearson VUE at least 24 hours in advance.

3. When you schedule the exam, you'll get instructions regarding all appointment and cancellation procedures, the ID requirements, and information about the testing-center location.

Tips for Taking Your CCNA Exam

The CCNA test contains about 50 to 65 questions, and must be completed in 90 minutes. This can change per exam. You must get a score of about 85% to pass this exam, but again, each exam can be different.

Many questions on the exam have answer choices that at first glance look identical—especially the syntax questions! Remember to read through the choices carefully, because close doesn't cut it. If you get commands in the wrong order or forget one measly character, you'll get the question wrong. So, to practice, do the hands-on exercises at the end of this book's chapters over and over again until they feel natural to you.

Also, never forget that the right answer is the Cisco answer. In many cases, more than one appropriate answer is presented, but the *correct* answer is the one that Cisco recommends. On the exam, it always tells you to pick one, two, or three, never "choose all that apply." The CCNA 640-801 exam includes the following test formats:

- Multiple-choice single answer
- Multiple-choice multiple answer
- Drag-and-drop
- Fill-in-the-blank
- Router simulations

In addition to multiple choice and fill-in response questions, Cisco Career Certifications exams may include performance simulation exam items.

RouterSim.com has created a perfect companion for the Sybex *CCNA: Cisco Certified Network Associate Study Guide, 4th Edition*, called the Cisco 801 CCNA CertSim exam, which matches perfectly to the new Cisco CCNA 801 exam objectives. Use the software included in this book, and for extra study material, check out the software at `www.routersim.com` that lets you design and configure an unlimited number of Cisco routers and switches running multiple routing protocols!

The software on the CD and at RouterSim.com provides step-by-step instruction on how to configure both Cisco routers and switches. However, router simulations in Cisco proctored exams will not show the steps to follow in completing a router interface configuration. They do allow partial command responses. For example, `show config` or `sho config` or `sh conf` would be acceptable. `Router#show ip protocol` or `router#show ip prot` would be acceptable.

Here are some general tips for exam success:

- Arrive early at the exam center, so you can relax and review your study materials.

- Read the questions *carefully*. Don't jump to conclusions. Make sure you're clear about *exactly* what each question asks.

- When answering multiple-choice questions that you're not sure about, use the process of elimination to get rid of the obviously incorrect answers first. Doing this greatly improves your odds if you need to make an educated guess.

- You can no longer move forward and backward through the Cisco exams, so double-check your answer before clicking Next since you can't change your mind.

After you complete an exam, you'll get immediate, online notification of your pass or fail status, a printed Examination Score Report that indicates your pass or fail status, and your exam results by section. (The test administrator will give you the printed score report.) Test scores are automatically forwarded to Cisco within five working days after you take the test, so you don't need to send your score to them. If you pass the exam, you'll receive confirmation from Cisco, typically within two to four weeks.

How to Contact the Author

You can reach Todd Lammle through GlobalNet Training Solutions, Inc. (`www.globalnettraining.com`), his training and systems Integration Company in Dallas, Texas—or through his software company (`www.routersim.com`) in Denver, Colorado, which creates both Cisco and Microsoft software simulation programs.

Assessment Test

1. What protocol does PPP use to identify the Network layer protocol?

   A. NCP

   B. ISDN

   C. HDLC

   D. LCP

2. You have ten users plugged into a hub running 10Mbps half-duplex. There is a server connected to the switch running 10Mbps half-duplex as well. How much bandwidth does each host have to the server?

   A. 100kbps

   B. 1Mbps

   C. 2Mbps

   D. 10Mbps

3. In a network with dozens of switches, how many root bridges would you have?

   A. 1

   B. 2

   C. 5

   D. 12

4. What does the command `routerA(config)#line cons 0` allow you to perform next?

   A. Set the Telnet password.

   B. Shut down the router.

   C. Set your console password.

   D. Disable console connections.

5. What ISDN command will bring up the second BRI at 50 percent load?

   A. `load balance 50`

   B. `load share 50`

   C. `dialer load-threshold 127`

   D. `dialer idle-timeout 125`

6. What PPP protocol provides dynamic addressing, authentication, and multilink?

   A. NCP

   B. HDLC

   C. LCP

   D. X.25

7. What command will display the line, protocol, DLCI, and LMI information of an interface?

   A. `sh pvc`

   B. `show interface`

   C. `show frame-relay pvc`

   D. `sho runn`

8. Which of the following is the valid host range for the subnet on which the IP address `192.168.168.188 255.255.255.192` resides?

   A. 192.168.168.129–190

   B. 192.168.168.129–191

   C. 192.168.168.128–190

   D. 192.168.168.128–192

9. What does the `passive` command provide to dynamic routing protocols?

   A. Stops an interface from sending or receiving periodic dynamic updates

   B. Stops an interface from sending periodic dynamic updates but still receives updates

   C. Stops the router from receiving any dynamic updates

   D. Stops the router from sending any dynamic updates

10. Which protocol does Ping use?

   A. TCP

   B. ARP

   C. ICMP

   D. BootP

11. How many collision domains are created when you segment a network with a 12-port switch?

   A. 1

   B. 2

   C. 5

   D. 12

12. Which of the following commands will allow you to set your Telnet password on a Cisco router?

   A. `line telnet 0 4`

   B. `line aux 0 4`

   C. `line vty 0 4`

   D. `line con 0`

13. Which router command allows you to view the entire contents of all access lists?

    A. `show all access-lists`

    B. `show access-lists`

    C. `show ip interface`

    D. `show interface`

14. What does a VLAN provide?

    A. The fastest port to all servers

    B. Multiple collision domains on one switch port

    C. Breaking up broadcast domains in a layer 2 switch internetwork

    D. Multiple broadcast domains within a single collision domain

15. If you wanted to delete the configuration stored in NVRAM, what would you type?

    A. `erase startup`

    B. `erase nvram`

    C. `delete nvram`

    D. `erase running`

16. Which protocol is used to send a Destination Network Unknown message back to originating hosts?

    A. TCP

    B. ARP

    C. ICMP

    D. BootP

17. Which class of IP address has the most host addresses available by default?

    A. A

    B. B

    C. C

    D. A and B

18. How often are BPDUs sent from a layer 2 device?

    A. Never

    B. Every two seconds

    C. Every 10 minutes

    D. Every 30 seconds

19. Which one of the following is true regarding VLANs?

    A. Two VLANs are configured by default on all Cisco switches.

    B. VLANs only work if you have a complete Cisco switched internetwork. No off-brand switches are allowed.

    C. You should not have more than 10 switches in the same VTP domain.

    D. VTP is used to send VLAN information to switches in a configured VTP domain.

20. What LAN switch mode keeps CRC errors to a minimum but still has a fixed latency rate?

    A. STP

    B. Store and forward

    C. Cut-through

    D. FragmentFree

21. How many broadcast domains are created when you segment a network with a 12-port switch?

    A. 1

    B. 2

    C. 5

    D. 12

22. What PDU is at the Transport layer?

    A. User data

    B. Session

    C. Segment

    D. Frame

23. What protocols are used to configure trunking on a switch? (Choose two answers.)

    A. VLAN Trunking Protocol

    B. VLAN

    C. 802.1Q

    D. ISL

24. What is a stub network?

    A. A network with more than one exit point

    B. A network with more than one exit and entry point

    C. A network with only one entry and no exit point

    D. A network that has only one entry and exit point

25. Where is a hub specified in the OSI model?

   A. Session layer

   B. Physical layer

   C. Data Link layer

   D. Application layer

26. If you wanted to configure ports on a Cisco switch, what are the different ways available to configure VLAN memberships? (Choose two answers.)

   A. Via a DHCP server

   B. Statically

   C. Dynamically

   D. Via a VTP database

27. What does the command `show controllers s 0` provide?

   A. The type of serial port connection (e.g., Ethernet or Token Ring)

   B. The type of connection (e.g., DTE or DCE)

   C. The configuration of the interface including the IP address and clock rate

   D. The controlling processor of that interface

28. What is a pre-10.3 IOS command that copies the contents of NVRAM to DRAM?

   A. `config t`

   B. `config net`

   C. `config mem`

   D. `wr mem`

29. What is the main reason the OSI model was created?

   A. To create a layered model larger than the DoD model

   B. So application developers can change only one layer's protocols at a time

   C. So different networks could communicate

   D. So Cisco could use the model

30. Which layer of the OSI model creates a virtual circuit between hosts before transmitting data?

   A. Application

   B. Session

   C. Transport

   D. Network

   E. Data Link

31. Which protocol does DHCP use at the Transport layer?

   A. IP

   B. TCP

   C. UDP

   D. ARP

32. How do you copy a router IOS to a TFTP host?

   A. `copy run starting`

   B. `copy start running`

   C. `copy running tftp`

   D. `copy flash tftp`

33. If your router is facilitating a CSU/DSU, which of the following commands do you need to use to provide the router with a 64000bps serial link?

   A. RouterA(config)#**bandwidth 64**

   B. RouterA(config-if)#**bandwidth 64000**

   C. RouterA(config)#**clockrate 64000**

   D. RouterA(config-if)#**clock rate 64**

   E. RouterA(config-if)#**clock rate 64000**

34. Which command is used to determine if an IP access-list is enabled on a particular interface?

   A. `show access-lists`

   B. `show interface`

   C. `show ip interface`

   D. `show interface access-lists`

35. Which of the following commands will set your prompt so you can set your Telnet password on a Cisco router?

   A. `line telnet 0 4`

   B. `line aux 0 4`

   C. `line vty 0 4`

   D. `line con 0`

36. What command do you use to set the enable secret password on a Cisco router to todd?

   A. RouterA(config)#**enable password todd**

   B. RouterA(config)#**enable secret todd**

   C. RouterA(config)#**enable secret password todd**

   D. RouterA(config-if)#**enable secret todd**

37. Which protocol is used to find an Ethernet address from a known IP address?

   A. IP

   B. ARP

   C. RARP

   D. BootP

38. Which command is used to upgrade an IOS on a Cisco router?

   A. `copy tftp run`

   B. `copy tftp start`

   C. `config net`

   D. `copy tftp flash`

39. If you want to copy a configuration from the router's DRAM to NVRAM, which command do you use?

   A. `copy run start`

   B. `copy start run`

   C. `config net`

   D. `config mem`

   E. `copy flash nvram`

40. If an interface is administratively down, what is the problem?

   A. The interface is bad.

   B. The interface is not connected to another device.

   C. There is no problem.

   D. The interface is looped.

Answers to Assessment Test

1. **A.** Network Control Protocol is used to help identify the Network layer protocol used in the packet. See Chapter 11 for more information.

2. **D.** Each device has 10Mpbs to the server. See Chapter 7 for more information.

3. **A.** You should have only one root bridge per network. See Chapter 7 for more information.

4. **C.** The command `line console 0` places you at a prompt where you can then set your console user-mode password. See Chapter 4 for more information.

5. **C.** The `dialer load-threshold 125` command tells the router to bring up the second BRI at 50 percent load. See Chapter 11 for more information.

6. **C.** Link Control Protocol in the PPP stack provides dynamic addressing, authentication, and multilink. See Chapter 11 for more information.

7. **B.** The `show interface` command shows the line, protocol, DLCI, and LMI information of an interface. See Chapter 11 for more information.

8. **A.** 256 − 192 = 64. 64 + 64 = 128. 128 + 64 = 192. The subnet is 128, the broadcast address is 191, and the valid host range is the numbers in between, or 129–190. See Chapter 3 for more information.

9. **B.** The `passive` command, short for `passive-interface`, stops regular updates from being sent out an interface. However, the interface can still receive updates. See Chapter 5 for more information.

10. **C.** ICMP is the protocol at the Network layer that is used to send echo requests and replies. See Chapter 2 for more information.

11. **D.** Layer 2 switching creates individual collision domains. See Chapter 7 for more information.

12. **C.** The command `line vty 0 4` places you in a prompt that will allow you to set or change your Telnet password. See Chapter 4 for more information.

13. **B.** To see the contents of all access lists, use the `show access-lists` command. See Chapter 9 for more information.

14. **C.** VLANs break up broadcast domains at layer 2. See Chapter 8 for more information.

15. **A.** The command `erase-startup-config` deletes the configuration stored in NVRAM. See Chapter 4 for more information.

16. **C.** ICMP is the protocol at the Network layer that is used to send messages back to an originating router. See Chapter 2 for more information.

17. **A.** Class A addressing provides 24 bits for hosts addressing. See Chapter 3 for more information.

18. **B.** Every two seconds, BPDUs are sent out from all active bridge ports by default. See Chapter 7 for more information.

19. D. Switches do not propagate VLAN information by default; you must configure the VTP domain. VLAN Trunking Protocol (VTP) is used to propagate VLAN information across a trunk link. See Chapter 8 for more information.

20. D. FragmentFree LAN switching checks into the data portion of the frame to make sure no fragmentation has occurred. See Chapter 7 for more information.

21. A. By default, switches break up collision domains but are one large broadcast domain. See Chapter 1 for more information.

22. C. Segmentation happens at the Transport layer. See Chapter 1 for more information.

23. C, D. VTP is not right because it has nothing to do with trunking, except that it sends VLAN information across a trunk link. 802.1Q and ISL are used to configure trunking on a port. See Chapter 8 for more information.

24. D. Stub networks have only one connection to an internetwork. Only default routes can be set on a stub network, or network loops may occur. See Chapter 5 for more information.

25. B. Hubs regenerate electrical signals, which are specified at the Physical layer. See Chapter 1 for more information.

26. B, C. You can configure VLAN memberships on a port either statically or dynamically. See Chapter 8 for more information.

27. B. The command `show controllers s 0` tells you what type of serial connection you have. If it is a DCE, you need to provide the clock rate. See Chapter 4 for more information.

28. C. The old command `config mem` was used to copy the configuration stored in NVRAM to RAM and append the file in DRAM, not replace it. The new command is `copy start run`. See Chapter 9 for more information.

29. C. The primary reason the OSI model was created was so that different networks could interoperate. See Chapter 1 for more information.

30. C. The Transport layer creates virtual circuits between hosts before transmitting any data. See Chapter 1 for more information.

31. C. User Datagram Protocol is a connection network service at the Transport layer, and DHCP uses this connectionless service. See Chapter 2 for more information.

32. D. The command used to copy a configuration from a router to a TFTP host is `copy flash tftp`. See Chapter 9 for more information.

33. E. The clock rate command is two words, and the speed of the line is in bps. See Chapter 4 for more information.

34. C. The `show ip interface` command will show you if any outbound or inbound interfaces have an access-list set. See Chapter 10 for more information.

35. C. The command `line vty 0 4` places you in a prompt that will allow you to set or change your Telnet password. See Chapter 4 for more information.

36. B.   The command enable secret todd sets the enable secret password to todd. See Chapter 4 for more information.

37. B.   If a device knows the IP address of where it wants to send a packet, but doesn't know the hardware address, it will send an ARP broadcast looking for the hardware or, in this case, Ethernet address. See Chapter 2 for more information.

38. D.   The copy tftp flash command places a new file in flash memory, which is the default location for the Cisco IOS in Cisco routers. See Chapter 9 for more information.

39. A.   The command to copy running-config, which is the file in DRAM, to NVRAM is copy running-config startup-config. See Chapter 9 for more information.

40. C.   If an interface is administratively shut down, it just means that the administrator needs to perform a no shutdown on the interface. See Chapter 4 for more information.

Chapter

1

Internetworking

THE CCNA EXAM TOPICS COVERED IN THIS CHAPTER INCLUDE THE FOLLOWING:

✓ **TECHNOLOGY**

- Describe network communications using layered models
- Compare and contrast key characteristics of LAN environments
- Describe the components of network devices
- Evaluate rules for packet control

Welcome to the exciting world of internetworking. This first chapter will really help you understand the basics of internetworking by focusing on how to connect networks together using Cisco routers and switches. First, you need to know exactly what an internetwork is, right? You create an internetwork when you take two or more LANs or WANs and connect them via a router, and configure a logical network addressing scheme with a protocol like IP.

I'll be covering these four topics in this chapter:

- Internetworking basics
- Network segmentation
- How bridges, switches, and routers are used to physically segment a network
- How routers are employed to create an internetwork

I'm also going to dissect the Open Systems Interconnection (OSI) model and describe each part to you in detail, because you really need a good grasp of it for the solid foundation you'll build your networking knowledge upon. The OSI model has seven hierarchical layers that were developed to enable different networks to communicate reliably between disparate systems. Since this book is centering upon all things CCNA, it's crucial for you to understand the OSI model as Cisco sees it, so that's how I'll be presenting the seven layers of the OSI model to you.

Since there's a bunch of different types of devices specified at the different layers of the OSI model, it's also very important to understand the many types of cables and connectors used for connecting all those devices to a network. We'll go over cabling Cisco devices, discussing how to connect to a router or switch along with Ethernet LAN technologies, and even how to connect a router or switch with a console connection.

Cisco makes a smorgasbord of router, hub, and switch products, so it follows that by understanding all that's available from Cisco, you can make a much more informed decision about exactly which product(s) will most strategically meet your networking needs. I'll help you with that by going over Cisco's product line of hubs, routers, and switches in a special section toward the end of this chapter.

We'll finish the chapter by discussing the Cisco three-layer hierarchical model that was developed by Cisco to help you design, implement, and troubleshoot internetworks.

After you finish reading this chapter, you'll encounter 20 review questions and three written labs. These are given to you to really lock the information from this chapter into your memory. So don't skip them!

Internetworking Basics

Before we explore internetworking models and the specifications of the OSI reference model, you've got to understand the big picture and learn the answer to the key question: "Why is it so important to learn Cisco internetworking?"

Networks and networking have grown exponentially over the last 15 years—understandably so. They've had to evolve at light speed just to keep up with huge increases in basic mission-critical user needs such as sharing data and printers, as well as more advanced demands such as video conferencing. Unless everyone who needs to share network resources is located in the same office area (an increasingly uncommon situation), the challenge is to connect the some-times many relevant networks together so all users can share the networks' wealth.

It's also likely that at some point, you'll have to break up one large network into a number of smaller ones because user response has dwindled to a trickle as the network grew and grew and LAN traffic congestion reached overwhelming proportions. Breaking up a larger network into a number of smaller ones is called *network segmentation*, and it's accomplished using *routers*, *switches*, and *bridges*.

Possible causes of LAN traffic congestion are:

- Too many hosts in a broadcast domain
- Broadcast storms
- Multicasting
- Low bandwidth

Routers are used to connect networks together and route packets of data from one network to another. Cisco became the de facto standard of routers because of their high-quality router products, great selection, and fantastic service. Routers, by default, break up a *broadcast domain*, which is the set of all devices on a network segment that hear all broadcasts sent on that seg-ment. Breaking up a broadcast domain is important because when a host or server sends a net-work broadcast, every device on the network must read and process that broadcast—unless you've got a router. When the router's interface receives this broadcast, it can respond by basi-cally saying "Thanks, but no thanks," and discard the broadcast without forwarding it on to other networks. Even though routers are known for breaking up broadcast domains by default, it's important to remember that they break up collision domains as well.

Two advantages of using routers in your network:

- They don't forward broadcasts by default.
- They can filter the network based on layer-3 (Network layer) information (i.e., IP address).

Conversely, switches aren't used to create internetworks, they're employed to add function-ality to an internetwork LAN. The main purpose of a switch is to make a LAN work better—to optimize its performance—providing more bandwidth for the LAN's users. And switches don't forward packets to other networks as routers do. Instead, they only "switch" frames from one port to another within the switched network. Okay, you may be thinking, "Wait a minute, what are frames and packets?" I'll tell you all about them later in this chapter, I promise!

By default, switches break up *collision domains*. This is an Ethernet term used to describe a network scenario wherein one particular device sends a packet on a network segment, forcing every other device on that same segment to pay attention to it. At the same time, a different device tries to transmit, leading to a collision, after which both devices must retransmit, one at a time. Not very efficient! This situation is typically found in a hub environment where each host segment connects to a hub that represents only one collision domain and only one broadcast domain. By contrast, each and every port on a switch represents its own collision domain.

NOTE   Switches create separate collision domains, but a single broadcast domain. Routers provide a separate broadcast domain for each interface.

The term *bridging* was introduced before routers and hubs were implemented, so it's pretty common to hear people referring to bridges as "switches." That's because bridges and switches basically do the same thing—break up collision domains on a LAN. So what this means is that a switch is basically just a multiple-port bridge with more brainpower, right? Well, pretty much, but there are differences. Switches do provide this function, but they do so with greatly enhanced management ability and features. Plus, most of the time, bridges only had two or four ports. Yes, you could get your hands on a bridge with up to 16 ports, but that's nothing compared to the hundreds available on some switches!

NOTE   You would use a bridge in a network to reduce collisions within broadcast domains and to increase the number of collision domains in your network, which provides more bandwidth for users.

Figure 1.1 shows how a network would look with all these internetwork devices in place. Remember that the router will not only break up broadcast domains for every LAN interface, but break up collision domains as well.

When you looked at Figure 1.1, did you notice that the router is found at center stage, and that it connects each physical network together? We have to use this layout because of the older technologies involved——bridges and hubs. Once we have only switches in our network, things change a lot! The LAN switches would then be placed at the center of the network world and the routers would be found connecting only logical networks together. If I've implemented this kind of setup, I've created virtual LANs (VLANs). Again don't stress— I'll go over VLANs thoroughly with you in Chapter 8, "Virtual LANs (VLANs)."

On the top network in Figure 1.1, you'll notice that a bridge was used to connect the hubs to a router. The bridge breaks up collision domains, but all the hosts connected to both hubs are still crammed into the same broadcast domain. Also, the bridge only created two collision domains, so each device connected to a hub is in the same collision domain as every other device connected to that same hub. This is actually pretty lame, but it's still better than having one collision domain for all hosts.

Notice something else: the three hubs at the bottom that are connected also connect to the router, creating one humongous collision domain and one humongous broadcast domain. This makes the bridged network look much better indeed!

FIGURE 1.1 Internetworking devices

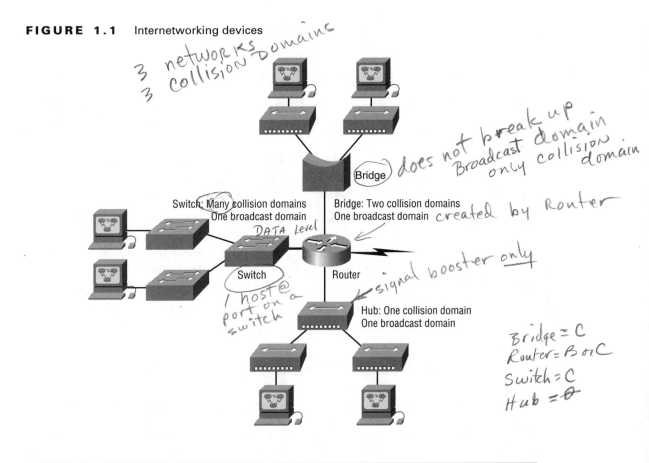

[handwritten annotations:] 3 networks 3 collision domains

Switch: Many collision domains
One broadcast domain

DATA level

Switch

1 host @ a port on a switch

Bridge: Two collision domains
One broadcast domain *created by Router*

Bridge *does not break up Broadcast domain only collision domain*

signal booster only

Router

Hub: One collision domain
One broadcast domain

Bridge = C
Router = B or C
Switch = C
Hub = Ø

Although bridges are used to segment networks, they will not isolate broadcast or multicast packets.

The best network connected to the router is the LAN switch network on the left. Why? Because each port on that switch breaks up collision domains. But it's not all good—all devices are still in the same broadcast domain. Remember why this can be a bad thing? Because all devices must listen to all broadcasts transmitted, that's why. And if your broadcast domains are too large, the users have less bandwidth and are required to process more broadcasts, and network response time will slow to a level that could cause office riots.

Obviously, the best network is one that's correctly configured to meet the business requirements of the company it serves. LAN switches with routers, correctly placed in the network, are the best network design. This book will help you understand the basics of routers and switches so you can make tight, informed decisions on a case-by-case basis.

So now that you've gotten an introduction to internetworking, and the various devices that live in an internetwork, it's time to head into internetworking models.

⊕ **Real World Scenario**

Should I just replace all my hubs with switches?

You're a Network Administrator at a large company in San Jose. The boss comes to you and says that he got your requisition to buy a switch and is not sure about approving the expense; do you really need it?

Well, if you can, sure—why not? Switches really add a lot of functionality to a network that hubs just don't have. But most of us don't have an unlimited budget. Hubs still can create a nice network—that is, of course, if you design and implement the network correctly.

Let's say that you have 40 users plugged into four hubs, 10 users each. At this point, the hubs are all connected together so that you have one large collision domain and one large broadcast domain. If you can afford to buy just one switch and plug each hub into a switch port, as well as the servers into the switch, then you now have four collision domains and one broadcast domain. Not great, but for the price of one switch, your network is a much better thing.

So, go ahead! Put that requisition in to buy all new switches. What do you have to lose?

Internetworking Models

When networks first came into being, computers could typically communicate only with computers from the same manufacturer. For example, companies ran either a complete DECnet solution or an IBM solution—not both together. In the late 1970s, the *Open Systems Interconnection (OSI) reference model* was created by the International Organization for Standardization (ISO) to break this barrier.

The OSI model was meant to help vendors create interoperable network devices and software in the form of protocols so that different vendor networks could work with each other. Like world peace, it'll probably never happen completely, but it's still a great goal.

The OSI model is the primary architectural model for networks. It describes how data and network information are communicated from an application on one computer, through the network media, to an application on another computer. The OSI reference model breaks this approach into layers.

In the following section, I am going to explain the layered approach and how we can use the layered approach in helping us troubleshoot our internetworks.

The Layered Approach

A *reference model* is a conceptual blueprint of how communications should take place. It addresses all the processes required for effective communication and divides these processes into logical groupings called *layers*. When a communication system is designed in this manner, it's known as *layered architecture*.

Think of it like this: You and some friends want to start a company. One of the first things you'll do is sit down and think through what tasks must be done, who will do them, what order they will be done in, and how they relate to each other. Ultimately, you might group these tasks into departments. Let's say you decide to have an order-taking department, an inventory department, and a shipping department. Each of your departments has its own unique tasks, keeping its staff members busy and requiring them to focus on only their own duties.

In this scenario, I'm using departments as a metaphor for the layers in a communication system. For things to run smoothly, the staff of each department will have to trust and rely heavily upon the others to do their jobs and competently handle their unique responsibilities. In your planning sessions, you would probably take notes, recording the entire process to facilitate later discussions about standards of operation that will serve as your business blueprint, or reference model.

Once your business is launched, your department heads, armed with the part of the blueprint relating to their department, will need to develop practical methods to implement their assigned tasks. These practical methods, or protocols, will need to be compiled into a standard operating procedures manual and followed closely. Each of the various procedures in your manual will have been included for different reasons and have varying degrees of importance and implementation. If you form a partnership or acquire another company, it will be imperative that its business protocols—its business blueprint—match yours (or at least be compatible with it).

Similarly, software developers can use a reference model to understand computer communication processes and see what types of functions need to be accomplished on any one layer. If they are developing a protocol for a certain layer, all they need to concern themselves with is the specific layer's functions, not those of any other layer. Another layer and protocol will handle the other functions. The technical term for this idea is *binding*. The communication processes that are related to each other are bound, or grouped together, at a particular layer.

Advantages of Reference Models

The OSI model is hierarchical, and the same benefits and advantages can apply to any layered model. The primary purpose of all such models, especially the OSI model, is to allow different vendors' networks to interoperate.

Advantages of using the OSI layered model include, but are not limited to, the following:

- Allows multiple-vendor development through standardization of network components
- Allows various types of network hardware and software to communicate
- Prevents changes in one layer from affecting other layers, so it does not hamper development

The OSI Reference Model

One of the greatest functions of the OSI specifications is to assist in data transfer between disparate hosts—meaning, for example, that they enable us to transfer data between a Unix host and a PC or a Mac.

FIGURE 1.2   The upper layers

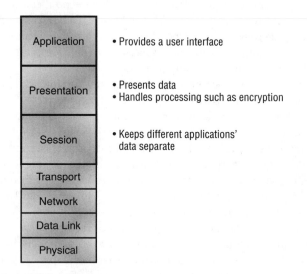

The OSI isn't a physical model, though. Rather, it's a set of guidelines that application developers can use to create and implement applications that run on a network. It also provides a framework for creating and implementing networking standards, devices, and internetworking schemes.

The OSI has seven different layers, divided into two groups. The top three layers define how the applications within the end stations will communicate with each other and with users. The bottom four layers define how data is transmitted end-to-end. Figure 1.2 shows the three upper layers and their functions, and Figure 1.3 shows the four lower layers and their functions.

When you study Figure 1.2, you can see that the user interfaces with the computer at the Application layer, and also that the upper layers are responsible for applications communicating between hosts. Remember that none of the upper layers knows anything about networking or network addresses. That's the responsibility of the four bottom layers.

In Figure 1.3, you can see that it's the four bottom layers that define how data is transferred through a physical wire or through switches and routers. These bottom layers also determine how to rebuild a data stream from a transmitting host to a destination host's application.

Network devices that operate at all seven layers of the OSI model include:

- Network management stations (NMS)

- Web and Application servers

- Gateways (not default gateways)

- Network hosts

Basically, the ISO is pretty much the Emily Post of the network protocol world. Just like Ms. Post, who wrote the book setting the standards—or protocols—for human social interaction, the ISO developed the OSI reference model as the precedent and guide for an open network protocol set. Defining the etiquette of communication models, it remains today the most popular means of comparison for protocol suites.

FIGURE 1.3　　The lower layers

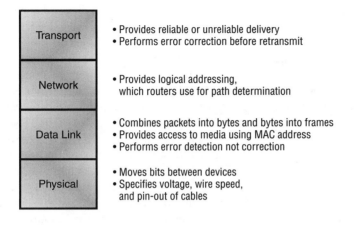

The OSI reference model has seven layers:

- Application layer
- Presentation layer
- Session layer
- Transport layer
- Network layer
- Data Link layer
- Physical layer

Figure 1.4 shows the functions defined at each layer of the OSI model. With this in hand, you're now ready to explore each layer's function in detail.

FIGURE 1.4　　Layer functions

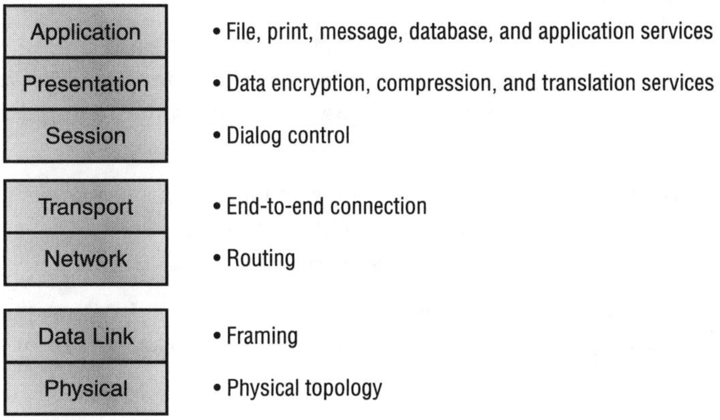

Application	• File, print, message, database, and application services
Presentation	• Data encryption, compression, and translation services
Session	• Dialog control
Transport	• End-to-end connection
Network	• Routing
Data Link	• Framing
Physical	• Physical topology

The Application Layer

The *Application layer* of the OSI model marks the spot where users actually communicate to the computer. This layer actually only comes into play when it's apparent that access to the network is going to be needed soon. Take the case of Internet Explorer. You could uninstall every trace of networking components from a system, such as TCP/IP, NIC card, etc., and you could still use Internet Explorer (IE) to view a local HTML document—no problem. But things would definitely get messy if you tried to do something like actually view an HTML document that must be retrieved using HTTP, or nab a file with FTP. That's because IE will respond to requests like those by attempting to access the Application layer. And what's actually happening is that the Application layer is acting as an interface between the actual application program—which isn't at all a part of the layered structure—and the next layer down, by providing ways for the application to send information down through the protocol stack. In other words, IE doesn't truly reside within the Application layer—it interfaces with Application-layer protocols when it needs to deal with remote resources.

The Application layer is also responsible for identifying and establishing the availability of the intended communication partner, and determining whether sufficient resources for the intended communication exist.

These tasks are important because computer applications sometimes require more than only desktop resources. Often, they'll unite communicating components from more than one network application. Prime examples are file transfers and e-mail, as well as enabling remote access, network management activities, client/server processes, and information location. Many network applications provide services for communication over enterprise networks, but for present and future internetworking, the need is fast developing to reach beyond the limits of current physical networking. Today, transactions and information exchanges between organizations are broadening to require internetworking applications such as the following:

World Wide Web (WWW)   Connects countless servers (the number seems to grow with each passing day) presenting diverse formats. Most are multimedia and can include graphics, text, video, and sound. (And as pressure to keep up the pace mounts, websites are only getting slicker and snappier. Keep in mind, the snazzier the site, the more resources it requires. You'll see why I mention this later.) Netscape Navigator and IE simplify both accessing and viewing websites.

E-mail gateways   Versatile; can use Simple Mail Transfer Protocol (SMTP) or the X.400 standard to deliver messages between different e-mail applications.

Electronic data interchange (EDI)   A composite of specialized standards and processes that facilitates the flow of tasks such as accounting, shipping/receiving, and order and inventory tracking between businesses.

Special interest bulletin boards   Include the many Internet chat rooms where people can "meet" (connect) and communicate with each other either by posting messages or by typing a live conversation. They can also share public-domain software.

Internet navigation utilities   Include applications such as Gopher and WAIS, as well as search engines such as Google and Yahoo!, which help users locate the resources and information they need on the Internet.

Financial transaction services   Target the financial community. They gather and sell information pertaining to investments, market trading, commodities, currency exchange rates, and credit data to their subscribers.

The Presentation Layer

The *Presentation layer* gets its name from its purpose: It presents data to the Application layer and is responsible for data translation and code formatting.

This layer is essentially a translator and provides coding and conversion functions. A successful data-transfer technique is to adapt the data into a standard format before transmission. Computers are configured to receive this generically formatted data and then convert the data back into its native format for actual reading (for example, EBCDIC to ASCII). By providing translation services, the Presentation layer ensures that data transferred from the Application layer of one system can be read by the Application layer of another one.

The OSI has protocol standards that define how standard data should be formatted. Tasks like data compression, decompression, encryption, and decryption are associated with this layer. Some Presentation layer standards are involved in multimedia operations too. The following serve to direct graphic and visual image presentation:

PICT   A picture format used by Macintosh programs for transferring QuickDraw graphics.

TIFF   Tagged Image File Format; a standard graphics format for high-resolution, bitmapped images.

JPEG   Photo standards brought to us by The Joint Photographic Experts Group.

Other standards guide movies and sound:

MIDI   Musical Instrument Digital Interface (sometimes called Musical Instrument Device Interface), used for digitized music.

MPEG   Increasingly popular Moving Picture Experts Group standard for the compression and coding of motion video for CDs. It provides digital storage and bit rates up to 1.5Mbps.

QuickTime   For use with Macintosh programs; manages audio and video applications.

RTF   Rich Text Format, a file format that lets you exchange text files between different word processors, even in different operating systems.

The Session Layer

The *Session layer* is responsible for setting up, managing, and then tearing down sessions between Presentation layer entities. This layer also provides dialogue control between devices, or nodes. It coordinates communication between systems, and serves to organize their communication by offering three different modes: *simplex*, *half duplex*, and *full duplex*. To sum up, the Session layer basically keeps different applications' data separate from other applications' data.

The following are some examples of Session layer protocols and interfaces (according to Cisco):

Network File System (NFS)   Developed by Sun Microsystems and used with TCP/IP and Unix workstations to allow transparent access to remote resources.

Structured Query Language (SQL)   Developed by IBM to provide users with a simpler way to define their information requirements on both local and remote systems.

Remote Procedure Call (RPC)   A broad client/server redirection tool used for disparate service environments. Its procedures are created on clients and performed on servers.

X Window   Widely used by intelligent terminals for communicating with remote Unix computers, allowing them to operate as though they were locally attached monitors.

AppleTalk Session Protocol (ASP)   Another client/server mechanism, which both establishes and maintains sessions between AppleTalk client and server machines.

Digital Network Architecture Session Control Protocol (DNA SCP)   A DECnet Session layer protocol.

The Transport Layer

The *Transport layer* segments and reassembles data into a data stream. Services located in the Transport layer both segment and reassemble data from upper-layer applications and unite it onto the same data stream. They provide end-to-end data transport services and can establish a logical connection between the sending host and destination host on an internetwork.

Some of you are probably familiar with TCP and UDP already. (But if you're not, no worries—I'll tell you all about them in Chapter 2, "Internet Protocols.") If so, you know that both work at the Transport layer, and that TCP is a reliable service and UDP is not. This means that application developers have more options because they have a choice between the two protocols when working with TCP/IP protocols.

The Transport layer is responsible for providing mechanisms for multiplexing upper-layer applications, establishing sessions, and tearing down virtual circuits. It also hides details of any network-dependent information from the higher layers by providing transparent data transfer.

   The term "reliable networking" can be used at the Transport layer. It means that acknowledgments, sequencing, and flow control will be used.

The Transport layer can be connectionless, or connection-oriented. However, Cisco is mostly concerned with you understanding the connection-oriented portion of the Transport layer. The following sections will provide the skinny on the connection-oriented (reliable) protocol of the Transport layer.

Flow Control

Data integrity is ensured at the Transport layer by maintaining *flow control* and by allowing users to request reliable data transport between systems. Flow control prevents a sending host on one side of the connection from overflowing the buffers in the receiving host—an event that can result in lost data. Reliable data transport employs a connection-oriented communications session between systems, and the protocols involved ensure that the following will be achieved:

▪   The segments delivered are acknowledged back to the sender upon their reception.

- Any segments not acknowledged are retransmitted.
- Segments are sequenced back into their proper order upon arrival at their destination.
- A manageable data flow is maintained in order to avoid congestion, overloading, and data loss.

Connection-Oriented Communication

In reliable transport operation, a device that wants to transmit sets up a connection-oriented communication with a remote device by creating a session. The transmitting device first establishes a connection-oriented session with its peer system, which is called a *call setup*, or a *three-way handshake*. Data is then transferred; when finished, a call termination takes place to tear down the virtual circuit.

Figure 1.5 depicts a typical reliable session taking place between sending and receiving systems. Looking at it, you can see that both hosts' application programs begin by notifying their individual operating systems that a connection is about to be initiated. The two operating systems communicate by sending messages over the network confirming that the transfer is approved and that both sides are ready for it to take place. After all of this required synchronization takes place, a connection is fully established and the data transfer begins.

FIGURE 1.5   Establishing a connection-oriented session

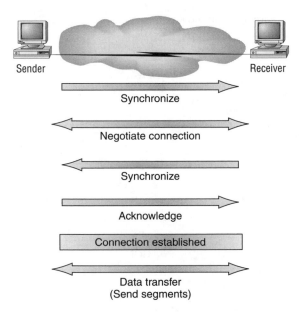

While the information is being transferred between hosts, the two machines periodically check in with each other, communicating through their protocol software to ensure that all is going well and that the data is being received properly.

Let me sum up the steps in the connection-oriented session—the three-way handshake—pictured in Figure 1.5:

- The first "connection agreement" segment is a request for synchronization.

- The second and third segments acknowledge the request and establish connection parameters—the rules—between hosts. The receiver's sequencing is also requested to be synchronized here, as well, so that a bi-directional connection is formed.

- The final segment is also an acknowledgment. It notifies the destination host that the connection agreement has been accepted and that the actual connection has been established. Data transfer can now begin.

Sounds pretty simple, but things don't always flow so smoothly. Sometimes during a transfer, congestion can occur because a high-speed computer is generating data traffic a lot faster than the network can handle transferring. A bunch of computers simultaneously sending datagrams through a single gateway or destination can also botch things up nicely. In the latter case, a gateway or destination can become congested even though no single source caused the problem. In either case, the problem is basically akin to a freeway bottleneck—too much traffic for too small a capacity. It's not usually one car that's the problem; there are simply too many cars on that freeway.

Okay, so what happens when a machine receives a flood of datagrams too quickly for it to process? It stores them in a memory section called a *buffer*. But this buffering action can only solve the problem if the datagrams are part of a small burst. If not, and the datagram deluge continues, a device's memory will eventually be exhausted, its flood capacity will be exceeded, and it will react by discarding any additional datagrams that arrive.

FIGURE 1.6   Transmitting segments with flow control

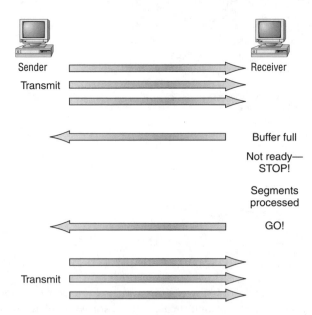

No huge worries here, though. Because of the transport function, network flood control systems actually work quite well. Instead of dumping resources and allowing data to be lost, the transport can issue a "not ready" indicator to the sender, or source, of the flood (as shown in Figure 1.6). This mechanism works kind of like a stop light, signaling the sending device to stop transmitting segment traffic to its overwhelmed peer. After the peer receiver processes the segments already in its memory reservoir—its buffer—it sends out a "ready" transport indicator. When the machine waiting to transmit the rest of its datagrams receives this "go" indictor, it resumes its transmission.

In fundamental, reliable, connection-oriented data transfer, datagrams are delivered to the receiving host in exactly the same sequence they're transmitted—and the transmission fails if this order is breached! If any data segments are lost, duplicated, or damaged along the way, a failure will transmit. This problem is solved by having the receiving host acknowledge that it has received each and every data segment.

 Connectionless transfer is covered in Chapter 2.

Windowing

Ideally, data throughput happens quickly and efficiently. And as you can imagine, it would be slow if the transmitting machine had to wait for an acknowledgment after sending each segment. But because there's time available *after* the sender transmits the data segment and *before* it finishes processing acknowledgments from the receiving machine, the sender uses the break as an opportunity to transmit more data. The quantity of data segments (measured in bytes) that the transmitting machine is allowed to send without receiving an acknowledgment for them is called a *window*.

 Windows are used to control the amount of outstanding, unacknowledged data segments.

So the size of the window controls how much information is transferred from one end to the other. While some protocols quantify information by observing the number of packets, TCP/IP measures it by counting the number of bytes.

As you can see in Figure 1.7, there are two window sizes—one set to 1, and one set to 3. When you've configured a window size of 1, the sending machine waits for an acknowledgment for each data segment it transmits before transmitting another. If you've configured a window size of 3, it's allowed to transmit three data segments before an acknowledgment is received. In our simplified example, both the sending and receiving machines are workstations. Reality is rarely that simple, and most often acknowledgments and packets will commingle as they travel over the network and pass through routers. Routing definitely complicates things! You'll learn about applied routing in Chapter 5, "IP Routing."

 If a TCP session is set up with a window size of 2 bytes, and during the transfer stage of the session the window size changes from 2 bytes to 3 bytes, the sending host must then transmit 3 bytes before waiting for an acknowledgment instead of the 2 bytes originally set up in the virtual circuit.

FIGURE 1.7   Windowing

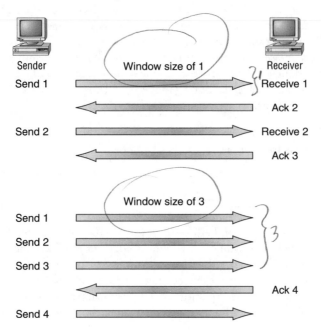

Acknowledgments

Reliable data delivery ensures the integrity of a stream of data sent from one machine to the other through a fully functional data link. It guarantees that the data won't be duplicated or lost. This is achieved through something called *positive acknowledgment with retransmission*— a technique that requires a receiving machine to communicate with the transmitting source by sending an acknowledgment message back to the sender when it receives data. The sender documents each segment it sends and waits for this acknowledgment before sending the next segment. When it sends a segment, the transmitting machine starts a timer and retransmits if it expires before an acknowledgment is returned from the receiving end.

In Figure 1.8, the sending machine transmits segments 1, 2, and 3. The receiving node acknowledges it has received them by requesting segment 4. When it receives the acknowledgment, the sender then transmits segments 4, 5, and 6. If segment 5 doesn't make it to the destination, the receiving node acknowledges that event with a request for the segment to be resent. The sending machine will then resend the lost segment and wait for an acknowledgment, which it must receive in order to move on to the transmission of segment 7.

The Network Layer

The *Network layer* (also called layer 3) manages device addressing, tracks the location of devices on the network, and determines the best way to move data, which means that the Network layer must transport traffic between devices that aren't locally attached. Routers (layer-3 devices) are specified at the Network layer and provide the routing services within an internetwork.

FIGURE 1.8   Transport layer reliable delivery

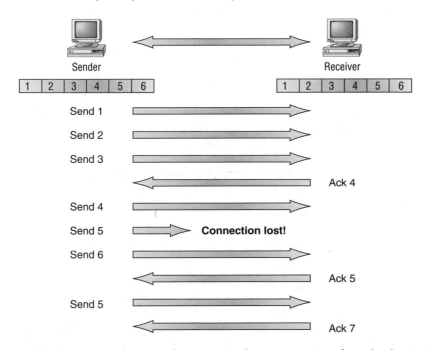

It happens like this: First, when a packet is received on a router interface, the destination IP address is checked. If the packet isn't destined for that particular router, it will look up the destination network address in the routing table. Once the router chooses an exit interface, the packet will be sent to that interface to be framed and sent out on the local network. If the router can't find an entry for the packet's destination network in the routing table, the router drops the packet.

Two types of packets are used at the Network layer: data and route updates.

Data packets   Used to transport user data through the internetwork. Protocols used to support data traffic are called *routed protocols*; examples of routed protocols are IP and IPX. You'll learn about IP addressing in Chapter 2 and Chapter 3, "IP Subnetting and Variable Length Subnet Masks (VLSM)."

Route update packets   Used to update neighboring routers about the networks connected to all routers within the internetwork. Protocols that send route update packets are called routing protocols; examples of some common ones are RIP, EIGRP, and OSPF. Route update packets are used to help build and maintain routing tables on each router.

In Figure 1.9, I've given you an example of a routing table. The routing table used in a router includes the following information:

Network addresses   Protocol-specific network addresses. A router must maintain a routing table for individual routing protocols because each routing protocol keeps track of a network with a different addressing scheme. Think of it as a street sign in each of the different languages spoken by the residents that live on a particular street. So, if there were American, Spanish, and French folks on a street named "Cat," the sign would read: Cat/Gato/Chat.

FIGURE 1.9   Routing table used in a router

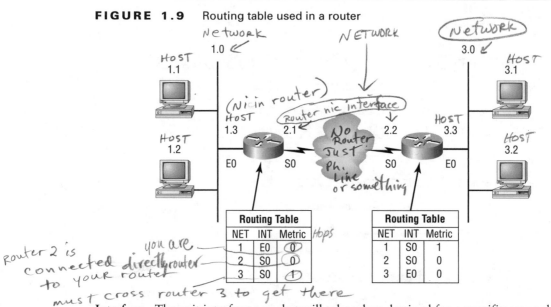

Interface   The exit interface a packet will take when destined for a specific network.

Metric   The distance to the remote network. Different routing protocols use different ways of computing this distance. I'm going to cover routing protocols in Chapter 5, but for now, know that some routing protocols use something called a *hop count* (the number of routers a packet passes through en route to a remote network), while others use bandwidth, delay of the line, or even tick count (1/18 of a second).

And as I mentioned earlier, routers break up broadcast domains, which means that by default, broadcasts aren't forwarded through a router. Do you remember why this is a good thing? Routers also break up collision domains, but you can also do that using layer-2 (Data Link layer) switches. Because each interface in a router represents a separate network, it must be assigned unique network identification numbers, and each host on the network connected to that router must use the same network number.

Here are some points about routers you should really commit to memory:

- Routers, by default, will not forward any broadcast or multicast packets.

- Routers use the logical address in a Network layer header to determine the next hop router to forward the packet to.

- Routers can use access lists, created by an administrator, to control security on the types of packets that are allowed to enter or exit an interface.

- Routers can provide layer-2 bridging functions if needed and can simultaneously route through the same interface.

- Layer-3 devices (routers in this case) provide connections between virtual LANs (VLANs).
- Routers can provide quality of service (QoS) for specific types of network traffic.

Switching and VLANs and are covered in Chapters 7 and 8.

The Data Link Layer

The *Data Link layer* provides the physical transmission of the data and handles error notification, network topology, and flow control. This means the Data Link layer will ensure that messages are delivered to the proper device on a LAN using hardware addresses, and translates messages from the Network layer into bits for the Physical layer to transmit.

The Data Link layer formats the message into pieces, each called a *data frame*, and adds a customized header containing the hardware destination and source address. This added information forms a sort of capsule that surrounds the original message in much the same way that engines, navigational devices, and other tools were attached to the lunar modules of the Apollo project. These various pieces of equipment were useful only during certain stages of space flight and were stripped off the module and discarded when their designated stage was complete. Data traveling through networks is similar.

Figure 1.10 shows the Data Link layer with the Ethernet and IEEE specifications. When you check it out, notice that the IEEE 802.2 standard is used in conjunction with and adds functionality to the other IEEE standards.

FIGURE 1.10   Data Link layer

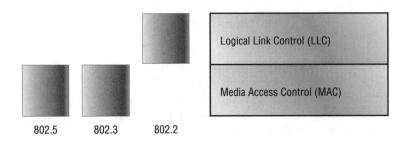

802.5   802.3   802.2

Logical Link Control (LLC)

Media Access Control (MAC)

It's important for you to understand that routers, which work at the Network layer, don't care at all about where a particular host is located. They're only concerned about where networks are located, and the best way to reach them—including remote ones. Routers are totally obsessive when it comes to networks. And for once, this is a good thing! It's the Data Link layer that's responsible for the actual unique identification of each device that resides on a local network.

For a host to send packets to individual hosts on a local network as well as transmitting packets between routers, the Data Link layer uses hardware addressing. Each time a packet is sent between routers, it's framed with control information at the Data Link layer, but that information is stripped off at the receiving router and only the original packet is left completely intact. This framing of the packet continues for each hop until the packet is finally delivered to the correct receiving host. It's really important to understand that the packet itself is never altered along the route; it's only encapsulated with the type of control information required for it to be properly passed on to the different media types.

The IEEE Ethernet Data Link layer has two sublayers:

Media Access Control (MAC) 802.3   Defines how packets are placed on the media. Contention media access is "first come/first served" access where everyone shares the same bandwidth—hence the name. Physical addressing is defined here, as well as logical topologies. What's a logical topology? It's the signal path through a physical topology. Line discipline, error notification (not correction), ordered delivery of frames, and optional flow control can also be used at this sublayer.

Logical Link Control (LLC) 802.2   Responsible for identifying Network layer protocols and then encapsulating them. An LLC header tells the Data Link layer what to do with a packet once a frame is received. It works like this: A host will receive a frame and look in the LLC header to find out where the packet is destined for—say, the IP protocol at the Network layer. The LLC can also provide flow control and sequencing of control bits.

The switches and bridges I talked about near the beginning of the chapter both work at the Data Link layer and filter the network using hardware (MAC) addresses. We will look at these in the following section.

Switches and Bridges at the Data Link Layer

Layer-2 switching is considered hardware-based bridging because it uses specialized hardware called an *application-specific integrated circuit (ASIC)*. ASICs can run up to gigabit speeds with very low latency rates.

Latency is the time measured from when a frame enters a port to the time it exits a port.

Bridges and switches read each frame as it passes through the network. The layer-2 device then puts the source hardware address in a filter table and keeps track of which port the frame was received on. This information (logged in the bridge's or switch's filter table) is what helps the machine determine the location of the specific sending device.

The real estate business is all about location, location, location, and it's the same way for both layer-2 and -3 devices. Though both need to be able to negotiate the network, it's crucial to remember that they're concerned with very different parts of it. Primarily, layer-3 machines (such as routers) need to locate specific networks, whereas layer-2 machines (switches and bridges) need to eventually locate specific devices. So, networks are to routers as individual devices are to switches and bridges. And routing tables that "map" the internetwork are for routers, as filter tables that "map" individual devices are for switches and bridges.

After a filter table is built on the layer-2 device, it will only forward frames to the segment where the destination hardware address is located. If the destination device is on the same segment as the frame, the layer-2 device will block the frame from going to any other segments. If the destination is on a different segment, the frame can only be transmitted to that segment. This is called *transparent bridging.*

When a switch interface receives a frame with a destination hardware address that isn't found in the device's filter table, it will forward the frame to all connected segments. If the unknown device that was sent the "mystery frame" replies to this forwarding action, the switch updates its filter table regarding that device's location. But in the event the destination address of the transmitting frame is a broadcast address, the switch will forward all broadcasts to every connected segment by default.

All devices that the broadcast is forwarded to are considered to be in the same broadcast domain. This can be a problem; layer-2 devices propagate layer-2 broadcast storms that choke performance, and the only way to stop a broadcast storm from propagating through an inter-network is with a layer-3 device—a router.

The biggest benefit of using switches instead of hubs in your internetwork is that each switch port is actually its own collision domain. (Conversely, a hub creates one large collision domain.) But even armed with a switch, you still can't break up broadcast domains. Neither switches nor bridges will do that. They'll typically simply forward all broadcasts instead.

Another benefit of LAN switching over hub-centered implementations is that each device on every segment plugged into a switch can transmit simultaneously. At least, they can as long as there is only one host on each port and a hub isn't plugged into a switch port. (Remember, each switch port is its own collision domain.) As you might have guessed, hubs only allow one device per network segment to communicate at a time.

Each network segment connected to the switch must have the same type of devices attached. What this means to you and me is that you can connect an Ethernet hub into a switch port and then connect multiple Ethernet hosts into the hub, but you can't mix Token Ring hosts in with the Ethernet gang on the same segment. Mixing hosts in this manner is called *media translation*, and Cisco says you've just got to have a router around if you need to provide this service, although I have found this not to be true in reality—but remember, we're studying for the CCNA exam here, right?

The Physical Layer

Finally arriving at the bottom, we find that the *Physical layer* does two things: It sends bits and receives bits. Bits come only in values of 1 or 0—a Morse code with numerical values. The Physical layer communicates directly with the various types of actual communication media. Different kinds of media represent these bit values in different ways. Some use audio tones, while others employ *state transitions*—changes in voltage from high to low and low to high. Specific protocols are needed for each type of media to describe the proper bit patterns to be used, how data is encoded into media signals, and the various qualities of the physical media's attachment interface.

The Physical layer specifies the electrical, mechanical, procedural, and functional require-ments for activating, maintaining, and deactivating a physical link between end systems. This layer is also where you identify the interface between the *data terminal equipment (DTE)* and the *data communication equipment (DCE)*. Some old-phone-company employees still call DCE data circuit-terminating equipment. The DCE is usually located at the service provider, while the DTE is the attached device. The services available to the DTE are most often accessed via a modem or *channel service unit/data service unit (CSU/DSU)*.

The Physical layer's connectors and different physical topologies are defined by the OSI as standards, allowing disparate systems to communicate. The CCNA exam is only interested in the IEEE Ethernet standards.

Hubs at the Physical Layer

A *hub* is really a multiple-port repeater. A repeater receives a digital signal and reamplifies or regenerates that signal, and then forwards the digital signal out all active ports without looking at any data. An active hub does the same thing. Any digital signal received from a segment on a hub port is regenerated or reamplified and transmitted out all ports on the hub. This means all devices plugged into a hub are in the same collision domain as well as in the same broadcast domain.

Hubs, like repeaters, don't actually examine any of the traffic as it enters and is then transmitted out to the other parts of the physical media. Every device connected to the hub, or hubs, must listen if a device transmits. A physical star network—where the hub is a central device and cables extend in all directions out from it—is the type of topology a hub creates. Visually, the design really does resemble a star, whereas Ethernet networks run a logical bus topology, meaning that the signal has to run from end to end of the network.

Ethernet Networking

Ethernet is a contention media access method that allows all hosts on a network to share the same bandwidth of a link. Ethernet is popular because it's readily scalable, meaning it's comparatively easy to integrate new technologies, such as FastEthernet and Gigabit Ethernet, into an existing network infrastructure. It's also relatively simple to implement in the first place, and with it, troubleshooting is reasonably straightforward. Ethernet uses both Data Link and Physical layer specifications, and this section of the chapter will give you both the Data Link and Physical layer information you need to effectively implement, troubleshoot, and maintain an Ethernet network.

Ethernet networking uses *Carrier Sense Multiple Access with Collision Detection (CSMA/CD)*, a protocol that helps devices share the bandwidth evenly without having two devices transmit at the same time on the network medium. CSMA/CD was created to overcome the problem of those collisions that occur when packets are transmitted simultaneously from different nodes. And trust me, good collision management is crucial because when a node transmits in a CSMA/CD network, all the other nodes on the network receive and examine that transmission. Only bridges and routers can effectively prevent a transmission from propagating throughout the entire network!

So, how does the CSMA/CD protocol work? Like this: When a host wants to transmit over the network, it first checks for the presence of a digital signal on the wire. If all is clear (no other host is transmitting), the host will then proceed with its transmission. But it doesn't stop there. The transmitting host constantly monitors the wire to make sure no other hosts begin transmitting. If the host detects another signal on the wire, it sends out an extended jam signal that causes all nodes on the segment to stop sending data (think, busy signal). The nodes respond to that jam signal by waiting a while before attempting to transmit again. Backoff algorithms determine when the colliding stations can retransmit. If collisions keep occurring after 15 tries, the nodes attempting to transmit will then time out. Pretty clean!

The effects of having a CSMA/CD network sustaining heavy collisions include:

- Delay
- Low throughput
- Congestion

NOTE Backoff on an 802.3 network is the retransmission delay that's enforced when a collision occurs.

In the following sections, I am going to cover Ethernet in detail at both the Data Link (layer 2) and the Physical layer (layer 1).

Half- and Full-Duplex Ethernet

Half-duplex Ethernet is defined in the original 802.3 Ethernet; Cisco says it uses only one wire pair with a digital signal running in both directions on the wire. Certainly, the IEEE specifications discuss the process of half-duplex somewhat differently, but what Cisco is talking about is a general sense of what is happening here with Ethernet.

It also uses the CSMA/CD protocol to help prevent collisions and to permit retransmitting if a collision does occur. If a hub is attached to a switch, it must operate in half-duplex mode because the end stations must be able to detect collisions. Half-duplex Ethernet—typically 10BaseT—is only about 30 to 40 percent efficient as Cisco sees it, because a large 10BaseT network will usually only give you 3 to 4Mbps—at most.

But full-duplex Ethernet uses two pairs of wires, instead of one wire pair like half duplex. And full duplex uses a point-to-point connection between the transmitter of the transmitting device and the receiver of the receiving device. This means that with full-duplex data transfer, you get a faster data transfer compared to half duplex. And because the transmitted data is sent on a different set of wires than the received data, no collisions will occur.

The reason you don't need to worry about collisions is because now it's like a freeway with multiple lanes instead of the single-lane road provided by half duplex. Full-duplex Ethernet is supposed to offer 100 percent efficiency in both directions—e.g., you can get 20Mbps with a 10Mbps Ethernet running full duplex, or 200Mbps for FastEthernet. But this rate is something known as an aggregate rate, which translates as "You're supposed to get" 100 percent efficiency. No guarantees, in networking as in life.

Full-duplex Ethernet can be used in three situations:

- With a connection from a switch to a host
- With a connection from a switch to a switch
- With a connection from a host to a host using a crossover cable

Full-duplex Ethernet requires a point-to-point connection when only two nodes are present.

Now, if it's capable of all that speed, why wouldn't it deliver? Well, when a full-duplex Ethernet port is powered on, it first connects to the remote end, and then negotiates with the other end of the FastEthernet link. This is called an *auto-detect mechanism*. This mechanism first decides on the exchange capability, which means it checks to see if it can run at 10 or 100Mbps. It then checks to see if it can run full duplex, and if it can't, it will run half duplex.

 Remember that half-duplex Ethernet shares a collision domain and provides a lower effective throughput than full-duplex Ethernet, which typically has a private collision domain and a higher effective throughput.

Ethernet at the Data Link Layer

Ethernet at the Data Link layer is responsible for Ethernet addressing, commonly referred to as hardware addressing or MAC addressing. Ethernet is also responsible for framing packets received from the Network layer and preparing them for transmission on the local network through the Ethernet contention media access method. There are four different types of Ethernet frames available:

- Ethernet_II
- IEEE 802.3
- IEEE 802.2
- SNAP

I'll go over all four of the available Ethernet frames in the upcoming sections.

Ethernet Addressing

Here's where we get into how Ethernet addressing works. It uses the *Media Access Control (MAC) address* burned into each and every Ethernet Network Interface Card (NIC). The MAC, or hardware address, is a 48-bit (6 byte) address written in a hexadecimal format.

Figure 1.11 shows the 48-bit MAC addresses and how the bits are divided.

FIGURE 1.11 Ethernet addressing using MAC addresses

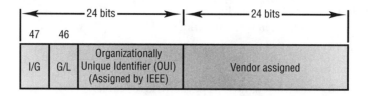

The *organizationally unique identifier (OUI)* is assigned by the IEEE to an organization. It's composed of 24 bits, or 3 bytes. The organization, in turn, assigns a globally administered address (24 bits, or 3 bytes) that is unique (supposedly, again—no guarantees) to each and every adapter they manufacture. Look closely at the figure. The high-order bit is the Individual/Group (I/G) bit. When it has a value of 0, we can assume that the address is actually the MAC address of a device and may well appear in the source portion of the MAC header. When it is a 1, we can assume that the address represents either a broadcast or multicast address in Ethernet, or a broadcast or functional address in TR and FDDI (who really knows about FDDI?). The next bit is the G/L bit (also known as U/L, where U means universal). When set to 0, this bit represents a globally administered address (as by the IEEE). When the bit is a 1, it represents an administratively locally governed address (as in DECnet). The low-order 24 bits of an Ethernet address represent a locally (if anything) administered or manufacturer-assigned code. This portion commonly starts with 24 0s for the first card made and continues in order until there are 24 1s for the last (16,777,216th) card made. You'll actually find that many manufacturers use these same six hex digits as the last six characters of their serial number on the same card.

Ethernet Frames

The Data Link layer is responsible for combining bits into bytes and bytes into frames. Frames are used at the Data Link layer to encapsulate packets handed down from the Network layer for transmission on a type of media access. There are three types of media access methods: contention (Ethernet), token passing (Token Ring and FDDI), and polling (IBM Mainframes and 100VG-AnyLAN).

The CCNA exam covers only Ethernet (contention) media access—so shall we.

The function of Ethernet stations is to pass data frames between each other using a group of bits known as a MAC frame format. This provides error detection from a cyclic redundancy check (CRC). But remember—this is error detection, not error correction. The 802.3 frames and Ethernet frame are shown in Figure 1.12.

The following details the different fields in the 802.3 and Ethernet frame types:

Preamble   An alternating 1,0 pattern provides a 5MHz clock at the start of each packet, which allows the receiving devices to lock the incoming bit stream. *Clock?*

Start Frame Delimiter (SFD)/Synch   The preamble is seven octets and the SFD is one octet (Synch). The SFD is 10101011, where the last pair of 1s allows the receiver to come into the alternating 1,0 pattern somewhere in the middle and still sync up and detect the beginning of the data.

FIGURE 1.12   802.3 and Ethernet frame formats

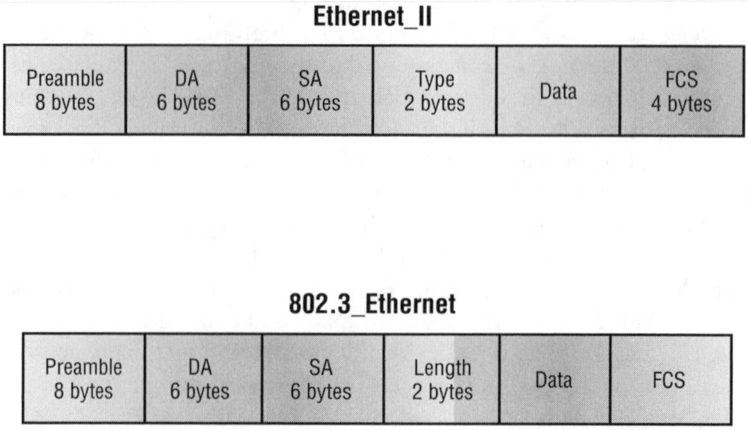

Ethernet_II

Preamble 8 bytes	DA 6 bytes	SA 6 bytes	Type 2 bytes	Data	FCS 4 bytes

802.3_Ethernet

Preamble 8 bytes	DA 6 bytes	SA 6 bytes	Length 2 bytes	Data	FCS

Destination Address (DA)   This transmits a 48-bit value using the least significant bit (LSB) first. The DA is used by receiving stations to determine whether an incoming packet is addressed to a particular node. The destination address can be an individual address, or a broadcast or multicast MAC address. Remember that a broadcast is all 1s (or Fs in hex) and is sent to all devices, but a multicast is sent only to a similar subset of nodes on a network.

> **NOTE**   Hex is short for hexadecimal, which is a numbering system that uses the first six letters of the alphabet (A through F) to extend beyond the available 10 digits in the decimal system. Hexadecimal has a total of 16 digits.

Source Address (SA)   The SA is a 48-bit MAC address used to identify the transmitting device, and it uses the LSB first. Broadcast and multicast address formats are illegal within the SA field.

Length or Type field   802.3 uses a Length field, but the Ethernet frame uses a Type field to identify the Network layer protocol. 802.3 cannot identify the upper-layer protocol and must be used with a proprietary LAN—IPX, for example.

Data   This is a packet sent down to the Data Link layer from the Network layer. The size can vary from 64 to 1500 bytes.

Frame Check Sequence (FCS)   FCS is a field at the end of the frame that's used to store the cyclic redundancy check (CRC).

Let's pause here for a minute and take a look at some frames caught on our trusty Etherpeek network analyzer. You can see that the frame below has only three fields: a Destination, Source, and Type (shown as Protocol Type on this analyzer) field:

```
Destination:    00:60:f5:00:1f:27
Source:         00:60:f5:00:1f:2c
Protocol Type: 08-00 IP
```

This is an Ethernet_II frame. Notice the type field is IP, or 08-00 in hexadecimal.

The next frame has the same fields, so it must be an Ethernet_II frame too:

```
Destination:    ff:ff:ff:ff:ff:ff Ethernet Broadcast
Source:         02:07:01:22:de:a4
Protocol Type: 81-37 NetWare
```

I included this one so you could see that the frame can carry more than just IP—it can also carry IPX, or 81-37h. Did you notice that this frame was a broadcast? You can tell because the destination hardware address is all 1s in binary, or all Fs in hexadecimal.

Now, pay special attention to the length field in the next frame; this must be an 802.3 frame:

```
Flags:          0x80 802.3
Status:         0x00
Packet Length: 64
Timestamp:      12:45:45.192000 06/26/1998
Destination:    ff:ff:ff:ff:ff:ff Ethernet Broadcast
Source:         08:00:11:07:57:28
Length:         34
```

The problem with this frame is this: How do you know which protocol this packet is going to be handed to at the Network layer? It doesn't specify in the frame, so it must be IPX. Why? Because when Novell created the 802.3 frame type (before the IEEE did and called it 802.3 Raw), Novell was pretty much the only LAN server out there. So, Novell assumed that if you were running a LAN, it must be IPX, and they didn't include any Network layer protocol field information in the 802.3 frame.

802.2 and SNAP

Since the 802.3 Ethernet frame cannot by itself identify the upper-layer (Network) protocol, it obviously needs some help. The IEEE defined the 802.2 LLC specifications to provide this function and more. Figure 1.13 shows the IEEE 802.3 with LLC (802.2) and the Subnetwork Access Protocol (SNAP) frame types.

Figure 1.13 shows how the LLC header information is added to the data portion of the frame. Now, let's take a look at an 802.2 frame and SNAP captured from our analyzer.

FIGURE 1.13 802.2 and SNAP

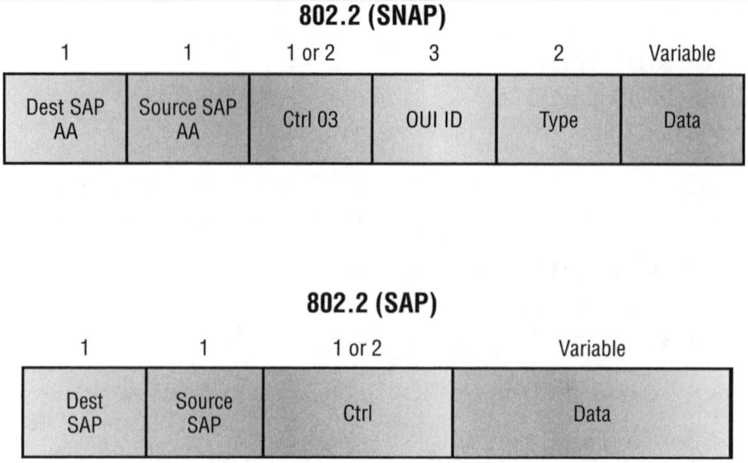

802.2 (SNAP)

1	1	1 or 2	3	2	Variable
Dest SAP AA	Source SAP AA	Ctrl 03	OUI ID	Type	Data

802.2 (SAP)

1	1	1 or 2	Variable
Dest SAP	Source SAP	Ctrl	Data

802.2 Frame

The following is an 802.2 frame captured with a protocol analyzer:

```
Flags:        0x80 802.3
Status:       0x02 Truncated
Packet Length:64
Slice Length: 51
Timestamp:    12:42:00.592000 03/26/1998
Destination:  ff:ff:ff:ff:ff:ff Ethernet Broadcast
Source:       00:80:c7:a8:f0:3d
LLC Length:   37
Dest. SAP:    0xe0 NetWare
Source SAP:   0xe0 NetWare Individual LLC
  SublayerManagement Function
Command:      0x03 Unnumbered Information
```

You can see that the first frame has a Length field, so it's probably an 802.3, right? Maybe. Look again. It also has a DSAP and an SSAP, so it's not an 802.3. It has to be an 802.2 frame. (Remember—an 802.2 frame is an 802.3 frame with the LLC information in the data field of the header so we know what the upper-layer protocol is.)

SNAP Frame

The SNAP frame has its own protocol field to identify the upper-layer protocol. This is really a way to allow an Ethernet_II Ether-Type field to be used in an 802.3 frame. Even though the following network trace shows a protocol field, it is actually an Ethernet_II type (Ether-Type) field:

```
Flags:          0x80 802.3
Status:         0x00
Packet Length:78
Timestamp:      09:32:48.264000 01/04/2000
802.3 Header
 Destination:   09:00:07:FF:FF:FF AT Ph 2 Broadcast
 Source:        00:00:86:10:C1:6F
 LLC Length:    60
802.2 Logical Link Control (LLC) Header
 Dest. SAP:     0xAA SNAP
 Source SAP:    0xAA SNAP
 Command:       0x03 Unnumbered Information
 Protocol:      0x080007809B AppleTalk
```

You can identify a SNAP frame because the DSAP and SSAP fields are always AA, and the Command field is always 3. This frame type was created because not all protocols worked well with the 802.3 Ethernet frame, which didn't have an Ether-Type field. To allow the proprietary protocols created by application developers to be used in the LLC frame, the IEEE defined the SNAP format that uses the exact same codes as Ethernet_II. Up until about 1997 or so, the SNAP frame was on its way out of the corporate market. However, the new 802.11 wireless LAN specification uses an Ethernet SNAP field to identify the Network layer protocol. Cisco also still uses a SNAP frame with their proprietary protocol Cisco Discovery Protocol (CDP)—something I'm going to talk about in Chapter 9, "Managing a Cisco Internetwork."

Ethernet at the Physical Layer

Ethernet was first implemented by a group called DIX (Digital, Intel, and Xerox). They created and implemented the first Ethernet LAN specification, which the IEEE used to create the IEEE 802.3 Committee. This was a 10Mbps network that ran on coax, and then eventually twisted-pair, and fiber physical media.

The IEEE extended the 802.3 Committee to two new committees known as 802.3u (FastEthernet) and 802.3ab (Gigabit Ethernet on Category 5) and then finally 802.3ae (10Gbps over fiber and coax).

Figure 1.14 shows the IEEE 802.3 and original Ethernet Physical layer specifications.

When designing your LAN, it's really important to understand the different types of Ethernet media available to you. Sure, it would be great to run Gigabit Ethernet to each desktop and 10Gbps between switches, and although this might happen one day, justifying the cost of that network today would be pretty difficult. But if you mix and match the different types of Ethernet media methods available today, you can come up with a cost-effective network solution that works great.

FIGURE 1.14 Ethernet Physical layer specifications

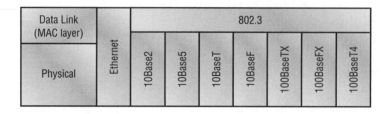

The EIA/TIA (Electronic Industries Association and the newer Telecommunications Industry Alliance) is the standards body that creates the Physical layer specifications for Ethernet. The EIA/TIA specifies that Ethernet uses a *registered jack (RJ) connector* with a 4 5 wiring sequence on *unshielded twisted-pair (UTP)* cabling (RJ-45). However, the industry is moving toward calling this just an 8-pin modular connector.

Each Ethernet cable type that is specified by the EIA/TIA has inherent attenuation, which is defined as the loss of signal strength as it travels the length of a cable and is measured in decibels (dB). The cabling used in corporate and home markets is measured in categories. A higher quality cable will have a higher rated category and lower attenuation. For example, category 5 is better than category 3 because category 5 cable has more wire twists per foot and therefore less crosstalk. Crosstalk is the unwanted signal interference from adjacent pairs in the cable.

Near End Crosstalk (NEXT) is crosstalk measured at the transmitting end of the cable. Far End Crosstalk (FEXT) is measured at the far end from where the signal was injected into the cable. Power Sum NEXT (PSNEXT) is basically a mathematical calculation that simulates all four pairs being energized at the same time. PSNEXT calculations are used to ensure that a cable will not exceed crosstalk noise performance requirements when all pairs are operating simultaneously. PSNEXT is typically used in Gigabit Ethernet, rather than 10BaseT or 100BaseT.

Here are the original IEEE 802.3 standards:

10Base2　10Mbps, baseband technology, up to 185 meters in length. Known as *thinnet* and can support up to 30 workstations on a single segment. Uses a physical and logical bus with AUI connectors. The 10 means 10Mbps, Base means baseband technology, and the 2 means almost 200 meters.10Base2 Ethernet cards use BNC (British Naval Connector, Bayonet Neill Concelman, or Bayonet Nut Connector) and T-connectors to connect to a network.

10Base5　10Mbps, baseband technology, up to 500 meters in length. Known as *thicknet*. Uses a physical and logical bus with AUI connectors. Up to 2500 meters with repeaters and 1024 users for all segments.

10BaseT　10Mbps using Category 3 UTP wiring. Unlike the 10Base2 and 10Base5 networks, each device must connect into a hub or switch, and you can only have one host per segment or wire. Uses an RJ-45 connector (8-pin modular connector) with a physical star topology and a logical bus.

The "Base" in the preceding network standards means "baseband," which is a signaling method for communication on the network.

Each of the 802.3 standards defines an Attachment Unit Interface (AUI), which allows a one-bit-at-a-time transfer to the Physical layer from the Data Link media access method. This allows the MAC to remain constant but means the Physical layer can support any existing and new technologies. The original AUI interface was a 15-pin connector, which allowed a transceiver (transmitter/receiver) that provided a 15-pin–to–twisted-pair conversion.

The thing is, the AUI interface cannot support 100Mbps Ethernet because of the high frequencies involved. So 100BaseT needed a new interface, and the 802.3U specifications created one called the Media Independent Interface (MII), which provides 100Mbps throughput. The MII uses a *nibble*, defined as 4 bits. Gigabit Ethernet uses a Gigabit Media Independent Interface (GMII) and is 8 bits at a time.

802.3u (FastEthernet) is compatible with 802.3 Ethernet because they share the same physical characteristics. FastEthernet and Ethernet use the same maximum transmission unit (MTU), same Media Access Control (MAC) mechanisms, and preserve the frame format that is used by 10BaseT Ethernet. Basically, FastEthernet is just based on an extension to the IEEE 802.3 specification, except that it offers a speed increase of 10 times that of 10BaseT.

Here are the expanded IEEE Ethernet 802.3 standards:

100BaseTX   EIA/TIA Category 5, 6, or 7 UTP two-pair wiring. One user per segment; up to 100 meters long. It uses an RJ-45 connector with a physical star topology and a logical bus.

100BaseFX   Uses fiber cabling 62.5/125-micron multimode fiber. Point-to-point topology; up to 412 meters long. It uses an ST or SC connector, which are media-interface connectors.

1000BaseCX   Copper twisted-pair called twinax (a balanced coaxial pair) that can only run up to 25 meters.

1000BaseT   Category 5, four-pair UTP wiring up to 100 meters long.

1000BaseSX   MMF using 62.5 and 50-micron core; uses a 850nano-meter laser and can go up to 220 meters with 62.5-micron, 550 meters with 50-micron.

1000BaseLX   Single-mode fiber that uses a 9-micron core and 1300nano-meter laser, and can go from 3 kilometers up to 10 kilometers.

100VG-AnyLAN is a twisted-pair technology that was the first 100Mbps LAN. But since it was incompatible with Ethernet signaling techniques (it used a demand priority access method), it wasn't very popular, and is now essentially dead.

Ethernet Cabling

Ethernet cabling is an important discussion, especially if you are planning on taking the Cisco CCNA exam. The types of Ethernet cables available are:

- Straight-through cable
- Crossover cable
- Rolled cable

We will look at each in the following sections.

 If you're studying for your CCNA exam, you'd better know your Ethernet cabling types!

Straight-Through Cable

The *straight-through cable* is used to connect:

- Host to switch or hub
- Router to switch or hub

Four wires are used in straight-through cable to connect Ethernet devices. It is relatively simple to create this type; Figure 1.15 shows the four wires used in a straight-through Ethernet cable.

FIGURE 1.15 Straight-through Ethernet cable

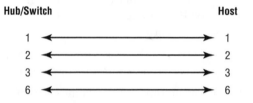

Notice that only pins 1, 2, 3, and 6 are used. Just connect 1 to 1, 2 to 2, 3 to 3, and 6 to 6, and you'll be up and networking in no time. However, remember that this would be an Ethernet-only cable and wouldn't work with Voice, Token Ring, ISDN, etc.

Crossover Cable

The *crossover cable* can be used to connect:

- Switch to switch
- Hub to hub
- Host to host
- Hub to switch
- Router direct to host

The same four wires are used in this cable as in the straight-through cable, but we just connect different pins together. Figure 1.16 shows how the four wires are used in a crossover Ethernet cable.

Notice that instead of connecting 1 to 1, etc., here we connect pins 1 to 3 and 2 to 6 on each side of the cable.

FIGURE 1.16 Crossover Ethernet cable

Rolled Cable

Although *rolled cable* isn't used to connect any Ethernet connections together, you can use a rolled Ethernet cable to connect a host to a router console serial communication (com) port.

If you have a Cisco router or switch, you would use this cable to connect your PC running Hyper-Terminal to the Cisco hardware. Eight wires are used in this cable to connect serial devices, although not all eight are used to send information, just as in Ethernet networking. Figure 1.17 shows the eight wires used in a rolled cable.

FIGURE 1.17   Rolled Ethernet cable

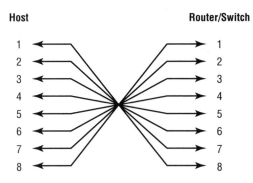

These are probably the easiest cables to make, because you just cut the end off on one side of a straight-through cable and reverse the end.

Once you have the correct cable connected from your PC to the Cisco router or switch, you can start HyperTerminal to create a console connection and configure the device. Set the configuration as follows:

1.   Open HyperTerminal and enter a name for the connection. It is irrelevant what you name it, but I always just use "Cisco." Then click OK.

2. Choose the communications port—either COM1 or COM2, whichever is open on your PC.

3. Now set the port settings. The default values (2400bps and no flow control) will not work; you must set the port settings as shown in Figure 1.18.

FIGURE 1.18 Port settings for a rolled cable connection

Notice that the bit rate is now set to 9600 and the flow control is set to none. At this point, you can click OK and press the Enter key, and you should be connected to your Cisco device console port.

Wireless Networking

No book on this subject today would be complete without mentioning wireless networking. That's because two years ago, it just wasn't all that common to find people using this technology—in 1996, a lot of people didn't even have an email address. Oh yeah—sure, some did, but now everyone does, and the same thing is happening in the wireless world. That's because wireless networking is just way too convenient not to use. I'm betting that some of you reading this probably have a wireless network at home. If not, you probably do at work. I do! For this reason, I'm now going to go over the various types of wireless networks as well as their speeds and distance limitations. Figure 1.19 shows some of the most popular types of wireless networks in use today (These are the ones you need to know for the new CCNA exam):

FIGURE 1.19 Wireless Networks

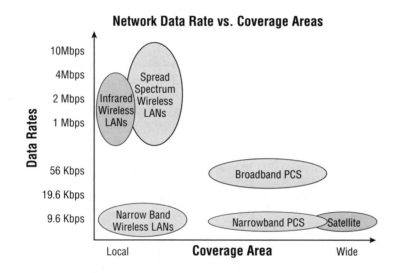

Okay, let's discuss these various types of wireless networks plus the speed and distance of each one.

Narrowband Wireless LANs Narrowband radio does as it's name suggests—it keeps the radio signal frequency as narrow as it possibly can and still be able to pass the information along. The problem of interference is avoided by directing different users onto different channel frequencies. The distance you get is decent, but the speeds available today just aren't adequate enough for corporate users. Plus, you've also got to have proprietary equipment to run it on, as well as buy an FCC license to run the frequency at each site!

Personal Communication Services (PCS) Personal Communication Service (PCS) includes a whole bunch of mobile, portable and auxiliary communications services for individuals and businesses. The Federal Communication Commission (FCC) roughly defined PCS as mobile and fixed communications options for both individuals and businesses that can be incorporated with various kinds of competing networks. Narrowband or broadband PCS is what's used today.

Narrowband PCS Again as the name implies, the narrowband PCS flavor requires a smaller serving size of the spectrum than broadband PCS does. With licenses for narrowband PCS, you get to access services like two-way paging and/or text-based messaging. Think about people with PDAs and keyboard attachments, etc. getting and sending wireless email—these subscribers are able to do this via microwave signals. With narrowband PCS you can also access cool services like wireless telemetry—the monitoring of mobile or stationary equipment remotely. Doing things like remotely monitoring utility meters of energy companies, commonly know as automatic meter reading, or AMR is accomplished using this technology.

Broadband PCS   Broadband Personal Communications Service (PCS) is used for a many kinds of wireless services—both mobile and fixed radio. The mobile broadband set includes both the voice and advanced two-way data features usually available to us via small, mobile, multifunction devices like digital camera/cell phones, etc. In the industry, these services are commonly referred to as Mobile Telephone Services and Mobile Data Services. Sources of these services include companies that rule huge amounts of broadband PCS spectrum like AT&T Wireless, Verizon and Sprint PCS.

Satellite   With satellite services, the speed you get is sweet—it's up to around 1Mbps upload and 2Mpbs download! But there's an annoying delay when connecting, so it doesn't work very well when you're dealing with bursty traffic. The good news is that speeds are increasing, but even so, they just can't compete with what you get via Wireless LAN's. The real upside to using a satellite-based network is that its geographic coverage area can be huge.

Infrared Wireless LAN's   Here we have pretty much the opposite. This technology works really well handling short, bursty traffic in the Personal Area Network (PAN) sector. And the speeds are increasing too, but the available range is still very short. It's commonly used for laptop-to-laptop and laptop to PDA transfers. The speed range we usually get is anywhere from 115kbps to 4Mbps, but a new specification called Very Fast Infrared (VFIR) says we'll see speeds up to 16Mbps in the future—we'll see!

Spread Spectrum Wireless LAN's   Your typical wireless LANs (WLANs) uses something called spread spectrum. It's a wideband radio frequency technique that the military came up with that's both reliable, and secure (that's debatable). The most popular WLAN in use today is 802.11b that runs up to 11Mbps, but the new 802.11g specifications can bump that figure up to around 22Mbps and more, depending on who made your equipment. Plus, the new 802.11a lives in the 5Ghz range and can run bandwidth around 50Mbps—and it's pledging over 100Mbps in the near future! But the distance is still less than what you get with the 802.11b and 802.11g 2.4Ghz range models (which is about 300 feet or so). So basically, you usually find 802.11b/g used indoors, and 802.11a in the shorter-distance outdoor market when more bandwidth is needed—but the market is still young and who knows what the future holds for these up and coming WLAN's.

Data Encapsulation

When a host transmits data across a network to another device, the data goes through *encapsulation:* it is wrapped with protocol information at each layer of the OSI model. Each layer communicates only with its peer layer on the receiving device.

To communicate and exchange information, each layer uses *Protocol Data Units (PDUs)*. These hold the control information attached to the data at each layer of the model. They are usually attached to the header in front of the data field but can also be in the trailer, or end, of it.

Each PDU is attached to the data by encapsulating it at each layer of the OSI model, and each has a specific name depending on the information provided in each header. This PDU information is read only by the peer layer on the receiving device. After it's read, it's stripped off, and the data is then handed to the next layer up.

Figure 1.20 shows the PDUs and how they attach control information to each layer. This figure demonstrates how the upper-layer user data is converted for transmission on the network. The data stream is then handed down to the Transport layer, which sets up a virtual circuit to the receiving device by sending over a synch packet. The data stream is then broken up into smaller pieces, and a Transport layer header (a PDU) is created and attached to the header of the data field; now the piece of data is called a segment. Each segment is sequenced so the data stream can be put back together on the receiving side exactly as it was transmitted.

FIGURE 1.20   Data encapsulation

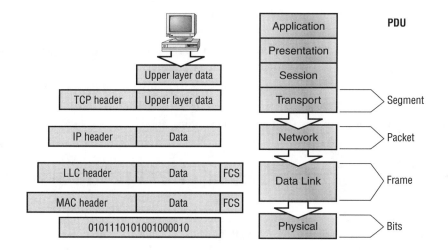

Each segment is then handed to the Network layer for network addressing and routing through the internetwork. Logical addressing (for example, IP) is used to get each segment to the correct network. The Network layer protocol adds a control header to the segment handed down from the Transport layer, and what we have now is called a *packet* or *datagram*. Remember that the Transport and Network layers work together to rebuild a data stream on a receiving host, but it's not part of their work to place their PDUs on a local network segment—which is the only way to get the information to a router or host.

It's the Data Link layer that's responsible for taking packets from the Network layer and placing them on the network medium (cable or wireless). The Data Link layer encapsulates each packet in a *frame*, and the frame's header carries the hardware address of the source and destination hosts. If the destination device is on a remote network, then the frame is sent to a router to be routed through an internetwork. Once it gets to the destination network, a new frame is used to get the packet to the destination host.

To put this frame on the network, it must first be put into a digital signal. Since a frame is really a logical group of 1s and 0s, the Physical layer is responsible for encoding these digits into a digital signal, which is read by devices on the same local network. The receiving devices will synchronize on the digital signal and extract (decode) the ones and zeros from the digital signal. At this point the devices build the frames, run a cyclic redundancy check (CRC), and then check their answer against the answer in the frame's FCS field. If it matches, the packet is pulled from the frame, and what's left of the frame is discarded. This process is called *de-encapsulation*. The packet is handed to the Network layer, where the address is checked. If the address matches, the segment is pulled from the packet, and what's left of the packet is discarded. The segment is processed at the Transport layer, which rebuilds the data stream and acknowledges to the transmitting station that it received each piece. It then happily hands the data stream to the upper-layer application.

At a transmitting device, the data encapsulation method works like this:

1. User information is converted to data for transmission on the network.

2. Data is converted to segments and a reliable connection is set up between the transmitting and receiving hosts.

3. Segments are converted to packets or datagrams, and a logical address is placed in the header so each packet can be routed through an internetwork.

4. Packets or datagrams are converted to frames for transmission on the local network. Hardware (Ethernet) addresses are used to uniquely identify hosts on a local network segment.

5. Frames are converted to bits, and a digital encoding and clocking scheme is used.

The Cisco Three-Layer Hierarchical Model

Most of us were exposed to hierarchy early in life. Anyone with older siblings learned what it was like to be at the bottom of the hierarchy. Regardless of where you first discovered hierarchy, today most of us experience it in many aspects of our lives. It is *hierarchy* that helps us understand where things belong, how things fit together, and what functions go where. It brings order and understandability to otherwise complex models. If you want a pay raise, for instance, hierarchy dictates that you ask your boss, not your subordinate. That is the person whose role it is to grant (or deny) your request. So basically, understanding hierarchy helps us discern where we should go to get what we need.

Hierarchy has many of the same benefits in network design that it does in other areas of life. When used properly, it makes networks more predictable. It helps us define which areas should perform certain functions. Likewise, you can use tools such as access lists at certain levels in hierarchical networks and avoid them at others.

Let's face it, large networks can be extremely complicated, with multiple protocols, detailed configurations, and diverse technologies. Hierarchy helps us summarize a complex collection of details into an understandable model. Then, as specific configurations are needed, the model dictates the appropriate manner to apply them.

The Cisco hierarchical model can help you design, implement, and maintain a scalable, reliable, cost-effective hierarchical internetwork. Cisco defines three layers of hierarchy, as shown in Figure 1.21, each with specific functions.

FIGURE 1.21   The Cisco hierarchical model

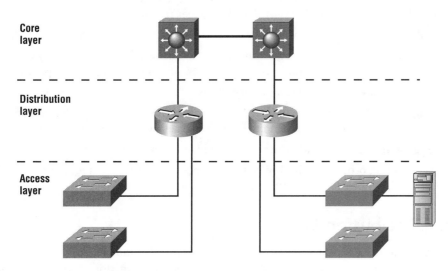

The following are the three layers and their typical functions:

- The core layer: Backbone
- The distribution layer: Routing
- The access layer: Switching

Each layer has specific responsibilities. Remember, however, that the three layers are logical and are not necessarily physical devices. Consider the OSI model, another logical hierarchy. The seven layers describe functions but not necessarily protocols, right? Sometimes a protocol maps to more than one layer of the OSI model, and sometimes multiple protocols communicate within a single layer. In the same way, when we build physical implementations of hierarchical networks, we may have many devices in a single layer, or we might have a single device performing functions at two layers. The definition of the layers is logical, not physical.

Now, let's take a closer look at each of the layers.

The Core Layer

The *core layer* is literally the core of the network. At the top of the hierarchy, the core layer is responsible for transporting large amounts of traffic both reliably and quickly. The only purpose of the network's core layer is to switch traffic as fast as possible. The traffic transported across the core is common to a majority of users. However, remember that user data is processed at the distribution layer, which forwards the requests to the core if needed.

If there is a failure in the core, *every single user* can be affected. Therefore, fault tolerance at this layer is an issue. The core is likely to see large volumes of traffic, so speed and latency are driving concerns here. Given the function of the core, we can now consider some design specifics. Let's start with some things we don't want to do:

- Don't do anything to slow down traffic. This includes using access lists, routing between virtual local area networks (VLANs), and packet filtering.

- Don't support workgroup access here.

- Avoid expanding the core (i.e., adding routers) when the internetwork grows. If performance becomes an issue in the core, give preference to upgrades over expansion.

Now, there are a few things that we want to do as we design the core. They include the following:

- Design the core for high reliability. Consider data-link technologies that facilitate both speed and redundancy, such as FDDI, Fast Ethernet (with redundant links), or even ATM.

- Design with speed in mind. The core should have very little latency.

- Select routing protocols with lower convergence times. Fast and redundant data-link connectivity is no help if your routing tables are shot!

The Distribution Layer

The *distribution layer* is sometimes referred to as the *workgroup layer* and is the communication point between the access layer and the core. The primary functions of the distribution layer are to provide routing, filtering, and WAN access and to determine how packets can access the core, if needed. The distribution layer must determine the fastest way that network service requests are handled—for example, how a file request is forwarded to a server. After the distribution layer determines the best path, it forwards the request to the core layer if needed. The core layer then quickly transports the request to the correct service.

The distribution layer is the place to implement policies for the network. Here you can exercise considerable flexibility in defining network operation. There are several actions that generally should be done at the distribution layer. They include the following:

- Routing

- Implementation of tools such as access lists, of packet filtering, and of queuing

- Implementation of security and network policies, including address translation and firewalls

- Redistribution between routing protocols, including static routing

- Routing between VLANs and other workgroup support functions

- Definitions of broadcast and multicast domains

Things to avoid at the distribution layer are limited to those functions that exclusively belong to one of the other layers.

The Access Layer

The *access layer* controls user and workgroup access to internetwork resources. The access layer is sometimes referred to as the *desktop layer*. The network resources most users need will be available locally. The distribution layer handles any traffic for remote services. The following are some of the functions to be included at the access layer:

- Continued (from distribution layer) access control and policies
- Creation of separate collision domains (segmentation)
- Workgroup connectivity into the distribution layer

Technologies such as DDR and Ethernet switching are frequently seen in the access layer. Static routing (instead of dynamic routing protocols) is seen here as well.

As already noted, three separate levels does not imply three separate routers. There could be fewer, or there could be more. Remember, this is a *layered* approach.

Summary

Phew! I know this seemed like the chapter that wouldn't end, but it did—and you made it! You're now armed with a ton of fundamental information; you're ready to build upon it, and well on your way to certification.

This chapter began with a discussion of the OSI model—the seven-layer model used to help application developers design applications that can run on any type of system or network. Each layer has its special jobs and select responsibilities within the model to ensure that solid, effective communications do, in fact, occur. I provided you with complete details of each layer and discussed how Cisco views the specifications of the OSI model.

In addition, each layer in the OSI model specifies different types of devices. I described the different types of devices, cables, and connectors used at each layer. Remember that hubs are Physical layer devices and repeat the digital signal to all segments except the one it was received from. Switches segment the network using hardware addresses and break up collision domains. Routers break up broadcast domains (and collision domains) and use logical addressing to send packets through an internetwork.

Lastly, this chapter covered the Cisco three-layer hierarchical model. I described in detail the three layers and how each is used to help design and implement a Cisco internetwork. We are now going to move on to IP addressing in the next chapter.

Exam Essentials

Remember the possible causes of LAN traffic congestion.   Too many hosts in a broadcast domain, broadcast storms, multicasting, and low bandwidth are all possible causes of LAN traffic congestion.

Understand the difference between a collision domain and a broadcast domain.   A collision domain is an Ethernet term used to describe a network collection of devices in which one particular device sends a packet on a network segment, forcing every other device on that same segment to pay attention to it. A broadcast domain is where a set of all devices on a network segment hear all broadcasts sent on that segment.

Understand the difference between a hub, a bridge, a switch, and a router.   Hubs create one collision domain and one broadcast domain. Bridges break up collision domains but create one large broadcast domain. They use hardware addresses to filter the network. Switches are really just multiple port bridges with more intelligence. They break up collision domains but create one large broadcast domain by default. Switches use hardware addresses to filter the network. Routers break up broadcast domains (and collision domains) and use logical addressing to filter the network.

Remember the Presentation layer protocols.   PICT, TIFF, JPEG, MIDI, MPEG, QuickTime, and RTF are examples of Presentation layer protocols.

Remember the difference between connection-oriented and connectionless network services.   Connection-oriented uses acknowledgments and flow control to create a reliable session. More overhead is used than in a connectionless network service. Connectionless services are used to send data with no acknowledgments or flow control. This is considered unreliable.

Remember the OSI layers.   You must remember the seven layers of the OSI model and what function each layer provides. The Application, Presentation, and Session layers are upper layers and are responsible for communicating from a user interface to an application. The Transport layer provides segmentation, sequencing, and virtual circuits. The Network layer provides logical network addressing and routing through an internetwork. The Data Link layer provides framing and placing of data on the network medium. The Physical layer is responsible for taking ones and zeros and encoding them into a digital signal for transmission on the network segment.

Remember the types of Ethernet cabling and when you would use them.   The three types of cables that can be created from an Ethernet cable are: straight-through (to connect a PC's or a router's Ethernet interface to a hub or switch), crossover (to connect hub to hub, hub to switch, switch to switch, or PC to PC), and rolled (for a console connection from a PC to a router or switch).

Understand how to connect a console cable from a PC to a router and start HyperTerminal.   Take a rolled cable and connect it from the COM port of the host to the console port of a router. Start HyperTerminal and set the BPS to 9600 and flow control to None.

Remember the three layers in the Cisco three-layer model.   The three layers in the Cisco hierarchical model are the core, distribution, and access layers.

Key Terms

Before you take the exam, be certain you are familiar with the following terms:

access layer	layers
Application layer	Media Access Control (MAC) address
application-specific integrated circuit (ASIC)	media translation
auto-detect mechanism	Network layer
binding	network segmentation
bridges	nibble
broadcast domain	Open Systems Interconnection (OSI) reference model
buffer	organizationally unique identifier (OUI)
call setup	packet
Carrier Sense Multiple Access with Collision Detection (CSMA/CD)	Physical layer
channel service unit/data service unit (CSU/DSU)	positive acknowledgment with retransmission
collision domains	Presentation layer
core layer	Protocol Data Units (PDUs)
crossover cable	reference model
data communication equipment (DCE)	registered jack (RJ) connector
data frame	rolled cable
Data Link layer	routed protocols
data terminal equipment (DTE)	routers
datagram	Session layer
de-encapsulation	simplex
desktop layer	state transitions
distribution layer	straight-through cable
encapsulation	switches
Ethernet	thicknet

flow control   thinnet

frame   three-way handshake

full duplex   transparent bridging

half duplex   Transport layer

hierarchy   tunneling

hop count   unshielded twisted-pair (UTP)

hub   window

layered architecture   workgroup layer

Written Lab 1

In this section, you'll complete the following labs to make sure you've got the information and concepts contained within them fully dialed in:

- Lab 1.1: OSI Questions
- Lab 1.2: Defining the OSI Layers and Devices
- Lab 1.3: Identifying Collision and Broadcast Domains

Written Lab 1.1: OSI Questions

Answer the following questions about the OSI model:

1. Which layer chooses and determines the availability of communicating partners, along with the resources necessary to make the connection; coordinates partnering applications; and forms a consensus on procedures for controlling data integrity and error recovery?

2. Which layer is responsible for converting data packets from the Data Link layer into electrical signals?

3. At which layer is routing implemented, enabling connections and path selection between two end systems?

4. Which layer defines how data is formatted, presented, encoded, and converted for use on the network?

5. Which layer is responsible for creating, managing, and terminating sessions between applications?

6. Which layer ensures the trustworthy transmission of data across a physical link and is primarily concerned with physical addressing, line discipline, network topology, error notification, ordered delivery of frames, and flow control?

7. Which layer is used for reliable communication between end nodes over the network and provides mechanisms for establishing, maintaining, and terminating virtual circuits; transport-fault detection and recovery; and controlling the flow of information?

8. Which layer provides logical addressing that routers will use for path determination?

9. Which layer specifies voltage, wire speed, and pinout cables and moves bits between devices?

10. Which layer combines bits into bytes and bytes into frames, uses MAC addressing, and provides error detection?

11. Which layer is responsible for keeping the data from different applications separate on the network?

12. Which layer is represented by frames?

13. Which layer is represented by segments?

14. Which layer is represented by packets?

15. Which layer is represented by bits?

16. Put the following in order of encapsulation:
    - Packets
    - Frames
    - Bits
    - Segments

17. Which layer segments and reassembles data into a data stream?

18. Which layer provides the physical transmission of the data and handles error notification, network topology, and flow control?

19. Which layer manages device addressing, tracks the location of devices on the network, and determines the best way to move data?

20. What is the bit length and expression form of a MAC address?

Written Lab 1.2: Defining the OSI Layers and Devices

Fill in the blanks with the appropriate layer of the OSI or hub, switch, or router device.

Description	Device or OSI Layer
This device sends and receives information about the Network layer.	
This layer creates a virtual circuit before transmitting between two end stations.	
This layer uses service access points.	
This device uses hardware addresses to filter a network.	
Ethernet is defined at these layers.	

This layer supports flow control and sequencing.

This device can measure the distance to a remote network.

Logical addressing is used at this layer.

Hardware addresses are defined at this layer.

This device creates one big collision domain and one large broadcast domain.

This device creates many smaller collision domains, but the network is still one large broadcast domain.

This device breaks up collision domains and broadcast domains.

Written Lab 1.3: Identifying Collision and Broadcast Domains

In the following exhibit, identify the number of collision domains and broadcast domains in each specified device. Each device is represented by a letter:

1. Hub
2. Bridge
3. Switch
4. Router

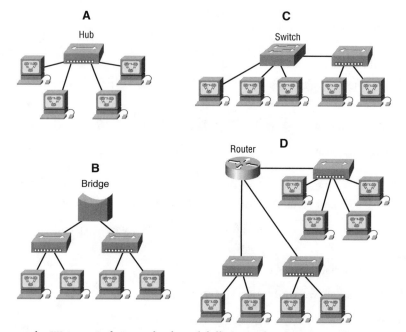

(The answers to the Written Lab 1 can be found following the answers to the Review Questions for this chapter.)

Review Questions

1. PDUs at the Network layer of the OSI are called what?

    A. Transport

    B. Frames

    C. Packets

    D. Segments

2. Which two statements about a reliable connection-oriented data transfer are true?

    A. Receiving hosts acknowledge receipt of data.

    B. When buffers are full, packets are discarded and are not retransmitted.

    C. Windowing is used to provide flow control and unacknowledged data segments.

    D. If the transmitting host's timer expires before receipt of an acknowledgment, the transmitting host drops the virtual circuit.

3. PDUs at the Data Link layer are named what?

    A. Transport

    B. Frames

    C. Packets

    D. Segments

4. Segmentation of a data stream happens at which layer of the OSI model?

    A. Physical

    B. Data Link

    C. Network

    D. Transport

5. You want to install a Wireless network in your corporate office, and need good speed but not more then about 250 feet of range. Which of the following wireless technologies should you install?

    A. Narrowband

    B. Narrowband PCS

    C. Broadband PCS

    D. Infrared

    E. Spread Spectrum

6. Which layer of the OSI provides translation of data?

   A. Application

   B. Presentation

   C. Session

   D. Transport

   E. Data Link

7. When data is encapsulated, which is the correct order?

   A. Data, frame, packet, segment, bit

   B. Segment, data, packet, frame, bit

   C. Data, segment, packet, frame, bit

   D. Data, segment, frame, packet, bit

8. Which of the following is not an advantage of a layered model?

   A. Allows multiple-vendor development through standardization of network components

   B. Allows various types of network hardware and software to communicate

   C. Allows changes to occur in all layers without having to change just one layer

   D. Prevents changes in one layer from affecting other layers, so it does not hamper development

9. What are two purposes for segmentation with a bridge?

   A. Add more broadcast domains.

   B. Create more collision domains.

   C. Add more bandwidth for users.

   D. Allow more broadcasts for users.

10. What does the term "Base" indicate in 100BaseTX?

    A. The maximum distance

    B. The type of wiring used

    C. A LAN switch method using half duplex

    D. A signaling method for communication on the network

11. What is the maximum distance of 100BaseT?

    A. 100 feet

    B. 1000 feet

    C. 100 meters

    D. 1000 meters

12. Which of the following would describe a Transport layer connection that would ensure reliable delivery?

   A. Routing

   B. Acknowledgments

   C. Switching

   D. System authentication

13. What are two reasons to segment a network with a bridge?

   A. Increase the amount of collision on a segment.

   B. Decrease the amount of broadcast on a segment.

   C. Reduce collisions within a broadcast domain.

   D. Increase the number of collision domains.

14. Which of the following types of connections can use full duplex? (Choose three options.)

   A. Hub to hub

   B. Switch to switch

   C. Host to host

   D. Switch to hub

   E. Switch to host

15. Which of the following are Presentation layer protocols? (Choose three options.)

   A. TFTP

   B. IP

   C. RTF

   D. QuickTime

   E. MIDI

16. Which of the following are considered some reasons for LAN congestion? (Choose three options.)

   A. Bill Gates

   B. Low bandwidth

   C. Too many users in a broadcast domain

   D. Broadcast storms

   E. Routers

   F. Multicasting

   G. Any Cisco competitor

17. Which of the following are reasons for breaking up a network into two segments with a router? (Choose two.)

A. To create fewer broadcast domains

B. To create more broadcast domains

C. To create one large broadcast domain

D. To stop one segment's broadcasts from being sent to the second segment

18. How do you connect to a router using HyperTerminal?

A. Connect the Ethernet port of your host to the Ethernet interface of the router using a rolled cable.

B. Connect the COM port of your host to the Ethernet port of your router using a straight-through cable.

C. Connect the Ethernet port of your host to the console port of the router using a rolled cable.

D. Connect the COM port of your host to the console port of the router using a crossover cable.

E. Connect the COM port of your host to the console port of the router using a rolled cable.

19. You want to use full-duplex Ethernet instead of half duplex. Which two of the following will be benefits on your network?

A. You will have more collision domains.

B. You'll have no collisions on each segment.

C. It should be faster.

D. It will be less expensive.

20. What is a reason you want to use switches in your network instead of hubs?

A. They are less expensive.

B. Switches are faster than hubs at reading frames.

C. Switches create more collision domains.

D. Switches do not forward broadcasts.

Answers to Review Questions

1. C. Protocol Data Units are used to define data at each layer of the OSI model. PDUs at the Network layer are called packets.

2. A, C. When a virtual circuit is created, windowing is used for flow control and acknowledgment of data.

3. B. Data is encapsulated with a media access method at the Data Link layer, and the Protocol Data Unit (PDU) is called a frame.

4. D. The Transport layer receives large data streams from the upper layers and breaks these up into smaller pieces called segments.

5. E. Spread spectrum LANs typically can run up to 11Mbps for about 300 feet depending on the environment, although the speeds are increasing to 20Mbps or higher.

6. B. The only layer of the OSI model that can actually change data is the Presentation layer.

7. C. The encapsulation method is: data, segment, packet, frame, bit.

8. C. The largest advantage of a layered model is that it can allow application developers to change the aspects of a program in just one layer of the layer model's specifications.

9. B, C. Bridges break up collision domains, which allows more bandwidth for users.

10. D. *Baseband* signaling is a technique that uses the entire bandwidth of a wire when transmitting. Broadband wiring uses many signals at the same time on a wire. These are both considered Ethernet signaling types.

11. C. 10BaseT and 100BaseT have a distance limitation of 100 meters.

12. B. A reliable Transport layer connection uses acknowledgments to make sure all data is transmitted and received reliably.

13. C, D. Bridges increase the number of collision domains in a network, which provides more bandwidth per user, which means less collision on a LAN.

14. B, C, E. Hubs cannot run full-duplex Ethernet. Full duplex must be used on a point-to-point connection between two devices capable of running full duplex. Switches and hosts can run full duplex between each other.

15. C, D, E. The Presentation layer defines many protocols; RTF, QuickTime, and MIDI are correct answers. IP is a Network layer protocol; TFTP is an Application layer protocol.

16. B, C, D, F. Although, Bill Gates is a good answer for me, and Cisco probably would like the last option, the answers are: not enough bandwidth, too many users, broadcast storms, and multicasting.

17. B, D. Routers, by default, break up broadcast domains, which means that broadcasts sent on one network would not be forwarded to another network by the router.

18. E. From a COM port of a PC or other host, connect a rolled cable to the console port of the router, start HyperTerminal, set the BPS to 9600 and flow control to None, then press Enter to connect.

19. B, C. No collision on a point-to-point full-duplex Ethernet segment should occur, and full-duplex Ethernet should be faster then half-duplex Ethernet.

20. C. Switches, which are really multiple-port bridges, break up collision domains on each port.

Answers to Written Lab 1

Answers to Written Lab 1.1

1. The Application layer is responsible for finding the network resources broadcast from a server and adding flow control and error control (if the application developer chooses).

2. The Physical layer takes frames from the Data Link layer and encodes the ones and zeros into a digital signal for transmission on the network medium.

3. The Network layer provides routing through an internetwork and logical addressing.

4. The Presentation layer makes sure that data is in a readable format for the Application layer.

5. The Session layer sets up, maintains, and terminates sessions between applications.

6. PDUs at the Data Link layer are called frames. As soon as you see "frame" in a question, you know the answer.

7. The Transport layer uses virtual circuits to create a reliable connection between two hosts.

8. The Network layer provides logical addressing, typically IP addressing and routing.

9. The Physical layer is responsible for the electrical and mechanical connections between devices.

10. The Data Link layer is responsible for the framing of data packets.

11. The Session layer creates sessions between different hosts' applications.

12. The Data Link layer frames packets received from the network layer.

13. The Transport layer segments user data.

14. The Network layer creates packets out of segments handed down from the Transport layer.

15. The Physical layer is responsible for transporting ones and zeros in a digital signal.

16. Segments, packets, frames, bits

17. Transport

18. Data Link

19. Network

20. 48 bits (6 bytes) expressed as a hexadecimal number

Answer to Written Lab 1.2

Description	Device or OSI Layer
This device sends and receives information about the Network layer.	Router
This layer can create a virtual circuit before transmitting between two end stations.	Transport
This layer uses service access points.	Data Link (LLC sublayer)
This device uses hardware addresses to filter a network.	Bridge or switch
Ethernet is defined at these layers.	Data Link and Physical
This layer supports flow control and sequencing.	Transport
This device can measure the distance to a remote network.	Router
Logical addressing is used at this layer.	Network
Hardware addresses are defined at this layer.	Data Link (MAC sublayer)
This device creates one big collision domain and one large broadcast domain.	Hub
This device creates many smaller collision domains but the network is still one large broadcast domain.	Switch or bridge
This device breaks up collision domains and broadcast domains.	Router

Answers to Written Lab 1.3

1. Hub: One collision domain, one broadcast domain
2. Bridge: Two collision domains, one broadcast domain
3. Switch: Four collision domains, one broadcast domain
4. Router: Three collision domains, three broadcast domains

Chapter 2

Internet Protocols

THE CCNA EXAM TOPICS COVERED IN THIS CHAPTER INCLUDE THE FOLLOWING:

✓ **TECHNOLOGY**

- Evaluate TCP/IP communication process and its associated protocols

The *Transmission Control Protocol/Internet Protocol (TCP/IP)* suite was created by the Department of Defense (DoD) to ensure and preserve data integrity, as well as maintain communications in the event of catastrophic war. So it follows that if designed and implemented correctly, a TCP/IP network can be a truly dependable and resilient one. In this chapter, I'll cover the protocols of TCP/IP, and throughout this book, you'll learn how to create a marvelous TCP/IP network—using Cisco routers, of course.

We'll begin by taking a look at the DoD's version of TCP/IP and then compare this version and its protocols with the OSI reference model discussed in Chapter 1, "Internetworking."

Once you understand the protocols used at the various levels of the DoD model, you'll learn how to convert between a binary number, hexadecimal number, and decimal number. Then I'll cover IP addressing and the different classes of addresses used in networks today.

Subnetting will be covered in Chapter 3, "IP Subnetting and Variable Length Subnet Masks (VLSM)."

Because broadcast addresses are so important to understanding IP addressing, subnetting, and VLSM; an understanding of the various flavors of broadcast addresses is critical. I'll cover the various types of broadcast addresses that you just must know. Lastly, I'll provide an introduction to Network Address Translation (NAT) and how Cisco uses NAT.

TCP/IP and the DoD Model

The DoD model is basically a condensed version of the OSI model—it's composed of four, instead of seven, layers:

- Process/Application layer
- Host-to-Host layer
- Internet layer
- Network Access layer

Figure 2.1 shows a comparison of the DoD model and the OSI reference model. As you can see, the two are similar in concept, but each has a different number of layers with different names.

FIGURE 2.1   The DoD and OSI models

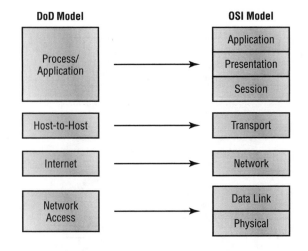

 When talking about the different protocols in the IP stack, the layers of the OSI and DoD models are interchangeable. In other words, the Internet layer and the Network layer describe the same thing, as do the Host-to-Host layer and the Transport layer.

A vast array of protocols combine at the DoD model's *Process/Application layer* to integrate the various activities and duties spanning the focus of the OSI's corresponding top three layers (Application, Presentation, and Session). We'll be looking closely at those protocols in the next part of this chapter. The Process/Application layer defines protocols for node-to-node application communication and also controls user-interface specifications.

The *Host-to-Host layer* parallels the functions of the OSI's Transport layer, defining protocols for setting up the level of transmission service for applications. It tackles issues such as creating reliable end-to-end communication and ensuring the error-free delivery of data. It handles packet sequencing and maintains data integrity.

The *Internet layer* corresponds to the OSI's Network layer, designating the protocols relating to the logical transmission of packets over the entire network. It takes care of the addressing of hosts by giving them an IP (Internet Protocol) address, and it handles the routing of packets among multiple networks.

At the bottom of the DoD model, the *Network Access layer* monitors the data exchange between the host and the network. The equivalent of the Data Link and Physical layers of the OSI model, the Network Access layer oversees hardware addressing and defines protocols for the physical transmission of data.

The DoD and OSI models are alike in design and concept and have similar functions in similar layers. Figure 2.2 shows the TCP/IP protocol suite and how its protocols relate to the DoD model layers.

FIGURE 2.2   The TCP/IP protocol suite

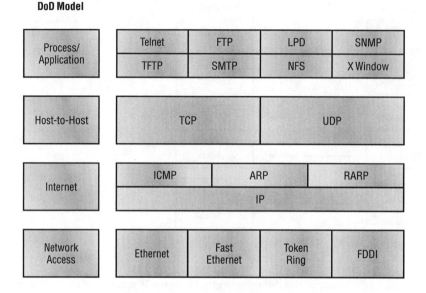

In the following sections, we will look at the different protocols in more detail, starting with the Process/Application layer protocols.

The Process/Application Layer Protocols

In this section, I'll describe the different applications and services typically used in IP networks. The different protocols and applications covered in this section include the following:

- Telnet
- FTP
- TFTP
- NFS
- SMTP
- LPD
- X Window
- SNMP
- DNS
- DHCP/BootP

Telnet

Telnet is the chameleon of protocols—its specialty is terminal emulation. It allows a user on a remote client machine, called the Telnet client, to access the resources of another machine, the Telnet server. Telnet achieves this by pulling a fast one on the Telnet server and making the client machine appear as though it were a terminal directly attached to the local network. This projection is actually a software image—a virtual terminal that can interact with the chosen remote host.

These emulated terminals are of the text-mode type and can execute refined procedures like displaying menus that give users the opportunity to choose options from them and access the applications on the duped server. Users begin a Telnet session by running the Telnet client software and then logging into the Telnet server.

The name *Telnet* comes from "telephone network," which is how most Telnet sessions used to occur.

File Transfer Protocol (FTP)

File Transfer Protocol (FTP) is the protocol that actually lets us transfer files, and it can accomplish this between any two machines using it. But FTP isn't just a protocol; it's also a program. Operating as a protocol, FTP is used by applications. As a program, it's employed by users to perform file tasks by hand. FTP also allows for access to both directories and files and can accomplish certain types of directory operations, such as relocating into different ones. FTP teams up with Telnet to transparently log you into the FTP server and then provides for the transfer of files.

Accessing a host through FTP is only the first step, though. Users must then be subjected to an authentication login that's probably secured with passwords and usernames implemented by system administrators to restrict access. But you can get around this somewhat by adopting the username "anonymous"—though what you'll gain access to will be limited.

Even when employed by users manually as a program, FTP's functions are limited to listing and manipulating directories, typing file contents, and copying files between hosts. It can't execute remote files as programs.

Trivial File Transfer Protocol (TFTP)

Trivial File Transfer Protocol (TFTP) is the stripped-down, stock version of FTP, but it's the protocol of choice if you know exactly what you want and where to find it, plus it's so easy to use and it's fast too! It doesn't give you the abundance of functions that FTP does, though. TFTP has no directory-browsing abilities; it can do nothing but send and receive files. This compact little protocol also skimps in the data department, sending much smaller blocks of data than FTP, and there's no authentication as with FTP, so it's insecure. Few sites support it because of the inherent security risks.

🌐 **Real World Scenario**

When should you use FTP?

Your San Francisco office needs a 50MB file e-mailed to them right away. What do you do? Most e-mail servers would reject the e-mail because they have size limits. Even if there's no size limit on the server, it still would take a while to send this big file to SF. FTP to the rescue!

If you need to give someone a large file or you need to get a large file from someone, FTP is a nice choice. Smaller files (less than 5MB) can just be sent via e-mail if you have the bandwidth of DSL or a cable modem. However, most ISPs don't allow files larger then 5MB to be e-mailed, so FTP is an option you should consider if you are in need of sending and receiving large files (who isn't these days?). To do this, you will need to set up an FTP server on the Internet so that the files can be shared. Besides, FTP is faster then e-mail, which is another reason to use FTP for sending or receiving large files. In addition, because it uses TCP and is connection-oriented, if the session dies, FTP can start up where it left off. Try that with your e-mail client!

Network File System (NFS)

Network File System (NFS) is a jewel of a protocol specializing in file sharing. It allows two different types of file systems to interoperate. It works like this: Suppose the NFS server software is running on an NT server, and the NFS client software is running on a Unix host. NFS allows for a portion of the RAM on the NT server to transparently store Unix files, which can, in turn, be used by Unix users. Even though the NT file system and Unix file system are unlike—they have different case sensitivity, filename lengths, security, and so on—both Unix users and NT users can access that same file with their normal file systems, in their normal way.

Simple Mail Transfer Protocol (SMTP)

Simple Mail Transfer Protocol (SMTP), answering our ubiquitous call to e-mail, uses a spooled, or queued, method of mail delivery. Once a message has been sent to a destination, the message is spooled to a device—usually a disk. The server software at the destination posts a vigil, regularly checking this queue for messages. When it detects them, it proceeds to deliver them to their destination. SMTP is used to send mail; POP3 is used to receive mail.

Line Printer Daemon (LPD)

The Line Printer Daemon (LPD) protocol is designed for printer sharing. The LPD, along with the LPR (Line Printer) program, allows print jobs to be spooled and sent to the network's printers using TCP/IP.

X Window

Designed for client-server operations, *X Window* defines a protocol for writing client/server applications based on a graphical user interface (GUI). The idea is to allow a program, called a client, to run on one computer and have it display things through a window server on another computer.

Simple Network Management Protocol (SNMP) *He has not used this,*

Simple Network Management Protocol (SNMP) collects and manipulates this valuable network information. It gathers data by polling the devices on the network from a management station at fixed or random intervals, requiring them to disclose certain information. When all is well, SNMP receives something called a *baseline*—a report delimiting the operational traits of a healthy network. This protocol can also stand as a watchdog over the network, quickly notifying managers of any sudden turn of events. These network watchdogs are called *agents*, and when aberrations occur, agents send an alert called a *trap* to the management station.

Domain Name Service (DNS)

Domain Name Service (DNS) resolves hostnames—specifically, Internet names, such as www.routersim.com. You don't have to use DNS; you can just type in the IP address of any device you want to communicate with. An IP address identifies hosts on a network and the Internet as well. However, DNS was designed to make our lives easier. Think about this: What would happen if you wanted to move your web page to a different service provider? The IP address would change and no one would know what the new one was. DNS allows you to use a domain name to specify an IP address. You can change the IP address as often as you want, and no one will know the difference.

DNS is used to resolve a *fully qualified domain name (FQDN)*—for example, www.lammle.com or todd.lammle.com. An FQDN is a hierarchy that can logically locate a system based on its domain identifier.

If you want to resolve the name "todd," you either must type in the FQDN of todd.lammle.com or have a device such as a PC or router add the suffix for you. For example, on a Cisco router, you can use the command ip domain-name lammle.com to append each request with the lammle.com domain. If you don't do that, you'll have to type in the FQDN to get DNS to resolve the name.

> An important thing to remember about DNS is that if you can ping a device with an IP address but cannot use its FQDN, then you might have some type of DNS configuration failure.

Dynamic Host Configuration Protocol (DHCP)/BootP (Bootstrap Protocol)

Dynamic Host Configuration Protocol (DHCP) gives IP addresses to hosts. It allows easier administration and works well in small-to-even-very-large network environments. All types of hardware can be used as a DHCP server, including a Cisco router.

DHCP differs from BootP in that BootP gives an IP address to a host, but the host's hardware address must be entered manually in a BootP table. You can think of DHCP as a dynamic BootP. But remember that BootP is also used to send an operating system that a host can boot from. DHCP can't do that.

But there is a lot of information a DHCP server can provide to a host when the host is requesting an IP address from the DHCP server. Here's a list of the information a DHCP server can provide:

- IP address
- Subnet mask
- Domain name
- Default gateway (routers)
- DNS
- WINS information

A DHCP server can give us even more information than this, but the items in that list are the most common.

The Host-to-Host Layer Protocols

The main purpose of the Host-to-Host layer is to shield the upper-layer applications from the complexities of the network. This layer says to the upper layer, "Just give me your data stream, with any instructions, and I'll begin the process of getting your information ready to send."

The following sections describe the two protocols at this layer:

- Transmission Control Protocol (TCP)
- User Datagram Protocol (UDP)

In addition, we'll look at some of the key host-to-host protocol concepts, as well as the port numbers.

Transmission Control Protocol (TCP)

Transmission Control Protocol (TCP) takes large blocks of information from an application and breaks them into segments. It numbers and sequences each segment so that the destination's TCP protocol can put the segments back into the order the application intended. After these segments are sent, TCP (on the transmitting host) waits for an acknowledgment of the receiving end's TCP virtual circuit session, retransmitting those that aren't acknowledged.

Before a transmitting host starts to send segments down the model, the sender's TCP protocol contacts the destination's TCP protocol to establish a connection. What is created is known as a *virtual circuit*. This type of communication is called *connection-oriented*. During this initial handshake, the two TCP layers also agree on the amount of information that's going to be sent before the recipient's TCP sends back an acknowledgment. With everything agreed upon in advance, the path is paved for reliable communication to take place.

TCP is a full-duplex, connection-oriented, reliable, and accurate protocol, but establishing all these terms and conditions, in addition to error checking, is no small task. TCP is very complicated and, not surprisingly, costly in terms of network overhead. And since today's networks are much more reliable than those of yore, this added reliability is often unnecessary.

TCP Segment Format

Since the upper layers just send a data stream to the protocols in the Transport layers, I'll demonstrate how TCP segments a data stream and prepares it for the Internet layer. The Internet layer then routes the segments as packets through an internetwork. The segments are handed to the receiving host's Host-to-Host layer protocol, which rebuilds the data stream to hand to the upper-layer applications or protocols.

Figure 2.3 shows the TCP segment format. The figure shows the different fields within the TCP header.

FIGURE 2.3 TCP segment format

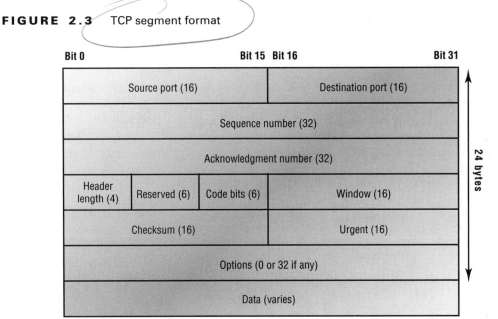

The TCP header is 20 bytes long, or up to 24 bytes with options. You need to understand what each field in the TCP segment is. The TCP segment contains the following fields:

Source port The port number of the application on the host sending the data. (Port numbers will be explained a little later in this section.)

Destination port The port number of the application requested on the destination host.

Sequence number Puts the data back in the correct order or retransmits missing or damaged data, a process called *sequencing*.

Acknowledgment number Defines which TCP octet is expected next.

Offset The number of 32-bit words in the TCP Header. This indicates where the data begins. The TCP header (even one including options) is an integral number of 32 bits in length.

Reserved Always set to zero.

Code bits   Control functions used to set up and terminate a session.

Window   The window size the sender is willing to accept, in octets.

Checksum   The cyclic redundancy check (CRC), because TCP doesn't trust the lower layers and checks everything. The CRC checks the header and data fields.

Urgent pointer   A valid field only if the Urgent pointer in the code bits is set. If so, this value indicates the offset from the current sequence number, in octets, where the first segment of non-urgent data begins.

Option   May be 0 or a multiple of 32 bits, if any. What this means is that no options have to be present (option size of 0). However, if any options are used that do not cause the option field to total a multiple of 32 bits, padding of 0s must be used to make sure the data begins on a 32-bit boundary.

Data   Handed down to the TCP protocol at the Transport layer, which includes the upper-layer headers.

Let's take a look at a TCP segment copied from a network analyzer:

```
TCP - Transport Control Protocol
 Source Port:       5973
 Destination Port: 23
 Sequence Number:  1456389907
 Ack Number:       1242056456
 Offset:           5
 Reserved:         %000000
 Code:             %011000
       Ack is valid
       Push Request
 Window:           61320
 Checksum:         0x61a6
 Urgent Pointer:   0
 No TCP Options
 TCP Data Area:
 vL.5.+.5.+.5.+.5  76 4c 19 35 11 2b 19 35 11 2b 19 35 11
   2b 19 35 +. 11 2b 19
Frame Check Sequence: 0x0d00000f
```

Did you notice that everything I talked about above is in the segment? As you can see from the number of fields in the header, TCP creates a lot of overhead. Application developers may opt for efficiency over reliability to save overhead, so User Datagram Protocol was also defined at the Transport layer as an alternative.

User Datagram Protocol (UDP)

If you were to compare *User Datagram Protocol (UDP)* with TCP, the former is basically the scaled-down economy model that's sometimes referred to as a thin protocol. Like a thin person on a park bench, a thin protocol doesn't take up a lot of room—or in this case, much bandwidth on a network.

UDP doesn't offer all the bells and whistles of TCP either, but it does do a fabulous job of transporting information that doesn't require reliable delivery—and it does so using far fewer network resources. (UDP is covered thoroughly in Request for Comments 768.)

> The Requests for Comments (RFCs) form a series of notes, started in 1969, about the Internet (originally the ARPAnet). The notes discuss many aspects of computer communication, focusing on networking protocols, procedures, programs, and concepts but also including meeting notes, opinion, and sometimes humor.

There are some situations where it would definitely be wise for developers to opt for UDP rather than TCP. Remember the watchdog SNMP up there at the Process/Application layer? SNMP monitors the network, sending intermittent messages and a fairly steady flow of status updates and alerts, especially when running on a large network. The cost in overhead to establish, maintain, and close a TCP connection for each one of those little messages would reduce what would be an otherwise healthy, efficient network to a dammed-up bog in no time!

Another circumstance calling for UDP over TCP is when reliability is already handled at the Process/Application layer. Network File System (NFS) handles its own reliability issues, making the use of TCP both impractical and redundant. But ultimately, it's up to the application developer who decides whether to use UDP or TCP, not the user who wants to transfer data faster.

UDP does *not* sequence the segments and does not care in which order the segments arrive at the destination. But after that, UDP sends the segments off and forgets about them. It doesn't follow through, check up on them, or even allow for an acknowledgment of safe arrival—complete abandonment. Because of this, it's referred to as an unreliable protocol. This does not mean that UDP is ineffective, only that it doesn't handle issues of reliability.

Further, UDP doesn't create a virtual circuit, nor does it contact the destination before delivering information to it. Because of this, it's also considered a *connectionless* protocol. Since UDP assumes that the application will use its own reliability method, it doesn't use any. This gives an application developer a choice when running the Internet Protocol stack: TCP for reliability or UDP for faster transfers.

UDP Segment Format

Figure 2.4 clearly illustrates UDP's markedly low overhead as compared to TCP's hungry usage. Look at the figure carefully—can you see that UDP doesn't use windowing or provide for acknowledgments in the UDP header?

FIGURE 2.4 UDP segment

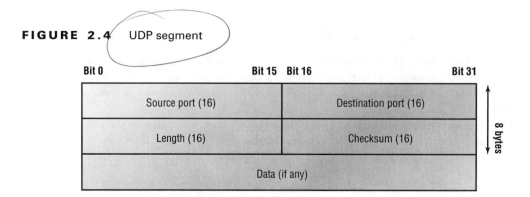

It's important for you to understand what each field in the UDP segment is. The UDP segment contains the following fields:

Source port   Port number of the application on the host sending the data.

Destination port   Port number of the application requested on the destination host.

Length of the segment   Length of UDP header and UDP data.

CRC   Checksum of both the UDP header and UDP data fields.

Data   Upper-layer data.

UDP, like TCP, doesn't trust the lower layers and runs its own CRC. Remember that the Frame Check Sequence (FCS) is the field that houses the CRC, which is why you can see the FCS information.

The following shows a UDP segment caught on a network analyzer:

```
UDP - User Datagram Protocol
 Source Port:      1085
 Destination Port: 5136
 Length:           41
 Checksum:         0x7a3c
 UDP Data Area:
 ..Z.............  00 01 5a 96 00 01 00 00 00 00 00 11 00
 00 00
 ...C..2...._C._C  2e 03 00 43 02 1e 32 0a 00 0a 00 80 43
 00 80
Frame Check Sequence: 0x00000000
```

Notice that low overhead! Try to find the sequence number, ack number, and window size in the UDP segment. You can't (I hope) because they just aren't there!

Key Concepts of Host-to-Host Protocols

Since you've seen both a connection-oriented (TCP) and connectionless (UDP) protocol in action, it would be good to summarize the two here. Table 2.1 highlights some of the key concepts that you should keep in mind regarding these two protocols. You should memorize this table.

TABLE 2.1   Key Features of TCP and UDP

TCP	UDP
Sequenced	Unsequenced
Reliable	Unreliable
Connection-oriented	Connectionless
Virtual circuit	Low overhead
Acknowledgments	No acknowledgment
Windowing flow control	No windowing or flow control

A telephone analogy could really help you understand how TCP works. Most of us know that before you speak to someone on a phone, you must first establish a connection with that other person—wherever they are. This is like a virtual circuit with the TCP protocol. If you were giving someone important information during your conversation, you might say, "You know?" or ask, "Did you get that?" Saying something like this is a lot like a TCP acknowledgment—it's designed to get you verification. From time to time (especially on cell phones), people also ask, "Are you still there?" They end their conversations with a "Goodbye" of some kind, putting closure on the phone call. TCP also performs these types of functions.

Alternately, using UDP is like sending a postcard. To do that, you don't need to contact the other party first. You simply write your message, address the postcard, and mail it. This is analogous to UDP's connectionless orientation. Since the message on the postcard is probably not a matter of life or death, you don't need an acknowledgment of its receipt. Similarly, UDP does not involve acknowledgments.

Port Numbers

TCP and UDP must use *port numbers* to communicate with the upper layers, because they're what keeps track of different conversations crossing the network simultaneously. Originating-source port numbers are dynamically assigned by the source host and will equal some number starting at 1024. 1023 and below are defined in RFC 3232 (or just see www.iana.org), which discusses what are called well-known port numbers.

Virtual circuits that don't use an application with a well-known port number are assigned port numbers randomly from a specific range instead. These port numbers identify the source and destination application or process in the TCP segment.

Figure 2.5 illustrates how both TCP and UDP use port numbers.

FIGURE 2.5   Port numbers for TCP and UDP

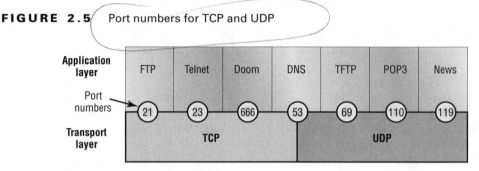

The different port numbers that can be used are explained next:

- Numbers below 1024 are considered well-known port numbers and are defined in RFC 3232.

- Numbers 1024 and above are used by the upper layers to set up sessions with other hosts, and by TCP to use as source and destination addresses in the TCP segment.

In the following sections we'll take a look at an analyzer output showing a TCP session.

TCP Session: Source Port

The following listing shows a TCP session captured with Etherpeek analyzer software:

```
TCP - Transport Control Protocol
 Source Port:       5973
 Destination Port: 23
 Sequence Number:   1456389907
 Ack Number:        1242056456
 Offset:            5
 Reserved:          %000000
 Code:              %011000
       Ack is valid
       Push Request
 Window:            61320
 Checksum:          0x61a6
 Urgent Pointer:    0
 No TCP Options
 TCP Data Area:
 vL.5.+.5.+.5.+.5   76 4c 19 35 11 2b 19 35 11 2b 19 35 11
   2b 19 35 +. 11 2b 19
Frame Check Sequence: 0x0d00000f
```

Notice that the source host makes up the source port and, in this case, is 5973. The destination port is 23, which is used to tell the receiving host the purpose of the intended connection (Telnet).

By looking at this session, you can see that the source host makes up the source port. But why does the source make up a port number? To differentiate between sessions with different hosts, my friend. How else would a server know where information is coming from if it didn't have a different number from a sending host? TCP and the upper layers don't use hardware and logical addresses to understand the sending host's address as the Data Link and Network layer protocols do. Instead, they use port numbers. And it's easy to imagine the receiving host getting thoroughly confused if all the hosts used the same port number to get to FTP!

TCP Session: Destination Port

You'll sometimes look at an analyzer and see that only the source port is above 1024 and the destination port is a well-known port, as shown in the following Etherpeek trace:

```
TCP - Transport Control Protocol
  Source Port:       1144
  Destination Port: 80 World Wide Web HTTP
  Sequence Number:   9356570
  Ack Number:        0
  Offset:            7
  Reserved:          %000000
  Code:              %000010
        Synch Sequence
  Window:            8192
  Checksum:          0x57E7
  Urgent Pointer:    0
  TCP Options:
   Option Type: 2 Maximum Segment Size
      Length:    4
      MSS:       536
   Option Type: 1 No Operation
   Option Type: 1 No Operation
   Option Type: 4
      Length:    2
      Opt Value:
  No More HTTP Data
Frame Check Sequence: 0x43697363
```

And sure enough, the source port is over 1024, but the destination port is 80, or HTTP service. The server, or receiving host, will change the destination port if it needs to.

In the preceding trace, a "syn" packet is sent to the destination device. The syn sequence is what's telling the remote destination device that it wants to create a session.

TCP Session: Syn Packet Acknowledgment

The next trace shows an acknowledgment to the syn packet:

```
TCP - Transport Control Protocol
  Source Port:       80 World Wide Web HTTP
  Destination Port: 1144
  Sequence Number:   2873580788
  Ack Number:        9356571
  Offset:            6
  Reserved:          %000000
  Code:              %010010
      Ack is valid
      Synch Sequence
  Window:            8576
  Checksum:          0x5F85
  Urgent Pointer:    0
  TCP Options:
   Option Type: 2 Maximum Segment Size
     Length:     4
     MSS:        1460
  No More HTTP Data
Frame Check Sequence: 0x6E203132
```

Notice the *Ack is valid*, which means the source port was accepted and the device agreed to create a virtual circuit with the originating host.

And here again, you can see that the response from the server shows the source is 80 and the destination is the 1144 sent from the originating host—all's well.

The Internet Layer Protocols

In the DoD model, there are two main reasons for the Internet layer's existence: routing, and providing a single network interface to the upper layers.

None of the other upper- or lower-layer protocols have any functions relating to routing—that complex and important task belongs entirely to the Internet layer. The Internet layer's second duty is to provide a single network interface to the upper-layer protocols. Without this layer, application programmers would need to write "hooks" into every one of their applications for each different Network Access protocol. This would not only be a pain in the neck, but it would lead to different versions of each application—one for Ethernet, another one for Token Ring, and so on. To prevent this, IP provides one single network interface for the upper-layer protocols. That accomplished, it's then the job of IP and the various Network Access protocols to get along and work together.

All network roads don't lead to Rome—they lead to IP. And all the other protocols at this layer, as well as all those at the upper layers, use it. Never forget that. All paths through the DoD model go through IP. The following sections describe the protocols at the Internet layer:

- Internet Protocol (IP)

- Internet Control Message Protocol (ICMP)

- Address Resolution Protocol (ARP)

- Reverse Address Resolution Protocol (RARP)

Internet Protocol (IP)

Internet Protocol (IP) essentially is the Internet layer. The other protocols found here merely exist to support it. IP holds the big picture and could be said to "see all," in that it's aware of all the interconnected networks. It can do this because all the machines on the network have a software, or logical, address called an IP address, which I'll cover more thoroughly later in this chapter.

IP looks at each packet's address. Then, using a routing table, it decides where a packet is to be sent next, choosing the best path. The protocols of the Network Access layer at the bottom of the DoD model don't possess IP's enlightened scope of the entire network; they deal only with physical links (local networks).

Identifying devices on networks requires answering these two questions: Which network is it on? And what is its ID on that network? The first answer is the *software address*, or *logical address* (the correct street). The second answer is the hardware address (the correct mailbox). All hosts on a network have a logical ID called an IP address. This is the software, or logical, address and contains valuable encoded information greatly simplifying the complex task of routing. (IP is discussed in RFC 791.)

IP receives segments from the Host-to-Host layer and fragments them into datagrams (packets) if necessary. IP then reassembles datagrams back into segments on the receiving side. Each datagram is assigned the IP address of the sender and of the recipient. Each router (layer 3 device) that receives a datagram makes routing decisions based on the packet's destination IP address.

Figure 2.6 shows an IP header. This will give you an idea of what the IP protocol has to go through every time user data is sent from the upper layers and is to be sent to a remote network.

The following fields make up the IP header:

Version IP version number.

Header Length (HLEN) Header length in 32-bit words.

ToS with IP Precedence Bits Type of Service tells how the datagram should be handled. The first 3 bits are the priority bits.

Total length Length of the packet including header and data.

Identifier Unique IP-packet value.

Flags Specifies whether fragmentation should occur.

FIGURE 2.6 IP header

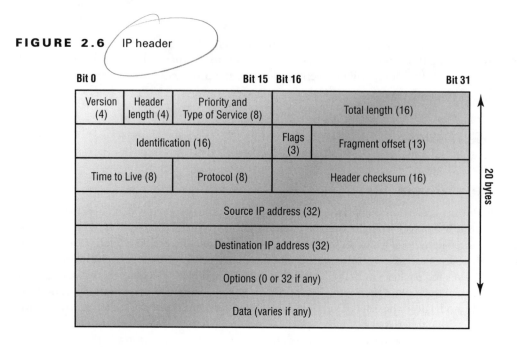

Frag offset Provides fragmentation and reassembly if the packet is too large to put in a frame. It also allows different maximum transmission units (MTUs) on the Internet.

TTL The time to live is set into a packet when it is originally generated. If it doesn't get to where it wants to go before the TTL expires, boom—it's gone. This stops IP packets from continuously circling the network looking for a home.

Protocol Port of upper-layer protocol (TCP is port 6 or UDP is port 17 [hex]). Also supports Network layer protocols.

Header checksum Cyclic redundancy check (CRC) on header only.

Source IP address 32-bit IP address of sending station.

Destination IP address 32-bit IP address of the station this packet is destined for.

IP option Used for network testing, debugging, security, and more.

Data After the IP option field will be the upper-layer data.

Here's a snapshot of an IP packet caught on a network analyzer (notice that all the header information discussed above appears here):

```
IP Header - Internet Protocol Datagram
  Version:          4
  Header Length:    5
  Precedence:       0
  Type of Service:  %000
```

```
Unused:                %00
Total Length:          187
Identifier:            22486
Fragmentation Flags:   %010 Do Not Fragment
Fragment Offset:       0
Time To Live:          60
IP Type:               0x06 TCP
Header Checksum:        0xd031
Source IP Address:     10.7.1.30
Dest. IP Address:      10.7.1.10
No Internet Datagram Options
```

Can you distinguish the logical, or IP, addresses in this header?

The Type field—it's typically a Protocol field, but this analyzer sees it as an IP Type field—is important. If the header didn't carry the protocol information for the next layer, IP wouldn't know what to do with the data carried in the packet. The example above tells IP to hand the segment to TCP.

Figure 2.7 demonstrates how the Network layer sees the protocols at the Transport layer when it needs to hand a packet to the upper-layer protocols.

FIGURE 2.7   The Protocol field in an IP header

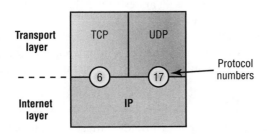

In this example, the Protocol field tells IP to send the data to either TCP port 6 or UDP port 17 (both hex addresses). But it will only be UDP or TCP if the data is part of a data stream headed for an upper-layer service or application. It could just as easily be destined for Internet Control Message Protocol (ICMP), Address Resolution Protocol (ARP), or some other type of Network layer protocol.

Table 2.2 is a list of some other popular protocols that can be specified in the Protocol field.

TABLE 2.2   Possible Protocols Found in the Protocol Field of an IP Header

Protocol	Protocol Number
ICMP	1

TABLE 2.2   Possible Protocols Found in the Protocol Field of an IP Header *(continued)*

Protocol	Protocol Number
IGRP	9
EIGRSP	88
OSPF	89
IPv6	41
GRE	47
IPX in IP	111
Layer 2 tunnel (L2TP)	115

Internet Control Message Protocol (ICMP)

Internet Control Message Protocol (ICMP) works at the Network layer and is used by IP for many different services. ICMP is a management protocol and messaging service provider for IP. Its messages are carried as IP datagrams. RFC 1256 is an annex to ICMP, which affords hosts' extended capability in discovering routes to gateways.

Periodically, router advertisements are announced over the network, reporting IP addresses for the router's network interfaces. Hosts listen for these network infomercials to acquire route information. A router solicitation is a request for immediate advertisements and may be sent by a host when it starts up.

> RFC 792 references ICMP and describes how ICMP must be implemented by all TCP/IP hosts.

The following are some common events and messages that ICMP relates to:

Destination Unreachable   If a router can't send an IP datagram any further, it uses ICMP to send a message back to the sender, advising it of the situation. For example, if a router receives a packet destined for a network that the router doesn't know about, it will send an ICMP Destination Unreachable message back to the sending station.

Buffer Full   If a router's memory buffer for receiving incoming datagrams is full, it will use ICMP to send out this message until the congestion abates.

Hops   Each IP datagram is allotted a certain number of routers, called hops, to pass through. If it reaches its limit of hops before arriving at its destination, the last router to receive that datagram deletes it. The executioner router then uses ICMP to send an obituary message, informing the sending machine of the demise of its datagram.

Ping   Ping (Packet Internet Groper) uses ICMP echo messages to check the physical and logical connectivity of machines on an internetwork.

Traceroute   Using ICMP timeouts, Traceroute is used to discover the path a packet takes as it traverses an internetwork.

> Both Ping and Traceroute (also just called Trace; Microsoft Windows uses tracert) allow you to verify address configurations in your internetwork.

The following data is from a network analyzer catching an ICMP echo request:

```
Flags:          0x00
 Status:         0x00
 Packet Length: 78
 Timestamp:      14:04:25.967000 12/20/03
Ethernet Header
 Destination: 00:a0:24:6e:0f:a8
 Source:      00:80:c7:a8:f0:3d
 Ether-Type:  08-00 IP
IP Header - Internet Protocol Datagram
 Version:              4
 Header Length:        5
 Precedence:           0
 Type of Service:      %000
 Unused:               %00
 Total Length:         60
 Identifier:           56325
 Fragmentation Flags:  %000
 Fragment Offset:      0
 Time To Live:         32
 IP Type:              0x01 ICMP
 Header Checksum:      0x2df0
 Source IP Address:    100.100.100.2
 Dest. IP Address:     100.100.100.1
 No Internet Datagram Options
ICMP - Internet Control Messages Protocol
 ICMP Type:      8 Echo Request
 Code:           0
 Checksum:       0x395c
 Identifier:     0x0300
 Sequence Number: 4352
 ICMP Data Area:
```

```
abcdefghijklmnop   61 62 63 64 65 66 67 68 69 6a 6b 6c 6d
qrstuvwabcdefghi   71 72 73 74 75 76 77 61 62 63 64 65 66
Frame Check Sequence: 0x00000000
```

Notice anything unusual? Did you catch the fact that even though ICMP works at the Internet (Network) layer, it still uses IP to do the Ping request? The Type field in the IP header is 0x01, which specifies the ICMP protocol.

The Ping program just uses the alphabet in the data portion of the packet as a payload, 100 bytes by default.

If you remember reading about the Data Link layer and the different frame types in Chapter 1, you should be able to look at the preceding trace and tell what type of Ethernet frame this is. The only fields are destination hardware address, source hardware address, and Ether-Type. The only frame that uses an Ether-Type field exclusively is an Ethernet_II frame. (SNAP uses an Ether-Type field also, but only within an 802.2 LLC field, which isn't present in the frame.)

Address Resolution Protocol (ARP)

Address Resolution Protocol (ARP) finds the hardware address of a host from a known IP address. Here's how it works: When IP has a datagram to send, it must inform a Network Access protocol, such as Ethernet or Token Ring, of the destination's hardware address on the local network. (It has already been informed by upper-layer protocols of the destination's IP address.) If IP doesn't find the destination host's hardware address in the ARP cache, it uses ARP to find this information.

As IP's detective, ARP interrogates the local network by sending out a broadcast asking the machine with the specified IP address to reply with its hardware address. So basically, ARP translates the software (IP) address into a hardware address—for example, the destination machine's Ethernet board address—and from it, deduces its whereabouts on LAN by broadcasting for this address. Figure 2.8 shows how an ARP looks to a local network.

ARP resolves IP addresses to Ethernet (MAC) addresses.

The following trace shows an ARP broadcast (notice that the destination hardware address is unknown, and is all Fs in hex (all 1s in binary), and a hardware address broadcast):

```
Flags:          0x00
Status:         0x00
Packet Length:  64
Timestamp:      09:17:29.574000 12/06/03
Ethernet Header
 Destination:    FF:FF:FF:FF:FF:FF Ethernet Broadcast
 Source:         00:A0:24:48:60:A5
```

```
Protocol Type: 0x0806 IP ARP
ARP - Address Resolution Protocol
  Hardware:                  1 Ethernet (10Mb)
  Protocol:                  0x0800 IP
  Hardware Address Length: 6
  Protocol Address Length: 4
  Operation:                 1 ARP Request
  Sender Hardware Address: 00:A0:24:48:60:A5
  Sender Internet Address: 172.16.10.3
  Target Hardware Address: 00:00:00:00:00:00 (ignored)
  Target Internet Address: 172.16.10.10
Extra bytes (Padding):
  ............... 0A 0A 0A 0A 0A 0A 0A 0A 0A 0A 0A 0A 0A
  0A 0A 0A 0A 0A
Frame Check Sequence: 0x00000000
```

FIGURE 2.8   Local ARP broadcast

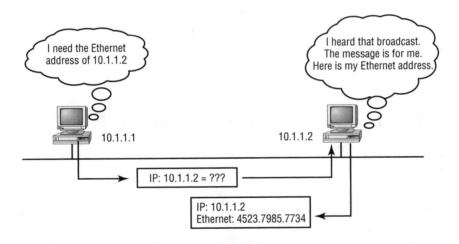

Reverse Address Resolution Protocol (RARP)

When an IP machine happens to be a diskless machine, it has no way of initially knowing its IP address. But it does know its MAC address. *Reverse Address Resolution Protocol (RARP)* discovers the identity of the IP address for diskless machines by sending out a packet that includes its MAC address and a request for the IP address assigned to that MAC address. A designated machine, called a *RARP server*, responds with the answer, and the identity crisis is over. RARP uses the information it does know about the machine's MAC address to learn its IP address and complete the machine's ID portrait.

RARP resolves Ethernet (MAC) addresses to IP addresses.

Figure 2.9 shows a diskless workstation asking for its IP address with a RARP broadcast:

FIGURE 2.9   RARP broadcast example

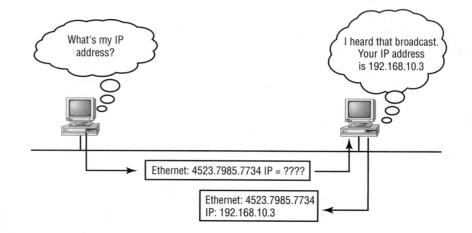

Binary to Decimal and Hexadecimal Conversion

Before we continue discussing the TCP/IP protocol stack and IP addressing, it's really important for you to truly understand the differences between binary, decimal, and hexadecimal numbers, and how to convert one format into the other.

So first, we're going to start with binary numbering. It's pretty simple, really. The digits used are limited to either a 1 (one) or a 0 (zero), with each digit being called one bit (short for binary digit). Typically, you count either 4 or 8 bits together, with these being referred to as a nibble or a byte, respectively.

What interests us in binary numbering is the value represented in a decimal format—the typical decimal format being our base 10 number scheme we've all used since kindergarten. The binary numbers are placed in a value spot; starting at the right and moving left, with each spot having double the value of the previous spot.

Table 2.3 shows the decimal values of each bit location in a nibble and a byte. Remember, a nibble is 4 bits and a byte is 8 bits.

TABLE 2.3   Binary Values

Nibble values	Byte values
8 4 2 1	128 64 32 16 8 4 2 1

What all this means is that if a one digit (1) is placed in a value spot, then the nibble or byte takes on that decimal value, and adds it to any other value spots that have a one. And if a zero (0) is placed in a bit spot, then you don't count that value.

Let me clarify things— if we have a 1 placed in each spot of our nibble, we would then add up 8 + 4 + 2 + 1, to give us a maximum value of 15. Another example for our nibble values would be 1010, which means that the 8 bit and the 2 bit are turned on, which equals a decimal value of 10. If we have a nibble binary value of 0110, then our decimal value would be 6, because the 4 and 2 bits are turned on.

But the byte values can add up to a value that's significantly higher than 15. This is how: If we counted every bit as a one (1), then the byte binary value would look like this (8 bits equal a byte):

11111111

We would then count up every bit spot because each is turned on. It would look like this:

128 + 64 + 32 + 16 + 8 + 4 + 2 + 1 = 255

which demonstrates the maximum value of a byte.

There are plenty of other decimal values that a binary number can equal. Let's work through a few examples:

10010110

Which bits are on? The 128, 16, 4, and 2 bits are on, so we'll just add them up: 128 + 16 + 4 + 2 = 150.

01101100

Which bits are on? The 64, 32, 8, and 4 bits are on, so we just need to add them up: 64 + 32 + 8 + 4 = 108.

11101000

Which bits are on? The 128, 64, 32 and 8 bits are on, so just add the values up: 128 + 64 + 32 + 8 = 232

Table 2.4 is a table you should memorize before braving the subnetting section in Chapter 3.

TABLE 2.4   Binary to Decimal Memorization Chart

Binary Value	Decimal Value
10000000	128

TABLE 2.4 Binary to Decimal Memorization Chart *(continued)*

Binary Value	Decimal Value
11000000	192
11100000	224
11110000	240
11111000	248
11111100	252
11111110	254
11111111	255

Perhaps it is needless to say (but just in case): You need to understand binary-to-decimal conversion before moving on to Chapter 3.

Hexadecimal addressing is completely different than binary or decimal—it's converted by reading nibbles, not bytes. By using a nibble, we can convert these bits to hex pretty simply. First, understand that the hexadecimal addressing scheme uses only the numbers 0 through 9. And since the numbers 10, 11, 12, etc. can't be used (because they are two digits), the letters A, B, C, D, E, and F are used to represent 10, 11, 12, 13, 14, and 15, respectively.

Table 2.5 shows both the binary value and decimal value for each hexadecimal digit.

TABLE 2.5 Hex to Binary to Decimal Chart

Hexadecimal Value	Binary Value	Decimal Value
0	0000	0
1	0001	1
2	0010	2
3	0011	3
4	0100	4
5	0101	5
6	0110	6

TABLE 2.5   Hex to Binary to Decimal Chart *(continued)*

Hexadecimal Value	Binary Value	Decimal Value
7	0111	7
8	1000	8
9	1001	9
A	1010	10
B	1011	11
C	1100	12
D	1101	13
E	1110	14
F	1111	15

Did you notice that the first 10 hexadecimal digits (0–9) are the same value as the decimal values? If not, look again. This handy fact makes those values super easy to convert.

So suppose you have something like this: 0x6A. (Sometimes Cisco likes to put 0x in front of characters so you know that they are a hex value. They don't have any other special meaning.) What are the binary and decimal values? All you have to remember is that each hex character is one nibble and two hex characters together make a byte. To figure out the binary value, we need to put the hex characters into two nibbles then put them together into a byte. 6 = 0110 and A (which is 10 in hex) = 1010, so the complete byte would be 01101010.

To convert from binary to hex, just take the byte and break it into nibbles. Here's what I mean:

Say you have the binary number 01010101. First, break it into nibbles—0101 and 0101— with the value of each nibble being 5, since the 1 and 4 bits are on. This makes the hex answer 55. Why? Because we're converting a whole byte. And in decimal format, the binary number is 01101010, which converts to 64 + 32 + 8 + 2 = 106.

Here's another binary number:

11001100

Your answer would be 1100 = 12 and 1100 = 12, (therefore it's converted to CC in hex). The decimal conversion answer would be 128 + 64 + 8 + 4 = 204.

One more example, then we've got to move on into IP Addressing. Suppose you had the following binary number:

10110101

The hex answer would be B5, since 1011 converts to B and 1010 converts to 5 in hex value. The decimal equivalent is 128 + 32 + 16 + 4 + 1 = 181.

IP Addressing

One of the most important topics in any discussion of TCP/IP is IP addressing. An *IP address* is a numeric identifier assigned to each machine on an IP network. It designates the specific location of a device on the network.

An IP address is a software address, not a hardware address—the latter is hard-coded on a Network Interface Card (NIC) and used for finding hosts on a local network. IP addressing was designed to allow a host on one network to communicate with a host on a different network, regardless of the type of LANs the hosts are participating in.

Before we get into the more complicated aspects of IP addressing, you need to understand some of the basics. First I'm going to explain some of the fundamentals of IP addressing and its terminology. Then you'll learn about the hierarchical IP addressing scheme and private IP addresses.

IP Terminology

Throughout this chapter you'll learn several important terms vital to your understanding of the Internet Protocol. Here are a few to get you started:

Bit   A *bit* is one digit; either a 1 or a 0.

Byte   A *byte* is 7 or 8 bits, depending on whether parity is used. For the rest of this chapter, always assume a byte is 8 bits.

Octet   An octet, made up of 8 bits, is just an ordinary 8-bit binary number. In this chapter the terms byte and octet are completely interchangeable.

Network address   This is the designation used in routing to send packets to a remote network—for example, 10.0.0.0, 172.16.0.0, and 192.168.10.0.

Broadcast address   The address used by applications and hosts to send information to all nodes on a network is called the *broadcast address*. Examples include 255.255.255.255, which is all networks, all nodes; 172.16.255.255, which is all subnets and hosts on network 172.16.0.0; and 10.255.255.255, which broadcasts to all subnets and hosts on network 10.0.0.0.

The Hierarchical IP Addressing Scheme

An IP address consists of 32 bits of information. These bits are divided into four sections, referred to as *octets* or bytes, each containing 1 byte (8 bits). You can depict an IP address using one of three methods:

- Dotted-decimal, as in 172.16.30.56
- Binary, as in 10101100.00010000.00011110.00111000
- Hexadecimal, as in AC.10.1E.38

All these examples truly represent the same IP address. Hexadecimal isn't used as often as dotted-decimal or binary when IP addressing is discussed, but you still might find an IP address stored in hexadecimal in some programs. The Windows Registry is a good example of a program that stores a machine's IP address in hex.

The 32-bit IP address is a structured or hierarchical address, as opposed to a flat or nonhierarchical address. Although either type of addressing scheme could have been used, *hierarchical addressing* was chosen for a good reason. The advantage of this scheme is that it can handle a large number of addresses, namely 4.3 billion (a 32-bit address space with two possible values for each position—either 0 or 1—gives you 232, or 4,294,967,296). The disadvantage of the flat addressing scheme, and the reason it's not used for IP addressing, relates to routing. If every address were unique, all routers on the Internet would need to store the address of each and every machine on the Internet. This would make efficient routing impossible, even if only a fraction of the possible addresses were used.

The solution to this problem is to use a two- or three-level, hierarchical addressing scheme that is structured by network and host, or network, subnet, and host.

This two- or three-level scheme is comparable to a telephone number. The first section, the area code, designates a very large area. The second section, the prefix, narrows the scope to a local calling area. The final segment, the customer number, zooms in on the specific connection. IP addresses use the same type of layered structure. Rather than all 32 bits being treated as a unique identifier, as in flat addressing, a part of the address is designated as the network address, and the other part is designated as either the subnet and host or just the node address.

In the following sections, I'm going to discuss IP network addressing and the different classes of address we can use to address our networks with.

Network Addressing

The *network address* (which can also be called the network number) uniquely identifies each network. Every machine on the same network shares that network address as part of its IP address. In the IP address 172.16.30.56, for example, 172.16 is the network address.

The *node address* is assigned to, and uniquely identifies, each machine on a network. This part of the address must be unique because it identifies a particular machine—an individual—as opposed to a network, which is a group. This number can also be referred to as a *host address*. In the sample IP address 172.16.30.56, the 30.56 is the node address.

The designers of the Internet decided to create classes of networks based on network size. For the small number of networks possessing a very large number of nodes, they created the rank *Class A network*. At the other extreme is the *Class C network*, which is reserved for the numerous networks with a small number of nodes. The class distinction for networks between very large and very small is predictably called the *Class B network*.

Subdividing an IP address into a network and node address is determined by the class designation of one's network. Figure 2.10 summarizes the three classes of networks—a subject I'll explain in much greater detail throughout this chapter.

To ensure efficient routing, Internet designers defined a mandate for the leading-bits section of the address for each different network class. For example, since a router knows that a Class A network address always starts with a 0, the router might be able to speed a packet on its way after reading only the first bit of its address. This is where the address schemes define the difference between a Class A, a Class B, and a Class C address. In the next sections, I'll discuss the differences between these three classes, followed by a discussion of the Class D and Class E addresses.

FIGURE 2.10   Summary of the three classes of networks

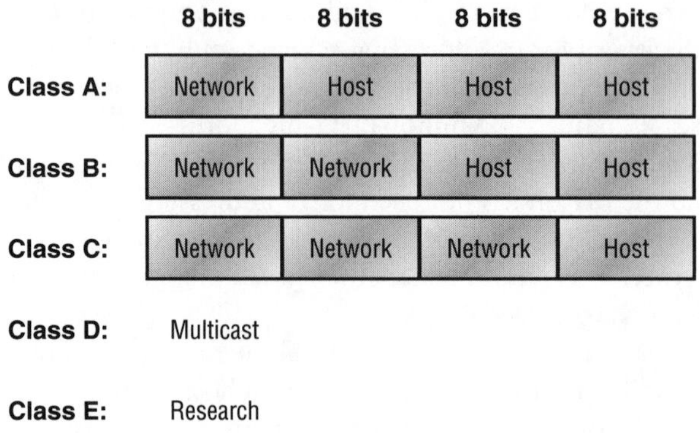

Network Address Range: Class A

The designers of the IP address scheme said that the first bit of the first byte in a Class A network address must always be off, or 0. This means a Class A address must be between 0 and 127 inclusive.

Consider the following network address:

0xxxxxxx

If we turn the other 7 bits all off and then turn them all on, we'll find the Class A range of network addresses:

00000000 = 0
01111111 = 127

So, a Class A network is defined in the first octet between 0 and 127, and it can't be less or more. (I'll talk about illegal addresses in a minute.)

Network Address Range: Class B

In a Class B network, the RFCs state that the first bit of the first byte must always be turned on, but the second bit must always be turned off. If you turn the other 6 bits all off and then all on, you will find the range for a Class B network:

10000000 = 128
10111111 = 191

As you can see, a Class B network is defined when the first byte is configured from 128 to 191.

Network Address Range: Class C

For Class C networks, the RFCs define the first 2 bits of the first octet as always turned on, but the third bit can never be on. Following the same process as the previous classes, convert from binary to decimal to find the range. Here's the range for a Class C network:

```
11000000 = 192
11011111 = 223
```

So, if you see an IP address that starts at 192 and goes to 223, you'll know it is a Class C IP address.

Network Address Ranges: Classes D and E

The addresses between 224 and 255 are reserved for Class D and E networks. Class D (224–239) is used for multicast addresses and Class E (240–255) for scientific purposes, but I'm not going into these types of addresses in this book (and you don't need to know them for the exam).

Network Addresses: Special Purpose

Some IP addresses are reserved for special purposes, so network administrators can't ever assign these addresses to nodes. Table 2.6 lists the members of this exclusive little club and the reasons why they're included in it.

T A B L E 2 . 6   Reserved IP Addresses

Address	Function
Network address of all 0s	Interpreted to mean "this network or segment."
Network address of all 1s	Interpreted to mean "all networks."
Network 127.0.0.1	Reserved for loopback tests. Designates the local node and allows that node to send a test packet to itself without generating network traffic.
Node address of all 0s	Interpreted to mean "network address" or any host on specified network.
Node address of all 1s	Interpreted to mean "all nodes" on the specified network; for example, 128.2.255.255 means "all nodes" on network 128.2 (Class B address).
Entire IP address set to all 0s	Used by Cisco routers to designate the default route. Could also mean "any network."
Entire IP address set to all 1s (same as 255.255.255.255)	Broadcast to all nodes on the current network; sometimes called an "all 1s broadcast" or limited broadcast.

Class A Addresses

In a Class A network address, the first byte is assigned to the network address, and the three remaining bytes are used for the node addresses. The Class A format is:

network.node.node.node

For example, in the IP address 49.22.102.70, the 49 is the network address, and 22.102.70 is the node address. Every machine on this particular network would have the distinctive network address of 49.

Class A network addresses are one byte long, with the first bit of that byte reserved and the 7 remaining bits available for manipulation (addressing). As a result, the maximum number of Class A networks that can be created is 128. Why? Because each of the 7 bit positions can be either a 0 or a 1, thus 2^7 or 128.

To complicate matters further, the network address of all 0s (0000 0000) is reserved to designate the default route (see Table 2.6 in the previous section). Additionally, the address 127, which is reserved for diagnostics, can't be used either, which means that you can really only use the numbers 1 to 126 to designate Class A network addresses. This means the actual number of usable Class A network addresses is 128 minus 2, or 126.

Each Class A address has three bytes (24-bit positions) for the node address of a machine. This means there are 2^{24}—or 16,777,216—unique combinations and, therefore, precisely that many possible unique node addresses for each Class A network. Because node addresses with the two patterns of all 0s and all 1s are reserved, the actual maximum usable number of nodes for a Class A network is 2^{24} minus 2, which equals 16,777,214. Either way, that's a huge amount of hosts on a network segment!

Class A Valid Host IDs

Here's an example of how to figure out the valid host IDs in a Class A network address:

- All host bits off is the network address: 10.0.0.0.
- All host bits on is the broadcast address: 10.255.255.255.

The valid hosts are the numbers in between the network address and the broadcast address: 10.0.0.1 through 10.255.255.254. Notice that 0s and 255s can be valid host IDs. All you need to remember when trying to find valid host addresses is that the host bits can't all be turned off or all be on at the same time.

Class B Addresses

In a Class B network address, the first two bytes are assigned to the network address and the remaining two bytes are used for node addresses. The format is:

network.network.node.node

For example, in the IP address 172.16.30.56, the network address is 172.16, and the node address is 30.56.

With a network address being two bytes (8 bits each), there would be 2^{16} unique combinations. But the Internet designers decided that all Class B network addresses should start with the binary digit 1, then 0. This leaves 14 bit positions to manipulate, therefore 16,384 (that is, 2^{14}) unique Class B network addresses.

A Class B address uses two bytes for node addresses. This is 2^{16} minus the two reserved patterns (all 0s and all 1s), for a total of 65,534 possible node addresses for each Class B network.

Class B Valid Host IDs

Here's an example of how to find the valid hosts in a Class B network:

- All host bits turned off is the network address: 172.16.0.0.
- All host bits turned on is the broadcast address: 172.16.255.255.

The valid hosts would be the numbers in between the network address and the broadcast address: 172.16.0.1 through 172.16.255.254.

Class C Addresses

The first three bytes of a Class C network address are dedicated to the network portion of the address, with only one measly byte remaining for the node address. The format is

network.network.network.node

Using the example IP address 192.168.100.102, the network address is 192.168.100, and the node address is 102.

In a Class C network address, the first three bit positions are always the binary 110. The calculation is: 3 bytes, or 24 bits, minus 3 reserved positions, leaves 21 positions. Hence, there are 2^{21}, or 2,097,152, possible Class C networks.

Each unique Class C network has one byte to use for node addresses. This leads to 28 or 256, minus the two reserved patterns of all 0s and all 1s, for a total of 254 node addresses for each Class C network.

Class C Valid Host IDs

Here's an example of how to find a valid host ID in a Class C network:

- All host bits turned off is the network ID: 192.168.100.0.
- All host bits turned on is the broadcast address: 192.168.100.255.

The valid hosts would be the numbers in between the network address and the broadcast address: 192.168.100.1 through 192.168.100.254.

Private IP Addresses

The people who created the IP addressing scheme also created what we call private IP addresses. These addresses can be used on a private network, but they're not routable through the Internet. This is designed for the purpose of creating a measure of well-needed security, but it also conveniently saves valuable IP address space.

If every host on every network had to have real routable IP addresses, we would have run out of IP addresses to hand out years ago. But by using private IP addresses, ISPs, corporations, and home users only need a relatively tiny group of bona fide IP addresses to connect their networks to the Internet. This is economical because they can use private IP addresses on their inside networks and get along just fine.

To accomplish this task, the ISP and the corporation—the end user, no matter who they are—need to use something called a *Network Address Translation (NAT)*, which basically takes a private IP address and converts it for use on the Internet. Many people can use the same real IP address to transmit out onto the Internet. Doing things this way saves megatons of address space—good for us all!

I'll provide an introduction to what NAT is in the section "Introduction to Network Address Translation (NAT)."

🌐 Real World Scenario

So, what private IP address should I use?

That's a really great question: Should you use Class A, Class B, or even Class C private addressing when setting up your network? Let's take Acme Corporation in SF, as an example. This company is moving into a new building and needs a whole new network (what a treat this is!). They have fourteen departments, with about 70 users in each. You could probably squeeze one or two class C addresses to use, or maybe you could use a class B, or even a class A, just for fun.

The rule of thumb in the consulting world is, when you're setting up a corporate network—regardless of how small it is—you should use a Class A network address because it gives you the most flexibility and growth options. For example, if you used the 10.0.0.0 network address with a /24 mask, then you'd have 65,534 networks, each with 254 hosts. Lots of room for growth with that network!

But if you're setting up a home network, you'd opt for a Class C address because it is the easiest for people to understand and configure. Using the default Class C mask gives you one network with 254 hosts—plenty for a home network.

With the Acme Corporation, a nice 10.1.x.0 with a /24 mask (the x is the subnet for each department) makes this easy to design, install and troubleshoot.

The reserved private addresses are listed in Table 2.7.

TABLE 2.7   Reserved IP Address Space

Address Class	Reserved address space
Class A	10.0.0.0 through 10.255.255.255
Class B	172.16.0.0 through 172.31.255.255
Class C	192.168.0.0 through 192.168.255.255

Broadcast Addresses

Even though I've referred to broadcast addresses throughout Chapters 1 and 2, I really haven't gone into their different terms and uses. Here are the four different types I'd like to define:

Layer 2 broadcasts   These are sent to all nodes on a LAN.

Broadcasts (layer 3)   These are sent to all nodes on the network.

Unicast   These are sent to a single destination host.

Multicast   These are packets sent from a single source, and transmitted to many devices on different networks.

First, understand that layer 2 broadcasts are also known as hardware broadcasts—they only go out on a LAN, and they usually don't go past the LAN boundary (router) unless they become a unicast packet (discussed in a minute). The typical hardware address is 6 bytes (48 bits) and looks something like 0c.43.a4.f3.12.c2. The broadcast would be all 1s in binary and all Fs in hexadecimal, as in FF.FF.FF.FF.FF.FF.

Then there's the plain old broadcast addresses at layer 3. Broadcast messages are meant to reach all hosts on a broadcast domain. These are the network broadcasts that have all host bits on. Here's an example that you're already familiar with: The network address of 172.16.0.0 255.255.0.0 would have a broadcast address of 172.16.255.255—all host bits on. Broadcasts can also be "all networks and all hosts," as indicated by 255.255.255.255. A good example of a broadcast message is an Address Resolution Protocol (ARP) request. When a host has a packet, it knows the logical address (IP) of the destination. To get the packet to the destination, the host needs to forward the packet to a default gateway if the destination resides on a different IP network. If the destination is on the local network, the source will forward the packet directly to the destination. Because the source doesn't have the MAC address it needs to forward the frame to, it sends out a broadcast, something that every device in the local broadcast domain will listen to. This broadcast says, in essence, "If you are the owner of IP address 192.168.2.3, please forward your MAC address to..." with the source giving the appropriate information.

A unicast is different because it's a broadcast that has an actual destination IP address—in other words, it's directed to a specific host, typically a DHCP server. Here's an example: Your host on a LAN sends out an FF.FF.FF.FF.FF.FF and 255.255.255.255 destination broadcast looking for a DHCP server on the LAN. The router will see that this is a broadcast meant for the DHCP server, and forward the request to the IP address of the DHCP server on another LAN. So, basically, if your DHCP server IP address is 172.16.10.1, your host just sends out a 255.255.255.255 broadcast, and the router changes that broadcast to the specific destination address of 172.16.10.1.

Multicast is a different beast entirely. At first glance, it appears to be a hybrid of unicast and broadcast communication, but that isn't quite the case. Multicast does allow point-to-multipoint communication, which is similar to broadcasts, but it happens in a different manner. The crux of *multicast* is that it enables multiple recipients to receive messages without flooding the messages to all hosts on a broadcast domain.

Multicast works by sending messages or data to IP *multicast group* addresses. Routers then forward copies of the packet out every interface that has hosts *subscribed* to that group address. This is where multicast differs from broadcast messages—with multicast communication, copies of packets, in theory, are sent only to subscribed hosts.

There are several different groups that users or applications can subscribe to. The range of multicast addresses starts with 224.0.0.0, and goes through 239.255.255.255. As you can see, this range of addresses falls within IP Class D address space based on classful IP assignment.

Introduction to Network Address Translation (NAT)

Whether your network is the home or the corporate type, if it uses the private IP addresses that I just talked about, you have to translate your private inside addresses to a global outside address by using NAT. The main idea is to conserve Internet global address space, but it also increases network security by hiding internal IP addresses from external networks. In NAT terminology, the *inside network* is the set of networks that are subject to translation. The *outside network* refers to all other addresses—usually those located on the Internet. However, just to help confuse you, it's important to understand that you can translate packets coming into the private network as well.

NAT operates on a Cisco router—generally only connecting two networks together—and translates your private (inside local) addresses within the internal network, into public (inside global) addresses before any packets are forwarded to another network. This functionality gives you the option to configure NAT so that it will advertise only a single address for your entire network to the outside world. Doing this effectively hides the internal network from the whole world really well, giving you some much needed additional security.

There are different flavors of NAT:

Static NAT   Designed to allow one-to-one mapping between local and global addresses. This flavor requires you to have one real Internet IP address for every host on your network.

Dynamic NAT   Designed to map an unregistered IP address to a registered IP address from out of a pool of registered IP addresses. You don't have to statically configure your router to map an inside to an outside address as in static NAT, but you do have to have enough real IP addresses for everyone who wants to send packets to and from the Internet.

Overloading   This is the most popular type of NAT configuration. Overloading is a form of dynamic NAT that maps multiple unregistered IP addresses to a single registered IP address (many-to-one) by using different ports. Therefore, it's also known as *port address translation (PAT)*. By using PAT (NAT Overload), you can have thousands of users connect to the Internet using only one real global IP address—pretty slick! NAT Overload is the reason we have not run out of valid IP address on the Internet.

Summary

If you made it this far and understood everything the first time through, you should be proud of yourself. We really covered a lot of ground in this chapter, but understand that the information in this chapter is key to being able to navigate through the rest of this book. And even if you didn't get a complete understanding the first time around, don't stress. It really wouldn't hurt you to read this chapter more than once. There are still lots of ground to cover, so make sure you've got it all down, and get ready for more

In this chapter, you learned about the Internet Protocol stack and the various protocols used at each layer of the DoD model. You then learned about translating binary to decimal to hex. I can't stress how important it is for you to truly understand the difference between the three types of addresses and how to translate each one.

After you learned about the DoD model and binary, decimal, and hex addressing, you learned the all-so-important IP addressing. I discussed in detail the difference between each class of address and how to find a network address, broadcast address, and valid host range, which is critical information to understand before going on to Chapter 3, "IP Subnetting and Variable Length Subnet Masks (VLSM)."

Lastly, I covered the private IP address range and Network Address Translation (NAT).

Since you've already come this far, there's no reason to stop now and waste all those brain-waves and new neurons. So don't stop—go through the written and review questions at the end of this chapter and make sure you understand each answer's explanation. The best is yet to come!

Exam Essentials

Remember the Process/Application layer protocols.   Telnet is a terminal emulation program that allows you to log into a remote host and run programs. File Transfer Protocol (FTP) is a connection-oriented service that allows you to transfer files. Trivial FTP (TFTP) is a connectionless file transfer program. Simple Mail Transfer Protocol (SMTP) is a send mail program.

Remember the Host-to-Host layer protocols.   Transmission Control Protocol (TCP) is a connection-oriented protocol that provides reliable network service by using acknowledgments and flow control. User Datagram Protocol (UDP) is a connectionless protocol that provides low overhead and is considered unreliable.

Remember the Internet layer protocols.   Internet Protocol (IP) is a connectionless protocol that provides network address and routing through an internetwork. Address Resolution Protocol (ARP) finds a hardware address from a known IP address. Reverse ARP (RARP) finds an IP address from a known hardware address. Internet Control Message Protocol (ICMP) provides diagnostics and unreachable messages.

Remember the Class A range.   The IP range for a Class A network is 1–126. This provides 8 bits of network addressing and 24 bits of host addressing by default.

Remember the Class B range.   The IP range for a Class B network is 128–191. Class B addressing provides 16 bits of network addressing and 16 bits of host addressing by default.

Remember the Class C range.   The IP range for a Class C network is 192–223. Class C addressing provides 24 bits of network addressing and 8 bits of host addressing by default.

Key Terms

Before you take the exam, be certain you are familiar with the following terms:

Address Resolution Protocol (ARP)	Network Access layer
bit	network address
broadcast address	Network Address Translation (NAT)
byte	Network File System (NFS)
Class A network	node address
Class B network	octets
Class C network	outside network
connectionless	port address translation (PAT)
connection-oriented	port numbers
Domain Name Service (DNS)	Process/Application layer
Dynamic Host Configuration Protocol (DHCP)	RARP server

File Transfer Protocol (FTP)

fully qualified domain name (FQDN)

hierarchical addressing

host address

Host-to-Host layer

inside network

Internet Control Message Protocol (ICMP)

Internet layer

Internet Protocol (IP)

IP address

logical address

multicast

multicast group

Reverse Address Resolution Protocol (RARP)

sequencing

Simple Mail Transfer Protocol (SMTP)

Simple Network Management Protocol (SNMP)

software address

Telnet

Transmission Control Protocol (TCP)

Transmission Control Protocol/Internet Protocol (TCP/IP)

Trivial File Transfer Protocol (TFTP)

User Datagram Protocol (UDP)

virtual circuit

X Window

Written Lab 2

1. What is the Class C address range in decimal and in binary?
2. What layer of the DoD model is equivalent to the Transport layer of the OSI model?
3. What is the valid range of a Class A network address?
4. What is the 127.0.0.1 address used for?
5. How do you find the network address from a listed IP address?
6. How do you find the broadcast address from a listed IP address?
7. What is the Class A private IP address space?
8. What is the Class B private IP address space?
9. What is the Class C private IP address space?
10. What are all the available characters that you can use in hexadecimal addressing?

(The answers to the Written Lab 2 can be found following the answers to the Review Questions for this chapter.)

Review Questions

1. What is the decimal and hexadecimal equivalent of the binary number 10101010?

   A. Decimal 100, hexadecimal 3ef2

   B. Decimal 150, hexadecimal AB

   C. Decimal 170, hexadecimal AA

   D. Decimal 180, hexadecimal FF

2. Which of the following statements are true? (Choose five options.)

   A. IP is connectionless and provides routing.

   B. ARP is used to find an IP address of a host.

   C. UDP is connectionless.

   D. TCP is connection oriented.

   E. TCP uses windowing as a flow control method.

   F. ICMP is used to manage data to routers.

   G. ARP is used to find a hardware address from a known IP address.

3. What is the address range of a Class C network address?

   A. 0–127

   B. 1–126

   C. 128–191

   D. 192–223

4. What protocol is used to find the hardware address of a local device?

   A. RARP

   B. ARP

   C. IP

   D. ICMP

   E. BootP

5. What are the two most common elements of a request/reply pair with ICMP messages when using the Ping program?

   A. Echo reply

   B. Echo request

   C. Destination unreachable

   D. Source quench

6. Which class of IP address provides a maximum of only 254 host addresses per network ID?

    A. Class A

    B. Class B

    C. Class C

    D. Class D

    E. Class E

7. Which two protocol tools use ICMP?

    A. Telnet

    B. Ping

    C. ARP

    D. Traceroute

8. Which of the following is a true statement?

    A. MAC address broadcasts are all zeros.

    B. MAC addresses are defined at the Physical layer.

    C. MAC addresses are used by bridges and switches to make forwarding/filtering decisions.

    D. IP addresses allow a flat address scheme, whereas MAC addresses are hierarchical.

9. What is the address range of a Class B network address?

    A. 0–127

    B. 1–126

    C. 128–191

    D. 192–223

10. What is the result of using a hierarchical addressing scheme?

    A. Increased number of addresses

    B. Decreased amount of routers needed

    C. Increased memory usage on routers

    D. No routing tables needed on routers

11. Which of the following statements are true? (Choose two.)

    A. TCP is connection-oriented but doesn't use flow control.

    B. IP is not necessary on all hosts that use TCP.

    C. ICMP must be implemented by all TCP/IP hosts.

    D. ARP is used to find a hardware address from a known IP address.

12. Which of the following are the Internet Protocol (IP) protocols used at the Application layer of the OSI model? (Choose three.)

   A. IP

   B. TCP

   C. Telnet

   D. FTP

   E. TFTP

13. You have the following binary number: 10110011. Which two of the following are equivalent to this?

   A. 128

   B. 179

   C. 184

   D. 0xAC

   E. 0x3C

   F. 0xB3

14. If you use either Telnet or FTP, which is the highest layer you are using to transmit data?

   A. Application

   B. Presentation

   C. Session

   D. Transport

15. The DoD model (also called the TCP/IP stack) has four layers. Which layer of the DoD model is equivalent to the Network layer of the OSI model?

   A. Application

   B. Host to Host

   C. Internet

   D. Network Access

16. You have the following binary number: 11000111. Which two of the following are equivalent to this?

   A. 228

   B. 179

   C. 199

   D. 0xC7

   E. 0x3C

   F. 0xB7

17. What layer in the TCP/IP stack is equivalent to the Transport layer of the OSI model?

    A. Application

    B. Host to Host

    C. Internet

    D. Network Access

18. What is the address range of a Class A network address in binary?

    A. 01$xxxxxx$

    B. 0$xxxxxxx$

    C. 10$xxxxxx$

    D. 110$xxxxx$

19. What is the address range of a Class B network address in binary?

    A. 01$xxxxxx$

    B. 0$xxxxxxx$

    C. 10$xxxxxx$

    D. 110$xxxxx$

20. Which of the following could be a unicast?

    A. 10.3.1.27/30

    B. 255.255.255.255

    C. 172.16.128.255/18

    D. 192.168.10.48/29

Answers to Review Questions

1. C. To turn a binary number into decimal, you just have to add the values of each bit that is a 1. The values of 10101010 are 128, 32, 8, and 2. 128 + 32 = 160 + 8 = 168 + 2 = 170. The decimal answer is 170. Hexadecimal is a base 16 number system. The values of hexadecimal are 0, 1, 2, 3, 4, 5, 6, 7, 8, 9, A, B, C, D, E, F—sixteen characters total, from which to create all the numbers you'll ever need. So, if 1010 in binary is 10, then the hexadecimal equivalent is A. Since we have 1010 and 1010, the hexadecimal answer is AA.

2. A, C, D, E, G. Both IP and UDP are connectionless, TCP is connection-oriented and uses windowing, and ARP is used to find a hardware address from a known IP address.

3. D. The address range of a Class C network is 192–223.

4. B. Address Resolution Protocol (ARP) is used to find the hardware address from a known IP address.

5. A, B. The Ping program uses ICMP echo request and echo replies to check a host on an internetwork.

6. C. A Class C network address has only 8 bits for defining hosts: $2^8 - 2 = 254$.

7. B, D. ICMP is used by both Ping and Traceroute.

8. C. MAC addresses are a flat address scheme and used by bridges/switches to make forwarding/filtering decisions. Routers use IP addresses, which are a hierarchical address scheme, to make routing decisions.

9. C. The address range for a Class B network address is 128–191.

10. A. The designers created a hierarchical addressing scheme when they created the IP address so that more addresses would be available to each network.

11. C, D. ICMP must be implemented by all TCP/IP hosts, and ARP is used to find a hardware address from a known IP address.

12. C, D, E. Telnet, File Transfer Protocol (FTP), and Trivial FTP are all Application layer protocols. IP is a Network layer protocol. Transmission Control Protocol (TCP) is a Transport layer protocol.

13. B, F. You need to find the decimal and hexadecimal equivalent to the listed binary number of 10110011. First, add the byte digits up: 128 + 32 + 16 + 2 + 1 = 179. Then, break the byte into nibbles and add those up as your hexadecimal answer: 1011 = 11, which is B in hex, and 0011, which is 3 in decimal and hex. So the answer is B3. However, Cisco likes to try to confuse you by adding the 0x in front, which just means that the following characters are hex characters.

14. A. Both FTP and Telnet use TCP at the Transport layer; however, they both are Application layer protocols, so the Application layer is the best answer for this question.

15. C. The four layers of the DoD model are Application/Process, Host to Host, Internet, and Network Access. The Internet layer is equivalent to the Network layer of the OSI model.

16. C, D. First, convert the binary number of 11000111 to a decimal address by adding up the bits that are ones (1s): 128 + 64 + 4 + 2 + 1 = 199. Now, to get our hexadecimal address, break the byte into nibbles: 1100 = 12 or C in hex and 0111 = 7 in both decimal and hex. However, Cisco likes to try to confuse you by adding the 0x in front, which just means that the following characters are hex characters.

17. B. The four layers of the TCP/IP stack (also called the DoD model) are Application/Process, Host to Host, Internet, and Network Access. The Host to Host layer is equivalent to the Transport layer of the OSI model.

18. B. The range of a Class A network address is 0–127, where only 1–126 are valid. This makes our binary range 0xxxxxxxx.

19. C. The range of a Class B network address is 128–191. This makes our binary range 10xxxxxx.

20. C. Understand that a Unicast is a broadcast that is forwarded to a specific host. Only answer C is a valid host; the rest are broadcast addresses. 172.16.128.255/18 is 255.255.192.0. The valid networks are 640 and128.0, where the broadcast address from 172.16.128.0 is 172.16.191.255 because the next block size of 64 is 192. You'll learn more about this in Chapter 3.

Answers to Written Lab 2

1. 192-223, 110xxxxx
2. Host to Host
3. 1–126
4. Loopback or diagnostics
5. Turn all host bits off.
6. Turn all host bits on.
7. 10.0.0.0 through 10.255.255.255
8. 172.16.0.0 through 172.31.255.255
9. 192.168.0.0 through 192.168.255.255
10. 0–9 and A, B, C, D, E and F

IP Subnetting and Variable Length Subnet Masks (VLSM)

THE CCNA EXAM TOPICS COVERED IN THIS CHAPTER INCLUDE THE FOLLOWING:

✓ **PLANNING & DESIGNING**

- Design a simple LAN using Cisco Technology
- Design an IP addressing scheme to meet design requirements
- Design a simple internetwork using Cisco technology

✓ **TECHNOLOGY**

- Evaluate TCP/IP communication process and its associated protocols

✓ **TROUBLESHOOTING**

- Perform LAN and VLAN troubleshooting
- Troubleshoot IP addressing and host configuration
- Troubleshoot a device as part of a working network

This chapter will pick up right where we left off in the last chapter. We will continue our discussion of IP addressing.

We will start with subnetting an IP network. You're going to have to really apply yourself, because subnetting takes time and practice in order to nail it, so be patient. Do whatever it takes to get this stuff dialed in. This chapter truly is very important—possibly the most important chapter in this book for you to understand.

I'll thoroughly cover IP subnetting from the very beginning. I know this might sound weird to you, but I think you'll be much better off if you can try to forget everything you've learned about subnetting before reading this chapter—especially if you've been to a Microsoft class!

After our discussion of IP subnetting, I'm going to tell you all about Variable Length Subnet Masks (VLSMs), as well as show you how to design and implement a network using VLSM networks.

I'm going to wrap up the chapter by going over IP address troubleshooting and take you through the steps Cisco recommends when troubleshooting an IP network.

So get psyched—you're about to go for quite a ride! This chapter will truly help you understand IP addressing and networking, so don't get discouraged or give up! If you stick with it, I promise—one day you'll look back on this and you'll be really glad you decided to hang on. It's one of those things that after you understand it, you'll wonder why you once thought it was so hard! So...ready? Let's go!

Subnetting Basics

In Chapter 2, you learned how to define and find the valid host ranges used in a Class A, Class B, and Class C network address by turning the host bits all off and then all on. This is very good, but here's the catch: You were only defining one network. What happens if you wanted to take one network address and create six networks from it? You would have to do something called *subnetting*, because that's what allows you to take one larger network and break it into a bunch of smaller networks.

There are loads of reasons in favor of subnetting. Some of the benefits include:

Reduced network traffic We all appreciate less traffic of any kind. Networks are no different. Without trusty routers, packet traffic could grind the entire network down to a near standstill. With routers, most traffic will stay on the local network; only packets destined for other networks will pass through the router. Routers create broadcast domains. The smaller broadcast domains you create, the less network traffic on that network segment.

Optimized network performance This is a result of reduced network traffic.

Simplified management   It's easier to identify and isolate network problems in a group of smaller connected networks than within one gigantic network.

Facilitated spanning of large geographical distances   Because WAN links are considerably slower and more expensive than LAN links, a single large network that spans long distances can create problems in every arena listed above. Connecting multiple smaller networks makes the system more efficient.

In the following sections, I am going to move to subnetting a network address. This is the good part...ready?

How to Create Subnets

To create subnetworks, you take bits from the host portion of the IP address and reserve them to define the subnet address. This means fewer bits for hosts, so the more subnets, the fewer bits available for defining hosts.

Later in this chapter, you'll learn how to create subnets, starting with Class C addresses. But before you actually implement subnetting, you need to determine your current requirements as well as plan for future conditions. Follow these steps:

1. Determine the number of required network IDs:
    - One for each subnet
    - One for each wide area network connection
2. Determine the number of required host IDs per subnet:
    - One for each TCP/IP host
    - One for each router interface
3. Based on the above requirement, create the following:
    - One subnet mask for your entire network
    - A unique subnet ID for each physical segment
    - A range of host IDs for each subnet

Understanding the Powers of 2

Powers of 2 are important to understand and memorize for use with IP subnetting. To review powers of 2, remember that when you see a number with another number to its upper right (called an exponent), this means you should multiply the number by itself as many times as the upper number specifies. For example, 2^3 is $2 \times 2 \times 2$, which equals 8. Here's a list of powers of 2 you should commit to memory:

$2^1 = 2$	$2^3 = 8$	$2^5 = 32$	$2^7 = 128$
$2^2 = 4$	$2^4 = 16$	$2^6 = 64$	$2^8 = 256$

Subnet Masks

For the subnet address scheme to work, every machine on the network must know which part of the host address will be used as the subnet address. This is accomplished by assigning a *subnet mask* to each machine. A subnet mask is a 32-bit value that allows the recipient of IP packets to distinguish the network ID portion of the IP address from the host ID portion of the IP address.

The network administrator creates a 32-bit subnet mask composed of 1s and 0s. The 1s in the subnet mask represent the positions that refer to the network or subnet addresses.

Not all networks need subnets, meaning they use the default subnet mask. This is basically the same as saying that a network doesn't have a subnet address. Table 3.1 shows the default subnet masks for Classes A, B, and C. These default masks cannot change. In other words, you can't make a Class B subnet mask read 255.0.0.0. If you try, the host will read that address as invalid and usually won't even let you type it in. For a Class A network, you can't change the first byte in a subnet mask; it must read 255.0.0.0 at a minimum. Similarly, you cannot assign 255.255.255.255, as this is all 1s—a broadcast address. A Class B address must start with 255.255.0.0, and a Class C has to start with 255.255.255.0.

TABLE 3.1   Default Subnet Mask

Class	Format	Default Subnet Mask
A	*network.node.node.node*	255.0.0.0
B	*network.network.node.node*	255.255.0.0
C	*network.network.network.node*	255.255.255.0

Classless Inter-Domain Routing (CIDR)

Another term you need to familiarize your self with is Classless Inter-Domain Routing (CIDR). It's basically the method that ISPs (Internet Service Providers) use to allocate an amount of addresses to a company, a home—a customer. They provide addresses in a certain block size—something I'll be going into in greater detail later in this chapter.

When you receive a block of addresses from an ISP, what you get will look something like this: 192.168.10.32/28. What this is telling you is what your subnet mask is. The slash notation (/) means how many bits are turned on (1s). Obviously, the maximum could only be /32 because a byte is 8 bits and there are four bytes in an IP address: ($4 \times 8 = 32$). But keep in mind that the largest subnet mask available (regardless of the class of address) can only be a /30 because you've got to keep at least 2 bits for host bits.

Take for example a Class A default subnet mask, which is 255.0.0.0. This means that the first byte of the subnet mask is all ones (1s) or 11111111. When referring to a slash notation, you need to count all the 1s bits to figure out your mask. The 255.0.0.0 is considered a /8 because it has 8 bits that are 1s—that is, 8 bits that are turned on.

A Class B default mask would be 255.255.0.0, which is a /16 because 16 bits are ones (1s): 11111111.11111111.00000000.00000000.

Table 3.2 has a listing of every available subnet mask and its equivalent CIDR slash notation.

TABLE 3.2   CIDR Values

Subnet Mask	CIDR Value
255.0.0.0	/8
255.128.0.0	/9
255.192.0.0	/10
255.224.0.0	/11
255.240.0.0	/12
255.248.0.0	/13
255.252.0.0	/14
255.254.0.0	/15
255.255.0.0	/16
255.255.128.0	/17
255.255.192.0	/18
255.255.224.0	/19
255.255.240.0	/20
255.255.248.0	/21
255.255.252.0	/22
255.255.254.0	/23
255.255.255.0	/24
255.255.255.128	/25
255.255.255.192	/26

T A B L E   3 . 2   CIDR Values *(continued)*

Subnet Mask	CIDR Value
255.255.255.224	/27
255.255.255.240	/28
255.255.255.248	/29
255.255.255.252	/30

No, you cannot configure a Cisco router using this slash format. Wouldn't that be nice?

Subnetting Class C Addresses

There are many different ways to subnet a network. The right way is the way that works best for you. First I'll show you how to use the binary method, and then we'll look at an easier way to do the same thing.

In a Class C address, only 8 bits are available for defining the hosts. Remember that subnet bits start at the left and go to the right, without skipping bits. This means that the only Class C subnet masks can be the following:

```
Binary     Decimal   Shorthand
--------------------------------------------------------
10000000 = 128      /25   (Not valid on the Cisco exams!)
11000000 = 192      /26
11100000 = 224      /27
11110000 = 240      /28
11111000 = 248      /29
11111100 = 252      /30
11111110 = 254      /31   (Not valid)
```

The RFCs say that you can't have only 1 bit for subnetting, since that would mean that the subnet bit would always be either off or on, which is illegal. So, the first subnet mask you can legally use is 192, and the last one is 252 because you need at least 2 bits for defining hosts.

In production, you can use 1 bit for assigning subnets. This is called *subnet-zero*. But know that Cisco doesn't consider subnet-zero valid on any of their certification exams!

In the following sections we are going to look at the binary way of subnetting, then move into the new, improved, easy to understand and implement, subnetting method!

The Binary Method: Subnetting a Class C Address

In this section, I'm going to teach you how to subnet a Class C address using the binary method. I'll start by using the first subnet mask available with a Class C address, which borrows 2 bits for subnetting. For this example, I'll be using 255.255.255.192.

192 = 11000000

The 1s represent the subnet bits, and the 0s represent the host bits available in each subnet. 192 provides 2 bits for subnetting and 6 bits for defining the hosts in each subnet.

What are the subnets? Since the subnet bits can't be both off or on at the same time, the only two valid subnets are these:

　　01000000 = 64 (all host bits off)

　　10000000 = 128 (all host bits off)

The valid hosts would be defined as the numbers between the subnets, minus the all-host-bits-off and all-host-bits-on numbers.

To find the hosts, first find your subnet by turning all the host bits off, then turn all the host bits on to find your broadcast address for the subnet. The valid hosts must be between those two numbers. Table 3.3 shows the 64 subnet, valid host range, and broadcast address. Table 3.4 shows the 128 subnet, valid host range, and broadcast address (The subnet and host bits equal to one byte).

TABLE 3.3　　Subnet 64

Subnet	Host	Meaning
01	000000 = 64	The network (do this first)
01	000001 = 65	The first valid host
01	111110 = 126	The last valid host
01	111111 = 127	The broadcast address (do this second)

TABLE 3.4   Subnet 128

Subnet	Host	Meaning
10	000000 = 128	The subnet address
10	000001 = 129	The first valid host
10	111110 = 190	The last valid host
10	111111 = 191	The broadcast address

Hopefully, you understood what I was trying to show you. The example I presented only used 2 subnet bits, so what if you had to subnet using 9, 10, or even 20 subnet bits? Try that with the binary method and see how long it takes you.

In the following section, I'm going to teach you an alternate method of subnetting that makes it easier to subnet larger numbers in no time.

Since the CCNA exam gives you just over a minute for each question, it's really important to know how much time you'll spend on a subnetting question. That's why committing as much as possible to memory as I suggested earlier in the chapter is vital. Using the binary method can take you way too long and you could fail the exam even if you know the material!

The Fast Way: Subnetting a Class C Address

When you've chosen a possible subnet mask for your network and need to determine the number of subnets, valid hosts, and broadcast addresses of a subnet that the mask provides, all you need to do is answer five simple questions:

- How many subnets does the chosen subnet mask produce?
- How many valid hosts per subnet are available?
- What are the valid subnets?
- What's the broadcast address of each subnet?
- What are the valid hosts in each subnet?

At this point it's important that you both understand and have memorized your powers of 2. Please refer to the sidebar earlier in this chapter if you need some help. Here's how you get the answers to those five big questions:

- *How many subnets?* $2^x - 2$ = number of subnets. x is the number of masked bits, or the 1s. For example, in 11000000, the number of ones gives us $2^2 - 2$ subnets. In this example, there are 2 subnets.

- *How many hosts per subnet?* $2^y - 2$ = number of hosts per subnet. y is the number of unmasked bits, or the 0s. For example, in 11000000, the number of zeros gives us $2^6 - 2$ hosts. In this example, there are 62 hosts per subnet.

- *What are the valid subnets?* 256 – subnet mask = block size, or base number. For example, 256 – 192 = 64. 64 is the first subnet. The next subnet would be the base number plus itself, or 64 + 64 = 128, (the second subnet). You keep adding the base number to itself until you reach the value of the subnet mask, which is not a valid subnet because all subnet bits would be turned on (1s).

- *What's the broadcast address for each subnet?* The broadcast address is all host bits turned on, which is the number immediately preceding the next subnet.

- *What are the valid hosts?* Valid hosts are the numbers between the subnets, omitting all 0s and all 1s.

I know this can truly seem confusing. But it really isn't as hard as it seems to be at first—just hang in there! Why not try a few and see for yourself?

Subnetting Practice Examples: Class C Addresses

Here's your opportunity to practice subnetting Class C addresses using the method I just described. We're going to start with the first Class C subnet mask and work through every subnet that we can using a Class C address. When we're done, I'll show you how easy this is with Class A and B networks too!

Practice Example #1C: 255.255.255.192 (/26)

Let's use the Class C subnet mask from the preceding example, 255.255.255.192, to see how much simpler this method is than writing out the binary numbers. We're going to subnet the network address 192.168.10.0 and subnet mask 255.255.255.192.

192.168.10.0 = Network address

255.255.255.192 = Subnet mask

Now, let's answer the big five:

- *How many subnets?* Since 192 is 2 bits on (**11**000000), the answer would be $2^2 - 2 = 2$. (The minus 2 is the subnet bits all on or all off, which are not valid by default.)

- *How many hosts per subnet?* We have 6 host bits off (11**000000**), so the equation would be $2^6 - 2 = 62$ hosts.

- *What are the valid subnets?* 256 – 192 = 64, which is the first subnet and our base number or block size. Keep adding the block size to itself until you reach the subnet mask. 64 + 64 = 128. 128 + 64 = 192, which is invalid because it is the subnet mask (all subnet bits turned on). Our two valid subnets are, then, 64 and 128.

- *What's the broadcast address for each subnet?* The number right before the value of the next subnet is all host bits turned on and equals the broadcast address.

- *What are the valid hosts?* These are the numbers between the subnet and broadcast address. The easiest way to find the hosts is to write out the subnet address and the broadcast address. This way the valid hosts are obvious. The following table shows the 64 and 128 subnets, the valid host ranges of each, and the broadcast address of both subnets:

The subnets (do this first)	64	128
Our first host (perform host addressing last)	65	129
Our last host	126	190
The broadcast address (do this second)	127	191

See? We really did come up with the same answers as when we did it the binary way, and this way is so much easier because you never have to do any binary-to-decimal conversions! About now, you might be thinking that it's not easier than the first method I showed you. And I'll admit, for the first subnet with only two subnet bits—you're right, it isn't that much easier. But remember, we're going after the gold: being able to subnet in your head. And to do that, you need one thing: practice!

Practice Example #2C: 255.255.255.224 (/27)

This time, we'll subnet the network address 192.168.10.0 and subnet mask 255.255.255.224.

192.168.10.0 = Network address

255.255.255.224 = Subnet mask

- *How many subnets?* 224 is 11100000, so our equation would be $2^3 - 2 = 6$.
- *How many hosts?* $2^5 - 2 = 30$.
- *What are the valid subnets?* 256 – 224 = 32. 32 + 32 = 64. 64 + 32 = 96. 96 + 32 = 128. 128 + 32 = 160. 160 + 32 = 192. 192 + 32 = 224, which is invalid because it is our subnet mask (all subnet bits on). Our subnets are 32, 64, 96, 128, 160, and 192.
- *What's the broadcast address for each subnet (always the number right before the next subnet)?*
- *What are the valid hosts (the numbers between the subnet number and the broadcast address)?*

To answer questions 4 and 5, first just write out the subnets, then write out the broadcast addresses—the number right before the next subnet. Lastly, fill in the host addresses. The following table gives you all the subnets for the 255.255.255.224 Class C subnet mask:

The subnet address	32	64	96	128	160	192
The first valid host	33	65	97	129	161	193
The last valid host	62	94	126	158	190	222
The broadcast address	63	95	127	159	191	223

Practice Example #3C: 255.255.255.240 (/28)

Let's practice on another one:

192.168.10.0 = Network address

255.255.255.240 = Subnet mask

- *Subnets?* 240 is 11110000 in binary. $2^4 - 2 = 14$.

- *Hosts?* 4 host bits, or $2^4 - 2 = 14$.

- *Valid subnets?* $256 - 240 = 16$. $16 + 16 = 32$. $32 + 16 = 48$. $48 + 16 = 64$. $64 + 16 = 80$. $80 + 16 = 96$. $96 + 16 = 112$. $112 + 16 = 128$. $128 + 16 = 144$. $144 + 16 = 160$. $160 + 16 = 176$. $176 + 16 = 192$. $192 + 16 = 208$. $208 + 16 = 224$. $224 + 16 = 240$, which is our subnet mask and therefore invalid. So, our valid subnets are 16, 32, 48, 64, 80, 96, 112, 128, 144, 160, 176, 192, 208, and 224.

- *Broadcast address for each subnet?*

- *Valid hosts?*

To answer questions 4 and 5, check out the following table. It gives you the subnets, valid hosts, and broadcast addresses for each subnet. First, find the broadcast address of each subnet (it's always the number right before the next valid subnet), then just fill in the host addresses. The following table shows the available subnets, hosts and broadcast addresses provided from a class C 255.255.255.240 mask.

Subnet	16	32	48	64	80	96	112	128	144	160	176	192	208	224
First host	17	33	49	65	81	97	113	129	145	161	177	193	209	225
Last host	30	46	62	78	94	110	126	142	158	174	190	206	222	238
Broadcast	31	47	63	79	95	111	127	143	159	175	191	207	223	239

Cisco has figured out the most people cannot count in sixteens and therefore have a hard time finding valid subnets, hosts and broadcast addresses with the class C 255.255.255.240 mask. You'd be wise to study this mask.

Practice Example #4C: 255.255.255.248 (/29)

Let's keep practicing:

192.168.10.0 = Network address

255.255.255.248 = Subnet mask

- *Subnets?* 248 in binary = 11111000. $2^5 - 2 = 30$.

- *Hosts?* $2^3 - 2 = 6$.

- *Valid subnets?* $256 - 248 = 8, 16, 24, 32, 40, 48, 56, 64, 72, 80, 88, 96, 104, 112, 120, 128, 136, 144, 152, 160, 168, 176, 184, 192, 200, 208, 216, 224, 232,$ and 240.

- *Broadcast address for each subnet?*

- *Valid hosts?*

Okay, take a look at the following table. It shows some of the subnets (first three and last three only), valid hosts, and broadcast addresses for the Class C 255.255.255.248 mask:

Subnet	8	16	24	...	224	232	240
First host	9	17	25	...	225	233	241
Last host	14	22	30	...	230	238	246
Broadcast	15	23	31	...	231	239	247

Practice Example #5C: 255.255.255.252 (/30)

Just a couple more:

> 192.168.10.0 = Network address
>
> 255.255.255.252 = Subnet mask

- *Subnets?* 62.
- *Hosts?* 2.
- *Valid subnets?* 4, 8, 12, etc., all the way to 248.
- *Broadcast address for each subnet?* (always the number right before the next subnet)
- *Valid hosts?* (the numbers between the subnet number and the broadcast address)

🌐 **Real World Scenario**

Should we really use this mask that provides only two hosts?

You are the network administrator for Acme corporation in San Francisco, with dozens of WAN links connecting to your corporate office. Right now your network is a classful network, which means all hosts, and router interfaces have the same subnet mask on each interface. You've read about classless routing where you can have different size masks, but don't know what to use on your point-to-point WAN links. Is the 255.255.255.252 a helpful mask in this situation?

Yes, this is a very helpful mask in wide area networks.

If you use the 255.255.255.0 mask, then each network would have 254 hosts, but you only use two addresses! That is a waste of 252 hosts per subnet. If you use the 255.255.255.252 mask, then each subnet has only two hosts and you don't waste precious addresses.

This is a really important subject, one that we'll address in a lot more detail in the VLSM network design section later in this chapter.

The following table shows you the subnet, valid host, and broadcast address of the first three and last three subnets in the 255.255.255.252 Class C subnet:

Subnet	4	8	12	...	240	244	248
First host	5	9	13	...	241	245	249
Last host	6	10	14	...	242	246	250
Broadcast	7	11	15	...	243	247	251

Practice Example #6C: 255.255.255.128 (/25)

I know I told you that using only 1 subnet bit was considered illegal in the original RFCs and that you ought not to do that. But aren't most rules meant to be broken? This mask can be used when you need two subnets, each with 126 hosts. But our trusty big five questions won't work with this one—it's special—so I'll just explain it to you. First, use the global configuration command `ip subnet-zero` to tell your router to break the rules and use a 1-bit subnet mask (this is a default command on all routers running the 12.x Cisco IOS).

Since 128 is 10000000 in binary, there is only 1 bit for subnetting. Since this bit can be either off or on, the two available subnets are 0 and 128. You can determine the subnet value by looking at the decimal value of the fourth octet. If the value of the fourth octet is below 128, then the host is in the 0 subnet. If the fourth octet value is above 128, then the host is in the 128 subnet.

The following table shows you the two subnets, valid host ranges, and broadcast addresses for the Class C 255.255.255.128 mask:

Subnet	0	128
First host	1	129
Last host	126	254
Broadcast	127	255

So, if you have an IP address of 192.168.10.5 using the 255.255.255.128 subnet mask, you know it's in the range of the 0 subnet and bit number 128 must be off. If you have an IP address of 192.168.10.189, then 128 must be on, and the host is considered to be in the 128 subnet. You'll see this again in a minute.

NOTE   Okay, this is a point of much confusion. Cisco says it is okay to use this mask in production, but then considers this invalid or illegal on the Cisco exams. Cisco is saying, "do as we say, not as we do." Remember for the exam that 1 subnet bit is considered invalid.

Subnetting in Your Head: Class C Addresses

It really is possible to subnet in your head. Even if you don't you believe me, I'll show you how. And it's not all that hard either—take the following example:

192.168.10.33 = Node address

255.255.255.224 = Subnet mask

First, determine the subnet and broadcast address of the above IP address. You can do this by answering question 3 of the big five questions: 256 – 224 = 32. 32 + 32 = 64. The address falls between the two subnets and must be part of the 192.168.10.32 subnet. The next subnet is 64, so the broadcast address is 63. (Remember that the broadcast address of a subnet is always the number right before the next subnet.) The valid host range is 33–62. This is too easy! No, it's not?

Okay, then let's try another one. We'll subnet another Class C address:

192.168.10.33 = Node address

255.255.255.240 = Subnet mask

What subnet and broadcast address is the above IP address a member of? 256 – 240 = 16. 16 + 16 = 32. 32 + 16 = 48. And bingo—the host address is between the 32 and 48 subnets. The subnet is 192.168.10.32, and the broadcast address is 47. The valid host range is 33–46.

Okay, we need to do more, just to make sure you have this down.

You have a node address of 192.168.10.174 with a mask of 255.255.255.240. What is the valid host range?

The mask is 240, so we'd do a 256 – 240 = 16. This is our block size. Just keep adding 16 until we pass the host address of 174: 16, 32, 48, 64, 80, 96, 112, 128, 144, 160, 176. The host address of 174 is between 160 and 176, so the subnet is 160. The broadcast address is 175, so the valid host range is 161–174. That was a tough one.

One more—just for fun. This is the easiest one of all Class C subnetting:

192.168.10.17 = Node address

255.255.255.252 = Subnet mask

What subnet and broadcast address is the above IP address a member of? 256 – 252 = 4, 8, 12, 16, 20 . You've got it! The host address is between the 16 and 20 subnets. The subnet is 192.168.10.16, and the broadcast address is 19. The valid host range is 17–18.

Now that you're all over Class C subnetting, let's move on to Class B subnetting.

Subnetting Class B Addresses

Before we dive into this, let's look at all the possible Class B subnet masks first. Notice that we have a lot more possible subnets than we do with a Class C network address:

255.255.128.0	(/17)	255.255.255.0	(/24)
255.255.192.0	(/18)	255.255.255.128	(/25)
255.255.224.0	(/19)	255.255.255.192	(/26)
255.255.240.0	(/20)	255.255.255.224	(/27)
255.255.248.0	(/21)	255.255.255.240	(/28)

```
255.255.252.0  (/22)      255.255.255.248  (/29)
255.255.254.0  (/23)      255.255.255.252  (/30)
```

We know the Class B network address has 16 bits available for host addressing. This means we can use up to 14 bits for subnetting because we have to leave at least 2 bits for host addressing.

> **NOTE** By the way, do you notice anything interesting about that list of subnet values—a pattern, maybe? Ah ha! That's exactly why I had you memorize the binary-to-decimal numbers at the beginning of this section. Since subnet mask bits start on the left, move to the right, and can't skip bits, the numbers are always the same regardless of the class of address. Memorize this pattern.

The process of subnetting a Class B network is pretty much the same as it is for a Class C, except that you just have more host bits. Use the same subnet numbers for the third octet with Class B that you used for the fourth octet with Class C, but add a zero to the network portion and a 255 to the broadcast section in the fourth octet. The following table shows you a host range of two subnets used in a Class B subnet:

First subnet	16.0	32.0
Second subnet	16.255	32.255

Just add the valid hosts between the numbers, and you're set!

Subnetting Practice Examples: Class B Addresses

This section will give you an opportunity to practice subnetting Class B addresses.

Practice Example #1B: 255.255.192.0 (/18)

172.16.0.0 = Network address

255.255.192.0 = Subnet mask

- *Subnets?* $2^2 - 2 = 2$.
- *Hosts?* $2^{14} - 2 = 16,382$. (6 bits in the third octet, and 8 in the fourth.)
- *Valid subnets?* $256 - 192 = 64$. $64 + 64 = 128$.
- *Broadcast address for each subnet?*
- *Valid hosts?*

The following table shows the two subnets available, the valid host range, and the broadcast address of each:

Subnet	64.0	128.0
First host	64.1	128.1
Last host	127.254	191.254
Broadcast	127.255	191.255

Notice that we just added the fourth octet's lowest and highest values and came up with the answers. Again, it's pretty much the same as it is for a Class C subnet—we just added 0 and 255 in the fourth octet.

Practice Example #2B: 255.255.240.0 (/20)

172.16.0.0 = Network address

255.255.240.0 = Subnet address

- *Subnets?* $2^4 - 2 = 14$.

- *Hosts?* $2^{12} - 2 = 4094$.

- *Valid subnets?* $256 - 240 = 16, 32, 48$, etc., up to 224. Notice that these are the same numbers as a Class C 240 mask.

- *Broadcast address for each subnet?*

- *Valid hosts?*

The following table shows the first three subnets, valid hosts, and broadcast addresses in a Class B 255.255.240.0 mask:

Subnet	16.0	32.0	48.0	...
First host	16.1	32.1	48.1	...
Last host	31.254	47.254	63.254	...
Broadcast	31.255	47.255	63.255	...

Practice Example #3B: 255.255.254.0 (/23)

172.16.0.0 = Network address

255.255.254.0 = Subnet address

- *Subnets?* $2^7 - 2 = 126$.

- *Hosts?* $2^9 - 2 = 510$.

- *Valid subnets?* $256 - 254 = 2, 4, 6, 8$, etc., up to 252.

- *Broadcast address for each subnet?*

- *Valid hosts?*

The following table shows the first four subnets, valid hosts, and broadcast addresses in a Class B 255.255.254.0 mask:

Subnet	2.0	4.0	6.0	8.0	...
First host	2.1	4.1	6.1	8.1	...
Last host	3.254	5.254	7.254	9.254	...
Broadcast	3.255	5.255	7.255	9.255	...

Practice Example #4B: 255.255.255.0 (/24)

Contrary to popular belief, 255.255.255.0 used with a Class B network address is not called a Class B network with a Class C subnet mask. It's amazing how many people see this mask used in a Class B network and think it's a Class C subnet mask. This is a Class B subnet mask with 8 bits of subnetting—it's considerably different from a Class C mask. Subnetting this address is fairly simple:

172.16.0.0 = Network address

255.255.255.0 = Subnet address

- *Subnets?* $2^8 - 2 = 254$.
- *Hosts?* $2^8 - 2 = 254$.
- *Valid subnets?* $256 - 255 = 1, 2, 3$, etc. all the way to 254.
- *Broadcast address for each subnet?*
- *Valid hosts?*

The following table shows the first three subnets and the last one, valid hosts, and broadcast addresses in a Class B 255.255.255.0 mask:

Subnet	1.0	2.0	3.0	...	254.0
First host	1.1	2.1	3.1	...	254.1
Last host	1.254	2.254	3.254	...	254.254
Broadcast	1.255	2.255	3.255	...	254.255

Practice Example #5B: 255.255.255.128 (/25)

Oh no! This one's got to be illegal, right? What type of mask is it? (Don't you wish it were illegal?) Well, it's a drag, but it's not illegal. It is one of the hardest subnet masks you can play with, though. And worse, it actually is a really good subnet to use in production because it creates over 500 subnets with 126 hosts for each subnet—a nice mixture. So, don't skip over it! (Cisco thinks it's nice too!)

172.16.0.0 = Network address

255.255.255.128 = Subnet address

- *Subnets?* $2^9 - 2 = 510$.
- *Hosts?* $2^7 - 2 = 126$.
- *Valid subnets?* Okay, now for the tricky part. $256 - 255 = 1, 2, 3$, etc., for the third octet. But you can't forget the one subnet bit used in the fourth octet. Remember when I showed you how to figure one subnet bit with a Class C mask? You figure this the same way. (Now you know why I showed you the 1-bit subnet mask in the Class C section—to make this part easier.) You actually get two subnets for each fourth octet value, hence the 510 subnets. For example, if the third octet is showing subnet 3, the two subnets would actually be 3.0 and 3.128.

- *Broadcast address for each subnet?*
- *Valid hosts?*

The following table shows how you can create subnets, valid hosts, and broadcast addresses using the Class B 255.255.255.128 subnet mask (the first seven subnets are shown, and then the last subnet):

Subnet	0.128	1.0	1.128	2.0	2.128	3.0	3.128	...	255.0
First host	0.129	1.1	1.129	2.1	2.129	3.1	3.129	...	255.1
Last host	0.254	1.126	1.254	2.126	2.254	3.126	3.254	...	255.126
Broadcast	0.255	1.127	1.255	2.127	2.255	3.127	3.255	...	255.127

Practice Example #6B: 255.255.255.192 (/26)

This one gets just a little tricky. Both the 0 subnet as well as the 192 subnet could be valid in the fourth octet. It just depends on what that third octet is doing.

172.16.0.0 = Network address

255.255.255.192 = Subnet address

- *Subnets?* $2^{10} - 2 = 1022$.
- *Hosts?* $2^6 - 2 = 62$.
- *Valid subnets?* 256 − 192 = 64 and 128. And as long as all the subnet bits on the third are not all off, then subnet 0 in the fourth octet is valid. Also, as long as all the subnet bits in the third octet are not all on, 192 is valid in the fourth octet as a subnet.
- *Broadcast address for each subnet?*
- *Valid hosts?*

The following table shows the first seven subnet ranges, valid hosts, and broadcast addresses:

Subnet	0.64	0.128	0.192	1.0	1.64	1.128	1.192	...
First host	0.65	0.129	0.193	1.1	1.65	1.129	1.193	...
Last host	0.126	0.190	0.254	1.62	1.126	1.190	1.254	...
Broadcast	0.127	0.191	0.255	1.63	1.127	1.191	1.255	...

Notice that for each subnet value in the third octet, you get subnets 0, 64, 128, and 192 in the fourth octet. This is true for every subnet in the third octet except 0 and 255. I just demonstrated the 0-subnet value in the third octet. But notice that for the 1 subnet in the third octet, the fourth octet has four subnets: 0, 64, 128, and 192.

Practice Example #7B: 255.255.255.224 (/27)

This is done the same way as the preceding subnet mask, except that we just have more subnets and fewer hosts per subnet available.

172.16.0.0 = Network address

255.255.255.224 = Subnet address

- *Subnets?* $2^{11} - 2 = 2046$.
- *Hosts?* $2^5 - 2 = 30$.
- *Valid subnets?* 256 − 224 = 32, 64, 96, 128, 160, 192. However, as demonstrated above, both the 0 and 224 subnets can be used as long as the third octet does not show a value of 0 or 255. Here's an example of having no subnet bits in the third octet.
- *Broadcast address for each subnet?*
- *Valid hosts?*

The following table shows the first seven subnets:

Subnet	0.32	0.64	0.96	0.128	0.160	0.192	0.224
First host	0.33	0.65	0.97	0.129	0.161	0.193	0.225
Last host	0.62	0.94	0.126	0.158	0.190	0.222	0.254
Broadcast	0.63	0.95	0.127	0.159	0.191	0.223	0.255

Let's take a look at a situation where a subnet bit is turned on in the third octet. The following table shows the full range of subnets available in the fourth octet:

Subnet	1.0	1.32	1.64	1.96	1.128	1.160	1.192	1.224
First host	1.1	1.33	1.65	1.97	1.129	1.161	1.193	1.225
Last host	1.30	1.62	1.94	1.126	1.158	1.190	1.222	1.254
Broadcast	1.31	1.63	1.95	1.127	1.159	1.191	1.223	1.255

This next table shows the last seven subnets:

Subnet	255.0	255.32	255.64	255.96	255.128	255.160	255.192
First host	255.1	255.33	255.65	255.97	255.129	255.161	255.193
Last host	255.30	255.62	255.94	255.126	255.158	255.190	255.222
Broadcast	255.31	255.63	255.95	255.127	255.159	255.191	255.223

Subnetting in Your Head: Class B Addresses

Are you nuts? Subnet Class B addresses in our heads? If you think easier equals crazy, then, yes, I'm a few sails short, but it's actually easier than writing it out—I'm not kidding! Let me show you how:

Question: What subnet and broadcast address is the IP address 172.16.10.33 255.255.255.224 a member of?

Answer: 256 – 224 = 32. 32 + 32 = 64. Bingo: 33 is between 32 and 64. However, remember that the third octet is considered part of the subnet, so the answer would be the 10.32 subnet. The broadcast is 10.63, since 10.64 is the next subnet.

Question: What subnet and broadcast address is the IP address 172.16.90.66 255.255.255.192 a member of?

Answer: 256 – 192 = 64. 64 + 64 = 128. The subnet is 172.16.90.64. The broadcast must be 172.16.90.127, since 90.128 is the next subnet.

Question: What subnet and broadcast address is the IP address 172.16.50.97 255.255.255.224 a member of?

Answer: 256 – 224 = 32, 64, 96, 128. The subnet is 172.16.50.96, and the broadcast must be 172.16.50.127 since 50.128 is the next subnet.

Question: What subnet and broadcast address is the IP address 172.16.10.10 255.255.255.192 a member of?

Answer: 256 – 192 = 64. This address must be in the 172.16.10.0 subnet, and the broadcast must be 172.16.10.63.

Question: What subnet and broadcast address is the IP address 172.16.10.10 255.255.255.252 a member of?

Answer: 256 – 252 = 4. The subnet is 172.16.10.8, with a broadcast of 172.16.10.11.

Subnetting Class A Addresses

Class A subnetting is not performed any differently from Classes B and C, but there are 24 bits to play with instead of the 16 in a Class B address and the 8 bits in a Class C address.

Let's start by listing all the Class A subnets:

255.128.0.0	(/9)	255.255.240.0 (/20)
255.192.0.0	(/10)	255.255.248.0 (/21)
255.224.0.0	(/11)	255.255.252.0 (/22)
255.240.0.0	(/12)	255.255.254.0 (/23)
255.248.0.0	(/13)	255.255.255.0 (/24)
255.252.0.0	(/14)	255.255.255.128 (/25)
255.254.0.0	(/15)	255.255.255.192 (/26)
255.255.0.0	(/16)	255.255.255.224 (/27)
255.255.128.0	(/17)	255.255.255.240 (/28)
255.255.192.0	(/18)	255.255.255.248 (/29)
255.255.224.0	(/19)	255.255.255.252 (/30)

That's it. You must leave at least 2 bits for defining hosts. And I hope you can see the pattern by now. Remember, we're going to do this the same way as a Class B or C subnet. It's just that, again, we simply have more host bits.

Subnetting Practice Examples: Class A Addresses

When you look at an IP address and a subnet mask, you must be able to distinguish the bits used for subnets from the bits used for determining hosts. This is imperative. If you're still struggling with this concept, please reread the preceding "IP Addressing" section. It shows you how to determine the difference between the subnet and host bits, and should help clear things up.

Practice Example #1A: 255.255.0.0 (/16)

Class A addresses use a default mask of 255.0.0.0, which leaves 22 bits for subnetting since you must leave 2 bits for host addressing. The 255.255.0.0 mask with a Class A address is using 8 subnet bits.

- *Subnets?* $2^8 - 2 = 254$.
- *Hosts?* $2^{16} - 2 = 65,534$.
- *Valid subnets?* $256 - 255 = 1, 2, 3$, etc. (all in the second octet). The subnets would be 10.1.0.0, 10.2.0.0, 10.3.0.0, etc., up to 10.254.0.0.
- *Broadcast address for each subnet?*
- *Valid hosts?*

The following table shows the first and last subnet, valid host range, and broadcast addresses:

Subnet	10.1.0.0	...	10.254.0.0
First host	10.1.0.1	...	10.254.0.1
Last host	10.1.255.254	...	10.254.255.254
Broadcast	10.1.255.255	...	10.254.255.255

Practice Example #2A: 255.255.240.0 (/20)

255.255.240.0 gives us 12 bits of subnetting and leaves us 12 bits for host addressing.

- *Subnets?* $2^{12} - 2 = 4094$.
- *Hosts?* $2^{12} - 2 = 4094$.
- *Valid subnets?* $256 - 240 = 16$. And since the second octet is 255, or all subnet bits on, we can start the third octet with 0 as long as a subnet bit is turned on in the second octet. So, the first valid subnets are 10.0.16.0, 10.0.32.0, and 10.0.48.0, all the way to 10.0.240.0. However, 10.0.0.0 and 10.255.240.0 are not valid subnet addresses by default. The next set of subnets would be 10.1.0.0, 10.1.16.0, 10.1.32.0, 10.1.48.0, all the way to 10.1.240.0. Notice that we can use 240 in the third octet as long as the subnet bits in the second octet are not all on (1s). In addition, we can use 0 in the third octet as long as the second octet is not a 0. In other words, 10.255.240.0 is invalid because all subnet bits are turned on. The last valid subnet would have to be 10.255.224.0.

- *Broadcast address for each subnet?*
- *Valid hosts?*

The following table shows some examples of the host ranges—the first, second, and last subnets:

Subnet	10.1.0.0	10.1.16.0	...	10.255.224.0
First host	10.1.0.1	10.1.16.1	...	10.255.224.1
Last host	10.1.15.254	10.1.31.254	...	10.255.239.254
Broadcast	10.1.15.255	10.1.31.255	...	10.255.239.255

Practice Example #3A: 255.255.255.192 (/26)

Let's do one more example using the second, third, and fourth octets for subnetting.

- *Subnets?* $2^{18} - 2 = 262,142$.
- *Hosts?* $2^6 - 2 = 62$.
- *Valid subnets?* Okay, now we need to add subnet numbers from the second, third, and fourth octets. In the second and third, they can range from 0 to 255, as long as all subnet bits in the second, third, and fourth octets are not all on or off at the same time. For the fourth octet, it will be $256 - 192 = 64$. And 0 will be valid as long as at least one other subnet bit is turned on in the second or third octet. Also, 192 will be valid as long as all the bits in the second and third octets are not turned on.
- *Broadcast address for each subnet?*
- *Valid hosts?*

The following table shows the first few subnets and their valid hosts and broadcast addresses in the Class A 255.255.255.192 mask:

Subnet	10.0.0.64	10.0.0.128	10.0.0.192	10.1.0.0
First host	10.0.0.65	10.0.0.129	10.0.0.193	10.1.0.1
Last host	10.0.0.126	10.0.0.190	10.0.0.254	10.1.0.62
Broadcast	10.0.0.127	10.0.0.191	10.0.0.255	10.1.0.63

The following table shows the last three subnets and their valid hosts and broadcast addresses:

Subnet	10.255.255.0	10.255.255.64	10.255.255.128
First host	10.255.255.1	10.255.255.65	10.255.255.129
Last host	10.255.255.62	10.255.255.126	10.255.255.190
Broadcast	10.255.255.63	10.255.255.127	10.255.255.191

Variable Length Subnet Masks (VLSMs)

You could easily devote an entire chapter to *Variable Length Subnet Masks (VLSMs)*, but instead I'm going to show you a simple way to take one network and create many networks using subnet masks of different lengths on different types of network designs. This is called VLSM networking, and does bring up another subject: classful and classless networking.

Neither RIPv1 nor IGRP routing protocols has a field for subnet information, so the subnet information gets dropped. What this means is that if a router running RIP has a subnet mask of a certain value, it assumes that *all* interfaces within the classful address space have the same subnet mask. This is called classful routing, and RIP and IGRP are both considered classful routing protocols. (I'll be talking more about RIP and IGRP in Chapter 5, "IP Routing.") If you mix and match subnet mask lengths in a network running RIP or IGRP, that network just won't work!

Classless routing protocols, however, do support the advertisement of subnet information. Therefore, you can use VLSM with routing protocols such as RIPv2, EIGRP, or OSPF. (EIGRP and OSPF will be discussed in detail in Chapter 6, "Enhanced IGRP and Open Shortest Path First (OSPF).") The benefit of this type of network is that you save a bunch of IP address space with it.

As the name suggests, with VLSMs we can have different subnet masks for different subnets. Look at Figure 3.1 to see an example of why VLSM networks are so beneficial.

FIGURE 3.1   Typical Classful Network

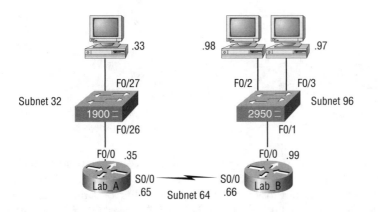

In this figure, you'll notice that we have two routers each with a LAN, and connected together with a WAN serial link. In a typical classful network design (RIP or IGRP routing protocols), we could subnet a network as follows:

192.168.10.0 = Network
255.255.255.224 = Mask

Our subnets would be (you know this part, right?) 32, 64, 96, 128, 160 and 192. We can then assign three subnets to our three networks. But how many hosts are available on each network? Well, as you should be well aware of by now, each subnet provides 30 hosts. This means that each LAN has 30 valid hosts, but the point-to-point WAN link also has 30 valid hosts. All hosts and router interfaces have the same subnet mask—again, this is called classful routing.

The only problem here is that the link between the two routers will never use more then two valid hosts! That wastes valuable IP address space, and it's the very reason we're going to talk about VLSM network design. Following our discussion of VLSM design, we will look at how to implement VLSM networks.

VLSM Design

It's time to jump into how to design and implement VLSM networks. First, let's take a look at a classful network, and then redesign the IP address scheme to work with VLSM. Check out Figure 3.2. It has a network with 14 subnets running only classful addressing.

FIGURE 3.2   Fourteen subnets with no VLSM applied

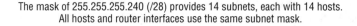

The mask of 255.255.255.240 (/28) provides 14 subnets, each with 14 hosts. All hosts and router interfaces use the same subnet mask.

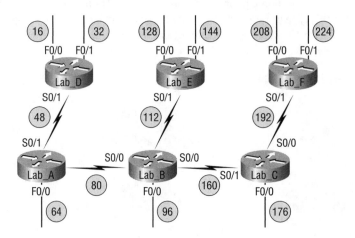

To figure out how many networks you have, you need to count the router interfaces in Figure 3.2. It's OK if you don't understand the difference between the f0/0, f0/1, s0/0, etc., in the figure, because you'll learn about those in the next chapter, "Introduction to the Cisco IOS." For now, just understand that the F0/0 is a FastEthernet LAN interface and the S0/0 is a WAN connection. Each interface is its own subnet or network. The WAN links between two routers are one subnet, and each router must have a valid host address on that configured subnet for the two routers to be able to communicate with each other.

The only IP subnet option for the network design in Figure 3.2 is to use the 255.255.255.240 mask, because this will give us 14 subnets, each with 14 hosts. In Figure 3.2, the circled numbers are the subnets assigned a router interface.

But the WAN links are point-to-point, and use only two IP addresses. So we're basically wasting 12 valid host addresses per WAN link! Let's take a look at Figure 3.3.

Remember, we can use different size masks on each interface. If we do that, we get 2 hosts per WAN interface and 14 hosts per LAN interface—nice! It makes a huge difference—not only can we get more hosts on a LAN, we still have room to add more WANs and LANs on the same network.

In Figure 3.3, each LAN has a /28 or 255.255.255.240 mask, which provides each LAN with 14 hosts, but each WAN used the /30 or 255.255.255.252 mask. Are you wondering why the subnets are listed as they are? Why the WAN links are subnets 4, 8, 12, 16, and 20, and the LANs start at subnet 32, and work in blocks of 16 up to subnet 160? Good! You're on the right track! The rest of the section will explain how all this came to be.

FIGURE 3.3   Fourteen subnets with VLSM applied

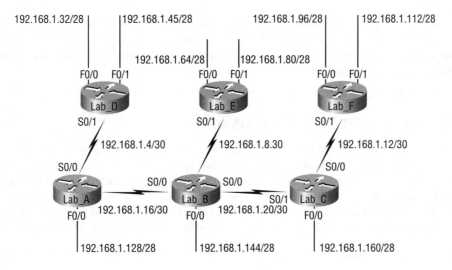

By using a VSLM design, we save address space!

Good question. There's a good answer too!

Because by creating contiguous blocks of addresses to specific areas of your network, you can then easily summarize your network and keep route updates with a routing protocol to a minimum. Why would anyone want to advertise hundreds of networks between buildings, when you can just send one summary route between buildings and achieve the same result?

If you're confused about what summary routes are, let me explain. Summarization, also called supernetting, provides route updates in the most efficient way possible by adverting many routes in one advertisement instead of individually. This saves a ton of bandwidth and minimizes router processing. As always, you use blocks of addresses (remember that block sizes are used in all sorts of networks) to configure your summary routes and watch your network's performance hum!

But know that summarization only works if you design your network carefully. If you carelessly hand out IP subnets to any location on the network, you'll notice straight up that you no longer have any summary boundaries. And you won't get very far with creating summary routes without those, so watch your step!

Implementing VLSM Networks

To create VLSMs quickly and efficiently, you need to understand how block sizes and charts work together to create the VLSM masks. Table 3.5 shows you the block sizes used when creating VLSMs with Class C networks. For example, if you need 25 hosts, then you'll need a block size of 32. If you need 11 hosts, you'll use a block size of 16. Need 40 hosts? Then you'll need a block of 64. You just cannot make up block sizes—they've got to be the block sizes shown in Table 3.5. So memorize the block sizes in this table—it's easy. They're the same numbers we used with subnetting!

TABLE 3.5   Block Sizes

Prefix	Mask	Hosts	Block Size
/26	192	62	64
/27	224	30	32
/28	240	14	16
/29	248	6	8
/30	252	2	4

The next step is to create a VLSM table. Figure 3.4 shows you the table used in creating a VLSM network. The reason we use this table is so we don't accidentally overlap networks.

FIGURE 3.4   The VLSM table

Variable Length Subnet Masks Worksheet

Subnet	Mask	Subnets	Hosts	Block
/26	192	2	62	64
/27	224	6	30	32
/28	240	14	14	16
/29	248	30	6	8
/30	252	62	2	4

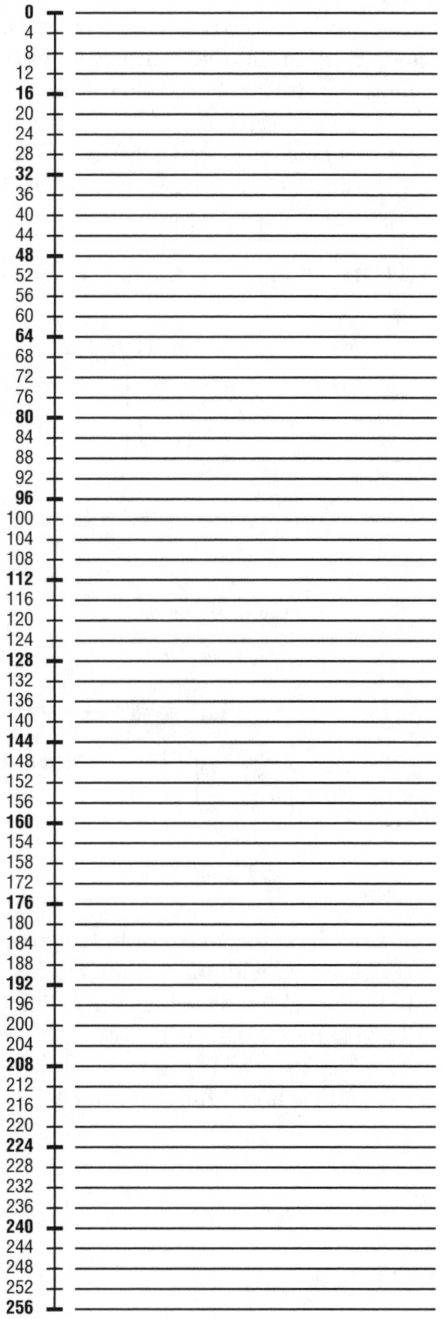

Class C Network   192.168.10.0

Network	Hosts	Block	Subnet	Mask
A				
B				
C				
D				
E				
F				
G				
H				
I				
J				
K				
L				
M				

```
0
4
8
12
16
20
24
28
32
36
40
44
48
52
56
60
64
68
72
76
80
84
88
92
96
100
104
108
112
116
120
124
128
132
136
140
144
148
152
156
160
154
158
172
176
180
184
188
192
196
200
204
208
212
216
220
224
228
232
236
240
244
248
252
256
```

You'll find the sheet shown in Figure 3.4 very valuable, because it lists every block size you can use for a network address. Notice the block sizes are listed starting from a block size of 4, all the way to a block size of 128. If you have two networks with block sizes of 128, you'll quickly see that you only can have two networks. With a block size of 64, you can only have four networks, and so on, all the way to having 64 networks if you only use block sizes of four. Remember that this takes into account that you are using subnet-zero in your network design.

Now, just fill in the chart in the lower-left corner, and then add the subnets to the worksheet and you're good to go.

So let's take what we've learned so far about our block sizes and VLSM table and create a VLSM using a Class C network address 192.168.10.0 for the network in Figure 3.5. Then, fill out the VLSM table, as shown in Figure 3.6.

FIGURE 3.5   A VLSM network, example one

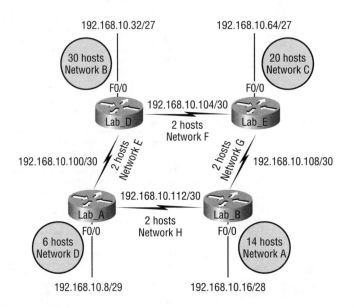

We still have plenty of room for growth with this VLSM network design. We never could accomplish that with one subnet mask.

In Figure 3.5, we have four WAN links and four LANs connected together. We need to create a VLSM network that will allow us to save address space. Looks like we have two block sizes of 32, a block size of 16, and a block size of 8, and our WANs each have a block size of 4. Take a look and see how I filled out our VLSM chart in Figure 3.6.

FIGURE 3.6   A VLSM table, example one

Variable Length Subnet Masks Worksheet

Subnet	Mask	Subnets	Hosts	Block
/26	192	2	62	64
/27	224	6	30	32
/28	240	14	14	16
/29	248	30	6	8
/30	252	62	2	4

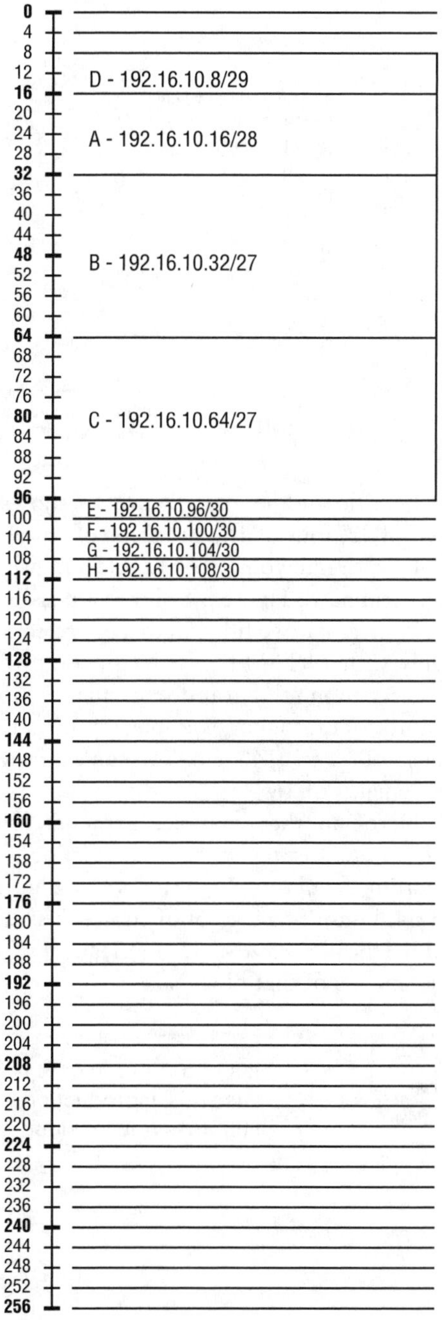

```
0
4
8
12      D - 192.16.10.8/29
16
20
24      A - 192.16.10.16/28
28
32
36
40
44
48      B - 192.16.10.32/27
52
56
60
64
68
72
76
80      C - 192.16.10.64/27
84
88
92
96
100     E - 192.16.10.96/30
104     F - 192.16.10.100/30
108     G - 192.16.10.104/30
112     H - 192.16.10.108/30
116
120
124
128
132
136
140
144
148
152
156
160
154
158
172
176
180
184
188
192
196
200
204
208
212
216
220
224
228
232
236
240
244
248
252
256
```

Class C Network   192.168.10.0

Network	Hosts	Block	Subnet	Mask
A	12	16	/28	240
B	20	32	/27	224
C	25	32	/27	224
D	4	8	/29	248
E	2	4	/30	252
F	2	4	/30	252
G	2	4	/30	252
H	2	4	/30	252

FIGURE 3.7 VLSM network, example two

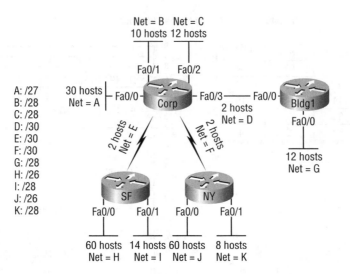

Let's do another one. Figure 3.7 shows a network with 11 networks, two block sizes of 64, two of 32, four of 16, and three of 4.

First, create your VLSM table and use your block size chart to fill in the table with the subnets you need. Figure 3.8 shows a possible solution.

Notice that we filled in this entire chart and only have room for one more block size of 4! Only with a VLSM network can you provide this type of address space savings.

Keep in mind that it doesn't matter where you start your block sizes as long as you always count from zero. For example, if you had a block size of 16, you must start at 0 and count from there—0, 16, 32, 48, etc. You can't start a block size of 16 from, say, 40 or anything other than increments of 16.

Here's another example. If you had block sizes of 32, you must start at zero like this: 0, 32, 64, 96, etc. Just remember that you don't get to start wherever you want, you must always start counting from zero. In the answer in Figure 3.8, I started at 64 and 128, with my two block sizes of 64. I didn't have a lot of choice, because my options are 0, 64, 128, and 192. However, I added the block size of 32, 16, 8, and 4 wherever I wanted just as long as they were in the correct increments of that block size.

It's important to note that I used subnet-zero in my network design. Although I use this in production and it does work, it is important to remember that Cisco still does not consider subnet-zero valid on their exams—yet.

FIGURE 3.8   VLSM table, example two

Variable Length Subnet Masks Worksheet

Subnet	Mask	Subnets	Hosts	Block
/26	192	2	62	64
/27	224	6	30	32
/28	240	14	14	16
/29	248	30	6	8
/30	252	62	2	4

Class C Network   192.168.10.0

Network	Hosts	Block	Subnet	Mask
A	30	32	32	224
B	10	16	0	240
C	12	16	16	240
D	2	4	244	252
E	2	4	248	252
F	2	4	252	252
G	12	16	208	240
H	60	64	64	192
I	14	16	192	240
J	60	64	128	192
K	8	16	224	240
L				
M				

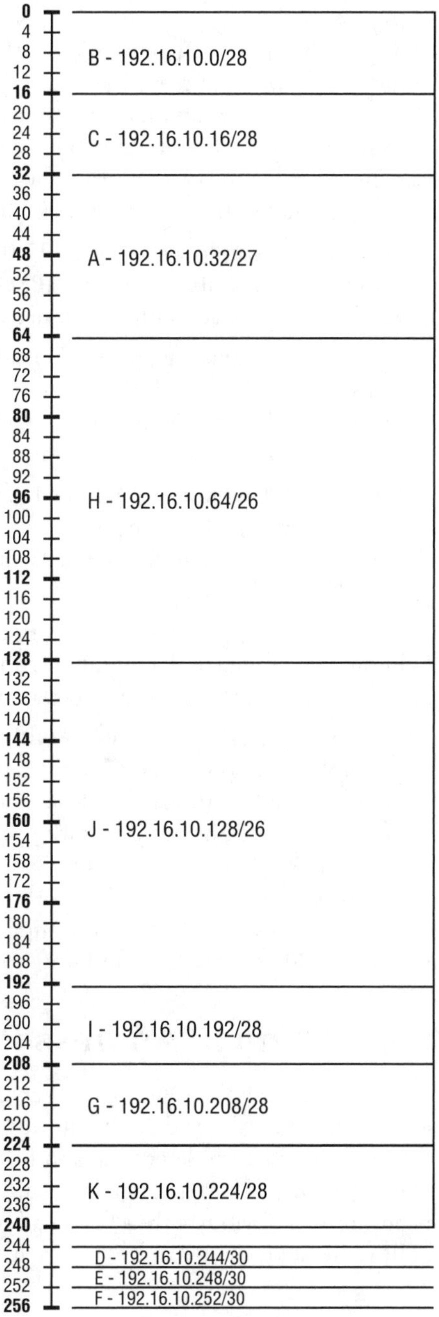

B - 192.16.10.0/28
C - 192.16.10.16/28
A - 192.16.10.32/27
H - 192.16.10.64/26
J - 192.16.10.128/26
I - 192.16.10.192/28
G - 192.16.10.208/28
K - 192.16.10.224/28
D - 192.16.10.244/30
E - 192.16.10.248/30
F - 192.16.10.252/30

Troubleshooting IP Addressing

Troubleshooting IP addressing is obviously an important section of this chapter and this book because trouble always happens—it's just a matter of time! And you must be able to determine and fix a problem on an IP network whether you're at work or at home. This section will teach you the "Cisco way" of troubleshooting IP addressing.

Let's go over the troubleshooting steps that Cisco uses first. These are pretty simple, but important nonetheless. Pretend you're at a customer host and they're complaining that their host cannot communicate to a server, which just happens to be on a remote network. Here are the four troubleshooting steps Cisco recommends:

1. Open a DOS window and ping 127.0.0.1. This is the diagnostic or loopback address, and if you get a successful ping, your IP stack is then considered to be initialized. If it fails, then you have an IP stack failure and need to reinstall TCP/IP on the host.

2. From the DOS window, ping the IP address of the local host. If that's successful, then your Network Interface Card (NIC) card is functioning. If it fails, then there is a problem with the NIC card. This doesn't mean that a cable is plugged into the NIC, only that the IP protocol stack on the host can communicate to the NIC.

3. From the DOS window, ping the default gateway (router). If the ping works, it means that the NIC is plugged into the network and can communicate on the local network. If it fails, then you have a local physical network problem that could be happening anywhere from the NIC to the router.

4. If steps 1 through 3 were successful, try to ping the remote server. If that works, then you know that you have IP communication between the local host and the remote server. You also know that the remote physical network is working.

If the user still can't communicate with the server after steps 1 through 4 are successful, then you probably have some type of name resolution problem, and need to check your Domain Name Server (DNS) settings. But if the ping to the remote server fails, then you know you have some type of remote physical network problem, and need to go to the server and work through steps 1 through 3 until you find the snag.

Once you've gone through all these steps, what do you do if you find a problem? How do you go about fixing an IP address configuration error? Let's move on and discuss how to determine the IP address problems and how to fix them.

Determining IP Address Problems

It's common for a host, router, or other network device to be configured with the wrong IP address, subnet mask, or default gateway. Because this happens way too often, I'm going to teach you how to both determine and fix IP address configuration errors.

Once you've worked through the four basic steps of troubleshooting and determined there's a problem, you obviously then need to find and fix it. It really helps to draw out the network and IP addressing scheme, unless you're lucky and it's already done. If so, go buy a lottery ticket, because though this should be done, it rarely is. And if it is, it's usually outdated or inaccurate anyway, but typically it is not done and you'll probably just have to bite the bullet and have to start from scratch.

 I'll show you how to draw out your network using CDP in Chapter 9: "Managing a Cisco Internetwork".

Once you have your network accurately drawn out, including the IP addressing scheme, you then need to verify each host's IP address, mask, and default gateway address to determine the problem (I'm assuming you don't have a physical problem, or if you did, you've already fixed it).

Let's check out the example illustrated in Figure 3.9. A user in the Sales department calls and tells you that she can't get to ServerA in the Marketing department. You ask her if she can get to ServerB in the Marketing department, but she doesn't know because she doesn't have rights to log on to that server. What do you do?

FIGURE 3.9   IP Address Problem 1

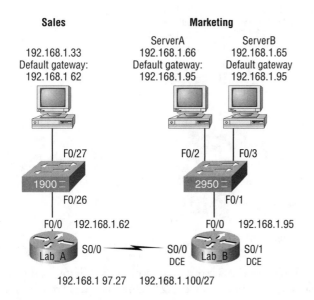

You ask the client to go through the four troubleshooting steps that we learned about in the above section. Steps 1 through 3 work, but step 4 fails. By looking at the figure, can you determine the problem? Look for clues in the network drawing. First, the WAN link between the Lab_A router and the Lab_B router shows the mask as a /27. You should already know this mask is 255.255.255.224 and then determine that all networks are using this mask. The network address is 192.168.1.0. What are our valid subnets and hosts? 256 - 224 = 32, so this makes our subnets 32, 64, 96, 128, etc. So, by looking at the figure, you can see that subnet 32 is being used by the Sales department, the WAN link is using subnet 96, and the Marketing department is using subnet 64.

Now you've got to determine what the valid host ranges are for each subnet. From what you learned at the beginning of this chapter, you should now be able to easily determine the subnet address, broadcast addresses, and valid host ranges. The valid hosts for the Sales LAN are 33 through 62—the broadcast address is 63 because the next subnet is 64, right? For the Marketing LAN, the valid hosts are 65 through 94 (broadcast 95), and for the WAN link, 97 through 126 (broadcast 127). By looking at the figure, you can determine that the default gateway on the Lab_B router is incorrect. That address is the broadcast address of the 64 subnet so there's no way it could be a valid host.

Did you get all that? Maybe we should try another one, just to make sure. Figure 3.10 has a network problem. A user in the Sales LAN can't get to ServerB. You have the user run through the four basic troubleshooting steps and find that the host can communicate to the local network, but not to the remote network. Find and define the IP addressing problem.

FIGURE 3.10   IP Address Problem 2

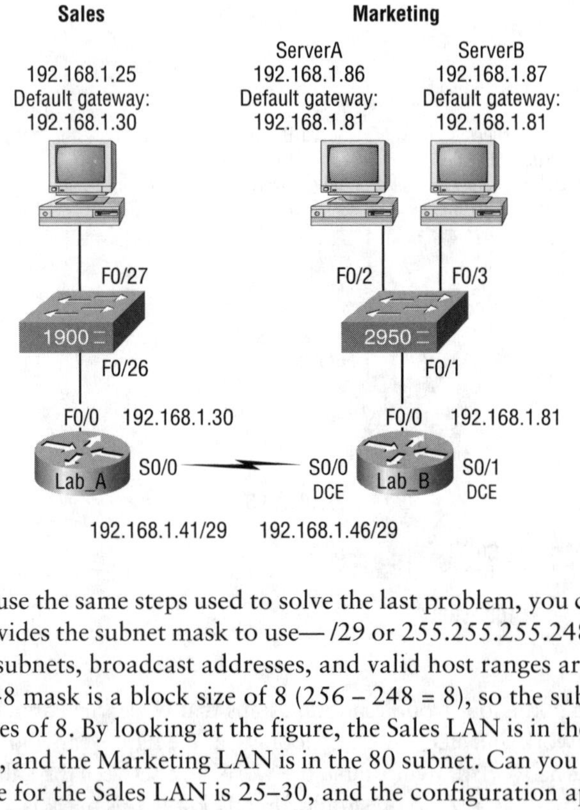

If you use the same steps used to solve the last problem, you can see first that the WAN link again provides the subnet mask to use— /29 or 255.255.255.248. You need to determine what the valid subnets, broadcast addresses, and valid host ranges are to solve this problem.

The 248 mask is a block size of 8 (256 − 248 = 8), so the subnets both start and increment in multiples of 8. By looking at the figure, the Sales LAN is in the 24 subnet, the WAN is in the 40 subnet, and the Marketing LAN is in the 80 subnet. Can you see the problem yet? The valid host range for the Sales LAN is 25–30, and the configuration appears correct. The valid host range for the WAN link is 41–46, and this also appears correct. The valid host range for the 80 subnet is 81–86, with a broadcast address of 87 because the next subnet is 88. ServerB has been configured with the broadcast address of the subnet.

Summary

Did you read Chapters 2 and 3 and understand everything on the first pass? If so, that is fantastic—congratulations! The thing is, you probably got lost a couple of times—and as I told you, that's what usually happens, so don't stress. So don't feel bad if you have to reread each chapter more than once, or even ten times before you're truly good to go.

This chapter provided you with an important understand of IP subnetting. After reading this chapter, you should be able to Subnet IP addresses in your head.

You should also know how to design and implement VLSM networks. Although I gave you a lot more information in this section than you'll find on the CCNA exam, having the background and understanding of VLSM networks is just that important. And it's really not all that difficult if you just understand the process of block sizes and how to use them.

You should also understand the Cisco troubleshooting methods. You must remember the four steps that Cisco recommends that you take when trying to narrow down exactly where a network problem/IP addressing problem is, and then know how to proceed systematically in order to fix the problem.

Exam Essentials

Remember the steps to subnet in your head.   Understand how IP addressing and subnetting work. First, determine your block size by using the 256-subnet mask math. Then count your subnets and determine the broadcast address of each subnet—it is always the number right before the next subnet. Your valid hosts are the numbers between the subnet address and the broadcast address.

Understand the various block sizes.   This is an important part of understanding IP addressing and subnetting. The valid block sizes are always 4, 8, 16, 32, 64, 128, etc. You can determine your block size by using the 256-subnet mask math.

Remember the four diagnostic steps.   The four simple steps that Cisco recommends for troubleshooting are: ping the loopback address; ping the NIC; ping the default gateway; and ping the remote device.

You must be able to find and fix an IP addressing problem.   Once you go through the four troubleshooting steps that Cisco recommends, you must be able to determine the IP addressing problem by drawing out the network and finding the valid and invalid hosts addressed in your network.

Key Terms

Before taking the exam, be sure you're familiar with the following terms:

broadcast address	loopback address
hierarchical addressing	network address
host address	subnet mask
Internet Protocol (IP)	subnetting
IP address	Variable Length Subnet Masks (VLSMs)

Written Lab 3

Write the subnet, broadcast address, and valid host range for each of the following:

1. 172.16.10.5 255.255.255.128
2. 172.16.10.33 255.255.255.224
3. 172.16.10.65 255.255.255.192
4. 172.16.10.17 255.255.255.252
5. 172.16.10.33 255.255.255.240
6. 192.168.100.25 255.255.255.252
7. 192.168.100.37 255.255.255.248
8. 192.168.100.66 255.255.255.224
9. 192.168.100.17 255.255.255.248
10. 10.10.10.5 255.255.255.252

(The answers to Written Lab 3 can be found following the answers to the Review Questions for this chapter.)

Review Questions

1. What valid host range is the IP address 172.16.10.22 255.255.255.240 a part of?
    A. 172.16.10.20 through 172.16.10.22
    B. 172.16.10.1 through 172.16.10.255
    C. 172.16.10.16 through 172.16.10.23
    D. 172.16.10.17 through 172.16.10.31
    E. 172.16.10.17 through 172.16.10.30

2. What is the broadcast address of the subnet address 172.16.8.159 255.255.255.192?
    A. 172.16.255.255
    B. 172.16.8.127
    C. 172.16.8.191
    D. 172.16.8.255

3. What is the broadcast address of the subnet address 192.168.10.33 255.255.255.248?
    A. 192.168.10.40
    B. 192.168.10.255
    C. 192.168.255.255
    D. 192.168.10.39

4. If you wanted to have 12 subnets with a Class C network ID, which subnet mask would you use?
    A. 255.255.255.252
    B. 255.255.255.248
    C. 255.255.255.240
    D. 255.255.255.255

5. If you need to have a Class B network address subnetted into exactly 510 subnets, what subnet mask would you assign?
    A. 255.255.255.252
    B. 255.255.255.128
    C. 255.255.255.0
    D. 255.255.255.192

6. If you are using a Class C network ID with two subnets and need 31 hosts per network, which of the following masks should you use?

   A. 255.255.255.0

   B. 255.255.255.192

   C. 255.255.255.224

   D. 255.255.255.248

7. How many subnets and hosts can you get from the network 192.168.254.0/26?

   A. 4 networks with 64 hosts

   B. 2 networks with 62 hosts

   C. 254 networks with 254 hosts

   D. 1 network with 254 hosts

8. You have the network 172.16.10.0/24. How many subnets and hosts are available?

   A. 1 subnet with 10 hosts

   B. 1 subnet with 254 hosts

   C. 192 subnets with 10 hosts

   D. 254 subnets with 254 hosts

9. What mask would you assign to the network ID of 172.16.0.0 if you needed about 100 subnets with about 500 hosts each?

   A. 255.255.255.0

   B. 255.255.254.0

   C. 255.255.252.0

   D. 255.255.0.0

10. You are the network administrator for RouterSim.com. A user cannot reach the corporate server from their remote office. The IP address of the host is 192.168.254.10/24, the default gateway of the host is 192.168.254.1, and the server is 192.168.10.10/24. You have the user type the following from a DOS prompt: `ping 192.168.254.10`; this is unsuccessful. You then have the user type: `ping 127.0.0.1`; this is also unsuccessful. What could the problem be?

   A. The router is down.

   B. The server is down.

   C. TCP/IP is not initialized on the host.

   D. The Ethernet cable is unplugged from the host.

11. You have a Class C 192.168.10.0/28 network. How many usable subnets and hosts do you have?

    A. 16 subnets, 16 hosts

    B. 14 subnets, 14 hosts

    C. 30 subnets, 6 hosts

    D. 62 subnets, 2 hosts

12. You have the network shown in the following graphic. Which classful subnet mask do you need in order to design and implement this network?

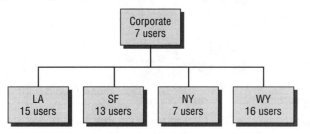

    A. 255.255.255.192

    B. 255.255.255.224

    C. 255.255.255.240

    D. 255.255.255.248

13. You have the network 192.168.10.0/24. How many subnets and hosts are available?

    A. 1 subnet with 10 hosts

    B. 1 subnet with 254 hosts

    C. 192 subnets with 10 hosts

    D. 254 subnets with 254 hosts

14. You have a 255.255.255.240 mask. Which two of the following are valid host IDs?

    A. 192.168.10.210

    B. 192.168.10.32

    C. 192.168.10.94

    D. 192.168.10.112

    E. 192.168.10.127

15. You have a Class B network ID and need about 450 IP addresses per subnet. What is the best mask for this network?

    A. 255.255.240.0

    B. 255.255.248.0

    C. 255.255.254.0

    D. 255.255.255.0

16. You have a network as shown in the following graphic. Why can't the host talk to the remote network?

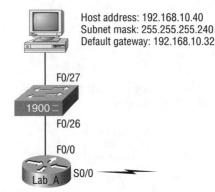

Host address: 192.168.10.40
Subnet mask: 255.255.255.240
Default gateway: 192.168.10.32

F0/27

1900

F0/26

F0/0

Lab_A   S0/0

   A. The default gateway is on another subnet.

   B. The host has the wrong IP address for the subnet.

   C. The host has an invalid default gateway address.

   D. The router and the host have different subnet masks.

17. Which of the following is a valid host for network 192.168.10.32/28?

   A. 192.168.10.39

   B. 192.168.10.47

   C. 192.168.10.14

   D. 192.168.10.54

18. You are the network administrator for RouterSim.com. A user cannot reach the corporate server from their remote office. The IP address of the host is 192.168.254.10/24, the default gateway of the host is 192.168.254.1, and the server is 192.168.10.10/24. You have the user type the following from a DOS prompt: `ping 127.0.0.1`; this is successful. You then have the user type `ping 192.168.254.10`; this is also successful. However, a ping to the default gateway is unsuccessful. What could the problem be?

   A. The PC is down.

   B. The server is down.

   C. TCP/IP is not initialized on the host.

   D. The Ethernet cable is unplugged from the host.

19. What is the valid host range that host 192.168.10.22/30 is a part of?

   A. 192.168.10.0

   B. 192.168.10.16

   C. 192.168.10.20

   D. 192.168.0.0

20. You are the network administrator for RouterSim.com, and a user cannot reach the corporate server from their remote office. The IP address of the host is 192.168.254.10/24, the default gateway of the host is 192.168.254.1, and the server is 192.168.10.10/24. You have the user type the following from a DOS prompt: **ping 127.0.0.1**; this is successful. You then have the user type **ping 192.168.254.10**; this is also successful. A ping to the default gateway is successful, but you cannot ping the remote server. What could the problem be?

   A. The router is down.

   B. There's a remote physical layer problem.

   C. TCP/IP is not initialized on the host.

   D. The Ethernet cable is unplugged from the host.

Answers to Review Questions

1. E. This is a Class B network address with 12 bits of subnetting—8 in the third octet and 4 in the fourth octet. The subnet in the third octet is 10, and the subnets in the fourth octet are 256 – 240 = 16, 32, 48, etc. Since the fourth octet is using 22, the host is in the 16 subnet, and since the next subnet is 32, the broadcast address for the 16 subnet is 31. The valid host range is the numbers in between, or 17–30.

2. C. This is a Class B network address with 10 bits of subnetting—8 in the third octet and 2 in the fourth octet. The subnet in the third octet is 8, and the subnets in the fourth octet are 256 – 192 = 64, and 128. However, as long as all the subnet bits in the third octet are not all on at once, the subnets in the fourth octet really can be 0, 64, 128 and 192. This means that the host is in the 128 subnet and since the next subnet is 192, our broadcast address is 8.191.

3. D. This is a Class C network address with 5 bits of subnetting. The valid subnets are 256 – 248 = 8, 16, 24, 32, 40, etc. Since the host ID is 33, we are in the 32 subnet. The next subnet is 40, so our broadcast address is 39.

4. C. Take a look at the answers and see which subnet mask will give you what you need for subnetting. 252 gives you 62 subnets, 248 gives you 30 subnets, 240 gives you 14 subnets, and 255 is invalid. Only the third option (240) gives you what you need.

5. B. If you use the mask 255.255.255.0, that only gives you 8 subnet bits, or 254 subnets. You are going to have to use 1 subnet bit from the fourth octet, or 255.255.255.128. This is 9 subnet bits $(2^9 – 2 = 510)$.

6. B. To answer this, you must be able to determine which Class C mask provides how many hosts and subnets. The 255.255.255.0 mask provides one network with 254 hosts. The 255.255.255.192 provides two subnets each with 62 hosts. The 255.255.255.224 provides 6 subnets, each with 30 hosts, and the 255.255.255.248 mask provides 30 subnets, each with 6 hosts.

7. B. The Class C mask of 255.255.255.192 provides two subnets (four if you are using subnet-zero—which Cisco is not!), each with 62 hosts.

8. B. The third octet is used for all subnets, and the fourth octet is used only for hosts. 8 bits for subnetting, 8 bits for hosts. However, a subnet is already listed, so you have one subnet with 254 hosts. If the question stated 172.16.0.0/24, then the answer would be 254 subnets each with 254 hosts.

9. B. This one takes some thought. 255.255.255.0 would give you 254 hosts each with 254 subnets. Doesn't work for this question. 255.255.254.0 would provide 126 subnets, each with 510 hosts; the second option looks good. 255.255.252.0 is 62 subnets, each with 1022 hosts. So 255.255.254.0 is the best answer.

10. C. 127.0.0.1 is called the loopback address and is used for diagnostics on a host. If you cannot ping the IP address 127.0.0.1, then you have an IP protocol stack failure on the host. Reinstall TCP/IP.

11. B. To answer this, you must know that /28 is 255.255.255.240. 256 – 240 = 16. You subtract 2 from this number for all subnet bits and host bits on/off, so the answer is 14 subnets with 14 hosts each.

12. B. You need 5 subnets, each with at least 16 hosts. The mask 255.255.255.240 provides 14 subnets with 14 hosts—this will not work. The mask 255.255.255.224 provides 6 subnets, each with 30 hosts. This is the best answer.

13. B. This is a Class C network using a default mask. This provides a simple single network with 254 hosts.

14. A, C. To answer this, just do 256 – 240 = 16. Keep adding 16 together until you reach the subnet mask value. 16 + 16 = 32. We'll keep adding 16 until we have all our subnets: 16, 32, 48, 64, 80, 96, 112, 128, 144, 160, 176, 192, 208, 224. The broadcast addresses for each subnet are the numbers right before the next subnet and are not valid hosts. The answers are 210 and 94.

15. C. Start with 255.255.255.0. This provides 254 subnets, each with 254 hosts. Move the subnet bits right if you need more subnets; move them left if you need more hosts. Since we need more hosts, we're going to take away subnet bits. The next mask then is 255.255.254.0, which provides 7 subnet bits and 9 host bits, or 126 subnets, each with 510 hosts.

16. C. The default gateway is the subnet address and not a valid host ID.

17. A. You have to know that /28 is 255.255.255.240. 256 – 240 = 16, 32, 48, etc. The host ID of 34 is in the 32 subnet; the next subnet is 48, so the broadcast address is 47. The valid host range is 33–46, so answer A is correct.

18. D. Although there could be many reasons why you cannot ping the default gateway, the best answer listed is that the Ethernet cable is unplugged. Remember, you can still ping the NIC if the cable is unplugged.

19. C. This is as easy as they get. A /30 is a 255.255.255.252 mask. 256 – 252 = 4, 8, 12, 16, 20, 24. This host is in the 20 subnet, the broadcast address is 23 and the valid host range is 21 and 22.

20. B. Although there could be many reasons why you cannot ping the remote server, the best answer listed in this question is that there is a remote physical layer problem.

Answers to Written Lab 3

1. 172.16.10.5 255.255.255.128: Subnet is 172.16.10.0, broadcast is 172.16.10.127, and valid host range is 172.16.10.1 through 126.
2. You need to ask yourself, "Is the subnet bit in the fourth octet on or off?" If the host address has a value of less than 128 in the fourth octet, then the subnet bit must be off. If the value of the fourth octet is higher than 128, then the subnet bit must be on. In this case, the host address is 10.5, and the bit in the fourth octet must be off. The subnet must be 172.16.10.0.
3. 172.16.10.33 255.255.255.224: Subnet is 172.16.10.32, broadcast is 172.16.10.63, and valid host range is 172.16.10.33 through 10.62.
4. 256 – 224 = 32. 32 + 32 = 64—bingo. The subnet is 10.32, and the next subnet is 10.64, so the broadcast address must be 10.63.
5. 172.16.10.65 255.255.255.192: Subnet is 172.16.10.64, broadcast is 172.16.10.127, and valid host range is 172.16.10.65 through 172.16.10.126.
6. 256 – 192 = 64. 64 + 64 = 128, so the network address must be 172.16.10.64, with a broadcast of 172.16.10.127.
7. 172.16.10.17 255.255.255.252: Subnet is 172.16.10.16, broadcast is 172.16.10.19, and valid hosts are 172.16.10.17 and 18.
8. 256 – 252 = 4. 4 + 4 = 8, plus 4 = 12, plus 4 = 16, plus 4 = 20—bingo. The subnet is 172.16.10.16, and the broadcast must be 10.19.
9. 172.16.10.33 255.255.255.240: Subnet is 172.16.10.32, broadcast is 172.16.10.47, and valid host range is 172.16.10.33 through 46.
10. 256 – 240 = 16. 16 + 16 = 32, plus 16 = 48. Subnet is 172.16.10.32; broadcast is 172.16.10.47.
11. 192.168.100.25 255.255.255.252: Subnet is 192.168.100.24, broadcast is 192.168.100.27, and valid hosts are 192.168.100.25 and 26.
12. 256 – 252 = 4. 4 + 4 = 8, plus 4 = 12, plus 4 = 16, plus 4 = 20, plus 4 = 24, plus 4 = 28. Subnet is 100.24; broadcast is 100.27.
13. 192.168.100.37 255.255.255.248: Subnet is 192.168.100.32, broadcast is 192.168.100.39, and valid host range is 192.168.100.33 through 38.
14. 256 – 248 = 8. 8 + 8 = 16, 24, 32, 40. Subnet is, then, 100.32, with a broadcast of 100.39 because 40 is the next subnet.
15. 192.168.100.66 255.255.255.224: Subnet is 192.168.100.64, broadcast is 192.168.100.95, and valid host range is 192.168.100.65 through 94.
16. 256 – 224 = 32. 32 + 32 = 64, plus 32 = 96. Subnet is 100.64, and broadcast is 100.95.
17. 192.168.100.17 255.255.255.248: Subnet is 192.168.100.16, broadcast is 192.168.100.23, and valid host range is 192.168.100.17 through 22.
18. 256 – 248 = 8. 8 + 8 = 16, plus 8 = 24. Subnet is 16, and broadcast is 23.
19. 10.10.10.5 255.255.255.252: Subnet is 10.10.10.4, broadcast is 10.10.10.7, and valid hosts are 10.10.10.5 and 6.
20. 256 – 252 = 4. 4 + 4 = 8.

Introduction to the Cisco IOS

THE CCNA EXAM TOPICS COVERED IN THIS CHAPTER INCLUDE THE FOLLOWING:

✓ **IMPLEMENTATION & OPERATION**

- Configure IP addresses, subnet masks, and gateway addresses on routers and hosts
- Configure a router for additional administrative functionality
- Implement a LAN
- Perform an initial configuration on a router
- Perform an initial configuration on a switch

It's now time to introduce you to the Cisco Internetwork Operating System (IOS). The IOS is what runs Cisco routers and also some Cisco switches, and it's what allows you to configure the devices as well.

In this chapter, you'll learn how to configure a Cisco IOS router using both the initial setup mode and the Cisco IOS command-line interface (CLI). Through the IOS interface, you can configure passwords, banners, and more. What's more, you'll also learn the basics of router configurations in this chapter. We will cover the following subjects in this chapter:

- Understanding and configuring the Cisco Internetwork Operating System (IOS)

- Connecting to a router

- Bringing up a router

- Logging into a router

- Understanding the router prompts

- Understanding the CLI prompts

- Performing editing and help features

- Gathering basic routing information

- Setting router passwords

- Setting router banners

- Performing interface configurations

- Setting router hostnames

- Setting interface descriptions

- Viewing and saving router configurations

- Verifying routing configurations

And just as it was with the preceding chapters, the fundamentals that you'll learn in this chapter are building blocks that should be in place before you go on to the next chapters in the book.

The Cisco Router User Interface

The *Cisco Internetwork Operating System (IOS)* is the kernel of Cisco routers and most switches. A kernel is the basic, indispensable part of an operating system that allocates resources and manages things such as low-level hardware interfaces and security. Cisco has created something called

CiscoFusion, which is supposed to make all Cisco devices run the same operating system. But they don't, because Cisco has acquired devices that they haven't designed and built themselves. Almost all Cisco routers run the same IOS, in contrast to only about half of their switches—but that number is growing fast.

In this section, I'll show you the Cisco IOS and how to configure a Cisco router step-by-step, using setup mode. In the next section, I'll show you how to do this using the command-line interface (CLI).

I'm going to save Cisco switch configurations for Chapter 7, "Layer 2 Switching".

Cisco Router IOS

The Cisco IOS was created to deliver network services and enable networked applications. It runs on most Cisco routers and on some Cisco Catalyst switches, such as the Catalyst 2950.

These are some of the important things the Cisco router IOS software is responsible for:

- Carrying network protocols and functions
- Connecting high-speed traffic between devices
- Adding security to control access and stop unauthorized network use
- Providing scalability for ease of network growth and redundancy
- Supplying network reliability for connecting to network resources

You can access the Cisco IOS through the console port of a router, from a modem into the auxiliary (or Aux) port, or even through Telnet. Access to the IOS command line is called an *EXEC session*.

Connecting to a Cisco Router

You can connect to a Cisco router to configure it, verify its configuration, and check statistics. There are different ways to do this, but most often, the first place you would connect to is the console port. The *console port* is usually an RJ-45 (8-pin Modular) connection located at the back of the router—by default, there's no password set.

See Chapter 1, "Internetworking," for an explanation on how to configure a PC to connect to a router console port.

You can also connect to a Cisco router through an *auxiliary port*—which is really the same thing as a console port, so it follows that you can use it as one. But this auxiliary port also allows you to configure modem commands so that a modem can be connected to the router. This is a cool feature—it lets you dial up a remote router and attach to the auxiliary port if the router is down and you need to configure it "out-of-band" (which means, basically, "out-of-the-network"). "In-band" means the opposite—configuring the router through the network.

The third way to connect to a Cisco router is in-band, through the program *Telnet*. Telnet is a terminal emulation program that acts as though it's a dumb terminal. You can use Telnet to connect to any active interface on a router like an Ethernet or serial port.

Figure 4.1 shows an illustration of a 2501 Cisco router. Pay special attention to all the different kinds of interfaces and connections.

FIGURE 4.1 A Cisco 2501 router

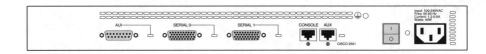

The 2501 router has two serial interfaces for WAN connection and one Attachment Unit Interface (AUI) connection for a 10Mbps Ethernet network connection. This router also has one console and one auxiliary connection via RJ-45 connectors.

A Cisco 2600 series router is a better router than those populating the 2500 series because it has a faster processor and can handle many more interfaces. Figure 4.2 shows a diagram of a Cisco 2600 modular router.

FIGURE 4.2 A Cisco 2600 router

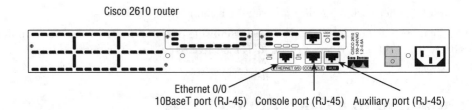

I'm mostly going to use 2600 routers throughout this book to show examples of configurations. This is because 2500 series machines just aren't capable of handling the demands of today's typical corporate network. You'll find 2600 or better in that kind of environment. The 2500 series still works great for home use, and when I do use them for an example, I'll point it out.

Bringing Up a Router

When you first bring up a Cisco router, it will run a power-on self-test (POST). If it passes, it will then look for and load the Cisco IOS from flash memory—if an IOS file is present. In case you don't know, flash memory is an electronically erasable programmable read-only memory—an EEPROM. The IOS then proceeds to load and looks for a valid configuration—the startup-config—that's stored by default in nonvolatile RAM, or NVRAM.

The following messages appear when you first boot or reload a router:

```
System Bootstrap, Version 12.2(13)T, RELEASE SOFTWARE (fc1)
Copyright (c) 2000 by cisco Systems, Inc.
C2600 platform with 32768 Kbytes of main memory
```

This is the first part of the router boot process output. It's information about the bootstrap program that first runs the POST, and then tells the router how to load, which by default is to find the IOS in flash memory.

The next part, shown below, shows us that the IOS is being decompressed into RAM:

```
program load complete, entry point: 0x80008000, size:
  0x43b7fc
Self decompressing the image :
###########################################################################
###########################################################################
###########################################################################
###########################################################################
###########################################################################
###########################################################################
################## [OK]
```

This step doesn't happen the same way for all routers. The output you're being shown is from my 2600. It's telling us that the IOS is being loaded into RAM. (The 2500 series router runs the IOS from flash memory—it doesn't load the IOS into RAM.)

After the IOS is decompressed into RAM, the IOS is then loaded and starts running the router, as shown below (notice that the IOS version is stated as version 12.1[13]):

```
Cisco Internetwork Operating System Software
IOS (tm) C2600 Software (C2600-I-M), Version 12.2(13),
  RELEASE SOFTWARE (fc1)
Copyright (c) 1986-2001 by cisco Systems, Inc.
Compiled Tue 17-Dec-03 04:55 by kellythw
Image text-base: 0x80008088, data-base: 0x8080853C
```

Once the IOS is loaded, the information learned from the POST will be displayed next, as shown here:

```
cisco 2621 (MPC860) processor (revision 0x101) with
  26624K/6144K bytes of memory.
Processor board ID JAD050697JB (146699779)
M860 processor: part number 0, mask 49
Bridging software.
X.25 software, Version 3.0.0.
2 FastEthernet/IEEE 802.3 interface(s)
1 Serial network interface(s)
```

```
32K bytes of non-volatile configuration memory.
8192K bytes of processor board System flash (Read/Write)
```

Once the IOS is loaded, and up and running, a valid configuration will be loaded from NVRAM. If there isn't a configuration in NVRAM, the router will go into *setup mode*—a step-by-step process to help you configure the router. You can also enter setup mode at any time from the command line by typing the command **setup** from something called privileged mode, which I'll get to in a minute. Setup mode only covers some very global commands, but it can be really helpful if you don't know how to configure certain protocols, such as bridging or DECnet.

Setup Mode

You actually have two options when using setup mode: *Basic Management* and *Extended Setup*. Basic Management only gives you enough configurations to allow connectivity to the router, but Extended Setup gives you the power to configure some global parameters as well as interface configuration parameters. To enter Setup mode, just say "yes" or "y" to the following question:

```
    --- System Configuration Dialog ---
Would you like to enter the initial configuration dialog?
  [yes/no]: y
```

```
At any point you may enter a question mark '?' for help.
Use ctrl-c to abort configuration dialog at any prompt.
Default settings are in square brackets '[]'.
```

Notice the two lines above that say you can use Ctrl+C to abort configuration dialog at any prompt, and that the default settings are in square brackets: [].

Basic Management setup configures only enough connectivity for management of the system. But since you can do so much more with Extended Setup, this mode will ask you to configure each interface on the system, as seen here:

```
Would you like to enter basic management setup?[yes/no]:n
```

```
First, would you like to see the current interface
  summary? [yes]:[Enter]
Any interface listed with OK? value "NO" does not have a
  valid configuration
```

```
Interface       IP-Address     OK? Method Status Protocol
FastEthernet0/0  unassigned    NO  unset  up     up
FastEthernet0/1  unassigned    NO  unset  up     up
```

```
Configuring global parameters:
  Enter host name [Router]: Todd
```

```
The enable secret is a password used to protect access
to privileged EXEC and configuration modes. This
password, after entered, becomes encrypted in the
configuration. Enter enable secret: todd

The enable password is used when you do not specify an
enable secret password, with some older software
versions, and some boot images.
Enter enable password: todd
% Please choose a password that is different from the
  enable secret
Enter enable password: todd1
```

There's something I want you to look at. Did you notice that setup mode asks you to configure two enable passwords? I'm going to cover passwords later in the chapter, but you should know that you really only use the enable secret password. The enable password is for pre-10.3 IOS routers (really old routers). Even so, you must configure the password when in setup mode, and it has to be different. It will never be used if the enable secret is configured, though.

By default, the enable secret is encrypted, and the enable password is not.

The next password is for setting up Telnet sessions to the router. The reason setup mode has you configure a Telnet (or VTY, which stands for Virtual TeleType) password is because you can't telnet into a router by default if a password for the VTY lines hasn't been set. Here is how you do that:

```
The virtual terminal password is used to protect
access to the router over a network interface.
Enter virtual terminal password: todd
Configure SNMP Network Management? [yes]:[Enter] or [no]
 Community string [public]:[no]
Configure DECnet? [no]:[Enter]
Configure AppleTalk? [no]:[Enter]
Configure IP? [yes]:[Enter]
 Configure IGRP routing? [yes]:no
 Configure RIP routing? [no]:[Enter]
Configure bridging? [no]:[Enter]
Configure IPX? [no]:[Enter]
```

The preceding commands can help you configure a protocol if you're not sure which commands you need to configure. But if you use the command-line interface (CLI) instead of setup mode, you'll have a lot more flexibility.

I'll show you the CLI in the next section.

If you have an Async modem card installed in your router, you can have setup mode config-ure the modems for you, as seen here:

```
Async lines accept incoming modems calls. If you will
have users dialing in via modems, configure these lines.
 Configure Async lines? [yes]:n
```

If your router has an ISDN BRI interface, you'll be prompted for the ISDN switch type to be configured. Take a look at the router output:

```
BRI interface needs isdn switch-type to be configured
Valid switch types are:
[0] none..........Only if you don't want to configure BRI
[1] basic-1tr6....1TR6 switch type for Germany
[2] basic-5ess....AT&T 5ESS switch type for the US/Canada
[3] basic-dms100..Northern DMS-100 switch type for
                  US/Canada
[4] basic-net3....NET3 switch type for UK and Europe
[5] basic-ni......National ISDN switch type
[6] basic-ts013...TS013 switch type for Australia
[7] ntt...........NTT switch type for Japan
[8] vn3...........VN3 and VN4 switch types for France
Choose ISDN BRI Switch Type [2]:2
```

The next section of the Extended Setup is configuring the interfaces. We only have two Fast Ethernet interfaces on this router: FastEthernet 0/0 and FastEthernet 0/1 (I'll go over various types of router interfaces later in this chapter):

```
Configuring interface parameters:

Do you want to configure FastEthernet0/0 interface?
  [yes]:[Enter]
 Use the 100 Base-TX (RJ-45) connector? [yes]:[Enter]
 Operate in full-duplex mode? [no]: y and [Enter]
 Configure IP on this interface? [yes]:[Enter]
  IP address for this interface: 1.1.1.1
  Subnet mask for this interface [255.0.0.0]: 255.255.0.0
  Class A network is 1.0.0.0, 16 subnet bits; mask is /16
```

```
Do you want to configure FastEthernet0/1 interface?
  [yes]:[Enter]
Use the 100 Base-TX (RJ-45) connector? [yes]:[Enter]
Operate in full-duplex mode? [no]:y and [Enter]
Configure IP on this interface? [yes]:[Enter]
  IP address for this interface: 2.2.2.2
  Subnet mask for this interface [255.0.0.0]: 255.255.0.0
  Class A network is 2.0.0.0, 16 subnet bits; mask is /16
```

This configuration is very basic, I know, but it will allow you to get a router up and running quickly. Notice the mask is displayed as /16, which means 16 out of 32 bits are being used.

See Chapter 3, "IP Subnetting and Variable Length Subnet Masks (VLSM)," if you need to review IP subnetting.

The Extended Setup will now show the running configuration created:

```
The following configuration command script was created:

hostname Todd
enable secret 5 $1$BOwu$5FOm/EDdtRkQ4vy4a8qwC/
enable password todd1
line vty 0 4
password todd
snmp-server community public
!
no decnet routing
no appletalk routing
ip routing
no bridge 1
no ipx routing
!
interface FastEthernet0/0
media-type 100BaseX
full-duplex
ip address 1.1.1.1 255.255.0.0
no mop enabled
!
interface FastEthernet0/1
media-type 100BaseX
full-duplex
```

```
ip address 2.2.2.2 255.255.0.0
no mop enabled
dialer-list 1 protocol ip permit
dialer-list 1 protocol ipx permit
!
end

[0] Go to the IOS command prompt without saving this
    config.
[1] Return back to the setup without saving this config.
[2] Save this configuration to nvram and exit.

Enter your selection [2]:0
```

The most interesting part of the Extended Setup is the options you get at the end. You can go to CLI mode and discard the running-config (0); you can go back to setup to do it all over again (1); or you can save this configuration to NVRAM, something known as startup-config (2). This file would then be loaded every time the router is rebooted.

I'm going to choose 0 to go to the IOS—we're not going to save the file we just created. Doing this will take us to the CLI, which we will discuss next.

   You can exit setup mode at any time by pressing Ctrl+C.

Command-Line Interface

Because it's so much more flexible, the *command-line interface (CLI)* truly is the best way to configure a router. I sometimes refer to the CLI as "Cash Line Interface" because if you can create advanced configurations on Cisco routers and switches using the CLI, then you'll get the cash!

To use the CLI, just say No to entering the initial configuration dialog. After you do that, the router will respond with messages that tell you all about the status of each and every one of the router's interfaces. Here's an example:

```
Would you like to enter the initial configuration dialog?
  [yes]:n
Would you like to terminate autoinstall? [yes]:[Enter]

Press RETURN to get started!
```

```
00:00:42: %LINK-3-UPDOWN: Interface FastEthernet0/0, changed
  state to up
00:00:42: %LINK-3-UPDOWN: Interface Serial0/0, changed
  state to down
00:00:42: %LINK-3-UPDOWN: Interface Serial0/1, changed
  state to down
00:00:42: %LINEPROTO-5-UPDOWN: Line protocol on Interface
  FastEthernet0/0, changed state to up
00:00:42: %LINEPROTO-5-UPDOWN: Line protocol on Interface
  Serial0/0, changed state to down
00:00:42: %LINEPROTO-5-UPDOWN: Line protocol on Interface
  Serial0/1, changed state to down
00:01:30: %LINEPROTO-5-UPDOWN: Line protocol on Interface
  FastEthernet0/0, changed state to down
00:01:31: %LINK-5-CHANGED: Interface Serial0/0, changed
  state to administratively down
00:01:31: %LINK-5-CHANGED: Interface FastEthernet0/0, changed
  state to administratively down
00:01:31: %LINK-5-CHANGED: Interface Serial0/1, changed
  state to administratively down
00:01:32: %IP-5-WEBINST_KILL: Terminating DNS process
00:01:38: %SYS-5-RESTART: System restarted --
Cisco Internetwork Operating System Software
IOS (tm) 2600 Software (2600-BIN-M), Version 12.2(13),
  RELEASE SOFTWARE (fc1)
Copyright (c) 1986-2003 by cisco Systems, Inc.
Compiled Tue 04-Jan-03 19:23 by dschwart
```

In the following sections, I am going to show you how to log in to a router and perform some basic administrative functions.

Logging into the Router

After the interface status messages appear and you press Enter, the Router> prompt will appear. This is called *user exec mode* (user mode) and is mostly used to view statistics, but it's also a stepping-stone to logging into privileged mode. You can only view and change the configuration of a Cisco router in *privileged exec mode* (privileged mode), which you get into with the enable command.

Here's how you would do that:

```
Router>
Router>enable
Router#
```

You now end up with a Router# prompt, which indicates you're in *privileged mode*, where you can both view and change the router's configuration. You can go back from privileged mode into user mode by using the disable command, as seen here:

```
Router#disable
Router>
```

At this point, you can type **logout** to exit the console:

```
Router>logout


Router con0 is now available
Press RETURN to get started.
```

Or you could just type **logout** or **exit** from the privileged-mode prompt to log out:

```
Router>en
Router#logout


Router con0 is now available
Press RETURN to get started.
```

Overview of Router Modes

To configure from a CLI, you can make global changes to the router by typing configure terminal (or **config t** for short), which puts you in global configuration mode and changes what's known as the running-config. A global command (a command run from global config) is one that is set once and affects the entire router.

You can type **config** from the privileged-mode prompt and then just press Enter to take the default of terminal, as seen here:

```
Router#config
Configuring from terminal, memory, or network
  [terminal]? [Enter]
Enter configuration commands, one per line. End with
  CNTL/Z.
Router(config)#
```

At this point, you make changes that affect the router as a whole, hence the term global configuration mode.

To change the running-config—the current configuration running in dynamic RAM (DRAM)—you use the configure terminal. To change the startup-config—the configuration stored in NVRAM—you use the configure memory command (or config mem for short). If you want to change a router configuration stored on a TFTP host (which is covered in Chapter 9, "Managing a Cisco Internetwork"), you use the configure network command (or config net for short).

However, you need to understand that for a router to actually make a change to a configuration, it needs to put that configuration in RAM. So, if you actually type config mem or config net, you'll replace the current running-config with the config stored in NVRAM or a configuration stored on a TFTP host. I'll be going over this in much greater detail in Chapter 9.

Configure terminal, configure memory, and configure network are all considered commands that are used to configure information into RAM on a router; however, typically only the configure terminal command is used.

CLI Prompts

It's really important that you understand the different prompts you can find when configuring a router. Knowing these well will help you navigate and recognize where you are at any time within configuration mode. In this section, I'm going to demonstrate the prompts that are used on a Cisco router. (Always check your prompts before making any changes to a router's configuration!)

I'm not going into every different command prompt offered. Doing that would be reaching beyond the scope of this exam. Instead, I'm going to describe all the different prompts you'll see throughout this chapter and the rest of the book. These command prompts are the ones you'll use most in your real life—and the ones you'll need to know for the exam.

It's not important that you understand what each of these command prompts accomplish at this time, because all of them will be explained later in great detail. At this point, you really need to concentrate on becoming familiar with the different prompts available.

Interfaces

To make changes to an interface, you use the interface command from global configuration mode:

```
Router(config)#interface ?
  Async           Async interface
  BVI             Bridge-Group Virtual Interface
  CTunnel         CTunnel interface
  Dialer          Dialer interface
  FastEthernet    FastEthernet IEEE 802.3
  Group-Async     Async Group interface
  Lex             Lex interface
  Loopback        Loopback interface
  MFR             Multilink Frame Relay bundle interface
```

```
Multilink          Multilink-group interface
Null               Null interface
Serial             Serial
Tunnel             Tunnel interface
Vif                PGM Multicast Host interface
Virtual-Template   Virtual Template interface
Virtual-TokenRing  Virtual TokenRing
range              interface range command
Router(config)#interface fastethernet 0/0
Router(config-if)#
```

Did you notice the prompt changed to Router(config-if)#? This tells you that you're in *interface configuration mode*. And wouldn't it be nice if the prompt also gave you an indication of what interface you were configuring? Well, at least for now we'll have to live without the prompt information because it doesn't. (Could this be one of the reasons Cisco administrators make more money than Windows administrators? Or is it just that we're smarter and better looking?) One thing is for sure: You really have to pay attention when configuring a router!

Subinterfaces

Subinterfaces allow you to create logical interfaces within the router. The prompt then changes to Router(config-subif)#:

```
Router(config)#int fastethernet0/0.?
 <0-4294967295> FastEthernet interface number
Router(config)#int fastethernet0/0.1
Router(config-subif)#
```

You can read more about subinterfaces in Chapters 8, "Virtual LANs (VLANs)," and 11, "Wide Area Networking Protocols," but don't skip ahead just yet!.

Line Commands

To configure user-mode passwords, use the line command. The prompt then becomes Router(config-line)#:

```
Router#config t
Enter configuration commands, one per line. End with
  CNTL/Z.
Router(config)#line ?
  <0-70>   First Line number
  aux      Auxiliary line
```

```
console   Primary terminal line
tty       Terminal controller
vty       Virtual terminal
x/y       Slot/Port for Modems

2600A(config)#line

Router(config)#line console 0
Router(config-line)#
```

The line console 0 command is known as a major command (also called a *global command*), and any command typed from the (config-line) prompt is known as a subcommand.

Routing Protocol Configurations

To configure routing protocols such as RIP and IGRP, use the prompt (config-router)#:

```
Router#config t
Enter configuration commands, one per line. End with
  CNTL/Z.
Router(config)#router rip
Router(config-router)#
```

Editing and Help Features

You can use the Cisco advanced editing features to help you configure your router. If you type in a question mark (**?**) at any prompt, you'll be given a list of all the commands available from that prompt:

```
Router#?
Exec commands:
 access-enable   Create a temporary Access-List entry
 access-profile  Apply user-profile to interface
 access-template Create a temporary Access-List entry
 bfe             For manual emergency modes setting
 clear           Reset functions
 clock           Manage the system clock
 configure       Enter configuration mode
 connect         Open a terminal connection
 copy            Copy configuration or image data
 debug           Debugging functions (see also 'undebug')
 disable         Turn off privileged commands
 disconnect      Disconnect an existing network connection
```

```
enable      Turn on privileged commands
erase       Erase flash or configuration memory
exit        Exit from the EXEC
help        Description of the interactive help system
lock        Lock the terminal
login       Log in as a particular user
logout      Exit from the EXEC
mrinfo      Request neighbor and version information
            from a multicast router
--More-
```

Plus, at this point, you can press the spacebar to get another page of information, or you can press Enter to go one command at a time. You can also press Q (or any other key for that matter) to quit and return to the prompt.

Here's a shortcut: To find commands that start with a certain letter, use the letter and the question mark with no space between them:

```
Router#c?
clear clock configure connect copy


Router#c
```

By typing **c?**, we received a response listing all the commands that start with *c*. Also notice that the Router# prompt reappears after the list of commands is displayed. This can be helpful when you have long commands and need the next possible command. It would be pretty lame if you had to retype the entire command every time you used a question mark!

To find the next command in a string, type the first command and then a question mark:

```
Router#clock ?
 set Set the time and date
Router#clock set ?
 hh:mm:ss Current Time
Router#clock set 10:30:10 ?
 <1-31> Day of the month
 MONTH  Month of the year
Router#clock set 10:30:10 28 ?
 MONTH  Month of the year
Router#clock set 10:30:10 28 august ?
 <1993-2035> Year
Router#clock set 10:30:10 28 august 2003 ?
 <cr>
Router#
```

By typing the **clock ?** command, you'll get a list of the next possible parameters and what they do. Notice that you should just keep typing a command, a space, and then a question mark until <cr> (carriage return) is your only option.

If you are typing commands and receive the following:

```
Router#clock set 10:30:10
% Incomplete command.
```

you'll know that the command string isn't yet done. Just press the Up arrow key to redisplay the last command entered, then continue with the command by using your question mark.

And if you receive the following error:

```
Router(config)#access-list 110 permit host 1.1.1.1
                              ^
% Invalid input detected at '^' marker.
```

you've entered a command incorrectly. See that little caret—the ^? It's a very helpful tool that marks the point where you have entered the command wrong.

Now if you receive this error:

```
Router#sh te
% Ambiguous command: "sh te"
```

it means there are multiple commands that begin with the string you entered and it is not unique. Use the question mark to find the command you need:

```
Router#sh te?
tech-support  template  terminal
```

Table 4.1 shows the list of the enhanced editing commands available on a Cisco router.

TABLE 4.1 Enhanced Editing Commands

Command	Meaning
Ctrl+A	Moves your cursor to the beginning of the line
Ctrl+E	Moves your cursor to the end of the line
Esc+B	Moves back one word
Ctrl+B	Moves back one character
Ctrl+F	Moves forward one character
Esc+F	Moves forward one word

TABLE 4.1 Enhanced Editing Commands *(continued)*

Command	Meaning
Ctrl+D	Deletes a single character
Backspace	Deletes a single character
Ctrl+R	Redisplays a line
Ctrl+U	Erases a line
Ctrl+W	Erases a word
Ctrl+Z	Ends configuration mode and returns to EXEC
Tab	Finishes typing a command for you

Another cool editing feature I want to show you is the automatic scrolling of long lines. In the following example, the command typed had reached the right margin and automatically moved 11 spaces to the left (the dollar sign [$] indicates that the line has been scrolled to the left):

```
Router#config t
Enter configuration commands, one per line. End with CNTL/Z.
Router(config)#$110 permit host 171.10.10.10 0.0.0.0 host
```

You can review the router-command history with the commands shown in Table 4.2:

TABLE 4.2 Router-Command History

Command	Meaning
Ctrl+P or up arrow	Shows last command entered
Ctrl+N or down arrow	Shows previous commands entered
show history	Shows last 10 commands entered by default
show terminal	Shows terminal configurations and history buffer size
terminal history size	Changes buffer size (max 256)

The following example demonstrates the show history command and how to change the history size, as well as how to verify it with the show terminal command.

First, use the show history command to see the last 10 commands that were entered on the router:

```
Router#sh history
 en
 sh history
 show terminal
 sh cdp neig
 sh ver
 sh flash
 sh int fa0
 sh history
 sh int s0/0
 sh int s0/1
```

Now you use the show terminal command to verify the terminal history size:

```
Router#sh terminal
Line 0, Location: "", Type: ""
[output cut]
History is enabled, history size is 10.
Full user help is disabled
Allowed transports are lat pad v120 telnet mop rlogin
  nasi. Preferred is lat.
No output characters are padded
No special data dispatching characters
Group codes:  0
```

The terminal history size command, used from privileged mode, can change the size of the history buffer:

```
Router#terminal history size ?
 <0-256> Size of history buffer
Router#terminal history size 25
```

Verify the change with the show terminal command.

```
Router#sh terminal
Line 0, Location: "", Type: ""
[output cut]
Editing is enabled.
History is enabled, history size is 25.
Full user help is disabled
Allowed transports are lat pad v120 telnet mop rlogin
```

```
nasi. Preferred is lat.
No output characters are padded
No special data dispatching characters
Group codes:  0
```

When do you use the Cisco editing features?

There are a couple of editing features that are used quite often, some not so much, if at all. Understand that Cisco didn't make these up; these are just old Unix commands. However, Ctrl+A is really helpful to negate a command.

For example, if you were to put in a long command and then decide you didn't want to use that command in your configuration or that it didn't work, then you can press your up arrow key to show the last command entered, press Ctrl+A, type **no** then a space, and press Enter, and poof! The command is negated. This doesn't work on every command, but it works on a lot of them.

Gathering Basic Routing Information

The show version command will provide basic configuration for the system hardware as well as the software version, the names and sources of configuration files, and the boot images. Here is an example:

```
Router#sh version
Cisco Internetwork Operating System Software
IOS (tm) C2600 Software (C2600-BIN-M), Version 12.2(13)T1,RELEASE SOFTWARE(fc1)
TAC Support: http://www.cisco.com/tac
Copyright (c) 1986-2003 by cisco Systems, Inc.
Compiled Sat 04-Jan-03 05:58 by ccai
Image text-base: 0x80008098, data-base: 0x80C4AD94
```

The preceding section of output describes the Cisco IOS running on the router. The following section describes the read-only memory (ROM) used, which is used to boot the router:

```
ROM: System Bootstrap, Version 11.3(2)XA4, RELEASE SOFTWARE (fc1)
```

The next section shows how long the router has been running, how it was restarted (if you see a "system restarted by bus-error," that is a very bad thing) as well as where the Cisco IOS was loaded from, plus the IOS name. Flash is the default:

```
Router uptime is 1 week, 2 hours, 39 minutes
System returned to ROM by reload
System image file is "flash:c2600-bin-mz.122-13.T1.bin"
```

And this next section displays the processor, the amount of DRAM and flash memory, and the interfaces the POST found on the router:

```
cisco 2621 (MPC860) processor (revision 0x101) with 27648K/5120K bytes of memory
Processor board ID JAB0402040J (2308906173)
M860 processor: part number 0, mask 49
Bridging software.
X.25 software, Version 3.0.0.
2 FastEthernet/IEEE 802.3 interface(s)
2 Serial network interface(s)
32K bytes of non-volatile configuration memory.
8192K bytes of processor board System flash (Read/Write)

Configuration register is 0x2102
```

The configuration register value is listed last—it's something I'll cover in Chapter 9.

Setting Passwords

There are five passwords used to secure your Cisco routers: console, auxiliary, telnet (VTY), enable password, and enable secret. Just as you learned earlier in the chapter, the first two passwords are used to set your enable password, which is used to secure privileged mode. This will prompt a user for a password when the enable command is used. The other three are used to configure a password when user mode is accessed either through the console port, the auxiliary port, or via Telnet.

We will look at each of these in the following sections.

Enable Passwords

You set the enable passwords from global configuration mode like this:

```
Router(config)#enable ?
 last-resort Define enable action if no TACACS servers
            respond
 password   Assign the privileged level password
 secret     Assign the privileged level secret
 use-tacacs Use TACACS to check enable passwords
```

The following points describe the enable password parameters:

Last-resort Allows you to still enter the router if you set up authentication through a TACACS server and it's not available. But it isn't used if the TACACS server is working.

Password Sets the enable password on older, pre-10.3 systems, and isn't ever used if an enable secret is set.

Secret Is the newer, encrypted password that overrides the enable password if it's set.

Use-tacacs   Tells the router to authenticate through a TACACS server. It's convenient if you have dozens or even hundreds of routers, because, well, would you like to face the fun of changing the password on 200 routers? If you go through the TACACS server, you only have to change the password once!

Here's an example of setting the enable passwords:

```
Router(config)#enable secret todd
Router(config)#enable password todd
The enable password you have chosen is the same as your
  enable secret. This is not recommended. Re-enter the
  enable password.
```

If you try to set the enable secret and enable passwords the same, the router will give you a nice, polite warning to change the second password. If you don't have older legacy routers, don't even bother to use the enable password.

User-mode passwords are assigned by using the line command:

```
Router(config)#line ?
  <0-70>   First Line number
  aux      Auxiliary line
  console  Primary terminal line
  tty      Terminal controller
  vty      Virtual terminal
  x/y      Slot/Port for Modems
```

Here are the lines we are concerned with:

aux   Sets the user-mode password for the auxiliary port. It's usually used for attaching a modem to the router, but it can be used as a console as well.

console   Sets a console user-mode password.

vty   Sets a Telnet password on the router. If this password isn't set, then Telnet can't be used by default.

To configure the user-mode passwords, you configure the line you want and use either the login or no login command to tell the router to prompt for authentication. The next section will provide a line-by-line example of each line configuration.

Auxiliary Password

To configure the auxiliary password, go into global configuration mode and type **line aux ?**. You can see that you only get a choice of 0–0 (that's because there's only one port):

```
Router#config t
Enter configuration commands, one per line. End with CNTL/Z.
Router(config)#line aux ?
```

```
<0-0> First Line number
Router(config)#line aux 0
Router(config-line)#login
Router(config-line)#password todd
```

It's important to remember the login command, or the auxiliary port won't prompt for authentication.

Okay, now watch what happens when I try to set the Aux on the "newer" IOS that Cisco has released:

```
2600A#config t
Enter configuration commands, one per line.  End with CNTL/Z.
2600A(config)#line aux 0
2600A(config-line)#login
% Login disabled on line 65, until 'password' is set
2600A(config-line)#
```

Cisco has begun this process of not letting you set the "login" command before a password is set on a line because if you set the login command under a line, and then don't set a password, the line won't be usable. And it will prompt for a password that doesn't exist. So this is a good thing—a feature, not a hassle!

Definitely remember that although Cisco has this new "password feature" on their routers starting in their newer IOS (12.2 and above), it's not in all their IOSes, and it is *not* on the Cisco CCNA exam.

Console Password

To set the console password, use the line console 0 command. But look at what happened when I tried to type line console 0 ? from the aux line configuration—I received an error. You can still type line console 0 and it will accept it, but the help screens just don't work from that prompt. Type **exit** to get back one level and you'll find that your help screens now work. This is a "feature." Really.

Here's the example:

```
Router(config-line)#line console ?
% Unrecognized command
Router(config-line)#exit
Router(config)#line console ?
 <0-0> First Line number
Router(config)#line console 0
Router(config-line)#login
Router(config-line)#password todd1
```

Since there's only one console port, I can only choose line console 0. You can set all your line passwords to the same password, but for security reasons, I'd recommend that you make them different.

There are a few other important commands to know for the console port.

For one, the exec-timeout 0 0 command sets the timeout for the console EXEC session to zero, which basically means to never time out. The default timeout is 10 minutes. (If you're feeling mischievous, try this on people at work: Set it to 0 1. That will make the console time out in 1 second! And to fix it, you have to continually press the down arrow key while changing the timeout time with your free hand!)

logging synchronous is a very cool command, and it should be a default command, but it's not. It stops annoying console messages from popping up and disrupting the input you're trying to type. The messages still pop up, but you are returned to your router prompt without your input interrupted. This makes your input messages oh-so-much easier to read.

Here's an example of how to configure both commands:

```
Router(config)#line con 0
Router(config-line)#exec-timeout ?
 <0-35791> Timeout in minutes
Router(config-line)#exec-timeout 0 ?
 <0-2147483> Timeout in seconds
 <cr>
Router(config-line)#exec-timeout 0 0
Router(config-line)#logging synchronous
```

Telnet Password

To set the user-mode password for Telnet access into the router, use the line vty command. Routers that aren't running the Enterprise edition of the Cisco IOS default to five VTY lines, 0 through 4. But if you have the Enterprise edition, you'll have significantly more. The best way to find out how many lines you have is to use that question mark:

```
Router(config-line)#line vty 0 ?
 <1-4> Last Line Number
 <cr>
Router(config-line)#line vty 0 4
Router(config-line)#login
Router(config-line)#password todd2
```

The CCNA exam only cares about lines 0 through 4 for the VTY lines. My routers actually have 70 lines, but no worries—I have demonstrated above all you need to know for the exam.

So what will happen if you try to telnet into a router that doesn't have a VTY password set? You'll receive an error stating that the connection is refused because, well, the password isn't set. But you can get around this and tell the router to allow Telnet connections without a password by using the `no login` command:

```
Router(config-line)#line vty 0 4
Router(config-line)#no login
```

After your routers are configured with an IP address, you can use the Telnet program to configure and check your routers instead of having to use a console cable. You can use the Telnet program by typing **telnet** from any command prompt (DOS or Cisco). Anything Telnet is covered more thoroughly in Chapter 9.

 If you can ping a router but are unable to telnet into it, the likely problem is that you didn't set the password on the VTY lines.

Encrypting Your Passwords

Because only the enable secret password is encrypted by default, you'll need to manually configure the user-mode and enable passwords for encryption.

Notice that you can see all the passwords except the enable secret when performing a `show running-config` on a router:

```
Router#sh running-config
[output cut]
!
enable secret 5 $1$rFbM$8.aXocHg6yHrM/zzeNkAT.
enable password todd1
!
[output cut]
line con 0
 password todd1
 login
line aux 0
 password todd
 login
line vty 0 4
 password todd2
 login
!
end

Router#
```

To manually encrypt your passwords, use the `service password-encryption` command. Here's an example of how to do it:

```
Router#config t
Enter configuration commands, one per line. End with CNTL/Z.
Router(config)#service password-encryption
Router(config)#^Z
Router#sh run
Building configuration...
[output cut]
!
enable secret 5 $1$rFbM$8.aXocHg6yHrM/zzeNkAT.
enable password 7 0835434A0D
!
[output cut]
!
line con 0
 password 7 111D160113
 login
line aux 0
 password 7 071B2E484A
 login
line vty 0 4
 password 7 0835434A0D
 login
line vty 5 197
 password 7 09463724B
 login
!
end
```

```
Router#config t
Router(config)#no service password-encryption
Router(config)#^Z
```

There you have it! The passwords will now be encrypted. You just encrypt the passwords, perform a show run, and then turn off the command. You can see that the enable password and the line passwords are all encrypted.

Banners

A good reason for having a *banner* is to add a security notice to users dialing or telnetting into your internetwork. You can set a banner on a Cisco router so that when either a user logs into the router or an administrator telnets into the router, the banner will give them the information you want them to have. There are four different banners available that you need to be aware of:

```
Router(config)#banner ?
  LINE     c banner-text c, where 'c' is a delimiting
           character
  exec     Set EXEC process creation banner
  incoming Set incoming terminal line banner
  login    Set login banner
  motd     Set Message of the Day banner
```

Message of the day (MOTD) is the most extensively used banner. It gives a message to every person dialing into or connecting to the router via Telnet or auxiliary port, or through a console port as seen here:

```
Router(config)#banner motd ?
LINE c banner-text c, where 'c' is a delimiting character
Router(config)#banner motd #
Enter TEXT message. End with the character '#'.
$ Acme.com network, then you must disconnect immediately.
#
Router(config)#^Z
Router#
00:25:12: %SYS-5-CONFIG_I: Configured from console by
  console
Router#exit

Router con0 is now available

Press RETURN to get started.

If you are not authorized to be in Acme.com network, then
  you must disconnect immediately.

Router>
```

The preceding MOTD banner essentially tells anyone connecting to the router that if they're not on the guest list, get lost! The part to understand is the delimiting character—the thing that's used to tell the router when the message is done. You can use any character you want for it, but you can't use the delimiting character in the message itself. Also, once the message is complete, press Enter, then the delimiting character, then Enter again. It'll still work if you don't do that, but if you have more than one banner, they'll be combined as one message and put on a single line.

These are the other banners:

Exec banner   You can configure a line-activation (exec) banner to be displayed when an EXEC process (such as a line-activation or incoming connection to a VTY line) is created. By simply starting a user exec session through a console port, you will activate the exec banner.

Incoming banner   You can configure a banner to be displayed on terminals connected to reverse Telnet lines. This banner is useful for providing instructions to users who use reverse Telnet.

Login banner   You can configure a login banner to be displayed on all connected terminals. This banner is displayed after the MOTD banner, but before the login prompts. The login banner can't be disabled on a per-line basis, so to globally disable it, you've got to delete it with the no banner login command.

Router Interfaces

Interface configuration is one of the most important router configurations, because without interfaces, a router is a totally useless thing. Plus, interface configurations must be exact to enable communication with other devices. Some of the configurations used to configure an interface are Network layer addresses, media type, bandwidth, and other administrator commands.

Different routers use different methods to choose the interfaces used on them. For instance, the following command shows a Cisco 2522 router with 10 serial interfaces, labeled 0 through 9:

```
Router(config)#int serial ?
 <0-9> Serial interface number
```

Now it's time to choose the interface you want to configure. Once you do that, you will be in interface configuration for that specific interface. The command to choose serial port 5, for example, would be:

```
Router(config)#int serial 5
Router(config)-if)#
```

The 2522 router has one Ethernet 10BaseT port, and typing **interface ethernet 0** can configure that interface, as seen here:

```
Router(config)#int ethernet ?
 <0-0> Ethernet interface number
Router(config)#int ethernet 0
Router(config-if)#
```

The 2500 router, as previously demonstrated, is a fixed configuration router, which means that when you buy that model, you're stuck with that physical configuration.

To configure an interface, you always use the interface *type number* sequence, but the 2600, 3600, 4000, and 7000 series routers use a physical slot in the router, with a port number on the module plugged into that slot. So on a 2600 router, the configuration would be interface *type slot/port*, as seen here:

```
Router(config)#int fastethernet ?
 <0-1> FastEthernet interface number
Router(config)#int fastethernet 0
% Incomplete command.
Router(config)#int fastethernet 0?
/
Router(config)#int fastethernet 0/?
 <0-1> FastEthernet interface number
```

And make note of the fact that you can't just type **int fastethernet 0**. You must type the full command: **type slot/port**, or **int fastethernet 0/0**, or **int fa 0/0**.

To set the type of connector used, use the media-type command (this is usually auto-detected):

```
Router(config)#int fa 0/0
Router(config-if)#media-type ?
 100BaseX Use RJ45 for -TX; SC FO for -FX
 MII     Use MII connector
```

In the following sections, I will continue with the router interface discussion, including how to bring up the interface and set an IP address on a router interface.

Bringing Up an Interface

You can turn an interface off with the interface command shutdown, and turn it on with the no shutdown command.

If an interface is shut down, it'll display administratively down when using the show interfaces (sh int for short) command:

```
Router#sh int ethernet0
Ethernet0 is administratively down, line protocol is down
[output cut]
```

Another way to check an interface's status is via the show running-config command. All interfaces are shut down by default.

You can bring up the interface with the no shutdown command (no shut for short):

```
Router#config t
Enter configuration commands, one per line. End with
  CNTL/Z.
Router(config)#int ethernet0
Router(config-if)#no shutdown
Router(config-if)#^Z
```

```
00:57:08: %LINK-3-UPDOWN: Interface Ethernet0, changed
   state to up
00:57:09: %LINEPROTO-5-UPDOWN: Line protocol on Interface
   Ethernet0, changed state to up
```

```
Router#sh int ethernet0
Ethernet0 is up, line protocol is up
[output cut]
```

Configuring an IP Address on an Interface

Even though you don't have to use IP on your routers, it's most often what people use. To configure IP addresses on an interface, use the ip address command from interface configuration mode:

```
Router(config)#int e0
Router(config-if)#ip address 172.16.10.2 255.255.255.0
Router(config-if)#no shut
```

Don't forget to turn on an interface with the no shutdown command. Remember to look at the command show interface e0 to see if it's administratively shut down or not. Show running-config will also give you this information.

   The ip address *address mask* command starts the IP processing on the interface.

If you want to add a second subnet address to an interface, you have to use the secondary parameter. If you type another IP address and press Enter, it will replace the existing IP address and mask. This is definitely a most excellent feature of the Cisco IOS.

So, let's try it. To add a secondary IP address, just use the secondary parameter:

```
Router(config-if)#ip address 172.16.20.2 255.255.255.0
   secondary
Router(config-if)#^Z
```

You can verify that both addresses are configured on the interface with the show running-config command (sh run for short):

```
Router#sh run
Building configuration...
Current configuration:
[output cut]
!
interface Ethernet0
 ip address 172.16.20.2 255.255.255.0 secondary
```

```
ip address 172.16.10.2 255.255.255.0
!
```

I really wouldn't recommend having multiple IP addresses on an interface because it's inefficient, but I showed you anyway just in case you someday find yourself dealing with an MIS manager who's in love with really bad network design and makes you administer it! And who knows? Maybe someone will ask you about it some day and you'll get to seem really smart because you know!

Serial Interface Commands

Before you jump in and configure a serial interface, there are a couple of things you need to know. First, the interface will usually be attached to a CSU/DSU type of device that provides clocking for the line to the router. But if you have a back-to-back configuration (for example, one that's used in a lab environment), one end—the data communication equipment (DCE) end of the cable—must provide clocking. By default, Cisco routers are all data terminal equipment (DTE) devices, so you must tell an interface to provide clocking if you need it to act like a DCE device.

You configure a DCE serial interface with the clock rate command:

```
Router#config t
Enter configuration commands, one per line. End with CNTL/Z.
Router(config)#int s0
Router(config-if)#clock rate ?
  Speed (bits per second)
 1200
 2400
 4800
 9600
 19200
 38400
 56000
 64000
 72000
 125000
 148000
 250000
 500000
 800000
 1000000
 1300000
 2000000
 4000000

 <300-4000000>  Choose clockrate from list above
```

```
Router(config-if)#clock rate 64000
%Error: This command applies only to DCE interfaces
Router(config-if)#int s1
Router(config-if)#clock rate 64000
```

It doesn't hurt anything to try to put a clock rate on an interface. Notice that the clock rate command is in bits per second. You can see if a router's serial interface has a DCE cable connected with the show controllers *int* command.

```
Router>sh controllers s 0
HD unit 0, idb = 0x297DE8, driver structure at 0x29F3A0
buffer size 1524  HD unit 0, V.35 DCE cable
```

The next command you need to get acquainted with is the bandwidth command. Every Cisco router ships with a default serial link bandwidth of T-1 (1.544Mbps). But this has nothing to do with how data is transferred over a link. The bandwidth of a serial link is used by routing protocols such as IGRP, EIGRP, and OSPF to calculate the best cost (path) to a remote network. So if you're using RIP routing, then the bandwidth setting of a serial link is irrelevant, since RIP uses only hop count to determine that. (Routing protocols and metrics are discussed in Chapter 5, "IP Routing.")

Here is an example of using the bandwidth command:

```
Router(config-if)#bandwidth ?
 <1-10000000> Bandwidth in kilobits
```

```
Router(config-if)#bandwidth 64
```

Did you notice that, unlike the clock rate command, the bandwidth command is configured in kilobits?

Hostnames

You can set the identity of the router with the hostname command. This is only locally significant, which means it has no bearing on how the router performs name lookups or how the router works on the internetwork.

Here is an example:

```
Router#config t
Enter configuration commands, one per line. End with
  CNTL/Z.
Router(config)#hostname Todd
Todd(config)#hostname Atlanta
Atlanta(config)#
```

Even though it's pretty tempting to configure the hostname after your own name, it's a better idea to name the router something pertinent to the location.

Descriptions

Setting descriptions on an interface is helpful to the administrator and, like the hostname, only locally significant. The `description` command is a helpful command because you can, for instance, use it to keep track of circuit numbers.

Here is an example:

```
Atlanta(config)#int e0
Atlanta(config-if)#description Sales Lan
Atlanta(config-if)#int s0
Atlanta(config-if)#desc Wan to Miami circuit:6fdda4321
```

You can view the description of an interface either with the `show running-config` command or the `show interface` command:

```
Atlanta#sh run
[cut]
interface Ethernet0
 description Sales Lan
 ip address 172.16.10.30 255.255.255.0
 no ip directed-broadcast
!
interface Serial0
 description Wan to Miami circuit:6fdda4321
 no ip address
 no ip directed-broadcast
 no ip mroute-cache
Atlanta#sh int e0
Ethernet0 is up, line protocol is up
 Hardware is Lance, address is 0010.7be8.25db (bia
  0010.7be8.25db)
 Description: Sales Lan
 [output cut]
Atlanta#sh int s0
Serial0 is up, line protocol is up
 Hardware is HD64570
 Description: Wan to Miami circuit:6fdda4321
[output cut]
Atlanta#
```

> ### 🌐 Real World Scenario
>
> #### description: **The Helpful Command**
>
> Bob, a Senior Network Administrator at Acme Corporation in San Francisco, has over 50 WAN links to various branches throughout the U.S. and Canada. Whenever an interface goes down, Bob spends a lot of time trying to figure out the circuit number as well as the phone number of the responsible provider of the WAN link.
>
> The interface description command would be very helpful to Bob because not only can he use this command on his LAN links so he knows where every router interface is connected to, but he would benefit the most by adding circuit numbers to each and every WAN interface, as well as the phone number of the responsible provider.
>
> By spending the few hours it would take to add this information to each and every router interface, Bob can save a lot of precious time when his WAN links go down (and they will!), and time is of the essence.

Viewing and Saving Configurations

If you run through setup mode, you'll be asked if you want to use the configuration you just created. If you say Yes, then it will copy the configuration running in DRAM, (known as the running-config), into NVRAM, and name the file startup-config.

You can manually save the file from DRAM to NVRAM by using the copy running-config startup-config command (you can use the shortcut copy run start also):

```
Atlanta#copy run start
Destination filename [startup-config]?[Enter]
Warning: Attempting to overwrite an NVRAM configuration
  previously written by a different version of the system
  image.
Overwrite the previous NVRAM configuration?[confirm][Enter]
Building configuration...
```

Notice that the message we received tells us we're trying to write over the older startup-config. The IOS had just been upgraded to version 12.2, and the last time the file was saved, 11.3 was running. Sometimes, when you see a question with an answer in [], it means that if you just press Enter, you're choosing the default answer.

Also, when the command asked for the destination filename, the default answer was startup-config. The "feature" aspect of this command output is that you can't even type anything else in or you'll get an error, as seen here:

```
Atlanta#copy run start
```

```
Destination filename [startup-config]?todd
%Error opening nvram:todd (No such file or directory)
Atlanta#
```

 Okay, you're right—it's weird! Why on earth do they even ask if you can't change it at all? Well, because this "feature" was first introduced with the release of the 12.*x* IOS, we're all pretty sure it will turn out to be relevant and important sometime in the future.

You can view the files by typing **show running-config** or **show startup-config** from privileged mode. The sh run command, which is a shortcut for show running-config, tells us that we are viewing the current configuration:

```
Atlanta#sh run
Building configuration...

Current configuration:
!
version 12.0
service timestamps debug uptime
service timestamps log uptime
no service password-encryption
!
hostname Atlanta
ip subnet-zero
frame-relay switching
!
[output cut]
```

The sh start command—one of the shortcuts for the show startup-config command—shows us the configuration that will be used the next time the router is reloaded. It also tells us how much NVRAM is being used to store the startup-config file. Here is an example:

```
Atlanta#sh start
Using 4850 out of 32762 bytes
!
version 12.0
service timestamps debug uptime
service timestamps log uptime
no service password-encryption
!
hostname Atlanta
```

```
!
!
ip subnet-zero
frame-relay switching
!
[output cut]
```

You can delete the startup-config file by using the **erase startup-config** command, after which you'll receive an error if you ever try to view the startup-config file:

```
Atlanta#erase startup-config
Erasing the nvram filesystem will remove all files!
  Continue? [confirm][Enter]
[OK]
Erase of nvram: complete
Atlanta#sh start
%% Non-volatile configuration memory is not present
Atlanta#reload
```

If you reload or power down and up the router after using the **erase startup-config** command, you'll be offered setup mode because there's no configuration saved in NVRAM. You can press Ctrl+C to exit setup mode at any time (the **reload** command can only be used from privileged mode).

At this point, you shouldn't use setup mode to configure your router. Setup mode was designed to help people who do not know how to use the Cash Line Interface (CLI), and this no longer applies to you!

Verifying Your Configuration

Obviously, **show running-config** would be the best way to verify your configuration, and **show startup-config** would be the best way to verify the configuration that'll be used the next time the router is reloaded—right?

Well, once you take a look at the running-config, if all appears well, you can verify your configuration with utilities such as Ping and Telnet. Ping is Packet Internet Groper, a program that uses ICMP echo requests and replies. (ICMP is discussed in Chapter 2, "Internet Protocols.") Ping sends a packet to a remote host, and if that host responds, you know that the host is alive. But you don't know if it's alive and also *well*—just because you can ping an NT server does not mean you can log in! Even so, Ping is an awesome starting point for troubleshooting an internetwork.

Did you know that you can ping with different protocols? You can, and you can test this by typing **ping ?** at either the router user-mode or privileged mode prompt:

```
Router#ping ?
  WORD      Ping destination address or hostname
  appletalk Appletalk echo
```

```
decnet    DECnet echo
ip        IP echo
ipx       Novell/IPX echo
srb       srb echo
<cr>
```

If you want to find a neighbor's Network layer address, either you need to go to the router or switch itself, or you can type **show cdp entry * protocol** to get the Network layer addresses you need for pinging. (Cisco Discovery Protocol [CDP] is covered in Chapter 9.)

Traceroute uses ICMP with IP Time To Live (TTL) timeouts to track the path a packet takes through an internetwork, in contrast to Ping, which just finds the host and responds. And Traceroute can also be used with multiple protocols.

```
Router#traceroute ?
WORD      Trace route to destination address or hostname
appletalk AppleTalk Trace
clns      ISO CLNS Trace
ip        IP Trace
oldvines  Vines Trace (Cisco)
vines     Vines Trace (Banyan)
<cr>
```

Telnet is the best tool since it uses IP at the Network layer and TCP at the Transport layer to create a session with a remote host. If you can telnet into a device, your IP connectivity just has to be good. You can only telnet to devices that use IP addresses, and you can use Windows hosts or router prompts to telnet to a remote device:

```
Router#telnet ?
WORD IP address or hostname of a remote system
<cr>
```

From the router prompt, you just type a hostname or IP address and it will assume you want to telnet—you don't need to type the actual command, `telnet`.

In the following sections, I am going to show you how to verify the interface statistics.

Verifying with the *show interface* Command

Another way to verify your configuration is by typing show interface commands, the first of which is show interface ?. That will reveal all the available interfaces to configure. The following output is from my 2600 routers:

```
Router#sh int ?
  Async         Async interface
  BVI           Bridge-Group Virtual Interface
  CTunnel       CTunnel interface
```

```
Dialer              Dialer interface
FastEthernet        FastEthernet IEEE 802.3
Loopback            Loopback interface
MFR                 Multilink Frame Relay bundle interface
Multilink           Multilink-group interface
Null                Null interface
Serial              Serial
Tunnel              Tunnel interface
Vif                 PGM Multicast Host interface
Virtual-Template    Virtual Template interface
Virtual-TokenRing   Virtual TokenRing
accounting          Show interface accounting
crb                 Show interface routing/bridging info
dampening           Show interface dampening info
description         Show interface description
irb                 Show interface routing/bridging info
mac-accounting      Show interface MAC accounting info
mpls-exp            Show interface MPLS experimental accounting info
precedence          Show interface precedence accounting info
rate-limit          Show interface rate-limit info
summary             Show interface summary
switching           Show interface switching
|                   Output modifiers
<cr>
```

The only "real" physical interfaces are FastEthernet, Serial, and async; the rest are all logical interfaces. In addition, the newer IOS shows the "possible" show commands that can be used to verify your router interfaces—a very new feature from Cisco.

The next command is show interface fastethernet 0/0. It reveals to us the hardware address, logical address, and encapsulation method, as well as statistics on collisions, as seen here:

```
Router#sh int fastethernet 0/0
FastEthernet0/0 is up, line protocol is up
  Hardware is AmdFE, address is 00b0.6483.2320 (bia 00b0.6483.2320)
  Description: connection to LAN 40
  Internet address is 192.168.1.33/27
  MTU 1500 bytes, BW 100000 Kbit, DLY 100 usec,
      reliability 255/255, txload 1/255, rxload 1/255
  Encapsulation ARPA, loopback not set
  Keepalive set (10 sec)
  Full-duplex, 100Mb/s, 100BaseTX/FX
  ARP type: ARPA, ARP Timeout 04:00:00
```

```
Last input never, output 00:00:04, output hang never
Last clearing of "show interface" counters never
Input queue: 0/75/0/0 (size/max/drops/flushes); Total output drops: 0
Queueing strategy: fifo
Output queue: 0/40 (size/max)
5 minute input rate 0 bits/sec, 0 packets/sec
5 minute output rate 0 bits/sec, 0 packets/sec
   0 packets input, 0 bytes
   Received 0 broadcasts, 0 runts, 0 giants, 0 throttles
   0 input errors, 0 CRC, 0 frame, 0 overrun, 0 ignored
   0 watchdog
   0 input packets with dribble condition detected
   84639 packets output, 8551135 bytes, 0 underruns
   0 output errors, 0 collisions, 16 interface resets
   0 babbles, 0 late collision, 0 deferred
   0 lost carrier, 0 no carrier
   0 output buffer failures, 0 output buffers swapped out
```

The most important statistic of the show interface command is the output of the line and data-link protocol status.

If the output reveals that FastEthernet 0/0 is up and the line protocol is up, then the interface is up and running:

```
Router#sh int fa0/0
FastEthernet0/0 is up, line protocol is up
```

The first parameter refers to the Physical layer, and it's up when it receives carrier detect. The second parameter refers to the Data Link layer, and it looks for keepalives from the connecting end. (Keepalives are used between devices to make sure connectivity has not dropped.)

Here is an example:

```
Router#sh int s0/0
Serial0/0 is up, line protocol is down
```

If you see the line is up but the protocol is down, as shown above, you are experiencing a clocking (keepalive) or framing problem. Check the keepalives on both ends to make sure that they match, the clock rate is set, if needed, and the encapsulation type is the same on both ends. The output above would be considered a Data Link layer problem.

```
Router#sh int s0/0
Serial0/0 is down, line protocol is down
```

If you discover that both the line interface and the protocol are down, it's a cable or interface problem. The output above would be considered a Physical layer problem.

If one end is administratively shut down (as shown next), the remote end would present as down and down:

```
Router#sh int s0/0
Serial0/0 is administratively down, line protocol is down
```

To enable the interface, use the command no shutdown from interface configuration mode.

The next show interface serial 0/0 command demonstrates the serial line and the maximum transmission unit (MTU)—1500 bytes by default. It also shows the default bandwidth (BW) on all Cisco serial links: 1.544Kbps. This is used to determine the bandwidth of the line for routing protocols such as IGRP, EIGRP, and OSPF.

Another important configuration to notice is the keepalive, which is 10 seconds by default. Each router sends a keepalive message to its neighbor every 10 seconds, and if both routers aren't configured for the same keepalive time, it won't work.

You can clear the counters on the interface by typing the command clear counters:

```
Router#sh int s0/0
Serial0/0 is up, line protocol is up
 Hardware is HD64570
 MTU 1500 bytes, BW 1544 Kbit, DLY 20000 usec,
   reliability 255/255, txload 1/255, rxload 1/255
 Encapsulation HDLC, loopback not set, keepalive set
 (10 sec)
 Last input never, output never, output hang never
 Last clearing of "show interface" counters never
 Queueing strategy: fifo
 Output queue 0/40, 0 drops; input queue 0/75, 0 drops
 5 minute input rate 0 bits/sec, 0 packets/sec
 5 minute output rate 0 bits/sec, 0 packets/sec
   0 packets input, 0 bytes, 0 no buffer
   Received 0 broadcasts, 0 runts, 0 giants, 0 throttles
   0 input errors, 0 CRC, 0 frame, 0 overrun, 0 ignored,
   0 abort
   0 packets output, 0 bytes, 0 underruns
   0 output errors, 0 collisions, 16 interface resets
   0 output buffer failures, 0 output buffers swapped out
   0 carrier transitions
   DCD=down DSR=down DTR=down RTS=down CTS=down


Router#clear counters ?
  Async                 Async interface
  BVI                   Bridge-Group Virtual Interface
```

```
CTunnel               CTunnel interface
Dialer                Dialer interface
FastEthernet          FastEthernet IEEE 802.3
Group-Async           Async Group interface
Line                  Terminal line
Loopback              Loopback interface
MFR                   Multilink Frame Relay bundle interface
Multilink             Multilink-group interface
Null                  Null interface
Serial                Serial
Tunnel                Tunnel interface
Vif                   PGM Multicast Host interface
Virtual-Template      Virtual Template interface
Virtual-TokenRing     Virtual TokenRing
<cr>
```

```
Router#clear counters s0/0
Clear "show interface" counters on this interface
  [confirm][Enter]
Router#
00:17:35: %CLEAR-5-COUNTERS: Clear counter on interface
  Serial0 by console
Router#
```

Verifying with the *show ip interface* Command

The show ip interface command will provide you with information regarding the layer 3 configurations of a router's interfaces:

```
Router#sh ip interface
FastEthernet0/0 is up, line protocol is up
  Internet address is 1.1.1.1/24
  Broadcast address is 255.255.255.255
  Address determined by setup command
  MTU is 1500 bytes
  Helper address is not set
  Directed broadcast forwarding is disabled
  Outgoing access list is not set
  Inbound  access list is not set
  Proxy ARP is enabled
  Security level is default
  Split horizon is enabled
[output cut]
```

The status of the interface, the IP address and mask, information on whether an access list is set on the interface, and basic IP information are included in this output.

Using the *show ip interface brief* Command

The show ip interface brief command is probably one of the most helpful commands that you can ever use on a Cisco router. This command provides a quick overview of the router's interfaces including the logical address and status:

```
Router#sh ip int brief
Interface         IP-Address      OK? Method Status                  Protocol
FastEthernet0/0   192.168.1.33    YES manual up                          up

FastEthernet0/1   10.3.1.88       YES manual up                          up

Serial0/0         10.1.1.1        YES manual up                          up

Serial0/1         unassigned      YES NVRAM  administratively down    down
```

Using the *show controllers* Command

The show controllers command displays information about the physical interface itself. It'll also give you the type of serial cable plugged into a serial port. Usually, this will only be a DTE cable that plugs into a type of data service unit (DSU).

```
Router#sh controllers serial 0/0
HD unit 0, idb = 0x1229E4, driver structure at 0x127E70
buffer size 1524 HD unit 0, V.35 DTE cable
cpb = 0xE2, eda = 0x4140, cda = 0x4000

Router#sh controllers serial 0/1
HD unit 1, idb = 0x12C174, driver structure at 0x131600
buffer size 1524 HD unit 1, V.35 DCE cable
cpb = 0xE3, eda = 0x2940, cda = 0x2800
```

Notice that serial 0/0 has a DTE cable, whereas the serial 0/1 connection has a DCE cable. Serial 0/1 would have to provide clocking with the clock rate command. Serial 0/0 would get its clocking from the DSU.

Summary

This was a fun chapter! I really showed you a lot about the Cisco IOS and I really hope you gained a lot of insight into the Cisco router world. This chapter started off by explaining the Cisco

Internetwork Operating System (IOS) and how you can use the IOS to run and configure Cisco routers. You learned how to bring a router up and what setup mode does. Oh, and by the way, since you can now basically configure Cisco routers, you should never use setup mode, right?

After I discussed how to connect to a router with a console and LAN connection, I covered the Cisco help features, and how to use the CLI to find commands and command parameters. In addition, I discussed some basic show commands to help you verify your configurations.

Setting router passwords is one of the most important configurations you can perform on your routers. I showed you the five passwords to set. In addition, I used the hostname, interface description, and banners to help you administer your router.

Well, that concludes your introduction to the Cisco Internetwork Operating System (IOS)! And, as usual, it's super-important for you to have the basics that we went over in this chapter before you move on to the following chapters.

Exam Essentials

Understand the sequence of what happens when you power on a router.   When you first bring up a Cisco router, it will run a power-on self-test (POST), and if that passes, it will then look for and load the Cisco IOS from flash memory, if a file is present. The IOS then proceeds to load and looks for a valid configuration in NVRAM called the startup-config. If no file is present in NVRAM, the router will go into setup mode.

Remember what setup mode provides.   Setup mode is automatically started if a router boots and no startup-config is in NVRAM. You can also bring up setup mode by typing **setup** from the privileged mode. Setup provides a minimum amount of configuration in an easy format for someone who does not understand how to configure a Cisco router from the command line.

Understand the difference between user mode and privileged mode.   User mode provides a command-line interface with very few available commands by default. User mode does not allow the configuration to be viewed or changed. Privileged mode allows a user to both view and change the configuration of a router. You can enter privileged mode by typing the command **enable** and entering the enable password or enable secret password, if set.

Remember what the command *show version* provides.   The show version command will provide basic configuration for the system hardware as well as the software version, the names and sources of configuration files, the config-register setting, and the boot images.

Remember how to set the hostname of a router.   The command sequence to set the hostname of a router is:

```
enable
config t
hostname Todd
```

Remember the difference between the enable password and enable secret password.   Both of these passwords are used to gain access into privileged mode. However, the enable secret is newer and is always encrypted by default. Also, if you set the enable password and then set the enable secret, only the enable secret will be used.

Remember how to set the enable secret on a router. To set the enable secret, you use the command enable secret. Do not use enable secret password *password*, or you will set your password to "password *password*". Here is an example:

```
enable
config t
enable secret todd
```

Remember how to set the console password on a router. To set the console password, the sequence is:

```
enable
config t
line console 0
login
password todd
```

Remember how to set the Telnet password on a router. To set the Telnet password, the sequence is:

```
enable
config t
line vty 0 4
login
password todd
```

Be able to understand how to troubleshoot a serial link problem. If you type show interface serial 0 and see that it is "down, line protocol is down," this will be considered a Physical layer problem. If you see it as "up, line protocol is down," then you have a Data Link layer problem.

Key Terms

Before you take the exam, be certain you are familiar with the following terms:

auxiliary port	global command
Basic Management Setup	interface configuration mode
Cisco Internetwork Operating System (IOS)	privileged mode
command-line interface (CLI)	setup mode

console port   Telnet

EXEC session   user mode

Extended Setup

Commands Used in This Chapter

The following list contains a summary of all the commands used in this chapter:

Command	Description
?	Gives you a help screen
Backspace	Deletes a single character
Bandwidth	Sets the bandwidth on a serial interface
Banner	Creates a banner for users who log into the router
clear counters	Clears the statistics from an interface
clock rate	Provides clocking on a serial DCE interface
config memory	Copies the startup-config to running-config
config network	Copies a configuration stored on a TFTP host to running-config
config terminal	Puts you in global configuration mode and allows changes to the running-config
copy run start	Short for `copy running-config startup-config`; places a configuration into NVRAM
Ctrl+A	Moves your cursor to the beginning of the line
Ctrl+D	Deletes a single character
Ctrl+E	Moves your cursor to the end of the line
Ctrl+B	Moves backward one character
Ctrl+F	Moves forward one character
Ctrl+R	Redisplays a line
Ctrl+U	Erases a line

Ctrl+W	Erases a word
Ctrl+Z	Ends configuration mode and returns to EXEC
Description	Sets a description on an interface
Disable	Takes you from privileged mode back to user mode
Enable	Puts you into privileged mode
Enable password	Sets the unencrypted enable password
Enable secret	Sets the encrypted enable secret password; supersedes the enable password if set
Erase startup	Deletes the startup-config
Esc+B	Moves back one word
Esc+F	Moves forward one word
exec-timeout	Sets the timeout in seconds and minutes for the line connections
Hostname	Sets the name of a router
Interface	Puts you in interface configuration mode; also used with show commands
Interface fastethernet 0/0	Puts you in interface configuration mode for a FastEthernet port; also used with show commands
Interface fastethernet 0/0.1	Creates a subinterface
Interface *int*	Puts you in configuration mode for the specified interface and can be used for show commands
ip address	Sets an IP address on an interface
line	Puts you in configuration mode to change or set your user mode passwords
line aux	Puts you in the auxiliary interface configuration mode
line console 0	Puts you in console configuration mode

`line vty`	Puts you in VTY (Telnet) interface configuration mode
`logging synchronous`	Stops console messages from overwriting your command-line input
`logout`	Logs you out of your console session
`media-type`	Sets the hardware media type on an interface
`no shutdown`	Turns on an interface
`ping`	Tests IP connectivity
`Reload`	Reboots the router
`router rip`	Puts you in router rip configuration mode
`service password-encryption`	Encrypts the user mode and enable passwords
`show controllers int`	Shows the DTE or DCE status of an interface
`show history`	Shows you the last 10 commands entered by default
`show interfaces int`	Shows the statistics of an interface
`show run`	Short for `show running-config`; shows the configuration currently running on the router in RAM.
`show start`	Short for `show startup-config`; shows the backup configuration stored in NVRAM
`show terminal`	Shows you your configured history size
`show version`	Shows you statistics, IOS name, and configuration register setting of the router
`shutdown`	Puts an interface in administratively-down mode
Tab	Finishes typing a command for you
`telnet`	Tests IP connectivity to allow you to configure a router
`terminal history size`	Changes your history size from the default of 10 up to 256
`traceroute`	Tests IP connectivity

Written Lab 4

Write out the command or commands for the following questions:

1.   What command is used to set a serial interface to provide clocking to another router at 64k?

2.   If you telnet into a router and get the response "connection refused, password not set," what would you do on the destination router to stop receiving this message and not be prompted for a password?

3.   If you type **show inter et 0** and notice the port is administratively down, what would you do?

4.   If you wanted to delete the configuration stored in NVRAM, what would you type?

5.   If you wanted to set a user-mode password for the console port, what would you type?

6.   If you wanted to set the enable secret password to *cisco*, what would you type?

7.   If you wanted to see if a serial interface needed to provide clocking, what command would you use?

8.   What command would you use to see the terminal history size?

9.   What old Cisco command will change a configuration stored on a TFTP host?

10. How would you set the name of a router to *Chicago*?

(The answers to Written Lab 4 can be found following the answers to the Review Questions for this chapter.)

Hands-on Labs

In this section, you will perform commands on a Cisco router that will help you understand what you learned in this chapter.

You'll need at least one Cisco router—two would be better, three would be outstanding. The hands-on labs in this section are included for use with real Cisco routers. If you are using software from RouterSim or Sybex, please use the hands-on labs found those programs.

The labs in this chapter include the following:

Lab 4.1: Logging into a Router

Lab 4.2: Using the Help and Editing Features

Lab 4.3: Saving a Router Configuration

Lab 4.4: Setting Your Passwords

Lab 4.5: Setting the Hostname, Descriptions, IP Address, and Clock Rate

Hands-on Lab 4.1: Logging into a Router

1.   Press Enter to connect to your router. This will put you into user mode.

2.   At the Router> prompt, type a question mark (**?**).

3. Notice the −more− at the bottom of the screen.

4. Press the Enter key to view the commands line by line.

5. Press the spacebar to view the commands a full screen at a time.

6. You can type **q** at any time to quit.

7. Type **enable** or **en** and press Enter. This will put you into privileged mode where you can change and view the router configuration.

8. At the Router# prompt, type a question mark (**?**). Notice how many options are available to you in privileged mode.

9. Type **q** to quit.

10. Type **config** and press Enter.

11. Press Enter to configure your router using your terminal.

12. At the Router(config)# prompt, type a question mark (**?**), then **q** to quit, or hit the spacebar to view the commands.

13. Type **interface e0** or **int e0**, (or even **int fa0/0**) and press Enter. This will allow you to configure interface Ethernet 0.

14. At the Router(config-if)# prompt, type a question mark (**?**).

15. Type **int s0** (**int s0/0**) or **interface s0** (same as the interface serial 0 command) and press Enter. This will allow you to configure interface serial 0. Notice that you can go from interface to interface easily.

16. Type **encapsulation ?**.

17. Type **exit**. Notice how this brings you back one level.

18. Press Ctrl+Z. Notice how this brings you out of configuration mode and places you back into privileged mode.

19. Type **disable**. This will put you into user mode.

20. Type **exit**, which will log you out of the router.

Hands-on Lab 4.2: Using the Help and Editing Features

1. Log into the router and go to privileged mode by typing **en** or **enable**.

2. Type a question mark (**?**).

3. Type **cl?** and then press Enter. Notice that you can see all the commands that start with *cl*.

4. Type **clock ?** and press Enter.

Notice the difference between Steps 3 and 4. Step 3 has you type letters with no space and a question mark, which will give you all the commands that start with *cl*. Step 4 has you type a command, space, and question mark. By doing this, you will see the next available parameter.

5. Set the router's clock by typing **clock ?** and, following the help screens, setting the router's time and date.

6. Type **clock ?**.

7. Type **clock set ?**.

8. Type **clock set 10:30:30 ?**.

9. Type **clock set 10:30:30 14 March ?**.

10. Type **clock set 10:30:30 14 March 2002**.

11. Press Enter.

12. Type **show clock** to see the time and date.

13. From privileged mode, type **show access-list 10**. Don't press Enter.

14. Press Ctrl+A. This takes you to the beginning of the line.

15. Press Ctrl+E. This should take you back to the end of the line.

16. Press Ctrl+A, then Ctrl+F. This should move you forward one character.

17. Press Ctrl+B, which will move you back one character.

18. Press Enter, then press Ctrl+P. This will repeat the last command.

19. Press the up arrow on your keyboard. This will also repeat the last command.

20. Type **sh history**. This shows you the last 10 commands entered.

21. Type **terminal history size ?**. This changes the history entry size. The "?" is the number of allowed lines.

22. Type **show terminal** to gather terminal statistics and history size.

23. Type **terminal no editing**. This turns off advanced editing. Repeat Steps 14–18 to see that the shortcut editing keys have no effect until you type **terminal editing**.

24. Type **terminal editing** and press Enter to re-enable advanced editing.

25. Type **sh run**, then press your Tab key. This will finish typing the command for you.

26. Type **sh start**, then press your Tab key. This will finish typing the command for you.

Hands-on Lab 4.3: Saving a Router Configuration

1. Log into the router and go into privileged mode by typing **en** or **enable**, then press Enter.

2. To see the configuration stored in NVRAM, type **sh start** and press Tab and Enter, or type **show startup-config** and press Enter. However, if no configuration has been saved, you will get an error message.

3. To save a configuration to NVRAM, which is known as startup-config, you can do one of the following:

   ▪ Type **copy run start** and press Enter.

   ▪ Type **copy running**, press Tab, type **start**, press Tab, and press Enter.

   ▪ Type **copy running-config startup-config** and press Enter.

4. Type **sh start**, press tab, then press Enter.

5. Type **sh run**, press tab, then press Enter.

6. Type **erase start**, press Tab, then press Enter.

7. Type **sh start**, press Tab, then press Enter. You should get an error message.

8. Type **reload**, then press Enter. Acknowledge the reload by pressing Enter. Wait for the router to reload.

9. Say no to entering setup mode, or just press Ctrl+C.

Hands-on Lab 4.4: Setting Your Passwords

1. Log into the router and go into privileged mode by typing **en** or **enable**.

2. Type **config t** and press Enter.

3. Type **enable ?**.

4. Set your enable secret password by typing **enable secret *password*** (the third word should be your own personalized password) and pressing Enter. Do not add the parameter `password` after the parameter `secret` (this would make your password the word *password*). An example would be `enable secret todd`.

5. Now let's see what happens when you log all the way out of the router and then log in. Log out by pressing Ctrl+Z, then type **exit** and press Enter. Go to privileged mode. Before you are allowed to enter privileged mode, you will be asked for a password. If you successfully enter the secret password, you can proceed.

6. Remove the secret password. Go to privileged mode, type **config t**, and press Enter. Type **no enable secret** and press Enter. Log out and then log back in again, and now you should not be asked for a password.

7. One more password used to enter privileged mode is called the enable password. It is an older, less secure password and is not used if an enable secret password is set. Here is an example of how to set it:

```
config t
enable password todd1
```

8. Notice that the enable secret and enable passwords are different. They cannot be the same.

9. Type **config t** to be at the right level to set your console and auxiliary passwords, then type **line ?**.

10. Notice that the parameters for the line commands is `auxiliary`, `vty`, and `console`. You will set all three.

11. To set the Telnet or VTY password, type **line vty 0 4** and then press Enter. The 0 4 is the range of the five available virtual lines used to connect with Telnet. If you have an enterprise IOS, the number of lines may vary. Use the question mark to determine the last line number available on your router.

12. The next command is used to set the authentication on or off. Type **login** and press Enter to prompt for a user-mode password when telnetting into the router. You will not be able to telnet into a router if the password is not set.

 You can use the no login command to disable the user-mode password prompt when using Telnet.

13. One more command you need to set for your VTY password is password. Type **password** *password* to set the password. (*password* is your password.)

14. Here is an example of how to set the VTY passwords:

```
config t
line vty 0 4
login
password todd
```

15. Set your auxiliary password by first typing **line auxiliary 0** or **line aux 0**.

16. Type **login**.

17. Type **password** *password*.

18. Set your console password by first typing **line console 0** or **line con 0**.

19. Type **login**.

20. Type **password** *password*. Here is an example of the last two commands:

```
config t
line con 0
login
password todd1
line aux 0
login
password todd
```

21. You can add the Exec-timeout 0 0 command to the console 0 line. This will stop the console from timing out and logging you out. The command will now look like this:

```
config t
line con 0
login
password todd2
exec-timeout 0 0
```

22. Set the console prompt to not overwrite the command you're typing with console messages by using the command logging synchronous.

```
config t
line con 0
logging synchronous
```

Hands-on Lab 4.5: Setting the Hostname, Descriptions, IP Address, and Clock Rate

1. Log into the router and go into privileged mode by typing **en** or **enable**.

2. Set your hostname on your router by using the `hostname` command. Notice that it is one word. Here is an example of setting your hostname:

   ```
   Router#config t
   Router(config)#hostname RouterA
   RouterA(config)#
   ```

   Notice that the hostname of the router changed as soon as you pressed Enter.

3. Set a banner that the network administrators will see by using the `banner` command.

4. Type **config t**, then **banner ?**.

5. Notice that you can set four different banners. For this exam we are only interested in the login and message of the day (MOTD) banners.

6. Set your MOTD banner, which will be displayed when a console, auxiliary, or Telnet connection is made to the router by typing:

   ```
   config t
   banner motd #
   This is an motd banner
   #
   ```

7. The preceding example used a # sign as a delimiting character. This tells the router when the message is done. You cannot use the delimiting character in the message.

8. You can remove the MOTD banner by typing:

   ```
   config t
   no banner motd
   ```

9. Set the login banner by typing

   ```
   config t
   banner login #
   This is a login banner
   #
   ```

10. The login banner will display immediately after the MOTD but before the user-mode password prompt. Remember that you set your user-mode passwords by setting the console, auxiliary, and VTY line passwords.

11. You can remove the login banner by typing:

    ```
    config t
    no banner login
    ```

12. You can add an IP address to an interface with the `ip address` command. You need to get into interface configuration mode first; here is an example of how you do that:

```
config t
int e0 (you can use int Ethernet 0 too)
ip address 1.1.1.1 255.255.0.0
no shutdown
```

Notice that the IP address (1.1.1.1) and subnet mask (255.255.0.0) are configured on one line. The no shutdown (or no shut for short) command is used to enable the interface. All interfaces are shut down by default.

13. You can add identification to an interface by using the `description` command. This is useful for adding information about the connection. Only administrators see this, not users. Here is an example:

```
config t
int s0
ip address 1.1.1.2 255.255.0.0
no shut
description Wan link to Miami
```

14. You can add the bandwidth of a serial link as well as the clock rate when simulating a DCE WAN link. Here is an example:

```
config t
int s0
bandwidth 64
clock rate 64000
```

Review Questions

1. Which of the following messages displays the code image running in router memory?

   A. `System Bootstrap, Version 12.1(3r)T2, RELEASE SOFTWARE (fc1)Copyright (c) 2000 by cisco Systems, Inc.C2600 platform with 32768 Kbytes of main memory`

   B. `program load complete, entry point: 0x80008000, size: 0x43b7fc. Self decompressing the image : ########################################################################## ######################################################### [OK]`

   C. `Cisco Internetwork Operating System Software IOS (tm) C2600 Software (C2600-I-M), Version 12.1(8), RELEASE C. SOFTWARE (fc1)Copyright (c) 1986-2001 by cisco Systems, Inc.Compiled Tue 19-Aug-03 04:55 by kellythw Image text-base: 0x80008088, data-base: 0x8080853C`

   D. `cisco 2621 (MPC860) processor (revision 0x101) with 26624K/6144K bytes of memory.Processor board ID JAD050697JB (146699779)M860 processor: part number 0, mask 49 Bridging software. X.25 software, Version 3.0.0.2 FastEthernet/IEEE 802.3 interface(s)1 Serial network interface(s)32K bytes of non-volatile configuration memory.8192K bytes of processor board System flash (Read/Write)`

2. Which of the following prompts indicates that you are in privileged mode?

   A. `>`

   B. `(config)#`

   C. `#`

   D. `!`

3. If you type a command and receive the error "% incomplete command" from a switch CLI, what would you do to get help?

   A. Type **history** to review the error.

   B. Re-enter the command followed by a question mark to view the keywords.

   C. Type **help**.

   D. Enter a question mark to see all of the console commands.

4. Which command will show you whether a DTE or DCE cable is plugged into serial 0?

   A. `sh int s0`

   B. `sh int serial 0`

   C. `sho controllers s 0`

   D. `sho serial 0 controllers`

5. What keystroke will terminate setup mode?
    A. Ctrl+Z
    B. Ctrl+^
    C. Ctrl+C
    D. Ctrl+Shift+^

6. Which of the following commands will display a backup configuration?
    A. `sh running-config`
    B. `show startup-config`
    C. `show version`
    D. `show backup-config`

7. Which of the following commands will configure all the default VTY ports on a router?
    A. Router#**line vty 0 4**
    B. Router(config)#**line vty 0 4**
    C. Router(config-if)#**line vty 0 4**
    D. Router(config)#**line vty all**

8. Which of the following commands sets the secret password to "Cisco"?
    A. `enable secret password Cisco`
    B. `enable secret cisco`
    C. `enable secret Cisco`
    D. `enable password Cisco`

9. If you wanted administrators to see a message when logging into the router, which command would you use?
    A. `message banner motd`
    B. `banner message motd`
    C. `banner motd`
    D. `message motd`

10. Which of the following commands will reload the router?
    A. Router>**reload**
    B. Router#**reset**
    C. Router#**reload**
    D. Router(config)#**reload**

11. What command do you type to save the configuration stored in RAM to NVRAM?

   A. Router(config)#**copy current to starting**

   B. Router#**copy starting to running**

   C. Router(config)#**copy running-config startup-config**

   D. Router#**copy run startup**

12. What command will display all the valid commands at the given mode?

   A. help

   B. help all

   C. ?

   D. list

13. Which command will delete the contents of NVRAM on a router?

   A. delete NVRAM

   B. delete startup-config

   C. erase NVRAM

   D. erase start

14. What is the problem with an interface if you type show interface serial 0 and receive the following message?

   Serial0 is administratively down, line protocol is down

   A. The keepalives are different times.

   B. The administrator has the interface shut down.

   C. The administrator is pinging from the interface.

   D. No cable is attached.

15. What do the square brackets indicate when in setup mode?

   A. That the router needs to be reloaded

   B. That the values entered are not saved

   C. Current or default settings

   D. Hard-coded values that cannot be changed

16. If you delete the contents of NVRAM and reboot the router, what mode will you be in?

   A. Privileged mode

   B. Global mode

   C. Setup mode

   D. NVRAM loaded mode

17. Which of the following is stored in RAM? (Choose all that apply.)

   A. Packet buffers

   B. Startup-config

   C. Cisco IOS

   D. ARP cache

   E. Routing table

   F. Running-config

   G. Configuration register

18. If you want to display all the commands in the history buffer, which command will you use?

   A. Ctrl+Shift+6, then X

   B. Ctrl+Z

   C. `show history`

   D. `show history buffer`

19. If you type **erase startup-config** and reboot your router, what router mode will you be in?

   A. Global config

   B. Interface config

   C. Setup

   D. User

20. What layer of the OSI model would you assume the problem is in if you type **show interface serial 1** and receive the following message?

   `Serial1 is a down, line protocol is down`

   A. Physical layer

   B. Data Link layer

   C. Network layer

   D. None; it is a router problem.

Answers to Review Questions

1. C. The only message that states the type of Cisco IOS running in memory is the third option.

2. C. The pound sign (#) indicates that you are in privileged mode.

3. B. If you receive the "% incomplete command" error, just press your up arrow key, then a question mark to see what the next available command is in the command string.

4. C. The show controllers serial 0 command will show you whether either a DTE or DCE cable is connected to the interface.

5. C. You can exit setup mode at any time by using the keystroke Ctrl+C.

6. B. The show startup-config command will display the configuration that will be loaded the next time the router is booted.

7. B. From global configuration mode, use the line vty 0 4 command to set all five default VTY lines.

8. C. The enable secret password is case sensitive, so the second option is wrong. To set the enable secret password, use the enable secret *password* command from global configuration mode.

9. C. The typical banner is a message of the day (MOTD) and is set by using the global configuration mode command banner motd.

10. C. To reload the router, use the command reload from privileged mode.

11. D. To copy the running-config to NVRAM so that it will be used if the router is restarted, use the copy running-config startup-config (copy run start, for short) command.

12. C. You can get a list of commands from any prompt by using the question mark (?).

13. D. The erase startup-config command erases the contents of NVRAM and will put you in setup mode if the router is restarted.

14. B. If an interface is shut down, the show interface command will show the interface as administratively shut down. (It is possible no cable is attached, but you can't tell that from this message.)

15. C. If you are using setup mode, which you really shouldn't be doing, the square brackets indicate the current or default commands.

16. C. If you delete the startup-config and reload the router, the router will automatically enter setup mode. You can also type **setup** from privileged mode at any time.

17. A, D, E, F. RAM is used to store the packet buffers, ARP cache, and routing tables as well as the running-config.

18. C. The show history command will display the last 10 commands entered by default. You can change the number of commands displayed with the terminal history size command.

19. C. You can enter setup mode by erasing the configuration and rebooting the router or by typing **setup** from privileged mode.

20. A. If you see that a serial interface and the protocol are both down, then you have a Physical layer problem.

Answers to Written Lab 4

1. `clock rate 64000`
2. `config t, line vty 0 4, no login`
3. `config t, int e0, no shut`
4. `erase startup-config`
5. `config t, line console 0, login, password todd`
6. `config t, enable secret cisco`
7. `show controllers int`
8. `show terminal`
9. `config net`
10. `config t, hostname Chicago`

IP Routing

THE CCNA EXAM TOPICS COVERED IN THIS CHAPTER INCLUDE THE FOLLOWING:

✓ **PLANNING & DESIGNING**

- Design a simple LAN using Cisco Technology
- Design an IP addressing scheme to meet design requirements
- Select an appropriate routing protocol based on user requirements
- Design a simple internetwork using Cisco technology

✓ **IMPLEMENTATION & OPERATION**

- Configure routing protocols given user requirements
- Configure IP addresses, subnet masks, and gateway addresses on routers and hosts
- Configure a router for additional administrative functionality
- Perform an initial configuration on a router
- Perform an initial configuration on a switch

✓ **TROUBLESHOOTING**

- Perform LAN and VLAN troubleshooting
- Troubleshoot routing protocols
- Troubleshoot IP addressing and host configuration
- Troubleshoot a device as part of a working network

✓ **TECHNOLOGY**

- Evaluate the characteristics of routing protocols
- Evaluate TCP/IP communication process and its associated protocols

In this chapter, I'm going to discuss the IP routing process. This is an important subject to understand, since it pertains to all routers and configurations that use IP. IP routing is the process of moving packets from one network to another network using routers. And as before, by routers I mean Cisco routers, of course!

But before you read this chapter, you must understand the difference between a routing protocol and a routed protocol. A *routing protocol* is used by routers to dynamically find all the networks in the internetwork and to ensure that all routers have the same routing table. Basically, a routing protocol determines the path of a packet through an internetwork. Examples of routing protocols are RIP, IGRP, EIGRP, and OSPF.

Once all routers know about all networks, a *routed protocol* can be used to send user data (packets) through the established enterprise. Routed protocols are assigned to an interface and determine the method of packet delivery. Examples of routed protocols are IP and IPX.

From what I've said so far, I'm pretty sure that I don't have to tell you that this is definitely important stuff to know. IP routing is basically what Cisco routers do, and they do it very well. Again, this chapter is dealing with truly fundamental material—these are things you must know if you want to understand the rest of the book!

In this chapter, you'll learn how to configure and verify IP routing with Cisco routers. I'll be covering the following:

- Static routing

- Default routing

- Dynamic routing

In Chapter 6, "Enhanced IGRP (EIGRP) and Open Shortest Path First (OSPF)," I'll be moving into more advanced, dynamic routing with EIGRP and OSPF. But first, let's start with some routing basics.

Routing Basics

Once you create an internetwork by connecting your WANs and LANs to a router, you'll need to configure logical network addresses, such as IP addresses, to all hosts on the internetwork so that they can communicate across that internetwork.

The term *routing* is used for taking a packet from one device and sending it through the network to another device on a different network. Routers don't really care about hosts—they only care about networks and the best path to each network. The logical network address of the destination host is used to get packets to a network through a routed network, then the hardware address of the host is used to deliver the packet from a router to the correct destination host.

If your network has no routers, then it should be apparent that you are not routing. Routers route traffic to all the networks in your internetwork. To be able to route packets, a router must know, at a minimum, the following:

- Destination address
- Neighbor routers from which it can learn about remote networks
- Possible routes to all remote networks
- The best route to each remote network
- How to maintain and verify routing information

The router learns about remote networks from neighbor routers or from an administrator. The router then builds a routing table that describes how to find the remote networks. If a network is directly connected, then the router already knows how to get to it. If a network isn't connected, the router must learn how to get to the remote network in two ways: by using static routing, meaning that someone must hand-type all network locations into the routing table, or through something called dynamic routing.

In *dynamic routing*, a protocol on one router communicates with the same protocol running on neighbor routers. The routers then update each other about all the networks they know about and place this information into the routing table. If a change occurs in the network, the dynamic routing protocols automatically inform all routers about the event. If *static routing* is used, the administrator is responsible for updating all changes by hand into all routers. Typically, in a large network, a combination of both dynamic and static routing is used.

The IP Routing Process

The IP routing process is fairly simple and doesn't change, regardless of the size network you have. For an example, we'll use Figure 5.1 to describe step by step what happens when Host_A wants to communicate with Host B on a different network.

FIGURE 5.1   IP routing example using two hosts and one router

In this example, a user on Host_A pings Host_B's IP address. Routing doesn't get simpler than this, but it still involves a lot of steps. Let's work through them:

1. Internet Control Message Protocol (ICMP) creates an echo request payload (which is just the alphabet in the data field).

2. ICMP hands that payload to Internet Protocol (IP), which then creates a packet. At a minimum, this packet contains an IP source address, an IP destination address, and a protocol field with 01h (remember that Cisco likes to use 0x in front of hex characters, so this could look like 0x01). All of that tells the receiving host to whom it should hand the payload when the destination is reached—in this example, ICMP.

3. Once the packet is created, IP determines whether the destination IP address is on the local network or a remote one.

4. Since IP determines this is a remote request, the packet needs to be sent to the default gateway so the packet can be routed to the remote network. The Registry in Windows is parsed to find the configured default gateway.

5. The default gateway of host 172.16.10.2 (Host_A) is configured to 172.16.10.1. To be able to send this packet to the default gateway, the hardware address of the router's interface Ethernet 0 (configured with the IP address of 172.16.10.1) must be known. Why? So the packet can be handed down to the Data Link layer, framed, and sent to the router's interface connected to the 172.16.10.0 network. Hosts communicate only via hardware addresses on the local LAN. It is important to understand that Host_A, in order to communicate to Host_B, must send the packets to the MAC address of the default gateway on the local network.

6. Next, the ARP cache is checked to see if the IP address of the default gateway has already been resolved to a hardware address:

   - If it has, the packet is then free to be handed to the Data Link layer for framing. (The hardware destination address is also handed down with that packet.)

   - If the hardware address isn't already in the ARP cache of the host, an ARP broadcast is sent out onto the local network to search for the hardware address of 172.16.10.1. The router responds to the request and provides the hardware address of Ethernet 0, and the host caches this address. The router also caches the hardware address of Host A in its ARP cache.

7. Once the packet and destination hardware address are handed to the Data Link layer, the LAN driver is used to provide media access via the type of LAN being used (in this example, Ethernet). A frame is then generated, encapsulating the packet with control information. Within that frame are the hardware destination and source addresses, plus in this case, an Ether-Type field that describes the Network layer protocol that handed the packet to the Data Link layer—in this case, IP. At the end of the frame is something called a Frame Check Sequence (FCS) field that houses the result of the cyclic redundancy check (CRC).

8. Once the frame is completed, it's handed down to the Physical layer to be put on the physical medium (in this example, twisted-pair wire) one bit at a time.

9. Every device in the collision domain receives these bits and builds the frame. They each run a CRC and check the answer in the FCS field. If the answers don't match, the frame is discarded.

   - If the CRC matches, then the hardware destination address is checked to see if it matches too (which, in this example, is the router's interface Ethernet 0).
   - If it's a match, then the Ether-Type field is checked to find the protocol used at the Network layer.

10. The packet is pulled from the frame, and what is left of the frame is discarded. The packet is handed to the protocol listed in the Ether-Type field—it's given to IP.

11. IP receives the packet and checks the IP destination address. Since the packet's destination address doesn't match any of the addresses configured on the receiving router itself, the router will look up the destination IP network address in its routing table.

12. The routing table must have an entry for the network 172.16.20.0, or the packet will be discarded immediately and an ICMP message will be sent back to the originating device with a "destination network unreachable" message.

13. If the router does find an entry for the destination network in its table, the packet is switched to the exit interface—in this example, interface Ethernet 1.

14. The router packet-switches the packet to the Ethernet 1 buffer.

15. The Ethernet 1 buffer needs to know the hardware address of the destination host and first checks the ARP cache.

   - If the hardware address of Host B has already been resolved, then the packet and the hardware address are handed down to the Data Link layer to be framed.
   - If the hardware address has not already been resolved, the router sends an ARP request out E1 looking for the hardware address of 172.16.20.2.

     Host_B responds with its hardware address, and the packet and destination hardware address are both sent to the Data Link layer for framing.

16. The Data Link layer creates a frame with the destination and source hardware address, Ether-Type field, and FCS field at the end of the frame. The frame is handed to the Physical layer to be sent out on the physical medium one bit at a time.

17. Host_B receives the frame and immediately runs a CRC. If the result matches what's in the FCS field, the hardware destination address is then checked. If the host finds a match, the Ether-Type field is then checked to determine the protocol that the packet should be handed to at the Network layer—IP, in this example.

18. At the Network layer, IP receives the packet and checks the IP destination address. Since there's finally a match made, the protocol field is checked to find out to whom the payload should be given.

19. The payload is handed to ICMP, which understands that this is an echo request. ICMP responds to this by immediately discarding the packet and generating a new payload as an echo reply.

20. A packet is then created including the source and destination address, protocol field, and payload. The destination device is now Host_A.

21. IP then checks to see whether the destination IP address is a device on the local LAN or on a remote network. Since the destination device is on a remote network, the packet needs to be sent to the default gateway.

22. The default gateway IP address is found in the Registry of the Windows device, and the ARP cache is checked to see if the hardware address has already been resolved from an IP address.

23. Once the hardware address of the default gateway is found, the packet and destination hardware address are handed down to the Data Link layer for framing.

24. The Data Link layer frames the packet of information and includes the following in the header:

   - The destination and source hardware address
   - The Ether-Type field with 0x800 (IP) in it
   - The FCS field with the CRC result in tow

25. The frame is now handed down to the Physical layer to be sent out over the network medium one bit at a time.

26. The router's Ethernet 1 interface receives the bits and builds a frame. The CRC is run, and the FCS field is checked to make sure the answers match.

27. Once the CRC is found to be okay, the hardware destination address is checked. Since the router's interface is a match, the packet is pulled from the frame and the Ether-Type field is checked to see what protocol at the Network layer the packet should be delivered to.

28. The protocol is determined to be IP, so it gets the packet. IP runs a CRC check on the IP header first, and then checks the destination IP address.

IP does not run a complete CRC as the Data Link layer does—it only checks the header for errors.

Since the IP destination address doesn't match any of the router's interfaces, the routing table is checked to see whether it has a route to 172.16.10.0. If it doesn't have a route over to the destination network, the packet will be discarded immediately. (This is the source point of confusion for a lot of administrators—when a ping fails, most people think the packet never reached the destination host. But as we see here, that's not *always* the case. All it takes is for just one of the remote routers to be lacking a route back to the originating host's network and POOF! The packet is dropped on the *return trip*, not on its way to the host.)

OK, just a quick note to mention that when the packet is lost on the way back to the originating host, you will typically see a "request timed out" message because it is an unknown error. If the error occurs because of a known issue, like if a route is not in the routing table on the way to the destination device, you will see a "destination unreachable" message. This should help you determine if the problem occurred on the way to the destination or on the way back.

29. But the router does know how to get to network 172.16.10.0—the exit interface is Ethernet 0—so the packet is switched to interface Ethernet 0.

30. The router checks the ARP cache to determine whether the hardware address for 172.16.10.2 has already been resolved.

31. Since the hardware address to 172.16.10.2 is already cached from the originating trip to Host B, the hardware address and packet are handed to the Data Link layer.

32. The Data Link layer builds a frame with the destination hardware address and source hardware address, and then puts IP in the Ether-Type field. A CRC is run on the frame, and the result is placed in the FCS field.

33. The frame is then handed to the Physical layer to be sent out onto the local network one bit at a time.

34. The destination host receives the frame, runs a CRC, checks the destination hardware address, and looks in the Ether-Type field to find out whom to hand the packet to.

35. IP is the designated receiver, and after the packet is handed to IP at the Network layer, it checks the protocol field for further direction. IP finds instructions to give the payload to ICMP, and ICMP determines the packet to be an ICMP echo reply.

36. ICMP acknowledges that it has received the reply by sending an exclamation point (!) to the user interface. ICMP then attempts to send four more echo requests to the destination host.

You've just experienced 36 easy steps to understanding IP routing. The key point to understand here is that if you had a much larger network, the process would be the *same*. In a really big internetwork, the packet just goes through more hops before it finds the destination host.

A very important point to remember is that when Host_A sends a packet to Host_B, the destination hardware address used is the default gateway Ethernet interface. This is because frames can't be placed on remote networks, only local networks, and packets destined for remote networks must go to the default gateway.

In the following section, we will look at how IP Routing is handled in a larger network.

IP Routing in a Larger Network

In the example I gave you in the previous section, the router already has both IP networks in its routing table because the networks are directly connected to it. But what if we add another router? Figure 5.2 shows three routers: Lab_A, Lab_B, and Lab_C. Remember—by default, these routers only know about networks that are directly connected to them.

Oh—and don't stress! We'll get to the switches shown in the figure later in Chapter 7, "Layer 2 Switching," and Chapter 8, "Virtual LANs (VLANs)."

FIGURE 5.2 IP routing example with more routers

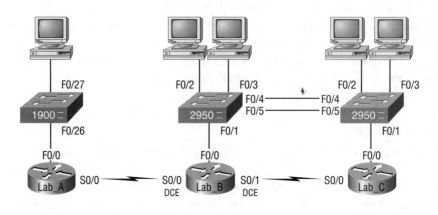

Figure 5.2 shows the three 2600 routers connected via a WAN. Each router also has an Ethernet network connected. The idea is that each router must know about all five networks.

The first step is to configure each router correctly. Table 5.1 shows the IP address scheme I'm going to use to configure the network. After we go over how the network is configured, I'll cover how to configure IP routing. Each network in the following table has a default Class C 24-bit subnet mask (255.255.255.0).

TABLE 5.1 Network Addressing for the IP Network

Router	Network Address	Interface	Address
Lab_A	192.168.10.0	fa0/0	192.168.10.1
Lab_A	192.168.20.0	s0/0	192.168.20.1
Lab_B	192.168.20.0	s0/0	192.168.20.2
Lab_B	192.168.40.0	s0/1	192.168.40.1
Lab_B	192.168.30.0	fa0/0	192.168.30.1
Lab_C	192.168.40.0	s0/0	192.168.40.2
Lab_C	192.168.50.0	fa0/0	192.168.50.1

Router configuration is really a pretty straightforward process, since you just need to add IP addresses to your interfaces and then perform a `no shutdown` on those interfaces. It will get a tad bit more complex later on, but first, let's configure the IP addresses in the network.

Lab_A Configuration

To configure the Lab_A router, you just need to add an IP address to interface FastEthernet 0/0 as well as the serial0/0. Configuring the hostnames of each router will make identification easier. And why not set the interface descriptions, banner, and router passwords, too? You really should get in the habit of configuring these commands on every router.

Here is how I did all that:

```
Router>en
Router#config t
Router(config)#hostname Lab_A
Lab_A(config)#enable secret todd
Lab_A(config)#interface fa0/0
Lab_A(config-if)#ip address 192.168.10.1 255.255.255.0
Lab_A(config-if)#description Lab_A LAN Connection
Lab_A(config-if)#no shut
Lab_A(config-if)#interface serial 0/0
Lab_A(config-if)#ip address 192.168.20.1 255.255.255.0
Lab_A(config-if)#description WAN Connection to Lab_B
Lab_A(config-if)#no shut
Lab_A(config-if)#exit
Lab_A(config)#line console 0
Lab_A(config-line)#password todd
Lab_A(config-line)#login
Lab_A(config-line)#line aux 0
Lab_A(config-line)#password todd
Lab_A(config-line)#login
Lab_A(config-line)#line vty 0 4
Lab_A(config-line)#password todd
Lab_A(config-line)#login
Lab_A(config-line)#exit
Lab_A(config)#banner motd #
This is the Lab_A router
#
Lab_A(config)#^z
Lab_A#copy running-config startup-config
Destination filename [startup-config]? [Enter]
Lab_A#
```

 If you have a hard time understanding this configuration process, refer back to Chapter 4, "Introduction to the Cisco IOS."

To view the IP routing tables created on a Cisco router, use the command show ip route. The command output is shown as follows:

```
Lab_A#sh ip route
Codes: C - connected, S - static, I - IGRP, R - RIP,
  M - mobile, B - BGP D - EIGRP, EX - EIGRP external, O -
  OSPF, IA - OSPF inter area N1 - OSPF NSS external type
  1, N2 - OSPF NSSA external type 2 E1 - OSPF external
  type 1, E2 - OSPF external type 2, E - EGP i - IS-IS,
  L1 - IS-IS level-1, L2 - IS-IS level-2, * - candidate
  default, U - per-user static route, o - ODR, P -
  periodic downloaded static route, T - traffic
  engineered route
Gateway of last resort is not set
C       192.168.10.0/24 is directly connected, FastEthernet0/0
C       192.168.20.0/24 is directly connected, Serial 0/0
Lab_A#
```

Notice that only the configured, directly connected networks are shown in the routing table. This means that the router only knows how to get to networks 192.168.10.0 and 192.168.20.0.

Did you notice the C? When you see it there, it means that the network is directly connected. The codes for each type of connection are listed at the top of the show ip route command with their abbreviations.

In the interest of brevity, the codes will be cut in the rest of this chapter.

Lab_B Configuration

It's now time to configure the next router. To configure Lab_B, we have three interfaces to deal with: FastEthernet 0/0, serial 0/0, and serial 0/1. Both serial interfaces are DCE. What that means to us is that we'll have to add the clock rate command to each interface.

If you'd like more information on the DCE interfaces and the clock rate command, just look it up in Chapter 4.

Let's make sure we don't forget to add our passwords, interface descriptions, and banner to the router configuration!

Here is the configuration I used:

```
Router>en
Router#config t
Router(config)#hostname Lab_B
```

```
Lab_B(config)#enable secret todd
Lab_B(config)#interface fa0/0
Lab_B(config-if)#ip address 192.168.30.1 255.255.255.0
Lab_B(config-if)#description Lab_B LAN Connection
Lab_B(config-if)#no shut
Lab_B(config-if)#interface serial 0/0
Lab_B(config-if)#ip address 192.168.20.2 255.255.255.0
Lab_B(config-if)#description WAN Connection to Lab_A
Lab_B(config-if)#clock rate 64000
Lab_B(config-if)#no shut
Lab_B(config-if)#interface serial 0/1
Lab_B(config-if)#ip address 192.168.40.1 255.255.255.0
Lab_B(config-if)#description WAN Connection to Lab_C
Lab_B(config-if)#clock rate 64000
Lab_B(config-if)#no shut
Lab_B(config-if)#exit
Lab_B(config)#line console 0
Lab_B(config-line)#password todd
Lab_B(config-line)#login
Lab_B(config-line)#line aux 0
Lab_B(config-line)#password todd
Lab_B(config-line)#login
Lab_B(config-line)#line vty 0 4
Lab_B(config-line)#password todd
Lab_B(config-line)#login
Lab_B(config-line)#exit
Lab_B(config)#banner motd #
This is the Lab_B router
#
Lab_B(config)#^z
Lab_B#copy running-config startup-config
Destination filename [startup-config]? [Enter]
Lab_B#
```

These commands configured serial 0/0 into network 192.168.20.0, serial 0/1 into network 192.168.40.0, and FastEthernet 0/0 into network 192.168.30.0. The show ip route command displays the following:

```
Lab_B#sh ip route
[output cut]
Gateway of last resort is not set
C       192.168.20.0/24 is directly connected, Serial0/0
```

```
C       192.168.40.0/24 is directly connected, Serial0/1
C       192.168.30.0 is directly connected FastEthernet 0/0
Lab_B#
```

Notice that router Lab_B knows how to get to networks 192.168.20.0, 192.168.30.0, and 172.16.40.0. Router Lab_A and Router Lab_B can now communicate because they're connected on the same WAN.

Lab_C Configuration

The configuration of Lab_C is similar to the other two routers (make sure we remember to add passwords, interface descriptions, and banner to the router configuration):

```
Router>en
Router#config t
Router(config)#hostname Lab_C
Lab_C(config)#enable secret todd
Lab_C(config)#interface fa0/0
Lab_C(config-if)#ip address 192.168.50.1 255.255.255.0
Lab_C(config-if)#description Lab_C LAN Connection
Lab_C(config-if)#no shut
Lab_C(config-if)#interface serial 0/0
Lab_C(config-if)#ip address 192.168.40.2 255.255.255.0
Lab_C(config-if)#description WAN Connection to Lab_B
Lab_C(config-if)#no shut
Lab_C(config-if)#exit
Lab_C(config)#line console 0
Lab_C(config-line)#password todd
Lab_C(config-line)#login
Lab_C(config-line)#line aux 0
Lab_C(config-line)#password todd
Lab_C(config-line)#login
Lab_C(config-line)#line vty 0 4
Lab_C(config-line)#password todd
Lab_C(config-line)#login
Lab_C(config-line)#exit
Lab_C(config)#banner motd #
This is the Lab_C router
#
Lab_C(config)# ^z
Lab_C#copy running-config startup-config
Destination filename [startup-config]? [Enter]
Lab_C#
```

The output of the following show ip route command displays the directly connected networks of 192.168.50.0 and 192.168.40.0, as seen here:

```
Lab_C#sh ip route
[output cut]
Gateway of last resort is not set
C       192.168.50.0/24 is directly connected, FastEthernet0/0
C       192.168.40.0/24 is directly connected, Serial0/0
Lab_C#
```

Routers Lab_A and Lab_B can communicate because they're on the same WAN network. And Lab_B and Lab_C can communicate too because they're connected with a WAN link. But Router Lab_A can't communicate with the Lab_C router because it does not know about networks 172.16.40.0 and 192.168.50.0—yet.

Configuring IP Routing in Our Network

Okay, our network is good to go—right? After all, it's been correctly configured with IP addressing! But how does a router send packets to remote networks when it can only send packets by looking at the routing table to find out how to get to the remote networks? Our configured routers only have information about directly connected networks in each routing table. And what happens when a router receives a packet for a network that isn't listed in the routing table? It doesn't send a broadcast looking for the remote network—the router just discards it. Period.

So we're not exactly ready to rock yet after all. But no worries—there are several ways to configure the routing tables to include all the networks in our little internetwork so that packets will be forwarded. And what's best for one network isn't necessarily what's best for another. Understanding the different types of routing will really help you come up with the best solution for your specific environment and business requirements.

The different types of routing you'll learn about in this section are:

- Static routing
- Default routing
- Dynamic routing

I'm going to start off by describing and implementing static routing on our network because if you can implement static routing, *and* make it work, it means you have a solid understanding of the internetwork. So let's get started.

Static Routing

Static routing occurs when you manually add routes in each router's routing table. There are pros and cons to static routing, but that's true for all routing processes.

Static routing has the following benefits:

- There is no overhead on the router CPU, which means you could possibly buy a cheaper router than if you were using dynamic routing.

- There is no bandwidth usage between routers, which means you could possibly save money on WAN links.

- It adds security, because the administrator can choose to allow routing access to certain networks only.

Static routing has the following disadvantages:

- The administrator must really understand the internetwork and how each router is connected in order to configure routes correctly.

- If a network is added to the internetwork, the administrator has to add a route to it on all routers—by hand.

- It's not feasible in large networks because maintaining it would be a full-time job in itself.

Okay—that said, here's the command syntax you use to add a static route to a routing table:

```
ip route [destination_network] [mask] [next-hop_address or exitinterface]
[administrative_distance] [permanent]
```

This list describes each command in the string:

ip route   The command used to create the static route.

destination_network   The network you're placing in the routing table.

mask   The subnet mask being used on the network.

next-hop_address   The address of the next-hop router that will receive the packet and forward it to the remote network. This is a router interface that's on a directly connected network. You must be able to ping the router interface before you add the route. If you type in the wrong next-hop address, or the interface to that router is down, the static route will show up in the router's configuration, but not in the routing table.

exitinterface   You can use it in place of the next-hop address if you want, but it's got to be on a point-to-point link, such as a WAN. This command won't work on a LAN such as Ethernet.

administrative_distance   By default, static routes have an administrative distance of 1 (or even 0 if you use an exit interface instead of a next hop address). You can change the default value by adding an administrative weight at the end of the command. I'll talk a lot more about this subject later in the chapter when we get to the section on dynamic routing.

permanent   If the interface is shut down, or the router can't communicate to the next-hop router, the route will automatically be discarded from the routing table. Choosing the permanent option keeps the entry in the routing table no matter what happens.

To help you understand how static routes work, I'll demonstrate the configuration on the internetwork shown previously in Figure 5.2.

Lab_A

Each routing table automatically includes directly connected networks. To be able to route to all networks in the internetwork, the routing table must include information that describes where these other networks are located and how to get there.

The Lab_A router is connected to networks 192.168.10.0 and 192.168.20.0. For the Lab_A router to be able to route to all networks, the following networks have to be configured in its routing table:

- 192.168.30.0
- 192.168.40.0
- 192.168.50.0

The following router output shows the configuration of static routes on the Lab_A router and the routing table after the configuration. For the Lab_A router to find the remote networks, an entry is placed in the routing table describing the network, the mask, and where to send the packets. Notice that each static route sends the packets to 192.168.20.2, which is the Lab_A router's next hop.

```
Lab_A(config)#ip route 192.168.30.0 255.255.255.0
   192.168.20.2
Lab_A(config)#ip route 192.168.40.0 255.255.255.0
   192.168.20.2
Lab_A(config)#ip route 192.168.50.0 255.255.255.0
   192.168.20.2
```

After the router is configured, you can type **show running-config** and **show ip route** to see the static routes:

```
Lab_A#sh ip route
[output cut]
S       192.168.50.0 [1/0] via 192.168.20.2
S       192.168.40.0 [1/0] via 192.168.20.2
S       192.168.30.0 [1/0] via 192.168.20.2
C       192.168.20.0 is directly connected, Serial 0/0
C       192.168.10.0 is directly connected, FastEthernet0/0
Lab_A#
```

Remember that if the routes don't appear in the routing table, it's because the router cannot communicate with the next-hop address you configured. You can use the **permanent** parameter to keep the route in the routing table even if the next-hop device can't be contacted.

The S in the routing table entries above means that the network is a static entry. The [1/0] is the administrative distance and metric, which I'll discuss below, to the remote network. Here the next hop interface is 0, indicating that it's directly connected.

The Lab_A router now has all the information it needs to communicate with the other remote networks. However, if the Lab_B and Lab_C routers are not configured with all the same information, the packets will be discarded at Lab_B and at Lab_C. We need to fix this with static routes.

Lab_B

The Lab_B router is connected to the networks 192.168.20.0, 192.168.30.0, and 192.168.40.0. The following static routes must be configured on the Lab_B router:

- 192.168.10.0
- 192.168.50.0

Here's the configuration for the Lab_B router:

```
Lab_B(config)#ip route 192.168.10.0 255.255.255.0
  192.168.20.1
Lab_B(config)#ip route 192.168.50.0 255.255.255.0
  192.168.40.2
```

By looking at the routing table, you can see that the Lab_B router now understands how to find each network:

```
Lab_B#sh ip route
[output cut]
S       192.168.50.0 [1/0] via 192.168.40.2
C       192.168.40.0 is directly connected, Serial0/1
C       192.168.30.0 is directly connected, FastEthernet 0/0
C       192.168.20.0 is directly connected, Serial0/0
S       192.168.10.0 [1/0] via 192.168.20.1
Lab_B#
```

The Lab_B router now has a complete routing table. As soon as the other routers in the internetwork have all the networks in their routing table, Lab_B can communicate to all remote networks.

Lab_C

The Lab_C router is directly connected to networks 192.168.40.0 and 192.168.50.0. Three routes need to be added:

- 192.168.30.0
- 192.168.20.0
- 192.168.10.0

Here's the configuration for the Lab_C router:

```
Lab_C(config)#ip route 192.168.30.0 255.255.255.0
  192.168.40.1
Lab_C(config)#ip route 192.168.20.0 255.255.255.0
  172.16.40.1
Lab_C(config)#ip route 192.168.10.0 255.255.255.0
  192.168.40.1
```

The following output shows the routing table on the Lab_C router:

```
Lab_C#sh ip route
[output cut]
C       192.168.50.0 is directly connected, FastEthernet0/0
C       192.168.40.0 is directly connected, Serial0/0
S       192.168.30.0 [1/0] via 192.168.40.1
S       192.168.20.0 [1/0[ via 192.168.40.1
S       192.168.10.0 [1/0] via 192.168.40.1
Lab_C#
```

Lab_C now shows all the networks in the internetwork and can communicate with all routers and networks. All the routers have the correct routing table, and all the routers and hosts should be able to communicate without a problem—for now. But if you add even one more network or another router to the internetwork, you'll have to update all routers' routing tables by hand. As I said, this isn't a problem at all if you've got a small network, but it's way too time-consuming a task if you're dealing with a large internetwork.

Verifying Your Configuration

Once all the routers' routing tables are configured, they need to be verified. The best way to do this, besides using the show ip route command, is with the Ping program. By pinging from routers Lab_A and Lab_C, the whole internetwork will be tested end-to-end.

 Really, the best test would be to use the Telnet program from one host to another, but we'll talk about that more in Chapter 9, "Managing a Cisco Internetwork." For now, Ping is king!

Here is the output of a ping to network 192.168.50.0 from the Lab_A router:

```
Lab_A#ping 192.168.50.1
Type escape sequence to abort.
Sending 5, 100-byte ICMP Echos to 172.16.50.1, timeout is 2 seconds:
!!!!!
Success rate is 80 percent (4/5), round-trip min/avg/max = 64/66/68 ms
Lab_A#
```

From Router Lab_C, a ping to 192.168.10.0 will test for good IP connectivity. Here is the router output:

```
Lab_C#ping 192.168.10.1
Type escape sequence to abort.
Sending 5, 100-byte ICMP Echos to 172.16.10.1, timeout is 2 seconds:
!!!!!
```

```
Success rate is 100 percent (5/5), round-trip min/avg/max
  = 64/67/72 ms
```

Since we can ping from end-to-end without a problem, our static route configuration was a success!

Default Routing

We use *default routing* to send packets with a remote destination network not in the routing table to the next-hop router. You can only use default routing on stub networks—those with only one exit path out of the network.

In the internetworking example used in the previous section, the only routers that are considered to be in a stub network are Lab_A and Lab_C. If you tried to put a default route on router Lab_B, packets wouldn't be forwarded to the correct networks because they have more than one interface routing to other routers. And even though router Lab_C has two connections, it doesn't have another router on the 192.168.50.0 network that needs packets sent to it. Lab_C will only send packets to 192.168.40.1, which is the serial 0/0 interface of Lab_B. Router Lab_A will only send packets to the 192.168.20.2 interface of Lab_A.

To configure a default route, you use wildcards in the network address and mask locations of a static route. In fact, you can just think of a default route as a static route that uses wildcards instead of network and mask information. In this section, you'll create a default route on the Lab_C router.

Router Lab_C is directly connected to networks 192.168.40.0 and 192.168.50.0. The routing table needs to know about networks 192.168.10.0, 192.168.20.0, and 192.168.30.0.

To configure the router to route to the other three networks, I placed three static routes in the routing table. By using a default route, you can just create one static route entry instead. You must first delete the existing static routes from the router, then add the default route.

```
Lab_C(config)#no ip route 192.168.10.0 255.255.255.0
  192.168.40.1
Lab_C(config)#no ip route 192.168.20.0 255.255.255.0
  192.168.40.1
Lab_C(config)#no ip route 192.168.30.0 255.255.255.0
192.168.40.1
Lab_C(config)#ip route 0.0.0.0 0.0.0.0 192.168.40.1
```

If you look at the routing table now, you'll see only the two directly connected networks plus an S*, which indicates that this entry is a candidate for a default route.

```
Lab_C#sh ip route
[output cut]
Gateway of last resort is 192.168.40.1 to network 0.0.0.0
C      192.168.50.0 is directly connected, FastEthernet0/0
C      192.168.40.0 is directly connected, Serial0/0
```

```
S*     0.0.0.0/0 [1/0] via 192.168.40.1
Lab_C#
```

Notice also in the routing table that the gateway of last resort is now set. Even so, there's one more command you must be aware of when using default routes: the `ip classless` command.

All Cisco routers are classful routers, meaning that they expect a default subnet mask on each interface of the router. When a router receives a packet for a destination subnet that's not in the routing table, it will drop the packet by default. If you're using default routing, you must use the `ip classless` command because it is possible that no remote subnets will be in the routing table.

Since I have version 12.*x* of the IOS on my routers, the `ip classless` command is on by default. If you're using default routing and this command isn't in your configuration, you would need to add it if you had subnetted networks on your routers (which we don't at this time). The command is shown here:

```
Lab_C(config)#ip classless
```

Notice that it's a global configuration mode command. The interesting part of the `ip classless` command is that default routing sometimes works without it, but sometimes doesn't. To be on the safe side, you should always turn on the `ip classless` command when you use default routing.

Dynamic Routing

Dynamic routing is when protocols are used to find networks and update routing tables on routers. True—this is easier than using static or default routing, but it'll cost you in terms of router CPU processes and bandwidth on the network links. A routing protocol defines the set of rules used by a router when it communicates routing information between neighbor routers.

The two routing protocols I'm going to talk about in this chapter are Routing Information Protocol (RIP) and Interior Gateway Routing Protocol (IGRP).

Enhanced Interior Gateway Routing Protocol (EIGRP) is an advanced distance-vector routing protocol and is Cisco proprietary. Open Shortest Path First (OSPF) is a non-proprietary link-state routing protocol limited to use with the TCP/IP stack. I'll talk about both EIGRP and OSPF in depth in Chapter 6.

There are two types of routing protocols used in internetworks: interior gateway protocols (IGPs) and exterior gateway protocols (EGPs).

IGPs are used to exchange routing information with routers in the same autonomous system (AS). An AS is a collection of networks under a common administrative domain, which basically means that all routers sharing the same routing table information are in the same AS.

EGPs are used to communicate between AS.

An example of an EGP is Border Gateway Protocol (BGP), which is discussed in the Sybex *CCNP: Building Scalable Cisco Internetworks Study Guide*, by Carl Timm, and Wade Edwards (Sybex, 2004)

Since routing protocols are so essential to dynamic routing, I'm going to give you the basic information you need to know about them next. Later on, we'll focus on RIP and IGRP in particular.

Routing Protocol Basics

There are some important things you should know about routing protocols before getting deeper into RIP. Specifically, you need to understand administrative distances, the three different kinds of routing protocols, and routing loops. We will look at each of these in more detail in the following sections.

Administrative Distances

The *administrative distance (AD)* is used to rate the trustworthiness of routing information received on a router from a neighbor router. An administrative distance is an integer from 0 to 255, where 0 is the most trusted and 255 means no traffic will be passed via this route.

If a router receives two updates listing the same remote network, the first thing the router checks is the AD. If one of the advertised routes has a lower AD than the other, then the route with the lowest AD will be placed in the routing table.

If both advertised routes to the same network have the same AD, then routing protocol metrics (such as *hop count* or bandwidth of the lines) will be used to find the best path to the remote network. The advertised route with the lowest metric will be placed in the routing table. But if both advertised routes have the same AD as well as the same metrics, then the routing protocol will load-balance to the remote network (which means that it sends packets down each link).

Table 5.2 shows the default administrative distances that a Cisco router uses to decide which route to take to a remote network.

TABLE 5.2 Default Administrative Distances

Route Source	Default AD
Connected interface	0
Static route	1
EIGRP	90
IGRP	100
OSPF	110
RIP	120

TABLE 5.2   Default Administrative Distances *(continued)*

Route Source	Default AD
External EIGRP	170
Unknown	255 (this route will never be used)

If a network is directly connected, the router will always use the interface connected to the network. If an administrator configures a static route, the router will believe that route over any other learned routes. You can change the administrative distance of static routes, but, by default, they have an AD of 1.

If you have a static route, a RIP-advertised route, and an IGRP-advertised route listing the same network, then by default, the router will always use the static route unless you change the AD of the static route.

Routing Protocols

There are three classes of routing protocols:

Distance vector   The *distance-vector protocols* find the best path to a remote network by judging distance. Each time a packet goes through a router, that's called a *hop*. The route with the least number of hops to the network is determined to be the best route. The vector indicates the direction to the remote network. Both RIP and IGRP are distance-vector routing protocols. They send the entire routing table to directly connected neighbors.

Link state   In *link-state protocols*, also called *shortest-path-first protocols*, the routers each create three separate tables. One of these tables keeps track of directly attached neighbors, one determines the topology of the entire internetwork, and one is used as the routing table. Link-state routers know more about the internetwork than any distance-vector routing protocol. OSPF is an IP routing protocol that is completely link state. Link state protocols send updates containing the state of their own links to all other routers on the network.

    I'm going to tell you much more about OSPF in Chapter 6.

Hybrid   *Hybrid protocols* use aspects of both distance vector and link state—for example, EIGRP. (Again, EIGRP will be covered in Chapter 6.)

There's no set way of configuring routing protocols for use with every business. This is something you really have to do on a case-by-case basis. If you understand how the different routing protocols work, you can make good, solid decisions that truly meet the individual needs of any business.

Distance-Vector Routing Protocols

The distance-vector routing algorithm passes complete routing table contents to neighboring routers, which then combine the received routing table entries with their own routing tables to complete the router's routing table. This is called routing by rumor, because a router receiving an update from a neighbor router believes the information about remote networks without actually finding out for itself.

It's possible to have a network that has multiple links to the same remote network, and if that's the case, the administrative distance is checked first. If the AD is the same, the protocol will have to use other metrics to determine the best path to use to that remote network.

RIP uses only hop count to determine the best path to a network. If RIP finds more than one link to the same remote network with the same hop count, it will automatically perform a round-robin load balancing. RIP can perform load balancing for up to six equal-cost links (four by default).

However, a problem with this type of routing metric arises when the two links to a remote network are different bandwidths but the same hop count. Figure 5.3, for example, shows two links to remote network 172.16.10.0.

FIGURE 5.3   Pinhole congestion

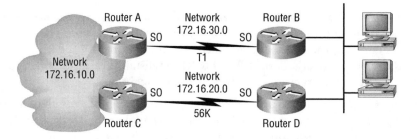

Since network 172.16.30.0 is a T1 link with a bandwidth of 1.544Mbps, and network 172.16.20.0 is a 56K link, you'd want the router to choose the T1 over the 56K link, right? But because hop count is the only metric used with RIP routing, the two links would be seen as being of equal cost. This little snag is called *pinhole congestion*.

It's important to understand what a distance-vector routing protocol does when it starts up. In Figure 5.4, the four routers start off with only their directly connected networks in the routing table. After a distance-vector routing protocol is started on each router, the routing tables are updated with all route information gathered from neighbor routers.

As shown in Figure 5.4, each router has only the directly connected networks in each routing table. Each router sends its complete routing table out to each active interface. The routing table of each router includes the network number, exit interface, and hop count to the network.

In Figure 5.5, the routing tables are complete because they include information about all the networks in the internetwork. They are considered *converged*. When the routers are converging, it is possible that no data will be passed. That's why fast convergence time is a serious plus. In fact, that's one of the problems with RIP—its slow convergence time.

FIGURE 5.4   The internetwork with distance-vector routing

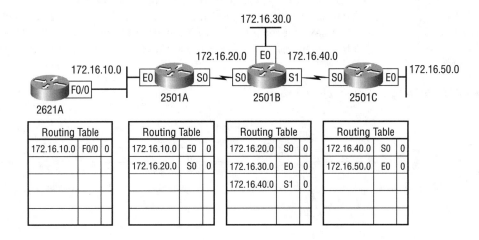

FIGURE 5.5   Converged routing tables

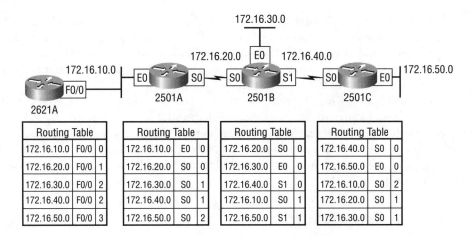

The routing table in each router keeps information regarding the remote network number, the interface to which the router will send packets to reach that network, and the hop count or metric to the network.

Routing Loops

Distance-vector routing protocols keep track of any changes to the internetwork by broadcasting periodic routing updates out all active interfaces. This broadcast includes the complete routing table. This works just fine, but it's expensive in terms of CPU process and link bandwidth. And if a network outage happens, real problems can occur. Plus, the slow convergence of distance-vector routing protocols can result in inconsistent routing tables and routing loops.

Routing loops can occur because every router isn't updated simultaneously, or even close to it. Here's an example—let's say that the interface to Network 5 in Figure 5.6 fails. All routers know about Network 5 from Router E. Router A, in its tables, has a path to Network 5 through Router B.

FIGURE 5.6   Routing loop example

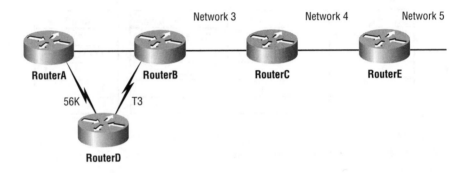

When Network 5 fails, Router E tells Router C. This causes Router C to stop routing to Network 5 through Router E. But Routers A, B, and D don't know about Network 5 yet, so they keep sending out update information. Router C will eventually send out its update and cause B to stop routing to Network 5, but Routers A and D are still not updated. To them, it appears that Network 5 is still available through Router B with a metric of 3.

The problem occurs when Router A sends out its regular 30-second "Hello, I'm still here—these are the links I know about" message, which includes the ability to reach Network 5 and now Routers B and D, then receive the wonderful news that Network 5 can be reached from Router A, so they send out the information that Network 5 is available. Any packet destined for Network 5 will go to Router A, to Router B, and then back to Router A. This is a routing loop—how do you stop it?

Maximum Hop Count

The routing loop problem just described is called *counting to infinity*, and it's caused by gossip and wrong information being communicated and propagated throughout the internetwork. Without some form of intervention, the hop count increases indefinitely each time a packet passes through a router.

One way of solving this problem is to define a *maximum hop count*. RIP permits a hop count of up to 15, so anything that requires 16 hops is deemed unreachable. In other words, after a loop of 15 hops, Network 5 will be considered down. Thus, the maximum hop count will control how long it takes for a routing table entry to become invalid or questionable.

Though this is a workable solution, it won't remove the routing loop itself. Packets will still go into the loop, but instead of traveling on unchecked, they'll just whirl around for 16 bounces and die.

Split Horizon

Another solution to the routing loop problem is called *split horizon*. This reduces incorrect routing information and routing overhead in a distance-vector network by enforcing the rule that routing information cannot be sent back in the direction from which it was received.

In other words, the routing protocol differentiates which interface a network route was learned on, and once this is determined, it won't advertise the route back out that same interface. This would have prevented Router A from sending the updated information it received from Router B back to Router B.

Route Poisoning

Another way to avoid problems caused by inconsistent updates and stop network loops is *route poisoning*. For example, when Network 5 goes down, Router E initiates route poisoning by advertising Network 5 as 16, or unreachable (sometimes referred to as *infinite*).

This poisoning of the route to Network 5 keeps Router C from being susceptible to incorrect updates about the route to Network 5. When Router C receives a route poisoning from Router E, it sends an update, called a *poison reverse*, back to Router E. This ensures all routes on the segment have received the poisoned route information.

Route poisoning and split horizon create a much more resilient and dependable distance-vector network than we'd have without them, and they serve us well in preventing network loops. But we're not done yet—this isn't all you need to know about loop prevention in distance-vector networks, so read on.

Holddowns

A *holddown* prevents regular update messages from reinstating a route that is going up and down (called *flapping*). Typically, this happens on a serial link that's losing connectivity and then coming back up. If there wasn't a way to stabilize this, the network would never converge, and that one flapping interface could bring the entire network down!

Holddowns prevent routes from changing too rapidly by allowing time for either the downed route to come back up or the network to stabilize somewhat before changing to the next best route. These also tell routers to restrict, for a specific time period, changes that might affect recently removed routes. This prevents inoperative routes from being prematurely restored to other routers' tables.

When a router receives an update from a neighbor indicating that a previously accessible network isn't working and is inaccessible, the holddown timer will start. If a new update arrives from a neighbor with a better metric than the original network entry, the holddown is removed and data is passed. But if an update is received from a neighbor router before the holddown timer expires and it has an equal or lower metric than the previous route, the update is ignored and the holddown timer keeps ticking. This allows more time for the network to stabilize before trying to converge.

Holddowns use triggered updates that reset the holddown timer to alert the neighbor routers of a change in the network. Unlike update messages from neighbor routers, triggered updates create a new routing update that is sent immediately to neighbor routers because a change was detected in the internetwork.

There are three instances when triggered updates will reset the holddown timer:

- The holddown timer expires.

- Another update is received with a better metric.

- A flush time, which is the time a route would be held before being removed, removes the route from the routing table when the timer expires.

Routing Information Protocol (RIP)

Routing Information Protocol (RIP) is a true distance-vector routing protocol. It sends the complete routing table out to all active interfaces every 30 seconds. RIP only uses hop count to determine the best way to a remote network, but it has a maximum allowable hop count of 15 by default, meaning that 16 is deemed unreachable. RIP works well in small networks, but it's inefficient on large networks with slow WAN links or on networks with a large number of routers installed.

RIP version 1 uses only *classful routing*, which means that all devices in the network must use the same subnet mask. This is because RIP version 1 doesn't send updates with subnet mask information in tow. RIP version 2 provides something called *prefix routing*, and does send subnet mask information with the route updates. This is called *classless routing*. I'm not going there, though. I'm only going to talk about RIP version 1 because that's what the CCNA objectives require.

In the following sections, we will discuss the RIP timers and then RIP configuration.

RIP Timers

RIP uses three different kinds of timers to regulate its performance:

Route update timer   Sets the interval (typically 30 seconds) between periodic routing updates, in which the router sends a complete copy of its routing table out to all neighbors.

Route invalid timer   Determines the length of time that must elapse (180 seconds) before a router determines that a route has become invalid. It will come to this conclusion if it hasn't heard any updates about a particular route for that period. When that happens, the router will send out updates to all its neighbors letting them know that the route is invalid.

Holddown timer   This sets the amount of time during which routing information is suppressed. Routes will enter into the holddown state when an update packet is received that indicated the route is unreachable. This continues until either an update packet is received with a better metric or until the holddown timer expires. The default is 180 seconds.

Route flush timer   Sets the time between a route becoming invalid and its removal from the routing table (240 seconds). Before it's removed from the table, the router notifies its neighbors of that route's impending demise. The value of the route invalid timer must be less than that of the route flush timer. This gives the router enough time to tell its neighbors about the invalid route before the local routing table is updated.

Configuring RIP Routing

To configure RIP routing, just turn on the protocol with the `router rip` command and tell the RIP routing protocol which networks to advertise. That's it. Let's configure our three-router internetwork (shown again in Figure 5.7) with RIP routing and practice that.

FIGURE 5.7   IP RIP routing example

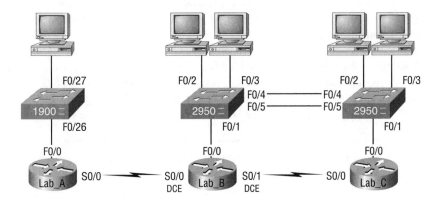

Lab_A

RIP has an administrative distance of 120. Static routes have an administrative distance of 1 by default and, since you currently have static routes configured, the routing tables won't be propagated with RIP information. So, the first thing you need to do is to delete the static routes off each router.

This is done with the `no ip route` command:

```
Lab_A(config)#no ip route 192.168.30.0 255.255.255.0
  192.168.20.2
Lab_A(config)#no ip route 192.168.40.0 255.255.255.0
  192.168.20.2
Lab_A(config)#no ip route 192.168.50.0 255.255.255.0
  192.168.20.2
```

Notice that in the preceding Lab_A router output, you must type the whole `ip route` command after the keyword `no` to delete the entry.

Once the static routes are deleted from the configuration, you can add the RIP routing protocol by using the `router rip` command and the `network` command. The `network` command tells the routing protocol which network to advertise.

Look at the next router configuration:

```
Lab_A(config)#router rip
Lab_A(config-router)#network 192.168.10.0
```

```
Lab_A(config-router)#network 192.168.20.0
Lab_A(config-router)#^Z
Lab_A#
```

Note the fact that you need to type in every directly connected network that you want RIP to advertise. But because they're not directly connected we're going to leave out networks 30, 40, and 50 because it's RIP's job to find them and populate the routing table.

That's it. Two or three commands, and you're done—sure makes your job a lot easier than when using static routes, doesn't it? However, keep in mind the extra router CPU process and bandwidth that you're consuming.

RIP and IGRP use the classful address when configuring the network address. Because of this, all subnet masks must be the same on all devices in the network (this is called classful routing). To clarify this, let's say you're using a Class B network address of 172.16.0.0/24 with subnets 172.16.10.0, 172.16.20.0 and 172.16.30.0. You would only type in the classful network address of 172.16.0.0 and let RIP find the subnets and place them in the routing table.

    Understand that RIP is configured with classful routing network addresses!

Lab_B

To configure RIP on the Lab_B router, you need to remove the two static routes you added from the earlier example. Once you make sure no routes are in the routing table with a better administrative distance than 120, you can add RIP. The Lab_B router has three directly connected networks and we want RIP to advertise them all so we will add three network statements.

Again, if you don't remove the static routes, RIP routes will never be found in the routing table even though RIP will still be running in the background causing a bunch of CPU processing on the routers and gobbling up precious bandwidth!

Here is what I did to configure RIP on the Lab_B:

```
Lab_B#config t
Enter configuration commands, one per line. End with CNTL/Z.
Lab_B(config)#no ip route 192.168.10.0 255.255.255.0
  192.168.20.1
Lab_B(config)#no ip route 192.168.50.0 255.255.255.0
  192.168.40.2

Lab_B(config)#router rip
Lab_B(config-router)#network 192.168.20.0
Lab_B(config-router)#network 192.168.30.0
Lab_B(config-router)#network 192.168.40.0
Lab_B(config-router)#^Z
Lab_B#
```

Lab_C

We've already removed the static routes on the Lab_C router because we placed a default route on it. So all that's needed here is to remove the default route from the Lab_C router. Once it's dust, you can turn on RIP routing for the two directly connected routes:

```
Lab_C#config t
Enter configuration commands, one per line. End with CNTL/Z.
Lab_C(config)#no ip route 0.0.0.0 0.0.0.0 192.168.40.1
Lab_C(config)#router rip
Lab_C(config-router)#network 192.168.40.0
Lab_C(config-router)#network 192.168.50.0
Lab_C(config-router)#^Z
Lab_C#
```

It's important to remember why we're doing this. Directly connected routes have an administrative distance of 0, static routes have an administrative distance of 1, and RIP has an administrative distance of 120. I call RIP the "gossip protocol" because it reminds me of junior high school, where if you hear a rumor (advertised route), it just has to be true without exception. And that pretty much sums up how RIP behaves on an internetwork—rumor mill as protocol!

Verifying the RIP Routing Tables

Each routing table should now have the routers' directly connected routes as well as RIP-injected routes received from neighboring routers.

This output shows us the contents of the Lab_A routing table:

```
Lab_A#sh ip route
[output cut]

R    192.168.50.0 [120/2] via 192.168.20.2, 00:00:23, Serial0/0
R    192.168.40.0 [120/1] via 192.168.20.2, 00:00:23, Serial0/0
R    192.168.30.0 [120/1] via 192.168.20.2, 00:00:23, Serial0/0
C    192.168.20.0 is directly connected, Serial0/0
C    192.168.10.0 is directly connected, FastEthernet0/0
Lab_A#
```

Looking at this, you can see that the routing table has the same entries that they had when we were using static routes, except for that R. The R means that the networks were added dynamically using the RIP routing protocol. The [120/1] is the administrative distance of the route (120) along with the number of hops to that remote network (1).

The following output displays Lab_B's routing table.

```
Lab_B#sh ip route
[output cut]

R   192.168.50.0 [120/1] via 172.16.40.2, 00:00:11, Serial0/1
C   192.168.40.0 is directly connected, Serial0/1
C   192.168.30.0 is directly connected, FastEthernet0/0
C   192.168.20.0 is directly connected, Serial0/0
R   192.168.10.0 [120/1] via 172.16.20.1, 00:00:21, Serial0/0
Lab_B#
```

Notice that here again the same networks are in the routing table and they weren't added manually.

Let's check out Lab_C's routing table:

```
Lab_C#sh ip route
[output cut]
Gateway of last resort is not set

C   192.168.50.0 is directly connected, FastEthernet0/0
C   192.168.40.0 is directly connected, Serial0/0
R   192.168.30.0 [120/1] via 192.168.40.1, 00:00:04, Serial0/0
R   192.168.20.0 [120/1] via 192.168.40.1, 00:00:26, Serial0/
R   192.168.10.0 [120/2] via 192.168.40.1, 00:00:04, Serial0/0
Lab_C#
```

So while yes, it's true that RIP has worked really well in our little internetwork, it's not the solution for every enterprise. That's because this technique has a maximum hop count of only 15 (16 is deemed unreachable) and it performs full routing-table updates every 30 seconds, both things that can wreak havoc in a larger internetwork.

There's one more thing I want to show you about RIP routing tables and the parameters used to advertise remote networks. Notice, as an example, that the following routing table shows [120/15] in the 192.168.10.0 network metric. This means that the administrative distance is 120, the default for RIP, but that the hop count is 15. Remember that each time a router receives an update from another router, it increments the hop count by one for each route.

```
Lab_C#sh ip route
[output cut]
Gateway of last resort is not set

C   192.168.50.0 is directly connected, FastEthernet0/0
C   192.168.40.0 is directly connected, Serial0/0
R   192.168.30.0 [120/1] via 192.168.40.1, 00:00:04, Serial0/0
R   192.168.20.0 [120/1] via 192.168.40.1, 00:00:26, Serial0/
R   192.168.10.0 [120/15] via 192.168.40.1, 00:00:04, Serial0/0
Lab_C#
```

So this [120/15] is really bad because the next router that receives the table from router Lab_C will just discard the route to network 192.168.10.0, since the hop count would then be 16, which is invalid. I know that in this example we don't have another router connected to the right of Lab_C, but you should be able to get my point here!

Holding Down RIP Propagations

You probably don't want your RIP network advertised everywhere on your LAN and WAN. There's not a whole lot to be gained by advertising your RIP network to the Internet, now, is there?

There are a few different ways to stop unwanted RIP updates from propagating across your LANs and WANs. The easiest one is through the `passive-interface` command. This command prevents RIP update broadcasts from being sent out a defined interface, but that same interface can still receive RIP updates.

Here's an example of how to configure a `passive-interface` on a router:

```
Lab_A#config t
Lab_A(config)#router rip
Lab_A(config-router)#network 192.168.10.0
Lab_A(config-router)#passive-interface serial 0/0
```

This command will stop RIP updates from being propagated out serial interface 0, but serial interface 0 can still receive RIP updates.

🌐 Real World Scenario

Should we really use RIP in an internetwork?

You have been hired as a consultant to install a couple of Cisco routers into a growing network. They have a couple of old Unix routers that they want to keep in the network. These routers do not support any routing protocol except RIP. I guess these means you just have to run RIP on the entire network.

Well, yes and no. You can run RIP on a router connecting that old network, but you certainly don't need to run RIP throughout the whole internetwork!

You can do what is called *redistribution*, which is basically translating from one type of routing protocol to another. This means that you can support those old routers using RIP but use Enhanced IGRP, for example, on the rest of your network.

This will stop RIP routes from being sent all over the internetwork and eating up all that precious bandwidth.

Redistribution is covered in detail in the Sybex *CCNP/CCIP: BSCI Study Guide*.

Interior Gateway Routing Protocol (IGRP)

Interior Gateway Routing Protocol (IGRP) is a Cisco-proprietary distance-vector routing protocol. This means that all your routers must be Cisco routers to use IGRP in your network. Cisco created this routing protocol to overcome the problems associated with RIP.

IGRP has a maximum hop count of 255 with a default of 100. This is helpful in larger networks and solves the problem of 15 hops being the maximum possible in a RIP network.

IGRP also uses a different metric than RIP. IGRP uses bandwidth and delay of the line by default as a metric for determining the best route to an internetwork. This is called a *composite metric*. Reliability, load, and maximum transmission unit (MTU) can also be used, although they are not used by default.

The main difference between RIP and IGRP configuration is that when you configure IGRP, you supply the autonomous system number. All routers must use the same number in order to share routing table information.

Here is a list of IGRP characteristics that you won't find in RIP:

- IGRP can be used in large Internetworks
- IGRP uses an Autonomous System number for activation
- IGRP gives a full route table update every 90 seconds
- IGRP uses bandwidth and delay of the line as metric (lowest composite metric)

In the following sections, we will discuss the IGRP timers and the configuration of IGRP.

IGRP Timers

To control performance, IGRP includes the following timers with default settings:

Update timers These specify how frequently routing-update messages should be sent. The default is 90 seconds.

Invalid timers These specify how long a router should wait before declaring a route invalid if it doesn't receive a specific update about it. The default is three times the update period.

Holddown timers These specify the holddown period. The default is three times the update timer period plus 10 seconds.

Flush timers These indicate how much time should pass before a route should be flushed from the routing table. The default is seven times the routing update period. If the update timer is 90 seconds by default, then $7 \times 90 = 630$ seconds elapse before a route will be flushed from the route table.

Configuring IGRP Routing

The command used to configure IGRP is the same as the one used to configure RIP routing with one important difference: you use an autonomous system (AS) number. All routers within an autonomous system must use the same AS number, or they won't communicate with routing information. Here's how to turn on IGRP routing:

```
Lab_A#config t
Lab_A(config)#router igrp 10
Lab_A(config-router)#network 192.168.10.0
```

Notice that the configuration in the above router commands is as simple as in RIP routing except that IGRP uses an AS number. This number advertises only to the specific routers you want to share routing information with.

> You absolutely *must* remember that you type a classful network number in when configuring IGRP!

IGRP can load-balance up to six unequal links. RIP networks must have the same hop count to load-balance, whereas IGRP uses bandwidth to determine how to load-balance. To load-balance over unequal-cost links, the `variance` command controls the load balancing between the best metric and the worst acceptable metric.

> Load balancing and traffic sharing are covered more in depth in Sybex's *CCNP: Building Scalable Cisco Internetworks Study Guide* (Sybex, 2004).

Configuring IGRP is pretty straightforward and not much different from configuring RIP. You do need to decide on an AS number before you configure your routers. Remember that all routers in your internetwork must use the same AS number if you want them to share routing information.

In the sample internetwork we've been using throughout this chapter, we'll use AS 10 to configure the routers.

Okay, let's configure our internetwork with IGRP routing.

Lab_A

The AS number, as shown in the router output below, can be any number from 1 to 65535. A router can be a member of as many AS as you need it to be.

```
Lab_A#config t
Enter configuration commands, one per line. End with CNTL/Z.
Lab_A(config)#router igrp ?
  <1-65535>  Autonomous system number
```

```
Lab_A(config)#router igrp 10
Lab_A(config-router)#netw 192.168.10.0
Lab_A(config-router)#netw 192.168.20.0
Lab_A(config-router)#^Z
Lab_A#
```

The `router igrp` command turns IGRP routing on in the router. As with RIP, you still need to add the network numbers you want to advertise. IGRP uses classful routing, which means that subnet mask information isn't sent along with the routing protocol updates.

 If you're using the 172.16.0.0/24 network, know that if you did type in the subnet **172.16.10.0**, the router would accept it and then change the configuration to a classful entry of 172.16.0.0. But don't do that—at least not on the exam! It's definitely not so forgiving and will simply mark your answer wrong if you type the wrong network number. I cannot stress this enough: **Think classful if you are using subnets!**

Lab_B

To configure the Lab_B router, all you need to do is turn on IGRP routing using AS 10 and then add the network numbers, as shown next:

```
Lab_B#config t
Enter configuration commands, one per line. End with CNTL/Z.
Lab_B(config)#router igrp 10
Lab_B(config-router)#netw 192.168.20.0
Lab_B(config-router)#netw 192.168.30.0
Lab_B(config-router)#netw 192.168.40.0
Lab_B(config-router)#^Z
Lab_B#
```

Lab_C

To configure Lab_C, once again you need to turn on IGRP using AS 10:

```
Lab_C#config t
Enter configuration commands, one per line. End with CNTL/Z.
Lab_C(config)#router igrp 10
Lab_C(config-router)#netw 192.168.40.0
Lab_C(config-router)#netw 192.168.50.0
Lab_C(config-router)#^Z
Lab_C#
```

Verifying the IGRP Routing Tables

Once the routers are configured, you need to verify the configuration with the show ip route command.

In all of the following router outputs, notice that the only routes to networks are either directly connected or IGRP-injected routes. Since we didn't turn off RIP, it's still running in the background and taking up both router CPU cycles and bandwidth. What's more, the routing tables will never use a RIP-found route because IGRP has a better administrative distance than RIP does.

The router output below is from the Lab_A router. Notice that all routes are in the routing table:

```
Lab_A#sh ip route
[output cut]
I       192.168.50.0 [100/170420] via 192.168.20.2, Serial0/0
I       192.168.40.0 [100/160260] via 192.168.20.2, Serial0/0
I       192.168.30.0 [100/158360] via 192.168.20.2, Serial0/0
C       192.168.20.0 is directly connected Serial0/0
C       192.168.10.0 is directly connected, FastEthernet0/0
```

The I means IGRP-injected routes. The 100 in [100/160360] is the administrative distance of IGRP. The 160360 is the composite metric. The lower the composite metric, the better the route.

 Remember that the composite metric is calculated by using the bandwidth and delay of the line by default. The delay of the line can also be referred to as the *cumulative interface delay*.

This is Lab_B's routing table:

```
Lab_B#sh ip route
[output cut]
I       192.168.50.0 [100/8576] via 192.168.40.2, 00:01:11, Serial0/1
C       192.168.40.0 is directly connected, Serial0/1
C       192.168.30.0 is directly connected, FastEthernet0/0
C       192.168.20.0 is directly connected, Serial0/0
I       192.168.10.0 [100/158350] via 192.168.20.1, 00:00:36, Serial0/0
Lab_B#
```

And here's Lab_C's routing table:

```
Lab_C#sh ip route
[output cut]
C       192.168.50.0 is directly connected, FastEthernet 0/0
```

```
C       192.168.40.0 is directly connected, Serial0/0
I       192.168.30.0 [100/143723] via 192.168.40.1, 00:00:42, Serial0/0
I       192.168.20.0 [100/152365] via 192.168.40.1, 00:00;52, Serial0/0
I       192.168.10.0 [100/158350] via 192.168.20.1, 00:00:36, Serial0/0
Lab_C#
```

If RIP isn't good for my network, then I should use IGRP, right?

The answer to this question is, "Well, no, not really." I know I said that RIP isn't exactly what anyone needs running in a large internetwork—or, actually, in any network—but that doesn't mean you should use IGRP instead.

You need to understand how RIP and IGRP work for the CCNA exam as well as for when you find yourself actually working in a production environment. By understanding information about all the various routing protocols, you can make decisions based on facts—on real knowledge of all protocols old and new—instead of just guessing about what's the best fit for the specific business requirements facing you.

But if what I'm telling you is that you really shouldn't use either RIP or IGRP on your internetwork if you can help it, then what should you use? If you have an all-Cisco router environment, the answer is for sure—you should use Enhanced IGRP. It's so much better a routing protocol than IGRP!

If you've got a mixed environment of router brands, then you likely should use OSPF. And lucky you—I'm going to cover both EIGRP and OSPF in the next chapter.

After all is said, though, I really can't recommend which protocols you should use in your network because each network truly is different. What I am recommending is that if you do have the option of using EIGRP over IGRP or RIP, use EIGRP. End of story.

Verifying Your Configurations

It's important to verify your configurations once you've completed them, or at least once you *think* you've completed them. The following list includes the commands you can use to verify the routed and routing protocols configured on your Cisco routers:

- `show ip route`
- `show protocols`
- `show ip protocols`
- `debug ip rip`

- debug ip igrp events
- debug ip igrp transactions

The first command was covered in the previous section—I'll go over the others in the sections below.

The *show protocols* Command

The show protocols command is useful because it displays all the routed protocols and the interfaces upon which the protocol is enabled.

The following output shows the IP address of the FastEthernet 0/0, serial 0/0, and serial 0/1 interfaces of the Lab_B router:

```
Lab_B#sh protocol
Global values:
  Internet Protocol routing is enabled
FastEthernet0 is up, line protocol is up
  Internet address is 192.168.30.1/24
Serial0/0 is up, line protocol is up
  Internet address is 192.168.20.2/24
Serial0/1 is up, line protocol is up
  Internet address is 192.168.40.1/24
Lab_B#
```

If IPX or AppleTalk were configured on the router, those network addresses would've appeared as well.

The *show ip protocols* Command

The show ip protocols command shows you the routing protocols that are configured on your router. Looking at the output below, you can see that both RIP and IGRP are still running on the router, but that only IGRP appears in the routing table because of its lower administrative distance (AD):

```
Lab_B#sh ip protocols
Routing Protocol is "rip"
  Sending updates every 30 seconds, next due in 6 seconds
  Invalid after 180 seconds, hold down 180, flushed after
  240
  Outgoing update filter list for all interfaces is
  Incoming update filter list for all interfaces is
  Redistributing: rip
  Default version control: send version 1, receive any
```

```
version
  Interface        Send  Recv   Key-chain
  FastEthernet0     1     1 2
  Serial0/0         1     1 2
  Serial0/1         1     1 2
Routing for Networks:
  192.168.10.0
  192.168.20.0
  192.168.30.0
Routing Information Sources:
  Gateway          Distance      Last Update
  192.168.40.2          120      00:00:21
  192.168.20.1          120      00:00:23
Distance: (default is 120)
```

The show ip protocols command also displays the timers used in the routing protocol. Notice in the output above that RIP is sending updates every 30 seconds, which is the default. Notice further down that RIP is routing for all directly connected networks , and the two neighbors it found are 192.168.40.2 and 192.168.20.1. The last entry is the default AD for RIP (120). The command output is continued below:

The following output shows the IGRP routing information (the default update timer is 90 seconds, and the administrative distance is 100):

```
Routing Protocol is "igrp 10"
  Sending updates every 90 seconds, next due in 42 seconds
  Invalid after 270 seconds, hold down 280, flushed after 630
  Outgoing update filter list for all interfaces is
  Incoming update filter list for all interfaces is
  Default networks flagged in outgoing updates
  Default networks accepted from incoming updates
  IGRP metric weight K1=1, K2=0, K3=1, K4=0, K5=0
  IGRP maximum hopcount 100
  IGRP maximum metric variance 1
  Redistributing: eigrp 10, igrp 10
  Routing for Networks:
    192.168.10.0
    192.168.20.0
    192.168.30.0
  Routing Information Sources:
    Gateway          Distance      Last Update
    192.168.40.2          100      00:00:47
    192.168.20.1          100      00:01:18
  Distance: (default is 100)
```

The information included in the show ip protocols command includes the AS, routing timers, networks being advertised, neighbors, and AD (100).

The invalid timer is set at 270 seconds (three times the update timer). If a route update is not received in three update periods, the route is considered invalid. The holddown timer is 280, about three times that of the update timer. This is the number of seconds a route is suppressed while waiting for a new or better update to be received. If a new or better update isn't received before the holddown timer and the flush timer expires, the route is removed (flushed) from the routing table.

The *debug ip rip* Command

The debug ip rip command sends routing updates as they are sent and received on the router to the console session. If you are telnetted into the router, you'll need to use the terminal monitor command to be able to receive the output from the debug commands.

We can see in this output that RIP is both sent and received on serial 0/0 and serial 0/1 interfaces (the metric is the hop count):

```
Lab_B#debug ip rip
RIP protocol debugging is on
Lab_B#
07:12:56: RIP: received v1 update from 192.168.40.2 on
  Serial0/1
07:12:56:       192.168.50.0 in 1 hops
07:12:56: RIP: received v1 update from 192.168.20.1 on
  Serial0/0
07:12:56:       192.168.10.0 in 1 hops
```

In the above debug output, notice the route updates received on the Lab_B serial 0/0 and serial 0/1 interfaces. These are from routers Lab_A and Lab_C, respectively. What you want to notice is that split horizon rules stop the Lab_A and C routers from advertising back routes that they learned from Lab_B. This means only network 192.168.50.0 is being advertised from Lab_C, and 192.168.10.0 is being advertised to Lab_B from Lab_A.

In the following output, split horizon rules only allow networks 192.168.30.0, 40, and 50 to be advertised to Lab_A:

```
07:12:58: RIP: sending v1 update to 255.255.255.255 via
  FastEthernet0/0 (192.168.30.1)
07:12:58:       subnet  192.168.50.0, metric 1
07:12:58:       subnet  192.168.40.0, metric 1
07:12:58:       subnet  192.168.20.0, metric 1
07:12:58:       subnet  192.168.10.0, metric 1
07:12:58: RIP: sending v1 update to 255.255.255.255 via
  Serial0/0 (172.16.20.2)
```

```
07:12:58:       subnet  192.168,50.0, metric 1
07:12:58:       subnet  192.168.40.0, metric 1
07:12:58:       subnet  192.168.30.0, metric 1
07:12:58: RIP: sending v1 update to 255.255.255.255 via
  Serial0/1 (172.16.40.1)
07:12:58:       subnet  192.168.30.0, metric 1
07:12:58:       subnet  192.168.20.0, metric 1
07:12:58:       subnet  192.168.10.0, metric 1
```

In the above output, Router Lab_B will not advertise the 192.168.10.0 network back to the Lab_A router, nor 192.168.50.0 back to Lab_C.

If the metric of a route shows 16, this is a route poison, and the route being advertised is unreachable.

To turn off debugging, use the undebug all or the no debug all command. Here is an example of using the undebug all command:

```
Lab_B#undebug all
All possible debugging has been turned off
Lab_B#
```

The *debug ip igrp* Command

With the debug ip igrp command, there are two options, events and transactions, as shown in this output:

```
Lab_B#debug ip igrp ?
  events        IGRP protocol events
  transactions  IGRP protocol transactions
```

The difference between these commands is explained in the following sections.

The *debug ip igrp events* Command

The debug ip igrp events command is a summary of the IGRP routing information that is running on the network. The following router output shows the source and destination of each update as well as the number of routers in each update:

```
Lab_B#debug ip igrp events
IGRP event debugging is on
07:13:50: IGRP: received request from 192.168.40.2 on
  Serial0/1
07:13:50: IGRP: sending update to 192.168.40.2 via Serial1
```

```
(192.168.40.1)
07:13:51: IGRP: Update contains 3 interior, 0 system, and
  0 exterior routes.
07:13:51: IGRP: Total routes in update: 3
07:13:51: IGRP: received update from 192.168.40.2 on
  Serial0/1
07:13:51: IGRP: Update contains 1 interior, 0 system, and
  0 exterior routes.
07:13:51: IGRP: Total routes in update: 1
```

Information about individual routes isn't something you'll get with this command.

You can turn the command off with the undebug ip igrp events or undebug all (or un all for short) command:

```
Lab_B#un all
All possible debugging has been turned off
```

The *debug ip igrp transactions* Command

The debug ip igrp transactions command shows message requests from neighbor routers asking for an update and the broadcasts sent from your router towards that neighbor router.

In the following output, a request was received from a neighbor router with an interface IP address of 192.168.40.2 to serial 0/1 of Router Lab_B, which responded with an update packet:

```
Lab_B#debug ip igrp transactions
IGRP protocol debugging is on
07:14:05: IGRP: received request from 192.168.40.2 on
  Serial1
07:14:05: IGRP: sending update to 192.168.40.2 via Serial1
  (172.16.40.1)
07:14:05:        subnet 192.168.30.0, metric=1100
07:14:05:        subnet 192.168.20.0, metric=158250
07:14:05:        subnet 192.168.10.0, metric=158350
07:14:06: IGRP: received update from 192.168.40.2 on
  Serial1
07:14:06:        subnet 192.168.50.0, metric 8576 (neighbor
  1100)
```

You can turn off the command with the undebug all command:

```
Lab_B#un all
All possible debugging has been turned off
```

Summary

This chapter covered IP routing in detail. It's extremely important that you really understand the basics we covered in this chapter, because everything that's done on a Cisco router typically will have some type of IP routing configured and running.

You learned in this chapter how IP routing uses frames to transport packets between routers and to the destination host. From there, we configured static routing on our routers and discussed the administrative distance used by IP to determine the past route to a destination network. If you have a stub network, you can configure default routing, which sets the gateway of last resort on a router.

After we finished with static routing, we turned our attention to dynamic routing where we discussed the timers and loop avoidance schemes used by RIP and IGRP. Once we understood how dynamic routing creates and maintains routing tables, we configured RIP and IGRP on our network.

Once we had RIP and IGRP running, we discussed how to verify the routing protocols by using the show ip route, show ip protocols, and especially the debugging commands used with RIP and IGRP.

Exam Essentials

Understand the basic IP routing process.   You need to remember that the frame changes at each hop, but that the packet is never changed or manipulated in any way until it reaches the destination device.

Understand how to configure RIP routing.   To configure RIP routing, first you must be in global configuration mode and then you type the command **router rip**. Then you add all directly connected networks, making sure to use the classful address.

Remember how to verify RIP routing.   Show ip route will provide you with the contents of the routing table. An R on the left side of the table indicates a RIP-found route. The debug ip rip command will show you RIP updates being sent and received on your router. If you see a route with a metric of 16, that route is considered down.

Understand how to configure IGRP routing.   IGRP is configured mostly like RIP, but with just one major difference: You must configure the autonomous system (AS).

Remember how to verify IGRP routing.   Show ip route will show you the routing table, and an I on the left side of the table indicates an IGRP-found route. The [100/123456] indicates the administrative distance—100 for IGRP, and the composite metric. The composite metric is determined by bandwidth and delay of the line, by default.

Key Terms

Before you take the exam, be certain you are familiar with the following terms:

administrative distance (AD)	hybrid protocols
classful routing	link-state protocols
classless routing	maximum hop count
composite metric	pinhole congestion
converged	poison reverse
counting to infinity	prefix routing
cumulative interface delay	redistribution
default routing	route poisoning
distance-vector protocols	routed protocol
dynamic routing	routing
flapping	routing protocol
holddown	shortest-path-first protocols
hop	split horizon
hop count	static routing

Commands Used in This Chapter

The following list contains a summary of all the commands used in this chapter:

Command	Description
show ip route	Displays the IP routing table
ip route	Creates static and default routes on a router
ip classless	Is a global configuration command used to tell a router to forward packets to a default route when the destination network is not in the routing table
router rip	Turns on IP RIP routing on a router
network	Tells the routing protocol what network to advertise

`no ip route`	Removes a static or default route
`router igrp` **`as`**	Turns on IP IGRP routing on a router
`show protocols`	Shows the routed protocols and network addresses configured on each interface
`show ip protocols`	Shows the routing protocols and timers associated with each routing protocol configured on a router
`debug ip rip`	Sends console messages displaying information about RIP packets being sent and received on a router interface
`debug ip igrp events`	Provides a summary of the IGRP routing information running on the network
`debug ip igrp transactions`	Shows message requests from neighbor routers asking for an update and the broadcasts sent from your router to that neighbor router

Written Lab 5

Write the answers to the following questions:

1. Create a static route to network 172.16.10.0/24 with a next-hop gateway of 172.16.20.1 and an administrative distance of 150.

2. Write the commands used to turn RIP routing on in a router and advertise network 10.0.0.0.

3. Write the commands to stop a router from propagating RIP information out serial 1.

4. Write the commands to create an AS 10 with IGRP in your 172.16.0.0 network.

5. Write the commands to configure a default route on a router to go to 172.16.50.3.

6. What works with triggered updates to help stop routing loops in distance-vector networks?

7. What stops routing loops in distance-vector networks by sending out a maximum hop count as soon as a link fails?

8. What stops routing loops in distance-vector networks by not resending information learned on an interface out that same interface?

9. What network number do you type to configure IGRP when a router is directly connected to subnets 172.16.10.0 and 172.16.35.0?

10. What command is used to send RIP routing updates as they are sent and received on the router to the console session?

(The answers to Written Lab 5 can be found following the answers to the Review Questions for this chapter.)

Hands-on Labs

In the following hands-on labs, you will configure a network with three 2501 routers and one 2621 router. These labs were meant for use with real Cisco routers.

The following labs will be covered:

Lab 5.1: Creating Static Routes

Lab 5.2: Dynamic Routing with RIP

Lab 5.3: Dynamic Routing with IGRP

Table 5.3 shows our IP addresses for each router (each interface uses a /24 mask).
Figure 5.8 will be used to configure all routers.

TABLE 5.3   Table 5.3: Our IP Addresses

Router	Interface	IP address
2621	F0/0	172.16.10.1
2501A	E0	172.16.10.2
2501A	S0	172.16.20.1
2501B	E0	172.16.30.1
2501B	S0	172.16.20.2
2501B	S1	172.16.40.1
2501C	S0	172.16.40.2
2501C	E0	172.16.50.1

FIGURE 5.8   Hands-on lab internetwork

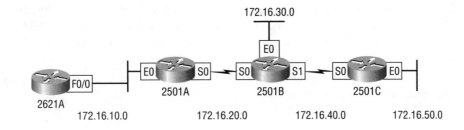

Hands-on Lab 5.1: Creating Static Routes

In this first lab, you will create a static route in all four routers so that the routers see all networks. Verify with the Ping program when complete.

1. The 2621A router is connected to network 172.16.10.0/24. It does not know about networks 172.16.20.0/24, 172.16.30.0/24, 172.16.40.0/24, and 172.16.50.0/24. The 2621A router fa0/0 interface has an IP address of 172.16.10.2/24, and the 2501A Ethernet 0 interface is 172.16.10.1/24. Create static routes so that the 2621A Router can see all networks, as shown here:

```
2621A#config t
2621A(config)#ip route 172.16.20.0 255.255.255.0
   172.16.10.1
2621A(config)#ip route 172.16.30.0 255.255.255.0
   172.16.10.1
2621A(config)#ip route 172.16.40.0 255.255.255.0
   172.16.10.1
2621A(config)#ip route 172.16.50.0 255.255.255.0
   172.16.10.1
```

2. Save the current configuration for the 2621A router by going to the privileged mode, typing **copy run start**, and pressing Enter.

3. On Router 2501A, which is already directly connected to networks 172.16.10.0/24 and 172.16.20.0/24, create a static route to see networks 172.16.30.0/24, 172.16.40.0/24, and 172.16.50.0/24, as shown here (the 2501B serial 0 interface IP address is 172.16.20.2/24, which we will use as our next hop address):

```
2501A#config t
2501A(config)#ip route 172.16.30.0 255.255.255.0
   172.16.20.2
2501A(config)#ip route 172.16.40.0 255.255.255.0
   172.16.20.2
2501A(config)#ip route 172.16.50.0 255.255.255.0
   172.16.20.2
```

These commands told Router 2501A to get to network 172.16.30.0/24 and use IP address 172.16.20.2, which is the closest neighbor interface connected to network 172.16.30.0/24, or Router 2501B. This is the same interface you will use to get to networks 172.16.40.0/24 and 172.16.50.0/24.

4. Save the current configuration for Router 2501A by going to the enabled mode, typing **copy run start**, and pressing Enter.

5. On Router 2501B, create a static route to see networks 172.16.10.0/24 and 172.16.50.0/24, which are not directly connected. Create static routes so that Router 2501B can see all networks, as shown here:

```
2501B#config t
2501B(config)#ip route 172.16.10.0 255.255.255.0
  172.16.20.1
2501B(config)#ip route 172.16.50.0 255.255.255.0
  172.16.40.2
```

The first command told Router 2501B that to get to network 172.16.10.0/24, it needs to use 172.16.20.1. The next command told Router 2501B to get to network 172.16.50.0/24 through 172.16.40.2, which is the 2501C serial 0 interface IP address.

Save the current configuration for Router 2501B by going to the enable mode, typing **copy run start**, and pressing Enter.

6. Router 2501C is connected to networks 172.16.50.0/24 and 172.16.40.0/24. It does not know about networks 172.16.30.0/24, 172.16.20.0/24, and 172.16.10.0/24. Create static routes so that Router 2501C can see all networks, as shown here (use the 2501B serial 1 interface address of 172.16.40.1):

```
2501C#config t
2501C(config)#ip route 172.16.30.0 255.255.255.0
  172.16.40.1
2501C(config)#ip route 172.16.20.0 255.255.255.0
  172.16.40.1
2501C(config)#ip route 172.16.10.0 255.255.255.0
  172.16.40.1
```

Save the current configuration for Router 2501C by going to the enable mode, typing **copy run start**, and pressing Enter.

7. Now ping from each router to your hosts and from each router to each router. If it is set up correctly, it will work.

Hands-on Lab 5.2: Dynamic Routing with RIP

In this lab, we will use the dynamic routing protocol RIP instead of static and default routing.

1. Remove any static routes or default routes configured on your routers by using the no ip route command. For example, here is how you would remove the static routes on the 2501A router:

```
2501A#config t
2501A(config)#no ip route 172.16.30.0 255.255.255.0
  172.16.20.2
2501A(config)#no ip route 172.16.40.0 255.255.255.0
```

```
    172.16.20.2
2501A(config)#no ip route 172.16.50.0 255.255.255.0
    172.16.20.2
```

Do the same thing for Routers 2501B and 2501C as well as the 2621A router. Type **sh run** and press Enter on each router to verify that all static and default routes are cleared.

2. After your static and default routes are clear, go into configuration mode on Router 2501A by typing **config t**.

3. Tell your router to use RIP routing by typing **router rip** and pressing Enter, as shown here:

```
config t
router rip
```

4. Add the network number you want to advertise by typing **network 172.16.0.0** and pressing Enter.

5. Press Ctrl+Z to get out of configuration mode.

6. Go to Routers 2501B and 2501C as well as the 2621A router and type the same commands, as shown here:

```
Config t
Router rip
network 172.16.0.0
```

7. Verify that RIP is running at each router by typing the following commands at each router:

```
show ip protocols
show ip route
show running-config or show run
```

8. Save your configurations by typing **copy run start** or **copy running-config startup-config** and pressing Enter at each router.

9. Verify the network by pinging all remote networks and hosts.

Hands-on Lab 5.3: Dynamic Routing with IGRP

In this lab, you will run the IGRP routing protocol simultaneously with RIP routing.

1. Log into your routers and go into privileged mode by typing **en** or **enable**.

2. Keep RIP running on your routers and verify that it is running on each router. If you want to remove RIP, you can use the no `router rip` global configuration command to remove it from each router. For example:

```
config t
no router rip
```

3. From the configuration mode on Router 2501A, type **router igrp ?**.

4. Notice that it asks for an autonomous system number. This is used to allow only routers with the same AS number to communicate. Type **10** and press Enter. Your router can be configured to be part of as many different AS as necessary.

5. At the config-router prompt, type **network 172.16.0.0**. Notice that we add the classful network boundary to advertise, rather than the subnet numbers.

6. Press Ctrl+Z to get out of configuration mode.

7. Go to Routers 2501B and 2501C as well as the 2621A router and type the commands shown here:

```
2501B(config)#router igrp 10
2501B(config-router)#network 172.16.0.0
```

8. Verify that IGRP is running by typing the following command at each router:

```
show ip protocols
```

Notice that this shows you your RIP and IGRP routing protocols and the update timers.

Then type this command:

```
sh ip route
```

This should let you see all five subnets: 10, 20, 30, 40, and 50. Some will be directly connected, and some will be I routes, which are IGRP-injected routes. RIP is still running, but if you look at the routing table, you'll notice the network entry has the following: [100/23456]. The first number (100) is the trustworthiness rating (administrative distance). Since RIP's default trustworthiness rating is 120, the IGRP route is used before a RIP route is used. The second number is the metric, or weight, of the route that is used to determine the best path to a network.

Next, type this command:

```
show running-config
```

This lets you see that RIP and IGRP are configured.

9. To save your configurations, type **copy running-config startup-config** or **copy run start** and press Enter at each router.

10. Verify the network by pinging all routers, switches, and hosts.

Review Questions

1. You are not able to ping a server on the 192.168.50.0 network as shown in the following graphic from the Lab_A router. However, from the console of the Lab_B router, you can ping the server on the 192.168.50.0 network. Looking at the following routing table, what could the problem be?

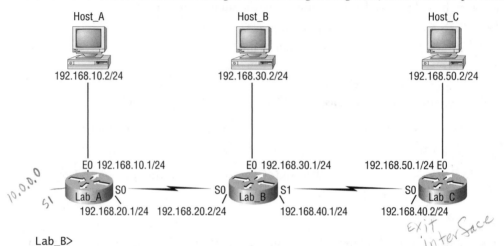

```
Lab_B>

Codes: C - connected, S - static, I - IGRP, R - RIP, M - mobile, B - BGP D -
EIGRP, EX - EIGRP external, O - OSPF,

IA - OSPF inter area N1 - OSPF NSSA external type 1, N2 - OSPF NSSA external
type 2 E1 - OSPF external type 1, E2 - OSPF external type 2, E - EGP i - IS-
IS, L1 - IS-IS level-1, L2 - IS-IS level-2, ia - IS-IS inter area
        * - candidate default, U - per-user static route, o - ODR
        P - periodic downloaded static route


Gateway of last resort is 10.1.1.1 to network 0.0.0.0

C    192.168.30.0/24 is directly connected, Ethernet0
C    192.168.40.0/24 is directly connected, Serial0
     172.16.0.0/24 is subnetted, 1 subnets
C       172.16.20.0 is directly connected, Loopback0
C    192.168.20.0/24 is directly connected, Serial0
R    10.0.0.0/8 [120/1] via 192.168.20.1, 00:00:16, Serial0
R    192.168.50.0/24 [120/1] via 192.168.40.2, 00:00:00, Serial0
R    192.168.30.0/24 [120/2] via 192.168.20.1, 00:00:16, Serial1
S*   0.0.0.0 [1/0] via 10.1.1.1
Lab_B>
```

A. The routing tables have not converged.

B. The RIP configuration is incorrect.

C. The static route is incorrect.

D. The LAN interface on Lab_C is shut down.

2. What command is used to stop RIP routing updates from exiting out an interface but still receive RIP route updates?

A. Router(config-if)#**no routing**

B. Router(config-if)#**passive-interface**

C. Router(config-router)#**passive-interface s0**

D. Router(config-router)#**no routing updates**

3. Which is true regarding how RIP routers share routing information? Please refer to the figure in question 1. (Choose two.)

A. Lab_A exchanges routing tables with Lab_C.

B. Lab_A exchanges routing tables with Lab_B.

C. Lab_B exchanges only with Lab_A.

D. Lab_C exchanges with Lab_B.

E. Lab_C exchanges with Lab_A.

4. In the following routing table, what does the [120/3] mean?

```
R     192.168.30.0/24 [120/1] via 192.168.40.1, 00:00:23, Serial0/0
C     192.168.40.0/24 is directly connected, Serial0/0
R     192.168.20.0/24 [120/1] via 192.168.40.1, 00:00:23, Serial/0
R     10.0.0.0/8 [120/2] via 192.168.40.1, 00:00:23, Serial0/0
C     192.168.50.0/24 is directly connected, FastEthernet0
R     192.168.3.0/24 [120/3] via 192.168.40.1, 00:00:23, Serial0/0
```

Admin Dist. of Rip / hops

A. The IP port number and packets sent

B. The administrative distance and metric

C. The metric and hop count

D. The bandwidth and update timer

5. Which of the following is true regarding the following output? (Choose two.)

```
04:06:16: RIP: received v1 update from 192.168.40.2 on Serial0/1
04:06:16:        192.168.50.0 in 16 hops (inaccessible)
04:06:40: RIP: sending v1 update to 255.255.255.255 via FastEthernet0/0
(192.168.30.1)
04:06:40: RIP: build update entries
04:06:40:        network 192.168.20.0 metric 1
04:06:40:        network 192.168.40.0 metric 1
```

```
04:06:40:        network 192.168.50.0 metric 2
04:06:40: RIP: sending v1 update to 255.255.255.255 via Serial0/1
(192.168.40.1)
```

A. There are three interfaces on the router participating in this update.

B. A ping to 192.168.50.1 will be successful.

C. There are at least two routers exchanging information.

D. A ping to 192.168.40.2 will be successful.

6. What is split horizon?

A. Information about a route should not be sent back in the direction from which the original update came.

B. It splits the traffic when you have a large bus (horizon) physical network.

C. It holds the regular updates from broadcasting to a downed link.

D. It prevents regular update messages from reinstating a route that has gone down.

7. What is poison reverse?

A. It sends back the protocol received from a router as a poison pill, which stops the regular updates.

B. It is information received from a router that can't be sent back to the originating router.

C. It prevents regular update messages from reinstating a route that has just come up.

D. It describes when a router sets the metric for a downed link to infinity.

8. Which Cisco IOS command can you use to see the IP routing table?

A. `sh ip config`

B. `sh ip arp`

C. `sh ip route`

D. `sh ip table`

9. Which two of the following are true regarding the distance-vector and link-state routing protocols? (Choose two.)

A. Link state sends its complete routing table out all active interfaces on periodic time intervals.

B. Distance vector sends its complete routing table out all active interfaces on periodic time intervals.

C. Link state sends updates containing the state of their own links to all routers in the internetwork.

D. Distance vector sends updates containing the state of their own links to all routers in the internetwork.

10. Which command displays RIP routing updates?

  A. `show ip route`

  B. `debug ip rip`

  C. `show protocols`

  D. `debug ip route`

11. Which of the following shows the correct parameters for configuring IGRP on the Lab_B router?

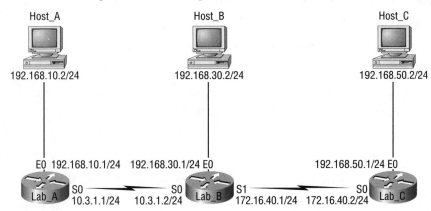

  A. `router igrp 10`
     `network 10.3.1.0`
     `network 192.168.0.0`

  B. `router igrp`
     `network 10.0.0.0`

  C. `router igrp 100`
     `network 10.0.0.0`
     `network 192.168.30.0`
     `network 172.16.0.0`

  D. `router igrp 100`
     `network 10.0.0.0`
     `network 192.168.30.0`
     `network 172.16.40.0`

12. What is the difference between routed and routing protocols? (Choose two.)

   A. Routed protocols update the routing tables of a router.

   B. Routing protocols determine the path of a packet through a network.

   C. Routed protocols are assigned to a router interface and determine the method of packet delivery.

   D. Routing protocols are assigned to a router interface and determine the method of packet delivery.

13. How is the 16300 calculated in the following? (Choose two.)

   ```
   I   192.168.10.0 [100/16300] via 192.168.20.1
   ```

   A. Maximum transmission unit

   B. Bandwidth

   C. Hop count

   D. Delay

   E. Administrative distance

14. If an IGRP advertised route has been determined to be invalid, when will the entry be removed from the routing table?

   A. 30 seconds

   B. 90 seconds

   C. 180 seconds

   D. 360 seconds

   E. 630 seconds

15. You type **debug ip rip** on your router console and see that 172.16.10.0 is being advertised with a metric of 16. What does this mean?

   A. The route is 16 hops away.

   B. The route has a delay of 16 microseconds.

   C. The route is inaccessible.

   D. The route is queued at 16 messages a second.

16. IGRP uses which of the following as default parameters for finding the best path to a remote network? (Choose two.)

   A. Hop count

   B. MTU

   C. Cumulative interface delay

   D. STP

   E. Path bandwidth value

17. An administrator is connected to the Lab_B router and can ping the s0/0 interface of Lab_C but not the f0/0 interface. Using the output below and the figure shown in question 1, which of the following could be the problem? (Choose two.)

```
Lab_C#sh ip protocols
Routing Protocol is "rip"
  Sending updates every 30 seconds, next due in 10 seconds
  Invalid after 180 seconds, hold down 180, flushed after 240
  Outgoing update filter list for all interfaces is
  Incoming update filter list for all interfaces is
  Redistributing: rip
  Default version control: send version 1, receive any version
    Interface    Send  Recv  Triggered RIP  Key-chain
    Ethernet0    1     1 2
    Serial 0     1     1 2
  Automatic network summarization is in effect
  Routing for Networks:
    192.168.40.0
   Routing Information Sources:
    Gateway         Distance      Last Update
    192.168.40.1          120      00:00:26
  Distance: (default is 120)
```

   A. The FastEthernet interface on the Lab_C router is shut down.

   B. The Lab_C router does not have the 192.168.50.0 network in the RIP configuration.

   C. RIP routing on the Lab_C router is not forwarding updates.

   D. The `clock rate` command was not entered on the Lab_B s0/1 interface.

18. If your routing table has a static, a RIP, and an IGRP route to the same network, which route will be used to route packets by default?

   A. Any available route

   B. RIP route

   C. Static route

   D. IGRP route

   E. They will all load-balance.

19. You have the following routing table. Which of the following networks will not be placed in the neighbor routing table?

```
R    192.168.30.0/24 [120/1] via 192.168.40.1, 00:00:12, Serial0
C    192.168.40.0/24 is directly connected, Serial0
     172.16.0.0/24 is subnetted, 1 subnets
C       172.16.30.0 is directly connected, Loopback0
```

```
R    192.168.20.0/24 [120/1] via 192.168.40.1, 00:00:12, Serial0
R    10.0.0.0/8 [120/15] via 192.168.40.1, 00:00:07, Serial0
C    192.168.50.0/24 is directly connected, Ethernet0
```

A. 172.16.30.0

B. 192.168.30.0

C. 10.0.0.0

D. All of them will be placed in the neighbors routing table.

20. What is the default administrative distance for IGRP?

A. 90

B. 100

C. 120

D. 220

Answers to Review Questions

1. C. The problem is that someone set a default route and they set it wrong as well!

2. C. The `(config-router)# passive-interface` command stops updates from being sent out an interface, but route updates are still received.

3. B, D. RIP routers (distance vector) only share routing information with directly attached neighbors. Lab_A can communicate with Lab_B, but not with Lab_C. Lab_B can communicate with Lab_A and Lab_C, but Lab_C can only communicate with Lab_B.

4. B. The [120/3] is administrative distance and hop count (metric).

5. C, D. The route to 192.168.50.0 is unreachable and only interfaces s0/1 and FastEthernet 0/0 are participating in the RIP update. Since a route update was received, at least two routers are participating in the RIP routing process.

6. A. A split horizon will not advertise a route back to the same router it learned the route from.

7. D. A poison reverse is used to communicate to a router that the link is down and that the hop count to that network is set to infinity or unreachable.

8. C. The command `show ip route` will show you the routing tables on each router it is run on.

9. B, C. Distance-vector routing protocol sends its complete routing table out all active interfaces on periodic time intervals. Link-state routing protocols sends updates containing the state of their own links to all routers in the internetwork

10. B. `Debug ip rip` is used to show the Internet Protocol (IP) Routing Information Protocol (RIP) updates being sent and received on the router.

11. C. You configure Interior Gateway Routing Protocol (IGRP) with an autonomous system number and then use the `network` command to tell the routing protocol which networks you want to advertise. The entry must be a classful entry, and contain all directly connected networks, which in this case is 10.0.0.0, 192.168.30.0, and 172.16.0.0

12. B, C. Routing protocols are used to update routing tables on routers, and routed protocols send user data through the internetwork. IP is an example of a routed protocol.

13. B, D. Interior Gateway Routing Protocol (IGRP) uses bandwidth and delay of the line, by default, to determine the best path to a remote network.

14. E. IGRP update timers are set by default at 90 seconds. After a route has been determined to be invalid, the routing table flushes the entry after 630 seconds.

15. C. You cannot have 16 hops on a RIP network by default. If you receive a route advertised with a metric of 16, this means it is inaccessible.

16. C, E. IGRP uses bandwidth and delay of the line, by default, to determine the best path to a remote network. Delay of the line can sometimes be called the cumulative interface delay.

17. B, C.   The interface can't be shut down because the output shows that RIP is being sent out two interfaces. However, this doesn't mean that RIP is actually working and forwarding RIP updates. Another good answer is that the network command for the 192.168.50.0 was not included in the RIP configuration. Remember, we are looking for the best answers here. The other answers are not correct.

18. C. Static routes have an administrative distance of one (1) by default. Unless you change this, a static route will always be used over any other found route. IGRP has an administrative distance of 100, and RIP has an administrative distance of 120, by default.

19. C. The network 10.0.0.0 cannot be placed in the next router's routing table because it already is at 15 hops. One more hop would make the route 16 hops, and that is not valid in RIP networking.

20. B. Interior Gateway Routing Protocol (IGRP)'s default administrative distance is 100; Routing Information Protocol (RIP)'s default administrative distance is 120.

Answers to Written Lab 5

1. `ip route 172.16.10.0 255.255.255.0 172.16.20.1 150`
2. `config t, router rip, network 10.0.0.0`
3. `config t, router rip, passive-interface serial 1`
4. `config t, router igrp 10, network 172.16.0.0`
5. `config t, ip route 0.0.0.0 0.0.0.0 172.16.50.3`
6. Holddown timers
7. Route poisoning
8. Split horizon
9. `172.16.0.0`
10. `debug ip rip`

Enhanced IGRP (EIGRP) and Open Shortest Path First (OSPF)

THE CCNA EXAM TOPICS COVERED IN THIS CHAPTER INCLUDE THE FOLLOWING:

✓ **PLANNING & DESIGNING**

 ▪ Select an appropriate routing protocol based on user requirements

 ▪ Design a simple internetwork using Cisco technology

✓ **IMPLEMENTATION & OPERATION**

 ▪ Configure routing protocols given user requirements

Enhanced Interior Gateway Routing Protocol (EIGRP) is a proprietary Cisco protocol that runs on Cisco routers and internal route processors found in the Cisco distribution and core layer switches. In this chapter, I'll show you the many features of EIGRP and describe how it works, with particular focus on the unique way it discovers, selects, and advertises routes.

I'm also going to introduce you to the Open Shortest Path First (OSPF) routing protocol. You'll build a solid foundation for understanding OSPF by first becoming familiar with the terminology and internal operation of it, and then learning about OSPF's advantages over RIP. Next, we'll explore the issues surrounding implementations of OSPF in broadcast and nonbroadcast networks of various types. I'll explain how to implement single-area OSPF in specific different networking environments and demonstrate how to verify that everything is running smoothly.

EIGRP Features and Operation

Enhanced IGRP (EIGRP) is a classless, enhanced distance-vector protocol that gives us a real edge over another Cisco proprietary protocol, Interior Gateway Routing Protocol (IGRP). That's basically why it's called Enhanced IGRP. Like IGRP, EIGRP uses the concept of an autonomous system to describe the set of contiguous routers that run the same routing protocol and share routing information. But unlike IGRP, EIGRP includes the subnet mask in its route updates. And as you now know, the advertisement of subnet information allows us to use VLSM and summarization when designing our networks!

EIGRP is sometimes referred to as a *hybrid routing protocol* because it has characteristics of both distance-vector and link-state protocols. For example, EIGRP doesn't send link-state packets as OSPF does; instead, it sends traditional distance-vector updates containing information about networks plus the cost of reaching them from the perspective of the advertising router. And EIGRP has link-state characteristics as well—it synchronizes routing tables between neighbors at startup, and then sends specific updates only when topology changes occur. This makes EIGRP suitable for very large networks. EIGRP has a maximum hop count of 255.

There are a number of powerful features that make EIGRP a real standout from IGRP and other protocols. The main ones are listed here:

- Support for IP, IPX, and AppleTalk via protocol-dependent modules
- Efficient neighbor discovery
- Communication via Reliable Transport Protocol (RTP)
- Best path selection via Diffusing Update Algorithm (DUAL)

Protocol-Dependent Modules

One of the most interesting features of EIGRP is that it provides routing support for multiple Network layer protocols: IP, IPX, and AppleTalk. The only other routing protocol that comes close and supports multiple network layer protocols is *Intermediate System-to-Intermediate System (IS-IS)*, but it only supports IP and *Connectionless Network Service (CLNS)*.

EIGRP supports different Network layer protocols through the use of *protocol-dependent modules (PDMs)*. Each EIGRP PDM will maintain a separate series of tables containing the routing information that applies to a specific protocol. What this means to you is that there will be IP/EIGRP tables, IPX/EIGRP tables, and AppleTalk/EIGRP tables.

OK, I know, I know, who cares about IPX and AppleTalk? Especially when studying for the new CCNA exam? But you know, in the real world, it's definitely possible that you'll still run into IPX or AppleTalk somewhere, and it's just important to understand that EIGRP can help you in this area if you do.

Neighbor Discovery

Before EIGRP routers are willing to exchange routes with each other, they must become neighbors. There are three conditions that must be met for neighborship establishment:

- Hello or ACK received

- AS numbers match

- Identical metrics (K values)

Link-state protocols tend to use Hello messages to establish neighborship because they normally do not send out periodic route updates, and there has to be some mechanism to help neighbors realize when a new peer has moved in, or an old one has left or gone down. To maintain the neighborship relationship, EIGRP routers must also continue receiving Hellos from their neighbors.

EIGRP routers that belong to different AS don't automatically share routing information and they don't become neighbors. This behavior can be a real benefit when used in larger networks to reduce the amount of route information propagated through a specific AS. The only catch is that you might have to take care of redistribution between the different AS manually.

The only time EIGRP advertises its entire routing table is when it discovers a new neighbor and forms an adjacency with it through the exchange of Hello packets. When this happens, both neighbors advertise their entire routing tables to one another. After each has learned its neighbor's routes, only changes to the routing table are propagated from then on.

When EIGRP routers receive their neighbors' updates, they store them in a local topology table. This table contains all known routes from all known neighbors, and serves as the raw material from which the best routes are selected and placed into the routing table.

More information on the EIGRP metrics and K values can be found in the Sybex *CCNP: Building Scalable Cisco Internetworks Study Guide*, by Carl Timm, and Wade Edwards (Sybex, 2004).

Let's define some terms before we move on:

Feasible Distance   This is the best metric along all paths to a remote network, including the metric to the neighbor that is advertising that remote network. This is the route that you will find in the routing table, because it is considered the best path. The metric of a feasible distance is the metric reported by the neighbor (called reported distance), plus the metric to the neighbor reporting the route.

Reported Distance   This is the metric of a remote network, as reported by a neighbor.

Feasible Successor   A feasible successor is a path whose reported distance is less than the feasible distance, and it is considered a backup route. EIGRP will keep up to six feasible successors in the topology table. Only the one with the best metric is placed in the routing table.

By using the feasible distance, and having feasible successors in the topology table as backup links, the network can converge instantly, and updates to any neighbor are the only traffic sent from EIGRP.

Reliable Transport Protocol (RTP)

EIGRP uses a proprietary protocol, called *Reliable Transport Protocol (RTP)*, to manage the communication of messages between EIGRP-speaking routers. And as the name suggests, reliability is a key concern of this protocol. Cisco has designed a mechanism that leverages multicasts and unicasts to deliver updates quickly, and to track the receipt of the data.

When EIGRP sends multicast traffic it uses the Class D address 224.0.0.10. As I said, each EIGRP router is aware of who its neighbors are, and for each multicast it sends out, it maintains a list of the neighbors who have replied. If EIGRP doesn't get a reply from a neighbor, it will switch to using unicasts to resend the same data. If it still doesn't get a reply after 16 unicast attempts, the neighbor is declared dead. People often refer to this process as *reliable multicast*.

Routers keep track of the information they send by assigning a sequence number to each packet. With this technique, it's possible for them to detect the arrival of old, redundant, or out-of-sequence information.

Being able to do these things is highly important because EIGRP is a quiet protocol. It depends upon its ability to synchronize routing databases at startup time and then maintain the consistency of databases over time by only communicating any changes. So the permanent loss of any packets, or the out-of-order execution of packets, can result in corruption of the routing database.

Diffusing Update Algorithm (DUAL)

EIGRP uses *Diffusing Update Algorithm (DUAL)* for selecting and maintaining the best path to each remote network. This algorithm allows for the following:

- Backup route determination if one is available
- Support of Variable-Length Subnet Masks (VLSMs)
- Dynamic route recoveries
- Sending out queries for an alternate route if no route can be found

DUAL provides EIGRP with possibly the fastest route convergence time among all protocols. The key to EIGRP's speedy convergence is twofold: First, EIGRP routers maintain a copy of all of their neighbors' routes, which they use to calculate their own cost to each remote network. If the best path goes down, it may be as simple as examining the contents of the topology table to select the best replacement route. Secondly, if there isn't a good alternative in the local topology table, EIGRP routers very quickly ask their neighbors for help finding one—they aren't afraid to ask directions! Relying on other routers and leveraging the information they provide accounts for the "diffusing" character of DUAL.

And as I said, the whole idea of the Hello protocol is to enable the rapid detection of new or dead neighbors. RTP answers this call by providing a reliable mechanism for conveying and sequencing messages. Building upon this solid foundation, DUAL is responsible for selecting and maintaining information about the best paths.

Using EIGRP to Support Large Networks

EIGRP includes a bunch of cool features that make it suitable for use in large networks:

- Support for multiple AS on a single router
- Support for VLSM and summarization
- Route discovery and maintenance

Each of these capabilities adds one small piece to the complex puzzle of supporting a huge amount of routers and multiple networks.

Multiple AS

EIGRP uses autonomous system numbers to identify the collection of routers that share route information. Only routers that have the same autonomous system numbers share routes. In large networks, you can easily end up with really complicated topology and route tables, and that can markedly slow convergence during diffusing computation operations.

So what's an administrator to do to mitigate the impact of managing really big networks? Well, it's possible to divide the network into multiple distinct EIGRP autonomous systems, or AS. Each AS is populated by a contiguous series of routers, and route information can be shared among the different AS via redistribution.

The use of redistribution within EIGRP leads us to another interesting feature. Normally, the administrative distance of an EIGRP route is 90, but this is true only for what is known as an *internal EIGRP route*. These are routes originated within a specific autonomous system by EIGRP routers that are members of the same autonomous system. The other type of route is called an *external EIGRP route* and has an administrative distance of 170, which is not so good. These routes appear within EIGRP route tables courtesy of either manual or automatic redistribution, and they represent networks that originated outside of the EIGRP autonomous system. And it doesn't matter if the routes originated from another EIGRP autonomous system or from another routing protocol such as OSPF—they're all considered to be external routes when redistributed within EIGRP.

VLSM Support and Summarization

As one of the more sophisticated classless routing protocols, EIGRP supports the use of Variable-Length Subnet Masks. This is really important because it allows for the conservation of address space through the use of subnet masks that more closely fit the host requirements such as using 30-bit subnet masks for point-to-point networks. And because the subnet mask is propagated with every route update, EIGRP also supports the use of discontiguous subnets, something that gives us a lot more flexibility when designing the network's IP address plan.

What's a discontiguous network? It's one that has two subnetworks of a classful network connected together by different networks. Figure 6.1 displays a typical discontiguous network.

The subnets 172.16.10.0 and 172.16.20.0 are connected together with a 10.3.1.0 network. Each router thinks it has the only 172.16.0.0 network by default.

FIGURE 6.1   A discontiguous network

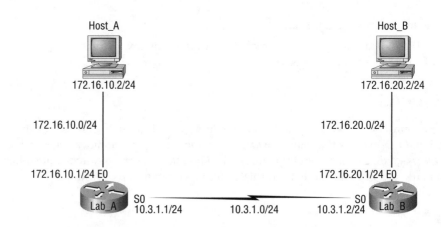

It's important to understand that discontiguous networks just won't work with RIPv1 or IGRP at all. And they don't work by default on RIPv2, EIGRP, or OSPF networks either, but no worries—there are ways to get them to work. I'll show you how to do that a bit later in this chapter.

EIGRP also supports the manual creation of summaries at any and all EIGRP routers, which can substantially reduce the size of the route table. However, EIGRP automatically summarizes networks at their classful boundaries, and Figure 6.2 shows how an EIGRP router would see the network plus the boundaries that it would auto summarize.

FIGURE 6.2   EIGRP auto summarization

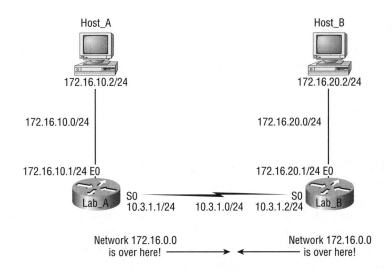

Obviously, this would never work by default! Make a note to yourself that RIP, RIPv2, and IGRP would also auto summarize these same boundaries by default, but OSPF won't.

Route Discovery and Maintenance

The hybrid nature of EIGRP is fully revealed in its approach to route discovery and maintenance. Like many link-state protocols, EIGRP supports the concept of neighbors that are discovered via a Hello process, and whose state is monitored. Like many distance-vector protocols, EIGRP uses the routing-by-rumor mechanism I talked about earlier that implies many routers never hear about a route update firsthand. Instead, they hear about it from another router that may also have heard about it from another one, and so on.

Given the huge amount of information that EIGRP routers have to collect, it makes sense that they have a place to store it, right? Well they do—EIGRP uses a series of tables to store important information about its environment:

- Neighborship table
- Topology table
- Route table

The *neighborship table* (usually referred to as the neighbor table) records information about routers with whom neighborship relationships have been formed.

The *topology table* stores the route advertisements about every route in the internetwork received from each neighbor.

The *route table* stores the routes that are currently used to make routing decisions. There would be separate copies of each of these tables for each protocol that is actively being supported by EIGRP, whether it's IP, IPX, or AppleTalk.

I am going to now discuss the EIGRP metrics and then move right into the *easy* configuration of EIGRP.

EIGRP Metrics

Another really sweet thing about EIGRP is that unlike many other protocols that use a single factor to compare routes and select the best possible path, EIGRP uses a combination of four:

- *Bandwidth*
- *Delay*
- *Load*
- *Reliability*

Like IGRP, EIGRP uses only bandwidth and delay of the line to determine the best path to a remote network by default. Cisco sometimes likes to call these path bandwidth value and cumulative line delay—go figure.

And it's worth noting that there's a fifth element, *maximum transmission unit (MTU)* size. This element has never been used in EIGRP calculations but it's a required parameter in some EIGRP-related commands, especially those involving redistribution. The value of the MTU element represents the smallest MTU value encountered along the path to the destination network.

Configuring EIGRP

Although EIGRP can be configured for IP, IPX, and AppleTalk, as a future Cisco Certified Network Associate, you really only need to focus on the configuration of IP.

There are two modes from which EIGRP commands are entered: router configuration mode and interface configuration mode. Router configuration mode enables the protocol, determines which networks will run EIGRP, and sets global characteristics. Interface configuration mode allows customization of summaries, metrics, timers, and bandwidth. This book, like the CCNA objectives, focuses on the global characteristics only.

To start an EIGRP session on a router, use the `router eigrp` command followed by the autonomous system number of your network. You then enter the network numbers connected to the router using the `network` command followed by the network number.

Let's look at an example of enabling EIGRP for autonomous system 20 on a router connected to two networks, with the network numbers being 10.3.1.0/24 and 172.16.10.0/24:

```
Router#config t
Router(config)#router eigrp 20
```

```
Router(config-router)#network 172.16.0.0
Router(config-router)#network 10.0.0.0
```

Remember—as with IGRP, you use the classful network address, which is all subnet and host bits turned off.

Say you need to stop EIGRP from working on a specific interface, such as a BRI interface or a serial connection to the Internet. To do that, you would flag the interface as passive using the `passive-interface` *interface* command. The following command shows you how to make interface Serial 0/1 a passive interface:

```
Router(config)#router eigrp 20
Router(config-router)#passive-interface serial 0/1
```

Doing this will prohibit the interface from sending or receiving Hello packets, and as a result, stop it from forming adjacencies. This means it won't send or receive route information on this interface.

> The impact of the `passive-interface` command depends upon the routing protocol under which the command is issued. For example, on an interface running RIP, the `passive-interface` command will prohibit the sending of route updates but allow their receipt. Thus, a RIP router with a passive interface will still learn about the networks advertised by other routers. This is different from EIGRP, where a `passive-interface` will neither send nor receive updates.

OK, let's configure that same network that we configured in the last chapter with RIP and IGRP. It doesn't matter that RIP and IGRP are already running—unless you're worried about bandwidth consumption and CPU cycles, of course, because EIGRP has an administrative distance of 90. Remember that IGRP is 100 and RIP is 120, so only EIGRP routes will populate the routing tables even if all three routing protocols are enabled.

Figure 6.3 shows the network that we've been working with—the same one we're going to use to configure with EIGRP.

FIGURE 6.3   Our internetwork

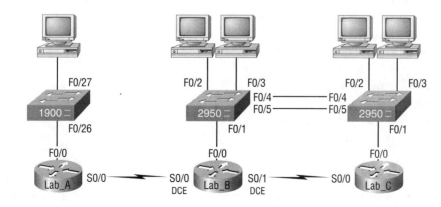

As a reminder, Table 6.1 contains the IP addresses we've been using on each interface:

TABLE 6.1   Network Addressing for the IP Network

Router	Network Address	Interface	Address
Lab_A	192.168.10.0	fa0/0	192.168.10.1
Lab_A	192.168.20.0	s0/0	192.168.20.1
Lab_B	192.168.20.0	s0/0	192.168.20.2
Lab_B	192.168.40.0	s0/1	192.168.40.1
Lab_B	192.168.30.0	fa0/0	192.168.30.1
Lab_C	192.168.40.0	s0/0	192.168.40.2
Lab_C	192.168.50.0	fa0/0	192.168.50.1

It's actually really easy to add EIGRP to our internetwork. I'll be using the same commands as I did with IGRP, only I'll add the "e."

Lab_A

The AS number, as shown in the router output below, can be any number from 1 to 65535. A router can be a member of as many AS as you want it to be, but for this book's purposes, we're just going to configure a single AS:

```
Lab_A#config t
Enter configuration commands, one per line. End with CNTL/Z.
Lab_A(config)#router eigrp ?
  <1-65535>  Autonomous system number

Lab_A(config)#router eigrp 10
Lab_A(config-router)#netw 192.168.10.0
Lab_A(config-router)#netw 192.168.20.0
Lab_A(config-router)#^Z
Lab_A#
```

The `router eigrp [as]` command turns EIGRP routing on in the router. As with RIP and IGRP, you still need to add the network numbers you want to advertise. But unlike IGRP,

EIGRP uses classless routing, which I'm sure you remember means that the subnet mask information is sent along with routing protocol updates.

Lab_B

To configure the Lab_B router, all you need to do is turn on EIGRP routing using AS 10 and then add the network numbers like this:

```
Lab_B#config t
Enter configuration commands, one per line. End with CNTL/Z.
Lab_B(config)#router eigrp 10
Lab_B(config-router)#netw 192.168.20.0
Lab_B(config-router)#netw 192.168.30.0
Lab_B(config-router)#netw 192.168.40.0
Lab_B(config-router)#^Z
Lab_B#
```

Lab_C

And to configure Lab_C, all you need to do is to again turn on EIGRP using AS 10:

```
Lab_C#config t
Enter configuration commands, one per line. End with CNTL/Z.
Lab_C(config)#router eigrp 10
Lab_C(config-router)#netw 192.168.40.0
Lab_C(config-router)#netw 192.168.50.0
Lab_C(config-router)#^Z
Lab_C#
```

That's it—really! Most routing protocols are pretty simple to set up, and EIGRP is no exception. But that's only for the basic configuration, of course!

Okay—let's take a look at our configuration with all three routing protocols configured on Lab_B:

```
!
```

```
router eigrp 10
 network 192.168.20.0
 network 192.168.30.0
 network 192.168.40.0
!
router rip
 network 192.168.20.0
 network 192.168.30.0
 network 192.168.40.0
!
router igrp 10
 network 192.168.20.0
 network 192.168.30.0
 network 192.168.40.0
!
```

Seems pretty harmless, but remember—only EIGRP routes are going to wind up in the routing table because it has the lowest administrative distance. So by having RIP and IGRP running in the background, we're not only using more memory and CPU cycles on the router, we're sucking up precious bandwidth across all our links! This can be nasty, so it's something you need to keep in mind.

There's one more configuration that you need to be aware of that has to do with auto summarization. Remember Figure 6.1 and how it demonstrated how EIGRP would auto summarize the boundaries on a discontiguous network? Look at that figure again, and then configure both routers with EIGRP:

In the figure, the Lab_A router is connected to a 172.16.10.0/24 network and the 10.3.1.0/24 backbone. The Lab_B router is connected to the 172.16.20.0/24 network and the 10.3.1.0/24 backbone. Both routers, by default, would auto summarize the classful boundaries. Here's the configuration that would make this network work:

```
Lab_A#config t
Lab_A(config)#router eigrp 100
Lab_A(config-router)#network 172.16.0.0
Lab_A(config-router)#network 10.0.0.0
Lab_A(config-router)#no auto-summary


Lab_B#config t
Lab_B(config)#router eigrp 100
Lab_B(config-router)#network 172.16.0.0
Lab_B(config-router)#network 10.0.0.0
Lab_B(config-router)#no auto-summary
```

By using the no auto-summary command, EIGRP won't advertise all networks between the two routers. If the networks were larger, you could then provide manual summarization on these same boundaries.

Verifying EIGRP

There are several commands that can be used on a router to help you troubleshoot and verify the EIGRP configuration. Table 6.2 contains all of the commands that are used in conjunction with verifying EIGRP operation, and offers a brief description of what each command does.

TABLE 6.2   EIGRP Troubleshooting Commands

Command	Description/Function
show ip route	Shows the entire routing table
show ip route eigrp	Shows only EIGRP entries in the routing table
show ip eigrp neighbors	Shows all EIGRP neighbors
show ip eigrp topology	Shows entries in the EIGRP topology table

I'll demonstrate how you would use the commands in Table 6.2 by using them on the internetwork that we just configured—not including the discontiguous network example.

The router output below is from the Lab_A router in our example:

```
Lab_A#sh ip route
[output cut]
Gateway of last resort is not set
D    192.168.30.0/24 [90/2172416] via 192.168.20.2,00:04:36, Serial0/0
C    192.168.10.0/24 is directly connected, FastEthernet0/0
D    192.168.40.0/24 [90/2681856] via 192.168.20.2,00:04:36, Serial0/0
C    192.168.20.0/24 is directly connected, Serial0/0
D    192.168.50.0/24 [90/2707456] via 192.168.20.2,00:04:35, Serial0/0
Lab_A#
```

You can see that all routes are there in the routing table. Notice that EIGRP routes are indicated with simply a *D* designation (DUAL), and that the administrative distance of these routes is 90. This represents internal EIGRP routes.

This output displays Lab_B's routing table:

```
Lab_B#sh ip route
[output cut]
Gateway of last resort is not set
C    192.168.30.0/24 is directly connected, FastEthernet0/0
D    192.168.10.0/24 [90/2195456] via 192.168.20.1, 00:06:30, Serial0/0
C    192.168.40.0/24 is directly connected, Serial0/1
C    192.168.20.0/24 is directly connected, Serial0/0
D    192.168.50.0/24 [90/2195456] via 192.168.40.2, 00:06:29, Serial0/1
Lab_B#
```

And here's Lab_C's routing table:

```
Lab_C#sh ip route
[output cut]
Gateway of last resort is not set
D    192.168.30.0/24 [90/2707456] via 192.168.40.1, Serial0/0
D    192.168.10.0/24 [90/2707456] via 192.168.40.1, 00:07:56, Serial0/0
C    192.168.40.0/24 is directly connected, Serial0/0
D    192.168.20.0/24 [90/2195456] via 192.168.40.1, Serial0/0
C    192.168.50.0/24 is directly connected, FastEthernet0/0
Lab_C#
```

Since we're on the Lab_C router, let's see what it shows us in the neighbor table:

```
Lab_C#show ip eigrp neighbor
H   Address Interface  Hold  Uptime    SRTT  RTO  Q   Seq Type
                       (sec)           (ms)      Cnt Num
0   192.168.40.1 Se0    12   00:13:24   26   200  0   7
```

We read the information in this output like this:

- The H field indicates the order in which the neighbor was discovered.

- The hold time is how long this router will wait for a Hello packet to arrive from a specific neighbor.

- The uptime indicates how long the neighborship has been established.

- The SRTT field is the smooth round-trip timer—an indication of the time it takes for a round-trip from this router to its neighbor and back. This value is used to determine how long to wait after a multicast for a reply from this neighbor. If a reply isn't received in time, the router will switch to using unicasts in an attempt to complete the communication. The time between multicast attempts is specified by the...

- Retransmission Time Out (RTO) field, is the amount of time EIGRP waits before retransmitting a packet from the retransmission queue to a neighbor.

- The Q value indicates whether there are any outstanding messages in the queue—consistently large values would indicate a problem.

- The Seq field indicates the sequence number of the last update from that neighbor—something that's used to maintain synchronization and avoid duplicate or out-of-sequence processing of messages.

Now let's see what's in the Lab_C topology table by using the show ip eigrp topology command:

```
Lab_C#show ip eigrp topology
Codes: P - Passive, A - Active, U - Update, Q - Query, R - Reply,
       r - reply Status, s - sia Status
P 192.168.40.0/24, 1 successors, FD is 2169856
        via Connected, Serial0
P 192.168.50.0/24, 1 successors, FD is 281600
        via Connected, Ethernet0
P 192.168.10.0/24, 1 successors, FD is 2707456
        via 192.168.40.1 (2707456/2195456), Serial0/0
P 192.168.30.0/24, 1 successors, FD is 2172416
        via 192.168.40.1 (2172416/28160), Serial0/0
P 192.168.20.0/24, 1 successors, FD is 2681856
        via 192.168.40.1 (2681856/2169856), Serial0/0
Lab_C#
```

Notice that every route is preceded by a *P*. What this means is that the route is in the *passive state,* which is good. Routes in the *active state* indicate that the router has lost its path to this network and is searching for a replacement. Each entry also indicates the feasible distance, or FD, to each remote network plus the next-hop neighbor through which packets will travel to this destination. Each entry also has two numbers in parentheses ( ). The first indicates the feasible distance, and the second the advertised distance to a remote network.

You've learned a lot about EIGRP so far, but stick around—you're not done with this chapter just yet! It's time now to get into the skinny on OSPF.

Open Shortest Path First (OSPF) Basics

Open Shortest Path First (OSPF) is an open standards routing protocol that's been implemented by a wide variety of network vendors, including Cisco. If you have multiple routers, and not all of them are Cisco (what!), then you can't use EIGRP, can you? So your remaining options are basically RIPv1, RIPv2, or OSPF. If it's a large network, then, really, your only options are OSPF or something called route redistribution—a translation service between routing protocols.

This works by using the Dijkstra algorithm. First, a shortest path tree is constructed, and then the routing table is populated with the resulting best paths. OSPF converges quickly, although perhaps not as quickly as EIGRP, and it supports multiple, equal-cost routes to the same destination. But unlike EIGRP, it only supports IP routing—not really a negative to using OSPF, if you ask me!

OSPF is the first link-state routing protocol that most people are introduced to, so it's useful to see how it compares to more traditional distance-vector protocols such as RIPv1. Table 6.3 gives you a comparison of these two protocols.

TABLE 6.3 OSPF and RIPv1 comparison

Characteristic	OSPF	RIPv1
Type of protocol	Link-state	Distance-vector
Classless support	Yes	No
VLSM support	Yes	No
Auto summarization	No	Yes
Manual summarization	Yes	No
Route propagation	Multicast on change	Periodic broadcast
Path metric	Bandwidth	Hops
Hop count limit	None	15
Convergence	Fast	Slow
Peer authentication	Yes	No
Hierarchical network	Yes (using areas)	No (flat only)
Route computation	Dijkstra	Bellman-Ford

OSPF has many features beyond the few I've listed in Table 6.3, and all of them contribute to a fast, scalable, and robust protocol that can be actively deployed in thousands of production networks.

OSPF is supposed to be designed in a hierarchical fashion, which basically means that you can separate the larger internetwork into smaller internetworks called areas. This is the best design for OSPF. The reasons for creating OSPF in a hierarchical design include:

- To decrease routing overhead
- To speed up convergence
- To confine network instability to single areas of the network

This does not make configuring OSPF easier, but more elaborate and difficult.

Figure 6.4 shows a typical OSPF simple design.

Notice how each router connects to the backbone—called area 0, or the backbone area. OSPF must have an area 0, and all routers should connect to this area if at all possible, but routers that connect other areas to the backbone within an AS are called Area Border Routers (ABRs). Still, at least one interface must be in area 0.

OSPF runs inside an autonomous system, but can also connect multiple autonomous systems together. The router that connects these AS together is called an Autonomous System Boundary Router (ASBR).

Ideally, you would create other areas of networks to help keep route updates to a minimum, and to keep problems from propagating throughout the network. But that's beyond the scope of this chapter. Just make note of it.

As in the section on EIGRP, I'll first cover the essential terminology you need to understand OSPF.

FIGURE 6.4   OSPF design example

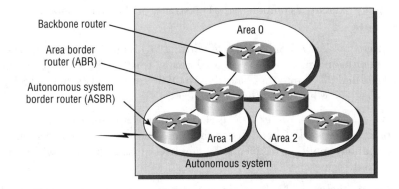

OSPF Terminology

Imagine how challenging it would be if you were given a map and compass but had no knowledge of east or west, north or south, river or mountain, lake or desert. You'd probably not get very far putting your new tools to good use without knowing about this stuff. For this reason, you'll begin your exploration of OSPF with a long list of terminology that will prevent you from getting lost in the later sections. The following are important OSPF terms to familiarize yourself with before you proceed:

Link   A *link* is a network or router interface assigned to any given network. When an interface is added to the OSPF process, it's considered by OSPF to be a link. This link, or interface, will have state information associated with it (up or down) as well as one or more IP addresses.

Router ID   The *Router ID (RID)* is an IP address used to identify the router. Cisco chooses the Router ID by using the highest IP address of all configured loopback interfaces. If no loopback interfaces are configured with addresses, OSPF will choose the highest IP address of all active physical interfaces.

Neighbors   *Neighbors* are two or more routers that have an interface on a common network, such as two routers connected on a point-to-point serial link.

Adjacency   An *adjacency* is a relationship between two OSPF routers that permits the direct exchange of route updates. OSPF is really picky about sharing routing information—unlike EIGRP, which directly shares routes with all of its neighbors. Instead, OSPF directly shares routes only with neighbors that have also established adjacencies. And not all neighbors will become adjacent—this depends upon both the type of network and the configuration of the routers.

Neighborship database   The *neighborship database* is a list of all OSPF routers for which Hello packets have been seen. A variety of details, including the Router ID and state, are maintained on each router in the neighborship database.

Topology database   The *topology database* contains information from all of the Link State Advertisement (LSA) packets that have been received for an area. The router uses the information from the topology database as input into the Dijkstra algorithm that computes the shortest path to every network.

Link State Advertisement   A *Link State Advertisement (LSA)* is an OSPF data packet containing link-state and routing information that's shared among OSPF routers. There are different types of LSA packets, and I'll go into these shortly. An OSPF router will exchange LSA packets only with routers to which it has established adjacencies.

Designated router   A *designated router (DR)* is elected whenever OSPF routers are connected to the same multi-access network. Cisco likes to call these "broadcast" networks, but really, they are networks that have multiple recipients. Try not to confuse multiaccess with multipoint, which can be easy to do sometimes.

A prime example is an Ethernet LAN. To minimize the number of adjacencies formed, a DR is chosen (elected) to disseminate/receive routing information to/from the remaining routers on the broadcast network or link. This ensures that their topology tables are synchronized. All routers on the shared network will establish adjacencies with the DR and backup designated router (BDR)—I'll define this next. The election is won by the router with the highest priority, and the Router ID is used as a tiebreaker if the priority of more than one router turns out to be the same.

Backup designated router   A *backup designated router (BDR)* is a hot standby for the DR on multi-access links (remember that Cisco sometimes likes to call these "broadcast" networks). The BDR receives all routing updates from OSPF adjacent routers, but doesn't flood LSA updates.

OSPF areas   An *OSPF area* is a grouping of contiguous networks and routers. All routers in the same area share a common Area ID. Because a router can be a member of more than one area at a time, the Area ID is associated with specific interfaces on the router. This would allow some interfaces to belong to area 1, while the remaining interfaces can belong to area 0. All of the routers within the same area have the same topology table. When configuring OSPF, you've got to remember that there must be an area 0, and that this is typically configured on the routers that connect to the backbone of the network. Areas also play a role in establishing a hierarchical network organization—something that really enhances the scalability of OSPF!

Broadcast (multi-access)   *Broadcast (multi-access) networks* such as Ethernet allow multiple devices to connect to (or access) the same network, as well as provide a *broadcast* ability in which a single packet is delivered to all nodes on the network. In OSPF, a DR and a BDR must be elected for each broadcast multi-access network.

Nonbroadcast multi-access   *Nonbroadcast multi-access (NBMA) networks* are types such as Frame Relay, X.25, and Asynchronous Transfer Mode (ATM). These networks allow for multi-access, but have no broadcast ability like Ethernet. So, NBMA networks require special OSPF configuration to function properly and neighbor relationships must be defined.

> DR and BDR are elected on broadcast and nonbroadcast multi-access networks.

Point-to-point   *Point-to-point* refers to a type of network topology consisting of a direct connection between two routers that provides a single communication path. The point-to-point connection can be physical, as in a serial cable directly connecting two routers, or it can be logical, as in two routers that are thousands of miles apart yet connected by a circuit in a Frame Relay network. In either case, this type of configuration eliminates the need for DRs or BDRs—but neighbors are discovered automatically.

Point-to-multipoint   *Point-to-multipoint* refers to a type of network topology consisting of a series of connections between a single interface on one router and multiple destination routers. All of the interfaces on all of the routers sharing the point-to-multipoint connection belong to the same network. As with point-to-point, no DRs or BDRs are needed.

All of these terms play an important part in understanding the operation of OSPF, so, again, make sure you're familiar with each of them. Reading through the rest of this chapter will help you to place the terms within their proper context.

SPF Tree Calculation

Within an area, each router calculates the best/shortest path to every network in that same area. This calculation is based upon the information collected in the topology database and an algorithm called *shortest path first (SPF)*. Picture each router in an area constructing a tree—much like a family tree—where the router is the root, and all other networks are arranged along the branches and leaves. This is the shortest path tree used by the router to insert routes into the routing table.

It's important to understand that this tree contains only networks that exist in the same area as the router itself does. If a router has interfaces in multiple areas, then separate trees will be constructed for each area. One of the key criteria considered during the route selection process of the SPF algorithm is the metric or cost of each potential path to a network. But this SPF calculation doesn't apply to routes from other areas.

OSPF uses a metric referred to as *cost*. A cost is associated with every outgoing interface included in an SPF tree. The cost of the entire path is the sum of costs of the outgoing interfaces along the path. Because cost is an arbitrary value as defined in RFC 2338, Cisco had to implement its own method of calculating the cost for each OSPF-enabled interface. Cisco uses a simple equation of 10^8/bandwidth. The bandwidth is the configured bandwidth for the interface. Using this rule, a 100Mbps Fast Ethernet interface would have a default OSPF cost of 1 and a 10Mbps Ethernet interface would have a cost of 10.

 An interface set with a bandwidth of 64000 would have a default cost of 1563.

This value may be overridden by using the `ip ospf cost` command. The cost is manipulated by changing the value to a number within the range of 1 to 65,535. Because the cost is assigned to each link, the value must be changed on the same interface that you want to change the cost on.

 Cisco bases link cost on bandwidth. Other vendors may use other metrics to calculate a given link's cost. When connecting links between routers from different vendors, you may have to adjust the cost to match another vendor's router. Both routers must assign the same cost to the link for OSPF to work.

Configuring OSPF

Configuring basic OSPF isn't as simple as RIP, IGRP, and EIGRP, and it can get can really complex once the many options that are allowed within OSPF are factored in. But that's okay—you're only interested in the basic single area OSPF configuration for the CCNA exam. The following sections describe how to configure single area OSPF.

These two elements are the basic elements of OSPF configuration:

- Enabling OSPF
- Configuring OSPF areas

Enabling OSPF

The easiest and also least scalable way to configure OSPF is to just use a single area. Doing this requires a minimum of two commands.

The command you use to activate the OSPF routing process is:

```
Lab_A(config)#router ospf ?
<1-65535>
```

A value in the range 1–65535 identifies the OSPF Process ID. It's a unique number on this router that groups a series of OSPF configuration commands under a specific running process. Different OSPF routers don't have to use the same Process ID in order to communicate. It's purely a local value that essentially has little meaning.

You can have more than one OSPF process running simultaneously on the same router if you want, but this isn't the same as running multi-area OSPF. The second process will maintain an entirely separate copy of its topology table and manage its communications independently of the first process. And because the CCNA objectives only cover single-area OSPF with each router running a single OSPF process, that's what I'm going to focus on in this book.

Configuring OSPF Areas

After identifying the OSPF process, you need to identify the interfaces that you want to activate OSPF communications on, as well as the area in which each resides. This will also configure the networks you're going to advertise to others. OSPF uses wildcards in the configuration—which are also used in access-list configurations (covered in Chapter 10).

Here's an OSPF basic configuration example for you:

```
Lab_A#config t
Lab_A(config)#router ospf 1
Lab_A(config-router)#network 10.0.0.0 0.255.255.255
 area ?
  <0-4294967295>  OSPF area ID as a decimal value
  A.B.C.D         OSPF area ID in IP address format
Lab_A(config-router)#network 10.0.0.0 0.255.255.255
 area 0
```

Remember, the OSPF Process ID number is irrelevant. It can be the same on every router on the network, or it can be different—doesn't matter. It's locally significant and just enables the OSPF routing on the router.

The arguments of the network command are the network number (10.0.0.0) and the wildcard mask (0.255.255.255). The combination of these two numbers identifies the interfaces that OSPF will operate on, and will also be included in its OSPF LSA advertisements. OSPF will use this command to find any interface on the router configured in the 10.0.0.0 network, and it will place any interface it finds into area 0. Notice that you can create about 4.2 billion areas (I doubt a router will let you actually create that many, but you can certainly name them using the numbers up to 4.2 billion). You can also label an area using an IP address format.

A quick review of wildcards: A 0 octet in the wildcard mask indicates that the corresponding octet in the network must match exactly. On the other hand, a 255 indicates that you don't care what the corresponding octet is in the network number. A network and wildcard mask combination of 1.1.1.1 0.0.0.0 would match 1.1.1.1 only, and nothing else. This is really useful if you want to activate OSPF on a specific interface in a very clear and simple way. If you insist on matching a range of networks, the network and wildcard mask combination of 1.1.0.0 0.0.255.255 would match anything in the range 1.1.0.0–1.1.255.255. Because of this, it's simpler and safer to stick to using wildcard masks of 0.0.0.0 and identify each OSPF interface individually.

The final argument is the area number. It indicates the area to which the interfaces identified in the network and wildcard mask portion belong. Remember that OSPF routers will only become neighbors if their interfaces share a network that's configured to belong to the same area number. The format of the area number is either a decimal value from the range 1–4294967295 or a value represented in standard dotted-decimal notation. For example, Area 0.0.0.0 is a legitimate area, and is identical to area 0.

Okay—now it's time for some fun! Let's configure our internetwork with OSPF using just area 0. Before we do that, we've got to remove IGRP and EIGRP, because OSPF has an administrative distance of 110. (IGRP is 100 and EIGRP is 90—but you already knew that, right?) And while we're at it, let's remove RIP too, just because we should.

There's a bunch of different ways to configure OSPF and, as I said, the simplest and easiest is to use the wildcard mask of 0.0.0.0. But I want to demonstrate that we can configure each router differently with OSPF and still come up with the exact same result. This is one reason why OSPF is more fun than other routing protocols—it gives us all a lot more ways to screw things up!

Lab_A

So here's the Lab_A router's configuration:

```
Lab_A#config t
Enter configuration commands, one per line.  End with CNTL/Z.
Lab_A(config)#no router eigrp 10
Lab_A(config)#no router igrp 10
Lab_A(config)#no router rip
Lab_A(config)#router ospf 132
Lab_A(config-router)#network 192.168.10.1 0.0.0.0 area 0
Lab_A(config-router)#network 192.168.20.1 0.0.0.0 area 0
Lab_A(config-router)#^Z
Lab_A#
```

Hmmmm—it seems we have a few things to discuss here. First, I removed EIGRP, IGRP, and RIP, then I added OSPF. So why did I use OSPF 132? It really doesn't matter—the number is irrelevant!

The two network commands are pretty straightforward. I typed in the IP address of each interface and used the wildcard mask of 0.0.0.0, which means that the IP address must match each octet exactly. Now, let's go on to Lab_B. We're going to use a different configuration.

Lab_B

The Lab_B router is directly connected to networks 20, 30, and 40. Instead of typing in each interface, I can use one network command and still make it work:

```
Lab_B#config t
Enter configuration commands, one per line.  End with CNTL/Z.
Lab_B(config)#no router eigrp 10
Lab_B(config)#no router igrp 10
Lab_B(config)#no router rip
Lab_B(config)#router ospf 1
Lab_B(config-router)#network 192.168.0.0 0.0.255.255 area0
                                                        ^
```

% Invalid input detected at '^' marker.

Lab_B(config-router)#**network 192.168.0.0 0.0.255.255 area 0**
Lab_B(config-router)#**^Z**
Lab_B#

Okay—other then my little typo, where I forgot to place a space between the area command and the area number, this is a fast, efficient configuration.

I first disabled the other routing protocols. Then I turned on OSPF routing process 1 and added the network command 192.168.0.0 with a wildcard of 0.0.255.255. What this said is just, "Find any interface that starts with 192.168, and place those interfaces into area 0." Quick and easy—slick!

Lab_C

Let's give the Lab_C router that's directly connected to networks 40 and 50 some attention:

Lab_C#**config t**
Enter configuration commands, one per line. End with CNTL/Z.
Lab_C(config)#**no router eigrp 10**

Lab_C(config)#**no router igrp 10**
Lab_C(config)#**no router rip**
Lab_C(config)#**router ospf 64999**
Lab_C(config-router)#**network 192.168.40.0 0.0.0.255 area 0**
Lab_C(config-router)#**network 192.168.50.0 0.0.0.255 area 0**
Lab_C(config-router)#**^Z**
Lab_C#

Cool! Now that we've configured all the routers with OSPF, what do we do next? ...Miller Time? Sorry—not yet. It's that verification thing again. We still have to make sure that OSPF is really working! We will do that in the next section.

Verifying OSPF Configuration

There are several ways to verify proper OSPF configuration and operation, and in the following sections I'll show you the OSPF show commands you need to know in order to do this. We're going to start by taking a quick look at the routing table of each router.

So, let's issue a show ip route command on the Lab_A router:

Lab_A#**sh ip route**
Gateway of last resort is not set
O   192.168.30.0/24 [110/65] via 192.168.20.2, 00:01:07, Serial0/0

```
C    192.168.10.0/24 is directly connected, FastEthernet0/0
O    192.168.40.0/24 [110/128] via 192.168.20.2, 00:01:07, Serial0/0
C    192.168.20.0/24 is directly connected, Serial0/0
O    192.168.50.0/24 [110/138] via 192.168.20.2, 00:01:07, Serial0/0
Lab_A#
```

The Lab_A router shows the OSPF found routes for networks 30, 40, and 50, with the O representing OSPF internet routes.

Now let's see what the Lab_B router found:

```
Lab_B#sh ip route
Gateway of last resort is not set
C    192.168.30.0/24 is directly connected, FastEthernet0/0
O    192.168.10.0/24 [110/74] via 192.168.20.1, 00:00:35, Serial0/2
C    192.168.40.0/24 is directly connected, Serial0/0
C    192.168.20.0/24 is directly connected, Serial0/2
O    192.168.50.0/24 [110/74] via 192.168.40.2, 00:00:35, Serial0/0
Lab_B#
```

The Lab_B router shows the OSPF found routes for 10 and 50—nice!

One more router to verify—Lab C:

```
Lab_C#sh ip route
Gateway of last resort is not set
O    192.168.30.0/24 [110/65] via 192.168.40.1, 00:00:02, Serial0
O    192.168.10.0/24 [110/138] via 192.168.40.1, 00:00:02, Serial0
C    192.168.40.0/24 is directly connected, Serial0
O    192.168.20.0/24 [110/128] via 192.168.40.1, 00:00:02, Serial0
C    192.168.50.0/24 is directly connected, Ethernet0
Lab_C#
```

The Lab_C router shows all the routes in the internetwork, so even though I configured each router differently with OSPF, notice that everything is working great.

In the following sections, I am going to show you the OSPF verification commands that you need to know.

The *show ip ospf* Command

The show ip ospf command is used to display OSPF information for one or all OSPF processes running on the router. Information contained therein includes the Router ID, area information, SPF statistics, and LSA timer information. Let's check out the output from the Lab_A router:

```
Lab_A#sho ip ospf
Routing Process "ospf 132" with ID 192.168.20.1
```

```
Supports only single TOS(TOS0) routes
Supports opaque LSA
SPF schedule delay 5 secs, Hold time between two SPFs 10 secs
Minimum LSA interval 5 secs. Minimum LSA arrival 1 secs
Number of external LSA 0. Checksum Sum 0x000000
Number of opaque AS LSA 0. Checksum Sum 0x000000
Number of DCbitless external and opaque AS LSA 0
Number of DoNotAge external and opaque AS LSA 0
Number of areas in this router is 1. 1 normal 0 stub 0 nssa
External flood list length 0
   Area BACKBONE(0)
       Number of interfaces in this area is 2
       Area has no authentication
       SPF algorithm executed 5 times
       Area ranges are
       Number of LSA 3. Checksum Sum 0x020E9A
       Number of opaque link LSA 0. Checksum Sum 0x000000
       Number of DCbitless LSA 0
       Number of indication LSA 0
       Number of DoNotAge LSA 0
       Flood list length 0
```

Notice the Router ID (RID) of 192.168.20.1, which is the highest IP address in the router.

The *show ip ospf database* Command

The information displayed by the show ip ospf database command indicates the number of links and the neighboring router's ID and is the topology database I mentioned earlier. The output is broken down by area. Here's a sample output, again from Lab A:

```
Lab_A#sh ip ospf database

        OSPF Router with ID (192.168.20.1) (Process ID 132)

            Router Link States (Area 0)

Link ID        ADV Router      Age     Seq#      Checksum Link count
192.168.20.1   192.168.20.1    648     0x80000003 0x005E2B 3
192.168.40.1   192.168.40.1    351     0x80000003 0x00E32F 5
192.168.40.2   192.168.40.2    192     0x80000003 0x00CD40 3
Lab_A#
```

The router output shows the link ID (remember that an interface is also a link) and the RID of the router on that link under the ADV router (advertising router).

The *show ip ospf interface* Command

The show ip ospf interface command displays all interface-related OSPF information. Data is displayed about OSPF information for all interfaces or for specified interfaces. The information displayed by this command includes:

- Interface IP address
- Area assignment
- Process ID
- Router ID
- Network type
- Cost
- Priority
- DR/BDR (if applicable)
- Timer intervals
- Adjacent neighbor information

Here's the output from the Lab_A router:

```
Lab_A#show ip ospf interface
Serial0/0 is up, line protocol is up
  Internet Address 192.168.20.1/24, Area 0
  Process ID 132, Router ID 192.168.20.1, Network Type POINT_TO_POINT, Cost: 64
  Transmit Delay is 1 sec, State POINT_TO_POINT,
  Timer intervals configured, Hello 10, Dead 40, Wait 40, Retransmit 5
    Hello due in 00:00:06
  Index 2/2, flood queue length 0
  Next 0x0(0)/0x0(0)
  Last flood scan length is 1, maximum is 1
  Last flood scan time is 0 msec, maximum is 0 msec
  Neighbor Count is 1, Adjacent neighbor count is 1
    Adjacent with neighbor 192.168.40.1
  Suppress hello for 0 neighbor(s)
FastEthernet0/0 is up, line protocol is up
  Internet Address 192.168.10.1/24, Area 0
  Process ID 132, Router ID 192.168.20.1, Network Type BROADCAST, Cost: 10
  Transmit Delay is 1 sec, State DR, Priority 1
  Designated Router (ID) 192.168.20.1, Interface address 192.168.10.1
  No backup designated router on this network
```

```
 Timer intervals configured, Hello 10, Dead 40, Wait 40, Retransmit 5
    Hello due in 00:00:04
 Index 1/1, flood queue length 0
 Next 0x0(0)/0x0(0)
 --More--
```

The *show ip ospf neighbor* Command

The show ip ospf neighbor command is super-useful because it summarizes the pertinent OSPF information regarding neighbors and the adjacency state. If a DR or BDR exists, that information will also be displayed. Here's a sample:

```
Lab_A#sh ip ospf neighbor

Neighbor ID   Pri  State      Dead Time  Address       Interface
192.168.40.1   1   FULL/  -   00:00:30   192.168.20.2  Serial0/0
Lab_A#
```

The *show ip protocols* Command

The show ip protocols command is also useful whether you're running OSPF, EIGRP, IGRP, RIP, BGP, IS-IS, or any other routing protocol that can be configured on your router. It provides an excellent overview of the actual operation of all currently running protocols.

Check out the output from the Lab_A router:

```
Lab_A#sh ip protocols
Routing Protocol is "ospf 132"
  Outgoing update filter list for all interfaces is not set
  Incoming update filter list for all interfaces is not set
  Router ID 192.168.20.1
  Number of areas in this router is 1. 1 normal 0 stub 0 nssa
  Maximum path: 4
  Routing for Networks:
    192.168.10.1 0.0.0.0 area 0
    192.168.20.1 0.0.0.0 area 0
  Routing Information Sources:
    Gateway          Distance     Last Update
    192.168.40.1          110     00:05:56
    192.168.40.2          110     00:05:56
    192.168.20.1          110     00:05:56
  Distance: (default is 110)

Lab_A#
```

Based upon this output, you can determine the OSPF Process ID, OSPF Router ID, type of OSPF area, networks and areas configured for OSPF, and OSPF Router IDs of neighbors—that's a lot. Read, efficient!

OSPF and Loopback Interfaces

Configuring loopback interfaces when using the OSPF routing protocol is important, and Cisco suggests using them whenever you configure OSPF on a router.

Loopback interfaces are logical interfaces, which means they are not real router interfaces. They can be used for diagnostic purposes as well as OSPF configuration. The reason you want to configure a loopback interface on a router is because if you don't, the highest IP address on a router will become that router's RID. The RID is used to advertise the routes as well as elect the DR and BDR.

Let's say that you are not using loopback interfaces and the serial interface of your router is the RID of the router because it has the highest IP address of active interfaces. If this interface goes down, then a re-election must occur on who is going to be the DR and BDR on the network. Not necessarily a big deal, but what happens if this is a flapping link (going up/down)? The routers will not converge because the election is never completed. This is obviously a problem with OSPF. Loopback interfaces solve this problem because they never go down and the RID of the router never changes.

In the following sections, you will see how to configure loopback interfaces, and how to verify loopback addresses and RIDs.

Configuring Loopback Interfaces

Configuring loopback interfaces rocks mostly because it's the easiest part of OSPF configuration, and we all need a break about now—right? So hang on, gang—we're in the home stretch!

First, let's see what the RID is on the Lab_A router with the show ip ospf command:

```
Lab_A#sh ip ospf
 Routing Process "ospf 132" with ID 192.168.20.1
[output cut]
```

We can see that the RID is 192.168.20.1, or the serial 0/0 interface of the router. So let's configure a loopback interface using a completely different IP addressing scheme:

```
Lab_A#config t
Enter configuration commands, one per line.  End with CNTL/Z.
Lab_A(config)#int loopback 0
Lab_A(config-if)#ip address 172.16.10.1 255.255.255.0
Lab_A(config-if)#no shut
Lab_A(config-if)#^Z
```

Lab_A#

The IP scheme really doesn't matter here, but each router has to be in a separate subnet. Let's configure Lab_B now:

```
Lab_B#config t
Enter configuration commands, one per line.  End with CNTL/Z.
Lab_B(config)#int lo0
Lab_B(config-if)#ip address 172.16.20.1 255.255.255.0
Lab_B(config-if)#no shut
Lab_B(config-if)#^Z
Lab_B#
```

Here is the configuration of the loopback interface on Lab_C:

```
Lab_C#config t
Enter configuration commands, one per line.  End with CNTL/Z.
Lab_C(config)#int lo0
Lab_C(config-if)#ip address 172.16.30.1 255.255.255.0
Lab_C(config-if)#no shut
Lab_C(config-if)#^Z
Lab_C#
```

The only question left to answer is whether you want to advertise the loopback interfaces under OSPF. There are pros and cons to using an address that won't be advertised, versus using an address that will be... Using an unadvertised address saves on real IP address space, but the address won't appear in the OSPF table, so you can't ping it. So basically, what you're faced with here is a choice that equals a trade-off between the ease of debugging the network and conservation of address space—what to do? A really tight strategy is to use a private IP address scheme as I did. Do this, and all will be good!

Verifying Loopbacks and RIDs

To verify your loopback addresses, use show running-config—it's the easiest way to do it:

```
Lab_C#show running-config
!
hostname Lab_C
!
interface Loopback0
 ip address 172.16.30.1 255.255.255.0
!
```

And to verify the new RIDs of each router, you can use the show ip ospf interface command, the show ip ospf database, or just the show ip ospf command. All three are shown below:

```
Lab_C#sho ip ospf database
          OSPF Router with ID (172.16.30.1) (Process ID 64999)
              Router Link States (Area 0)
Link ID          ADV Router      Age  Seq# Checksum Link count
172.16.10.1      172.16.10.1     689  0x80000002 0xB404  3
172.16.20.1      172.16.20.1     139  0x8000000A 0x4AB1  5
172.16.30.1      172.16.30.1     138  0x80000002 0x2B14  3
```

The show ip ospf database shows the RID in the first line of output. The show ip ospf interface also displays this information, but you have to dig for it a little more:

```
Lab_C#show ip ospf interface
FastEthernet0/0 is up, line protocol is up
  Internet Address 192.168.50.1/24, Area 0
  Process ID 64999, Router ID 172.16.30.1, Network Type BROADCAST, Cost: 10
  Transmit Delay is 1 sec, State DR, Priority 1
  Designated Router (ID) 172.16.30.1, Interface address 192.168.50.1
  No backup designated router on this network
[output cut]
```

The show ip ospf command shows the RID in the first line of output:

```
Lab_C#show ip ospf
Routing Process "ospf 64999" with ID 172.16.30.1 and Domain ID 0.0.253.231
 [output cut]
```

An important thing to keep in mind is that the new RIDs didn't show up after setting the loopback interface on each router until I rebooted the routers!

> **NOTE** It's important to remember that although the IP address on the interface is higher than the loopback's address, the highest loopback address always beats any physical interface.

Summary

I know—this chapter has been, you could say, a touch on the extensive side. But it's really important! EIGRP, the main focus of the chapter, is a hybrid of link-state routing and distance-vector protocols. It allows for unequal-cost load balancing, controlled routing updates, and formal neighbor adjacencies.

EIGRP uses the capabilities of the Reliable Transport Protocol (RTP) to communicate between neighbors and utilizes the Diffusing Update Algorithm (DUAL) to compute the best path to each remote network.

EIGRP also supports large networks through features such as support for VLSM, discontiguous networks, and summarization. The ability to configure EIGRP behavior over NBMA networks also makes it a really hot protocol for large networks.

I also went over the configuration of EIGRP, and explored a number of troubleshooting commands.

This chapter provided you with a great deal of information about OSPF. It's really difficult to include everything about OSPF because so much of it falls outside the scope of this chapter and book, but know that I've given you the info you need for the exam, plus a few tips here and there, so you're good to go. As long as you make sure you've got what I presented to you dialed in, that is!

I talked about a lot of OSPF topics, including terminology, operations, configuration as well as verification and monitoring.

Each of these topics encompasses quite a bit of information—the terminology section just scratched the surface of OSPF. But again, you've got the goods for the exam—things like configuring single area OSPF. Finally, I gave you a tight survey of commands useful in observing the operation of OSPF so you can verify that things are moving along as they should. So eat it all up, and you're set!

Exam Essentials

Know EIGRP features.   EIGRP is a classless, advanced distance-vector protocol that supports IP, IPX, and AppleTalk. EIGRP uses a unique algorithm, called DUAL, to maintain route information and uses RTP to communicate with other EIGRP routers reliably.

Know how to configure EIGRP.   Be able to configure basic EIGRP. This is configured the same as IGRP with classful addresses.

Know how to verify EIGRP operation.   Know all of the EIGRP show commands and be familiar with their output and the interpretation of the main components of their output.

Compare OSPF and RIPv1.   OSPF is a link-state protocol that supports VLSM and classless routing; RIPv1 is a distance-vector protocol that does not support VLSM and supports only classful routing.

Know how OSPF routers become neighbors and/or adjacent.   OSPF routers become neighbors when each router sees the other's Hello packets.

Know the different OSPF NBMA network types.   There are five different OSPF network types that Cisco routers can be configured to support. Two of these are non-proprietary based (nonbroadcast and point-to-multipoint) and three are Cisco proprietary (broadcast, point-to-point, and point-to-multipoint nonbroadcast). Each network type is further characterized by how routers become adjacent and whether they require the election of a DR/BDR.

Be able to configure single area OSPF. A minimal single-area configuration involves only two commands: `router ospf` *process-id* *and* `network` *x.x.x.x* *y.y.y.y* `area` *Z*.

Be able to verify operation of OSPF. There are many `show` commands that provide useful details on OSPF, and it is useful to be completely familiar with the output of each: `show ip ospf`, `show ip ospf database`, `show ip ospf interface`, `show ip ospf neighbor`, and `show ip protocols`.

Key Terms

Before you take the exam, be certain you are familiar with the following terms:

active state	neighbors
adjacency	neighborship database
backup designated router (BDR)	neighborship table
bandwidth	nonbroadcast multi-access (NBMA) networks
broadcast (multi-access) networks	Open Shortest Path First (OSPF)
Connectionless Network Service (CLNS)	OSPF area
delay	passive state
designated router (DR)	point-to-multipoint
Diffusing Update Algorithm (DUAL)	point-to-point
Enhanced IGRP (EIGRP)	protocol-dependent modules (PDMs)
external EIGRP route	reliability
hybrid routing protocol	reliable multicast
Intermediate System-to-Intermediate System (IS-IS)	Reliable Transport Protocol (RTP)
internal EIGRP route	route table
link	Router ID (RID)
Link State Advertisement (LSA)	shortest path first (SPF)
load	topology database
Loopback interfaces	topology table
maximum transmission unit (MTU)	

Commands Used in This Chapter

The following list contains a summary of all the commands used in this chapter:

Command	Description
`router eigrp as`	Starts EIGRP processes on a router using a specific autonomous system number.
`network ip-address`	Enables EIGRP on the local interfaces that reside on the specified networks. EIGRP is configured with a classful address.
`passive-interface interface-type interface-number`	Identifies interfaces that do not participate in EIGRP updates.
`no auto-summary`	Turns off the automatic summarization of routes at classful boundaries.
`show ip eigrp neighbors`	Shows all EIGRP neighbors.
`show ip route eigrp`	Shows all EIGRP routes.
`show ip eigrp topology`	Shows entries in the EIGRP topology table.
`show ip eigrp traffic`	Shows the packet count for EIGRP packets sent and received.
`router ospf process-id`	Activates the OSPF routing process and identifies the process-id under which it will run. Process-id is in the range 1–65535.
`network network-number wild-card area area-id`	Enables OSPF on a specific interface or set of interfaces that reside on the specified network. These interfaces will reside in the specified area.
`show ip ospf`	Summarizes all relative OSPF information, such as OSPF processes, Router ID, area assignments, authentication, and SPF statistics.
`show ip ospf process-id`	Shows the same information as the `show ip ospf` command, but only for the specified process.
`show ip ospf database`	Displays the link-state topology database.
`show ip ospf interface`	Displays interface OSPF parameters and other OSPF information specific to the interface.

`show ip ospf neighbor`	Displays each OSPF neighbor and adjacency status.
`show ip protocols`	Displays status and configuration summary for all active routing protocols.

Written Lab 6

1. What three routed protocols are supported by EIGRP?
2. When is redistribution required for EIGRP?
3. What command would be used to enable EIGRP with an autonomous system number of 300?
4. What command will tell EIGRP that it is connected to network 172.10.0.0?
5. What type of EIGRP interface will neither send nor receive Hello packets?
6. Write the command that will enable OSPF process 101 on a router.
7. Write the command that will display details of all OSPF routing processes enabled on a router.
8. Write the command that will display interface-specific OSPF information.
9. Write the command that will display all OSPF neighbors.
10. Write the command that will display all different OSPF route types that are currently known by the router.

(The answers to Written Lab 6 can be found following the answers to the Review Questions for this chapter.)

Hands-On Labs

In this section, you will use the same network that you configured in Chapter 5, but just add EIGRP and OSPF routing. The network configuration is shown in the following graphic.

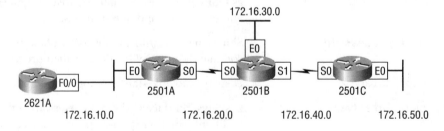

The first lab below (Lab 6.1) requires you to configure three routers for EIGRP and then view the configuration. In the last four labs, you will be asked to enable OSPF routing on the same network. Note that the labs in this chapter were written to be used with real equipment.

 You must remove EIGRP and IGRP before starting Labs 6.2–6.4 because they have a lower administrative distance than OSPF.

The labs in this chapter are:

Lab 6.1: Configuring and Verifying EIGRP

Lab 6.2: Enabling the OSPF Process

Lab 6.3 Configuring OSPF Neighbors

Lab 6.4: Verifying OSPF Operation

Table 6.4 shows our IP addresses for each router (each interface uses a /24 mask).

TABLE 6.4 Our IP Addresses

router	Interface	IP address
2621	F0/0	172.16.10.1
2501A	E0	172.16.10.2
2501A	S0	172.16.20.1
2501B	E0	172.16.30.1
2501B	S0	172.16.20.2
2501B	S1	172.16.40.1
2501C	S0	172.16.40.2
2501C	E0	172.16.50.1

Lab 6.1: Configuring and Verifying EIGRP

1. Implement EIGRP on 2621A:

```
2621A#conf t
Enter configuration commands, one per line.
  End with CNTL/Z.
2621A(config)#router eigrp 100
```

```
2621A(config-router)#network 172.16.0.0
2621A(config-router)#^Z
2621A#
```

2. Implement EIGRP on 2501A:

```
2501A#conf t
Enter configuration commands, one per line.
  End with CNTL/Z.
2501A(config)#router eigrp 100
2501A(config-router)#network 172.16.0.0
2501A(config-router)#exit
2501A#
```

3. Implement EIGRP on 2501B:

```
2501B#conf t
Enter configuration commands, one per line.
  End with CNTL/Z.
2501B(config)#router eigrp 100
2501B(config-router)#network 172.16.0.0
2501B(config-router)#^Z
2501B#
```

4. Implement EIGRP on 2501C:

```
2501C#conf t
Enter configuration commands, one per line.
  End with CNTL/Z.
2501C(config)#router eigrp 100
2501C(config-router)#network 172.16.0.0
2501C(config-router)#^Z
2501C#
```

5. Display the topology table for 2501B:

```
2501B#show ip eigrp topology
```

6. Display the routing table on the 2501B router:

```
2501B#show ip route
```

7. Display the neighbor table on the 2501B router:

```
2501B#show ip eigrp topology
```

Lab 6.2: Enabling the OSPF Process

1. Enable OSPF process 100 on 2621A:

```
2621A#conf t
Enter configuration commands, one per line.
  End with CNTL/Z.
2621A(config)#router ospf 100
2621A(config-router)#^Z
```

2. Enable OSPF process 101 on 2501A:

```
2501A#conf t
Enter configuration commands, one per line.
  End with CNTL/Z.
2501A(config)#router ospf 101
2501A(config-router)#^Z
```

3. Enable OSPF process 102 on 2501B:

```
2501B#conf t
Enter configuration commands, one per line.
  End with CNTL/Z.
2501B(config)#router ospf 102
2501B(config-router)#^Z
```

4. Enable OSPF process 103 on 2501C:

```
2501C#conf t
Enter configuration commands, one per line.
  End with CNTL/Z.
Router(config)#router ospf 103
2501C(config-router)#^Z
```

Lab 6.3: Configuring OSPF Neighbors

1. Configure the network between 2621A and 2501A. Assign it to Area 0:

```
2621A#conf t
Enter configuration commands, one per line.
  End with CNTL/Z.
2621A(config)#router ospf 100
2621A(config-router)#network 172.16.10.1 0.0.0.0 area 0
2621A(config-router)#^Z
2621A#
```

2. Configure the networks on the 2501A router. Assign it to Area 0:

```
2501A#conf t
Enter configuration commands, one per line.
  End with CNTL/Z.
2501A(config)#router ospf 101
2501A(config-router)#network 172.16.10.2 0.0.0.0 area 0
2501A(config-router)#network 172.16.20.1 0.0.0.0
  area 0
2501A(config-router)#^Z
2501A#
```

3. Configure the networks on the 2501B router. Assign them to Area 0:

```
2501B#conf t
Enter configuration commands, one per line.
  End with CNTL/Z.
2501B(config)#router ospf 102
2501B(config-router)#network 172.16.20.2 0.0.0.0 area 0
2501B(config-router)#network 172.16.30.1 0.0.0.0 area 0
2501B(config-router)#network 172.16.40.1 0.0.0.0 area 0
2501B(config-router)#^Z
2501B#
```

4. Configure the networks on the 2501C router. Assign them to Area 0:

```
2501C#conf t
Enter configuration commands, one per line.
  End with CNTL/Z.
2501C(config)#router ospf 103
2501C(config-router)#network 172.16.40.2 0.0.0.0 area 0
2501C(config-router)#network 172.16.50.1 0.0.0.0 area 0
2501C(config-router)#^Z
2501C#
```

Lab 6.4: Verifying OSPF Operation

1. Execute a show ip ospf neighbors command from the 2621 router and view the results:

```
2621A#sho ip ospf neig
```

2. Execute a show ip route command to verify that all other routers are learning all routes:

```
2621A#sho ip route
```

Review Questions

1. What are the three tables that EIGRP uses? (Choose three.)

    A. Route

    B. Broadcast

    C. Topology

    D. Neighbor

    E. Update

2. What are benefits of using a link-state routing protocol? (Choose two.)

    A. It uses the Hello protocol to establish adjacencies.

    B. It uses several components to calculate the metric of a route.

    C. Updates are sent only when changes occur in the network.

    D. It is always a better solution to implement than a distance-vector protocol.

3. How is EIGRP implemented on a router?

    A. `ip router eigrp as`

    B. `router ip eigrp as`

    C. `router eigrp process-id`

    D. `router eigrp as`

4. When the `show ip route` command is used, which of the following codes indicate an EIGRP learned route?

    A. D

    B. R

    C. S

    D. I

5. You want to use a routing protocol that utilizes the benefits of both distance vector and link state. Which routing protocol will you use?

    A. IP

    B. RIP

    C. EIGRP

    D. OSPF

6. You get a call from a network administrator who tells you that he typed the following into his router:

```
Router#ospf 1
Router(config-router)#network 10.0.0.0 255.0.0.0 area 0
```

He tells you he still can't see any routes in the routing table. What configuration error did the administrator make?

   A. The wildcard mask is incorrect.

   B. The OSPF area is wrong.

   C. The OSPF process ID is incorrect.

   D. The AS configuration is wrong.

7. Which of the following are used by default by EIGRP to calculate the best path to a destination network? (Choose two.)

   A. Bandwidth

   B. Load

   C. Delay

   D. Reliability

8. Which of the following is true regarding OSPF areas? (Choose three.)

   A. You must have separate loopback interfaces configured in each area

   B. The numbers you can assign an area go up to 65535

   C. The backbone area is also called area 0

   D. If your design is hierarchical, then you don't need multiple areas

   E. All areas must connect to area 0

   F. If you have only one area, it must be called area 1

9. Which of the following network types have a designated router and a backup designated router assigned? (Choose two.)

   A. Broadcast

   B. Point-to-point

   C. NBMA broadcast

   D. NBMA point-to-point

   E. NBMA point-to-multipoint

10. Which of the following OSPF terms refers to a connected (or adjacent) router that is running an OSPF process, with the adjacent interface assigned to the same area?

   A. Link

   B. Neighbor

   C. LSA

   D. STP

11. What OSPF term refers to a network or router interface?

    A. Link

    B. Area

    C. LSA

    D. STP

12. Which of the following are advantages of OSPF over RIPv1? (Choose three.)

    A. Has higher convergence speed

    B. Is simple to configure

    C. Has support for VLSMs

    D. Has greater scalability

13. A network is being advertised from a neighbor EIGRP router, but your router has stopped receiving hello updates from this router, but the topology table has a feasible successor listed. What will EIGRP do?

    A. Flood the network telling everyone that the advertised network is down

    B. Use the feasible distance as the new route, place it in the routing table, and start routing immediately

    C. Use the feasible successor as the new route, place it in the routing table and start routing immediately

    D. Place a holddown on the network

14. Which type of OSPF network will elect a backup designated router? (Choose two.)

    A. Broadcast Multiaccess

    B. Non-broadcast multi-access

    C. Point-to-point

    D. Broadcast multipoint

15. Which two of the following commands will place network 10.2.3.0/24 into Area 0?

    A. `router eigrp 10`

    B. `router ospf 10`

    C. `router rip`

    D. `network 10.0.0.0`

    E. `network 10.2.3.0 255.255.255.0 area 0`

    F. `network 10.2.3.0 0.0.0.255 area0`

    G. `network 10.2.3.0 0.0.0.255 area 0`

16. What does EIGRP use to deliver routing information throughout the internetwork?

   A. DUAL

   B. RTP

   C. RTMP

   D. PDM

17. What are three reasons for creating OSPF in a hierarchical design?

   A. To decrease routing overhead

   B. To speed up convergence

   C. To confine network instability to single areas of the network

   D. To make configuring OSPF easier

18. What is the administrative distance of OSPF?

   A. 90

   B. 100

   C. 110

   D. 120

19. Which of the following commands will display the RID? (Choose two.)

   A. `show ip route`

   B. `show ip ospf`

   C. `show ip ospf interface`

   D. `show protocols`

20. Which of the following will become the RID of a router by default if a router contains both logical and physical interfaces?

   A. The lowest IP address of any physical interface

   B. The highest IP address of any physical interface

   C. The lowest IP address of any logical interface

   D. The highest IP address of any logical interface

Answers to Review Questions

1. A, C, D. Unlike IGRP and RIP, OSPF uses three different tables to maintain routing information. The neighbor table, which is a table of all directly connected neighbors. A topology table, which lists all links and all paths to each network, and the route table which lists the best path (and the one IP will use to get to a remote network).

2. A, C. Link-state routing protocols use the Hello protocol to establish adjacency, which is an advantage because these packets are small and more efficient than full routing table updates. They update neighbors only when changes occur, and they send only the changed information and not the entire routing table. Using several components to calculate metrics is not an advantage of link-state protocols. Some distance-vector protocols, such as IGRP, use multiple components to calculate routes whereas some link-state protocols, such as OSPF, use only one. It is also not always true that it is better to use a link-state protocol. RIP and IGRP are well suited for small environments, are easy to configure, and have relatively low overhead.

3. D. The command `router eigrp` followed by the autonomous system number is used to implement EIGRP. Process numbers are not used by EIGRP. All of the other command options had radically incorrect command syntax.

4. A. EIGRP uses D, RIP uses R, S identifies a static route, and I indicated IGRP.

5. C. EIGRP is a routing protocol that utilizes the benefits of both distance vector and link state.

6. A. The administrator typed in the wrong wildcard mask configuration. The wildcard should have been 0.0.0.255.

7. A, C. Bandwidth and delay are the only parameters used by default to calculate the metric of a route. Reliability and load are legitimate parameters that may also be used in the metric calculation, but they are not used by default.

8. C, D, E. Loopback interfaces are created on a router and the highest IP address on a loopback (logical) interface becomes the RID of the router, but has nothing to do with areas, so option A is wrong. The numbers you can create an area with are from 0 to 4294967295, option B is wrong. The backbone area is called area 0, so option C is correct. All areas must connect to area 0, so option E is correct. If you have only one area, it must be called area 0, so option F is incorrect. This leaves option D, which must be correct, but doesn't make much sense.

9. A, C. No DR is assigned on any type of point-to-point link. No DR/BDR is assigned on the NBMA point-to-multipoint due to the hub/spoke topology.

10. B. Found via Hello packets, a neighbor is an adjacent OSPF router. Note that no routing information is exchanged with neighbors unless adjacencies are formed.

11. A. Within OSPF, *link* is synonymous with *interface*.

12. A, C, D. Although OSPF has more configuration complexity than RIP, it does offer far speedier convergence, the support of VLSMs, and greater scalability (overcoming RIP's 15 hop-count limitation).

13. C. EIGRP places any routes that do not have metrics that are as good as the route in the routing table in the topology table as feasible successor. These basically become backup links.

14. A, B. No DR is assigned on any type of point-to-point link. No DR/BDR is assigned on the NBMA point-to-multipoint due to the hub/spoke topology.

15. B, G. To configure OSPF, you must first start the process with the `router ospf process_id`. Then you must add the networks with the network command and wildcards. There must also be a space after the area parameter and the configured area number.

16. A. Explanation: EIGRP uses the Diffusing Update Algorithm (DUAL) to find routes and make sure the network is loop free.

17. A, B, C. OSPF hierarchical design, if done correctly, can help decrease routing protocol overhead as well as speed up convergence time of the network. If a problem occurs, the whole network isn't flooded with information; only routers within the troublesome area would be affected. This design is a much more difficult configuration.

18. C. The administrative distance of OSPF is 110. If you are running EIGRP or IGRP, then you must disable EIGRP/IGRP if you want to have OSPF populate the routing table because EIGRP has an administrative distance of 90 and IGRP is 100. RIP is 120.

19. B, C. The command `show ip route` shows the routing table and the command show protocols shows the routed information configured on each interface. The commands `show ip ospf` and `show ip ospf interface` will show you the RID of a router. In addition, the command `show ip protocols` will display the RID.

20. D. The RID of a router is the highest IP address configured on the router, unless you have a loopback interface configured with an IP address, and then this will automatically become the RID of the router. If you have multiple logical interfaces, then the one with the highest IP address will become the RID.

Answers to Written Lab 6

1. The three routed protocols supported by EIGRP are IP, IPX, and AppleTalk.

2. Redistribution is required when more than one EIGRP session or process is running and they are identified with different ASNs. Redistribution shares topology information between EIGRP sessions.

3. `router eigrp 300`

4. `network 172.10.0.0`

5. Passive interface

6. `router ospf 101`

7. `show ip ospf`

8. `show ip ospf interface`

9. `show ip ospf neighbor`

10. `show ip ospf database`

Layer 2 Switching

**THE CCNA EXAM TOPICS COVERED IN THIS
CHAPTER INCLUDE THE FOLLOWING:**

✓ **TECHNOLOGY**

  ▪ Describe the Spanning Tree process

When Cisco discusses switching, they're talking about layer 2 switching unless they say otherwise. Layer 2 switching is the process of using the hardware address of devices on a LAN to segment a network. Since you've got the basic ideas down, I'm now going to focus on the particulars of layer 2 switching and nail down how it works.

Okay, you know that switching breaks up large collision domains into smaller ones, and that a collision domain is a network segment with two or more devices sharing the same bandwidth. A hub network is a typical example of this type of technology. But since each port on a switch is actually its own collision domain, you can make a much better Ethernet LAN network just by replacing your hubs with switches!

Switches truly have changed the way networks are designed and implemented. If a pure switched design is properly implemented, it absolutely will result in a clean, cost-effective, and resilient internetwork. In this chapter, we'll survey and compare network design before and after switching technologies were introduced.

Routing protocols (such as RIP, which you learned about in Chapter 5, "IP Routing") have processes for stopping network loops from occurring at the Network layer. However, if you have redundant physical links between your switches, routing protocols won't do a thing to stop loops from occurring at the Data Link layer. That's exactly the reason Spanning Tree Protocol was developed—to put a stop to loops in a layer 2 switched internetwork. The essentials of this vital protocol, as well as how it works within a switched network, are also important subjects this chapter will cover thoroughly.

When frames traverse a switched network, the LAN switch type determines how a frame is forwarded to an exit port on a switch. There are three different types of LAN switch methods, and each one handles frames differently as they are forwarded through a switch. This chapter will discuss the three methods used by Cisco switches.

I'll wrap this chapter up by showing you how to provide basic configuration to the 1900 and 2950 Cisco Catalyst switches. And in the next chapter, "Virtual LANs (VLANs)," you'll learn how to configure the switches with VLANs.

Before Layer 2 Switching

Let's go back in time a bit and take a look at the condition of networks before switches and how switches have helped segment the corporate LAN. Before LAN switching, the typical network design looked like the network in Figure 7.1.

FIGURE 7.1   Before switching

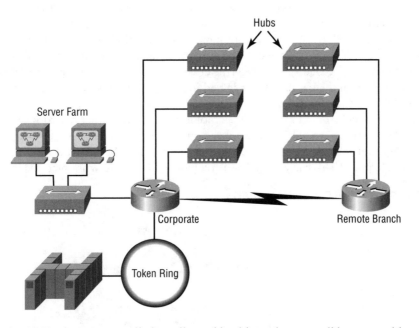

The design in Figure 7.1 was called a collapsed backbone because all hosts would need to go to the corporate backbone to reach any network services—both LAN and mainframe.

Going back even further, before networks like the one shown in Figure 7.1 had physical segmentation devices such as routers and hubs, there was the mainframe network. This network included the mainframe (IBM, Honeywell, Sperry, DEC, etc.), controllers, and dumb terminals that connected into the controller. Any remote sites were connected to the mainframe with bridges.

And then the PC began its rise to stardom, and the mainframe was connected to the Ethernet or to a Token Ring LAN where the servers were installed. These servers were usually O/S2 or LAN Manager because this was "pre-NT." Each floor of a building ran either coax or twisted-pair wiring to the corporate backbone, and was then connected to a router. PCs ran an emulating software program that allowed them to connect to the mainframe services, giving those PCs the ability to access services from the mainframe and LAN simultaneously. Eventually the PC became robust enough to allow application developers to port applications more effectively than they could ever before—an advance that markedly reduced networking prices and enabled businesses to grow at a much faster rate.

When Novell became more popular in the late 1980s and early 1990s, O/S2 and LAN Manager servers were by and large replaced with NetWare servers. This made the Ethernet network even more popular, because that's what Novell 3.*x* servers used to communicate with client/server software.

So that's the story about how the network in Figure 7.1 came into being. There was only one problem—the corporate backbone grew and grew, and as it grew, network services became slower. A big reason for this was that, at the same time this huge burst in growth was taking place, LAN services needed even faster service, and the network was becoming totally saturated. Everyone was dumping the Macs and dumb terminals used for the mainframe service in favor of those slick new PCs so they could more easily connect to the corporate backbone and network services.

All this was taking place before the Internet's momentous popularity (Al Gore was still inventing it?), so everyone in the company needed to access the corporate network's services. Why? Because without the Internet, all network services were internal—exclusive to the company network. This created a screaming need to segment that one humongous and plodding corporate network, connected with sluggish old routers. At first, Cisco just created faster routers (no doubt about that), but more segmentation was needed, especially on the Ethernet LANs. The invention of FastEthernet was a very good and helpful thing too, but it didn't address that network segmentation need at all.

But devices called bridges did, and they were first used in the network to break up collision domains. Bridges were sorely limited by the amount of ports and other network services they could provide, and that's when layer 2 switches came to the rescue. These switches saved the day by breaking up collision domains on each and every port—like a bridge, and switches could provide hundreds of ports! This early, switched LAN looked like the network pictured in Figure 7.2:

FIGURE 7.2 The first switched LAN

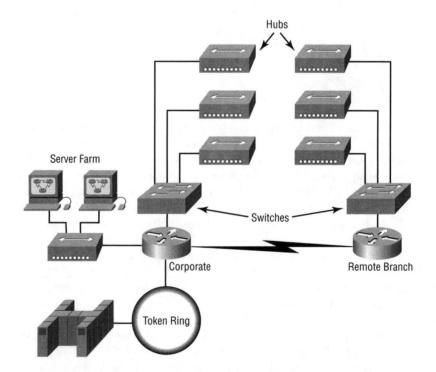

Each hub was placed into a switch port, an innovation that vastly improved the network. Now, instead of each building being crammed into the same collision domain, each hub became its own separate collision domain. But there was a catch—switch ports were still very new, hence unbelievably expensive. Because of that, simply adding a switch into each floor of the building just wasn't going to happen—at least, not yet. Thanks to whomever you choose to thank for these things, the price has dropped dramatically, so now having every one of your users plugged into a switch port is both good and feasible.

So there it is—if you're going to create a network design and implement it, including switching services is a must. A typical contemporary network design would look something like Figure 7.3, a complete switched network design and implementation.

"But I still see a router in there," you say! Yes, it's not a mirage—there *is* a router in there. But its job has changed. Instead of performing physical segmentation, it now creates and handles logical segmentation. Those logical segments are called VLANs, and I promise I'll explain them thoroughly—both in the duration of this chapter and in Chapter 8, where they'll be given a starring role.

FIGURE 7.3   The typical switched network design

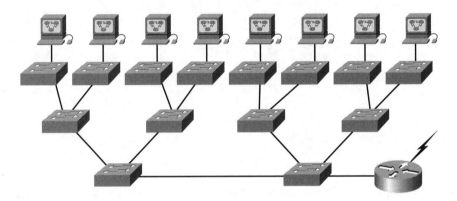

Switching Services

Unlike bridges that use software to create and manage a filter table, switches use application-specific integrated circuits (ASICs) to build and maintain their filter tables. But it's still okay to think of a layer 2 switch as a multiport bridge because their basic reason for being is the same: to break up collision domains.

Layer 2 switches and bridges are faster than routers because they don't take up time looking at the Network layer header information. Instead, they look at the frame's hardware addresses before deciding to either forward the frame or drop it.

Switches create private dedicated collision domains and provide independent bandwidth on each port, unlike a hub. Figure 7.4 shows five hosts connected to a switch—all running 10Mbps half-duplex to the server:

Unlike a hub, each host has 10Mbps dedicated communication to the server.

Layer 2 switching provides the following:

- Hardware-based bridging (ASIC)
- Wire speed
- Low latency
- Low cost

What makes layer 2 switching so efficient is that no modification to the data packet takes place. The device only reads the frame encapsulating the packet, which makes the switching process considerably faster and less error-prone than routing processes are.

FIGURE 7.4   Switches create private domains

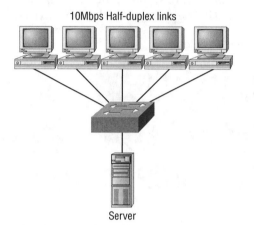

10Mbps Half-duplex links

Server

And if you use layer 2 switching for both workgroup connectivity and network segmentation (breaking up collision domains), you can create a flatter network design with more network segments than you can with traditional routed networks.

Plus, layer 2 switching increases bandwidth for each user because, again, each connection (interface) into the switch is its own collision domain. This feature makes it possible for you to connect multiple devices to each interface.

In the following sections, I will dive deeper into the layer 2 switching technology.

Limitations of Layer 2 Switching

Since we commonly stick layer 2 switching into the same category as bridged networks, we also tend to think it has the same hang-ups and issues that bridged networks do. Keep in mind that bridges are good and helpful things if we design the network correctly, keeping their features as well as their limitations in mind. And to design well with bridges, the two most important considerations are:

- We absolutely must break up the collision domains correctly.

- The right way to create a functional bridged network is to make sure that its users spend 80 percent of their time on the local segment.

Bridged networks break up collision domains, but remember, that network is still one large broadcast domain. Neither layer 2 switches nor bridges break up broadcast domains by default—something that not only limits your network's size and growth potential, but can also reduce its overall performance.

Broadcasts and multicasts, along with the slow convergence time of spanning trees, can give you some major grief as your network grows. These are the big reasons why layer 2 switches and bridges cannot completely replace routers (layer 3 devices) in the inter-network.

Bridging vs. LAN Switching

It's true—layer 2 switches really are pretty much just bridges that give us a lot more ports, but there are some important differences you should always keep in mind:

- Bridges are software based, while switches are hardware based because they use ASIC chips to help make filtering decisions.

- A switch can be viewed as a multiport bridge.

- Bridges can only have one spanning-tree instance per bridge, while switches can have many. (I'm going to tell you all about spanning trees in a bit.)

- Switches have a higher number of ports than most bridges.

- Both bridges and switches forward layer 2 broadcasts.

- Bridges and switches learn MAC addresses by examining the source address of each frame received.

- Both bridges and switches make forwarding decisions based on layer 2 addresses.

Three Switch Functions at Layer 2

There are three distinct functions of layer 2 switching (you need to remember these!): *address learning*, *forward/filter decisions*, and *loop avoidance*.

Address learning   Layer 2 switches and bridges remember the source hardware address of each frame received on an interface, and they enter this information into a MAC database called a forward/filter table.

Forward/filter decisions   When a frame is received on an interface, the switch looks at the destination hardware address and finds the exit interface in the MAC database. The frame is only forwarded out the specified destination port.

Loop avoidance   If multiple connections between switches are created for redundancy purposes, network loops can occur. Spanning Tree Protocol (STP) is used to stop network loops while still permitting redundancy.

I'm going to talk about address learning, forward/filtering decisions, and loop avoidance in detail in the next sections.

Address Learning

When a switch is first powered on, the MAC forward/filter table is empty, as shown in Figure 7.5:

When a device transmits and an interface receives a frame, the switch places the frame's source address in the MAC forward/filter table, allowing it to remember which interface the sending device is located on. The switch then has no choice but to flood the network with this frame out of every port except the source port because it has no idea where the destination device is actually located.

FIGURE 7.5   Empty forward/filter table on a switch

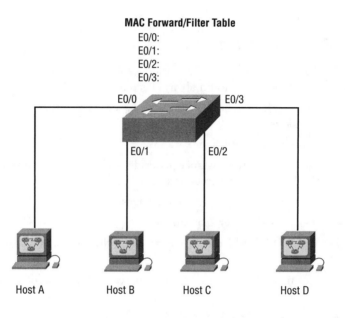

MAC Forward/Filter Table
E0/0:
E0/1:
E0/2:
E0/3:

FIGURE 7.6   How switches learn hosts' locations

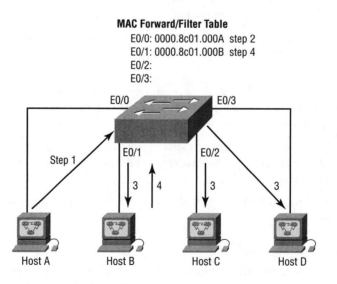

MAC Forward/Filter Table
E0/0: 0000.8c01.000A step 2
E0/1: 0000.8c01.000B step 4
E0/2:
E0/3:

If a device answers this flooded frame and sends a frame back, then the switch will take the source address from that frame and place that MAC address in its database as well, associating this address with the interface that received the frame. Since the switch now has both of the relevant

MAC addresses in its filtering table, the two devices can now make a point-to-point connection. The switch doesn't need to flood the frame as it did the first time, because now the frames can and will be forwarded only between the two devices. This is exactly the thing that makes layer 2 switches better than hubs. In a hub network, all frames are forwarded out all ports every time—no matter what! Figure 7.6 shows the processes involved in building a MAC database:

In this figure, you can see four hosts attached to a switch. When the switch is powered on, it has nothing in its MAC address forward/filter table, just as in Figure 7.5. But when the hosts start communicating, the switch places the source hardware address of each frame in the table along with the port that the frame's address corresponds to.

Let me give you an example of how a forward/filter table is populated:

1.   Host A sends a frame to Host B. Host A's MAC address is 0000.8c01.000A; Host B's MAC address is 0000.8c01.000B.

2.   The switch receives the frame on the E0/0 interface and places the source address in the MAC address table.

3.   Since the destination address is not in the MAC database, the frame is forwarded out all interfaces—except the source port.

4.   Host B receives the frame and responds to Host A. The switch receives this frame on interface E0/1 and places the source hardware address in the MAC database.

5.   Host A and Host B can now make a point-to-point connection and only the two devices will receive the frames. Hosts C and D will not see the frames, nor are their MAC addresses found in the database because they haven't yet sent a frame to the switch.

If Host A and Host B don't communicate to the switch again within a certain amount of time, the switch will flush their entries from the database to keep it as current as possible.

Forward/Filter Decisions

When a frame arrives at a switch interface, the destination hardware address is compared to the forward/filter MAC database. If the destination hardware address is known and listed in the database, the frame is only sent out the correct exit interface. The switch doesn't transmit the frame out any interface except for the destination interface. This preserves bandwidth on the other network segments and is called *frame filtering*.

But if the destination hardware address is not listed in the MAC database, then the frame is flooded out all active interfaces except the interface the frame was received on. If a device answers the flooded frame, the MAC database is updated with the device's location (interface).

If a host or server sends a broadcast on the LAN, the switch will flood the frame out all active ports except the source port by default. Remember, the switch only creates smaller collision domains, but it's still one large broadcast domain by default.

Loop Avoidance

Redundant links between switches are a good idea because they help prevent complete network failures in the event one link stops working.

Sounds great, but even though redundant links can be extremely helpful, they often cause more problems than they solve. This is because frames can be flooded down all redundant links simultaneously, creating network loops as well as other evils. Here's a list of some of the ugliest problems:

- If no loop avoidance schemes are put in place, the switches will flood broadcasts endlessly throughout the internetwork. This is sometimes referred to as a *broadcast storm*. (But most of the time it's referred to in ways we're not permitted to repeat in print!) Figure 7.7 illustrates how a broadcast can be propagated throughout the network. Observe how a frame is continually being flooded through the internetwork's physical network media:

FIGURE 7.7 Broadcast storm

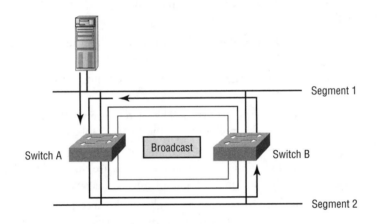

- A device can receive multiple copies of the same frame, since that frame can arrive from different segments at the same time. Figure 7.8 demonstrate how a whole bunch of frames can arrive from multiple segments simultaneously. The server in the figure sends a unicast frame to Router C. Since it's a unicast frame, Switch A forwards the frame, and Switch B provides the same service—it forwards the broadcast. This is bad because it means that Router C receives that unicast frame twice, causing additional overhead on the network.

- You may have thought of this one: The MAC address filter table will be totally confused about the device's location because the switch can receive the frame from more than one link. And what's more, the bewildered switch could get so caught up in constantly updating the MAC filter table with source hardware address locations that it will fail to forward a frame! This is called thrashing the MAC table.

- One of the nastiest things that can happen is multiple loops generating throughout a network. This means that loops can occur within other loops, and if a broadcast storm were to also occur, the network wouldn't be able to perform frame switching—period!

All of these problems spell disaster (or at least close to it) and are decidedly evil situations that must be avoided, or at least fixed somehow. That's where the Spanning Tree Protocol comes into the game. It was developed to solve each and every one of the problems I just told you about.

FIGURE 7.8 Multiple frame copies

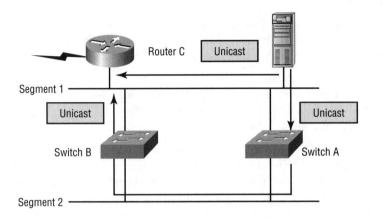

Spanning Tree Protocol (STP)

Back before it was purchased and renamed Compaq, a company called Digital Equipment Corporation (DEC) created the original version of *Spanning Tree Protocol (STP)*. The IEEE later created its own version of STP called 802.1D. All Cisco switches run the IEEE 802.1D version of STP, which isn't compatible with the DEC version.

STP's main task is to stop network loops from occurring on your layer 2 network (bridges or switches). It vigilantly monitors the network to find all links, making sure that no loops occur by shutting down any redundant links. STP uses the spanning-tree algorithm (STA) to first create a topology database, then search out and destroy redundant links. With STP running, frames will only be forwarded on the premium, STP-picked links.

In the following sections, I am going to hit the nitty-gritty of the Spanning Tree Protocol.

Spanning Tree Terms

Before I get into describing the details of how STP works in the network, you need to understand some basic ideas and terms and how they relate within the layer 2 switched network:

STP Spanning Tree Protocol (STP) is a bridge protocol that uses the STA to find redundant links dynamically and create a spanning-tree topology database. Bridges exchange BPDU messages with other bridges to detect loops, and then remove them by shutting down selected bridge interfaces.

Root bridge The *root bridge* is the bridge with the best bridge ID. With STP, the key is for all the switches in the network to elect a root bridge that becomes the focal point in the network. All other decisions in the network—such as which port is to be blocked and which port is to be put in forwarding mode—are made from the perspective of this root bridge.

BPDU All the switches exchange information to use in the selection of the root switch, as well as in subsequent configuration of the network. Each switch compares the parameters in the

Bridge Protocol Data Unit (BPDU) that they send to one neighbor with the one that they receive from another neighbor.

Bridge ID The bridge ID is how STP keeps track of all the switches in the network. It is determined by a combination of the bridge priority (32,768 by default on all Cisco switches) and the base MAC address. The bridge with the lowest bridge ID becomes the root bridge in the network.

Nonroot bridge These are all bridges that are not the root bridge. Nonroot bridges exchange BPDUs with all bridges and update the STP topology database on all switches, preventing loops and providing a measure of defense against link failures.

Root port The root port is always the link directly connected to the root bridge, or the shortest path to the root bridge. If more than one link connects to the root bridge, then a port cost is determined by checking the bandwidth of each link. The lowest cost port becomes the root port. If multiple links have the same cost, the bridge with the lower advertising bridge ID is use. Since multiple links can be from the same device, the lowest port number will be used.

Designated port A port that has been determined as having the best (lower) cost—a *designated port* will be marked as a forwarding port.

Port cost Port cost determines when multiple links are used between two switches and none are root ports. The cost of a link is determined by the bandwidth of a link.

Nondesignated port Port with a higher cost than the designated port that will be put in blocking mode—a *nondesignated port* is not a forwarding port.

Forwarding port A forwarding port forwards frames.

Blocked port A blocked port is the port that will not forward frames, in order to prevent loops. However, a blocked port will always listen to frames.

Spanning Tree Operations

As I've said before, STP's job is to find all links in the network and shut down any redundant ones, thereby preventing network loops from occurring. STP does this by first electing a root bridge that will preside over network topology decisions. Once all switches agree on who the root bridge is, every bridge must find the root port. If there are multiple links between switches, there must be one and only one designated port.

Things tend to go a lot more smoothly when you don't have more than one person making a navigational decision, and so, there can only be one root bridge in any given network. I'll discuss the root bridge election process more completely in the next section.

Selecting the Root Bridge

The bridge ID is used to elect the root bridge in the STP domain as well as to determine the root port. This ID is 8 bytes long, and includes both the priority and the MAC address of the device. The default priority on all devices running the IEEE STP version is 32,768.

To determine the root bridge, the priority of each bridge is combined with its MAC address. If two switches or bridges happen to have the same priority value, then the MAC address becomes

/Default priority.

the tie breaker for figuring out which one has the lowest (best) ID. It's like this: If two switches—I'll name them A and B—both use the default priority of 32,768, then the MAC address will be used instead. If Switch A's MAC address is 0000.0c00.1111 and Switch B's MAC address is 0000.0c00.2222, then Switch A would become the root bridge. Just remember that the lower value is the better one when it comes to electing a root bridge.

BPDUs are sent every 2 seconds, by default, out all active ports on a bridge/switch, and the bridge with the lowest (best) bridge ID is elected the root bridge. You can change the bridge's ID by lowering its priority so that it will become a root bridge automatically. Being able to do that is important in a large switched network—it ensures that the best paths are chosen.

Changing STP parameters is beyond the scope of this book, but it's covered in *CCNP: Building Cisco Multilayer Switched Networks Study Guide*, (Sybex, 2003).

Selecting the Designated Port

If more than one link is connected to the root bridge, then port cost becomes the factor used to determine which port will be the root port. So, to determine the port that will be used to communicate with the root bridge, you must first figure out the path's cost. The STP cost is an accumulated total path cost based on the available bandwidth of each of the links. Table 7.1 shows the typical costs associated with various Ethernet networks.

TABLE 7.1   Typical Costs of Different Ethernet Networks

Speed	New IEEE Cost	Original IEEE Cost
10Gbps	2	1
1Gbps	4	1
100Mbps	19	10
10Mbps	100	100

The IEEE 802.1D specification has recently been revised to handle the new higher-speed links. The IEEE 802.1D specification assigns a default port cost value to each port based on bandwidth.

Spanning-Tree Port States

The ports on a bridge or switch running STP can transition through five different states:

Blocking   A blocked port won't forward frames; it just listens to BPDUs. The purpose of the blocking state is to prevent the use of looped paths. All ports are in blocking state by default when the switch is powered up.

Listening The port listens to BPDUs to make sure no loops occur on the network before passing data frames. A port in listening state prepares to forward data frames without populating the MAC address table.

Learning The switch port listens to BPDUs and learns all the paths in the switched network. A port in learning state populates the MAC address table but doesn't forward data frames.

Forwarding The port sends and receives all data frames on the bridged port. If the port is still a designated or root port at the end of the Learning state, it enters this state.

Disabled A port in the disabled state (administratively) does not participate in the frame forwarding or STP. A port in the disabled state is virtually nonoperational.

Switch ports are most often in either the blocking or forwarding state. A forwarding port is one that has been determined to have the lowest (best) cost to the root bridge. But when and if the network experiences a topology change (because of a failed link or because someone adds in a new switch), you'll find the ports on a switch in listening and learning state.

As I mentioned, blocking ports is a strategy for preventing network loops. Once a switch determines the best path to the root bridge, then all other ports will be in blocking mode. Blocked ports can still receive BPDUs—they just don't send out any frames.

If a switch determines that a blocked port should now be the designated or root port because of a topology change, it will go into listening mode and check all BPDUs it receives to make sure that it won't create a loop once the port goes to forwarding mode.

Convergence

Convergence occurs when all ports on bridges and switches have transitioned to either the forwarding or blocking modes. No data is forwarded until convergence is complete. Before data can be forwarded again, all devices must be updated. Convergence is important to make sure all devices have the same database, but it does cost you some time. It usually takes 50 seconds to go from blocking to forwarding mode, and I don't recommend changing the default STP timers. (But you can adjust those timers if necessary.) Forward delay means the time it takes to transition a port from listening to learning mode or vice versa.

Spanning Tree Example

It's time to begin using and not just reading about this stuff. It's important to see how a spanning tree works in an internetwork, because it will really help you understand it better. So in this section, I'll give you a chance to observe what you've learned as it takes place in a live network.

In Figure 7.9, you can assume that all five switches have the same priority of 32,768. But now study the MAC address of each switch. By looking at the priority and MAC addresses of each device, you should be able to determine the root bridge:

Once you've established which switch has got to be the root bridge, look at the figure again and try to figure out which is the root port on each of the switches. (Hint: Root ports are always forwarding ports, which means they will always be in forwarding mode.) Okay, next try to establish which of the ports will be in blocking mode.

FIGURE 7.9   Spanning tree example

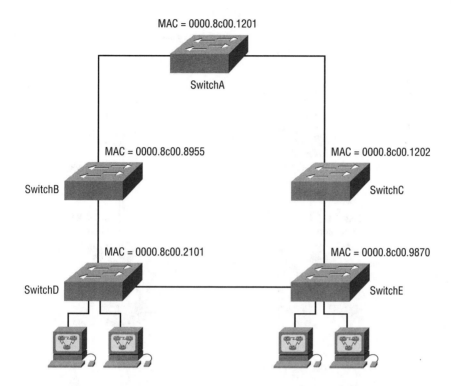

MAC = 0000.8c00.1201

SwitchA

MAC = 0000.8c00.8955

SwitchB

MAC = 0000.8c00.1202

SwitchC

MAC = 0000.8c00.2101

SwitchD

MAC = 0000.8c00.9870

SwitchE

Figure .7.10 has the answers for each of the port states for each switch.

Since Switch A has the lowest MAC address, and all five switches use the default priority, Switch A gets to be the root bridge. And remember this: A root bridge always has every port in forwarding mode (designated ports).

To determine the root ports on Switch B and Switch C, just follow the connection to the root bridge. Each direct connection to the root bridge will be a root port, so it will become forwarding. On Switches D and E, the ports connected to Switches B and C are Switches D and E's closest ports to the root bridge (lowest cost), so those ports are root ports and in forwarding mode.

Take another look at the Figure 7.10. Can you tell which of the ports between Switch D and E must be shut down so a network loop doesn't occur? Let's work it out: Since the connection from Switches D and E to Switches B and C are root ports, those can't be shut down. Next, the bridge ID is used to determine designated and nondesignated ports; so, because Switch D has the lowest (best) bridge ID, Switch E's port to Switch D will become nondesignated (blocking), and Switch D's connection to Switch E will be designated (forwarding).

FIGURE 7.10 Spanning tree example answers

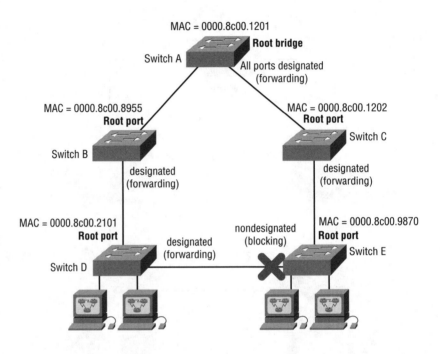

Real World Scenario

When should I worry about spanning tree?

Bob, a Senior Network Administrator at Acme Corporation in San Francisco, is concerned about all the new switches his bosses just asked him to install, which will bring the total number of switches in his network to 20. He is concerned about STP and isn't sure if he should even think about it since it seems to work OK with the few switches he has installed. Bob calls you for advice. What should you tell Bob when he calls?

If you have fewer than six switches in your internetwork and no more than about 100 users in your network, you would usually just let STP do its job and not worry about it. Understand that each network may vary, but with Bob ending up with about 20 switches, he has to think about STP!

But if you have dozens of switches and hundreds of users in your network, then it's time to pay attention to how STP is running. That's because if you don't set the root switch in this larger switched network, your STP may never converge between switches—a nasty situation that could bring your network down.

Setting the timers and root switch are covered in the Sybex *CCNP: Building Cisco Multilayer Switched Networks Study Guide*.

LAN Switch Types

LAN switch types decide how a frame is handled when it's received on a switch port. Latency—the time it takes for a frame to be sent out an exit port once the switch receives the frame—depends on the chosen switching mode. There are three switching modes:

Cut-through (FastForward)   When in this mode, the switch only waits for the destination hardware address to be received before it looks up the destination address in the MAC filter table. Cisco sometimes calls this the FastForward method.

FragmentFree (modified cut-through)   This is the default mode for the Catalyst 1900 switch, and it's sometimes referred to as modified cut-through. In FragmentFree mode, the switch checks the first 64 bytes of a frame before forwarding it for fragmentation, thus guarding against forwarding runts, which are caused by collisions.

Store-and-forward   Herein, the complete data frame is received on the switch's buffer, a CRC is run, and then the switch looks up the destination address in the MAC filter table.

Figure 7.11 delimits the different points where the switching mode takes place in the frame:

FIGURE 7.11   Different switching modes within a frame

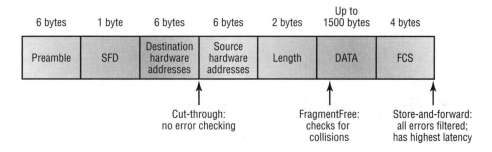

Let's now discuss these three switching modes in more detail.

Cut-Through (Real Time)

You may see Cisco call this Cut-Through, FastForward, or even Real time. With the *cut-through* switching method, the LAN switch reads only the destination address (the first six bytes following the preamble) onto its onboard buffers. That done, it then looks up the hardware destination address in the MAC switching table, determines the outgoing interface, and proceeds to forward the frame toward its destination.

A cut-through switch really helps to reduce latency because it begins to forward the frame as soon as it reads the destination address and determines the outgoing interface.

With some switches, you get an extra super-cool feature: the flexibility to perform cut-through switching on a per-port basis until a user-defined error threshold is reached. At the point that threshold is attained, the ports automatically change over to store-and-forward mode so they will stop forwarding the errors. And when the error rate on the port falls back below the threshold, the port automatically changes back to cut-through mode.

FragmentFree (Modified Cut-Through)

FragmentFree is a modified form of cut-through switching in which the switch waits for the collision window (64 bytes) to pass before forwarding. This is because if a packet has a collision error, it almost always occurs within the first 64 bytes. It means each frame will be checked into the data field to make sure no fragmentation has occurred.

FragmentFree mode provides better error checking than the cut-through mode with practically no increase in latency. It's the default switching method for the 1900 switches.

Store-and-Forward

Store-and-forward switching is Cisco's primary LAN switching method. When in *store-and-forward*, the LAN switch copies the entire frame onto its onboard buffers and then computes the cyclic redundancy check (CRC). Because it copies the entire frame, latency through the switch varies with frame length.

The frame is discarded if it contains a CRC error—if it's too short (less than 64 bytes including the CRC) or if it's too long (more than 1518 bytes including the CRC). If the frame doesn't contain any errors, the LAN switch looks up the destination hardware address in its forwarding or switching table to find the correct outgoing interface. When it does, out goes the frame toward its destination.

Configuring the Catalyst 1900 and 2950 Switches

The 1900 switch is the Cisco Catalyst switch family's low-end model. In fact, there are actually two different models associated with the Catalyst 1900 switch: the 1912 and the 1924. The 1912 switches have 12 10BaseT ports and the 1924 switches have 24 10BaseT ports as well as each switch having a DIX port on the back. Each has two 100Mbps uplinks—either twisted-pair or fiber.

The 2950 comes in many flavors, and runs 10Mbps all the way up to 1Gbps switched ports, with either twisted-pair or fiber. These switches have more intelligence to offer than a 1900 series switch does—they can provide basic data, video, and voice services. If you're faced with buying a switch of this type, you'll find yourself choosing one of the dozen models Cisco has available, all of which can be found on the Cisco website.

In this section, you will learn how to start up and configure both the Cisco Catalyst 1900 and 2950 switches using the command-line interface (CLI). I'll teach you the basic configuration commands to use on each type of switch.

After you get the basic commands down, I will show you how to configure Virtual LANs (VLANs), plus ISL routing and Virtual Trunk Protocol (VTP).

Here's a list of the basic tasks we'll be covering:

- Setting the passwords
- Setting the hostname
- Configuring the IP address and subnet mask
- Setting a description on the interfaces
- Erasing the switch configurations
- Configuring VLANs
- Adding VLAN memberships to switch ports
- Creating a VTP domain
- Configuring trunking

1900 and 2950 Switch Startup

When the 1900 switch is first powered on, it runs through a power-on self-test (POST). At first, all port LEDs are green, and if upon completion the POST determines that all ports are in good shape, all the LEDs blink and then turn off. But if the POST finds a port that has failed, both the System LED and the port's LED turn amber.

If you have a console cable connected to the switch, the menu shown below appears after the POST.

By pressing K, you can use the command-line interface, and when you press M, you'll be allowed to configure the switch through a menu system. Pressing I allows you to configure the IP configuration of the switch, but you can also do this through the menu or CLI at any time. And once the IP configuration is set, the I selection no longer appears.

This is what the switch's output looks like on the console screen after the switch is powered up:

```
1 user(s) now active on Management Console.


        User Interface Menu

    [M] Menus
    [K] Command Line
    [I] IP Configuration

Enter Selection:  K


        CLI session with the switch is open.
        To end the CLI session, enter [Exit].

>
```

When you power on a 2950 switch, it's just like a Cisco router—the switch comes up into setup mode. However, unlike a router, the switch is actually usable in fresh-out-of-the-box condition. You can just plug the switch into your network and connect network segments together without any configuration! This is because switch ports are enabled by default, and you don't need an IP address on a switch to make it work in a network—unless you want to manage the switch via the network.

Here's the 2950 switch's initial output:

```
--- System Configuration Dialog ---
Would you like to enter the initial configuration dialog? [yes/no]: no

Press RETURN to get started!

00:04:53: %LINK-5-CHANGED: Interface Vlan1, changed state to
    administratively down
00:04:54: %LINEPROTO-5-UPDOWN: Line protocol on Interface Vlan1,
    changed state to down
Switch>
```

Setting the Passwords

The first thing we're going to configure—that you always want to configure first on a switch—is the password. Why? You don't want unauthorized users connecting to the switch.

You can set both the user mode and privileged mode passwords just as you can for a router.

The login (user mode) password can be used to verify authorization on the switch, including accessing any line and the console. The enable password is used to allow access to the switch so the configuration can be viewed or changed. Again, this is the same as it is with any Cisco router.

Even though the 1900 switch uses a CLI running an IOS, the commands for the user mode and enable mode passwords are different than the ones you use for routers. Yes, you do use the command enable password, which is the same, but you choose different access levels. These are optional on a Cisco router but not on the 1900 switch. The 2950 is done exactly like a router, though.

In the following sections, you'll learn how to set the user mode and enable mode passwords, as well as how to set the enable secret password.

Setting the User Mode and Enable Mode Passwords

You use the same command to set the user mode password and enable mode password on the 1900 switch, but you do use different level commands to control the type of access that each password provides.

To configure the user mode and enable mode password, press K at the switch console output. You get into enable mode by using the enable command, then you enter global configuration mode by using the config t command.

Once you're in global configuration mode, you can set both the user mode and enable mode passwords by using the `enable password` command.

The following output shows the configuration of both the user mode and enable mode passwords:

```
(config)#enable password ?
  level  Set exec level password
(config)#enable password level ?
  <1-15>  Level number
```

To enter the user mode password, use level number 1. To enter the enable mode password, use level mode 15. The password must be at least four characters, but no longer than eight.

The switch output below shows the user mode password being set and denied because it's more than eight characters:

```
(config)#enable password level 1 toddlammle
Error: Invalid password length.
Password must be between 4 and 8 characters
```

This output is an example of how to set both the user mode and enable mode passwords on the 1900 switch:

```
(config)#enable password level 1 todd
(config)#enable password level 15 toddl
(config)#exit
#exit
CLI session with the switch is now closed.
Press any key to continue.
```

To set the user mode passwords for the 2950 switch, you configure the lines just as you would on a router:

```
Switch>enable
Switch#config t
Enter configuration commands, one per line.  End with CNTL/Z.
Switch(config)#line ?
  <0-16>   First Line number
  console  Primary terminal line
  vty      Virtual terminal

Switch(config)#line vty ?
  <0-15>  First Line number

Switch(config)#line vty 0 15
```

```
Switch(config-line)#login
Switch(config-line)#password telnet
Switch(config-line)#line con 0
Switch(config-line)#login
Switch(config-line)#password todd
Switch(config-line)#exit
Switch(config)#exit
Switch#
```

You've just learned how to set the user mode passwords and the enable password on the 1900, but there's still one more password that needs attention on each switch: the enable secret.

Setting the Enable Secret Password

The enable secret password is a more secure password and it supersedes the enable password if you set it. This means that if you have enable secret password set, you don't need to bother setting the enable mode password. You set the enable secret password the same way you do on a router:

```
(config)#enable secret todd2
```

You can make the `enable password` and `enable secret` commands the same on the 1900 switch, but on a router you are not allowed to do this. And on the 2950, the enable password and enable secret must be different, as shown below:

```
Switch(config)#enable password todd
Switch(config)#enable secret todd
The enable secret you have chosen is the same as your enable password.
This is not recommended.  Re-enter the enable secret.

Switch(config)#enable secret todd1
Switch(config)#
```

Again, you don't really need to set the enable password since the enable secret supersedes it anyway.

Setting the Hostname

As it is with a router, the hostname on a switch is only locally significant. This means that it doesn't have any function on the network or with name resolution. (The only exception to this is with PPP authentication, which will be discussed in Chapter 11.) But it's still helpful to set a hostname on a switch so that you can identify the switch when connecting to it. A good rule of thumb is to name the switch after the location it is serving.

From the 1900 switch, just set the hostname as you would on a router:

```
#config t
Enter configuration commands, one per line.  End with CNTL/Z
```

```
(config)#hostname Todd1900
Todd1900(config)#
```

From the 2950, use the same hostname command, as seen here:

```
Switch(config)#hostname Todd2950
Todd2950(config)#
```

Setting IP Information

Remember, you don't have to set any IP configuration on the switch to make it work. You can just plug it in. But there are two reasons you probably do want to set the IP address information on the switch:

- To manage the switch via Telnet or other management software
- To configure the switch with different VLANs and other network functions

By default, no IP address or default-gateway information is set. You would set both of these on a layer 2 switch just as you would on any host. By using the command show ip (or sh ip), you can see the 1900's default IP configuration:

```
Todd1900#sh ip
IP Address: 0.0.0.0
Subnet Mask: 0.0.0.0
Default Gateway: 0.0.0.0
Management VLAN:  1
Domain name:
Name server 1: 0.0.0.0
Name server 2: 0.0.0.0
HTTP server : Enabled
HTTP port :  80
RIP : Enabled
```

You'll notice that no IP address, default gateway, or other IP parameters are configured. You use the ip address command to set the IP address on a 1900 switch, and the ip default-gateway command to set the default gateway.

This output shows an example of how to set the IP address and default gateway:

```
Todd1900#config t
Enter configuration commands, one per line.  End with CNTL/Z
Todd1900(config)#ip address 172.16.10.16 255.255.255.0
Todd1900(config)#ip default-gateway 172.16.10.1
Todd1900(config)#
```

The IP address is configured differently on the 2950 switch than it is on the 1900, or on any router—you actually configure it under the VLAN1 interface! Remember that every port on every switch is a member of VLAN1 by default. This really confuses a lot of people—you'd think that you would set an IP address under a switch interface—but no, that's not where it goes. Remember that you set an IP address "for" the switch so you can manage the thing in-band (through the network). Check out this output:

```
Todd2950#config t
Enter configuration commands, one per line.  End with CNTL/Z.
Todd2950(config)#int vlan1
Todd2950(config-if)#ip address 172.16.10.17 255.255.255.0
Todd2950(config-if)#no shut
Todd2950(config-if)#exit
00:22:01: %LINK-3-UPDOWN: Interface Vlan1, changed state to up
00:22:02: %LINEPROTO-5-UPDOWN: Line protocol on Interface Vlan1, changed state
to up
Todd2950(config)#ip default-gateway 172.16.10.1
Todd2950(config)#
```

Notice that I set the IP address for the 2950 switch under the VLAN 1 interface. And notice that I also had to enable the interface with the no shutdown command. The default gateway command is deployed from global configuration mode.

Configuring Interface Descriptions

You can administratively set a name for each interface on the switches, and as with the hostname, the descriptions are only locally significant.

For the 1900 and 2950 series switches, use the description command. You can't use spaces with this command on the 1900, but you can use underscores if you need to.

To set the descriptions, you've first got to be in interface configuration mode. From interface configuration mode, use the description command to describe each interface. Your descriptions can be more than one word, but remember, you can't use spaces.

Here's an example—in it, I used underscores instead of spaces:

```
Todd1900#config t
Enter configuration commands, one per line.  End with CNTL/Z
Todd1900(config)#int e0/1
Todd1900(config-if)#description Finance_VLAN
Todd1900(config-if)#int f0/26
Todd1900(config-if)#description trunk_to_Building_4
Todd1900(config-if)#
```

I set descriptions on both a 10Mbps port and a 100Mbps port on the 1900 switch.

When you set descriptions on a 2950 switch, you can use spaces:

```
Todd2950(config)#int fastEthernet 0/?
  <0-12>  FastEthernet interface number

Todd2950(config)#int fastEthernet 0/1
Todd2950(config-if)#description Sales Printer
Todd2950(config-if)#int f0/12
Todd2950(config-if)#description Connection to backbone
Todd2950(config-if)#^Z
Todd2950#
```

All of the ports on my 2950 switch are 10/100 ports. You can see by looking at this output that I set the interface descriptions on ports 0/1 and 0/12.

Once you've got your descriptions neatly configured on each interface, you can take a look at them any time you want with either the show interface command or the show running-config command.

Erasing the Switch Configuration

As is true on routers, both the 1900's and 2950's configurations are stored in NVRAM. You don't get to check out the startup-config or the contents of NVRAM on the 1900—you can only look at the running-config.

When you make a change to the switch's running-config, the switch will automatically copy the configuration on itself over to NVRAM. This is a big difference from a router where you have to type **copy running-config startup-config**. You just can't do that on a 1900!

But the 2950 switch has a running-config and a startup-config. You save the configuration with the copy run start command, and you can erase the contents of NVRAM with the erase startup-config command.

Check out the 1900 switch output below, and notice that there are two options: nvram and vtp. I want to delete the contents of NVRAM to the factory default settings.

```
Todd1900#delete ?
  nvram  NVRAM configuration
  vtp    Reset VTP configuration to defaults
Todd1900#delete nvram
This command resets the switch with factory defaults.  All system
  parameters will revert to their default factory settings.  All static
  and dynamic addresses will be removed.
Reset system with factory defaults, [Y]es or [N]o?  Yes
```

Notice the message the 1900 gave me when I used the delete nvram command—once you say yes, the configuration is gone!

To delete the 2950, you just type **erase startup-config** from the privileged mode prompt like this:

```
Todd2950#erase startup-config
Erasing the nvram filesystem will remove all files! Continue? [confirm] (enter)
[OK]
Erase of nvram: complete
Todd2950#
```

Unlike the 1900, when you erase the configuration on the 2950, you have to reload the switch before the running-config will actually be deleted.

Summary

You can think of this as the layer 2 switching background chapter because the information I presented in it was designed to give you everything you need before continuing on to Chapter 8.

In this chapter, I talked about the differences between switches and bridges and how they both work at layer 2 and create a MAC address forward/filter table in order to make decisions on whether to forward or flood a frame.

I also discussed problems that can occur if you have multiple links between bridges (switches) and how to solve these problems by using the Spanning Tree Protocol (STP).

LAN Switch types were also discussed in detail and how each one works through a switch. I ended this chapter by showing you basic configurations of both 1900 and 2950 switches.

These concepts are both fundamental and progressive, and if you're a little confused at this point, you'll probably just get even more frustrated if you move on to Chapter 8 without really understanding them. It will only take a few minutes, and it's worth going over again to make the rest of the course clearer and easier to understand!

We're moving on to considerably more advanced theory and configuration next: VLANS.

Exam Essentials

Remember the three switch functions. Address learning, forward/filter decisions, and loop avoidance are the functions of a switch.

Understand the main purpose of the spanning tree in a switched LAN. The main purpose of STP is to prevent switching loops in a network with redundant switched paths.

Remember the states of STP. The purpose of the blocking state is to prevent the use of looped paths. A port in listening state prepares to forward data frames without populating the MAC address table. A port in learning state populates the MAC address table but doesn't forward data frames. The port in forwarding state sends and receives all data frames on the bridged port. Lastly, a port in the disabled state is virtually nonoperational.

Remember the three LAN switch methods.   The three LAN switch methods are cut-through (also called FastForward), FragmentFree (also known as modified cut-through), and store-and-forward.

Understand how the cut-through LAN switch method works.   When in this mode, the switch waits only for the destination hardware address to be received before it looks up the address in the MAC filter table.

Understand how the FragmentFree LAN switch method works.   The FragmentFree LAN switch method checks the first 64 bytes of a frame before forwarding it for fragmentation.

Understand how the store-and-forward LAN switch method works.   Store-and-forward first receives the complete data frame on the switch's buffer; a CRC is run, and then the switch looks up the destination address in the MAC filter table.

Key Terms

Before taking the exam, be sure you're familiar with the following terms:

address learning	frame filtering
Bridge Protocol Data Unit (BPDU)	loop avoidance
broadcast storm	nondesignated port
cut-through	root bridge
designated port	Spanning Tree Protocol (STP)
forward/filter decisions	store-and-forward
FragmentFree	

Commands Used in This Chapter

The following list contains a summary of all the commands used in this chapter:

Command	Description
enable password level 1 password	Sets the user mode password on a 1900 switch
enable password level 15 password	Sets the enable password on a 1900 switch
Enable secret password	Sets the enable password on a 1900 and 2950 switch
hostname name	Sets the name of the device

`sh ip`	Shows the IP configuration information on a 1900 switch
`ip address ip_address mask`	Sets the IP address on a device
`ip default-gateway ip_address`	Sets the default gateway on a 1900 and 2950 switch
`int vlan1`	Chooses the default VLAN on a 2950 switch
`description description`	Sets a description on an interface
`delete nvram`	Erase the configuration on a 1900 switch
`Copy running-config startup-config`	Saves the configuration on a 2950 switch

Written Lab 7

Write the answers to the following questions:

1. Which LAN switch method has the highest latency?
2. Which LAN switch method only reads the hardware destination address before forwarding the frame?
3. What are the three switch functions at layer 2?
4. Which LAN switch type reads into the data field of the frame before forwarding the frame?
5. What is used at layer 2 to prevent switching loops?
6. Which LAN switch method receives the complete frame before beginning to forward it?
7. Which two LAN switch methods have a constant latency?
8. What LAN switch method is also known as "modified cut-through"?
9. What is used to prevent switching loops in a network with redundant switched paths?
10. Which LAN switch method runs a CRC on every frame the switch receives?

    (The answers to Written Lab 7 can be found following the Review Questions for this chapter.)

Hands-on Labs

In this section, you'll configure the three switches in the following graphic to work in the internetworking environment. This lab will assume that you have at least one 2950 switch and a 1900 enterprise edition switch. If you only have one 2950 at this time, that is sufficient.

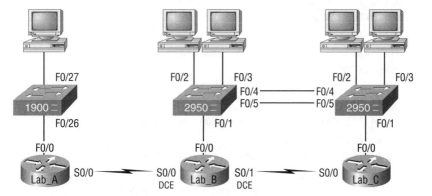

The labs in this chapter include the following:

Lab 7.1: Switch Basic Administrative Configurations

Lab 7.2: Verifying the Switch Configurations

Hands-on Lab 7.1: Switch Basic Administrative Configurations

This lab will also assume that you have configured the internetworking lab in Chapter 6, that OSPF or EIGRP is running, and that all routers are up and communicating. We'll configure our switches with the following, based on the router configurations from the previous chapters:

- 1900: IP address 192.168.10.10/24

- 2900B: (connected to Lab_B router) 192.168.30.10/24

- 2900C: (connected to Lab_C router) 192.168.50.10/24

Don't worry about the two connections between the 2950 switches; we'll get to those in the next chapter. However, we can set descriptions for the interfaces, just for fun.

At this point, we just want to provide basic administrative configuration on the switches and verify their configuration. Let's start by adding hostnames, passwords, banner, interface description, and IP addresses to each switch.

1. The first switch we'll configure is the 2950 connected to the Lab_C router:

```
Switch>en
Switch#config t
  Enter configuration commands, one per line.  End with CNTL/Z.
Switch(config)#hostname 2950C
```

```
2950C(config)#enable secret todd
2950C(config)#line con 0
2950C(config-line)#login
2950C(config-line)#password console
2950C(config-line)#line vty 0 15
2950C(config-line)#login
2950C(config-line)#password telnet
2950C(config-line)#banner motd #
  Enter TEXT message.  End with the character '#'.
  This is my 2950C switch
  #
2950C(config)#int f0/1
2950C(config-if)#description Connection to router
2950C(config-if)#interface f0/4
2950C(config-if)#description Connection to 2950B
2950C(config-if)#int f0/5
2950C(config-if)#description 2nd connection to 2950B
2950C(config-if)#int vlan1
2950C(config-if)#ip address 192.168.50.10 255.255.255.0
2950C(config-if)#no shut
2950C(config-if)#exit
2950C(config)#ip default-gateway 192.168.50.1
2950C(config)#^Z
2950C#copy run start
Destination filename [startup-config]? (return)
  Building configuration...
  [OK]
  2950C#
```

2. Now let's continue on with the 2950B switch:

```
Switch>en
Switch#config t
  Enter configuration commands, one per line.  End with CNTL/Z.
Switch(config)#hostname 2950B
2950B(config)#enable secret todd
2950B(config)#line con 0
2950B(config-line)#login
2950B(config-line)#password console
2950B(config-line)#line vty 0 15
2950B(config-line)#login
2950B(config-line)#password telnet
```

```
2950B(config-line)#banner motd #
 Enter TEXT message.  End with the character '#'.
 This is my 2950B switch
 #
 2950B(config)#
2950B(config)#int f0/4
2950B(config-if)#desc connection to 2950C
2950B(config-if)#int f0/5
2950B(config-if)#desc 2nd connection to 2950C
2950B(config-if)#int vlan 1
2950B(config-if)#ip address 192.168.30.10 255.255.255.0
2950B(config-if)#no shut
2950B(config-if)#exit
2950B(config)#ip default-gateway 192.168.30.1
2950B(config)#exit
2950B#copy run start
Destination filename [startup-config]? (return)
 Building configuration...
 [OK]
 2950B#
```

3. Now, let's configure the 1900 switch connected to the Lab_A router:

```
>enable
#config t
(config)#enable password level 1 todd
(config)#enable password level 15 todd1
(config)#enable secret globalnet
(config)#hostname 1900A
1900A(config)#ip address 192.168.10.10 255.255.255.0
1900A(config)#ip default-gateway 192.168.10.1
1900A(config)#banner motd #

 This is the 1900A switch

 #
1900A(config)#int fa0/26
1900A(config-if)#desc Connection to Lab_A router
1900A(config-if)#^z

 1900A#
```

Hands-on Lab 7.2: Verifying the Switch Configurations

To verify the configurations, the show running-config command can be used on both the 1900 and 2950 Catalyst switches. However, to test that the switches are working in the internetwork, Ping is a great tool to use.

1. From the 1900 switch, ping the Lab_A router:

    1900A#**ping 192.168.10.1**

2. From the 1900 switch, ping the two 2950 switches:

    1900A#**ping 192.168.30.10**
    1900A#**ping 192.168.50.10**

3. From the 2950B switch, ping the 1900A switch and the 2950C switch:

    2950B#**ping 192.168.10.10**
    2950B#**ping 192.168.50.10**

4. From the 2950C switch, ping the 1900A switch and the 2950B switch:

    2950C#**ping 192.168.10.10**
    2950C#**ping 192.168.30.10**

Review Questions

1. Which LAN switch method runs a CRC on every frame?

   A. Cut-through

   B. Store-and-forward

   C. FragmentCheck

   D. FragmentFree

2. You have 10 hosts plus a server connected to a switch. Each device is running 10Mbps half-duplex. What is the bandwidth available for each device when it communicates to the server?

   A. 1Mpbs

   B. 2Mbps

   C. 10Mbps

   D. 100Mbps

3. What is the result of segmenting a network with a bridge (switch)? (Choose two options.)

   A. It increases the number of collision domains.

   B. It decreases the number of collision domains.

   C. It increases the number of broadcast domains.

   D. It decreases the number of broadcast domains.

   E. It makes smaller collision domains.

   F. It makes larger collision domains.

4. Layer 2 switching provides which of the following? (Choose two options.)

   A. Hardware-based bridging (MAC)

   B. Wire speed

   C. High latency

   D. High cost

5. If your network is currently congested and you are using only hubs in your network, what would be the best solution to decrease congestion on your network?

   A. Cascade your hubs.

   B. Replace your hubs with switches.

   C. Replace your hubs with routers.

   D. Add faster hubs.

6. Which LAN switch method is also known as a modified version of cut-through?

   A. Cut-throughout

   B. FragmentFree

   C. Store-and-forward

   D. Store-and-release

7. Which of the following are true regarding store-and-forward? (Choose two options.)

   A. The latency time varies with frame size.

   B. The latency time is constant.

   C. The frame is transmitted only after the complete frame is received.

   D. The frame is transmitted as soon as the header of the frame is read.

8. What are the three distinct functions of layer 2 switching that increase available bandwidth on the network? (Choose three options.)

   A. Address learning

   B. Routing

   C. Forwarding and filtering

   D. Creating network loops

   E. Loop avoidance

   F. IP addressing

9. You are working on a network design and determine that a new testing application requires multiple hosts that must be capable of sharing data between each host and server running 10Mbps. Other departments use applications that require less than 3Mbps to the server. What should you recommend?

   A. Replace the 10Mbps Ethernet hub with a 100Mbps Ethernet hub.

   B. Install a router between departments.

   C. Use a switch with a 100Mbps uplink to the server and 10Mbps to the hosts.

   D. Use a bridge to break up collision domains.

10. What technology is used by Catalyst switches to resolve topology loops and ensure that data flows properly through a single network path?

    A. RIP

    B. STP

    C. IGRP

    D. Store-and-forward

    E. Cut-through

11. Which of the following statements is true?

    A. A switch creates a single collision domain and a single broadcast domain. A router creates a single collision domain.

    B. A switch creates separate collision domains but one broadcast domain. A router provides a separate broadcast domain.

    C. A switch creates a single collision domain and separate broadcast domains. A router provides a separate broadcast domain as well.

    D. A switch creates separate collision domains and separate broadcast domains. A router provides separate collision domains.

12. Which of the following is true regarding layer 2 switches? (Choose two options.)

    A. A switch is a hub with more ports.

    B. A switch is a multi-port bridge.

    C. Switches learn IP addresses from each frame and filter the network using these addresses.

    D. Switches learn MAC addresses by examining the source address of each frame.

13. What does a switch do when a frame is received on an interface and the destination hardware address is unknown or not in the filter table?

    A. Forwards the switch to the first available link

    B. Drops the frame

    C. Floods the network with the frame looking for the device

    D. Sends back a message to the originating station asking for a name resolution

14. Which LAN switch type waits for the collision window to pass before looking up the destination hardware address in the MAC filter table and forwarding the frame?

    A. Cut-through

    B. Store-and-forward

    C. FragmentCheck

    D. FragmentFree

15. What statement about switching methods is true?

    A. Store-and-forward has the lowest latency.

    B. Cut-through latency time varies by packet size.

    C. The modified version holds the packet in memory until 50% of the packet reaches the switch.

    D. The modified version holds the packet in memory until the data portion of the packet reaches the switch.

16. Which layer 2 device enables high-speed data exchange?

    A. Repeater

    B. Hub

    C. Switch

    D. Router

17. What purpose in a switched LAN does STP perform?

    A. Prevent routing loops in a network with redundant paths.

    B. Prevent switching loops in a network with redundant switched paths.

    C. Allow VLAN information to be passed in a trunked link.

    D. Create multiple broadcast domains in a layer 2 switched network.

18. Which of the following is a characteristic of having a network segment on a switch?

    A. The segment is many collision domains.

    B. The segment can translate from one media to a different media.

    C. All devices on a segment are part of a different broadcast domain.

    D. One device per segment can send frames to the switch at a time.

19. What could happen on a network if no loop avoidance schemes are put in place? (Choose two options.)

    A. Faster convergence times.

    B. Broadcast storms.

    C. Multiple frame copies.

    D. IP routing will cause flapping on a serial link.

20. Which of the following is true in regard to bridges?

    A. Bridges do not isolate broadcast domains.

    B. Bridges broadcast packets into the same collision domain they were received from.

    C. Bridges use IP addresses to filter the network.

    D. Bridges can translate from one media to a different media.

Answers to Review Questions

1. B. Store-and-forward LAN switching checks every frame for CRC errors. It has the highest latency of any LAN switch type.

2. C. Each device has a dedicated connection running 10Mbps. If the devices were connected to a hub, then they would all have to share the bandwidth.

3. A, E. Bridges break up collision domains, which would increase the number of collision domains in a network and also make smaller collision domains.

4. A, B. Layer 2 switching uses ASICs to provide frame filtering and is considered hardware based. Layer 2 switching also provides wire-speed frame transfers, with low latency.

5. B. Layer 2 switches break up collision domains and will decrease congestion on your network.

6. B. The modified version of cut-through is called FragmentFree.

7. A, C. Store-and-forward latency (delay) will always vary because the complete frame must be received before the frame is transmitted back out the switch.

8. A, C, E. Layer 2 features that increase available bandwidth include address learning, forwarding and filtering of the network, and loop avoidance.

9. C. By adding a switch, you can effectively segment the network and provide 100Mbps to the server and 10 Mbps to the hosts.

10. B. Spanning Tree Protocol (STP) will make sure that no network loops occur at layer 2.

11. B. Switches break up collision domains, and routers break up broadcast domains.

12. B, D. A switch is really just a multi-port bridge with more intelligence. Switches (and bridges) build their filter table by examining the source MAC address of each frame.

13. C. Switches flood all frames that have an unknown destination address. If a device answers the frame, the switch will update the MAC address table to reflect the location of the device.

14. D. FragmentFree looks at the first 64 bytes of a frame to make sure a collision has not occurred. It is sometimes referred to as modified cut-through.

15. D. The last option is the best answer because the FragmentFree LAN switch method reads into the data field of every frame.

16. C. Layer 2 switches are used to enable high-speed data exchange on a LAN.

17. B. Spanning Tree Protocol (STP) stops loops at layer 2; in this question, the best answer is to stop loops in a switched network because switches work at layer 2. Routing protocols (RIP, IGRP, etc.) are used to stop loops at layer 3 (routing).

18. D. Only one device on a network segment connected to a switch can send frames to the switch at a time. A switch cannot translate from one media type to another on the same segment.

19. B, C. Broadcast storms and multiple frame copies are typically found in a network that has multiple links to remote locations without some type of loop-avoidance scheme.

20. A. A bridge breaks up collision domains, but it is one large broadcast domain by default.

Answers to Written Lab 7

1. Store-and-forward

2. Cut-through

3. Address learning, filter/forward, loop avoidance

4. FragmentFree

5. Spanning Tree Protocol (STP)

6. Store-and-forward

7. Cut-through, FragmentFree

8. FragmentFree

9. Spanning Tree Protocol (STP)

10. Store-and-forward

Virtual LANs (VLANs)

THE CCNA EXAM TOPICS COVERED IN THIS CHAPTER INCLUDE THE FOLLOWING:

✓ **IMPLEMENTATION & OPERATION**

- Configure a switch with VLANS and inter-switch communication
- Implement a LAN
- Customize a switch configuration to meet specified network requirements

✓ **TROUBLESHOOTING**

- Perform LAN and VLAN troubleshooting

I know I keep telling you this, but I've just got to be sure you never forget it, so here I go one last time: By default, switches break up collision domains and routers break up broadcast domains. Okay, I feel better! Now let's move on.

In contrast to the networks of yesterday, which were based on collapsed backbones, today's network design is characterized by a flatter architecture—thanks to switches. So now what? How do we break up broadcast domains in a pure switched internetwork? By creating a virtual local area network (VLAN), that's how. A VLAN is a logical grouping of network users and resources connected to administratively defined ports on a switch. When you create VLANs, you are given the ability to create smaller broadcast domains within a layer 2 switched inter-network by assigning different ports on the switch to different subnetworks. A VLAN is treated like its own subnet or broadcast domain, which means that frames broadcast onto the network are only switched between the ports logically grouped within the same VLAN.

So, does this mean we no longer need routers? Maybe yes; maybe no. It really depends on what you want to do. By default, all hosts in a specific VLAN cannot communicate with any other hosts that are members of another VLAN, so if you want inter-VLAN communication, the answer is yes—you still need a router.

In this chapter, you're going to learn exactly what a VLAN is and how VLAN memberships are used in a switched internetwork. Also, I'm going to tell you all about how VLAN Trunk Protocol (VTP) is used to update switch databases with VLAN information, and how trunking is used to send information from all VLANs across one link. And then I'll wrap things up by discussing how you can make inter-VLAN communication happen by introducing a router into your switched internetwork.

VLAN Basics

As shown in Figure 8.1, layer 2 switched networks are typically designed as flat networks. Every broadcast packet transmitted is seen by every device on the network, regardless of whether the device needs to receive that data.

By default, routers allow broadcasts only within the originating network, but switches forward broadcasts to all segments. The reason it's called a *flat network* is because it's one *broadcast domain*, not because its design is physically flat.

In Figure 8.1 we see Host A sending a broadcast and all ports on all switches forwarding this broadcast, except the port that originally received it. Now look at Figure 8.2, which pictures a switched network. It shows Host A sending a frame with Host D as its destination, and as you can see, that frame is only forwarded out the port where Host D is located. This is a huge improvement over the old hub networks, unless having one *collision domain* by default is what you really want.

FIGURE 8.1   Flat network structure

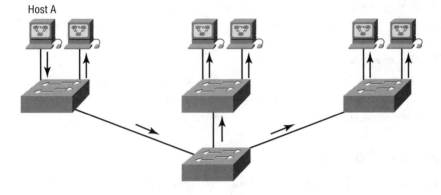

Now you already know that the largest benefit gained by having a layer 2 switched network is that it creates individual collision domain segments for each device plugged into each port on the switch. This scenario frees us from the Ethernet distance constraints, so now larger networks can be built. But with each new advance, we often encounter new issues—the larger the number of users and devices, the more broadcasts and packets each switch must handle!

FIGURE 8.2   The benefit of a switched network

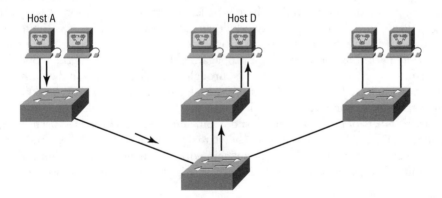

And here's another one—security! This one's a real problem because within the typical layer 2 switched internetwork, all users can see all devices by default. And you can't stop devices from broadcasting, nor users from trying to respond to broadcasts. Your security options are dismally limited to placing passwords on the servers and other devices.

But not if you create a *virtual LAN (VLAN)*. You can solve many of the problems associated with layer 2 switching with VLANs—as you'll soon see.

There are several ways that VLANs simplify network management:

- Network adds, moves, and changes are achieved by configuring a port into the appropriate VLAN.

- A group of users needing high security can be put into a VLAN so that no users outside of the VLAN can communicate with them.

- As a logical grouping of users by function, VLANs can be considered independent from their physical or geographic locations.

- VLANs can enhance network security.

- VLANs increase the number of broadcast domains while decreasing their size.

In the following sections, I am going to discuss switching characteristics and how switches provide better network services then hubs do in our networks.

Broadcast Control

Broadcasts occur in every protocol, but how often they occur depends upon three things:

- Type of protocol
- The application(s) running on the internetwork
- How these services are used

Some older applications have been rewritten to reduce their bandwidth needs, but there's a new generation of applications that are incredibly bandwidth-greedy, consuming all they can find. These bandwidth abusers are multimedia applications that use broadcasts and multicasts extensively. Faulty equipment, inadequate segmentation, and poorly designed firewalls only serve to compound the problems that these broadcast-intensive applications create. All of this has truly added a new dimension to network design, as well as generating new challenges for an administrator. Making sure the network is properly segmented in order to isolate one segment's problems and keep those problems from propagating throughout the internetwork is imperative. The most effective way of doing this is through strategic switching and routing.

Since switches have become more cost-effective lately, many companies are replacing their flat hub networks with a pure switched network and VLAN environment. All devices in a VLAN are members of the same broadcast domain and receive all broadcasts. The broadcasts, by default, are filtered from all ports on a switch that are not members of the same VLAN. This is great because it offers all the benefits you gain with a switched design without the serious anguish you would experience if all your users were in the same broadcast domain!

Security

But it seems there's always a catch, so let's get back to those security issues. A flat internetwork's security used to be tackled by connecting hubs and switches together with routers. So it was basically the router's job to maintain security. This arrangement was pretty ineffective for several reasons: First, anyone connecting to the physical network could access the network resources located on that physical LAN. Secondly, all anyone had to do to observe any and all traffic happening in that network was to simply plug a network analyzer into the hub. And in that same vein, users could join a workgroup by just plugging their workstations into the existing hub. So basically, this was non-security!

This is why VLANs are so cool. By building them and creating multiple broadcast groups, administrators can now have control over each port and user! The days when users could just plug their workstations into any switch port and gain access to network resources are history, because the administrator is now awarded control over each port and whatever resources that port can access.

Also, because VLANs can be created in accordance with the network resources a user requires, switches can be configured to inform a network management station of any unauthorized access to network resources. And if you need inter-VLAN communication, you can implement restrictions on a router to achieve it. You can also place restrictions on hardware addresses, protocols, and applications—now we're talking security!

Flexibility and Scalability

If you were paying attention to what you've read so far, you know that layer 2 switches only read frames for filtering—they don't look at the Network layer protocol. And by default, switches forward all broadcasts. But if you create and implement VLANs, you're essentially creating smaller broadcast domains at layer 2.

This means that broadcasts sent out from a node in one VLAN won't be forwarded to ports configured to be in a different VLAN. So by assigning switch ports or users to VLAN groups on a switch or group of connected switches, you gain the flexibility to add only the users you want into that broadcast domain regardless of their physical location! This setup can also work to block broadcast storms caused by a faulty Network Interface Card (NIC), as well as prevent an intermediate device from propagating the storms throughout the entire internetwork. Those evils can still happen on the VLAN where the problem originated, but the disease will just be quarantined to that one ailing VLAN.

Another advantage is that when a VLAN gets too big, you can create more VLANs to keep the broadcasts from consuming too much bandwidth—the fewer users in a VLAN, the fewer users affected by broadcasts. This is well and good, but you absolutely need to keep network services in mind and understand how the users connect to these services when you create your VLAN. It's a good move to try and keep all services, except for the e-mail and Internet access that everyone needs, local to all users when possible.

To understand how a VLAN looks to a switch, it's helpful to begin by first looking at a traditional network. Figure 8.3 shows how a network was created by connecting physical LANs using hubs to a router.

Here you can see that each network was attached with a hub port to the router (each segment also had its own logical network number, though this is not obvious from the figure). Each node attached to a particular physical network had to match that network number in order to be able to communicate on the internetwork. Notice that each department had its own LAN, so if you needed to add new users to Sales, for example, you would just plug them into the Sales LAN and they would automatically be part of the Sales collision and broadcast domain. This design really did work well for many years.

FIGURE 8.3 Physical LANs connected to a router

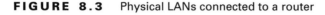
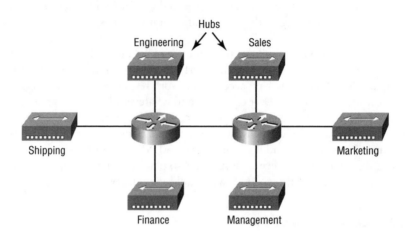

But there was one major flaw: what happens if the hub for Sales is full and you need to add another user to the Sales LAN? Or, what do we do if there's no more physical space in the location where the Sales team is located for this new employee? Well, let's say there just happens to be plenty of room in the Finance section of the building. That new Sales team member will just have to sit on the same side of the building as the Finance people, and we'll just plug the poor soul into the hub for Finance.

Doing this obviously makes the new user part of the Finance LAN, which is bad for many reasons. First and foremost, we now have a security issue, because this new user is a member of the Finance broadcast domain and can therefore see all the same servers and network services that the Finance folks can. Secondly, for this user to access the Sales network services they need to get the job done, they would need to go through the router to log in to the Sales server—not exactly efficient!

Now let's look at what a switch accomplishes. Figure 8.4 demonstrates how switches remove the physical boundary to solve our problem.

Figure 8.4 shows how six VLANs (numbered 2 through 7) were used to create a broadcast domain for each department. Each switch port is then administratively assigned a VLAN membership, depending on the host and which broadcast domain it must be in.

So now, if I needed to add another user to the Sales VLAN (VLAN 7), I could just assign the port used to VLAN 7, regardless of where the new Sales team member is physically located—nice! This illustrates one of the sweetest advantages to designing your network with VLANs over the old collapsed backbone design. Now, cleanly and simply, each host that needs to be in the Sales VLAN is merely assigned to VLAN 7.

Notice that I started assigning VLANs with VLAN number 2. The number is irrelevant, but you might be wondering: What happened to VLAN 1? That VLAN is an administrative VLAN, and even though it can be used for a workgroup, Cisco recommends that you use this for administrative purposes only. You can't delete or change the name of VLAN 1, and by default, all ports on a switch are members of VLAN 1 until you change them.

FIGURE 8.4   Switches removing the physical boundary

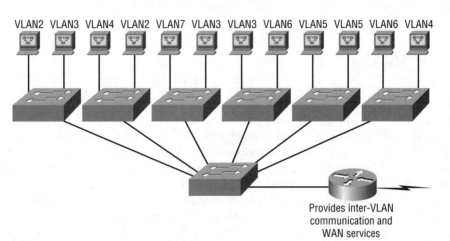

Marketing	VLAN2	172.16.20.0/24	
Shipping	VLAN3	172.16.30.0/24	
Engineering	VLAN4	172.16.40.0/24	
Finance	VLAN5	172.16.50.0/24	
Management	VLAN6	172.16.60.0/24	
Sales	VLAN7	172.16.70.0/24	

Each VLAN is considered a broadcast domain, so it must also have its own subnet number, as shown in Figure 8.4. And if you're also using IPX, then each VLAN must also be assigned its own IPX network number.

Now let's get back to that "because of switches, we don't need routers anymore" misconception. In Figure 8.4, notice that there are seven VLANs or broadcast domains, counting VLAN 1. The nodes within each VLAN can communicate with each other, but not with anything in a different VLAN, because the nodes in any given VLAN "think" that they're actually in a collapsed backbone as in Figure 8.3.

And what handy little tool do we need to enable the hosts in Figure 8.4 to communicate to a node or host on a different VLAN? You guessed it—a router! Those nodes positively need to go through a router, or some other layer 3 device, just like when they're configured for inter-network communication (as shown in Figure 8.3). It's the same as if we were trying to connect different physical networks. Communication between VLANs must go through a layer 3 device. So don't expect routers to disappear anytime soon!

VLAN Memberships

VLANs are usually created by an administrator, who then assigns switch ports to each VLAN. Such a VLAN is called a *static VLAN*. If the administrator wants to do a little more work up front and assign all the host devices' hardware addresses into a database, the switches can be configured to assign VLANs dynamically whenever a host is plugged into a switch. This is called a *dynamic VLAN*. We will look at both static and dynamic VLANs in the following sections.

Static VLANs

Static VLANs are the usual way of creating VLANs, and they're also the most secure. The switch port that you assign a VLAN association to always maintains that association until an administrator manually changes that port assignment.

This type of VLAN configuration is comparatively easy to set up and monitor, and it works well in a network where the movement of users within the network is controlled. And although it can be helpful to use network management software to configure the ports, it's not mandatory.

In Figure 8.4, each switch port was configured with a VLAN membership by an administrator based on which VLAN the host needed to be a member of—the device's actual physical location doesn't matter. The broadcast domain the hosts will become a member of is an administrative choice. Remember that each host must also have the correct IP address information. For example, each host in VLAN 2 must be configured into the 172.16.20.0/24 network. It is also important to remember that, if you plug a host into a switch, you must verify the VLAN membership of that port. If the membership is different than what is needed for that host, the host will not be able to reach the needed network services, such as a workgroup server.

Dynamic VLANs

A dynamic VLAN determines a node's VLAN assignment automatically. Using intelligent management software, you can base VLAN assignments on hardware (MAC) addresses, protocols, or even applications to create dynamic VLANs.

It's up to you! For example, suppose MAC addresses have been entered into a centralized VLAN management application. If a node is then attached to an unassigned switch port, the VLAN management database can look up the hardware address and assign and configure the switch port to the correct VLAN. This is very cool—it makes management and configuration easier because if a user moves, the switch will assign them to the correct VLAN automatically. But you have to do a lot more work initially setting up the database.

Cisco administrators can use the VLAN Management Policy Server (VMPS) service to set up a database of MAC addresses that can be used for dynamic addressing of VLANs. A VMPS database maps MAC addresses to VLANs.

Identifying VLANs

As frames are switched throughout the network, switches must be able to keep track of all the different types, plus understand what to do with them depending on the hardware address. And remember, frames are handled differently according to the type of link they are traversing.

FIGURE 8.5   Access and trunk links in a switched network

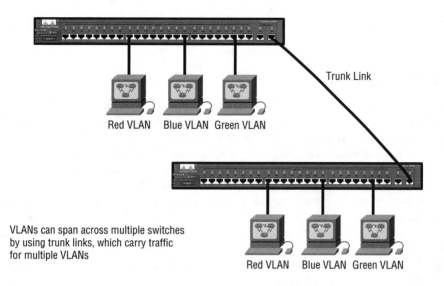

Trunk Link

Red VLAN   Blue VLAN   Green VLAN

VLANs can span across multiple switches
by using trunk links, which carry traffic
for multiple VLANs

Red VLAN   Blue VLAN   Green VLAN

There are two different types of links in a switched environment:

Access links   This type of link is only part of one VLAN, and it's referred to as the *native VLAN* of the port. Any device attached to an *access link* is unaware of a VLAN membership—the device just assumes it's part of a broadcast domain, but it has no understanding of the physical network.

Switches remove any VLAN information from the frame before it's sent to an access-link device. Access-link devices cannot communicate with devices outside their VLAN unless the packet is routed.

Trunk links   Trunks can carry multiple VLANs and originally gained their name after the telephone system trunks that carry multiple telephone conversations.

A *trunk link* is a 100- or 1000Mbps point-to-point link between two switches, between a switch and router, or between a switch and server. These carry the traffic of multiple VLANs—from 1 to 1005 at a time.

Trunking allows you to make a single port part of multiple VLANs at the same time. This can be a real advantage. For instance, you can actually set things up to have a server in two broadcast domains simultaneously, so that your users won't have to cross a layer 3 device (router) to log in and access it. Another benefit to trunking is when you're connecting switches. Trunk links can carry some or all VLAN information across the link, but if the links between your switches aren't trunked, only VLAN 1 information will be switched across the link by default.

All VLANs are configured on a trunked link unless cleared by an administrator by hand.

Figure 8.5 shows how the different links are used in a switched network. All hosts connected to the switches can communicate to all ports in all VLANs because of the trunk link between them. And remember, using an access link only allows one VLAN to be used across the link. As you can see, these hosts are using access links to connect to the switch, so that means they're communicating in one VLAN only.

In the following sections, I am going to discuss frame tagging and the VLAN identification methods used in frame tagging.

Frame Tagging

As mentioned, you can create your VLANs to span more than one connected switch. In Figure 8.4, hosts from various VLANs are spread across many switches. This flexible, power-packed capability is probably the main advantage to implementing VLANs!

But this can get kind of complicated—even for a switch—so there needs to be a way for each one to keep track of all the users and frames as they travel the switch fabric and VLANs. (Remember, a switch fabric is basically a group of switches sharing the same VLAN information.) This is where *frame tagging* comes in. This frame identification method uniquely assigns a user-defined ID to each frame. Sometimes people refer to it as a "VLAN ID" or "color."

Here's how it works: Each switch that the frame reaches must first identify the VLAN ID from the frame tag, then it finds out what to do with the frame by looking at the information in the filter table. If the frame reaches a switch that has another trunked link, the frame will be forwarded out the trunk-link port.

Once the frame reaches an exit to an access link matching the frames VLAN ID, the switch removes the VLAN identifier. This is so the destination device can receive the frames without having to understand their VLAN identification.

VLAN Identification Methods

So VLAN identification is what switches use to keep track of all those frames as they're traversing a switch fabric. It's how switches identify which frames belong to which VLANs, and there's more than one trunking method:

Inter-Switch Link (ISL)   This is proprietary to Cisco switches, and it's used for Fast Ethernet and Gigabit Ethernet links only. *ISL routing* can be used on a switch port, router interfaces, and server interface cards to trunk a server. This is a very good approach if you're creating functional VLANs and you don't want to break the 80/20 rule.

Wait a minute—what's the 80/20 rule? Well, it's a formula that says 80 percent (or more) of the data traffic should stay on the local segment while 20 percent (or less) crosses a segmentation device. A trunked server is part of all VLANs (broadcast domains) simultaneously, so users don't have to cross a layer 3 device to access it.

IEEE 802.1Q   Created by the IEEE as a standard method of frame tagging, it actually inserts a field into the frame to identify the VLAN. If you're trunking between a Cisco switched link and a different brand of switch, you have to use 802.1Q for the trunk to work.

It works like this: You must designate each 802.1Q port to be associated with a specific VLAN ID. The ports that populate the same trunk create a group that's known as a native VLAN, and each port gets tagged with an identification number that reflects its native VLAN—the default being VLAN 1.

The basic purpose of ISL and 802.1Q frame-tagging methods is to provide inter-switch VLAN communication.

Inter-Switch Link (ISL) Protocol

Inter-Switch Link (ISL) is a way of explicitly tagging VLAN information onto an Ethernet frame. This tagging information allows VLANs to be multiplexed over a trunk link through an external encapsulation method (ISL), which allows the switch to identify the VLAN membership of a frame over the trunked link.

By running ISL, you can interconnect multiple switches and still maintain VLAN information as traffic travels between switches on trunk links. ISL functions at layer 2 by encapsulating a data frame with a new header and cyclic redundancy check (CRC).

 Cisco created the ISL protocol, and it's proprietary to Cisco devices only. If you need a non-proprietary VLAN protocol, use the 802.1Q.

Because ISL is an external tagging process, the original frame isn't altered—it's only encapsulated with a new 26-byte ISL header. It also adds a second 4-byte Frame Check Sequence (FCS) field at the end of the frame. Because the frame has been encapsulated by ISL with information, only ISL-aware devices can read it. These frames can be up to a whopping 1522 bytes long!

On multi-VLAN (trunk) ports, each frame is tagged as it enters the switch. ISL network interface cards (NICs) allow servers to send and receive frames tagged with multiple VLANs so they can traverse multiple VLANs without going through a router. This is good because it reduces latency. ISL makes it easy for users to access servers quickly and efficiently without having to go through a router every time they need to communicate with a resource. This technology can also be used with probes and certain network analyzers, and administrators can use it to include file servers in multiple VLANs simultaneously.

ISL VLAN information is added to a frame only if the frame is forwarded out a port configured as a trunk link. The ISL encapsulation is removed from the frame if the frame is forwarded out an access link—this is a really important ISL fact, so make a mental note, and don't forget it!

VLAN Trunking Protocol (VTP)

Cisco created this one too, but this time it isn't proprietary. The basic goals of *VLAN Trunking Protocol (VTP)* are to manage all configured VLANs across a switched internetwork and to maintain consistency throughout that network. VTP allows an administrator to add, delete, and rename VLANs—information that is then propagated to all other switches in the VTP domain.

Here's a list of some of the benefits VTP has to offer:

- Consistent VLAN configuration across all switches in the network
- Allows VLANs to be trunked over mixed networks, such as Ethernet to ATM LANE or even FDDI
- Accurate tracking and monitoring of VLANs
- Dynamic reporting of added VLANs to all switches in the VTP domain
- Plug-and-Play VLAN adding

Very cool—yes, but before you can get VTP to manage your VLANs across the network, you have to create a VTP server. All servers that need to share VLAN information must use the same domain name, and a switch can be in only one domain at a time. So, this means that a switch can only share VTP domain information with other switches if they're configured into the same VTP domain. You can use a VTP domain if you have more than one switch connected in a network, but if you've got all your switches in only one VLAN, you don't need to use VTP. VTP information is sent between switches via a trunk port.

Switches advertise VTP-management domain information, as well as a configuration revision number and all known VLANs with any specific parameters. And there's also something called *VTP transparent mode*. In it, you can configure switches to forward VTP information through trunk ports, but not to accept information updates or update their VTP databases.

If you find yourself having problems with users adding switches to your VTP domain, you can include passwords, but don't forget—every switch must be set up with the same password, and this can be difficult.

Switches detect the additional VLANs within a VTP advertisement and then prepare to receive information on their trunk ports with the newly defined VLAN in tow. Updates are sent out as revision numbers that are the notification plus 1. Any time a switch sees a higher revision number, it knows the information that it's receiving is more current, and it will overwrite the current database with that new information.

In the following sections, I will continue my discussion of VTP with VTP modes and VTP pruning.

VTP Modes of Operation

There are three different modes of operation within a VTP domain. Figure 8.6 shows you all three:

Server This is the default for all Catalyst switches. You need at least one server in your VTP domain to propagate VLAN information throughout the domain. The switch must be in server mode to be able to create, add, or delete VLANs in a VTP domain. Changing VTP information must also be done in server mode, and any change made to a switch in server mode will be advertised to the entire VTP domain.

Client In client mode, switches receive information from VTP servers, and they also send and receive updates. But they can't make any changes. Plus, none of the ports on a client switch can be added to a new VLAN before the VTP server notifies the client switch of the new VLAN. Here's a hint: If you want a switch to become a server, first make it a client so it receives all the correct VLAN information, then change it to a server—much easier!

FIGURE 8.6   VTP modes

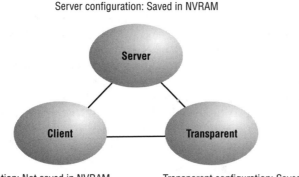

Server configuration: Saved in NVRAM

Client configuration: Not saved in NVRAM   Transparent configuration: Saved in NVRAM

Transparent   Switches in transparent mode don't participate in the VTP domain, but they'll still forward VTP advertisements through any configured trunk links. These switches can't add and delete VLANs because they keep their own database—one they do not share with other switches. The VLAN database in Transparent mode is really considered locally significant only.

🌐 Real World Scenario

When do I need to worry about VTP?

Bob, a Senior Network Administrator at Acme Corporation in San Francisco has about 25 switches all connected together, and he wants to configure VLANs to break up broadcast domains. When should he start to think about using VTP?

Whenever you have more than one switch and you have multiple VLANs. If you have only one switch, then VTP is irrelevant. It also isn't important if you're not configuring VLANs in your network. However, if you do have multiple switches that use multiple VLANs, then you'd better configure your VTP server and clients correctly!

When you first bring up your switched network, verify that your main switch is a VTP server and all others are VTP clients. When you create VLANs on the main VTP server, all switches will receive the VLAN database.

If you have an existing switched network and you want to add a new switch, make sure to configure it as a VTP client before you install it. Because if you don't, it's possible—okay, likely—that this new switch will send out a new VTP database to all your other switches, effectively wiping out all your existing VLANs! And no one needs that!

VTP Pruning

VTP provides a way for you to preserve bandwidth by configuring it to reduce the amount of broadcasts, multicasts, and unicast packets. This is called *pruning*. VTP pruning only sends broadcasts to trunk links that truly must have the information. Here's an example: If Switch A doesn't have any ports configured for VLAN 5, and a broadcast is sent throughout VLAN 5, that broadcast would not traverse the trunk link to Switch A. By default, VTP pruning is disabled on all switches.

When you enable pruning on a VTP server, you enable it for the entire domain. By default, VLANs 2 through 1005 are pruning-eligible, but VLAN 1 can never prune because it's an administrative VLAN.

Routing between VLANs

Hosts in a VLAN live in their own broadcast domain and can communicate freely. VLANs create network partitioning and traffic separation at layer 2 of the OSI, and as I said when I told you why we still need routers, if you want hosts or any other IP addressable device to communicate between VLANs, a layer 3 device is absolutely necessary.

For this, you can use a router that has an interface for each VLAN or a router that supports ISL routing. The least expensive router that supports ISL routing is the 2600 series router. The 1600, 1700, and 2500 series don't support ISL routing.

As shown in Figure 8.7, if you had only a few VLANs (two or three), you could get a router with two or three 10BaseT or Fast Ethernet connections. And 10BaseT is okay, but I'd recommend Fast Ethernet—that will work really well.

FIGURE 8.7   Router with individual VLAN associations

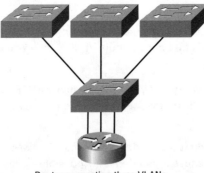

Router connecting three VLANs
together for inter-VLAN communication,
one interface for each VLAN.

What we see in Figure 8.7 is that each router interface is plugged into an access link. This means that each of the routers' interface IP addresses would then become the default gateway address for each host in each VLAN.

If you have more VLANs available than router interfaces, you can either run ISL trunking on one Fast Ethernet interface or buy a layer 3 switch such as the Cisco 3550.

Instead of using a router interface for each VLAN, you use one Fast Ethernet interface and run ISL or 802.1Q trunking. Figure 8.8 shows how a Fast Ethernet interface on a router will look when configured with ISL or 802.1Q trunking. This allows all VLANs to communicate through one interface. Cisco calls this a "router on a stick."

FIGURE 8.8   Router-on-a-stick

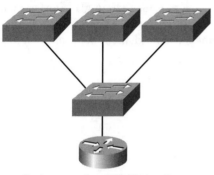

Router connecting all VLANs together
allowing for inter-VLAN communication,
using only one router interface
(Router on a stick).

Configuring VLANs

Configuring VLANs is actually pretty easy. Figuring out which users you want in each VLAN is not. It's super time-consuming, but once you've decided on the number of VLANs you want to create, and established the users you want to belong to each one, it's time to bring your first VLAN into existence!

To configure VLANs on a 1900 switch, use the vlan *vlan#* name *name* [*vlan#*] command. In the following example, I am going to demonstrate how to configure VLANs on the 1900 switch by creating three VLANs for three different departments (VLAN 1 is the native and administrative VLAN):

```
>en
#config t
Enter configuration commands, one per line.  End with CNTL/Z
```

```
(config)#hostname 1900
1900(config)#vlan 2 name sales
1900(config)#vlan 3 name marketing
1900(config)#vlan 4 name mis
1900(config)#exit
```

After you create the VLANs that you want, you can use the show vlan command to see them. But notice that by default, all ports on the switch are in VLAN 1. To change the VLAN associated with a port, you need to go to each interface and tell it which VLAN to be a part of.

 Remember that a created VLAN is unused until it is assigned to a switch port or ports, and that all ports are always assigned in VLAN 1 unless set otherwise.

Once the VLANs are created, verify your configuration with the show vlan command (sh vlan for short):

```
1900#sh vlan

VLAN Name              Status      Ports
----------------------------------------
1    default           Enabled     1-12, AUI, A, B
2    sales             Enabled
3    marketing         Enabled
4    mis               Enabled
1002 fddi-default      Suspended
1003 token-ring-defau  Suspended
1004 fddinet-default   Suspended
1005 trnet-default     Suspended
----------------------------------------

[output cut]
```

Creating VLANs for the 2950 switch is very different. You configure them in what is called a VLAN database. Here's how:

```
Switch#vlan database
Switch(vlan)#?
VLAN database editing buffer manipulation commands:
  abort  Exit mode without applying the changes
  apply  Apply current changes and bump revision number
  exit   Apply changes, bump revision number, and exit mode
  no     Negate a command or set its defaults
  reset  Abandon current changes and reread current database
  show   Show database information
```

```
vlan    Add, delete, or modify values associated with a single VLAN
vtp     Perform VTP administrative functions.
Switch(vlan)#
```

Notice that to create VLANs on the 2950 you have to enter the VLAN database through privileged mode, not configuration mode. Here's an example of creating three VLANs on the 2950 switch. Notice that when I tried to change VLAN 1 to a name of Sales, it returned an error:

```
Switch(vlan)#vlan 1 name Sales
A default VLAN may not have its name changed.
Switch(vlan)#vlan 2 name Marketing
VLAN 2 modified:
    Name: Marketing
Switch(vlan)#vlan 3 name Accounting
VLAN 3 added:
    Name: Accouting
Switch(vlan)#Vlan 4 name Shipping
VLAN 4 added:
    Name: Shipping
Switch(vlan)#apply
APPLY completed.
Switch(vlan)#control+c
Switch#
```

Notice that you have to apply the changes with the apply command or the changes won't take effect. Also, in the first line where I tried to change VLAN 1, I received an error. That's because it's the default VLAN, which you can't change. It's the native VLAN of all switches by default, and Cisco recommends that you use this as your administrative VLAN. Native VLAN basically means that any packets that aren't specifically assigned to a different VLAN will be sent down the native VLAN.

To see the VLAN database, use the show vlan command or the show vlan brief command:

```
Switch#sh vlan brief

VLAN Name                             Status    Ports
---- -------------------------------- --------- ---------------------------
1    default                          active    Fa0/1, Fa0/2, Fa0/3, Fa0/4
                                                Fa0/5, Fa0/6, Fa0/7, Fa0/8,
                                                Fa0/9, Fa0/10, Fa0/11, Fa0/12
2    Marketing                        active
3    Accounting                       active
4    Shipping                         active
21   VLAN0021                         active
22   VLAN0022                         active
```

```
51   VLAN0051                      active
52   VLAN0052                      active
1002 fddi-default                  active
1003 token-ring-default            active
1004 fddinet-default               active
1005 trnet-default                 active
Switch#
```

Now that we can see the VLANs created, we can assign switch ports to specific ones. Each port can be part of only one VLAN. With the trunking I mentioned earlier you can make a port available to traffic from all VLANs. I'll cover that below.

Assigning Switch Ports to VLANs

You can configure each port on a 1900 switch to be in a VLAN by using the vlan-membership command. You can only configure VLANs one port at a time. There's no command available with the 1900 switch that lets you assign more than one port to a VLAN at a time.

Remember that you can configure either static memberships or dynamic memberships on a port. Even so, I'm only going to cover the static flavor in this book.

In the following example, I configure interface 2 to VLAN 2, interface 4 to VLAN 3, and interface 5 to VLAN 4:

```
1900#config t
Enter configuration commands, one per line.  End with CNTL/Z
1900(config)#int e0/2
1900(config-if)#vlan-membership ?
  dynamic  Set VLAN membership type as dynamic
  static   Set VLAN membership type as static
1900(config-if)#vlan-membership static ?
  <1-1005>  ISL VLAN index
1900(config-if)#vlan-membership static 2
1900(config-if)#int e0/4
1900(config-if)#vlan-membership static 3
1900(config-if)#int e0/5
1900(config-if)#vlan-membership static 4
1900(config-if)#exit
1900(config)#exit
```

Now, type **show vlan** again to see the ports assigned to each VLAN:

```
1900#sh vlan

VLAN Name             Status      Ports
-------------------------------------------
1    default          Enabled     1, 3, 6-12, AUI, A, B
```

```
2    sales            Enabled   2
3    marketing        Enabled   4
4    mis              Enabled   5
1002 fddi-default     Suspended
1003 token-ring-defau Suspended
1004 fddinet-default  Suspended
1005 trnet-default    Suspended
----------------------------------------
```

[output cut]

And of course it's really different for the 2950. Here's how to configure a 2950 with VLANs:

```
Switch(config-if)#int f0/2
Switch(config-if)#switchport access vlan 2
Switch(config-if)#int f0/3
Switch(config-if)#switchport access vlan 3
Switch(config-if)#int f0/4
Switch(config-if)#switchport access vlan 4
Switch(config-if)#
```

If you want to verify your configuration, just use the show vlan or show vlan brief command to show you the VLANs with port assignments:

```
Switch#sh vlan brief
```

VLAN	Name	Status	Ports
1	default	active	Fa0/1, Fa0/5, Fa0/6, Fa0/7, Fa0/8, Fa0/9, Fa0/10, Fa0/11, Fa0/12
2	Marketing	active	Fa0/2
3	Accounting	active	Fa0/3
4	Shipping	active	Fa0/4

That's it. Well, sort of. If you plugged devices into each VLAN port, they can only talk to other devices in the same VLAN. We want to enable inter-VLAN communication and we're going to do that, but first, you need to learn about trunking.

Configuring Trunk Ports

The 1900 switch only runs the Dynamic Inter-Switch Link (DISL) encapsulation method. To configure trunking on a FastEthernet port, use the interface command trunk [parameter].

The following switch output shows the trunk configuration on interface 26 as set to trunk on:

```
1900#config t
Enter configuration commands, one per line.  End with CNTL/Z
1900(config)#int f0/26
1900(config-if)#trunk ?
  auto        Set DISL state to AUTO
  desirable   Set DISL state to DESIRABLE
  nonegotiate Set DISL state to NONEGOTIATE
  off         Set DISL state to OFF
  on          Set DISL state to ON
1900(config-if)#trunk on
```

The following list describes the different options available when setting a trunk interface:

Auto   The interface will become trunked only if the connected device is set to on or desirable.

Desirable   If a connected device is on either desirable or auto, it will negotiate to become a trunk port. Nonegotiate, when mated with desirable, will result in a trunk link, as well.

Nonegotiate   The interface becomes a permanent ISL trunk port and will not negotiate with any attached device.

Off   The interface is disabled from running trunking and tries to convert any attached device to be trunked as well.

On   The interface becomes a permanent ISL trunk port. It can negotiate with a connected device to convert the link to trunk mode.

On the 2950, you use the switchport command:

```
Switch#config t
Enter configuration commands, one per line.  End with CNTL/Z.
Switch(config)#int f0/12
Switch(config-if)#switchport mode trunk
Switch(config-if)#^Z
Switch#
```

To disable trunking on an interface, use the switchport mode access command. You can verify your configuration with the show running-config command:

```
[output cut]
!
interface FastEthernet0/2
 switchport access vlan 2
 no ip address
!
interface FastEthernet0/3
```

```
 switchport access vlan 3
 no ip address
!
interface FastEthernet0/4
 switchport access vlan 4
 no ip address
!
interface FastEthernet0/12
 switchport mode trunk
 no ip address
!
```
[output cut]

Now, let's get a look at connecting a router to our network and configuring inter-VLAN communication.

Configuring Inter-VLAN Routing

By default, only hosts that are members of the same VLAN can communicate. To change this and allow inter-VLAN communication to be possible, you need a router or a layer 3 switch. We're going to take the router approach and use one to connect to both a 1900 and a 2950 switch to make inter-VLAN communication happen.

To support ISL or 802.1Q routing on a FastEthernet interface, the router's interface is divided into logical interfaces—one for each VLAN. These are called *subinterfaces*.

It's important to understand that you cannot provide trunking between the 1900 and 2950 switch by default because the 1900 switch only supports ISL routing and the 2950 switch only supports 802.1Q routing. And these two trunking methods aren't compatible by default. What's more, it's really weird that Cisco doesn't support ISL on their 2950 switch, since ISL is a Cisco proprietary frame-tagging method—go figure!

Anyway, from a FastEthernet or Gigabit interface, you can set the interface to trunk with the encapsulation command. For a connection to a 1900 trunk port (ISL), use the following command:

```
2600#config t
2600(config)#int f0/0.1
2600(config-subif)#encapsulation isl vlan#
```

The configuration above chooses a subinterface, then sets the encapsulation used for a particular VLAN. The subinterface number is locally significant only, so it doesn't matter at all how the subinterface numbers are configured on the router. Most of the time, I'll configure a subinterface with the same number as the VLAN I want to route. It's easy to remember that way, and since the subinterface number is used only for administrative purposes, it's good to remember it.

For a router trunk connection to a 2950 switch (802.1Q), use the following command:

```
2600(config)#int f0/0.1
2600(config-subif)#encapsulation dotlq vlan#
```

It's important to understand that each VLAN is a separate subnet. True, I know—they don't *have* to be. But it really is a good idea to configure your VLANs as separate subnets, so just do that. After I show you how to configure VTP, we'll go through the switches in our internetwork and configure inter-VLAN routing on the Lab_C router.

Configuring VTP

Both the Catalyst 1900 and 2950 switches—actually, all switches—are configured to be VTP servers by default. To configure VTP, first you have to configure the domain name you want to use. And of course, once you configure the VTP information on a switch, you need to verify it.

When you create the VTP domain, you have a number of options, including setting the domain name, password, operating mode, and pruning capabilities of the switch. Use the vtp global configuration mode command to set all this information. In the following example, I set the switch to a vtp server, the VTP domain to Lammle, and the VTP password to todd:

```
1900(config)#vtp ?
  client       VTP client
  domain       Set VTP domain name
  password     Set VTP password
  pruning      VTP pruning
  server       VTP server
  transparent  VTP transparent
  trap         VTP trap
1900(config)#vtp server
1900(config)#vtp domain lammle
1900(config)#vtp password todd
```

Please remember that all switches are set to VTP server mode by default, and if you want to change any VLAN information on a switch, you must be in VTP server mode.

After you configure the VTP information, you can verify it with the show vtp command:

```
1900#sh vtp
    VTP version: 1
    Configuration revision: 0
    Maximum VLANs supported locally: 1005
    Number of existing VLANs: 5
    VTP domain name        : lammle
```

```
    VTP password              : todd
    VTP operating mode        : Server
    VTP pruning mode          : Disabled
    VTP traps generation      : Enabled
    Configuration last modified by: 0.0.0.0 at 00-00-0000 00:00:00
1900#
```

The preceding switch output shows the VTP domain, the VTP password, and the switch's mode.

To configure VTP on the 2950 switch, you again configure the domain name you want to use first. Again, once you configure the VTP information on a switch, you need to verify it. You use the vtp global configuration mode command to set this information.

In the following example, I'll set the switch to a vtp server, (which it already is by default), and then set the VTP domain to routersim:

```
Switch(config)#vtp mode ?
    client       Set the device to client mode.
    server       Set the device to server mode.
    transparent  Set the device to transparent mode.

Switch(config)#vtp mode server
    Device mode already VTP SERVER.

Switch(config)#vtp domain ?
    WORD  The ascii name for the VTP administrative domain.

Switch(config)#vtp domain routersim
    Changing VTP domain name from NULL to routersim
Switch(config)#
```

After you configure the VTP information, you can verify it with the **show vtp** command:

```
SwitchA#sh vtp ?
  counters  VTP statistics
  status    VTP domain status


SwitchA#sh vtp status
VTP Version                     : 2
Configuration Revision          : 1
Maximum VLANs supported locally : 64
Number of existing VLANs        : 7
VTP Operating Mode              : Server
VTP Domain Name                 : routersim
VTP Pruning Mode                : Disabled
```

VTP V2 Mode	: Disabled
VTP Traps Generation	: Disabled
MD5 digest	: 0x4C 0x60 0xA6 0x5D 0xD7 0x41 0x8C 0x37

Configuration last modified by 172.16.10.1 at 3-1-94 06:40:09
Local updater ID is 172.16.10.1 on interface Vl1 (lowest numbered VLAN interface found)

Configuring Switching in Our Sample Internetwork

You've configured the routers in our internetwork for the last few chapters, and now it's time to get to those switches. Figure 8.9 shows the network that we've been configuring so far:

FIGURE 8.9 Our Internetwork

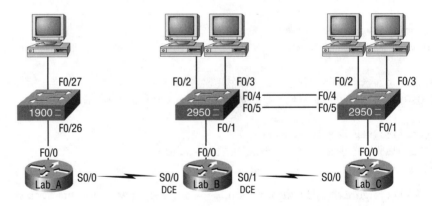

Our internetwork has two 2950s interconnected and ready for us to configure VLANs. I'll name the 2950 connected to the Lab_C router 2950C and the 2950 connected to the Lab_B router 2950B.

For the management VLAN (VLAN 1), I'll use the 172.16.10.0/24 network, with the fa0/0 interface of Lab_B being the router port I'll use to configure inter-VLAN routing. Each switch must have an IP address in the 172.16.10.0 subnet configured to be able to communicate.

I'll also create two more VLANs: VLAN 2 will have the subnet 172.16.20.0/24 and VLAN 3 will have the subnet 172.16.30.0/24.

Let's start by adding hostnames, passwords, banner, interface description, and IP addresses to each switch:

```
Switch>en
Switch#config t
```

```
Enter configuration commands, one per line.  End with CNTL/Z.
Switch(config)#hostname 2950C
2950C(config)#enable secret todd
2950C(config)#line con 0
2950C(config-line)#login
2950C(config-line)#password console
2950C(config-line)#line vty 0 15
2950C(config-line)#login
2950C(config-line)#password telnet
2950C(config-line)#banner motd #
Enter TEXT message.  End with the character '#'.
This is my 2950C switch
#
2950C(config)#int f0/1
2950C(config-if)#description Connection to router
2950C(config-if)#interface f0/4
2950C(config-if)#description Connection to 2950B
2950C(config-if)#int f0/5
2950C(config-if)#description 2nd connection to 2950B
2950C(config-if)#int vlan1
2950C(config-if)#ip address 172.16.10.2 255.255.255.0
2950C(config-if)#no shut
2950C(config-if)#exit
2950C(config)#ip default-gateway 172.16.10.1
2950C(config)#^Z
2950C#copy run start
Destination filename [startup-config]? [Press Enter]
Building configuration...
[OK]
2950C#
```

That should do if for the 2950C switch. Let's continue on with the 2950B switch:

```
Switch>en
Switch#config t
Enter configuration commands, one per line.  End with CNTL/Z.
Switch(config)#hostname 2950B
2950B(config)#enable secret todd
2950B(config)#line con 0
2950B(config-line)#login
2950B(config-line)#password console
```

```
2950B(config-line)#line vty 0 15
2950B(config-line)#login
2950B(config-line)#password telnet
2950B(config-line)#banner motd #
Enter TEXT message.  End with the character '#'.
This is my 2950B switch
#
2950B(config)#
2950B(config)#int f0/4
2950B(config-if)#desc connection to 2950C
2950B(config-if)#int f0/5
2950B(config-if)#desc 2nd connection to 2950C
2950B(config-if)#int vlan 1
2950B(config-if)#ip address 172.16.10.3 255.255.255.0
2950B(config-if)#no shut
2950B(config-if)#exit
2950B(config)#ip default-gateway 172.16.10.1
2950B(config)#exit
2950B#copy run start
Destination filename [startup-config]? [Press Enter]
Building configuration...
[OK]
2950B#
2950B#ping 172.16.10.2

Type escape sequence to abort.
Sending 5, 100-byte ICMP Echos to 172.16.10.2, timeout is 2 seconds:
.!!!!
Success rate is 80 percent (4/5), round-trip min/avg/max = 1/3/4 ms
2950B#
```

Now that the two switches are configured with all the basic administrative information and can ping each other, let's set the trunking on the ports connecting each switch together. I'm going to set trunking up on the port connecting to the router, too:

```
2950B#config t
2950B(config)#int f0/1
2950B(config-if)#switchport mode trunk
2950B(config-if)#int f0/4
2950B(config-if)#switchport mode trunk
2950B(config-if)#int fa0/5
2950B(config-if)#switchport mode trunk
2950B(config-if)#
```

```
2950C#config t
Enter configuration commands, one per line.  End with CNTL/Z.
2950C(config)#int fa0/4
2950C(config-if)#switchport mode trunk
2950C(config-if)#int fa0/5
2950C(config-if)#switchport mode trunk
2950C(config-if)#
```

We can verify our trunk information on each switch with the show interface trunk command:

```
2950B#sh int trunk

Port      Mode      Encapsulation  Status       Native vlan
Fa0/1     on        802.1q         trunking     1
Fa0/4     on        802.1q         trunking     1
Fa0/5     on        802.1q         trunking     1
[output cut]
```

We've configured both switches with administrative information and set the trunk ports, and verified it all. So what's next? If you were thinking that we haven't configured the VTP information, set the VLANs, or assigned ports to the VLANs, you're right. On the 2950C switch, let's set the VTP information and then create two VLANs:

```
2950C#config t
Enter configuration commands, one per line.  End with CNTL/Z.
2950C(config)#vtp mode server
Device mode already VTP SERVER.
2950C(config)#vtp domain RouterSim
2950C(config)#^z
2950C#vlan database
2950C(vlan)#vlan 2 name Sales
VLAN 2 added:
   Name: Sales
2950C(vlan)#vlan 3 name Marketing
VLAN 3 added:
   Name: Marketing
2950C(vlan)#apply
APPLY completed.
2950C(vlan)#
```

In the above configuration, the VTP information has to be set before we create our VLANs because we could end up with a problem with the VTP database. We can easily verify that our changes took effect by using the show vlan brief command:

2950C#**sh vlan brief**

```
VLAN Name              Status    Ports
---- ---------------   --------- ------------------------------
1    default           active    Fa0/1, Fa0/2, Fa0/3, Fa0/4
                                 Fa0/7, Fa0/8, Fa0/11, Fa0/12

2    Sales             active
3    Marketing         active
[output cut]
```

There's one more configuration on the 2950C switch: setting the interfaces to the VLAN memberships. Interface fa0/2 will be in VLAN 2, and int fa0/3 will be in VLAN 3. Remember that all ports are in VLAN 1 unless set otherwise! Here is how you do that:

2950C#**config t**
2950C(config)#**int fa0/2**
2950C(config-if)#**switchport access vlan 2**
2950C(config-if)#**int fa0/3**
2950C(config-if)#**switchport access vlan 3**

Let's verify our VLAN information on the 2950C switch:

2950C#**sh vlan brief**

```
VLAN Name              Status    Ports
---- ------------------ --------- ---------------------------
1    default           active    Fa0/1, Fa0/4, Fa0/5, Fa0/6
                                 Fa0/7, Fa0/8, Fa0/9, Fa0/10

2    Sales             active    Fa0/2
3    Marketing         active    Fa0/3
```

We still have to configure our 2950B switch with VTP information and assign the ports. Remember that the purpose of setting the VTP information is to ensure that all switches share the same VLAN database. This means you only set your VLANs once and all switches will build their VLAN databases from the VTP server. 2950B is a VTP client. Here is what you would do:

2950B#**config t**
Enter configuration commands, one per line. End with CNTL/Z.
2950B(config)#**vtp domain RouterSim**
Device mode set to VTP CLIENT.

```
2950B(config)#vtp mode client
2950B(config)#^z
2950B#
```

Noticed that I had to set the domain information before changing the switch from VTP server mode to client mode. Let's check and make sure our 2950B switch has received the VLAN information from the VTP server (2950C):

```
2950B#sh vlan brief
```

VLAN	Name	Status	Ports
1	default	active	Fa0/1, Fa0/2, Fa0/3, Fa0/4
			Fa0/7, Fa0/8, Fa0/11, Fa0/12
2	Sales	active	
3	Marketing	active	

[output cut]

Yes, the 2950B switch knows about the VLANs. We still need to set the VLAN memberships, then move onto the router configuration:

```
2950B#config
2950B(config)#int fa0/2
2950B(config-if)#switchport access vlan 2
2950B(config-if)#int fa0/3
2950B(config-if)#switchport access vlan 3
```

And let's verify our VLAN information on the 2950B switch:

```
2950B#sh vlan brief
```

VLAN	Name	Status	Ports
1	default	active	Fa0/1, Fa0/4, Fa0/5, Fa0/6
			Fa0/7, Fa0/8, Fa0/9, Fa0/10
2	Sales	active	Fa0/2
3	Marketing	active	Fa0/3

Both switches are completely configured, and we verified that it's all good. The hosts can only communicate with hosts that are members of the same VLAN, right? Right. So what this means to us is that the hosts in ports fa0/2 can communicate only with each other—same with the hosts in ports fa0/3. We're not done yet! We want it all, and if we want to have all our hosts talking, we need a router or layer 3 switch to make that happen.

In this example, we're going to use the Lab_B router to configure inter-VLAN communication. Here's how:

```
Router>enable
Router#config t
Enter configuration commands, one per line.  End with CNTL/Z.
Router(config)#hostname Trunkrouter
Trunkrouter(config)#int f0/0
Trunkrouter(config-if)#no ip address
Trunkrouter(config-if)#no shutdown
Trunkrouter(config-if)#int f0/0.1
Trunkrouter(config-subif)#ip address 172.16.10.1 255.255.255.0
Configuring IP routing on a LAN subinterface is only allowed if that
subinterface is already configured as part of an IEEE 802.10, IEEE 802.1Q, or
ISL VLAN.
Trunkrouter(config-subif)#encapsulation dot1q 1
Trunkrouter(config-subif)#ip address 172.16.10.1 255.255.255.0
Trunkrouter(config-subif)#int f0/0.2
Trunkrouter(config-subif)#encap dot1q 2
Trunkrouter(config-subif)#ip address 172.16.20.1 255.255.255.0
Trunkrouter(config-subif)#int f0/0.3
Trunkrouter(config-subif)#encap dot1q 3
Trunkrouter(config-subif)#ip address 172.16.30.1 255.255.255.0
Trunkrouter(config-subif)#exit
```

When configuring this router, I created three subinterfaces—one for each VLAN. Remember that the subinterface number isn't really important except for administration, but I did match it to each VLAN number so it's easy to remember. Also, notice that when I tried to set an IP address on the first subinterface, it gave me the following error message until I set the encapsulation type:

```
Configuring IP routing on a LAN subinterface is only allowed if that
subinterface is already configured as part of an IEEE 802.10, IEEE 802.1Q, or
ISL VLAN.
```

Let's check out our router configuration now:

```
Trunkrouter#show run
!
interface FastEthernet0/0
 no ip address
 no ip directed-broadcast
!
interface FastEthernet0/0.1
 encapsulation dot1Q 1
```

```
 ip address 172.16.10.1 255.255.255.0
 no ip directed-broadcast
!
interface FastEthernet0/0.2
 encapsulation dot1Q 2
 ip address 172.16.20.1 255.255.255.0
 no ip directed-broadcast
!
interface FastEthernet0/0.3
 encapsulation dot1Q 3
 ip address 172.16.30.1 255.255.255.0
 no ip directed-broadcast
!
```

Looking good—all of our hosts should now be able to communicate freely. Yes!

Summary

This chapter introduced you to the world of virtual LANs and described how Cisco switches can use them. We talked about how VLANs break up broadcast domains in a switched internetwork—a very important and necessary thing because layer 2 switches only break up collision domains and, by default, all switches make up one large broadcast domain. I also described trunked VLANs across a Fast Ethernet link.

Trunking is a crucial technology to understand well when you're dealing with a network with multiple switches running several VLANs. I also talked at length about VLAN Trunk Protocol (VTP), which, in reality, has nothing to do with trunking. You learned that it does send VLAN information down a trunked link, but that the trunk configuration in and of itself isn't part of VTP.

I finished the chapter off by providing examples of VTP, trunking, and VLAN configurations.

Exam Essentials

Understand the term "frame tagging."   Frame tagging refers to VLAN identification; this is what switches use to keep track of all those frames as they're traversing a switch fabric. It's how switches identify which frames belong to which VLANs.

Understand the ISL VLAN identification method.   Inter-Switch Link (ISL) is a way of explicitly tagging VLAN information onto an Ethernet frame. This tagging information allows VLANs to be multiplexed over a trunk link through an external encapsulation method, which allows the switch to identify the VLAN membership of a frame over the link. ISL is a Cisco-proprietary frame-tagging method that can only be used with Cisco switches and routers.

Understand the 802.1Q VLAN identification method.   This is a nonproprietary IEEE method of frame tagging. If you're trunking between a Cisco switched link and a different brand of switch, you have to use 802.1Q for the trunk to work.

Remember how to set a trunk port on a 2950 switch.   To set a port to trunking on a 2950, use the `switchport mode trunk` command.

Remember to check a switch port's VLAN assignment when plugging in a new host.   If you plug a new host into a switch, then you must verify the VLAN membership of that port. If the membership is different than what is needed for that host, the host will not be able to reach the needed network services, such as a workgroup server.

Key Terms

Before you take the exam, be certain you are familiar with the following terms:

access link	pruning
broadcast domain	static VLAN
collision domain	subinterfaces
dynamic VLAN	switch fabric
flat network	trunk link
frame tagging	virtual LAN (VLAN)
ISL routing	VLAN Trunking Protocol (VTP)
native VLAN	VTP transparent mode

Commands Used in This Chapter

The following list contains a summary of all the commands used in this chapter:

Command	Description
`vlan 2 name` *name*	Creates and names a VLAN
`sh vlan`	Shows the VLAN database
`vlan database`	Puts you into the VLAN database on a 2950 switch
`sh vlan brief`	Shows a brief overview of the VLAN database

`vlan-membership static vlan#`	Sets a port on a 1900 to a specific VLAN membership
`switchport access vlan vlan#`	Sets a port on a 2950 to a specific VLAN membership
`trunk on`	Sets a port on a 1900 to trunking mode
`switchport mode trunk`	Sets a port on a 2950 to trunking mode
`encapsulation isl vlan#`	Sets the encapsulation on a routers trunk port to isl encapsulation
`encapsulation dot1q vlan#`	Sets the encapsulation on a routers trunk port to 802.1Q encapsulation
`vtp server`	Sets the VTP mode on the switch to server
`vtp client`	Sets the VTP mode on the switch to client
`vtp transparent`	Sets the VTP mode on the switch to transparent
`vtp domain name`	Sets the vtp domain on a switch to the specified name
`vtp password password`	Sets the VTP password. All switches that want to participate in the domain must have the same password.
`sh vtp`	Displays the vtp configured information on a switch

Written Lab 8

In this section, write the answers to the following questions:

1. What VTP mode can only accept VLAN information and not change VLAN information?
2. What VLAN identification method is proprietary to Cisco routers?
3. VLANs break up _____ domains.
4. Switches, by default, only break up _____ domains.
5. What is the default VTP mode?
6. What does trunking provide?
7. What is frame tagging?

8. True/False: The ISL encapsulation is removed from the frame if the frame is forwarded out an access link.

9. What type of link is only part of one VLAN and is referred to as the "native VLAN" of the port?

10. What type of Cisco tagging information allows VLANs to be multiplexed over a trunk link through an external encapsulation method?

(The answers to Written Lab 8 can be found following the answers to the Review Questions for this chapter.)

Review Questions

1. Which of the following are true regarding VLANs?

   A. You must have at least two VLANs defined in every Cisco switched network.

   B. All VLANs are configured at the fastest switch and, by default, propagate this information to all other switches.

   C. You should not have more than 10 switches in the same VTP domain.

   D. VTP is used to send VLAN information to switches in a configured VTP domain.

2. How does inter-VLAN communication take place?

   A. Using a layer 2 switch

   B. Using a router

   C. Using a hub

   D. Using a repeater

3. Which two statements about frame tagging are true?

   A. A filtering table is loaded into each switch.

   B. Frame tagging assigns a user-defined ID to each frame.

   C. A unique identifier is placed in the header of each frame as it is forwarded between switches.

   D. It is used by switches to control broadcasts.

4. How are dynamic VLANs configured?

   A. Statically

   B. By an administrator

   C. Via a DHCP server

   D. Via a VLAN Management Policy Server

5. Which of the following protocols are used to configure trunking on a switch? (Choose two options.)

   A. VLAN Trunk Protocol

   B. VLAN

   C. Trunk

   D. ISL

6. What is Cisco's proprietary frame-tagging method?

    A. 802.1Q

    B. 802.3

    C. ISL

    D. VTP

7. Which switching technology reduces the size of a broadcast domain?

    A. ISL

    B. 802.1Q

    C. VLANs

    D. STP

8. What VTP allows you to change VLAN information on the switch?

    A. Client

    B. STP

    C. Server

    D. Transparent

9. What is the main purpose of creating VLANs?

    A. Break up collision domains at layer 2

    B. Break up collision domains at layer 3

    C. Break up broadcast domains at layer 2

    D. Break up broadcast domains at layer 3

10. Which of the following is true regarding VTP?

    A. All switches are VTP servers by default.

    B. All switches are VTP transparent by default.

    C. VTP is on by default with a domain name of Cisco on all Cisco switches.

    D. All switches are VTP clients by default.

11. Which of the following is true regarding trunked links?

    A. They are configured by default on all switch ports.

    B. They only work with a type of Ethernet network—not with Token Ring, FDDI, or ATM.

    C. You can set trunk links on any 10-, 100-, and 1000Mbps ports.

    D. You must clear the unwanted VLANs by hand.

12. Which of the following commands sets a trunk port on a 2950 switch?

    A. `trunk on`

    B. `trunk all`

    C. `switchport trunk on`

    D. `switchport mode trunk`

13. Which of the following is an IEEE standard for frame tagging?

    A. ISL

    B. 802.3Z

    C. 802.1Q

    D. 802.3U

14. You connect a host to a switch port, but the new host cannot log into the server that is plugged into the same switch. What could the problem be? (Choose the most likely answer.)

    A. The router is not configured for the new host.

    B. The VTP configuration on the switch is not updated for the new host.

    C. The host has an invalid MAC address.

    D. The switch port the host is connected to is not configured to the correct VLAN membership.

15. When is frame tagging used?

    A. When VLANs are traversing an access link

    B. When VLANs are traversing a trunked link

    C. When ISL is used on an access link

    D. When 802.1Q is used on an access link

16. When talking about frame tagging with VLAN ID, which of the following would be used to describe this?

    A. VTP with multiple switches and VLANs

    B. VLAN color and placement

    C. Identifying VLAN memberships over trunked links

    D. Connecting an access port to a switch a router with ISL

17. Which of the following provide inter-switch VLAN communication? (Choose two.)

    A. ISL

    B. VTP

    C. 802.1Q

    D. 802.3Z

18. You have two switches connected with a trunked link running two VLANs. VLAN 1 is assigned to ports 1 through 3 of each switch and VLAN 2 has been assigned to ports 8 through 12 of each switch. HostA and HostB are in VLAN 1. HostG and HostH are in VLAN 2. There is *no* inter-VLAN routing. What should you do to verify proper VLAN and trunk operations? (Choose three.)

    A. Verify that HostA can ping HostB.

    B. Verify that HostA can ping HostG.

    C. Verify that HostG can ping HostH.

    D. Verify that HostG cannot ping HostA.

    E. Verify that HostA cannot ping HostB.

19. You need to add a new VLAN named ROUTERSIM to your switched network. Which of the following are true regarding configuration of this VLAN? (Choose all that apply.)

    A. You must name the VLAN.

    B. You must assign ports on a switch for this VLAN.

    C. You must add this VLAN to the VTP domain.

    D. The VLAN must be created.

    E. You must add an IP address for the ROUTERSIM VLAN.

20. Which of the following protocols is used to exchange VLAN configuration information between switches?

    A. 802.10

    B. VLAN Trunking Protocol (VTP)

    C. Inter-Switch Link (ISL)

    D. 802.1Q

Answers to Review Questions

1. D. Switches do not propagate VLAN information by default; you must configure the VTP domain. VLAN Trunk Protocol (VTP) is used to propagate VLAN information across a trunked link.

2. B. Inter-VLAN communication must take place with a router or layer 3 switch.

3. B, C. Frame tagging is used to keep track of frames as they traverse a switched fabric.

4. D. A VMPS server must be configured with the hardware addresses of all hosts on the networks.

5. C, D. VTP is not right because it has nothing to do with trunking, except that it sends VLAN information across a trunked link. 802.1Q and ISL are used to configure trunking on a port.

6. C. The Cisco proprietary frame-tagging method is Inter-Switch Link (ISL) trunking.

7. C. Virtual LANs break up broadcast domains in layer 2 switched internetworks.

8. C. Only in server mode can you change VTP information on a switch.

9. C. Virtual LANs were created so that broadcast domains can be broken up in a layer 2 switched network.

10. A. All Cisco switches are VTP servers by default. No other VTP information is configured on a Cisco switch by default.

11. D. By default, if you create a trunked link, all VLANs are allowed on that trunked link. You must delete any unwanted VLANs by hand.

12. D. To set a switch port to trunk mode, which allows all VLAN information to pass down the link, use the `switchport mode trunk` command.

13. C. 802.1Q was created to allow trunked links between disparate switches.

14. D. This question is a little vague, but the best answer is that the VLAN membership for the port is not configured.

15. B. Cisco created frame tagging to be used when an Ethernet frame traverses a trunked link.

16. C. Frame tagging is the process of identifying frames as they traverse a trunked link. Cisco uses the proprietary ISL version, where 802.1Q is a nonproprietary version.

17. A, C. ISL is a Cisco proprietary frame-tagging method. IEEE 802.1Q is the nonproprietary version of frame tagging.

18. A, C, D. If you are not providing a type of inter-VLAN routing, then hosts not in the same VLAN will not be able to communicate. HostA and HostB can communicate, and HostG and HostH can communicate, but HostA and B cannot communicate to HostG and HostH.

19. A, B, D. To establish a VLAN, you must first create the VLAN, name it, and then add the VLAN to the desired ports of a switch. Since the Network layer protocol is irrelevant to the VLAN, the IP address answer is not correct.

20. B. VLAN Trunking Protocol is responsible for distributing and synchronizing information about configured VLANs between switches throughout the network. VTP manages additions, deletions, and name changes for network VLANs.

Answers to Written Lab 8

1. Client
2. Inter-Switch Link (ISL)
3. Broadcast
4. Collision
5. Server
6. Trunking allows you to make a single port part of multiple VLANs at the same time.
7. Frame identification (frame tagging) uniquely assigns a user-defined ID to each frame. This is sometimes referred to as a VLAN ID or color.
8. True
9. Access link
10. Inter-Switch Link (ISL)

Managing a Cisco Internetwork

THE CCNA EXAM TOPICS COVERED IN THIS CHAPTER INCLUDE THE FOLLOWING:

✓ **IMPLEMENTATION & OPERATION**

- Manage system image and device configuration files

✓ **TROUBLESHOOTING**

- Utilize the OSI model as a guide for systematic network troubleshooting
- Perform LAN and VLAN troubleshooting
- Troubleshoot IP addressing and host configuration
- Troubleshoot a device as part of a working network

In this chapter, I'm going to show you how to manage Cisco routers on an internetwork. The Internetwork Operating System (IOS) and configuration files reside in different locations in a Cisco device, and it's important to understand where these files are located and how they work.

You'll learn about the main components of a router, the router boot sequence, and the configuration register, including how to use the configuration register for password recovery. After that, you'll find out how to manage routers by performing the following tasks:

- Backing up and restoring the Cisco IOS

- Backing up and restoring the Cisco configuration

- Gathering information about neighbor devices through CDP and Telnet

- Resolving hostnames

- Using the `ping` and `traceroute` commands to test network connectivity

The Internal Components of a Cisco Router

In order to configure and troubleshoot a Cisco internetwork, you need to know the major components of Cisco routers and understand what each one does. Table 9.1 describes the major Cisco router components.

TABLE 9.1   Cisco Router Components

Component	Description
Bootstrap	Stored in the microcode of the ROM, the bootstrap is used to bring a router up during initialization. It will boot the router and then load the IOS.
POST (power-on self-test)	Stored in the microcode of the ROM, the POST is used to check the basic functionality of the router hardware and determines which interfaces are present.
ROM monitor	Stored in the microcode of the ROM, the ROM monitor is used for manufacturing, testing, and troubleshooting

TABLE 9.1   Cisco Router Components *(continued)*

Component	Description
Mini-IOS	Called the RXBOOT or bootloader by Cisco, the mini-IOS is a small IOS in ROM that can be used to bring up an interface and load a Cisco IOS into flash memory. The mini-IOS can also perform a few other maintenance operations.
RAM (random-access memory)	Used to hold packet buffers, ARP cache, routing tables, and also the software and data structures that allow the router to function. Running-config is stored in RAM, and the IOS can also be run from RAM in some routers.
ROM (read-only memory)	Used to start and maintain the router.
Flash memory	Used on the router to hold the Cisco IOS. Flash memory is not erased when the router is reloaded. It is EEPROM (electronically erasable programmable read-only memory) created by Intel.
NVRAM (nonvolatile RAM)	Used to hold the router and switch configuration. NVRAM is not erased when the router or switch is reloaded.
Configuration register	Used to control how the router boots up. This value can be seen with the show version command and typically is 0x2102, which tells the router to load the IOS from flash memory as well as tell the router to load the configuration from NVRAM.

The Router Boot Sequence

When a router boots up, it performs a series of steps, called the *boot sequence*, to test the hardware and load the necessary software. The boot sequence consists of the following steps:

1. The router performs a POST. The POST tests the hardware to verify that all components of the device are operational and present. For example, the POST checks for the different interfaces on the router. The POST is stored in and run from *ROM (read-only memory)*.

2. The bootstrap looks for and loads the Cisco IOS software. The bootstrap is a program in ROM that is used to execute programs. The bootstrap program is responsible for finding where each IOS program is located and then loading the file. By default, the IOS software is loaded from flash memory in all Cisco routers.

3. The IOS software looks for a valid configuration file stored in NVRAM. This file is called startup-config and is only there if an administrator copies the running-config file into NVRAM.

4. If a startup-config file is in NVRAM, the router will load and run this file. The router is now operational. If a startup-config file is not in NVRAM, the router will start the setup mode configuration upon bootup.

Managing Configuration Registers

All Cisco routers have a 16-bit software register that's written into NVRAM. By default, the *configuration register* is set to load the Cisco IOS from *flash memory* and to look for and load the startup-config file from NVRAM. In the following sections I am going to discuss the configuration register settings, and how to use these settings to provide password recovery on your routers.

Understanding the Configuration Register Bits

The 16 bits of the configuration register are read from 15 to 0, from left to right. The default configuration setting on Cisco routers is 0x2102. This means that bits 13, 8, and 1 are on, as shown in Table 9.2. Notice that each set of 4 bits is read in binary with a value of 8, 4, 2, 1:

TABLE 9.2   The Configuration Register Bit Numbers

Configuration Register			2					1				0			2	
Bit number	15	14	13	12	11	10	9	8	7	6	5	4	3	2	1	0
Binary	0	0	1	0	0	0	0	1	0	0	0	0	0	0	1	0

Add the prefix 0x to the configuration register address. The 0x means that the digits that follow are in hexadecimal.

Table 9.3 lists the software configuration bit meanings. Notice that bit 6 can be used to ignore the NVRAM contents. This bit is used for password recovery—something I'll go over with you soon in the "Recovering Passwords" section of this chapter.

Remember that in hex, the scheme is 0–9 and A–F (A = 10, B = 11, C = 12, D = 13, E = 14, and F = 15). This means that a 210F setting for the configuration register is actually 210(15), or 1111 in binary.

T A B L E   9 . 3   Software Configuration Meanings

Bit	Hex	Description
0–3	0x0000–0x000F	Boot field (see Table 9.4)
6	0x0040	Ignore NVRAM contents
7	0x0080	OEM bit enabled
8	0x101	Break disabled
10	0x0400	IP broadcast with all zeros
5, 11–12	0x0800–0x1000	Console line speed
13	0x2000	Boot default ROM software if network boot fails
14	0x4000	IP broadcasts do not have net numbers
15	0x8000	Enable diagnostic messages and ignore NVRAM contents

The boot field, which consists of bits 0–3 in the configuration register, controls the router boot sequence. Table 9.4 describes the boot field bits.

T A B L E   9 . 4   The Boot Field (Configuration Register Bits 00–03)

Boot Field	Meaning	Use
00	ROM monitor mode	To boot to ROM monitor mode, set the configuration register to 2100. You must manually boot the router with the b command. The router will show the rommon> prompt.
01	Boot image from ROM	To boot an IOS image stored in ROM, set the configuration register to 2101. The router will show the router(boot)> prompt.
02–F	Specifies a default boot file name	Any value from 2102 through 210F tells the router to use the boot commands specified in NVRAM.

Checking the Current Configuration Register Value

You can see the current value of the configuration register by using the show version command (sh version or show ver for short), as demonstrated here:

```
Router#sh version
Cisco Internetwork Operating System Software
IOS (tm) C2600 Software (C2600-I-M), Version 12.1(8)T3,
  RELEASE SOFTWARE (fc1)
[output cut]
Configuration register is 0x2102
```

The last information given from this command is the value of the configuration register. In this example, the value is 0x2102—the default setting. The configuration register setting of 0x2102 tells the router to look in NVRAM for the boot sequence.

Notice that the show version command also provides the IOS version, and in the example above, it shows the IOS version as 12.1(8)T3.

The show version command will display system hardware configuration information, software version, and the names and sources of configuration files and boot images on a router.

Changing the Configuration Register

You can change the configuration register value to modify how the router boots and runs. The following is the possible reasons for changing the configuration register:

- Force the system into the ROM monitor mode.
- Select a boot source and default boot filename.
- Enable or disable the Break function.
- Control broadcast addresses.
- Set the console terminal baud rate.
- Load operating software from ROM.
- Enable booting from a Trivial File Transfer Protocol (TFTP) server.

Before you change the configuration register, make sure you know the current configuration register value. Use the show version command to get this information.

And you can change the configuration register by using the `config-register` command. Here's an example. The following commands tell the router to boot a small IOS from ROM monitor mode and then show the current configuration register value:

```
Router(config)#config-register 0x101
Router(config)#^Z
Router#sh ver
[output cut]
Configuration register is 0x2102 (will be 0x0101 at next
   reload)
```

Notice that the `show version` command shows the current configuration register value, as well as what it will be when the router reboots. Any change to the configuration register won't take effect until the router is reloaded. The 0x0101 will load the IOS from ROM the next time the router is rebooted. You may see it listed as 0x101; that's basically the same thing, and it can be written either way.

Recovering Passwords

If you're locked out of a router because you forgot the password, you can change the configuration register to help you get back on your feet. As I said earlier, bit 6 in the configuration register is used to tell the router whether to use the contents of NVRAM to load a router configuration.

The default configuration register value is 0x2102, meaning that bit 6 is off. With the default setting, the router will look for and load a router configuration stored in NVRAM (startup-config). To recover a password, you need to turn on bit 6. Doing this will tell the router to ignore the NVRAM contents. The configuration register value to turn on bit 6 is 0x2142.

Here are the main steps to password recovery:

1. Boot the router and interrupt the boot sequence by performing a break.

2. Change the configuration register to turn on bit 6 (with the value 0x2142).

3. Reload the router.

4. Enter privileged mode.

5. Copy the startup-config file to running-config.

6. Change the password.

7. Reset the configuration register to the default value.

8. Save the router configuration.

9. Reload the router.

I'm going to cover these steps in more detail in the following sections, and I'll show you the commands to restore access to 2600 and 2500 series routers.

Interrupting the Router Boot Sequence

Your first step is to boot the router and perform a break. This is usually done by pressing the Ctrl+Break key combination when using HyperTerminal and while the router first reboots.

> **WARNING**   The Windows NT or 2000 default HyperTerminal program won't perform the break. You've got to upgrade the HyperTerminal program or use Windows 95/98 instead.

After you've performed a break, you should see something like this:

```
System Bootstrap, Version 11.3(2)XA4, RELEASE SOFTWARE (fc1)
Copyright (c) 1999 by cisco Systems, Inc.
TAC:Home:SW:IOS:Specials for info
PC = 0xfff0a530, Vector = 0x500, SP = 0x680127b0
C2600 platform with 32768 Kbytes of main memory
PC = 0xfff0a530, Vector = 0x500, SP = 0x80004374
monitor: command "boot" aborted due to user interrupt
rommon 1 >
```

Notice the line "boot" aborted due to user interrupt. At this point, you will be at the rommon 1> prompt on some routers.

Changing the Configuration Register

As I explained earlier, you can change the configuration register by using the config-register command. To turn on bit 6, use the configuration register value 0x2142.

> **NOTE**   Remember that if you change the configuration register to 0x2142, then the startup-config will be bypassed and the router will load into setup mode.

Cisco 2600 Series Commands

To change the bit value on a Cisco 2600 series router, you just enter the command at the rommon 1> prompt:

```
rommon 1 > confreg 0x2142
You must reset or power cycle for new config to take effect
```

Cisco 2500 Series Commands

To change the configuration register on a 2500 series router, type **o** after creating a break sequence on the router. This brings up a menu of configuration register option settings. To change the configuration register, enter the command **o/r**, followed by the new register value. Here's an example of turning on bit 6 on a 2501 router:

```
System Bootstrap, Version 11.0(10c), SOFTWARE
Copyright (c) 1986-1996 by cisco Systems
2500 processor with 14336 Kbytes of main memory
Abort at 0x1098FEC (PC)
>o
Configuration register = 0x2102 at last boot
Bit#    Configuration register option settings:
15      Diagnostic mode disabled
14      IP broadcasts do not have network numbers
13      Boot default ROM software if network boot fails
12-11   Console speed is 9600 baud
10      IP broadcasts with ones
08      Break disabled
07      OEM disabled
06      Ignore configuration disabled
03-00   Boot file is cisco2-2500 (or 'boot system' command)
>o/r 0x2142
```

Notice that the last entry in the router output is 03-00. This tells the router what the IOS boot file is. By default, the router will use the first file found in the flash memory, so if you want to boot a different file name, you can either change the configuration register or use the **boot system** *ios_name* command.

Another way is to load an IOS image from a TFTP server by using the command boot system *tftp ios_name ip_address* from global configuration mode.

Reloading the Router and Entering Privileged Mode

At this point, you need to reset the router like this:

- From the 2600 series router, type **reset**.
- From the 2500 series router, type **I** (for initialize).

The router will reload and ask if you want to use setup mode (because no startup-config is used). Answer No to entering setup mode, press Enter to go into user mode, and then type **enable** to go into privileged mode.

Viewing and Changing the Configuration

Now you're past the point where you would need to enter the user mode and privileged mode passwords in a router. Copy the startup-config file to the running-config file:

```
copy startup-config running-config
```

or use the shortcut:

```
copy start run
```

The configuration is now running in *random access memory (RAM)*, and you're in privileged mode, meaning that you can now view and change the configuration. But you can't view the `enable secret` setting for the password. To change the password, do this:

```
config t
enable secret todd
```

Resetting the Configuration Register and Reloading the Router

After you're finished changing passwords, set the configuration register back to the default value with the `config-register` command:

```
config t
config-register 0x2102
```

Finally, save the new configuration with a `copy running-config startup-config` and reload the router.

Backing Up and Restoring the Cisco IOS

Before you upgrade or restore a Cisco IOS, you really should copy the existing file to a *TFTP host* as a backup just in case the new image crashes and burns.

And you can use any TFTP host to accomplish this. By default, the flash memory in a router is used to store the Cisco IOS. In the following sections, I'll describe how to check the amount of flash memory, copy the Cisco IOS from flash memory to a TFTP host, and then show you how to copy the IOS from a TFTP host to flash memory.

But before you back up an IOS image to a network server, you've got to do these three things:

- Make sure you can access the network server.

- Ensure that the network server has adequate space for the code image.

- Verify the file naming and path requirement.

Verifying Flash Memory

Before you attempt to upgrade the Cisco IOS on your router with a new IOS file, it's a good idea to verify that your flash memory has enough room to hold the new image. You verify the amount of flash memory and the file or files being stored in flash memory by using the `show flash` command (`sh flash` for short):

```
Router#sh flash
```

```
System flash directory:
File  Length    Name/status
  1   8121000   c2500-js-1.112-18.bin
[8121064 bytes used, 8656152 available, 16777216 total]
16384K bytes of processor board System flash (Read ONLY)
Router#
```

Notice that the filename in this example is c2500-js-1.112-18.bin. The name of the file is platform-specific and derived as follows:

- c2500 is the platform.

- j indicates that the file is an enterprise image.

- s indicates that the file contains extended capabilities.

- 1 indicates that the file can be moved from flash memory if needed and is not compressed.

- 11.2-18 is the revision number.

- .bin indicates that the Cisco IOS is a binary executable file.

The last line in the router output shows that the flash is 16,384KB (or 16MB). So if the new file that you want to use is, say, 10MB in size, you know that there's plenty of room for it. And once you've verified that flash memory can hold the IOS you want to copy, you're free to continue with your backup operation.

Backing Up the Cisco IOS

To back up the Cisco IOS to a TFTP server, you use the copy flash tftp command. It's a straightforward command that requires only the source filename and the IP address of the TFTP server.

The key to success in this backup routine is to make sure that you've got good, solid connectivity to the TFTP server. Check this by pinging the device from the router console prompt like this:

```
Router#ping 192.168.0.120
Type escape sequence to abort.
Sending 5, 100-byte ICMP Echos to 192.168.0.120, timeout
  is 2 seconds:
!!!!!
Success rate is 100 percent (5/5), round-trip min/avg/max
  = 4/4/8 ms
```

The *Packet Internet Groper (Ping)* utility is used to test network connectivity, and I use it in some of the examples in this chapter. I'll be talking about it in more detail in the "Checking Network Connectivity" section later in the chapter.

After you ping the TFTP server to make sure that IP is working, you can use the copy flash tftp command to copy the IOS to the TFTP server as shown next:

```
Router#copy flash tftp
System flash directory:
File  Length    Name/status
  1   8121000   c2500-js-1.112-18.bin
[8121064 bytes used, 8656152 available, 16777216 total]
Address or name of remote host [255.255.255.255]?
  192.168.0.120
Source file name?c2500-js-1.112-18.bin
Destination file name [c2500-js-1.112-18.bin]?[Enter]
Verifying checksum for 'c2500-js-1.112-18.bin')file #1)
...OK
Copy '/c2500-js-1.112-18' from Flash to server
  as '/c2500-js-1.112-18'? [yes/no]y
!!!!!!!!!!!!!!!!!!!!!!!!!!!!!!!!!!!!!!!!!!!!!!!!!!!!!!!!!!!!
  !!!!!!!!!!!!!!!!!!!! [output cut]
Upload to server done
Flash copy took 00:02:30 [hh:mm:ss]
Router#
```

Look at the output—you can see that after you enter the command, the name of the file in flash memory is displayed. This is very cool because it makes things easy for you. Just copy the filename and then paste it when prompted for the source filename.

In the example above, the content of flash memory was copied successfully to the TFTP server. The address of the remote host is the IP address of the TFTP server, and the source filename is the file in flash memory.

The copy flash tftp command won't prompt you for the location of any file, or ask you where to put the file. TFTP is just a "grab it and place it" program in this situation. This means that the TFTP server must have a default directory specified, or it won't work!

Restoring or Upgrading the Cisco Router IOS

What happens if you need to restore the Cisco IOS to flash memory to replace an original file that has been damaged, or if you want to upgrade the IOS? You can download the file from a TFTP server to flash memory by using the copy tftp flash command. This command requires the IP address of the TFTP server and the name of the file you want to download.

But before you begin, make sure that the file you want to place in flash memory is in the default TFTP directory on your host. When you issue the command, TFTP won't ask you where the file is, so if the file you want to restore isn't in the default directory of the TFTP server, this just won't work.

 WARNING   Copying the IOS from the TFTP server to flash memory requires a router reboot. So, instead of upgrading or restoring the IOS at 9 a.m. on Monday morning, you should probably wait until lunchtime, right?!

After you enter the `copy tftp flash` command, you'll see a message informing you that the router must reboot and run a ROM-based IOS image to perform this operation:

```
Router#copy tftp flash
                **** NOTICE ****
Flash load helper v1.0
This process will accept the copy options and then
terminate the current system image to use the ROM based
image for the copy. Routing functionality will not be
available during that time. If you are logged in via
telnet, this connection will terminate. Users with
console access can see the results of the copy operation.
                ---- ******** ----
Proceed? [confirm][Enter]
```

After you press Enter to confirm that you truly understand that the router needs to reboot, you'll be presented with the following router output:

```
System flash directory:
File  Length    Name/status
  1   8121000   /c2500-js-1.112-18
[8121064 bytes used, 8656152 available, 16777216 total]
Address or name of remote host [192.168.0.120]?[Enter]
```

Once the router has used the TFTP server, it will remember the address, and just prompt you to press Enter:

The next prompt is for the name of the file you want to copy to flash memory (and remember—this file must be in your TFTP server's default directory):

```
Source file name?c2500-js56i-1.120-9.bin
Destination file name [c2500-js56i-1.120-9.bin]?[Enter]
Accessing file 'c2500-js56i-1.120-9.bin' on 192.168.0.120
...
Loading c2500-js56i-1.120-9.bin from 192.168.0.120
  (via Ethernet0): ! [OK]
```

After you tell the router the filename and where the file is, it will ask you to confirm that you understand that the contents of flash memory will be erased.

If you don't have enough room in flash memory to store both copies, or if the flash memory is new and no file has been written to it before, the router will ask to erase the contents of flash memory before writing the new file into flash memory.

You are prompted three times just to make sure that you really want to proceed with erasing flash memory. If you haven't issued a copy run start command, you'll be prompted to do so because the router needs to reboot:

```
Erase flash device before writing? [confirm][Enter]
Flash contains files. Are you sure you want to erase?
  [confirm][Enter]

System configuration has been modified. Save? [yes/no]: y
Building configuration...
[OK]
Copy 'c2500-js56i-1.120-9.bin' from server
  as 'c2500-js56i-1.120-9.bin' into Flash WITH erase?
  [yes/no] y
```

After you say yes three times to erasing flash memory, the router must reboot to load a small IOS from ROM memory. (You can't delete the flash file if it's in use.) This done, the contents of flash memory are erased, and the file from the TFTP server is accessed and copied to flash memory:

This done, the contents of flash memory are erased, and the file from the TFTP server is accessed and copied to flash memory:

```
%SYS-5-RELOAD: Reload requested
%FLH: c2500-js56i-1.120-9.bin from 192.168.0.120 to flash
...
System flash directory:
File  Length   Name/status
  1   8121000  /c2500-js-1.112-18
[8121064 bytes used, 8656152 available, 16777216 total]
Accessing file 'c2500-js56i-1.120-9.bin' on 192.168.0.120
...
Loading c2500-js56i-1.120-9.bin .from 192.168.0.120
  (via Ethernet0): ! [OK]

Erasing device... eeeeeeeeeeeeeeeeeeeeeeeeeeeeeeeeeeeeeeeee
  eeeeeeeeeeeeeeeeeeeeee
Loading c2500-js56i-1.120-9.bin from 192.168.0.120
```

```
(via Ethernet0):
!!!!!!!!!!!!!!!!!!!!!!!!!!!!!!!!!!!!!!!!!!!!!!!!!!!!!!!!!!
!!!!!!!!!!!!!!!!!!!!!!!!!!!!!!!!!!!! [output cut]
```

The row of **e** characters shows the contents of flash memory being erased. Each exclamation point (!) means that one UDP segment has been successfully transferred.

Once the copy is complete, you should receive this message:

```
[OK - 10935532/16777216 bytes]

Verifying checksum...  OK (0x2E3A)
Flash copy took 0:06:14 [hh:mm:ss]
%FLH: Re-booting system after download
```

After the file is loaded into flash memory and a checksum is performed, the router is rebooted to run the new IOS file.

A Cisco router can become a TFTP-server host for a router system image that's run in flash memory. The global configuration command is `tftp-server flash tftp: ios_name`.

Backing Up and Restoring the Cisco Configuration

Any changes that you make to the router configuration are stored in the running-config file. And if you don't enter a `copy run start` command after you make a change to running-config, that change will go poof if the router reboots or gets powered down. So, you probably want to make another backup of the configuration information just in case the router or switch completely dies on you. Even if your machine is healthy and happy, it's good to have for reference and documentation reasons.

In the following sections, I'll describe how to copy the configuration of a router and a switch to a TFTP server and how to restore that configuration.

Backing Up the Cisco Router Configuration

To copy the router's configuration from a router to a TFTP server, you can use either the `copy running-config tftp` or the `copy startup-config tftp` command. Either one will back up the router configuration that's currently running in DRAM, or that's stored in NVRAM.

Verifying the Current Configuration

To verify the configuration in DRAM, use the show running-config command (sh run for short) like this:

```
Router#sh run
Building configuration...

Current configuration:
!
version 12.0
```

The current configuration information indicates that the router is now running version 12.0 of the IOS.

Verifying the Stored Configuration

Next, you should check the configuration stored in NVRAM. To see this, use the show startup-config command (sh start for short) like this:

```
Router#sh start
Using 366 out of 32762 bytes
!
version 11.2
```

The second line shows you how much room your backup configuration is using. Here, we can see that NVRAM is 32KB and that only 366 bytes of it are used. Also notice that the version of configuration in NVRAM is 11.2. That's because I haven't copied running-config to startup-config since upgrading the router.

If you're not sure that the files are the same, and the running-config file is what you want to use, then use the copy running-config startup-config. This will help you verify that both files are in fact the same. I'll go through this with you in the next section.

Copying the Current Configuration to NVRAM

By copying running-config to NVRAM as a backup, as shown in the following output, you're assured that your running-config will always be reloaded if the router gets rebooted. In the new IOS version 12.0, you're prompted for the filename you want to use. And since the version of IOS was 11.2 the last time a copy run start was performed, the router will tell us that it's going to replace that file with the new 12.0 version:

```
Router#copy run start
Destination filename [startup-config]?[Enter]
Warning: Attempting to overwrite an NVRAM configuration
  previously written by a different version of the system
  image.
```

```
Overwrite the previous NVRAM configuration?
  [confirm][Enter]
Building configuration...
[OK]
```

Now when you run show startup-config, the version shows 12.0:

```
Router#sh start
Using 487 out of 32762 bytes
!
version 12.0
```

Copying the Configuration to a TFTP Server

Once the file is copied to NVRAM, you can make a second backup to a TFTP server by using the copy running-config tftp command (copy run tftp for short), like this:

```
Router#copy run tftp
Address or name of remote host []?192.168.0.120
Destination filename [router-confg]?todd1-confg
!!
487 bytes copied in 12.236 secs (40 bytes/sec)
Router#
```

Notice that this took only two exclamation points (!!)—which means that 20 packets have been transferred (ten for each exclamation point). In the above example, I named the file todd1-confg because I had not set a hostname for the router. If you have a hostname already configured, the command will automatically use the hostname plus the extension -confg as the name of the file.

Restoring the Cisco Router Configuration

If you've changed your router's running-config file and want to restore the configuration to the version in the startup-config file, the easiest way to do this is to use the copy startup-config running-config command (copy start run for short). You can also use the older Cisco command config mem to restore a configuration. Of course, this will work only if you first copied running-config into NVRAM before making any changes!

If you did copy the router's configuration to a TFTP server as a second backup, you can restore the configuration using the copy tftp running-config command (copy tftp run for short) or the copy tftp startup-config command (copy tftp start for short), as shown below (remember that the old command that provides this function is config net):

```
Router#copy tftp run
Address or name of remote host []?192.168.0.120
```

```
Source filename []?toddl-confg
Destination filename [running-config]?[Enter]
Accessing tftp://192.168.0.120/toddl-confg...
Loading toddl-confg from 192.168.0.120 (via Ethernet0):
!!
[OK - 487/4096 bytes]
487 bytes copied in 5.400 secs (97 bytes/sec)
Router#
00:38:31: %SYS-5-CONFIG: Configured from
  tftp://192.168.0.120/toddl-confg
Router#
```

The configuration file is an ASCII text file, meaning that before you copy the configuration stored on a TFTP server back to a router, you can make changes to the file with any text editor.

 It is important to remember that when you copy or merge a configuration from a TFTP server to a router's RAM, the interfaces are shut down by default and you must manually go and enable each interface with the no shutdown command.

Erasing the Configuration

To delete the startup-config file on a Cisco router, use the command erase startup-config, like this:

```
Router#erase startup-config
Erasing the nvram filesystem will remove all files!
  Continue? [confirm][Enter]
[OK]
Erase of nvram: complete
Router#
```

This command deletes the contents of NVRAM on the router, so the next time the router boots, it'll run the setup mode.

Using Cisco Discovery Protocol (CDP)

Cisco Discovery Protocol (CDP) is a proprietary protocol designed by Cisco to help administrators collect information about both locally attached and remote devices. By using CDP, you can gather hardware and protocol information about neighbor devices, which is useful info for troubleshooting and documenting the network!

In the following sections I am going to discuss the CDP timer and CDP commands used to verify your network.

Getting CDP Timers and Holdtime Information

The show cdp command (sh cdp for short) gives you information about two CDP global parameters that can be configured on Cisco devices:

- *CDP timer* is how often CDP packets are transmitted to all active interfaces.
- *CDP holdtime* is the amount of time that the device will hold packets received from neighbor devices.

Both Cisco routers and Cisco switches use the same parameters.

The output on a router looks like this:

```
Router#sh cdp
Global CDP information:
        Sending CDP packets every 60 seconds
        Sending a holdtime value of 180 seconds
Router#
```

Use the global commands cdp holdtime and cdp timer to configure the CDP holdtime and timer on a router:

```
Router#config t
Enter configuration commands, one per line.  End with
  CNTL/Z.
Router(config)#cdp ?
  holdtime  Specify the holdtime (in sec) to be sent in
            packets
  timer     Specify the rate at which CDP packets are
            sent (in sec)
  run

Router(config)#cdp timer 90
Router(config)#cdp holdtime 240
Router(config)#^Z
```

You can turn off CDP completely with the no cdp run command from the global configuration mode of a router. To turn CDP off or on for an interface, use the no cdp enable and cdp enable commands. Be patient—I'll work through these with you in a second.

Gathering Neighbor Information

The show cdp neighbor command (sh cdp nei for short) delivers information about directly connected devices. It's important to remember that CDP packets aren't passed through a Cisco switch, and that you only see what's directly attached. So this means that if your router is connected to a switch, you won't see any of the devices hooked up to that switch.

The following output shows the show cdp neighbor command used on a 2509 router:

```
Todd2509#sh cdp nei
Capability Codes: R - Router, T - Trans Bridge,
  B - Source Route Bridge, S - Switch, H - Host,
  I - IGMP, r - Repeater
Device ID  Local Intrfce Holdtme Capability Platform Port ID
1900Switch    Eth 0       238      T S        1900     2
2500B         Ser 0       138      R          2500     Ser 0
Todd2509#
```

Okay, you are directly connected with a console cable to the 2509 router and the 2509 router is directly connected to a switch with a hostname of 1900Switch, and a 2500 router with a hostname of 2500B. Notice that no devices connected to the 1900Switch and the 2500B router show up in the CDP table on the 2509 router. All you get to see are directly connected devices.

Table 9.5 summarizes the information displayed by the show cdp neighbor command for each device:

TABLE 9.5   Output of the *show cdp neighbor* Command

Field	Description
Device ID	The hostname of the device directly connected.
Local Interface	The port or interface on which you are receiving the CDP packet.
Holdtime	The amount of time the router will hold the information before discarding it if no more CDP packets are received.
Capability	The neighbor's capability, such as router, switch, or repeater. The capability codes are listed at the top of the command output.
Platform	The type of Cisco device. In the above output, a Cisco 2509, Cisco 2511, and Catalyst 5000 are attached to the switch. The 2509 only sees the switch and the 2501 router connected through its serial 0 interface.
Port ID	The neighbor device's port or interface on which the CDP packets are multicast.

Another command that'll deliver the goods on neighbor information is the show cdp neighbor detail command (show cdp nei de for short). This command can be run on both routers and switches, and it displays detailed information about each device connected to the device you're running the command on. Check out this router output for an example:

```
Todd2509#sh cdp neighbor detail
-------------------------
Device ID: 1900Switch
Entry address(es):
  IP address: 0.0.0.0
Platform: cisco 1900,  Capabilities: Trans-Bridge Switch
Interface: Ethernet0,  Port ID (outgoing port): 2
Holdtime : 166 sec
Version :
V9.00

-------------------------
Device ID: 2501B
Entry address(es):
  IP address: 172.16.10.2
Platform: cisco 2500,  Capabilities: Router
Interface: Serial0,  Port ID (outgoing port): Serial0
Holdtime : 154 sec
Version :
Cisco Internetwork Operating System Software
IOS (tm) 3000 Software (IGS-J-L), Version 11.1(5),
  RELEASE SOFTWARE (fc1)Copyright (c) 1986-1996 by cisco
  Systems, Inc.Compiled Tue 05-Aug-03 11:48 by mkamson
Todd2509#
```

What are we being shown here? First, we're given the hostname and IP address of all directly connected devices. In addition to the same information displayed by the show cdp neighbor command (see Table 9.5), the show cdp neighbor detail command also gives us the IOS version of the neighbor device.

The show cdp entry * command displays the same information as the show cdp neighbor details command. Here's an example of the router output using the show cdp entry * command:

```
Todd2509#sh cdp entry *
-------------------------
Device ID: 1900Switch
Entry address(es):
  IP address: 0.0.0.0
```

```
Platform: cisco 1900,  Capabilities: Trans-Bridge Switch
Interface: Ethernet0,  Port ID (outgoing port): 2
Holdtime : 223 sec
Version :
V9.00
------------------------
Device ID: 2501B
Entry address(es):
  IP address: 172.16.10.2
Platform: cisco 2500,  Capabilities: Router
Interface: Serial0,  Port ID (outgoing port): Serial0
Holdtime : 151 sec
Version :
Cisco Internetwork Operating System Software
IOS (tm) 3000 Software (IGS-J-L), Version 11.1(5),
  RELEASE SOFTWARE (fc1)Copyright (c) 1986-1996 by cisco
  Systems, Inc.Compiled Tue 05-Aug-03 11:48 by mkamson
Todd2509#
```

Gathering Interface Traffic Information

The show cdp traffic command displays information about interface traffic, including the number of CDP packets sent and received and the errors with CDP.

The following output shows the show cdp traffic command used on the 2509 router:

```
Todd2509#sh cdp traffic
CDP counters:
        Packets output: 13, Input: 8
        Hdr syntax: 0, Chksum error: 0, Encaps failed: 0
        No memory: 0, Invalid packet: 0, Fragmented: 0
Todd2509#
```

This is not really the most important information you can gather from a router, but it does show how many CDP packets are sent and received on a device.

Gathering Port and Interface Information

The show cdp interface command gives you the CDP status on router interfaces or switch ports.

As I said earlier, you can turn off CDP completely on a router by using the no cdp run command. But, remember that you can also turn off CDP on a per-interface basis with the no cdp enable command. You enable a port with the cdp enable command. All ports and interfaces default to cdp enable.

On a router, the show cdp interface command displays information about each interface using CDP, including the encapsulation on the line, the timer, and the holdtime for each interface. Here's an example of this command's output on the 2509 router:

```
Todd2509#sh cdp interface
Ethernet0 is up, line protocol is up
  Encapsulation ARPA
  Sending CDP packets every 60 seconds
  Holdtime is 180 seconds
Serial0 is administratively down, line protocol is down
  Encapsulation HDLC
  Sending CDP packets every 60 seconds
  Holdtime is 180 seconds
Serial1 is administratively down, line protocol is down
  Encapsulation HDLC
  Sending CDP packets every 60 seconds
  Holdtime is 180 seconds
```

To turn off CDP on one interface on a router, use the no cdp enable command from interface configuration mode:

```
Todd2509#config t
Enter configuration commands, one per line.  End with
  CNTL/Z.
Router(config)#int s0
Router(config-if)#no cdp enable
Router(config-if)#^Z
```

Verify the change with the show cdp interface command:

```
Todd2509#sh cdp int
Ethernet0 is up, line protocol is up
  Encapsulation ARPA
  Sending CDP packets every 60 seconds
  Holdtime is 180 seconds
Serial1 is administratively down, line protocol is down
  Encapsulation HDLC
  Sending CDP packets every 60 seconds
  Holdtime is 180 seconds
Todd2509#
```

Notice above that serial 0 isn't listed in the router output. To get that, you'd have to perform a cdp enable on serial 0. It would then show up in the output.

🌐 Real World Scenario

CDP can save lives!

Karen was just hired as a Senior Network Consultant at a large hospital in Dallas, Texas. She is expected to be able to take care of any problem that comes up, but no stress here; she only has to worry about people possibly not getting the right health care if the network goes down! Talk about a potential life-or-death situation!

Karen starts her job, happily, and then of course, the network has some problems. She asks one of the Junior administrators for a network map so she can troubleshoot the network. This person tells her that the old Senior Administrator (who just got fired) had them with him and now no one can find them…ouch!

Doctors are calling every couple minutes because they can't get the necessary information they need to take care of their patients. What should she do?

CDP to the rescue! Thank God this hospital has all Cisco routers and switches, and that CDP is enabled by default on all Cisco devices. Also, luckily the disgruntled administrator who just got fired didn't turn off CDP on any devices before he left.

All Karen has to do now is to use the `show cdp neighbor detail` command to find all the information she needs about each device to help draw out the hospital network and save lives!

The only snag to nailing this comes at you if you don't know the passwords of all those devices. Your only hope then is to somehow find out the access passwords or to perform password recovery on them.

So, use CDP— you never know when you may end up saving someone's life!

P.S. This is a true story.

Using Telnet

Telnet, part of the TCP/IP protocol suite, is a virtual terminal protocol that allows you to make connections to remote devices, gather information, and run programs.

After your routers and switches are configured, you can use the Telnet program to reconfigure and/or check up on your routers and switches without using a console cable. You run the Telnet program by typing **telnet** from any command prompt (DOS or Cisco). You need to have VTY passwords set on the routers for this to work.

Remember, you can't use CDP to gather information about routers and switches that aren't directly connected to your device. But you can use the Telnet application to connect to your neighbor devices, then run CDP on those remote devices to get information on them.

You can issue the `telnet` command from any router prompt like this:

```
Todd2509#telnet 172.16.10.2
Trying 172.16.10.2 ... Open

Password required, but none set

[Connection to 172.16.10.2 closed by foreign host]
Todd2509#
```

As you can see, I didn't set my passwords—how embarrassing! Remember that the VTY ports on a router are configured as `login`, meaning that we have to either set the VTY passwords or use the `no login` command. (You can review setting passwords in Chapter 4, "Introduction to the Cisco IOS," if you need to.)

On a Cisco router, you don't need to use the `telnet` command; you can just type in an IP address from a command prompt, and the router will assume that you want to telnet to the device. Here's how that looks:

```
Todd2509#172.16.10.2
Trying 172.16.10.2 ... Open

Password required, but none set

[Connection to 172.16.10.2 closed by foreign host]
Todd2509#
```

At this point, it would be a great idea to set those VTY passwords on the router I want to telnet into. Here's what I did on the remote router:

```
2501B#config t
Enter configuration commands, one per line.  End with
  CNTL/Z.
2501B(config)#line vty 0 4
2501B(config-line)#login
2501B(config-line)#password todd
2501B(config-line)#^Z
2501B#
%SYS-5-CONFIG_I: Configured from console by console
```

Now, let's try this again. Here, I'm connecting to the router from the 2509's console:

```
Todd2509#172.16.10.2
Trying 172.16.10.2 ... Open
```

```
User Access Verification

Password:
2501B>
```

Remember that the VTY password is the user-mode password, not the enable-mode password. Watch what happens when I try to go into privileged mode after telnetting into router 2501B:

```
2501B>en
% No password set
2501B>
```

It is basically saying "no way!" This is a really good security feature, because you don't want anyone telnetting into your device and being able to just type the enable command to get into privileged mode. You've got to set your enable mode password or enable secret password to use Telnet to configure remote devices!

In the following examples, I am going to show you how to telnet into multiple devices simultaneously, then show you how to use hostnames instead of IP addresses.

Telnetting into Multiple Devices Simultaneously

If you telnet to a router or switch, you can end the connection by typing exit at any time. But what if you want to keep your connection to a remote device but still come back to your original router console? To do that, you can press the Ctrl+Shift+6 key combination, release it, and then press X.

Here's an example of connecting to multiple devices from my Todd2509 router console:

```
Todd2509#telnet 172.16.10.2
Trying 172.16.10.2 ... Open

User Access Verification

Password:
2501B>[Cntl+Shift+6, then X]
Todd2509#
```

In the example above, I telnetted to the 2501B router then typed the password to enter user mode. I next pressed Ctrl+Shift+6, then X (but you can't see that because it doesn't show on the screen output). Notice that my command prompt is now back at the Todd2509 router.

You can also telnet into a 1900 switch, but to get away with that you must set the enable mode password to level 15, or the enable secret password on the switch, before you can gain access via the Telnet application.

In the following example, I telnetted into a 1900 switch that responded by giving me the console output of the switch:

```
Todd2509#telnet 192.168.0.148
Trying 192.168.0.148 ... Open


Catalyst 1900 Management Console
Copyright (c) Cisco Systems, Inc.  1993-1999
All rights reserved.
Enterprise Edition Software
Ethernet Address:       00-B0-64-75-6B-C0

PCA Number:             73-3122-04
PCA Serial Number:      FAB040131E2
Model Number:           WS-C1912-A
System Serial Number:   FAB0401U0JQ
Power Supply S/N:       PHI033108SD
PCB Serial Number:      FAB040131E2,73-3122-04
-------------------------------------------------

1 user(s) now active on Management Console.


      User Interface Menu

   [M] Menus
   [K] Command Line

Enter Selection:
```

At this point, I pressed Ctrl+Shift+6, then X, which took me back to my Todd2509 router console:

```
Todd2509#
```

Checking Telnet Connections

To see the connections made from your router to a remote device, use the show sessions command.

```
Todd2509#sh sessions
Conn Host            Address          Byte Idle Conn Name
   1 172.16.10.2     172.16.10.2       0    0  172.16.10.2
*  2 192.168.0.148   192.168.0.148     0    0  192.168.0.148
Todd2509#
```

See that asterisk (*) next to connection 2? It means that session 2 was your last session. You can return to your last session by pressing Enter twice. You can also return to any session by typing the number of the connection and pressing Enter twice.

Checking Telnet Users

You can list all active consoles and VTY ports in use on your router with the show users command:

```
Todd2509#sh users
     Line     User     Host(s)          Idle Location
*    0 con 0            172.16.10.2      00:07:52
                        192.168.0.148    00:07:18
```

In the command's output, con represents the local console. In this example, the console is connected to two remote IP addresses, or, in other words, two devices.

In the next example, I typed **sh users** on the 2501B router that the Todd2509 router had telnetted into:

```
2501B>sh users
     Line     User     Host(s)          Idle Location
     0 con 0            idle             9
*    2 vty 0
```

This output shows that the console is active and that VTY port 2 is being used. The asterisk represents the current terminal session from which the show user command was entered.

Closing Telnet Sessions

You can end Telnet sessions a few different ways—typing exit or disconnect is probably the easiest and quickest.

To end a session from a remote device, use the exit command:

```
Todd2509#[Enter] and again [Enter]
[Resuming connection 2 to 192.168.0.148 ... ]

1900Switch>exit

[Connection to 192.168.0.148 closed by foreign host]
Todd2509#
```

Since the 1900Switch was my last session, I just pressed Enter twice to return to that session.

To end a session from a local device, use the disconnect command:

```
Todd2509#disconnect ?
  <1-2>  The number of an active network connection
```

```
 WORD    The name of an active network connection
 <cr>
```

```
Todd2509#disconnect 1
Closing connection to 172.16.10.2 [confirm]
Todd2509#
```

In this example, I used the session number 1 because that was the connection to the 2501B router that I wanted to end. As I said, you can use the show sessions command to see the connection number.

If you want to end a session of a device attached to your local device through Telnet, you should first check to see if any devices are attached to your router. Use the show users command to get that information like this:

```
2501B#sh users
    Line     User     Host(s)          Idle Location
*   0 con 0            idle             0
    1 aux 0            idle             0
    2 vty 0            idle             0 172.16.10.1
```

This output shows that VTY 0 has IP address 172.16.10.1 connected. That's the Todd2509 router.

To clear the connection, use the clear line # command:

```
2501B#clear line 2
[confirm]
 [OK]
```

Then verify that the user has been disconnected with the show users command:

```
2501B#sh users
    Line     User     Host(s)          Idle Location
*   0 con 0            idle             0
    1 aux 0            idle             1
```

```
2501B#
```

This output confirms that the line has been cleared.

Resolving Hostnames

In order to use a hostname rather than an IP address to connect to a remote device, the device that you are using to make the connection must be able to translate the hostname to an IP address.

There are two ways to resolve hostnames to IP addresses: building a host table on each router or building a Domain Name System (DNS) server, which is similar to a dynamic host table.

Building a Host Table

A host table provides name resolution only on the router that it was built upon. The command to build a host table on a router is:

ip host *host_name tcp_port_number ip_address*

The default is TCP port number 23, but you can create a session using Telnet with a different TCP port number if you want. You can also assign up to eight IP addresses to a hostname.

Here's an example of configuring a host table with two entries to resolve the names for the 2501B router and the switch:

```
Todd2509#config t
Enter configuration commands, one per line.  End with
  CNTL/Z.
Todd2509(config)#ip host ?
  WORD  Name of host

Todd2509(config)#ip host 2501B ?
  <0-65535>  Default telnet port number
  A.B.C.D    Host IP address (maximum of 8)

Todd2509(config)#ip host 2501B 172.16.10.2 ?
  A.B.C.D  Host IP address (maximum of 8)
  <cr>
Todd2509(config)#ip host 2501B 172.16.10.2
Todd2509(config)#ip host 1900Switch 192.168.0.148
Todd2509(config)#^Z
```

And to see the newly built host table, just use the show hosts command:

```
Todd2509#sh hosts
Default domain is not set
Name/address lookup uses domain service
Name servers are 255.255.255.255

Host            Flags     Age Type   Address(es)
2501B           (perm, OK)  0   IP     172.16.10.2
1900Switch      (perm, OK)  0   IP     192.168.0.148
Todd2509#
```

You can see the two hostnames plus their associated IP addresses in the preceding router output. The perm in the Flags column means that the entry is manually configured. If it said temp, it would be an entry that was resolved by DNS.

To verify that the host table resolves names, try typing the hostnames at a router prompt. Remember that if you don't specify the command, the router assumes you want to telnet. In the following example, I used the hostnames to telnet into the remote devices, and then pressed Ctrl+Shift+6, then X to return to the main console of the Todd2509 router:

```
Todd2509#2501b
Trying 2501B (172.16.10.2)... Open

User Access Verification

Password:
2501B>
Todd2509#[Ctrl+Shift+6, then X]
Todd2509#1900switch
Trying 1900switch (192.168.0.148)... Open

Catalyst 1900 Management Console
Copyright (c) Cisco Systems, Inc.   1993-1999
All rights reserved.
Enterprise Edition Software
Ethernet Address:       00-B0-64-75-6B-C0

PCA Number:             73-3122-04
PCA Serial Number:      FAB040131E2
Model Number:           WS-C1912-A
System Serial Number:   FAB0401U0JQ
Power Supply S/N:       PHI033108SD
PCB Serial Number:      FAB040131E2,73-3122-04
-------------------------------------------------


1 user(s) now active on Management Console.

        User Interface Menu

    [M] Menus
    [K] Command Line

Enter Selection:[Ctrl+Shift+6, then X]
Todd2509#
```

I successfully used entries in the host table to create a session to two devices, and used the names to telnet into both devices. Notice that the entries in the show sessions output below now display the hostnames and IP addresses instead of just the IP addresses:

```
Todd2509#sh sess
Conn Host          Address         Byte  Idle Conn Name
   1 1900switch    192.168.0.148      0     0 switch
*  2 2501b         172.16.10.2        0     0 2501b
Todd2509#
```

If you want to remove a hostname from the table, just use the no ip host command like this:

```
RouterA(config)#no ip host routerb
```

The problem with the host table method is that you would need to create a host table on each router to be able to resolve names. And if you have a whole bunch of routers and want to resolve names, using DNS is a much better choice!

Using DNS to Resolve Names

So if you have a lot of devices and don't want to create a host table in each device, you can use a DNS server to resolve hostnames.

Any time a Cisco device receives a command it doesn't understand, it will try to resolve it through DNS by default. Watch what happens when I type the special command **todd** at a Cisco router prompt:

```
Todd2509#todd
Translating "todd"...domain server (255.255.255.255)
% Unknown command or computer name, or unable to find
  computer address
Todd2509#
```

It doesn't know my name or what command I am trying to type, so it tries to resolve this through DNS. This is really annoying for two reasons: first, because it doesn't know my name <grin> and second, because I need to hang out and wait for the name lookup to time out. You can get around this and prevent a time-consuming DNS lookup by using the no ip domain-lookup command on your router from global configuration mode.

If you have a DNS server on your network, you need to add a few commands to make DNS name resolution work:

- The first command is ip domain-lookup, which is turned on by default. It only needs to be entered if you previously turned it off (with the no ip domain-lookup command).

- The second command is ip name-server. This sets the IP address of the DNS server. You can enter the IP addresses of up to six servers.

- The last command is ip domain-name. Although this command is optional, it really should be set. It appends the domain name to the hostname you type in. Since DNS uses a fully qualified domain name (FQDN) system, you must have a full DNS name, in the form domain.com.

Here's an example of using these three commands:

```
Todd2509#config t
Enter configuration commands, one per line.  End with
  CNTL/Z.
Todd2509(config)#ip domain-lookup
Todd2509(config)#ip name-server ?
  A.B.C.D  Domain server IP address (maximum of 6)
Todd2509(config)#ip name-server 192.168.0.70
Todd2509(config)#ip domain-name lammle.com
Todd2509(config)#^Z
Todd2509#
```

After the DNS configurations are set, you can test the DNS server by using a hostname to ping or telnet a device like this:

```
Todd2509#ping 2501b
Translating "2501b"...domain server (192.168.0.70) [OK]
Type escape sequence to abort.
Sending 5, 100-byte ICMP Echos to 172.16.10.2, timeout is
  2 seconds:
!!!!!
Success rate is 100 percent (5/5), round-trip min/avg/max
  = 28/31/32 ms
```

Notice that the router uses the DNS server to resolve the name.

After a name is resolved using DNS, use the show hosts command to see that the device cached this information in the host table:

```
Todd2509#sh hosts
Default domain is lammle.com
Name/address lookup uses domain service
Name servers are 192.168.0.70

Host                 Flags       Age Type  Address(es)
2501b.lammle.com     (temp, OK)  0   IP    172.16.10.2
1900switch           (perm, OK)  0   IP    192.168.0.148
Todd2509#
```

🌐 **Real World Scenario**

Should you use a host table or DNS server?

Karen has finally finished drawing out her network by using CDP and the doctors are much happier. However, Karen is having a difficult time administering the network because she has to keep looking at the network drawing to find an IP address every time she needs to telnet to a remote router.

Karen was thinking about putting host tables on each router, but with literally hundreds of routers, this is a daunting task.

Most networks have a DNS server now anyway, so adding a hundred or so hostnames into it would be an easy way to go—certainly easier then adding these hostnames to each and every router! Just add the three commands on each router and blammo—you're resolving names!

Using a DNS server makes it easy to update any old entries too—remember, even one little change, and off you go to each and every router to manually update its table if you're using static host tables.

Keep in mind that this has nothing to do with name resolution on the network, and nothing to do with what a host on the network is trying to accomplish. This is only used when you're trying to resolve names from the router console.

The entry that was resolved is shown as `temp`, but the 1900 switch device is still `perm`, meaning that it's a static entry. Notice that the hostname is a full domain name. If I hadn't used the `ip domain-name lammle.com` command, I would have needed to type in **ping 2501b.lammle.com**, which is a pain.

Checking Network Connectivity

You can use the `ping` and `traceroute` commands to test connectivity to remote devices, and both of them can be used with many protocols, not just IP.

Using the *ping* Command

So far, you've seen many examples of pinging devices to test IP connectivity and name resolution using the DNS server. To see all the different protocols that you can use with the `ping` program, type **ping ?**:

```
Todd2509#ping ?
  WORD      Ping destination address or hostname
```

```
apollo     Apollo echo
appletalk  Appletalk echo
clns       CLNS echo
decnet     DECnet echo
ip         IP echo
ipx        Novell/IPX echo
srb        srb echo
tag        Tag encapsulated IP echo
vines      Vines echo
xns        XNS echo
<cr>
```

The ping output displays the minimum, average, and maximum times it takes for a ping packet to find a specified system and return. Here's an example:

```
Todd2509#ping todd2509
Translating "todd2509"...domain server (192.168.0.70)[OK]
Type escape sequence to abort.
Sending 5, 100-byte ICMP Echos to 192.168.0.121, timeout
  is 2 seconds:
!!!!!
Success rate is 100 percent (5/5), round-trip min/avg/max
  = 32/32/32 ms
Todd2509#
```

You can see that the DNS server was used to resolve the name, and the device was pinged in 32ms (milliseconds).

 The ping command can be used in user and privileged mode, but not configuration mode.

Using the *traceroute* Command

Traceroute (the traceroute command, or trace for short) shows the path a packet takes to get to a remote device. To see the protocols that you can use with the traceroute command, type **traceroute ?**:

```
Todd2509#traceroute ?
  WORD       Trace route to destination address or
             hostname
  appletalk  AppleTalk Trace
```

```
clns       ISO CLNS Trace
ip         IP Trace
ipx        IPX Trace
oldvines   Vines Trace (Cisco)
vines      Vines Trace (Banyan)
<cr>
```

The `trace` command shows the hop or hops that a packet traverses on its way to a remote device. Here's an example:

```
Todd2509#trace 2501b
Type escape sequence to abort.
Tracing the route to 2501b.lammle.com (172.16.10.2)

  1 2501b.lammle.com (172.16.10.2) 16 msec *   16 msec
Todd2509#
```

You can see that the packet went through only one hop to find the destination.

Do not get confused on the exam. You can't use the `tracert` command—it's a Windows command. For a router, use the `traceroute` command!

Summary

In this chapter, you learned how Cisco routers are configured and how to manage those configurations.

This chapter covered the internal components of a router, which included the ROM, RAM, NVRAM, and Flash.

In addition, I covered what happens when a router boots and which files are loaded. The configuration register tells the router how to boot and where to find files, and we learned in this chapter how to change and verify the configuration register settings for password recovery purposes.

Next, you learned how to back up and restore a Cisco IOS image, as well as how to back up and restore the configuration of a Cisco router. Then you learned how to use CDP and Telnet to gather information about remote devices. Finally, the chapter covered how to resolve hostnames and use the `ping` and `trace` commands to test network connectivity.

Exam Essentials

Remember the various configuration register commands and settings. The 0x2102 setting is the default on all Cisco routers and tells the router to look in NVRAM for the boot sequence. 0x2101 tells the router to boot from ROM, and 0x2142 tells the router to not load the startup-config in NVRAM to provide password recovery.

Remember how to back up an IOS image. By using the privileged-mode command `copy flash tftp`, you can back up a file from flash memory to a TFTP (network) server.

Remember how to restore or upgrade an IOS image. By using the privileged-mode command `copy tftp flash`, you can restore or upgrade a file from a TFTP (network) server to flash memory.

Remember what you must complete before you back up an IOS image to a network server. Make sure that you can access the network server, ensure that the network server has adequate space for the code image, and verify the file naming and path requirement.

Remember how to save the configuration of a router. There are a couple ways to do this, but the most common, as well as most tested, method is `copy running-config startup-config`.

Remember how to erase the configuration of a router. Type the privileged-mode command `erase startup-config` and reload the router.

Understand when to use CDP. Cisco Discovery Protocol can be used to help you document your network as well as troubleshoot your network.

Remember the output from the `show cdp neighbors` command. The `show cdp neighbors` command provides the following information: device ID, local interface, holdtime, capability, platform, and port ID (remote interface).

Understand how to telnet into a router, keep your connection, but return to your originating console. If you telnet to a router or switch, you can end the connection by typing **exit** at any time. However, if you want to keep your connection to a remote device but still come back to your original router console, you can press the Ctrl+Shift+6 key combination, release it, and then press X.

Remember the command to verify your Telnet sessions. The command `show sessions` will provide you with all the sessions your router has with other routers.

Remember how to build a static host table on a router. By using the global configuration mode command `ip host host_name ip_address`, you can build a static host table on your router. You can apply multiple IP addresses against the same host entry.

Remember how to verify your host table on a router. You can verify the host table with the `show hosts` command.

Understand when to use the `ping` command. Packet Internet Groper (Ping) uses ICMP echo request and ICMP echo replies to verify an active IP address on a network.

Remember how to ping a valid host ID. You can ping an IP address from a router's user mode or privileged mode, but not from configuration mode. You must ping a valid address, such as 1.1.1.1. Examples of invalid addresses are 192.168.10.0, 192.168.10.255, and

192.168.10.256. (See Chapter 3, "IP Subnetting and Variable Length Subnet Masks (VLSM)," for information on IP addressing if you do not understand this.)

Key Terms

Before you take the exam, be certain you are familiar with the following terms:

boot sequence	random access memory (RAM)
CDP holdtime	read-only memory (ROM)
CDP timer	Telnet
configuration register	TFTP server
flash memory	Traceroute
Packet Internet Groper (Ping)	

Commands Used in This Chapter

The following list contains a summary of all the commands used in this chapter:

Command	Description
cdp enable	Turns on CDP on an individual interface
cdp holdtime	Changes the holdtime of CDP packets
cdp run	Turns on CDP on a router
cdp timer	Changes the CDP update timer
clear line	Clears a connection connected via Telnet to your router
config-register	Tells the router how to boot and to change the configuration register setting
confreg	Changes the configure register of a router from Rom monitor mode (2600 series is an example).
copy flash tftp	Copies a file from flash memory to a TFTP server
copy run start	Copies the running-config file to the startup-config file
copy run tftp	Copies the running-config file to a TFTP server

`copy tftp flash`	Copies a file from a TFTP server to flash memory
`copy tftp run`	Copies a configuration from a TFTP server to the `running-config`.
Ctrl+Shift+6, then X	Returns you to the originating router when you telnet to other devices and your sessions remains established.
`disconnect`	Disconnects a connection to a remote router from the originating router
`erase startup-config`	Deletes the contents of NVRAM on a router
`exit`	Disconnects a connection to a remote router via Telnet from the remote router.
`ip domain-lookup`	Turns on DNS lookup (which is on by default)
`ip domain-name`	Appends a domain name to a DNS lookup
`ip host`	Creates a host table on a router
`ip name-server`	Sets the IP address of up to six DNS servers
`no cdp enable`	Turns off CDP on an individual interface
`no cdp run`	Turns off CDP completely on a router
`no ip domain-lookup`	Turns off DNS lookup
`no ip host`	Removes a hostname from a host table
`o/r 0x2142`	Changes a 2500 series to boot without using the contents of NVRAM
`ping`	Tests IP connectivity to a remote device
`show cdp`	Displays the CDP timer and holdtime frequencies
`show cdp entry *`	Same as `show cdp neighbor detail`, but does not work on a 1900 switch
`show cdp interface`	Shows the individual interfaces enabled with CDP
`show cdp neighbor`	Shows the directly connected neighbors and some limited information about them
`show cdp neighbor detail`	Shows the IP address and IOS version and type, and includes all of the information from the `show cdp neighbor` command
`show cdp traffic`	Shows the CDP packets sent and received on a device and any errors

`show flash`	Shows the files in flash memory
`show hosts`	Shows the contents of the host table
`show running-config`	Displays the `running-config` file
`show sessions`	Shows your connections via Telnet to remote devices
`show start`	Displays the `startup-config` file
`show users`	Displays the users that are telnetted into your device
`show version`	Displays the IOS type and version as well as the configuration register
`telnet`	Connects, views, and runs programs on a remote device
`tftp-server flash:ios-name`	Creates a TFTP-server host for a router system image that is run in flash memory
`traceroute`	Tests a connection to a remote device and shows the path it took through the internetwork to find the remote device

Written Lab 9

Write the answers to the following questions:

1. What is the command to copy a Cisco IOS to a TFTP server?
2. What is the command to copy a Cisco `startup-config` file to a TFTP server?
3. What is the command to copy the `startup-config` file to DRAM?
4. What is an older command that you can use to copy the startup-config file to DRAM?
5. What command can you use to see the neighbor router's IP address from your router prompt?
6. What command can you use to see the hostname, local interface, platform, and remote port of a neighbor router?
7. What keystrokes can you use to telnet into multiple devices simultaneously?
8. What command will show you your active Telnet connections to neighbor and remote devices?
9. What command can you use to upgrade a Cisco IOS?
10. What command can you use to create a host table entry for Bob, using IP addresses 172.16.10.1 and 172.16.20.2?

(The answers to Written Lab 9 can be found following the answers to the Review Questions for this chapter.)

Hands-on Labs

To complete the labs in this section, you need at least one router (three are best) and at least one PC running as a TFTP server. Remember that the labs listed here were created for use with real routers.

Here is a list of the labs in this chapter:

Hands-on Lab 9.1: Backing Up Your Router IOS

1. Log into your router and go into privileged mode by typing **en** or **enable**.
2. Make sure you can connect to the TFTP server that is on your network by pinging the IP address from the router console.
3. Type **show flash** to see the contents of flash memory.
4. Type **show version** at the router privileged mode prompt to get the name of the IOS currently running on the router. If there is only one file in flash memory, the show flash and show version commands show the same file. Remember that the show version command shows you the file that is currently running, and the show flash command shows you all of the files in flash memory.
5. Once you know you have good Ethernet connectivity to the TFTP server, and you also know the IOS filename, back up your IOS by typing **copy flash tftp**. This command tells the router to copy the contents of flash memory (this is where the IOS is stored by default) to a TFTP server.
6. Enter the IP address of the TFTP server and the source IOS filename. The file is now copied and stored in the TFTP server's default directory.

Hands-on Lab 9.2: Upgrading or Restoring Your Router IOS

1. Log into your router and go into privileged mode by typing **en** or **enable**.
2. Make sure you can connect to the TFTP server by pinging the IP address of the server from the router console.
3. Once you know you have good Ethernet connectivity to the TFTP server, issue the copy tftp flash command.
4. Confirm that the router is not functioning during the restore or upgrade by following the prompts provided on the router console.

5. Enter the IP address of the TFTP server.

6. Enter the IOS filename you want to restore or upgrade.

7. Confirm that you understand that the contents of flash memory will be erased.

8. Watch in amazement as your IOS is deleted out of flash memory, and your new IOS is copied to flash memory.

   If the file that was in flash memory is deleted, but the new version wasn't copied to flash memory, the router will boot from ROM monitor mode. You'll need to figure out why the copy operation did not take place.

Hands-on Lab 9.3: Backing Up the Router Configuration

1. Log into your router and go into privileged mode by typing **en** or **enable**.

2. Ping the TFTP server to make sure you have IP connectivity.

3. From Router B, type **copy run tftp**.

4. Type the IP address of the TFTP server (for example, 172.16.30.2) and press Enter.

5. The router will prompt you for a filename. The hostname of the router is followed by the suffix -confg (yes, I spelled that correctly). You can use any name you want.

    ```
    Name of configuration file to write [RouterB-confg]?
    ```

    Press Enter to accept the default name.

    ```
    Write file RouterB-confg on host 172.16.30.2? [confirm]
    ```

    Press Enter.

Hands-on Lab 9.4: Using the Cisco Discovery Protocol (CDP)

1. Log into your router and go into privileged mode by typing **en** or **enable**.

2. From the router, type **sh cdp** and press Enter. You should see that CDP packets are being sent out to all active interfaces every 60 seconds and the holdtime is 180 seconds (these are the defaults).

3. To change the CDP update frequency to 90 seconds, type **cdp timer 90** in global configuration mode.

    ```
    RouterC#config t
    Enter configuration commands, one per line.  End with
      CNTL/Z.
    RouterC(config)#cdp timer ?
      <5-900>  Rate at which CDP packets are sent (in sec)
    RouterC(config)#cdp timer 90
    ```

4. Verify that your CDP timer frequency has changed by using the command show cdp in privileged mode.

```
RouterC#sh cdp
Global CDP information:
Sending CDP packets every 90 seconds
Sending a holdtime value of 180 seconds
```

5. Now, use CDP to gather information about neighbor routers. You can get the list of available commands by typing **sh cdp ?**.

```
RouterC#sh cdp ?
  entry     Information for specific neighbor entry
  interface CDP interface status and configuration
  neighbors CDP neighbor entries
  traffic   CDP statistics
  <cr>
```

6. Type **sh cdp int** to see the interface information plus the default encapsulation used by the interface. It also shows the CDP timer information.

7. Type **sh cdp entry** * to see the CDP information received from all device.

8. Type **show cdp neighbors** to gather information about all connected neighbors. (You should know the specific information output by this command.)

9. Type **show cdp neighbors detail**. Notice that it produces the same output as show cdp entry *.

Hands-on Lab 9.5: Using Telnet

1. Log into your router and go into privileged mode by typing **en** or **enable**.

2. From RouterA, telnet into your remote router by typing **telnet *ip_address*** from the command prompt.

3. Type in RouterB's IP address from RouterA's command prompt. Notice that the router automatically tries to telnet to the IP address you specified. You can use the telnet command or just type in the IP address.

4. From RouterB, press Ctrl+Shift+6, then X to return to RouterA's command prompt. Now telnet into your third router, RouterC. Press Ctrl+Shift+6, then X to return to RouterA.

5. From RouterA, type **show sessions**. Notice your two sessions. You can press the number displayed to the left of the session and press Enter twice to return to that session. The asterisk shows the default session. You can press Enter twice to return to that session.

6. Go to the session for your RouterB. Type **show users**. This shows the console connection and the remote connection. You can use the disconnect command to clear the session, or just type **exit** from the prompt to close your session with RouterB.

7. Go to the RouterC's console port by typing **show sessions** on the first router and using the connection number to return to RouterC. Type **show user** and notice the connection to your first router, RouterA.

8. Type **clear line** to disconnect the Telnet session.

Hands-on Lab 9.6: Resolving Hostnames

1. Log into your router and go into privileged mode by typing **en** or **enable**.

2. From RouterA, type **todd** and press Enter at the command prompt. Notice the error you receive and the delay. The router is trying to resolve the hostname to an IP address by looking for a DNS server. You can turn this feature off by using the no ip domain-lookup command from global configuration mode.

3. To build a host table, you use the ip host command. From RouterA, add a host table entry for RouterB and RouterC by entering the following commands:

    ```
    ip host routerb ip_address
    ip host routerc ip_address
    ```

    Here is an example:

    ```
    ip host routerb 172.16.20.2
    ip host routerc 172.16.40.2
    ```

4. Test your host table by typing **ping routerb** from the command prompt (not the config prompt).

    ```
    RouterA#ping routerb
    Type escape sequence to abort.
    Sending 5, 100-byte ICMP Echos to 172.16.20.2, timeout
      is 2 seconds:
    !!!!!
    Success rate is 100 percent (5/5), round-trip
      min/avg/max = 4/4/4 ms
    ```

5. Test your host table by typing **ping routerc**.

    ```
    RouterA#ping routerc
    Type escape sequence to abort.
    Sending 5, 100-byte ICMP Echos to 172.16.40.2, timeout
      is 2 seconds:
    !!!!!
    Success rate is 100 percent (5/5), round-trip
      min/avg/max = 4/6/8 ms
    ```

6. Keep your session to RouterB open, and then return to RouterA by pressing Ctrl+Shift+6, then X.

7. Telnet to RouterC by typing **routerc** at the command prompt.

8. Return to RouterA and keep the session to RouterC open by pressing Ctrl+Shift+6, then X.

9. View the host table by typing **show hosts** and pressing Enter.

```
Default domain is not set
Name/address lookup uses domain service
Name servers are 255.255.255.255
Host                Flags       Age Type  Address(es)
routerb             (perm, OK)  0   IP    172.16.20.2
routerc             (perm, OK)  0   IP    172.16.40.2
```

Review Questions

1. Which command will show you the hostname resolved to the IP address on a router?

   A. sh router

   B. sho hosts

   C. sh ip hosts

   D. sho name resolution

2. Which command will copy the IOS to a backup host on your network?

   A. transfer IOS to 172.16.10.1

   B. copy run start

   C. copy tftp flash

   D. copy start tftp

   E. copy flash tftp

3. Which command will copy a router configuration stored on a TFTP server to the router's NVRAM?

   A. transfer IOS to 172.16.10.1

   B. copy run start

   C. copy tftp startup

   D. copy tftp run

   E. copy flash tftp

4. You copy a configuration from a network host to a router's RAM. The configuration looks correct, yet it is not working at all. What could the problem be?

   A. You copied the wrong configuration into RAM.

   B. You copied the configuration into flash memory instead.

   C. The copy did not override the shutdown command in running-config.

   D. The IOS became corrupted after the copy command was initiated.

5. Which memory in a Cisco router stores packet buffers, ARP cache, and routing tables?

   A. Flash

   B. RAM

   C. ROM

   D. NVRAM

6. Which of the following is the correct command to create a host table on a Cisco router?

A. `bob ip host 172.16.10.1`

B. `host 172.16.10.1 bob`

C. `ip host bob 172.16.10.1 172.16.10.2`

D. `host bob 172.16.10.1`

7. Which command loads a new version of the Cisco IOS into a router?

A. `copy flash ftp`

B. `copy ftp flash`

C. `copy flash tftp`

D. `copy tftp flash`

8. Which command will show you the IOS version running on your router?

A. `sh IOS`

B. `sh flash`

C. `sh version`

D. `sh running-config`

9. Which of the following saves the configuration stored in RAM to NVRAM?

A. `copy running-config startup-config`

B. `copy tftp running-config`

C. `copy startup-config running-config`

D. `copy active backup`

10. To copy a configuration from the Cisco router's DRAM to a TFTP server on your network, what command can you use?

A. `config netw`

B. `config mem`

C. `config term`

D. `copy run tftp`

E. `copy start tftp`

11. If you want to have more than one Telnet session open at the same time, what keystroke combination would you use?

A. Tab+spacebar

B. Ctrl+X, then 6

C. Ctrl+Shift+X, then 6

D. Ctrl+Shift+6, then X

12. Which of the following commands will load an image named "beta" from a network server at 1.1.1.1 during the next router reload?

   A. `load system tftp beta 1.1.1.1`

   B. `load system tftp 1.1.1. beta`

   C. `boot system tftp beta 1.1.1.1`

   D. `load system tftp 1.1.1.1 beta`

13. Which exec command displays system hardware config information, software version, and the names and sources of config files and boot images on a router?

   A. `show flash`

   B. `show running-config`

   C. `show version`

   D. `show config`

14. Which three commands can be used to check LAN connectivity problems on a router?

   A. `show interfaces`

   B. `show ip route`

   C. `tracert`

   D. `ping`

   E. `dns lookups`

15. Which command is used to find the path a packet takes through an internetwork?

   A. `ping`

   B. `trace`

   C. `rip`

   D. `sap`

16. Which two commands can be used to test IP through your network and verify address configuration?

   A. `ping`

   B. `trace`

   C. `rip`

   D. `sap`

17. Which command displays the configuration register setting?

   A. `show ip route`

   B. `show boot version`

   C. `show version`

   D. `show flash`

18. In what two modes can the ICMP `ping` command be used?

    A. User

    B. Privileged

    C. Global configuration

    D. Interface configuration

19. Which of the following should be done before you back up an IOS on a network server? (Choose three.)

    A. Make sure you are logged in as root.

    B. Make sure the TFTP server has enough space for the image.

    C. Make sure you can access the server.

    D. Verify the IOS name and path requirements.

    E. Make sure the server can run the IOS code.

20. The configuration register setting of 0x2102 provides what function to a router?

    A. Tells the router to boot into ROM monitor mode

    B. Provides password recovery

    C. Tells the router to look in NVRAM for the boot sequence

    D. Boots the IOS from a TFTP server

    E. Boots an IOS image stored in ROM

Answers to Review Questions

1. B. The command to see the host table, which resolves hostnames to IP addresses, is `show host` or `show hosts`.

2. E. To copy the IOS to a backup host, which is stored in flash memory by default, use the `copy flash tftp` command.

3. C. To copy a configuration of a router stored on a TFTP server to a router's NVRAM, use the `copy tftp startup-config` command.

4. C. Since the configuration looks correct, you probably didn't screw the copy job up. However, when you perform a copy from a network host to a router, the interfaces are automatically shut down and need to manually be enabled with the `no shutdown` command.

5. B. RAM is used to store packet buffers and routing tables, among other things.

6. C. The command `ip host hostname ip_addresses` is used to create a host table on a Cisco router. The second IP address will only be tried if the first one does not work.

7. D. The command `copy tftp flash` will allow you to copy a new IOS into flash memory on your router.

8. C. The best answer is `show version`, which shows you the IOS file running currently on your router. The `show flash` shows you the contents of flash memory, not which file is running.

9. A. The `copy running-config startup-config` command copies the configuration stored in RAM to NVRAM.

10. D. To copy a configuration of a router from DRAM to a TFTP server, use the `copy running-config tftp` command.

11. D. To keep open one or more Telnet sessions, use the Ctrl+Shift+6, then X keystroke combination.

12. C. The command `boot system tftp IOS-name TFTP_server_address` will load an IOS image file from a TFTP server when the router is reloaded.

13. C. The `show version` command will show you the IOS names and the source from which the IOS files was loaded, the configuration register setting, and the software version.

14. A, B, D. The `tracert` command is a Windows command and will not work on a router! A router uses the `traceroute` command.

15. B. The `trace` command displays the path a packet takes to find a remote destination by using ICMP time exceeded messages.

16. A, B. The `ping` and `trace` commands can both be used to test IP connectivity in an internetwork.

17. C. The `show version` command provides you with the current configuration register setting.

18. A, B. The `ping` and `traceroute` commands can be used from user mode or privileged mode only.

19. B, C, D. Before you back up an IOS image to a network server (TFTP), make sure you can ping the server, that the server has enough space to hold the file, and that you know the IOS name.

20. C. The default configuration setting of 0x2102 tells the router to look in NVRAM for the boot sequence.

Answers to Written Lab 9

1. `copy flash tftp`
2. `copy start tftp`
3. `copy start run`
4. `config mem`
5. `show cdp neighbor detail` or `show cdp entry *`
6. `show cdp neighbor`
7. Ctrl+Shift+6, then X
8. `show sessions`
9. `copy tftp flash`
10. `ip host bob 172.16.10.1 172.16.20.2`

Managing Traffic with Access Lists

THE CCNA EXAM TOPICS COVERED IN THIS CHAPTER INCLUDE THE FOLLOWING:

✓ **PLANNING & DESIGNING**

  ▪ Develop an access list to meet user specifications

✓ **IMPLEMENTATION & OPERATION**

  ▪ Implement access lists

✓ **TROUBLESHOOTING**

  ▪ Troubleshoot an access list

✓ **TECHNOLOGY**

  ▪ Evaluate rules for packet control

The proper use and configuration of access lists is a vital part of router configuration because access lists are such versatile networking accessories. Contributing mightily to the efficiency and operation of your network, access lists give network managers a huge amount of control over traffic flow throughout the enterprise. With access lists, managers can gather basic statistics on packet flow and security policies can be implemented. Sensitive devices can also be protected from unauthorized access.

Access lists can be used to permit or deny packets moving through the router, permit or deny Telnet (VTY—also known as Virtual TeleType) access to or from a router, and create dial-on-demand interesting traffic that triggers dialing to a remote location.

In this chapter, we'll discuss access lists for TCP/IP and cover some of the tools available to test and monitor the functionality of applied access lists.

Introduction to Access Lists

An *access list* is essentially a list of conditions that categorize packets. They can be really helpful when you need to exercise control over network traffic. An access list would be your tool of choice for decision-making in these situations.

One of the most common and easiest to understand uses of access lists is filtering unwanted packets when implementing security policies. For example, you can set them up to make very specific decisions about regulating traffic patterns so that they'll only allow certain hosts to access WWW resources on the Internet while restricting others. With the right combination of access lists, network managers arm themselves with the power to enforce nearly any security policy they can invent.

Access lists can even be used in other situations that don't necessarily involve blocking packets too. For example, you can use them to control which networks will or won't be advertised by dynamic routing protocols. How you configure the access list is the same. The difference here is simply how you apply it—to a routing protocol instead of an interface. When you apply an access list in this way, it's called a distribute list, and it doesn't stop routing advertisements, it just controls their content. You can also use access lists to categorize packets for queuing or QOS-type services, and for controlling which types of traffic can activate a pricey ISDN link.

The CCNA exam focuses on both IP access lists as well as using access lists as packet filters, so that's what we're going to zero in on too!

Creating access lists is really a lot like programming a series of `if-then` statements—if a given condition is met, then a given action is taken. If the specific condition isn't met, nothing happens, and the next statement is evaluated. Access-list statements are basically packet filters that packets are compared against, categorized by, and acted upon accordingly. Once the lists are built, they can be applied to either inbound or outbound traffic on any interface. Applying an access list causes the router to analyze every packet crossing that interface in the specified direction and take the appropriate action.

There are a few important rules that a packet follows when it's being compared with an access list:

- It's always compared with each line of the access list in sequential order—i.e., it'll always start with the first line of the access list, then go to line 2, then line 3, and so on.

- It's compared with lines of the access list only until a match is made. Once the packet matches the condition on a line of the access list, the packet is acted upon, and no further comparisons take place.

- There is an implicit "deny" at the end of each access list—this means that if a packet doesn't match the condition on any of the lines in the access list, the packet will be discarded.

Each of these rules has some powerful implications when filtering IP packets with access lists. So keep in mind that creating effective access lists truly takes some practice.

There are two main types of access lists:

Standard access lists   These use only the source IP address in an IP packet as the condition test. All decisions are made based on source IP address. This means that standard access lists basically permit or deny an entire suite of protocols. They don't distinguish between any of the many types of IP traffic such as WWW, Telnet, UDP, etc.

Extended access lists   Extended access lists can evaluate many of the other fields in the layer 3 and layer 4 headers of an IP packet. They can evaluate source and destination IP addresses, the protocol field in the Network layer header, and port number at the Transport layer header. This gives extended access lists the ability to make much more granular decisions when controlling traffic.

Named access lists   Hey, wait a minute—I said two types of access lists but listed three! Well, technically there really are only two since *named access lists* are either standard or extended and not actually a new type. I'm just distinguishing them because they're created and referred to differently than standard and extended access lists. But they're functionally the same.

We will look at these types of access lists in more depth later in the chapter.

Once you create an access list, it's not really going to do anything until you apply it. Yes, they're there on the router, but they're inactive until you tell that router what to do with them. To use an access list as a packet filter, you need to apply it to an interface on the router where you want the traffic filtered. And you've got to specify which direction of traffic you want the access list applied to. There's a good reason for this—you may want different controls in place for traffic leaving your enterprise destined for the Internet than you'd want for traffic coming into your enterprise from the Internet. So, by specifying the direction of traffic, you can—and frequently, you'll need to—use different access lists for inbound and outbound traffic on a single interface:

Inbound access lists   When an access list is applied to inbound packets on an interface, those packets are processed through the access list before being routed to the outbound interface. Any packets that are denied won't be routed because they're discarded before the routing process is invoked.

Outbound access lists   When an access list is applied to outbound packets on an interface, those packets are routed to the outbound interface and then processed through the access list before being queued.

There are some general access-list guidelines that should be followed when creating and implementing access lists on a router:

- You can assign only one access list per interface per protocol per direction. This means that when creating IP access lists, you can only have one inbound access list and one outbound access list per interface.

When you consider the implications of the implicit deny at the end of any access list, it makes sense that you can't have multiple access lists applied on the same interface in the same direction for the same protocol. That's because any packets that don't match some condition in the first access list would be denied, and there wouldn't be any packets left over to compare against a second access list.

- Organize your access lists so that the more specific tests are at the top of the access list.

- Any time a new entry is added to the access list, it will be placed at the bottom of the list. Using a text-editor for access-lists is highly suggested.

- You cannot remove one line from an access list. If you try to do this, you will remove the entire list. It is best to copy the access list to a text editor before trying to edit the list. The only exception is when using named access lists.

You can delete a single line from a named access list. I'll show this to you shortly.

- Unless your access list ends with a `permit any` command, all packets will be discarded if they do not meet any of the lists' tests. Every list should have at least one `permit` statement, or it will deny all traffic.

- Create access lists and then apply them to an interface. Any access list applied to an interface without an access list present will not filter traffic.

- Access lists are designed to filter traffic going through the router. They will not filter traffic that has originated from the router.

- Place IP standard access lists as close to the destination as possible. This is the reason we don't really want to use standard access lists in our networks. You cannot put a standard access list close to the source host or network because you can only filter based on source address and nothing would be forwarded.

- Place IP extended access lists as close to the source as possible. Since extended access lists can filter on very specific addresses and protocols, you don't want your traffic to traverses the entire network and then be denied. By placing this list as close to the source address as possible, you can filter traffic before it uses up your precious bandwidth.

Standard Access Lists

Standard IP access lists filter network traffic by examining the source IP address in a packet. You create a *standard IP access list* by using the access-list numbers 1–99 or 1300-1999 (expanded range). Access list types are generally differentiated using a number. Based on the number used when the access list is created, the router knows which type of syntax to expect as the list is entered. By using numbers 1–99 or 1300–1999, you're telling the router that you want to create a standard IP access list, so the router will expect syntax specifying only the source IP address in the test lines.

Below is an example of the many access-list number ranges that you can use to filter traffic on your network (the protocols for which you can specify access lists depend on your IOS version):

```
Lab_A(config)#access-list ?
  <1-99>       IP standard access list
  <100-199>    IP extended access list
  <1000-1099>  IPX SAP access list
  <1100-1199>  Extended 48-bit MAC address access list
  <1200-1299>  IPX summary address access list
  <1300-1999>  IP standard access list (expanded range)
  <200-299>    Protocol type-code access list
  <2000-2699>  IP extended access list (expanded range)
  <300-399>    DECnet access list
  <600-699>    Appletalk access list
  <700-799>    48-bit MAC address access list
  <800-899>    IPX standard access list
  <900-999>    IPX extended access list
```

As you can see, there's a bunch of different types of access lists you can create. But for the CCNA exam, we'll focus exclusively on IP access lists.

Let's take a look at the syntax used when creating a standard access list:

```
Lab_A(config)#access-list 10 ?
  deny    Specify packets to reject
  permit  Specify packets to forward
```

As I said, by using the access-list numbers between 1–99 or 1300–1999, you're telling the router that you want to create a standard IP access list.

After you choose the access-list number, you need to decide whether you're creating a permit or deny statement. For this example, you will create a deny statement:

```
Lab_A(config)#access-list 10 deny ?
  Hostname or A.B.C.D  Address to match
  any                  Any source host
  host                 A single host address
```

The next step requires a more detailed explanation. There are three options available. You can use the any parameter to permit or deny any host or network; you can use an IP address to specify either a single host or a range of them; or you can use the host command to specify a specific host only. The any command is pretty obvious—any source address matches the statement, so every packet compared against this line will match. The host command is relatively simple. Here's an example using it:

```
Lab_A(config)#access-list 10 deny host 172.16.30.2
```

This tells the list to deny any packets from host 172.16.30.2. The default parameter is host. In other words, if you type **access-list 10 deny 172.16.30.2**, the router assumes you mean host 172.16.30.2.

But there's another way to specify either a particular host or a range of hosts—you can use wildcard masking. In fact, to specify any range of hosts, you have to use wildcard masking in the access list.

What's wildcard masking? You'll learn all about it using a standard access list example, as well as how to control access to a virtual terminal, in the following sections.

Wildcard Masking

Wildcards are used with access lists to specify an individual host, a network, or a certain range of a network or networks. To understand a *wildcard*, you need to understand what a *block size* is; they're used to specify a range of addresses. Some of the different block sizes available are 64, 32, 16, 8, and 4.

When you need to specify a range of addresses, you choose the next-largest block size for your needs. For example, if you need to specify 34 networks, you need a block size of 64. If you want to specify 18 hosts, you need a block size of 32. If you only specify two networks, then a block size of 4 would work.

Wildcards are used with the host or network address to tell the router a range of available addresses to filter. To specify a host, the address would look like this:

172.16.30.5 0.0.0.0

The four zeros represent each octet of the address. Whenever a zero is present, it means that octet in the address must match exactly. To specify that an octet can be any value, the value of 255 is used. As an example, here's how a /24 subnet is specified with a wildcard:

172.16.30.0 0.0.0.255

This tells the router to match up the first three octets exactly, but the fourth octet can be any value.

Now, that was the easy part. What if you want to specify only a small range of subnets? This is where the block sizes come in. You have to specify the range of values in a block size. In other words, you can't choose to specify 20 networks. You can only specify the exact amount as the block size value. For example, the range would have to be either 16 or 32, but not 20.

Let's say that you want to block access to part of network that is in the range from 172.16.8.0 through 172.16.15.0. That is a block size of 8. Your network number would be 172.16.8.0, and the wildcard would be 0.0.7.255. Whoa! What is that? The 7.255 is what the router uses to determine the block size. The network and wildcard tell the router to start at 172.16.8.0 and go up a block size of eight addresses to network 172.16.15.0.

Seriously—it really is easier than it looks—really! I could certainly go through the binary math for you, but no one needs that. Because, actually, all you have to do is remember that the wildcard is always one number less than the block size. So, in our example, the wildcard would be 7 since our block size is 8. If you used a block size of 16, the wildcard would be 15. Easy, huh?

But just in case, we'll go through some examples to help you nail it. The following example tells the router to match the first three octets exactly but that the fourth octet can be anything:

Lab_A(config)#**access-list 10 deny 172.16.10.0 0.0.0.255**

The next example tells the router to match the first two octets and that the last two octets can be any value:

Lab_A(config)#**access-list 10 deny 172.16.0.0
0.0.255.255**

Try to figure out this next line:

Lab_A(config)#**access-list 10 deny 172.16.16.0 0.0.3.255**

The above configuration tells the router to start at network 172.16.16.0 and use a block size of 4. The range would then be 172.16.16.0 through 172.16.19.0.

The example below shows an access list starting at 172.16.16.0 and going up a block size of 8 to 172.16.23.0:

Lab_A(config)#**access-list 10 deny 172.16.16.0 0.0.7.255**

The next example starts at network 172.16.32.0 and goes up a block size of 32 to 172.16.63.0:

Lab_A(config)#**access-list 10 deny 172.16.32.0**
  0.0.31.255

The last example starts at network 172.16.64.0 and goes up a block size of 64 to 172.16.127.0:

Lab_A(config)#**access-list 10 deny 172.16.64.0**
  0.0.63.255

Here are two more things to keep in mind when working with block sizes and wildcards:

- Each block size must start at 0 or a multiple of the block size. For example, you can't say that you want a block size of 8 and then start at 12. You must use 0–7, 8–15, 16–23, etc. For a block size of 32, the ranges are 0–31, 32–63, 64–95, etc.

- The command any is the same thing as writing out the wildcard 0.0.0.0 255.255.255.255.

 Wildcard masking is a crucial skill to master when creating IP access lists. It's used identically when creating standard and extended IP access lists.

Standard Access List Example

In this section, you'll learn how to use a standard access list to stop specific users from gaining access to the Finance department LAN.

In Figure 10.1, a router has three LAN connections and one WAN connection to the Internet. Users on the Sales LAN should not have access to the Finance LAN, but they should be able to access the Internet and the marketing department. The Marketing LAN needs to access the Finance LAN for application services.

On the router in the figure, the following standard IP access list is configured:

Lab_A#**config t**
Lab_A(config)#**access-list 10 deny 172.16.40.0 0.0.0.255**
Lab_A(config)#**access-list 10 permit any**

It's very important to know that the any command is the same thing as saying the following using wildcard masking:

Lab_A(config)#**access-list 10 permit 0.0.0.0**
  255.255.255.255

Since the wildcard mask says that none of the octets are to be evaluated, every address matches the test condition. So this is functionally the same as using the any keyword.

FIGURE 10.1   IP access list example with three LANs and a WAN connection

At this point, the access list is configured to deny source addresses from the Sales LAN access to the Finance LAN, and allow everyone else. But remember, no action will be taken until the access list is applied on an interface in a specific direction. But where should this access list be placed? If you place it as an incoming access list on E0, you might as well shut down the Ethernet interface because all of the Sales LAN devices will be denied access to all networks attached to the router. The best place to apply this access list is on the E1 interface as an outbound list:

```
Lab_A(config)#int e1
Lab_A(config-if)#ip access-group 10 out
```

This completely stops traffic from 172.16.40.0 from getting out Ethernet 1. It has no effect on the hosts from the Sales LAN accessing the Marketing LAN and the Internet, since traffic to those destinations doesn't go through interface E1. Any packet trying to exit out E1 will have to go through the access list first. If there were an inbound list placed on E0, then any packet trying to enter interface E0 would have to go through the access list before being routed to an exit interface.

Controlling VTY (Telnet) Access

You'll probably have a difficult time trying to stop users from telnetting to a large router because any active interface on a router is fair game for VTY access. You could try to create an extended IP access list that limits Telnet access to every IP address on the router. But if you did that, you'd have to apply it inbound on every interface, and that really wouldn't scale well to a large router with tens, even hundreds, of interfaces, would it? Here's a much better solution: Use a standard IP access list to control access to the VTY lines themselves.

Why does this work? Because when you apply an access list to the VTY lines, you don't need to specify the Telnet protocol, since access to the VTY implies terminal access. You also don't need to specify a destination address, since it really doesn't matter which interface address the user used as a target for the Telnet session. You really only need to control where the user is coming from—their source IP address.

🌐 Real World Scenario

Should you secure your Telnet lines on a router?

You're monitoring your network and notice that someone has telnetted into your core router by using the show users command. You use the disconnect command and they are disconnected from the router, but you notice they are back into the router a few minutes later. You are thinking about putting an access list on the router interfaces, but don't want to add a lot of latency on each interface since your router is already pushing a lot of packets. You are considering putting an access list on the VTY lines themselves, but not having done this before you are not sure if this is a safe alternative to putting an access list on each interface. Is putting an access-list on the VTY lines a good idea for this network?

Yes, absolutely, and the access-class command illustrated above is the best way to do this. Why? Because it doesn't use an access list that just sits on an interface looking at every packet that is coming and going. This can cause overhead on the packets trying to be routed.

By putting the access-class command on the VTY lines, only packets trying to telnet into the router will be looked at and compared. This provides a nice, easy-to-configure security for your router.

To perform this function, follow these steps:

1. Create a standard IP access list that permits only the host or hosts you want to be able to telnet into the routers.

2. Apply the access list to the VTY line with the access-class command.

Here is an example of allowing only host 172.16.10.3 to telnet into a router:

```
Lab_A(config)#access-list 50 permit 172.16.10.3
Lab_A(config)#line vty 0 4
Lab_A(config-line)#access-class 50 in
```

Because of the implied deny any at the end of the list, the access list stops any host from telnetting into the router except the host 172.16.10.3, regardless of which individual IP address on the router is used as a target.

Extended Access Lists

In the standard IP access list example above, notice how you had to block all access from the Sales LAN to the Finance department. What if you needed Sales to gain access to a certain server on the

Finance LAN but not to other network services, for security reasons? With a standard IP access list, you can't allow users to get to one network service and not another. Said another way, when you need to make decisions based on both source and destination addresses, a standard access list won't allow you to do that since it only makes decisions based on source address.

But an *extended access list* will hook you up. That's because extended access lists allow you to specify source and destination address as well as the protocol and port number that identify the upper-layer protocol or application. By using extended access lists, you can effectively allow users access to a physical LAN and stop them from accessing specific hosts—or even specific services on those hosts.

Here's an example of an extended IP access list:

```
Lab_A(config)#access-list ?
  <1-99>       IP standard access list
  <100-199>    IP extended access list
  <1000-1099>  IPX SAP access list
  <1100-1199>  Extended 48-bit MAC address access list
  <1200-1299>  IPX summary address access list
  <1300-1999>  IP standard access list (expanded range)
  <200-299>    Protocol type-code access list
  <2000-2699>  IP extended access list (expanded range)
  <300-399>    DECnet access list
  <600-699>    Appletalk access list
  <700-799>    48-bit MAC address access list
  <800-899>    IPX standard access list
  <900-999>    IPX extended access list
```

The first command shows the access-list numbers available. You'll use the extended access-list range from 100 to 199. Be sure to notice that the range 2000–2699 is also available for extended IP access lists.

At this point, you need to decide what type of list entry you are making. For this example, you'll choose a deny list entry.

```
Lab_A(config)#access-list 110 ?
  deny      Specify packet
  dynamic   Specify a DYNAMIC list of PERMITs or DENYs
  permit    Specify packets to forward
```

Once you choose the access-list type, you then need to select a protocol field entry.

```
Lab_A(config)#access-list 110 deny ?
  <0-255>  An IP protocol number
  eigrp    Cisco's EIGRP routing protocol
  gre      Cisco's GRE tunneling
  icmp     Internet Control Message Protocol
  igmp     Internet Gateway Message Protocol
```

```
igrp    Cisco's IGRP routing protocol
ip      Any Internet Protocol
ipinip  IP in IP tunneling
nos     KA9Q NOS compatible IP over IP tunneling
ospf    OSPF routing protocol
tcp     Transmission Control Protocol
udp     User Datagram Protocol
```

 If you want to filter by Application layer protocol, you have to choose the appropriate layer 4 transport protocol here. For example, to filter Telnet or FTP, you choose TCP since both Telnet and FTP use TCP at the Transport layer. If you were to choose IP, you wouldn't be allowed to specify a specific application protocol later.

Here, you'll choose to filter an Application layer protocol that uses TCP by selecting TCP as the protocol. You'll specify the specific TCP port later. Next, you will be prompted for the source IP address of the host or network (you can choose the any command to allow any source address):

```
Lab_A(config)#access-list 110 deny tcp ?
  A.B.C.D  Source address
  any      Any source host
  host     A single source host
```

After the source address is selected, the destination address is chosen:

```
Lab_A(config)#access-list 110 deny tcp any ?
  A.B.C.D Destination address
  any     Any destination host
  eq      Match only packets on a given port number
  gt      Match only packets with a greater port number
  host    A single destination host
  lt      Match only packets with a lower port number
  neq     Match only packets not on a given port number
  range   Match only packets in the range of port numbers
```

In the example below, any source IP address that has a destination IP address of 172.16.30.2 has been denied.

```
Lab_A(config)#access-list 110 deny tcp any host  172.16.30.2 ?
  eq           Match only packets on a given port number
  established  Match established connections
  fragments    Check fragments
  gt           Match only packets with a greater port
               number
```

```
log            Log matches against this entry
log-input      Log matches against this entry,including
               input interface
lt             Match only packets with a lower port
               number
neq            Match only packets not on a given port
               number
precedence     Match packets with given precedence value
range          Match only packets in the range of port
               numbers
tos            Match packets with given TOS value
<cr>
```

You can press Enter here and leave the access list as is. But if you do that, all TCP traffic to host 172.16.30.2 will be denied, regardless of destination port You can be even more specific: once you have the host addresses in place, just specify the type of service you are denying. The following help screen shows you the available options. You can choose a port number, or use the application or protocol name:

```
Lab_A(config)#access-list 110 deny tcp any host  172.16.30.2 eq ?
  <0-65535>    Port number
  bgp          Border Gateway Protocol (179)
  chargen      Character generator (19)
  cmd          Remote commands (rcmd, 514)
  daytime      Daytime (13)
  discard      Discard (9)
  domain       Domain Name Service (53)
  echo         Echo (7)
  exec         Exec (rsh, 512)
  finger       Finger (79)
  ftp          File Transfer Protocol (21)
  ftp-data     FTP data connections (20, 21)
  gopher       Gopher (70)
  hostname     NIC hostname server (101)
  ident        Ident Protocol (113)
  irc          Internet Relay Chat (194)
  klogin       Kerberos login (543)
  kshell       Kerberos shell (544)
  login        Login (rlogin, 513)
  lpd          Printer service (515)
  nntp         Network News Transport Protocol (119)
```

```
pim-auto-RP  PIM Auto-RP
pop2         Post Office Protocol v2 (109)
pop3         Post Office Protocol v3 (110)
smtp         Simple Mail Transport Protocol (25)
sunrpc       Sun Remote Procedure Call (111)
syslog       Syslog (514)
tacacs       TAC Access Control System (49)
talk         Talk (517)
telnet       Telnet (23)
time         Time (37)
uucp         Unix-to-Unix Copy Program (540)
whois        Nicname (43)
www          World Wide Web (HTTP, 80)
```

At this point, let's block Telnet (port 23) to host 172.16.30.2 only. If the users want to FTP, fine, that's allowed. The log command is used to log messages every time the access list is hit. This can be an extremely cool way to monitor inappropriate access attempts. Here is how to do this:

Lab_A(config)#**access-list 110 deny tcp any host**
172.16.30.2 eq 23 log

You need to keep in mind that the next line is an implicit deny any by default. If you apply this access list to an interface, you might as well just shut the interface down, since by default there is an implicit deny all at the end of every access list. You've got to follow up the access list with the following command:

Lab_A(config)#**access-list 110 permit ip any any**

Remember, the 0.0.0.0 255.255.255.255 is the same command as any, so the command could look like this:

Lab_A(config)#**access-list 110 permit ip 0.0.0.0**
255.255.255.255 0.0.0.0 255.255.255.255

Once the access list is created, you need to apply it to an interface (it's the same command as the IP standard list):

Lab_A(config-if)#**ip access-group 110 in**

or

Lab_A(config-if)#**ip access-group 110 out**

In the following section, we'll look at an example of how to use an extended access list.

Extended Access List Example

Using Figure 10.1 from the IP standard access list example above, let's use the same network and deny access to a host at 172.16.30.5 on the Finance department LAN for both Telnet and FTP services. All other services on this and all other hosts are acceptable for the sales and marketing departments to access.

The following access list should be created:

```
Lab_A#config t
Lab_A(config)#access-list 110 deny tcp any host
  172.16.30.5 eq 21
Lab_A(config)#access-list 110 deny tcp any host
  172.16.30.5 eq 23
Lab_A(config)#access-list 110 permit ip any any
```

The access-list 110 tells the router you are creating an extended IP access list. The tcp is the protocol field in the Network layer header. If the list doesn't say tcp here, you cannot filter by port numbers 21 and 23 as shown in the example. (These are FTP and Telnet, and they both use TCP for connection-oriented services.) The any command is the source, which means any IP address, and the host is the destination IP address.

After the list is created, it needs to be applied to the Ethernet 1 interface outbound. This applies the policy we created to all hosts, and effectively blocks all FTP and Telnet access to 172.16.30.5 from outside the local LAN. If this list were created to only block access from the Sales LAN, then we'd have put this list closer to the source, or on Ethernet interface 0. So, in this situation, we'd apply the list to inbound traffic. Let's go ahead and apply the list to interface E1 and block all outside FTP and Telnet access to the host:

```
Lab_A(config-if)#ip access-group 110 out
```

Named Access Lists

As I said earlier, named access lists are just another way to create standard and extended access lists. In medium to large enterprises, management of access lists can become, well, a real hassle over time. For example, when you need to make a change to an access list, a frequent practice is to copy the access list to a text editor, change the number, edit the list, then paste the new list back into the router. With this done, you can simply change the access-list number on the interface from the old to the new access list, and there is never a time on the network where an access list isn't in place.

This would work pretty well if it weren't for what I call "packrat" mentality. The question becomes, what do I do with the old access list? Delete it? Or should I save it in case I find a problem with the new list and need to back out of the change? So what happens is over time—through this and countless other scenarios—you can end up with a whole bunch of unapplied access lists building up on a router. What were they for? Are they important? Do I need them? All good questions and named access lists could be your answer.

This can also apply to access lists that are up and running. Let's say that you come into an existing network and are looking at access lists on a router. Suppose you find an access list 177 (which is an extended access list) that is 33 lines long. This could cause you much needless existential questioning—what is it for? Why is it here? Instead, wouldn't an access list called, say, finance LAN be more descriptive than one that's named 177?

Named access lists allow you to use names to both create and apply either standard or extended access lists. There is nothing new or different about these access lists aside from being able to refer to them in a way that makes sense to humans. But there are some subtle changes to the syntax, so let's re-create the standard access list we created earlier for our test network in Figure 10.1 using a named access list:

```
Lab_A#config t
Enter configuration commands, one per line.  End with CNTL/Z.
Lab_A(config)#ip access-list ?
  extended  Extended Acc
  logging   Control access list logging
  standard  Standard Access List
```

Notice that I started by typing **ip access-list**, not **access-list**. This allows me to enter a named access list. Next, I'll need to specify that it's to be a standard access list:

```
Lab_A(config)#ip access-list standard ?
  <1-99>  Standard IP access-list number
  WORD    Access-list name
```

```
Lab_A(config)#ip access-list standard BlockSales
Lab_A(config-std-nacl)#
```

I've specified a standard access list, then added a name BlockSales. Notice that I could've used a number for a standard access list, but instead, I chose to use a descriptive name. Also, notice that after entering the name, I hit Enter, and the router prompt changed. I'm now in named access list configuration mode, and am entering the named access list:

```
Lab_A(config-std-nacl)#?
Standard Access List configuration commands:
  default  Set a command to its defaults
  deny     Specify packets to reject
  exit     Exit from access-list configuration mode
  no       Negate a command or set its defaults
  permit   Specify packets to forward
```

```
Lab_A(config-std-nacl)#deny 172.16.40.0 0.0.0.255
```

```
Lab_A(config-std-nacl)#permit any
Lab_A(config-std-nacl)#exit
Lab_A(config)#^Z
Lab_A#
```

I enter the access list, and then exit out of configuration mode. Next, I'll take a look at the running configuration to verify that the access list is indeed in the router:

```
Lab_A#show running-config
...
!
ip access-list standard BlockSales
 deny    172.16.40.0 0.0.0.255
 permit any
!
...
```

The BlockSales access list has truly been created and is in the running-config of the router. Next, I'll need to apply the access list to an interface:

```
Lab_A#config t
Enter configuration commands, one per line.  End with CNTL/Z.
Lab_A(config)#int e1
Lab_A(config-if)#ip access-group BlockSales out
Lab_A(config-if)#^Z
Lab_A#
```

All right! At this point, we've re-created the work done earlier using named access lists.

Monitoring Access Lists

It's important to be able to verify the configuration on a router. Table 10.1 lists the commands that can be used to verify the configuration

TABLE 10.1   Commands Used to Verify Access List Configuration.

Command	Effect
show access-list	Displays all access lists and their parameters configured on the router. This command does not show you which interface the list is set on.

TABLE 10.1 Commands Used to Verify Access List Configuration. *(continued)*

Command	Effect
show access-list 110	Shows only the parameters for the access list 110. This command does not show you the interface the list is set on.
show ip access-list	Shows only the IP access lists configured on the router.
show ip interface	Shows which interfaces have access lists set.
show running-config	Shows the access lists and which interfaces have access lists set.

We've already used the show running-config to verify that a named access list was in the router. So now let's take a look at the output from some of the other commands.

The show access-list command will list all access lists on the router, whether they're applied to an interface or not:

```
Lab_A#show access-list
Standard IP access list 10
    deny    172.16.40.0, wildcard bits 0.0.0.255
    permit any
Standard IP access list BlockSales
    deny    172.16.40.0, wildcard bits 0.0.0.255
    permit any
Extended IP access list 110
    deny tcp any host 172.16.30.5 eq ftp
    deny tcp any host 172.16.30.5 eq telnet
    permit ip any any
Lab_A#
```

First, notice that both access list 10 and our named access list appear on this list. Second, notice that even though I entered actual numbers for TCP ports in access list 110, the show command gives us the protocol names rather than TCP ports for readability (hey, not everyone has them all memorized!).

Okay—here's the output of the show ip interface command:

```
Lab_A#show ip interface e1
Ethernet1 is up, line protocol is up
  Internet address is 172.16.30.1/24
  Broadcast address is 255.255.255.255
  Address determined by non-volatile memory
```

```
MTU is 1500 bytes
Helper address is not set
Directed broadcast forwarding is disabled
Outgoing access list is BlockSales
Inbound  access list is not set
Proxy ARP is enabled
Security level is default
Split horizon is enabled
ICMP redirects are always sent
ICMP unreachables are always sent
ICMP mask replies are never sent
IP fast switching is disabled
IP fast switching on the same interface is disabled
IP Null turbo vector
IP multicast fast switching is disabled
IP multicast distributed fast switching is disabled
Router Discovery is disabled
IP output packet accounting is disabled
IP access violation accounting is disabled
TCP/IP header compression is disabled
RTP/IP header compression is disabled
Probe proxy name replies are disabled
Policy routing is disabled
Network address translation is disabled
Web Cache Redirect is disabled
BGP Policy Mapping is disabled
Lab_A#
```

Be sure to notice the bold line indicating that the outgoing list on this interface is BlockSales, but the inbound access list isn't set.

Summary

In this chapter, I covered how to configure standard access lists so they filter IP traffic. You learned what a standard access list is and how to apply it to a Cisco router to add security to your network. In addition, you learned how to configure extended access lists to filter IP traffic. I also discussed difference between a standard and an extended access list and how to apply these lists to Cisco routers.

New to this version of this book is how to configure named access lists, and apply them to interfaces on the router. Named access lists offer the advantage of being readily identifiable and, therefore, simpler to administer than access lists referred to exclusively by obscure numbers.

Lastly, we covered how to monitor and verify selected access-list operations on the router. We went over some basic monitoring commands to verify IP access lists.

Exam Essentials

Remember the standard and extended IP access-list number ranges. The numbered ranges you can use to configure a standard IP access list are 1–99 and 1300-1999. The numbered ranges for an extended IP access list are 100–199 and 2000-2699.

Understand the term "implicit deny." At the end of every access list is an implicit deny. What this means is that if a packet does not match any of the lines in the access list, then it will be discarded. Also, if you have nothing but deny statements in your list, then the list will not permit any packets.

Understand the standard IP access-list configuration command. To configure a standard IP access list, use the access-list numbers 1–99 or 1300–1999 in global configuration mode. Choose permit or deny, then choose the source IP address you want to filter on using one of the three techniques covered earlier.

Understand the extended IP access-list configuration command. To configure an extended IP access list, use the access-list numbers 100–199 or 2000–2699 in global configuration mode. Choose permit or deny, the Network layer protocol field, the source IP address you want to filter on, the destination address you want to filter on, and finally the Transport layer protocol (if selected).

Remember the command to verify an access list on an interface. To see whether an access list is set on an interface and in which direction it is filtering, use the show ip interface command. This command will not show you the contents of the access list, merely which access lists are applied on the interface.

Remember the command to verify the access-lists configuration. To see the configured access lists on your router, use the show access-list command. This command will not show you which interfaces have an access list set.

Key Terms

Before you take the exam, be certain you're familiar with the following terms:

access list	named access list
block size	standard IP access list
extended access list	wildcard

Commands Used in This Chapter

The following list contains a summary of all the commands used in this chapter:

Command	Description
0.0.0.0 255.255.255.255	A wildcard command; same as the any parameter
access-class	Applies an access list to a VTY line
access-list	Creates a list of tests to filter network traffic
any	Specifies any host or any network; same as the 0.0.0.0 255.255.255.255 parameter
host	Specifies a single host address
ip access-group	Applies an IP access list to an interface
show access-lists	Shows all the access lists configured on the router
show access-lists 110	Shows only access list 110
show ip access-lists	Shows only the IP access lists
show ip interface	Shows which interfaces have IP access lists applied

Written Lab 10

In this section, write the answers to the following questions:

1. Write the command you would use to configure a standard IP access list to prevent all machines on network 172.16.0.0 from accessing your Ethernet network.
2. Write the command to apply the access list you created in question 1 to an Ethernet interface.
3. Write the command you would use to create an access list that denies host 192.168.15.5 access to an Ethernet network.
4. Write the command to verify that you've entered the access list correctly.
5. Write the two commands that verify that the access list was properly applied to the Ethernet interface.
6. Write the command you would use to create an extended access list that stops host 172.16.10.1 from telnetting to host 172.16.30.5.
7. Write the command to set an access list on a VTY line.
8. From question number 1 above, write the same standard IP access list as a named access list.

9. From number 2 above, write the command to apply the named access list you created to an interface.

10. Write the command to verify the placement and direction of an access list.

(The answers to Written Lab 10 can be found following the answers to the Review Questions for this chapter.)

Hands-on Labs

In this section, you will complete two labs. To complete these labs, you will need at least three 2600 series routers and three Ethernet switches. If you are using the RouterSim or Sybex software programs, please use the labs found in those programs.

Lab 10.1: Standard IP Access Lists

Lab 10.2: Extended IP Access Lists

All of the labs will use the following graphic for configuring the routers.

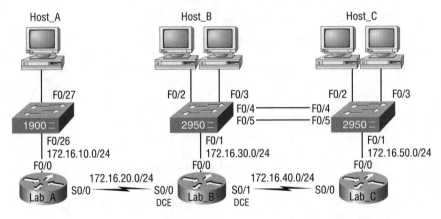

Hands-on Lab 10.1: Standard IP Access Lists

In this lab, you will allow only packets from Host B from network 172.16.30.0 to enter network 172.16.10.0.

1. Go to Lab_A and enter global configuration mode by typing **config t**.

2. From global configuration mode, type **access-list ?** to get a list of all the different access lists available.

3. Choose an access-list number that will allow you to create an IP standard access list. This is a number between 1 and 99, or 1300 and 1399.

4. Choose to permit host 172.16.30.2, which is Host B's address:

```
Lab_A(config)#access-list 10 permit 172.16.30.2 ?
  A.B.C.D  Wildcard bits
  <cr>
```

To specify only host 172.16.30.2, use the wildcards 0.0.0.0:

```
Lab_A(config)#access-list 10 permit 172.16.30.2
  0.0.0.0
```

5. Now that the access list is created, you must apply it to an interface to make it work:

```
Lab_A(config)#int f0/0
Lab_A(config-if)#ip access-group 10 out
```

6. Verify your access lists with the following commands:

```
Lab_A#sh access-list
Standard IP access list 10
    permit 172.16.30.2
Lab_A#sh run
[output cut]
interface FastEthernet0/0
 ip address 172.16.10.1 255.255.255.0
 ip access-group 10 out
```

7. Test your access list by pinging from Host B (172.16.30.2) to Host A (172.16.10.2).

8. Ping from Lab_B and Lab_C to Host A (172.16.10.2); this should fail if your access list is correct.

Hands-on Lab 10.2: Extended IP Access Lists

In this lab, you will use an extended IP access list to stop host 172.16.10.2 from creating a Telnet session to router Lab_B (172.16.20.2). However, the host still should be able to ping the Lab_B router. IP extended lists should be placed close to the source, so add the extended list on router Lab_A.

1. Remove any access lists on Lab_A and add an extended list to Lab_A.

2. Choose a number to create an extended IP list. The IP extended lists use 100–199, or 2000–2699.

3. Use a deny statement (you'll add a permit statement in step 7 to allow other traffic to still work).

```
Lab_A(config)#access-list 110 deny ?
  <0-255>  An IP protocol number
  ahp      Authentication Header Protocol
```

```
eigrp      Cisco's EIGRP routing protocol
esp        Encapsulation Security Payload
gre        Cisco's GRE tunneling
icmp       Internet Control Message Protocol
igmp       Internet Gateway Message Protocol
igrp       Cisco's IGRP routing protocol
ip         Any Internet Protocol
ipinip     IP in IP tunneling
nos        KA9Q NOS compatible IP over IP tunneling
ospf       OSPF routing protocol
pcp        Payload Compression Protocol
tcp        Transmission Control Protocol
udp        User Datagram Protocol
```

4. Since you are going to deny Telnet, you must choose TCP as a Transport layer protocol:

```
Lab_A(config)#access-list 110 deny tcp ?
A.B.C.D  Source address
any      Any source host
host     A single source host
```

5. Add the source IP address you want to filter on, then add the destination host IP address. Use the host command instead of wildcard bits.

```
Lab_A(config)#access-list 110 deny tcp host
172.16.10.2 host 172.16.20.2 ?
ack          Match on the ACK bit
eq           Match only packets on a given port
             number
established  Match established connections
fin          Match on the FIN bit
fragments    Check fragments
gt           Match only packets with a greater
             port number
log          Log matches against this entry
log-input    Log matches against this entry,
             including input interface
lt           Match only packets with a lower port
             number
neq          Match only packets not on a given
             port number
precedence   Match packets with given precedence
             value
```

```
psh          Match on the PSH bit
range        Match only packets in the range of
             port numbers
rst          Match on the RST bit
syn          Match on the SYN bit
tos          Match packets with given TOS value
urg          Match on the URG bit
<cr>
```

6. At this point, you can add the `eq telnet` command to filter host 172.16.10.2 from telnetting to 172.16.20.2. The `log` command can also be used at the end of the command so that whenever the access-list line is hit, a log will be generated on the console.

```
Lab_A(config)#access-list 110 deny tcp host
   172.16.10.2 host 172.16.20.2 eq telnet log
```

7. It is important to add this line next to create a `permit` statement. (Remember that 0.0.0.0 255.255.255.255 is the same as the any command)

```
Lab_A(config)#access-list 110 permit ip any 0.0.0.0
   255.255.255.255
```

8. You must create a `permit` statement; if you just add a `deny` statement, nothing will be permitted at all. Please see the sections earlier in this chapter for more detailed information on the `permit` command.

9. Apply the access list to the FastEthernet0/0 on Lab_A to stop the Telnet traffic as soon as it hits the first router interface.

```
Lab_A(config)#int f0/0
Lab_A(config-if)#ip access-group 110 in
Lab_A(config-if)#^Z
```

10. Try telnetting from host 172.16.10.2 to Lab_A using the destination IP address of 172.16.20.2. The following messages should be generated on Lab_A's console; however, the `ping` command should work:

```
From host 172.16.10.2: C:\>telnet 172.16.20.2
```

On Lab_A's console, this should appear as follows:

```
01:11:48: %SEC-6-IPACCESSLOGP: list 110 denied tcp
   172.16.10.2(1030) -> 172.16.20.2(23), 1 packet
01:13:04: %SEC-6-IPACCESSLOGP: list 110 denied tcp
   172.16.10.2(1030) -> 172.16.20.2(23), 3 packets
```

Review Questions

1. Which of the following is an example of a standard IP access list?

   A. `access-list 110 permit host 1.1.1.1`

   B. `access-list 1 deny 172.16.10.1 0.0.0.0`

   C. `access-list 1 permit 172.16.10.1 255.255.0.0`

   D. `access-list standard 1.1.1.1`

2. Extended IP access lists use which of the following as a basis for permitting or denying packets?

   A. Source address

   B. Destination address

   C. Protocol

   D. Port

   E. All of the above

3. To specify all hosts in the Class B IP network 172.16.0.0, which wildcard access-list mask would you use?

   A. 255.255.0.0

   B. 255.255.255.0

   C. 0.0.255.255

   D. 0.255.255.255

   E. 0.0.0.255

4. Which of the following are valid ways to refer only to host 172.16.30.55 in an IP access list? (Choose two options.)

   A. `172.16.30.55 0.0.0.255`

   B. `172.16.30.55 0.0.0.0`

   C. `any 172.16.30.55`

   D. `host 172.16.30.55`

   E. `0.0.0.0 172.16.30.55`

   F. `ip any 172.16.30.55`

5. Which of the following access lists will allow only WWW traffic into network 196.15.7.0?

A. `access-list 100 permit tcp any 196.15.7.0 0.0.0.255 eq www`

B. `access-list 10 deny tcp any 196.15.7.0 eq www`

C. `access-list 100 permit 196.15.7.0 0.0.0.255 eq www`

D. `access-list 110 permit ip any 196.15.7.0 0.0.0.255`

E. `access-list 110 permit www 196.15.7.0 0.0.0.255`

6. What router command allows you to determine whether an IP access list is enabled on a particular interface?

A. `show ip port`

B. `show access-lists`

C. `show ip interface`

D. `show access-lists interface`

7. Which router command allows you to view the entire contents of all access lists?

A. `Router#show interface`

B. `Router>show ip interface`

C. `Router#show access-lists`

D. `Router>show all access-lists`

8. If you wanted to deny all Telnet connections to network 192.168.10.0, which command could you use?

A. `access-list 100 deny tcp 192.168.10.0 255.255.255.0 eq telnet`

B. `access-list 100 deny tcp 192.168.10.0 255.255.255.0 eq telnet`

C. `access-list 100 deny tcp any 192.168.10.0 0.0.0.255 eq 23`

D. `access-list 100 deny 192.168.10.0 0.0.0.255 any eq 23`

9. If you wanted to deny FTP access from network 200.200.10.0 to network 200.199.11.0, but allow everything else, which of the following command strings is valid?

A. `access-list 110 deny 200.200.10.0 to network 200.199.11.0 eq ftp`
`access-list 111 permit ip any 0.0.0.0 255.255.255.255`

B. `access-list 1 deny ftp 200.200.10.0 200.199.11.0 any any`

C. `access-list 100 deny tcp 200.200.10.0 0.0.0.255 200.199.11.0 0.0.0.255 eq ftp`

D. `access-list 198 deny tcp 200.200.10.0 0.0.0.255 200.199.11.0 0.0.0.255 eq ftp`
`access-list 198 permit ip any 0.0.0.0 255.255.255.255`

10. Which of the following commands will show extended access list 187? Select two options.

A. sh ip int

B. sh ip access-list

C. sh access-list 187

D. sh access-list 187 extended

11. Which command would you use to apply an access list to a router interface?

A. ip access-list 101 out

B. access-list ip 101 in

C. ip access-group 101 in

D. access-group ip 101 in

12. Which command is used to display both the placement and the direction of an IP access control list on a router?

A. sh int

B. sh ip interface

C. sh nvram

D. sh access-list

13. Which access configuration allows only traffic from network 172.16.0.0 to enter interface s0?

A. access-list 10 permit 172.16.0.0 0.0.255.255
int s0
ip access-list 10 in

B. access-group 10 permit 172.16.0.0 0.0.255.255
int s0
ip access-list 10 out

C. access-list 10 permit 172.16.0.0 0.0.255.255
int s0
ip access-group 10 in

D. access-list 10 permit 172.16.0.0 0.0.255.255
int s0
ip access-group 10 out

14. Which of the following commands connect access list 110 inbound to interface ethernet0?

A. Router(config)#**ip access-group 110 in**

B. Router(config)#**ip access-list 110 in**

C. Router(config-if)#**ip access-group 110 in**

D. Router(config-if)#**ip access-list 110 in**

15. What command will permit SMTP mail to only host 1.1.1.1?

   A. `access-list 10 permit smtp host 1.1.1.1`

   B. `access-list 110 permit ip smtp host 1.1.1.1`

   C. `access-list 10 permit tcp any host 1.1.1.1 eq smtp`

   D. `access-list 110 permit tcp any host 1.1.1.1 eq smtp`

16. If you configure the following access list:

```
access-list 110 deny tcp 10.1.1.128 0.0.0.63 any eq smtp
access-list 110 deny any any eq 23
int ethernet 0
ip access-group 110 out
```

   What will the result of this access list be?

   A. E-mail and Telnet will be allowed out E0.

   B. E-mail and Telnet will be allowed in E0.

   C. Everything but e-mail and Telnet will be allowed out E0.

   D. No IP traffic will be allowed out E0.

17. Which of the following series of commands will restrict Telnet access to the router?

   A. Lab_A(config)#**access-list 10 permit 172.16.1.1**
       Lab_A(config)#**line con 0**
       Lab_A(config-line)#**ip access-group 10 in**

   B. Lab_A(config)#**access-list 10 permit 172.16.1.1**
       Lab_A(config)#**line vty 0 4**
       Lab_A(config-line)#**access-class 10 out**

   C. Lab_A(config)#**access-list 10 permit 172.16.1.1**
       Lab_A(config)#**line vty 0 4**
       Lab_A(config-line)#**access-class 10 in**

   D. Lab_A(config)#**access-list 10 permit 172.16.1.1**
       Lab_A(config)#**line vty 0 4**
       Lab_A(config-line)#**ip access-group 10 in**

18. Which of the following is true regarding access lists applied to an interface?

   A. You can place as many access lists as you want on any interface until you run out of memory.

   B. You can apply only one access list on any interface.

   C. One access list may be configured, per direction, for each layer 3 protocol configured on an interface.

   D. You can apply two access lists to any interface.

19. You are working on a router that has established privilege levels that restrict access to certain functions. You discover that you are not able to execute the command show running-configuration. How can you view and confirm the access lists that have been applied to the Ethernet 0 interface on your router?

A. show access-lists

B. show interface Ethernet 0

C. show ip access-lists

D. show ip interface Ethernet 0

20. You have created a named access list called Blocksales. Which of the following is a valid command for applying this to packets trying to enter interface s0 of your router?

A. (config)#ip access-group 110 in

B. (config-if)#ip access-group 110 in

C. (config-if)#ip access-group Blocksales in

D. (configt-if)#blocksales ip access-list in

Answers to Review Questions

1. B. Standard IP access lists use the numbers 1–99 and filter based on source IP address only.

2. E. IP extended lists use source and destination IP addresses, Network layer protocol field, and port fields in the Transport layer header.

3. C. The mask 0.0.255.255 tells the router to match the first two octets and that the last two octets can be any value.

4. B, D. The wildcard 0.0.0.0 tells the router to match all four octets. The wildcard command can be replaced with the host command.

5. A. The first thing to check in a question like this is the access-list number. Right away, you can see that the second option is wrong because it is using a standard IP access-list number. The second thing to check is the protocol. If you are filtering by upper-layer protocol, then you must be using either UDP or TCP; this eliminates the fourth option. The second and last answers have the wrong syntax.

6. C. Only the show ip interface command will tell you which ports have access lists applied. show access-lists will not show you which interfaces have an access list applied.

7. C. The show access-lists command will allow you to view the entire contents of all access lists, but will not show you to which interfaces the access lists are applied.

8. C. The extended access list range is 100–199 and 2000-2699, so the access-list number of 100 is valid. Telnet uses TCP, so the protocol TCP is valid. Now, you just need to look for the source and destination address. Only the third option has the correct sequence of commands.

9. D. Extended IP access lists use numbers from 100-199 and 2000-2699, and filter based on source and destination IP address, protocol number, and port number. The last option is correct because of the second line that specifies "permits ip any any" (I used 0.0.0.0 255.255.255.255, which is the same as the any option). The third option does not have this, so would deny access, but not allow everything else.

10. B, C. You can see the access lists with the show ip access-list command or the show access-list # command.

11. C. To apply an access list, the proper command is: ip access-group 101 in.

12. B. The command show ip interface will show you whether an access list is set on an interface and in which direction it is filtering.

13. C. This is a standard IP access list that only filters on source IP addresses. The number range for IP access list is 1–99. The command to place an IP access list on an interface is ip access-group. Since the question specified incoming traffic, only the third option works.

14. C. To place an access list on an interface, use the ip access-group command.

15. D. When trying to find the best answer to an access-list question, always check the access-list number and then the protocol. When filtering to an upper-layer protocol, you must use an extended list, numbers 100–199 and 2000-2699. Also, when you filter to an upper-layer protocol, you must use either `tcp` or `udp` in the protocol field. If it says `ip` in the protocol field, you cannot filter to an upper-layer protocol.

16. D. If you add an access list to an interface and you do not have at least one `permit` statement, then you will effectively shut down the interface because of the implicit `deny any` at the end of every list.

17. C. Telnet access to the router is restricted by using either a standard or extended IP access list to the VTY lines on the router. The command `access-class` is used to apply the access list to the VTY lines.

18. C. A Cisco router has rules regarding the placement of access lists on a router interface. You can place one access list per direction for each layer 3 protocol configured on an interface.

19. D. The only command that shows which access lists have been applied to an interface is `show ip interface Ethernet 0`. The command `show access-lists` displays all configured access lists, and `show ip access-lists` displays all configured IP access lists, but neither command indicates whether the displayed access lists have been applied to an interface.

20. C. By using a named access list, this just replaces the number used when applying the list to the router's interface. `IP access-group Blocksales in` is correct.

Answers to Written Lab 10

1. access-list 10 deny 172.16.0.0 0.0.255.255
   access-list 10 permit any

2. ip access-group 10 out

3. access-list 10 deny host 196.22.15.5
   access-list 10 permit any

4. show access-lists

5. show running-config
     sh ip interface

6. access-list 110 deny tcp host 172.16.10.1 host
     172.16.30.5 eq 23
     access-list 110 permit ip any any

7. access-class
   ip access-group 110 in

8. ip access-list No172Net
   deny 172.16.0.0 0.0.255.255
   permit any

9. ip access-group No172Net out

10. show ip interfaces

11

Wide Area Networking Protocols

THE CCNA EXAM TOPICS COVERED IN THIS CHAPTER INCLUDE THE FOLLOWING:

✓ **PLANNING & DESIGNING**

   ▪ Choose WAN services to meet customer requirements

✓ **IMPLEMENTATION & OPERATION**

   ▪ Implement simple WAN protocols

✓ **TROUBLESHOOTING**

   ▪ Perform simple WAN troubleshooting

✓ **TECHNOLOGY**

   ▪ Evaluate key characteristics of WANs

The Cisco IOS WAN supports many different WAN protocols that can help you extend your LANs to other LANs at remote sites. Connecting company sites together so information can be exchanged is imperative in today's economy. But it wouldn't exactly be cost-effective to put in your own cable or connections to connect all of your company's remote locations yourself. A better way to go about it is to use service providers that will lease or share connections they already have installed and save huge amounts of money and time.

I'm not going to cover every type of Cisco WAN support in this chapter—again, this book's purpose is mainly to give you everything you need to pass the exam. For that reason, I'm going to focus on the HDLC, PPP, Frame Relay, and ISDN protocols. But first, we will look at the WAN basics, including cabling a WAN.

Introduction to Wide Area Networks

So what is it that makes something a *wide area network (WAN)* instead of a local area network (LAN)? Distance is the first thing that comes to mind, but these days, wireless LANs can cover some serious turf! So is it bandwidth? Here again, really big pipes can be had for a price in many places, so that's not it either. Well, what then? Perhaps one of the best ways to tell a WAN from a LAN is that you generally own a LAN infrastructure, but you generally lease WAN infrastructure from a service provider. While modern technologies will blur even this definition, it applies well in the context of the CCNA exam. I've already talked about a data link that you usually own (Ethernet), but now we're going to take a look at the data links you most often don't own, but instead lease from a service provider.

The key to understanding WAN technologies is to be familiar with the different WAN terms and connection types often used by service providers to join your networks together.

Defining WAN Terms

Before ordering a WAN service type, it would be a good idea to understand the following terms, commonly used by service providers:

Customer premises equipment (CPE)   *Customer premises equipment (CPE)* is equipment that's owned by the subscriber and located on the subscriber's premises.

Demarcation point   The *demarcation point* is the spot where the service provider's responsibility ends and the CPE begins. It's generally a device in a telecommunications closet owned and installed by the telecommunications company (telco). The customer is responsible to cable (extended demarc) from this box to the CPE, which is usually a connection to a CSU/DSU or ISDN interface.

Local loop   The *local loop* connects the demarc to the closest switching office, called a central office.

Central office (CO)   This point connects the customers to the provider's switching network. A *central office (CO)* is sometimes referred to as a *point of presence (POP)*.

Toll network   The *toll network* is a trunk line inside a WAN provider's network. This network is a collection of switches and facilities owned by the ISP.

It is important to familiarize yourself with these terms, as they are crucial to understanding WAN technologies.

WAN Connection Types

A WAN can use a number of different connection types and this section will provide you with an introduction to the various types of WAN connections you'll find on the market today. Figure 11.1 shows the different WAN connection types that can be used to connect your LANs together (DTE) over a DCE network.

The following list explains the WAN connection types:

Leased lines   Typically, these are referred to as a *point-to-point connection* or dedicated connection. A *leased line* is a pre-established WAN communications path from the CPE, through the DCE switch, to the CPE of the remote site, allowing DTE networks to communicate at any time with no setup procedures before transmitting data. When cost is no object, it's really the best choice. It uses synchronous serial lines up to 45Mbps. HDLC and PPP encapsulations are frequently used on leased lines, and I'll go over them with you in detail in a bit.

Circuit switching   When you hear the term circuit switching, think phone call. The big advantage is cost—you only pay for the time you actually use. No data can transfer before an end-to-end connection is established. *Circuit switching* uses dial-up modems or ISDN, and is used for low-bandwidth data transfers.

Packet switching   This is a WAN switching method that allows you to share bandwidth with other companies to save money. *Packet switching* can be thought of as a network that's designed to look like a leased line, yet charges you (and costs) more like circuit switching. There is a downside: If you need to transfer data constantly, forget about this option. Just get yourself a leased line. Packet switching will only work well if your data transfers are bursty in nature. Frame Relay and X.25 are packet-switching technologies. Speeds can range from 56Kbps to T3 (45Mbps).

FIGURE 11.1   WAN connection types

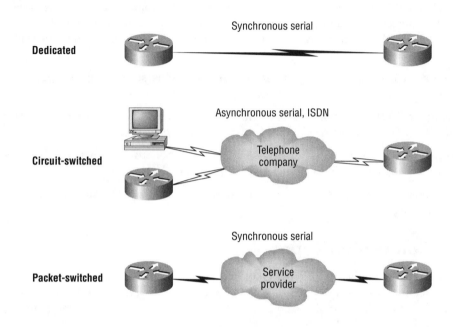

WAN Support

In this section, we will define the most prominent WAN protocols used today—Frame Relay, ISDN, LAPB, HDLC, PPP, and ATM:

  I'll dedicate the rest of the chapter to explaining in depth how WAN protocols work and how to configure them with Cisco routers. I'm only going to mention LAPB and ATM here briefly because they're not part of the CCNA exam.

Frame Relay   A packet-switched technology that emerged in the early 1990s, *Frame Relay* is a Data Link and Physical layer specification that provides high performance. Frame Relay is a successor to X.25, except that much of the technology in X.25 used to compensate for physical errors (noisy lines) has been eliminated. Frame Relay can be more cost-effective than point-to-point links, and can typically run at speeds of 64Kbps up to 45Mbps (T3). Frame Relay provides features for dynamic bandwidth allocation and congestion control.

ISDN   *Integrated Services Digital Network (ISDN)* is a set of digital services that transmit voice and data over existing phone lines. ISDN can offer a cost-effective solution for remote users who need a higher-speed connection than analog dial-up links offer. ISDN is also a good choice as a backup link for other types of links such as Frame Relay or a T-1 connection.

LAPB   *Link Access Procedure, Balanced (LAPB)* was created to be a connection-oriented protocol at the Data Link layer for use with X.25. It can also be used as a simple data link transport. LAPB causes a tremendous amount of overhead because of its strict timeout and windowing techniques.

HDLC   *High-Level Data-Link Control (HDLC)* was derived from Synchronous Data Link Control (SDLC), which was created by IBM as a Data Link connection protocol. HDLC is a protocol at the Data Link layer, and it has very little overhead compared to LAPB. HDLC wasn't intended to encapsulate multiple Network layer protocols across the same link. The HDLC header carries no identification of the type of protocol being carried inside the HDLC encapsulation. Because of this, each vendor that uses HDLC has their own way of identifying the Network layer protocol, which means that each vendor's HDLC is proprietary for their equipment.

PPP   *Point-to-Point Protocol (PPP)* is an industry-standard protocol. Because all multi-protocol versions of HDLC are proprietary, PPP can be used to create point-to-point links between different vendors' equipment. It uses a Network Control Protocol field in the Data Link header to identify the Network layer protocol. It allows authentication and multilink connections and can be run over asynchronous and synchronous links.

ATM   Asynchronous Transfer Mode (ATM) was created for time-sensitive traffic, providing simultaneous transmission of voice, video, and data. ATM uses cells instead of packets that are a fixed 53 bytes long. It also can use isochronous clocking (external clocking) to help the data move faster.

⊕ Real World Scenario

Which of the listed WAN services is the best?

You are a network administrator in San Francisco for Acme Corporation and you need to install a remote connection. Which one do you use?

A leased line is almost always the choice if money is no object. But in today's economy, cost is almost always a consideration. Services such as Frame Relay are hugely popular.

One of the newer WAN services that Cisco doesn't list as a WAN service in the CCNA objectives is a wireless connection. You can get from 1Mbps to over 50Mbps, depending on the service, and it actually works too! For the speed you get, it is relatively inexpensive. If you want to connect two buildings together, then you should consider a wireless solution. Of course, Cisco handily sells everything you need to do this—and at a pretty decent price compared to a wired solution.

You can even use a wireless solution for connecting your business to the Internet. The problem with wireless ISPs (WISPs) is that they come and go—they're in business one day and gone the next. Make sure you have a backup solution in the wings if you decide on a WISP, because they just might not answer the phone tomorrow. Eventually, things will mellow out and become better as technology develops, and we'll see wireless carriers sticking around for more than a week!

Cabling the Wide Area Network

There are a couple of things that you need to know in order to connect your WAN. For starters, you've got to understand the WAN Physical layer implementation provided by Cisco, and you must be familiar with the various types of WAN serial connectors.

Cisco serial connections support almost any type of WAN service. The typical WAN connections are dedicated leased lines using HDLC, PPP, Integrated Services Digital Network (ISDN), and Frame Relay. Typical speeds run at anywhere from 2400bps to 45Mbps (T3).

HDLC, PPP, and Frame Relay can use the same Physical layer specifications, but ISDN has different pinouts and specifications at the Physical layer.

In the following sections, we'll discuss the various types of connections, and then move into the nitty-gritty of the WAN protocols specified in the CCNA objectives.

Serial Transmission

WAN serial connectors use *serial transmission*, which takes place one bit at a time over a single channel.

 Parallel transmission can pass at least 8 bits at a time, but all WANs use serial transmission.

Cisco routers use a proprietary 60-pin serial connector that you must get from Cisco or a provider of Cisco equipment. Cisco also has a new, smaller proprietary serial connection that is about 1/10 the size of the 60-pin basic serial cable. This is called the "smart-serial," for some reason, and you have to make sure you have the right type of interface in your router before using this cable connector. The type of connector you have on the other end of the cable depends on your service provider or end-device requirements. The different ends available are:

- EIA/TIA-232
- EIA/TIA-449
- V.35 (used to connect to a CSU/DSU)
- X.21 (used in X.25)
- EIA-530

Serial links are described in frequency or cycles-per-second (hertz). The amount of data that can be carried within these frequencies is called *bandwidth*. Bandwidth is the amount of data in bits-per-second that the serial channel can carry.

Data Terminal Equipment and Data Communication Equipment

Router interfaces are, by default, *data terminal equipment (DTE)*, and they connect into *data communication equipment (DCE)*—for example a *channel service unit/data service unit (CSU/*

DSU). The CSU/DSU then plugs into a demarcation location (demarc) and is the service provider's last responsibility. Most of the time, the demarc is a jack that has an RJ-45 (8-pin modular) female connector located in a telecommunications closet.

You may have heard of demarcs if you've ever had the glorious experience of reporting a problem to your service provider—they'll always tell you it tests fine up to the demarc, and that the problem must be the CPE, or customer premises equipment. In other words, it's your problem, not theirs.

The idea behind a WAN is to be able to connect two DTE networks together through a DCE network. The DCE network includes the CSU/DSU, through the provider's wiring and switches, all the way to the CSU/DSU at the other end. The network's DCE device provides clocking to the DTE-connected interface (the router's serial interface).

 Terms such as EIA/TIA-232, V.35, X.21, and HSSI (High-Speed Serial Interface) describe the physical layer between the DTE (router) and DCE device (CSU/DSU).

Fixed and Modular Interfaces

Some of the routers Cisco sells have fixed interfaces, while others are modular. The fixed routers, such as the 2500 series, have set interfaces that can't be changed. The 2501 router has two serial connections and one 10BaseT AUI interface. If you need to add a third serial interface, you need to buy a new router—ouch! However, the 1600, 1700, 2600, 3600, and higher routers have modular interfaces that allow you to buy what you need now and add almost any type of interface you may need later. The 1600 and 1700 are limited and have both fixed and modular ports, but the 2600 and up provide many serials, FastEthernet, and even voice-module availability.

Let's move on and start talking about the various WAN protocols, so we can get on with configuring our Cisco routers.

High-Level Data-Link Control (HDLC) Protocol

The High-Level Data-Link Control (HDLC) protocol is a popular ISO-standard, bit-oriented Data Link layer protocol. It specifies an encapsulation method for data on synchronous serial data links using frame characters and checksums. HDLC is a point-to-point protocol used on leased lines. No authentication can be used with HDLC.

In byte-oriented protocols, control information is encoded using entire bytes. On the other hand, bit-oriented protocols, may use single bits to represent control information. Bit-oriented protocols include SDLC, LLC, HDLC, TCP, IP, and others.

HDLC is the default encapsulation used by Cisco routers over synchronous serial links. Cisco's HDLC is proprietary—it won't communicate with any other vendor's HDLC implementation. But don't give Cisco grief for it—*everyone's* HDLC implementation is proprietary. Figure 11.2 shows the Cisco HDLC format:

FIGURE 11.2   Cisco HDLC frame format

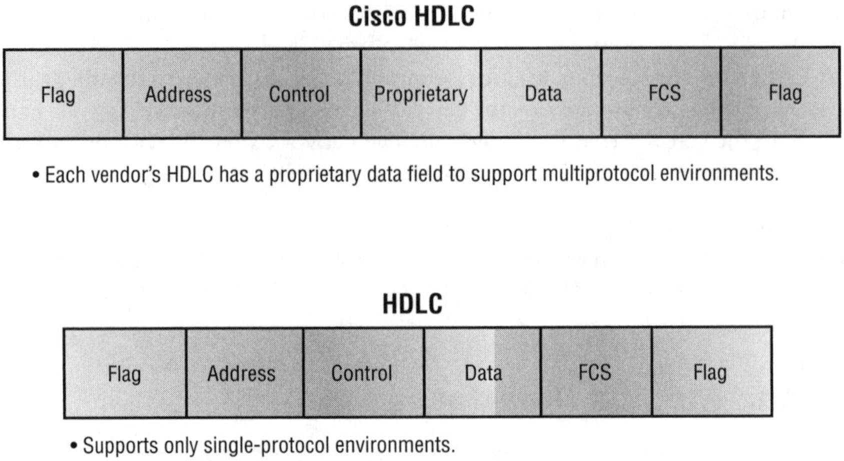

Cisco HDLC

Flag	Address	Control	Proprietary	Data	FCS	Flag

• Each vendor's HDLC has a proprietary data field to support multiprotocol environments.

HDLC

Flag	Address	Control	Data	FCS	Flag

• Supports only single-protocol environments.

As shown in the figure, the reason that every vendor has a proprietary HDLC encapsulation method is that each vendor has a different way for the HDLC protocol to encapsulate multiple Network layer protocols. If the vendors didn't have a way for HDLC to communicate the different layer 3 protocols, then HDLC would only be able to carry one protocol. This proprietary header is placed in the data field of the HDLC encapsulation.

Let's say you only have one Cisco router, and you need to connect to a Bay router because your other Cisco router is on order. What would you do? You couldn't use the default HDLC serial encapsulation because it wouldn't work. Instead, you would use something like PPP, an ISO-standard way of identifying the upper-layer protocols. In addition, you can check RFC 1661 for more information on the origins and standards of PPP.

Point-to-Point Protocol (PPP)

Point-to-Point Protocol (PPP) is a Data Link layer protocol that can be used over either asynchronous serial (dial-up) or synchronous serial (ISDN) media. It uses the LCP (Link Control Protocol) to build and maintain data-link connections.

The basic purpose of PPP is to transport layer 3 packets across a Data Link layer point-to-point link. Figure 11.3 shows the protocol stack compared to the OSI reference model.

FIGURE 11.3   Point-to-point protocol stack

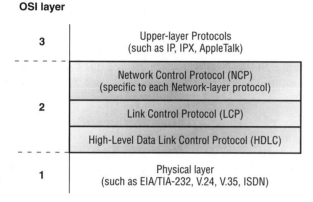

OSI layer

Layer	
3	Upper-layer Protocols (such as IP, IPX, AppleTalk)
2	Network Control Protocol (NCP) (specific to each Network-layer protocol)
	Link Control Protocol (LCP)
	High-Level Data Link Control Protocol (HDLC)
1	Physical layer (such as EIA/TIA-232, V.24, V.35, ISDN)

PPP contains four main components:

EIA/TIA-232-C, V.24, V.35, and ISDN   A Physical layer international standard for serial communication.

HDLC   A method for encapsulating datagrams over serial links.

LCP   A method of establishing, configuring, maintaining, and terminating the point-to-point connection.

NCP   A method of establishing and configuring different Network layer protocols. NCP is designed to allow the simultaneous use of multiple Network layer protocols. Some examples of protocols here are IPCP (Internet Protocol Control Protocol) and IPXCP (Internetwork Packet Exchange Control Protocol).

It is important to understand that the PPP protocol stack is specified at the Physical and Data Link layers only. NCP is used to allow communication of multiple Network layer protocols by encapsulating the protocols across a PPP data link.

Remember that if you have a Cisco router and a non-Cisco router connected with a serial connection, you must configure PPP or another encapsulation method, such as Frame Relay, because the HDLC default won't work!

In the following sections, I'll discuss the options for LCP and PPP session establishment.

Link Control Protocol (LCP) Configuration Options

Link Control Protocol (LCP) offers different PPP encapsulation options, including the following:

Authentication   This option tells the calling side of the link to send information that can identify the user. The two methods are PAP and CHAP.

Compression This is used to increase the throughput of PPP connections by compressing the data or payload prior to transmission. PPP decompresses the data frame on the receiving end.

Error detection PPP uses Quality and Magic Number options to ensure a reliable, loop-free data link.

Multilink Starting in IOS version 11.1, multilink is supported on PPP links with Cisco routers. This option allows several separate physical paths to appear to be one logical path at layer 3. For example, two T1s running multilink PPP would appear as a single 3Mbps path to a layer 3 routing protocol.

PPP callback PPP can be configured to call back after successful authentication. *PPP callback* can be a good thing for you because you can keep track of usage based upon access charges, for accounting records, or a variety of other reasons. With callback enabled, a calling router (client) will contact a remote router (server) and authenticate as described in the previous section. Both routers must be configured for the callback feature. Once authentication is completed, the remote router will terminate the connection and then re-initiate a connection to the calling router from the remote router.

> If you have Microsoft devices in your PPP callback, be aware that Microsoft uses a proprietary callback, Microsoft Callback Control Protocol (MSCP), and is supported in IOS release 11.3(2)T and later.

PPP Session Establishment

When PPP connections are started, the links go through three phases of session establishment:

Link-establishment phase LCP packets are sent by each PPP device to configure and test the link. These packets contain a field called the Configuration Option that allows each device to see the size of the data, compression, and authentication. If no Configuration Option field is present, then the default configurations are used.

Authentication phase If required, either CHAP or PAP can be used to authenticate a link. Authentication takes place before Network layer protocol information is read. It is possible that link-quality determination may occur at this same time.

Network layer protocol phase PPP uses the *Network Control Protocol (NCP)* to allow multiple Network layer protocols to be encapsulated and sent over a PPP data link. Each Network layer protocol (i.e. IP, IPX, AppleTalk, which are routed protocols) establishes a service with NCP.

PPP Authentication Methods

There are two methods of authentication that can be used with PPP links:

Password Authentication Protocol (PAP) The *Password Authentication Protocol (PAP)* is the less secure of the two methods. Passwords are sent in clear text, and PAP is only performed upon the initial link establishment. When the PPP link is first established, the remote node sends back to the originating router the username and password until authentication is acknowledged. That's it.

Challenge Handshake Authentication Protocol (CHAP)   The *Challenge Handshake Authentication Protocol (CHAP)* is used at the initial startup of a link and at periodic checkups on the link to make sure the router is still communicating with the same host.

After PPP finishes its initial link-establishment phase, the local router sends a challenge request to the remote device. The remote device sends a value calculated using a one-way hash function called MD5. The local router checks this hash value to make sure it matches. If the values don't match, the link is immediately terminated.

Configuring PPP on Cisco Routers

Configuring PPP encapsulation on an interface is a fairly straightforward process. To configure it, follow these router commands:

```
Router#config t
Enter configuration commands, one per line. End with CNTL/Z.
Router(config)#int s0
Router(config-if)#encapsulation ppp
Router(config-if)#^Z
Router#
```

Of course, PPP encapsulation must be enabled on both interfaces connected to a serial line to work, and there are several additional configuration options available by using the help command.

Configuring PPP Authentication

After you configure your serial interface to support PPP encapsulation, you can configure authentication using PPP between routers. First set the hostname of the router if it's not already set. Then set the username and password for the remote router connecting to your router.

Here is an example:

```
Router#config t
Enter configuration commands, one per line. End with CNTL/Z.
Router(config)#hostname RouterA
RouterA(config)#username RouterB password cisco
```

When using the hostname command, remember that the username is the hostname of the remote router connecting to your router. And it's case sensitive. Also, the password on both routers must be the same. It's a plain-text password that you can see with a show run command. And you can encrypt the password by using the command service password-encryption. You must have a username and password configured for each remote system you plan to connect to. The remote routers must also be configured with usernames and passwords.

After you set the hostname, usernames, and passwords, choose the authentication type, either CHAP or PAP:

```
RouterA#config t
Enter configuration commands, one per line. End with CNTL/Z.
RouterA(config)#int s0
RouterA(config-if)#ppp authentication chap pap
RouterA(config-if)#^Z
RouterA#
```

If both methods are configured on the same line as is shown here, then only the first method will be used during link negotiation—the second is a backup in case the first method fails.

See Hands-on Lab 11.1 for further examples of PPP authentication.

Verifying PPP Encapsulation

Now that PPP encapsulation is enabled, let's see how to verify that it's up and running. You can verify the configuration with the show interface command:

```
RouterA#show int s0
Serial0 is up, line protocol is up
 Hardware is HD64570
 Internet address is 172.16.20.1/24
 MTU 1500 bytes, BW 1544 Kbit, DLY 20000 usec, rely
  255/255, load 1/255
 Encapsulation PPP, loopback not set, keepalive set (10 sec)
 LCP Open
 Listen: IPXCP
 Open: IPCP, CDPCP, ATCP
[output cut]
```

Notice that the sixth line lists encapsulation as PPP, and the seventh tells us that LCP is open. Remember that LCP's job is to build and maintain connections. The ninth line tells us that IPCP, CDPCP, and ATCP are open. This shows the IP, CDP, and AppleTalk support from their associated NCPs. The eighth line reports that we're listening for IPXCP.

You can verify the PPP authentication configuration by using the debug ppp authentication command.

Frame Relay

Frame Relay has become one of the most popular WAN services deployed over the past decade. There are good reasons for this, but primarily it has to do with cost. Frame Relay technology frequently saves money over alternatives, and very few network designs ignore the cost factor.

Frame Relay has at its roots a technology called X.25. Frame Relay essentially incorporates the components of X.25 relevant to today's reliable and relatively "clean" telecommunications networks and leaves out the error-correction components that aren't needed anymore. It's substantially more complex than the simple leased-line networks you learned about in our discussion of the HDLC and PPP protocols. These leased-line networks are easy to conceptualize. Not so with Frame Relay. It can be significantly more complex and versatile, which is why it's often represented as a "cloud" in networking graphics. I'll get to that in a minute—for right now, I'm going to introduce Frame Relay in concept and show you how it differs from simpler leased-line technologies.

With your introduction to this technology, you get a virtual dictionary of all the new terminology you'll need in order to get a grip on the basics of Frame Relay. After that, I'll guide you through some simple Frame Relay implementations.

Introduction to Frame Relay Technology

As a CCNA, you need to understand the basics of the Frame Relay technology and be able to configure it in simple scenarios. You need to realize that I'm merely introducing Frame Relay here in this chapter—this technology gets much deeper than what we'll be dealing with here.

Frame Relay is a packet-switched technology. From everything you've learned so far, just telling you this should make you immediately realize several things about it:

- You won't be using the `encapsulation hdlc` or `encapsulation ppp` commands to configure it.

- Frame Relay doesn't work like a point-to-point leased line (although it can be made to look like one).

- Frame Relay will in many cases be less expensive than a leased line, but there are some sacrifices made in order to gain that savings.

To help you understand, here's an example of how packet-switching versus leased-line networks work:

Let's say you have a router in Miami and a router in Denver that you want to connect. With a leased line, you pay a telecommunications company to provide a T1 line between them for you. Basically, this means that they'll provide the T1 and install a piece of equipment in each of your facilities that represents the demarcation point. You would plug this into your CSU/DSU and into your routers, select HDLC or PPP encapsulation, and proceed to configure and troubleshoot the connection.

When buying a technology like this, you can expect the telco to provide you with a full T1 between your two sites. You can transmit at 1.544Mbps (full capacity) continuously if you want, and the telco has to deliver the packets. This is kind of like buying every seat to every showing of your favorite movie—you can see it whenever you want, as many times as you want—it's always available to you because, well, you paid for it.

So what happens if you skip a few showings at the theatre? Do you get a refund just because you failed to show up? Nope. Likewise, if you choose to transmit at less than 1.544Mbps continuously, you don't get to enjoy any cost savings on a leased line. You're paying for the full T1 whether you use it or not. Yes, the infrastructure is always there for you, but you're going to pay for that availability whether you use it or not!

Let's go back to that connection between Miami and Denver. Suppose you had a way to get a connection that looked like a T1 and acted like a T1, but allowed you to pay for whatever portion of that T1 you actually used, without charging you for data you could've sent but didn't. Sound like a deal? That's essentially what packet-switched networks do. However, if you don't use your bandwidth, don't think that you'll be getting a refund check! You are contractually guaranteed to able to use your agreed-upon bandwidth (called a Committed Information Rate or CIR)—you may possibly even burst to more bandwidth if someone isn't using their bandwidth, but that is not guaranteed.

This works because it's quite possible that your telecommunications company has hundreds, even thousands, of customers who have locations in both Miami and Denver. And they've installed a significant amount of infrastructure at both cities, as well as at many sites in between. So if you buy a T1 from Miami to Denver, they have to carve you out a T1 from Miami to Denver, and reserve it for you all the time, just as in our movie theatre analogy. But if you're willing to share their infrastructure with some of their other customers, you get to save some serious cash.

Sometimes you'll find that you're transmitting at full T1 speeds, but other times you'll be transmitting hardly any bits at all. You may average only 25% of a full T1 over time. If the telco has 1000 customers in Miami, and each customer only averages 25% of a full T1, and these customers agree to share the telco's infrastructure (Frame Relay), the telco does not need 1000 T1s in Miami. Statistically, they can get away with a lot fewer than that because they only need enough to meet the peak demand of all their customers combined. And since probability says that all their customers will never need full capacity simultaneously, the telco needs fewer T1 lines than if each customer had their very own leased-line. Fewer T1 lines = less infrastructure = big money saved.

This concept is called oversubscription. The telco sells the same infrastructure to a whole bunch of customers at a discount knowing that it's highly unlikely that there will come a time where all their customers need simultaneous access. Telcos have been doing this for years with voice networks—ever gotten an All Circuits Busy message on Mother's Day? They're pretty good at installing just enough but not too much. With Frame Relay, many customers share the telco's backbone frame network, and since the customers agree to share this infrastructure (oversubscribe), they get a better price than if they each opted for dedicated leased lines. It's this win-win concept that amounts to huge savings for both customer and provider, and that makes Frame Relay so popular.

In the following sections I am going to cover the Frame Relay technology information you need to know when studying the CCNA objectives.

Frame Relay Technology

To better introduce you to the Frame Relay terminology, let's take a preliminary look at how the technology works. Figure 11.4 is labeled with the various terms used to describe different parts of a Frame Relay network.

FIGURE 11.4   Frame Relay technology and terms

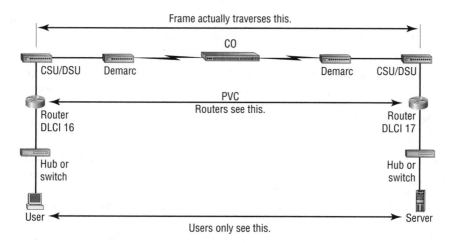

The basic idea behind Frame Relay networks is to allow users to communicate between two DTE devices (in this case, routers) through DCE devices. The users shouldn't see a difference between connecting to and gathering resources from a local server and a server at a remote site connected with Frame Relay other than a potential change in speed. Figure 11.4 illustrates everything that must happen in order for two DTE devices to communicate. Here is how the process works:

1. The user's network host sends a frame out on the local area network. The hardware address of the router (default gateway) will be in the header of the frame.

2. The router picks up the frame, extracts the packet, and discards what is left of the frame. It then looks at the destination IP address within the packet and checks to see whether it knows how to get to the destination network by looking into the routing table.

3. The router then forwards the data out the interface that it thinks can find the remote network. (If it can't find the network in its routing table, it will discard the packet.) Because this will be a serial interface encapsulated with Frame Relay, the router puts the packet onto the Frame Relay network encapsulated within a Frame Relay frame.

4. The channel service unit/data service unit (CSU/DSU) receives the digital signal and encodes it into the type of digital signaling that the switch at the packet switching exchange (PSE) can understand. For example, it may alter it from the encoding used in V.35 to the encoding of the access line, which might be B8ZS over a T1. The PSE receives the digital signal and extracts the ones and zeros from the line.

5. The CSU/DSU is connected to a demarcation (demarc) installed by the service provider, and its location is the service provider's first point of responsibility (last point on the receiving end). The demarc is typically just an RJ-45 (8-pin modular) jack installed close to the router and CSU/DSU (sometimes called a Smart Jack).

6. The demarc is typically a twisted-pair cable that connects to the local loop. The local loop connects to the closest central office (CO), sometimes called a point of presence (POP). The local loop can connect using various physical mediums; twisted-pair or fiber is common.

7. The CO receives the frame and sends it through the Frame Relay "cloud" to its destination. This cloud can be dozens of switching offices—or more!

8. Once the frame reaches the switching office closest to the destination office, it's sent through the local loop. The frame is received at the demarc, and is then sent to the CSU/DSU. Finally, the router extracts the packet, or datagram, from the frame and puts the packet in a new LAN frame to be delivered to the destination host. The frame on the LAN will have the final destination hardware address in the header. This was found in the router's ARP cache, or an ARP broadcast was performed.

The user and server do not need to know, nor should they know, everything that happens as the frame makes its way across the Frame Relay network. The remote server should be as easy to use as a locally connected resource.

There are several things that make the Frame Relay circuit different than a leased line. With a leased line, you typically specify the bandwidth you desire (T1, fractional T1, DS3, etc.). But with Frame Relay, you specify both an access rate (port speed) and a CIR. I'll talk about this next.

Committed Information Rate (CIR)

Frame Relay provides a packet-switched network to many different customers at the same time. This is a great idea because it spreads the cost of the switches, etc., among many customers. But remember, Frame Relay is based on the assumption that all customers will never need to transmit constant data all at the same time.

Frame Relay works by providing a portion of dedicated bandwidth to each user, and also allowing the user to exceed their guaranteed bandwidth if resources on the telco network are available. So basically, Frame Relay providers allow customers to buy a lower amount of bandwidth than what they really use. There are two separate bandwidth specifications with Frame Relay:

Access rate   The maximum speed at which the Frame Relay interface can transmit.

CIR   The maximum bandwidth of data guaranteed to be delivered. However, in reality, this is the average amount that the service provider will allow you to transmit.

If these two values are the same, the Frame Relay connection is pretty much just like a leased line. However, they can also be set to different values. Here's an example: Let's say that you buy an access rate of T1 (1.544Mbps) and a CIR of 256Kbps. By doing this, the first 256Kbps of traffic you send is guaranteed to be delivered. Anything beyond that is called a "burst," which is a transmission that exceeds your guaranteed 256Kbps, and can be any amount up to the T1 access rate (if that amount is in your contract). If your combined committed burst (the basis for your CIR) and excess burst sizes (which when combined are known as the MBR or maximum burst rate) exceed the access rate, you can pretty much be guaranteed that your additional traffic will be dropped, although it depends on the subscription level of the particular service provider. In a perfect world, this always works beautifully—but remember that little word *guarantee*? As in guaranteed rate—of 256Kbps, to be exact? This means that any burst of data you send that exceeds your guaranteed 256Kbps rate will be delivered on something called a "best effort" basis of delivery. Or maybe not—if your telco's equipment doesn't have the capacity to deliver at the time you transmitted, then your frames will be discarded and the DTE will be notified. Timing is everything—you can scream data out at six times your guaranteed rate of 256Kbps (T1), *only if* your telco has the capacity available on their equipment at that moment! Remember that "oversubscription" we talked about? Well, here it is in action!

 The CIR is the rate, in bits per second, at which the Frame Relay switch agrees to transfer data.

Therefore, you should choose a CIR based on realistic, anticipated traffic rates. Some Frame Relay providers allow you to purchase a CIR of zero. You can use a zero CIR to save money if retransmitting packets is acceptable to you. Doing that is a real gamble, though, because it means that every packet you send is eligible to be discarded in the provider's network!

Frame Relay Encapsulation Types

When configuring Frame Relay on Cisco routers, you need to specify it as an encapsulation on serial interfaces. As I said earlier, you can't use HDLC or PPP with Frame Relay. When you configure Frame Relay, you specify an encapsulation of Frame Relay (as shown below). But unlike HDLC or PPP, with Frame Relay there are two encapsulation types: Cisco and IETF (which stands for Internet Engineering Task Force). The following router output shows these two different encapsulation methods when choosing Frame Relay on your Cisco router:

```
RouterA(config)#int s0
RouterA(config-if)#encapsulation frame-relay ?
  ietf  Use RFC1490 encapsulation
  <cr>
```

The default encapsulation is Cisco unless you manually type in **ietf**, and Cisco is the type used when connecting two Cisco devices. You'd opt for the IETF-type encapsulation if you needed to connect a Cisco device to a non-Cisco device with Frame Relay. Whichever you choose, make sure that the Frame Relay encapsulation is the same on both ends.

Virtual Circuits

Frame Relay operates using *virtual circuits*, as opposed to real circuits that leased lines use. These virtual circuits are what link together the thousands of devices connected to the provider's "cloud." Referring back to the Miami and Denver example, you want these routers to connect to each other. That is, you want a circuit between them. Frame Relay provides a virtual circuit to be established between your two DTE devices making them appear to be connected via a circuit, when in reality they are dumping their frames into a large, shared infrastructure. You never see the complexity of what is happening inside the cloud because you have a virtual circuit.

There are two types of virtual circuits—permanent and switched. Permanent Virtual Circuits (PVCs) are by far the most common type in use today. What permanent means is that the telco creates the mappings inside their gear, and as long as you pay the bill, they will remain in place.

Switched Virtual Circuits (SVCs) are more like a phone call. The virtual circuit is established when data needs to be transmitted, then is taken down when data transfer is complete.

I have never seen a Frame Relay service using SVCs actually offered by a telco in North America. However, I do understand that it has been used mainly in private FR networks.

Data Link Connection Identifiers (DLCIs)

Frame Relay PVCs are identified to DTE end devices using *Data Link Connection Identifiers (DLCIs)*. A Frame Relay service provider typically assigns DLCI values, which are used on Frame Relay interfaces to distinguish between different virtual circuits. Because many virtual circuits can be terminated on one multipoint Frame Relay interface, many DLCIs are often affiliated with it.

This statement bears some explanation. Suppose you have a central HQ with three branch offices. If you were to connect each branch office to HQ using a T1, you would need three serial interfaces on your router at HQ, one for each T1. Simple, huh? Well, suppose you use Frame Relay PVCs. You could have a T1 at each branch connected to a service provider, and only a *single* T1 at HQ. There would be three PVCs on the single T1 at HQ, one going to each branch. Even though there's only a single interface and a single CSU/DSU, the three PVCs function as three separate circuits. Remember what I said about saving money? How much for two additional T1 interfaces and a pair of CSU/DSUs? Answer: a lot of money! So, just go ahead and ask for a percentage of the savings in your bonus.

Let's talk about DLCIs for another minute. Yes, they're locally significant—global significance requires the buy-in of the entire network to use the LMI extensions that give us global significance. Therefore, you're likely to see global DLCIs only in private networks.

However, the DLCI does not have to be globally significant for it to be functional in getting a frame across the network. Here's how it works. When Router A wants to send a frame to Router B, it looks up the InARP or manual mapping of the DLCI to the IP address it's trying to get to. Armed with the DLCI, it sends the frame out with the DLCI value it found in the DLCI field of the FR header. The provider's ingress switch gets this frame and does a lookup on the DLCI/physical-port combination it observes. Associated with that combination, it finds a new "locally significant" (between it and the next-hop switch) DLCI to use in the header, and in the same entry in its table, it finds an outgoing physical port. This happens all the way to Router B. Therefore, you actually can say that the DLCI that Router A knows identifies the entire virtual circuit to Router B, even though every DLCI between every pair of devices could be completely different. The point is that Router A is unaware of these differences. That's what makes the DLCI locally significant. Note, then, that DLCIs really are used by the telco to "find" the other end of your PVC.

DLCI numbers, used to identify a PVC, are typically assigned by the provider and start at 16. You configure a DLCI number to be applied to an interface like this:

```
RouterA(config-if)#frame-relay interface-dlci ?
  <16-1007> Define a DLCI as part of the current
            subinterface
RouterA(config-if)#frame-relay interface-dlci 16
```

Local Management Interface (LMI)

Local Management Interface (LMI) is a signaling standard used between your router and the first Frame Relay switch it's connected to. It allows for passing information about the operation and status of the virtual circuit between the provider's network and the DTE (your router). It communicates information about the following:

Keepalives   These verify that data is flowing.

Multicasting   This is an optional extension of the LMI specification that allows, for example, the efficient distribution of routing information and ARP requests over a Frame Relay network. Multicasting uses the reserved DLCIs from 1019 through 1022.

Global addressing   This provides global significance to DLCIs, allowing the Frame Relay cloud to work exactly like a LAN.

Status of virtual circuits   This provides DLCI status. These status inquiries and status messages are used as keepalives when there is no regular LMI traffic to send.

Remember, LMI is not communication between your routers—it's communication between your router and the nearest Frame Relay switch. So it's entirely possible that the router on one end of a PVC is actively receiving LMI, while the router on the other end of the PVC is not. (Of course, PVCs won't work with one end down. I just said this to illustrate the local nature of LMI communications.)

There are three different types of LMI message formats: Cisco, ANSI, and Q.933A. The different kinds depend on the type and configuration of the telco's switching gear. It's imperative to configure your router for the correct one, which should be provided by the telco.

Beginning with IOS version 11.2, the LMI type is auto-sensed. This enables the interface to determine the LMI type supported by the switch. If you're not going to use the auto-sense feature, you'll need to check with your Frame Relay provider to find out which type to use instead.

On Cisco equipment, the default type is Cisco, but you may need to change to ANSI or Q.933A, depending on what your service provider tells you. The three different LMI types are depicted in the following router output:

```
RouterA(config-if)#frame-relay lmi-type ?
  cisco
```

```
ansi
q933a
```

As seen in the output, all three standard LMI signaling formats are supported. Here's a listing of each:

Cisco   LMI defined by the Gang of Four (default). The Local Management Interface (LMI) was developed in 1990 by Cisco Systems, StrataCom, Northern Telecom, and Digital Equipment Corporation and became known as the Gang-of-Four LMI or Cisco LMI.

ANSI   Annex D included with ANSI standard T1.617.

ITU-T (q933a)   Annex A included in the ITU-T standard and defined by using the Q.933 command keyword.

Routers receive LMI information from the service provider's Frame Relay switch on a frame-encapsulated interface and update the virtual circuit status to one of three different states:

Active state   Everything is up, and routers can exchange information.

Inactive state   The router's interface is up and working with a connection to the switching office, but the remote router is not working.

Deleted state   No LMI information is being received on the interface from the switch. It could be a mapping problem or a line failure.

Frame Relay Congestion Control

Remember back to our talk about CIR? From that, it should be obvious that the lower your CIR is set, the greater the risk that your data will become toast. This can be easily avoided if you have just one key piece of information—when to transmit or not to transmit that burst! So our questions are: Is there any way for us to find out when our telco's shared infrastructure is free and clear and when it's, well, crammed and clogged? And if there is, how do we go about it? In this next section, I'm going to talk about how the Frame Relay switch notifies the DTE of congestion problems and address those very important questions.

Here are the three congestion bits and their meanings:

Discard Eligibility (DE)   As you know, when you burst (transmit packets beyond the CIR of a PVC), any packets exceeding the CIR are eligible to be discarded if the provider's network is congested at the time. Because of this, the excessive bits are marked with a *Discard Eligibility (DE)* bit in the Frame Relay header. And if the provider's network is congested, the Frame Relay switch will discard the packets with the first DE bit set. So if your bandwidth is configured with a Committed Information Rate (CIR) of zero, the DE will always be on.

Forward Explicit Congestion Notification (FECN)   When the Frame Relay network recognizes congestion in the cloud, the switch will set the *Forward Explicit Congestion Notification (FECN)* bit to 1 in a Frame Relay packet header. This will indicate to the destination DTE that the path the frame just traversed is congested.

Backward Explicit Congestion Notification (BECN)   When the switch detects congestion in the Frame Relay network, it'll set the *Backward Explicit Congestion Notification (BECN)* bit in a Frame Relay packet that's destined for the source router. This notifies the router that congestion is being encountered ahead. Cisco routers do not necessarily take action on this congestion information unless you tell them to. For further information on this, search on "Frame Relay Traffic Shaping" on Cisco's website.

Frame Relay Implementation and Monitoring

As I've said, there's a ton of Frame Relay commands and configuration options, but I'm going to zero in on the ones you really need to know for the CCNA exam. I'm going to start with one of the simplest configuration options—two routers with a single PVC between them. Next, I'll show you a more complex configuration using subinterfaces, and demonstrate some of the monitoring commands available to verify the configuration.

Single Interface

Let's get started by looking at a simple example. Suppose that we just want to connect two routers with a single PVC. Here's how that configuration would look:

```
RouterA#config t
Enter configuration commands, one per line.  End with CNTL/Z.
RouterA(config)#int s0/0
RouterA(config-if)#encapsulation frame-relay
RouterA(config-if)#ip address 172.16.20.1 255.255.255.0
RouterA(config-if)#frame-relay lmi-type ansi
RouterA(config-if)#frame-relay interface-dlci 101
RouterA(config-if)#^Z
RouterA#
```

The first step is to specify the encapsulation as Frame Relay. Note that since I didn't specify a specific encapsulation type—Cisco or IETF—the Cisco default type was used. If the other router were non-Cisco, I would've specified IETF. Next, I assigned an IP address to the interface, then specified the LMI type of ANSI (the default was Cisco) based on information provided by the telecommunications provider. Finally, I added the DLCI of 101, which indicates the PVC we wish to use (given to me by my ISP)—assuming there's only one PVC on this physical interface.

That's all there is to it. Assuming that both sides are configured correctly, the circuit will come up.

> Please see Hands-on Lab 11.3 for a complete example of this type of configuration, including instructions on creating your own Frame Relay switch from a router!

Subinterfaces

As I said earlier, you can have multiple virtual circuits on a single serial interface and yet treat each as a separate interface. This is accomplished by creating *subinterfaces*. Think of a subinterface as a logical interface defined by the IOS software. Several subinterfaces will share a single hardware interface, yet for configuration purposes, they operate as if they were separate physical interfaces (called multiplexing).

You define subinterfaces using the int s0.*subinterface number*. You must first set the encapsulation on the physical serial interface, then you can define the subinterfaces, generally one subinterface per PVC. Here is an example:

```
RouterA(config)#int s0
RouterA(config-if)#encapsulation frame-relay
RouterA(config-if)#int s0.?
  <0-4294967295>  Serial interface number
RouterA(config-if)#int s0.16 ?
  multipoint       Treat as a multipoint link
  point-to-point  Treat as a point-to-point link
RouterA(config-if)#int s0.16 point-to-point
```

You can define an almost limitless number of subinterfaces on a given physical interface, keeping in mind that there are only about a thousand available DLCIs. In the above example, I chose to use subinterface 16 because that represents the DLCI number assigned to that PVC by the carrier. There are two types of subinterfaces:

Point-to-point   Used when a single virtual circuit connects one router to another. Each point-to-point subinterface requires its own subnet.

Multipoint   Used when the router is the center of a star of virtual circuits. Uses a single subnet for all routers' serial interfaces connected to the frame switch. This is most often implemented with the hub router in this mode and the spoke routers in physical interface (always point-to-point) or point-to-point subinterface mode.

Next, I'll show you an example of a production router running multiple subinterfaces. In the output below, notice that the subinterface number matches the DLCI number (this isn't a requirement, but it helps with the administration of the interfaces):

```
interface Serial0
 no ip address
 no ip directed-broadcast
 encapsulation frame-relay
!
interface Serial0.102 point-to-point
 ip address 10.1.12.1 255.255.255.0
 no ip directed-broadcast
 appletalk cable-range 12-12 12.65
 appletalk zone wan2
 appletalk protocol eigrp
 no appletalk protocol rtmp
```

```
 ipx network 12
 frame-relay interface-dlci 102
!
interface Serial0.103 point-to-point
 ip address 10.1.13.1 255.255.255.0
 no ip directed-broadcast
 appletalk cable-range 13-13 13.174
 appletalk zone wan3
 appletalk protocol eigrp
 no appletalk protocol rtmp
 ipx network 13
 frame-relay interface-dlci 103
!
interface Serial0.104 point-to-point
 ip address 10.1.14.1 255.255.255.0
 no ip directed-broadcast
 appletalk cable-range 14-14 14.131
 appletalk zone wan4
 appletalk protocol eigrp
 no appletalk protocol rtmp
 ipx network 14
 frame-relay interface-dlci 104
!
interface Serial0.105 point-to-point
 ip address 10.1.15.1 255.255.255.0
 no ip directed-broadcast
 appletalk cable-range 15-15 15.184
 appletalk zone wan5
 appletalk protocol eigrp
 no appletalk protocol rtmp
 ipx network 15
 frame-relay interface-dlci 105
!
```

Notice that there's no LMI type defined. This means that the routers are running either the Cisco default or using autodetect (if running Cisco IOS version 11.2 or newer). This configuration was taken from one of my customers' production routers—used with permission, of course! Notice that each interface is defined as a separate subnet, separate IPX network, and separate AppleTalk cable range. (IPX and AppleTalk configuration are beyond the scope of this book and the exam).

Monitoring Frame Relay

There are several commands frequently used to check the status of your interfaces and PVCs once you have Frame Relay encapsulation set up and running. To list them, use the show frame ? command, as seen here:

```
RouterA>sho frame ?
end-to-end      Frame-relay end-to-end VC information
fragment        show frame relay fragmentation information
ip              show frame relay IP statistics
lapf            show frame relay lapf status/statistics
lmi             show frame relay lmi statistics
map             Frame-Relay map table
pvc             show frame relay pvc statistics
qos-autosense   show frame relay qos-autosense information
route           show frame relay route
svc             show frame relay SVC stuff
traffic         Frame-Relay protocol statistics
vofr            Show frame-relay VoFR statistics
```

Let's take a look at the most frequently used commands and the information they provide:

The *show frame relay lmi* Command

The show frame relay lmi command will give you the LMI traffic statistics exchanged between the local router and the Frame Relay switch. Here is an example:

```
Router#sh frame lmi

LMI Statistics for interface Serial0 (Frame Relay DTE)
LMI TYPE = CISCO
   Invalid Unnumbered info 0      Invalid Prot Disc 0
   Invalid dummy Call Ref 0       ˙Invalid Msg Type 0
   Invalid Status Message 0       Invalid Lock Shift 0
   Invalid Information ID 0        Invalid Report IE Len 0
   Invalid Report Request 0       Invalid Keep IE Len 0
   Num Status Enq. Sent 0         Num Status msgs Rcvd 0
   Num Update Status Rcvd 0        Num Status Timeouts 0
Router#
```

The router output from the show frame relay lmi command shows you any LMI errors, as well as the LMI type.

The *show frame pvc* Command

The show frame pvc command will list all configured PVCs and DLCI numbers. It provides the status of each PVC connection and traffic statistics. It will also give you the number of BECN and FECN packets received on the router per PVC.

Here is an example:

```
RouterA#sho frame pvc

PVC Statistics for interface Serial0 (Frame Relay DTE)

DLCI = 16,DLCI USAGE = LOCAL,PVC STATUS =ACTIVE,
INTERFACE = Serial0.1
 input pkts 50977876    output pkts 41822892
  in bytes 3137403144
 out bytes 3408047602   dropped pkts 5
  in FECN pkts 0
 in BECN pkts 0      out FECN pkts 0      out BECN pkts 0
 in DE pkts 9393     out DE pkts 0
 pvc create time 7w3d, last time pvc status changed 7w3d

DLCI = 18,DLCI USAGE =LOCAL,PVC STATUS =ACTIVE,
INTERFACE = Serial0.3
 input pkts 30572401    output pkts 31139837
  in bytes 1797291100
 out bytes 3227181474   dropped pkts 5
  in FECN pkts 0
 in BECN pkts 0      out FECN pkts 0      out BECN pkts 0
 in DE pkts 28       out DE pkts 0
 pvc create time 7w3d, last time pvc status changed 7w3d
```

To see information about only PVC 16, you can type the command **show frame-relay pvc 16**.

The *show interface* Command

You can use the show interface command to check for LMI traffic. The show interface command displays information about the encapsulation as well as layer 2 and layer 3 information. It also displays line, protocol, DLCI, and LMI information. Here is an example:

```
RouterA#sho int s0
Serial0 is up, line protocol is up
 Hardware is HD64570
```

```
MTU 1500 bytes, BW 1544 Kbit, DLY 20000 usec, rely
 255/255, load 2/255
Encapsulation FRAME-RELAY, loopback not set, keepalive
 set (10 sec)
LMI enq sent 451751,LMI stat recvd 451750,LMI upd recvd
 164,DTE LMI up
LMI enq recvd 0, LMI stat sent 0, LMI upd sent 0
LMI DLCI 1023 LMI type is CISCO frame relay DTE
Broadcast queue 0/64, broadcasts sent/dropped 0/0,
 interface broadcasts 839294
```

The LMI DLCI above is used to define the type of LMI being used. If it's 1023, it's the default LMI type of Cisco. If LMI DLCI is zero, then it's the ANSI LMI type (q933a uses 0 as well). If LMI DLCI is anything other than 0 or 1023, call your provider—they have a definite problem!

The *show frame map* Command

The show frame map command displays the Network layer–to–DLCI mappings. Here is an example:

```
RouterB#show frame map
Serial0 (up): ipx 20.0007.7842.3575 dlci 16(0x10,0x400),
              dynamic, broadcast,, status defined, active
Serial0 (up): ip 172.16.20.1 dlci 16(0x10,0x400),
              dynamic, broadcast,, status defined, active
Serial1 (up): ipx 40.0007.7842.153a dlci 17(0x11,0x410),
              dynamic, broadcast,, status defined, active
Serial1 (up): ip 172.16.40.2 dlci 17(0x11,0x410),
              dynamic, broadcast,, status defined, active
```

Notice that the serial interfaces have two mappings, one for IP and one for IPX. Also, notice that the Network layer addresses were resolved with the dynamic protocol Inverse ARP (IARP). After the DLCI number is listed, you can see some numbers in parentheses. Notice that the first number is 0x10. That's the hex equivalent for the DLCI number 16, used on serial 0. The 0x11 is the hex for DLCI 17 used on serial 1. The second numbers, 0x400 and 0x410, are the DLCI numbers configured in the Frame Relay frame. They're different because of the way the bits are spread out in the frame.

The *debug frame lmi* Command

The debug frame lmi command will show output on the router consoles by default (as with any debug command). The information from this command will allow you to verify and troubleshoot the Frame Relay connection by helping you to determine whether the router and switch are exchanging the correct LMI information. Here is an example:

```
Router#debug frame-relay lmi
Serial3/1(in): Status, myseq 214
```

```
RT IE 1, length 1, type 0
KA IE 3, length 2, yourseq 214, myseq 214
PVC IE 0x7 , length 0x6 , dlci 130, status 0x2 , bw 0
Serial3/1(out): StEnq, myseq 215, yourseen 214, DTE up
datagramstart = 0x1959DF4, datagramsize = 13
FR encap = 0xFCF10309
00 75 01 01 01 03 02 D7 D6

Serial3/1(in): Status, myseq 215
RT IE 1, length 1, type 1
KA IE 3, length 2, yourseq 215, myseq 215
Serial3/1(out): StEnq, myseq 216, yourseen 215, DTE up
datagramstart = 0x1959DF4, datagramsize = 13
FR encap = 0xFCF10309
00 75 01 01 01 03 02 D8 D7
```

Integrated Services Digital Network (ISDN)

Integrated Services Digital Network (ISDN) is a digital service designed to run over existing telephone networks. ISDN can support both data and voice—a telecommuter's dream. But ISDN applications require bandwidth. Typical ISDN applications and implementations include high-speed image applications (such as Group IV facsimile), high-speed file transfer, videoconferencing, and multiple links into homes of telecommuters.

ISDN is actually a set of communication protocols proposed by telephone companies that allows them to carry a group of digital services that simultaneously convey data, text, voice, music, graphics, and video to end users, and it was designed to achieve this over the telephone systems already in place. ISDN is referenced by a suite of ITU-T standards that encompass the OSI model's Physical, Data Link, and Network layers.

 The ISDN standards define the hardware and call-setup schemes for end-to-end digital connectivity.

PPP is typically used with ISDN to provide data transfer, link integrity, and authentication. So don't think of ISDN as a replacement for PPP, HDLC, or Frame Relay, because it's really an underlying infrastructure that any of these could use. And as I said, PPP is the most common encapsulation across ISDN connections.

These are the benefits of ISDN:

- It can carry voice, video, and data simultaneously.
- Call setup is faster than with an analog modem.

- Data rates are faster than on an analog modem connection.

- Full-time connectivity across the ISDN is spoofed by the Cisco IOS routers using dial-on-demand (DDR) routing.

- Small office and home office sites can be economically supported with ISDN BRI services.

- ISDN can be used as a backup service for a leased-line connection between the remote and central offices.

- Modem racking and cabling can be eliminated by integration of digital modem cards on Cisco IOS Network Access Server (NAS).

In the following sections, I am going to dive further into the ISDN technology. But don't be dismayed—remember, this is the last chapter in the book!

ISDN Connections

Integrated Services Digital Network (ISDN) *Basic Rate Interface (BRI)* is two B (Bearer) channels of 64k each, and one D (Data) channel of 16k for signaling.

ISDN BRI routers come with either a U interface or something known as an S/T interface. The difference between the two is that the U interface is already a two-wire ISDN convention that can plug right into the ISDN local loop. Conversely, the S/T interface is a four-wire interface that basically needs an adapter—a Network Termination type 1 (NT 1)—to convert from a four-wire to the two-wire ISDN specification.

The U interface has a built-in NT 1 device. If your service provider uses an NT 1 device, then you need to buy a router that has an S/T interface. Most Cisco router BRI interfaces are marked with a U or an S/T. When in doubt, ask Cisco or the salesperson you bought it from.

Primary Rate Interface (PRI) provides T-1 speeds (1.544Mbps) in the U.S. and E-1 speeds (2.048) in Europe, but I'm not going to tell you all about it in this book because it's not relevant to the CCNA course.

The ISDN BRI interface uses an RJ-45, straight-through cable. It's important to avoid plugging a console cable or other LAN cable into a BRI interface on a router, because it will probably ruin the interface. At least, that's what Cisco says—though my students do it every week and I haven't lost one yet.

ISDN Components

The components used with ISDN include functions and reference points. Figure 11.5 shows how the different types of terminal and reference points can be used in an ISDN network:

FIGURE 11.5   ISDN functions and reference points

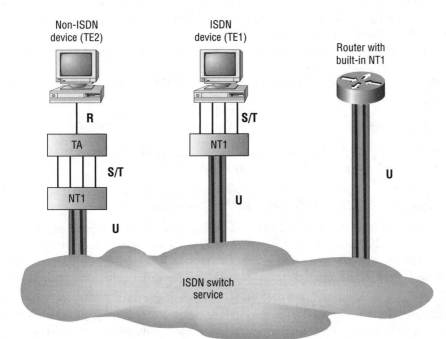

FIGURE 11.6   ISDN BRI reference points and terminal equipment

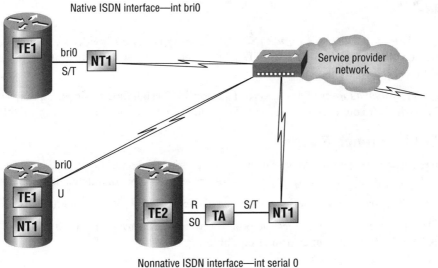

In North America, ISDN uses a two-wire connection, called a U reference point, into a home or office. The NT1 device is used to convert the typical four-wire connection to a two-wire connection that is used by ISDN phones and terminal adapters (TAs). Most routers can now be purchased with a built-in NT1 (U) interface.

Figure 11.6 shows the different reference points and terminal equipment that can be used with Cisco ISDN BRI interfaces:

In the following sections, I'm going to discuss the ISDN terminals, reference points, protocols, and ISDN switch types.

ISDN Terminals

Devices connecting to the ISDN network are known as terminal equipment (TE) and *network termination (NT)* equipment. There are two types of each:

TE1   A *terminal equipment type 1 (TE1)* device refers to those terminals that understand ISDN standards and can plug right into an ISDN network.

TE2   A *terminal equipment type 2 (TE2)* device refers to those that predate ISDN standards (are not natively ISDN-compliant). To use a TE2, you have to use a terminal adapter (TA) to be able to plug into an ISDN network. An example of a TE2 device would be a serial interface on a router, a standard PC, or even the modular interface of a common analog phone.

NT1   The *network termination 1 (NT1)* device implements the ISDN Physical layer specifications and connects the user devices to the ISDN network by converting the network from a four-wire to the two-wire network used by ISDN. Basically, we'll call this a U reference point that connects into the telco.

 We'll talk about reference points next.

NT2   The *network termination 2 (NT2)* device is typically a provider's equipment, such as a switch or PBX. It also provides Data Link and Network layer implementation. It's very rare to find these on a customer's premises.

TA   A *terminal adapter (TA)* converts TE2 non-ISDN signaling to signaling that's used by the ISDN switch. It connects into an NT1 device for conversion into a two-wire ISDN network.

ISDN Reference Points

Reference points are a series of specifications that define the connection between the various equipment used in an ISDN network. ISDN has four reference points that define logical interfaces:

R   The *R reference point* defines the point between non-ISDN equipment (TE2) and a TA.

S   The *S reference point* defines the point between the customer router and an NT2. Enables calls between the different customer equipment.

T The *T reference point* defines the point between NT1 and NT2 devices. S and T reference points are electrically the same and can perform the same function. Because of this, they're sometimes referred to as an S/T reference point.

U The *U reference point* defines the point between NT1 devices and local-termination equipment in a carrier network. (This is only in North America, where the NT1 function isn't provided by the carrier network.)

ISDN Protocols

ISDN protocols are defined by the ITU-T, and there are several series of protocols dealing with diverse issues (see `www.itu.int` for more info, but it is not needed for the exam):

- Protocols beginning with the letter *E* deal with using ISDN on the existing telephone network.

- Protocols beginning with the letter *I* deal with concepts, aspects, and services.

- Protocols beginning with the letter *Q* cover switching and signaling. These are the protocols that are used to connect to an ISDN network and to troubleshoot it. The Q.921 protocol describes the ISDN Data Link process of the Link Access Procedure on the D channel (LAPD). The Q.931 specifies the OSI reference model Layer 3 functions. Q.931 passes between the DTE and the provider's switch on the D-channel over Q.921-specified LAPD frames to set up, maintain, and tear down calls.

ISDN Switch Types

We can credit AT&T and Nortel for the majority of the ISDN switches in place today, but other companies also make them.

In Table 11.1, you'll find the keyword to use along with the `isdn switch-type` command to configure a router for the variety of switches it's going to connect to. If you don't know which switch your provider is using at their central office, call them to find out.

TABLE 11.1   ISDN Switch Types

Switch Type	Keyword
AT&T basic rate switch	`basic-5ess`
Nortel DMS-100 basic rate switch	`basic-dms100`
National ISDN-1 switch	`basic-ni1`
AT&T 4ESS (ISDN PRI only)	`primary-4ess`
AT&T 5ESS (ISDN PRI only)	`primary-5ess`
Nortel DMS-100 (ISDN PRI only)	`primary-dms100`

Basic Rate Interface (BRI)

ISDN Basic Rate Interface (BRI) service, also known as 2B+D, provides two B channels and one D channel. The BRI B-channel service operates at 64Kbps and carries data, while the BRI D-channel service operates at 16Kbps and usually carries control and signaling information. The total bandwidth for ISDN BRI is then 144Kbps (64 + 64 + 16 = 144).

The D-channel signaling protocols (Q.921 and Q.931) span the OSI reference model's Physical, Data Link, and Network layers. The D channel carries signaling information to set up and control calls. The D channel can also be used for other functions, such as an alarm system for a building or anything else that doesn't need much bandwidth, since it's only giving you a whopping 16K. D channels work with LAPD at the Data Link layer for reliable connections.

When configuring ISDN BRI, you'll need to obtain service profile identifiers (SPIDs), and you should have one SPID for each B channel. The SPID is a unique number, often based on the directory number (DN), which is the dialable number of the ISDN subscriber, of which there are normally two provided on a 2B+D implementation.

The ISDN device gives the SPID to the ISDN switch, which then allows the device to access the network for BRI service. Without a SPID, many ISDN switches don't allow an ISDN device to place a call on the network.

To set up a BRI call, four events must take place:

1. The D channel between the router and the local ISDN switch comes up.

2. The ISDN switch uses the SS7 signaling technique to set up a path to a remote switch.

3. The remote switch sets up the D-channel link to the remote router.

4. The B channels are then connected end-to-end.

Primary Rate Interface (PRI)

In North America and Japan, the ISDN *Primary Rate Interface (PRI)*—also known as 23B+D—service delivers 23 64Kbps B channels and one 64Kbps D channel, for a total bit rate of 1.544Mbps.

In Europe, Australia, and other parts of the world, ISDN provides 30 64Kbps B channels and one 64Kbps D channel, for a total bit rate of 2.048Mbps.

ISDN with Cisco Routers

Accessing ISDN with a Cisco router means that you'll need to either purchase a router with a built-in NT1 (U reference point), or get an ISDN modem (called a terminal adapter, or TA). If your router has a BRI interface, you're ready to rock. Otherwise, if you can get hold of a TA you can use one of your router's serial interfaces. A router with a BRI interface is called a TE1 (terminal equipment type 1), and one that requires a TA is called a TE2 (terminal equipment type 2).

When configuring ISDN, you'll need to know the type of switch that your service provider is using. To see which switches your router will support, use the `isdn switch-type ?` command in global configuration mode or interface configuration mode.

For each ISDN BRI interface, you need to specify the SPIDs that are configured for the circuit by the service provider using the `isdn spid1` and `isdn spid2` interface subcommands. These are provided by the ISDN provider and identify you on the switch, sort of like a telephone number. Some providers no longer require SPIDs to be configured on the router. Check with yours to be sure.

The second part of the SPID configuration is the local directory number for that SPID. It's optional, but some switches need to have those set on the router in order to use both B channels simultaneously.

Here's an example:

```
RouterA#config t
Enter configuration commands, one per line. End with CNTL/Z.
RouterA(config)#isdn switch-type basic-ni
RouterA(config)#int bri0
RouterA(config-if)#encap ppp (optional)
RouterA(config-if)#isdn spid1 086506610100 8650661
RouterA(config-if)#isdn spid2 086506620100 8650662
```

The `isdn switch-type` command can be configured in either global configuration or interface configuration mode. Configuring the switch type globally will set the switch type for all BRI interfaces in the router. If you only have one interface, it doesn't matter where you use the `isdn switch-type` command.

If you are not using DDR (discussed next), the three basic commands that Cisco says you need to configure when bringing up an ISDN link are:

```
RouterA(config)#isdn switch-type basic-ni
RouterA(config)#isdn dialer map ip address name name connection number
RouterA(config-if)#ip address address mask
```

The `isdn switch-type` command has already been discussed, and we will talk about the `isdn dial map` command (which is very important if you are studying for the CCNA exam) in the DDR section. However, you still just need to remember what Cisco says are the "three basic ISDN commands."

🌐 Real World Scenario

Should we really still use ISDN?

You work for a large communication company in San Francisco called Acme Corporation. You need to set up a remote location for access to your corporate network. The local ISP called and said they can provide ISDN as a connection.

Should you go for it?

Only if you can't get anything else! If your only other option is a 56Kbps dial-up modem, then yes, ISDN will be better. Since it's a true 128Kbps data service, it will provide much better performance than any modem will.

But if you can get DSL, a cable modem, Frame Relay, or even a wireless connection, you'll be much better off!

Dial-on-Demand Routing (DDR)

Dial-on-demand routing (DDR) is used to allow two or more Cisco routers to dial an ISDN dial-up connection on an as-needed basis. DDR is only used for low-volume, periodic network connections using either a Plain Old Telephone Service (POTS) or ISDN connection. This was designed to reduce WAN costs if you have to pay on a per-minute or per-packet basis.

DDR works when a packet received on an interface meets the requirements of an access list defined by an administrator, which defines interesting traffic. The following five steps give a basic description of how DDR works when an interesting packet is received in a router interface:

1. The route to the destination network is determined to be across the dial-up connection.

2. Interesting packets dictate a DDR call.

3. Dialer information is looked up and the call is placed.

4. Traffic is transmitted.

5. Call is terminated when no more interesting traffic is being transmitted over a link and the idle-timeout period ends.

In the following sections I am going to discuss Dial on Demand Routing (DDR), which is a very important section to pay attention to—that is, if you are studying the CCNA exam objectives!

Configuring DDR

To configure DDR, you need to perform three tasks:

1. Define static routes, which specify how to get to the remote networks and what interface to use to get there.

2. Specify the traffic that is considered interesting to the router.

3. Configure the dialer information that will be used to dial the interface to get to the remote network.

We will see how to perform each of these steps in the following sections.

Configuring Static Routes

To forward traffic across the ISDN link, you configure static routes in each of the routers. You certainly can configure dynamic routing protocols to run on your ISDN link, but then the link will never drop. The suggested routing method is static routes. Keep the following in mind when creating static routes:

- All participating routers must have static routes defining all routes of known networks.

- Default routing can be used if the network is a stub network.

Here's an example of static routing with ISDN:

```
RouterA(config)#ip route 172.16.50.0 255.255.255.0
  172.16.60.2
RouterA(config)#ip route 172.16.60.2 255.255.255.255 bri0
```

What this does is tell the router how to get to network 172.16.50.0 through 172.16.60.2. The second line tells the router how to get to 172.16.60.2. This second IP route command is vital, as you'll soon see; together with the `dialer map` command, it lets ISDN know where to place the call.

Specifying Interesting Traffic

After setting the route tables in each router, you need to configure the router to determine what brings up the ISDN line. An administrator using the `dialer-list` global configuration command defines interesting packets.

The command to turn on all IP traffic is shown as follows:

```
804A(config)#dialer-list 1 protocol ip permit
804A(config)#int bri0
804A(config-if)#dialer-group 1
```

The `dialer-group` command sets the access list on the BRI interface. Extended access lists can be used with the `dialer-list` command to define interesting traffic to just certain applications. I'll cover that in a minute.

> If you use the `dialer-list` command, you must enter the `dialer-group` command on an interface before this will work!

Configuring the Dialer Information

There are five steps to configuring the dialer information:

1. Choose the interface.
2. Set the IP address.
3. Configure the encapsulation type.
4. Link interesting traffic to the interface.
5. Configure the number or numbers to dial.

Here's how to configure those five steps:

```
804A#config t
804A(config)#int bri0
804A(config-if)#ip address 172.16.60.1 255.255.255.0
804A(config-if)#no shut
804A(config-if)#encapsulation ppp
804A(config-if)#dialer-group 1
804A(config-if)#dialer string 8350661
```

Instead of the `dialer string` command, you can use a `dialer map` command. It provides more security. Here is an example:

```
804A(config-if)#dialer map ip 172.16.60.2 name 804B
  8350661
```

The `dialer map` command can be used with the `dialer-group` command and its associated access list to initiate dialing. The `dialer map` command uses the IP address of the next hop router, the hostname of the remote router for authentication, and then the number to dial to get there.

The five basic Dialer Map steps that you must be aware of are:

1. Dialer
2. Map
3. Protocol

4. Next hop

5. Dial string

Now, you may be wondering what is so special about the `dialer map` command and why I broke the actual command down into the steps listed above. It's important that you understand that I don't make this stuff up (although I'm sure some of you wonder about that sometimes) and I place technical information into this book so you can study for and pass your CCNA exam. So, to help you remember this important command sequence, I will put the commands back into the typical command string as shown:

804A#**dialer map [protocol] [next hop address] [dial string]**

> Remember, the `dialer map` command is used to associate an ISDN phone number with the next hop router address.

Take a look at the following configuration of an 804 router:

```
804B#sh run
Building configuration...
Current configuration:
!
version 12.0
no service pad
service timestamps debug uptime
service timestamps log uptime
no service password-encryption
!
hostname 804B
!
ip subnet-zero
!
isdn switch-type basic-ni
!
interface Ethernet0
 ip address 172.16.50.10 255.255.255.0
 no ip directed-broadcast
!
interface BRI0
 ip address 172.16.60.2 255.255.255.0
 no ip directed-broadcast
```

```
encapsulation ppp
dialer idle-timeout 300
dialer string 8358661
dialer load-threshold 2 either
dialer-group 1
isdn switch-type basic-ni
isdn spid1 0835866201 8358662
isdn spid2 0835866401 8358664
hold-queue 75 in
!
ip classless
ip route 172.16.30.0 255.255.255.0 172.16.60.1
ip route 172.16.60.1 255.255.255.255 BRI0
!
dialer-list 1 protocol ip permit
!
```

What can you determine by looking at this output? Well, first, the BRI interface is running the PPP encapsulation, and it has a timeout value of 300 seconds. The dialer `load-threshold` command makes both BRI interfaces come up immediately (which is great; I feel that if I am paying for both, I want them both up all the time!). The one thing you really want to notice is the `dialer-group 1` command. That number must match the dialer-list number. The `hold-queue 75 in` command tells the router that when it receives an interesting packet, it should queue up to 75 packets while it's waiting for the BRI to come up. If there are more than 75 packets queued before the link comes up, the additional packets will be dropped.

Optional Commands

There are two other commands that you should configure on your BRI interface:

- `dialer load-threshold`
- `dialer idle-timeout`

The `dialer load-threshold` command tells the BRI interface when to bring up the second B channel. The range is from 1 to 255, where 255 tells the BRI to bring up the second B channel only when the first channel is 100 percent loaded. The second option for that command is inbound, outbound, or either. This calculates the actual load on the interface either on outbound traffic, inbound traffic, or combined. The default is outbound.

The `dialer idle-timeout` command specifies the number of seconds before a call is disconnected after the last interesting traffic is sent. The default is 120 seconds.

Here is an example using both commands:

```
RouterA(config-if)#dialer load-threshold 125 either
RouterA(config-if)#dialer idle-timeout 180
```

The `dialer load-threshold 125` tells the BRI interface to bring up the second B channel if either the inbound or outbound traffic load is 45 percent. The `dialer idle-timeout 180` changes the default disconnect time from 120 to 180 seconds.

DDR with Access Lists

You can use access lists to be more specific about what is, or is not, interesting traffic. In the preceding example we just set the dialer list to allow any IP traffic to bring up the line. That's great if you're testing, but it can defeat the purpose of why you use a DDR line in the first place. You can use extended access lists to set the restriction, for instance, to only e-mail or Telnet.

Here's how you define the dialer list to use an access list:

```
804A(config)#dialer-list 1 protocol ip list 110
804A(config)#access-list 110 permit tcp any any eq smtp
804A(config)#access-list 110 permit tcp any any eq telnet
804A(config)#int bri0
804A(config-if)#dialer-group 1
```

I configured the `dialer-list` command to look at an access list. This doesn't have to be IP—it can be used with any protocol. Create your dialer list, then apply it to the BRI interface with the `dialer-group` command.

Now, if you don't create your access list correctly, you can end up keeping your link up all the time because of broadcasts. Take a look at the following example:

```
Access-list 150 deny tcp 10.10.10.0 0.0.0.255 host 192.168.10.1 eq www
Access-list 150 permit ip any any
Dialer-list 1 protocol ip list 150
```

In the example above, the first line denies port 80 (www) from bringing up the BRI line if it is coming from network 10.10.10.0 and headed to host 192.168.10.1. However, the second line allows all other traffic to bring up the BRI interface. Any broadcast from any host to any destination could bring up the line.

Verifying the ISDN Operation

Table 11.2 commands can be used to verify DDR and ISDN.

TABLE 11.2   ISDN Verification Commands

Command	Description
ping and telnet	Great IP tools for any network. However, your interesting traffic restriction must dictate that Ping and Telnet are acceptable as interesting traffic in order to bring up a link. Once a link is up, you can ping or telnet to your remote router regardless of your interesting traffic lists.
show dialer	Gives good diagnostic information about your dialer and shows the number of times the dialer string has been reached, the idle-timeout values of each B channel, the length of the call, and the name of the router to which the interface is connected.
show isdn active	Shows the number called and whether a call is in progress.
show isdn status	A good command to use before trying to dial. Shows if your SPIDs are valid and if you are connected and communicating with layers 1 through 3 information to the provider's switch.
sho ip route	Shows all routes the router knows about.
debug isdn q921	Used to see layer 2 information only.
debug isdn q931	Used to see layer 3 information, including call setup and teardown.
debug dialer	Gives you call setup and teardown activity.
isdn disconnect int bri0	Clears the interface and drops the connection. Performing a shutdown on the interface can give you the same results.

Summary

In this chapter, we covered the following key points:

This chapter covered the difference between the following WAN services: X.25/LAPB, Frame Relay, ISDN/LAPD, SDLC, HDLC, and PPP.

You must understand High-Level Data Link Control (HDLC) and how to verify with the show interface command that HDLC is enabled. This chapter provided this important HDLC information to you as well as how the Point-to-point (PPP) is used if you need more features then HDLC or you are using two different brands of routers because HDLC is proprietary and won't work between two different vendor routers.

In the discussion of PPP, I discussed the various LCP options as well as the two types of authentication that can be used: PAP and CHAP.

Frame Relay and the two different encapsulation methods used with Frame Relay were discussed in detail. This chapter also discussed the LMI options, Frame Relay maps and subinterface configurations. In addition to the Frame Relay terms and features discussed, Frame Relay configuration and verification was covered in detail.

Lastly, I covered ISDN network and the relevant use and context for ISDN. You also learned in this chapter how to identify ISDN protocol, function groups, reference points and channels. You also learned how to verify and debug ISDN networking.

Exam Essentials

Remember the default serial encapsulation on Cisco routers.   Cisco routers use a proprietary High-Level Data-Link Control (HDLC) encapsulation on all their serial links by default.

Understand what the LMI is in Frame Relay.   The LMI is a signaling standard between a CPE device (router) and a frame switch. The LMI is responsible for managing and maintaining status between these devices. This also provides transmission keepalives to ensure that the PVC does not shut down because of inactivity.

Understand the different Frame Relay encapsulations.   Cisco uses two different Frame Relay encapsulation methods on their routers. Cisco is the default, and means that the router is connected to a Cisco Frame Relay switch; Internet Engineering Task Force (IETF) means that your router is connecting to anything but a Cisco Frame Relay switch.

Remember what the CIR is in Frame Relay.   The CIR is the average rate, in bits per second, at which the Frame Relay switch agrees to transfer data.

Remember the commands for verifying Frame Relay.   The show frame relay lmi command will give you the LMI traffic statistics exchanged between the local router and the Frame Relay switch. The show frame pvc command will list all configured PVCs and DLCI numbers.

Remember the PPP Data Link layer protocols.   The three Data Link layer protocols are: Network Control Protocol (NCP), which defines the Network layer protocols; Link Control Protocol (LCP), a method of establishing, configuring, maintaining, and terminating the point-to-point connection; and High-Level Data-Link Control (HDLC), the MAC layer protocol that encapsulates the packets.

Understand what the basic standards of ISDN provide.   The ISDN standards define the hardware and call-setup schemes for end-to-end digital connectivity.

Remember what the total bandwidth of BRI provides.   Basic Rate Interface provides two 64Kbps bearer (B) channels and one data (D) channel of 16K, for a total of 144Kbps.

Remember what the command show isdn status provides.   The show isdn status command shows whether your SPIDs are valid and whether you are connected and communicating with layers 1 through 3 information to the provider's switch.

Key Terms

Before you take the exam, be certain you are familiar with the following terms:

Backward Explicit Congestion Notification (BECN)

Network Control Protocol (NCP)

bandwidth

network termination (NT)

Basic Rate Interface (BRI)

network termination 1 (NT1)

central office (CO)

network termination 2 (NT2)

Challenge Handshake Authentication Protocol (CHAP)

packet switching

channel service unit/data service unit (CSU/DSU)

Password Authentication Protocol (PAP)

circuit switching

point of presence (POP)

Customer premises equipment (CPE)

point-to-point connection

data communication equipment (DCE)

Point-to-Point Protocol (PPP)

Data Link Connection Identifiers (DLCIs)

PPP callback

data terminal equipment (DTE)

Primary Rate Interface (PRI)

demarcation point

R reference point

Dial-on-demand routing (DDR)

S reference point

Discard Eligibility (DE)

serial transmission

Forward Explicit Congestion Notification (FECN)

subinterfaces

Frame Relay

T reference point

High-Level Data-Link Control (HDLC)

terminal adapter (TA)

Integrated Services Digital Network (ISDN)

terminal equipment type 1 (TE1)

leased line

terminal equipment type 2 (TE2)

Link Access Procedure, Balanced (LAPB)

toll network

Link Control Protocol (LCP)

U reference point

local loop

virtual circuits

Local Management Interface (LMI)

wide area network (WAN)

Commands Used in This Chapter

The following list contains a summary of all the commands used in this chapter:

Command	Description
`debug dialer`	Shows you the call setup and teardown procedures.
`debug frame-relay lmi`	Shows the LMI exchanges between the router and the Frame Relay switch.
`debug isdn q921`	Shows layer 2 processes.
`debug isdn q931`	Shows layer 3 processes.
`dialer idle-timeout` *number*	Tells the BRI line when to drop if no interesting traffic is found.
`Dialer list` *number* `protocol` *protocol permit/deny*	Specifies interesting traffic for a DDR link.
`Dialer load-threshold` *number* *inbound/outbound/either*	Sets the parameters that describe when the second BRI comes up on an ISDN link.
`Dialer` *next hop address* `name` *hostname dial string*	Used instead of a dialer string to provide more security in an ISDN network.
`dialer string`	Sets the phone number to dial for a BRI interface.
`Encapsulation frame-relay`	Changes the encapsulation to Frame Relay on a serial link and sets the default Cisco proprietary encapsulation.
`Encapsulation frame-relay ietf`	Sets the Frame Relay encapsulation type to the Internet Engineering Task Force (IETF).Connects Cisco routers to off-brand routers.
`Encapsulation hdlc`	Restores the default encapsulation of HDLC on a serial link.
`Encapsulation ppp`	Changes the encapsulation on a serial link to PPP.
`frame-relay interface-dlci`	Configures the PVC address on a serial interface or subinterface.
`frame-relay lmi-type`	Configures the LMI type on a serial link.

`frame-relay map` *`protocol`* *`address DLCI`*	Creates a static mapping for use with a Frame Relay network.
`interface s0.16 multipoint`	Creates a multipoint subinterface on a serial link that can be used with Frame Relay networks.
`interface s0.16 point-to-point`	Creates a point-to-point subinterface on a serial link that can be used with Frame Relay.
`isdn spid1`	Sets the number that identifies the first B-channel to the ISDN switch.
`isdn spid2`	Sets the number that identifies the second B-channel to the ISDN switch.
`isdn switch-type`	Sets the type of ISDN switch that the router will communicate with. Can be set at interface level or global configuration mode.
`no inverse-arp`	Turns off the dynamic IARP used with Frame Relay. Static mappings must be configured.
`ppp authentication chap`	Tells PPP to use CHAP authentication.
`ppp authentication pap`	Tells PPP to use PAP authentication.
`show dialer`	Shows the number of times the dialer string has been reached, the idle-timeout values of each B channel, the length of call, and the name of the router to which the interface is connected.
`show frame-relay lmi`	Shows the LMI stats on a per-interface basis.
`show frame-relay map`	Shows the static and dynamic Network layer–to–PVC mappings.
`show frame-relay pvc`	Shows the configured PVCs and DLCI numbers configured on a router.
`show ip route`	Shows the IP routing table.
`show isdn active`	Shows the number called and whether a call is in progress.
`show isdn status`	Shows if your SPIDs are valid and if you are connected and communicating with the provider's switch.
`username` *`name`* `password` *`password`*	Creates usernames and passwords for authentication on a Cisco router.

Written Lab 11

Write the answers to the following questions:

1. Write the command to see the encapsulation method on serial 0 of a Cisco router.

2. Write the commands to configure s0 to PPP encapsulation.

3. Write the commands to configure a username of *todd* and password of *cisco* that is used on a Cisco router.

4. Write the commands to enable CHAP authentication on a Cisco BRI interface (assume PPP is the encapsulation type).

5. Write the commands to configure the DLCI numbers for two serial interfaces, 0 and 1. Use 16 for s0 and 17 for s1.

6. Write the commands to configure a remote office using a point-to-point subinterface. Use DLCI 16 and IP address 172.16.60.1/24.

7. Write the commands to set the switch type of basic-ni1 on a Cisco router BRI interface.

8. Set the switch type on a Cisco router at the interface level.

9. Write the command that will specify interesting traffic to bring up the ISDN link. Choose all IP traffic.

10. Write the commands necessary to apply the command that you specified in Question 9 to a Cisco router.

11. Write the commands to configure the dialer information on a Cisco router.

12. Write the commands to set the dialer load-threshold to 180 and the idle-time percentage to about 40%.

13. Write the commands that will set the queue for packets at 75 when a packet is found interesting and needs a place to wait for the ISDN link to come up.

14. Write out the five steps in the configuration of the dialer information.

15. Write out the five steps that give a basic description of how DDR works when an interesting packet is received in a router interface.

(The answers to Written Lab 11 can be found following the answers to Review Questions for this chapter.)

Hands-on Labs

In this section, you will configure Cisco routers in four different WAN labs using the figure supplied in each lab. (These labs are included for use with real Cisco routers.)

Lab 11.1: Configuring PPP Encapsulation and Authentication

Lab 11.2: Configuring and Monitoring HDLC

Lab 11.3: Configuring Frame Relay and Subinterfaces

Lab 11.4: Configuring ISDN and BRI Interfaces

Hands-on Lab 11.1: Configuring PPP Encapsulation and Authentication

By default, Cisco routers use High-Level Data-Link Control (HDLC) as a point-to-point encapsulation method on serial links. If you are connecting to non-Cisco equipment, then you can use the PPP encapsulation method to communicate.

The lab you will configure is shown in the following graphic:

RouterA   RouterB

1. Type **sh int s0** on Routers A and B to see the encapsulation method.

2. Make sure that each router has the hostname assigned:

    RouterA#**config t**

    RouterA(config)#**hostname RouterA**

    RouterB#**config t**

    RouterB(config)#**hostname RouterB**

3. To change the default HDLC encapsulation method to PPP on both routers, use the encapsulation command at interface configuration. Both ends of the link must run the same encapsulation method.

    RouterA#**Config t**

    RouterA(config)#**int s0**

    RouterA(config-if)#**Encap ppp**

4. Now go to Router B and set serial 0 to PPP encapsulation.

    RouterB#**config t**

    RouterB(config)#**int s0**

    RouterB(config-if)#**encap ppp**

5. Verify the configuration by typing **sh int s0** on both routers.

6. Notice the IPCP, IPXCP, and CDPCP. This is the information used to transmit the upper-layer (Network layer) information across the HDLC at the MAC sublayer.

7. Define a username and password on each router. Notice that the username is the name of the remote router. Also, the password must be the same.

```
RouterA#config t
RouterA(config)#username RouterB password todd

RouterB#config t
RouterB(config)#username RouterA password todd
```

8. Enable CHAP or PAP authentication on each interface.

```
RouterA(config)#int s0
RouterA(config-if)#ppp authentication chap

RouterB(config)#int s0
RouterB(config-if)#ppp authentication chap
```

9. Verify the PPP configuration on each router by using these two commands:

```
sh int s0
debug ppp authentication
```

Hands-on Lab 11.2: Configuring and Monitoring HDLC

There is no configuration for HDLC, but if you completed Lab 11.1, then the PPP encapsulation would be set on both routers. This is why I put the PPP lab first. This lab allows you to actually configure HDLC encapsulation on a router.

 NOTE   This second lab will use the same configuration as Lab 11.1 used.

1. Set the encapsulation for each serial interface by using the encapsulation hdlc command.

```
RouterA#config t
RouterA(config)#int s0
RouterA(config-if)#encapsulation hdlc

RouterB#config t
RouterB(config)#int s0
RouterB(config-if)#encapsulation hdlc
```

2. Verify the HDLC encapsulation by using the show interface s0 command on each router.

Hands-on Lab 11.3: Configuring Frame Relay and Subinterfaces

In this lab, you will use the following graphic to configure Frame Relay configurations.

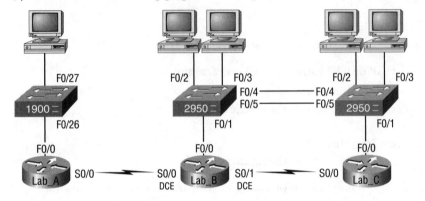

In this lab, you will configure the Lab _B router to be a Frame Relay switch. You will then configure the Lab_A and Lab_C routers to use the switch to bring up the PVC.

1. Set the hostname, `frame-relay switching` command, and the encapsulation of each serial interface on the Frame Relay switch.

   Router#**config t**
   Router(config)#**hostname Lab_B**
   Lab_B(config)#**frame-relay switching** *[makes the router a FR switch]*
   Lab_B(config)#**int s0**
   Lab_B(config-if)#**encapsulation frame-relay**
   Lab_B(config-if)#**int s1**
   Lab_B(config-if)#**encapsulation frame-relay**

2. Configure the Frame Relay mappings on each interface. You do not have to have IP addresses on these interfaces, as they are only switching one interface to another with Frame Relay frames.

   Lab_B(config-if)#**int s0**
   Lab_B(config-if)#**frame intf-type dce** *[makes this a FR DCE interface, which is different than a routers interface being DCE]*
   Lab_B(config-if)#**frame-relay route 102 interface**
     Serial0/1 201
   Lab_B(config-if)#**clock rate 64000** *[if you have this as DCE, which is different from a FR DCE]*
   Lab_B(config-if)#**int s1**
   Lab_B(config-if)#**frame intf-type dce**
   Lab_B(config-if)#**frame-relay route 201 interface**

```
Serial0/0 102
Lab_B(config-if)#clock rate 64000 [if you have this as DCE]
```

This is not as hard as it looks. The route command just says that if you receive frames from PVC 102, send them out int s0/1 using PVC 201. The second mapping on serial 0/1 is just the opposite. Anything that comes in int s0/1 is routed out serial0/ 0 using PVC 102.

3. Configure your Router A with a point-to-point subinterface.

```
Router#config t
Router(config)#hostname Lab_A
Lab_A(config)#int s0
Lab_A(config-if)#encapsulation frame-relay
Lab_A(config-if)#int s0.102 point-to-point
Lab_A(config-if)#ip address 172.16.10.1
   255.255.255.0
Lab_A(config-if)#frame-relay interface-dlci 102
```

4. Configure Router C with a point-to-point subinterface.

```
Router#config t
Router(config)#hostname Lab_C
Lab_C(config)#int s0
Lab_C(config-if)#encapsulation frame-relay
Lab_C(config-if)#int s0.201 point-to-point
Lab_C(config-if)#ip address 172.16.10.2
   255.255.255.0
Lab_C(config-if)#frame-relay interface-dlci 201
```

5. Verify your configurations with the following commands:

```
Lab_A>sho frame ?
  ip        show frame relay IP statistics
  lmi       show frame relay lmi statistics
  map       Frame-Relay map table
  pvc       show frame relay pvc statistics
  route     show frame relay route
  traffic   Frame-Relay protocol statistics
```

6. Also, use Ping and Telnet to verify connectivity.

Hands-on Lab 11.4: Configuring ISDN and BRI Interfaces

In this lab, you will use the following graphic as a reference for configuring and monitoring ISDN on Cisco routers. In this lab, you will configure routers 804A and 804B to dial ISDN between the networks 172.16.30.0 and 172.16.50.0, using network 172.16.60.0 on the ISDN BRI interfaces.

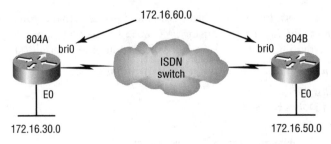

1. Go to 804B and set the hostname and ISDN switch type.

   ```
   Router#config t
   Router(config)#hostname 804B
   804B(config)#isdn switch-type basic-ni
   ```

2. Set the hostname and then set the switch type on 804A at the interface level. The point of steps 1 and 2 is to show you that you can configure the switch type either through global configuration mode or interface level.

   ```
   Router#config t
   Router(config)#hostname 804A
   804A(config)#int bri0
   804A(config-if)#isdn switch-type basic-ni
   ```

3. On 804A, set the SPID numbers on BRI 0 and make the IP address 171.16.60.1/24. If you have either a real connection into an ISDN network or an ISDN simulator, put your SPID numbers in.

   ```
   804A#config t
   804A(config)#int bri0
   804A(config-if)#isdn spid 1 0835866101 8358661
   804A(config-if)#isdn spid 2 0835866301 8358663
   804A(config-if)#ip address 172.16.60.1 255.255.255.0
   804A(config-if)#no shut
   ```

4. Set the SPIDs on 804B and make the IP address of the interface 172.16.60.2/24.

   ```
   804B#config t
   804B(config)#int bri0
   804B(config-if)#isdn spid 1 0835866201 8358662
   804B(config-if)#isdn spid 2 0835866401 8358664
   804B(config-if)#ip address 172.16.60.2 255.255.255.0
   804B(config-if)#no shut
   ```

5. Create static routes on the routers to use the remote ISDN interface. Dynamic routing will create two problems: (1) the ISDN line may always stay up, and (2) a network loop will occur because of multiple links between the same location. Static routes are recommended with ISDN.

    ```
    804A(config)#ip route 172.16.50.0 255.255.255.0
      172.16.60.2
    804A(config)#ip route 172.16.60.2 255.255.255.255 bri0

    804B(config)#ip route 172.16.30.0 255.255.255.0
      172.16.60.1
    804B(config)#ip route 172.16.60.1 255.255.255.255 bri0
    ```

6. Specify interesting traffic to bring up the ISDN link. Let's choose all IP traffic. This is a global configuration mode command.

    ```
    804A(config)#dialer-list 1 protocol ip permit
    804B(config)#dialer-list 1 protocol ip permit
    ```

7. Under the BRI interface of both routers, add the command `dialer-group 1`, which matches the dialer-list number.

    ```
    804A(config)#config t
    804A(config)#int bri0
    804A(config-if)#dialer-group 1
    804B(config)#config t
    804B(config)#int bri0
    804B(config-if)#dialer-group 1
    ```

8. Configure the dialer information on both routers.

    ```
    804A#config t
    804A(config)#int bri0
    804A(config-if)#dialer string 8358662

    804B#config t
    804B(config)#int bri0
    804B(config-if)#dialer string 8358661
    ```

9. Set the `dialer load-threshold` and `multilink` commands, as well as the idle-time percentage on both 804 routers.

    ```
    804A#config t
    804A(config)#int bri0
    804A(config-if)#dialer load-threshold 125 either
    804A(config-if)#dialer idle-timeout 180
    ```

```
804B#config t
804B(config)#int bri0
804B(config-if)#dialer load-threshold 125 either
804B(config-if)#dialer idle-timeout 180
```

10. Set the hold queue for packets when they are found interesting and need a place to wait for the ISDN link to come up.

```
804A#config t
804A(config)#int bri0
804A(config-if)#hold-queue 75 output

804B#config t
804B(config)#int bri0
804B(config-if)#hold-queue 75 output
```

11. Verify the ISDN connection.

```
ping
telnet
show dialer
show isdn status
sh ip route
```

Review Questions

1. Which of the following connects a "U" reference point to a telco?

    A. NT1

    B. NT2

    C. TE1

    D. TE1

2. Which of the following can be negotiated by PPP when establishing a connection? (Choose three.)

    A. callback

    B. multilink

    C. bandwidth

    D. PAP or CHAP authentication

    E. TCP

3. Suppose that you have a customer who has a central HQ and six branch offices. They antic-ipate adding six more branches in the near future. They wish to implement a WAN technol-ogy that will allow the branches to economically connect to HQ. Which of the following would you recommend?

    A. PPP

    B. HDLC

    C. Frame Relay

    D. ISDN

4. If you wanted to view the DLCI numbers configured for your Frame Relay network, which com-mand or commands would you use? (Choose two.)

    A. `sh frame-relay`

    B. `show frame-relay map`

    C. `sh int s0`

    D. `sh frame-relay dlci`

    E. `sh frame-relay pvc`

5. Suppose that you had a working Frame Relay connection, but had a router failure. Someone on site replaced the failed router with a non-Cisco router. What are you most likely going to have to change to bring the circuit back up?

    A. LMI type

    B. Frame Relay encapsulation type

    C. IP addressing information

    D. DLCI

6. What does the ISDN Basic Rate Interface (BRI) provide?

    A. Twenty-three B channels and one 64Kbps D channel

    B. Total bit rate of up to 1.544Mbps

    C. Two 56Kbps B channels and one 64Kbps D channel

    D. Two 64Kbps B channels and one 16Kbps D channel

7. What is true about Frame Relay DLCI?

    A. DLCI is optional in a Frame Relay network.

    B. DLCI represents a single physical circuit.

    C. DLCI identifies a logical connection between DTE devices.

    D. DLCI is used to tag the beginning of a frame when using LAN switching.

8. By looking at the following output, what protocols are active on the serial 0 interface?

    ```
    RouterA#show int s0
    Serial0 is up, line protocol is up
     Hardware is HD64570
     Internet address is 172.16.20.1/24
     MTU 1500 bytes, BW 1544 Kbit, DLY 20000 usec, rely
      255/255, load 1/255
     Encapsulation PPP, loopback not set, keepalive set (10 sec)
     LCP Open
     Closed: IPXCP
     Open: IPCP, CDPCP
    ```

    A. IP, IPX and CDP

    B. IP and CDP

    C. IP and IPX

    D. None

9. What is the default encapsulation on point-to-point links between two Cisco routers?

    A. SDLC

    B. HDLC

    C. Cisco

    D. ANSI

10. You are using a WAN service that provides two Data Link layer encapsulations, one for data and one for signaling. What service are you using?

   A. Frame Relay

   B. HDLC

   C. ISDN

   D. LAPD

11. Which of the following is true regarding PPP? (Choose three options.)

   A. Converts layer 2 to layer 3 addresses

   B. Supports IP only

   C. Provides error correction

   D. Can be used on analog

   E. Encapsulates several routed protocols

12. Which of the following are valid PPP authentication methods? (Choose two.)

   A. LCP

   B. PAP

   C. CHAP

   D. MD5

13. In Frame Relay, what identifies the PVC?

   A. NCP

   B. LMI

   C. IARP

   D. DLCI

14. Suppose that you have a leased T1 line connected to a Cisco router and a non-Cisco router. Which of the following encapsulation types will you most likely use?

   A. SLIP

   B. HDLC

   C. Frame Relay

   D. PPP

15. Which of the following is an ISDN Data Link layer signaling standard?

   A. NCP

   B. LAPB

   C. LAPD

   D. TE2

16. Which of the following are the five basic steps to set up a `dialer map` command string?

   A. dial string, dialer, map, protocol, next hop

   B. dialer, dial string, map, protocol, next hop

   C. dialer, map, protocol, next hop, dial string

   D. dialer, map, next hop, protocol, dial string

17. If you have a remote router with a hostname of "Bob" and you want to set up a PPP authentication link using the password "Cisco" to a local router with a hostname "Todd," which of the following commands is correct?

   A. `username bob password cisco`

   B. `username Bob password Cisco`

   C. `username todd password cisco`

   D. `username Todd password Cisco`

18. The following ISDN command verifies which of the following?

   `show isdn status`

   A. Shows that a router has established layer 1 and layer 2 connectivity to the telephone company ISDN switch

   B. Shows the number called and whether a call is in progress

   C. Shows the idle-timeout values of each B channel, the length of the call, and the name of the router to which the interface is connected

   D. Shows the dialer diagnostic information and the number of times the dialer string has been reached, the idle-timeout values of each B channel, the length of the call, and the name of the router to which the interface is connected

19. What is the default encapsulation type for Frame Relay in a Cisco router?

   A. HDLC

   B. IETF

   C. Cisco

   D. PPP

   E. Ansi

   F. Q933i

20. The Local Management Interface (LMI) is responsible for which of the following?

   A. For keeping routers up and running with less memory overhead

   B. For telling the switch what type of router is running on each end

   C. For broadcasting IP routing protocol information

   D. For transmitting keepalives to ensure that the PVC does not shut down because of inactivity

Answers to Review Questions

1. A. The best answer is NT1, which converts a 4-wire to a 2-wire and can connect the now "U" interface into the telco.

2. A, B, D. PPP can negotiate multilink, callback, or authentication using PAP or CHAP.

3. C. Frame Relay will provide the most scalable and cost-effective solution in this situation.

4. B, E. You can use the `show frame-relay map` and `show frame-relay pvc` commands to see the DLCI numbers configured on your router.

5. B. The default Frame Relay encapsulation type of Cisco will likely need to be changed on the other router should the failed router be replaced with a non-Cisco device.

6. D. BRI is two B-channels, which are 64Kbps each. It also has one data channel of 16Kbps to provide signaling.

7. C. DLCI is required to be used on each circuit with Frame Relay. The DLCI number identifies the PVC of each logical circuit. PVCs are logical links between two DTE devices.

8. B. The very last line in this router output shows IPCP and CDPCP, which are the NCP encapsulations of IP and CDP.

9. B. Cisco uses a proprietary HDLC as the default encapsulation on all their serial interfaces.

10. C. ISDN works at the Physical, Data Link, and Network layers. It uses two encapsulations at the Data Link layer, one for Data and one for signaling.

11. C, D, E. PPP can be used on both point-to-point and analog dialup lines, provides error correction and can encapsulate several routed protocols, not just IP.

12. B, C. PAP and CHAP are valid authentication methods available to PPP authentication.

13. D. Data Link Connection Identifiers (DLCIs) are used to identify a permanent virtual circuit.

14. D. PPP is your only option since HDLC is proprietary. Serial connections must have the same encapsulation on each end. Frame Relay is not an encapsulation used for leased lines; it is used for circuit-switched networks.

15. C. LAPD is used at the Data Link layer to provide signaling for ISDN circuits.

16. C. The five basic Dialer Map steps that you must be aware of are:

1. Dialer

2. Map

3. Protocol

4. Next hop

5. Dial string

17. B. To set up authentication, you must use the `username` command with the hostname of the remote router. Both the username and password are case sensitive. The password is the same on both routers.

18. A. The command `show isdn status` shows that a router has established layer 1 and layer 2 connectivity, and even layer 3, to the telephone company ISDN switch.

19. C. If you just type `encapsulation frame-relay` from interface configuration mode, the encapsulation type will be Cisco.

20. D. The LMI provides keepalives between the router and the frame switch to verify that the link and connection are still active.

Answers to Written Lab 11

1. `sh int s0`

2. `config t`
   `int s0`
   `encap ppp`

3. `config t`
   `username todd password cisco`

4. `config t`
   `int bri0`
   `ppp authentication chap`

5. `config t`
   `int s0`
   `frame interface-dlci 16`
   `int s1`
   `frame interface-dlci 17`

6. `config t`
   `int s0`
   `encap frame`
   `int s0.16 point-to-point`
   `ip address 172.16.60.1 255.255.255.0`

   `frame interface-dlci 16`

7. `config t`
   `isdn switch-type basic-ni1`

8. `config t`
   `interface bri 0`
   `isdn switch-type basic-ni`

9. `Router(config)#`**`dialer-list 1 protocol ip permit`**

10. `config t`
    `int bri0`
    `dialer-group 1`

11. `config t`
    `int bri0`
    `dialer string 8358662`

12. `config t`
    `int bri0`
    `dialer load-threshold 125 either`
    `dialer idle-timeout 180`

13. ```
    config t
    int bri0
    hold-queue 75 in
    ```

14. These are the steps you should take to configure the dialer information:

    1. Choose the interface.

    2. Set the IP address.

    3. Configure the encapsulation type.

    4. Link interesting traffic to the interface.

    5. Configure the number or numbers to dial.

15. These are the steps that DDR follows when an interesting packet is received in a router interface:

    1. The route to the destination network is determined.

    2. Interesting packets dictate a DDR call.

    3. Dialer information is looked up and the call is made.

    4. Traffic is transmitted.

    5. Call is terminated when no more interesting traffic is being transmitted over a link and the idle-timeout period ends.
    ```

Appendix A

Commands in This Study Guide

This appendix is a compilation of all the "Commands Used in This Chapter" sections at the end of the chapters.

Command	Description	Chapter
?	Gives you a help screen	4
0.0.0.0 255.255.255.255	A wildcard command; same as the any command	10
access-class	Applies a standard IP access list to a VTY line	10
access-list	Creates a list of tests to filter the networks	10
any	Specifies any host or any network; same as the 0.0.0.0 255.255.255.255 command	10
Backspace	Deletes a single character	4
bandwidth	Sets the bandwidth on a serial interface	4
banner	Creates a banner for users who log into the router	4
cdp enable	Turns on CDP on an individual interface	9
cdp holdtime	Changes the holdtime of CDP packets	9
cdp run	Turns on CDP on a router	9
cdp timer	Changes the CDP update timer	9
clear counters	Clears the statistics from an interface	4
clear line	Clears a connection connected via Telnet to your router	9
clock rate	Provides clocking on a serial DCE interface	4
config memory	Copies the startup-config to running-config	4
config network	Copies a configuration stored on a TFTP host to running-config	4
config terminal	Puts you in global configuration mode and changes the running-config	4

Command	Description	Chapter
config-register	Tells the router how to boot and to change the configuration register setting	9
confreg	Changes the configure register of a router from Rom monitor mode (2600 series is an example).	9
copy flash tftp	Copies a file from flash memory to a TFTP host	9
copy run start	Short for copy running-config startup-config; places a configuration into NVRAM	4, 9
copy run tftp	Copies the running-config file to a TFTP host	9
copy running-config startup-config	Saves the configuration on a 2950 switch	9
copy tftp flash	Copies a file from a TFTP host to flash memory	9
copy tftp run	Copies a configuration from a TFTP host to the running-config file	9
Ctrl+A	Moves your cursor to the beginning of the line	4
Ctrl+D	Deletes a single character	4
Ctrl+E	Moves your cursor to the end of the line	4
Ctrl+F	Moves forward one character	4
Ctrl+R	Redisplays a line	4
Ctrl+Shift+6, then X(keyboard combination)	Returns you to the originating router when you telnet to numerous routers	9
Ctrl+U	Erases a line	4
Ctrl+W	Erases a word	4
Ctrl+Z	Ends configuration mode and returns to EXEC	4
debug dialer	Shows you the call setup and teardown procedures	11
debug frame-relay lmi	Shows the lmi exchanges between the router and the Frame Relay switch	11
debug ip igrp events	Provides a summary of the IGRP routing information running on the network	5

Command	Description	Chapter
debug ip igrp transactions	Shows message requests from neighbor routers asking for an update and the broadcasts sent from your router to that neighbor router	5
debug ip rip	Sends console messages displaying informa-tion about RIP packets being sent and received on a router interface	5
debug isdn q921	Shows layer-2 processes	11
debug isdn q931	Shows layer-3 processes	11
delete nvram	Deletes the contents of NVRAM on a 1900 switch	7
description	Sets a description on an interface	4
dialer idle-timeout number	Tells the BRI line when to drop if no interesting traffic is found	11
dialer list number protocol protocol permit/ deny	Specifies interesting traffic for a DDR link	11
dialer load-threshold number inbound/outbound/ either	Sets the parameters that describe when the second BRI comes up on an ISDN link	11
dialer map protocol address name hostname number	Used instead of a dialer string to provide more security in an ISDN network	11
dialer next hop address name hostname dial string	Used instead of a dialer string to provide more security in an ISDN network.	11
dialer string	Sets the phone number to dial for a BRI interface	11
disable	Takes you from privileged mode back to user mode	4
disconnect	Disconnects a connection to a remote router from the originating router	7
enable	Puts you into privileged mode	4
enable password	Sets the unencrypted enable password	4
enable password level 1 password	Sets the usermode password on a 1900 switch	7

Command	Description	Chapter
enable password level 15 password	Sets the enable password on a 1900 switch	7
enable secret	Sets the encrypted enable secret password. Supersedes the enable password if set	4
enable secret password	Sets the enable password on a 1900 and 2950 switch	7
encapsulation	Sets the frame type used on an interface	8
encapsulation dot1q *vlan#*	Sets the encapsulation on a routers trunk port to 802.1Q encapsulation	8
encapsulation frame-relay	Changes the encapsulation to Frame Relay on a serial link	11
encapsulation frame-relay ietf	Sets the encapsulation type to the Internet Engineering Task Force (IETF); connects Cisco routers to off-brand routers	11
encapsulation hdlc	Restores the default encapsulation of HDLC on a serial link	11
encapsulation isl *vlan#*	Sets the encapsulation on a routers trunk port to isl encapsulation	8
encapsulation ppp	Changes the encapsulation on a serial link to PPP	11
erase startup	Deletes the startup-config	4
erase startup-config	Deletes the contents of NVRAM on a router	9
Esc+B	Moves back one word	4
Esc+F	Moves forward one word	4
exec-timeout	Sets the timeout in seconds and minutes for the console connection	4
exit	Disconnects a connection to a remote router via Telnet	9
frame-relay interface-dlci	Configures the PVC address on a serial interface or subinterface	11
frame-relay lmi-type	Configures the LMI type on a serial link	11
frame-relay map *protocol address DLCI*	Creates a static mapping for use with a Frame Relay network	11

Command	Description	Chapter
host	Specifies a single host address	11
hostname *name*	Sets the name of a router or a switch	4
int vlan1	Chooses the default VLAN on a 2950 switch	7
interface	Puts you in interface configuration mode; also used with show commands	4
interface fastethernet0/0	Puts you in interface configuration mode for a Fast Ethernet port; also used with show commands	4
interface fastethernet0/0.1	Creates a subinterface	4
interface *int*	Puts you in configuration mode for the specified interface and can be used for show commands.	4
interface s0.16 multipoint	Creates a multipoint subinterface on a serial link that can be used with Frame Relay networks	11
interface s0.16 point-to-point	Creates a point-to-point subinterface on a serial link that can be used with Frame Relay	11
interface serial 5	Puts you in configuration mode for interface serial 5 and can be used for show commands	4
ip access-group	Applies an IP access list to an interface	10
ip address	Sets an IP address on an interface or a switch	4
ip address ip_address mask	Sets the IP address on a device	7
ip classless	A global configuration command used to tell a router to forward packets to a default route when the destination network is not in the routing table	5
ip default-gateway ip_address	Sets the default gateway on a 1900 and 2950 switch	7
ip domain-lookup	Turns on DNS lookup (which is on by default)	7
ip domain-name	Appends a domain name to a DNS lookup	7
ip host	Creates a host table on a router	7
ip name-server	Sets the IP address of up to six DNS servers	7
ip route	Creates static and default routes on a router	5

Command	Description	Chapter
isdn spid1	Sets the number that identifies the first DS0 to the ISDN switch	11
isdn spid2	Sets the number that identifies the second DS0 to the ISDN switch	11
isdn switch-type	Sets the type of ISDN switch that the router will communicate with; can be set at interface level or global configuration mode	11
line	Puts you in configuration mode to change or set your user mode passwords	4
line aux	Puts you in the auxiliary interface configuration mode	4
line console 0	Puts you in console configuration mode	4
line vty	Puts you in VTY (Telnet) interface configuration mode	4
logging synchronous	Stops console messages from overwriting your command-line input	4
logout	Logs you out of your console session	4
media-type	Sets the hardware media type on an interface	4
network	Tells the routing protocol what network to advertise	5
network *ip-address*	Enables EIGRP on the local interfaces that reside on the specified networks. EIGRP is configured with a classful address.	6
network *network-number wild-card* area *area-id*	Enables OSPF on a specific interface or set of interfaces that reside on the specified network. These interfaces will reside in the specified area.	6
no auto-summary	Turns off the automatic summarization of routes at classful boundaries.	6
no cdp enable	Turns off CDP on an individual interface	9
no cdp run	Turns off CDP completely on a router	9
no inverse-arp	Turns off the dynamic IARP used with Frame Relay; static mappings must be configured	11

Command	Description	Chapter
`no ip domain-lookup`	Turns off DNS lookup	9
`no ip host`	Removes a hostname from a host table	9
`No ip route`	Removes a static or default route	5
`no shutdown`	Turns on an interface	4
`o/r 0x2142`	Changes a 2501 to boot without using the contents of NVRAM	9
`passive-interface interface-type interface-number`	Identifies interfaces that do not participate in EIGRP updates.	6
`ping`	Tests IP connectivity to a remote device	4, 9
`ppp authentication chap`	Tells PPP to use CHAP authentication	11
`ppp authentication pap`	Tells PPP to use PAP authentication	11
`reload`	Reboots the router	4
`router eigrp as`	Starts EIGRP processes on a router using a specific autonomous system number.	6
`router igrp as`	Turns on IP IGRP routing on a router	5
`router ospf process-id`	Activates the OSPF routing process and identifies the process-id under which it will run. Process-id is in the range 1-65535.	6
`router rip`	Puts you in router rip configuration mode	4, 5
`Service password-encryption`	Encrypts the user mode and enable password	4
`sh ip`	Shows the IP configuration information on a 1900 switch	7
`sh vlan`	Shows the VLAN database	8
`sh vlan brief`	Shows a brief overview of the VLAN database	8
`sh vtp`	Displays the VTP configured information on a switch	8
`show access-lists`	Shows all the access lists configured on the router	10
`show access-lists 110`	Shows only access list 110	10

Command	Description	Chapter
show cdp	Displays the CDP timer and holdtime frequencies	9
show cdp entry *	Same as show cdp neighbor detail, but does not work on a 1900 switch	9
show cdp interface	Shows the individual interfaces enabled with CDP	9
show cdp neighbor	Shows the directly connected neighbors and the details about them	9
show cdp neighbor detail	Shows the IP address and IOS version and type, and includes all of the information from the show cdp neighbor command	9
show cdp traffic	Shows the CDP packets sent and received on a device and any errors	9
show controllers *int*	Shows the DTE or DCE status of an interface.	4
show controllers s 0	Shows the DTE or DCE status of an interface	4
show dialer	Shows the number of times the dialer string has been reached, the idle-timeout values of each B channel, the length of call, and the name of the router to which the interface is connected	11
show flash	Shows the files in flash memory	9
show frame-relay lmi	Shows the LMI type on a serial interface	11
show frame-relay map	Shows the static and dynamic Network layer–to–PVC mappings	11
show frame-relay pvc	Shows the configured PVCs and DLCI numbers configured on a router	11
show history	Shows you the last 10 commands entered by default	4
show hosts	Shows the contents of the host table	9
show interface s0	Shows the statistics of interface serial 0	4
show interfaces *int*	Shows the statistics of an interface.	4
show ip access-lists	Shows only the IP access lists	10
show ip eigrp neighbors	Shows all EIGRP neighbors.	6
show ip eigrp topology	Shows entries in the EIGRP topology table.	6

Command	Description	Chapter
show ip eigrp traffic	Shows the packet count for EIGRP packets sent and received.	6
show ip interface	Shows which interfaces have IP access lists applied	10
show ip ospf	Summarizes all relative OSPF information, such as OSPF processes, Router ID, area assignments, authentication, and SPF statistics.	6
show ip ospf database	Displays the link-state topology database.	6
show ip ospf interface	Displays interface OSPF parameters and other OSPF information specific to the interface.	6
show ip ospf neighbor	Displays each OSPF neighbor and adjacency status.	6
show ip ospf *process-id*	Shows the same information as the show ip ospf command, but only for the specified process.	6
show ip protocols	Shows the routing protocols and timers associated with each routing protocol configured on a router	5, 6
show ip route	Displays the IP routing table	5, 11
show isdn active	Shows the number called and whether a call is in progress	11
show isdn status	Shows if your SPIDs are valid and if you are connected and communicating with the provider's switch	11
show protocols	Shows the routed protocols and network addresses configured on each interface	5, 8
show running-config	Also abbreviated to show run; shows the configuration currently running on the router	4, 9
show sessions	Shows your connections via Telnet to remote devices	9
show start	Short for show startup-config; shows the backup configuration stored in NVRAM	4, 9
show terminal	Shows you your configured history size	4
show users	Displays the users that are telnetted into your device.	9

Command	Description	Chapter
show version	Gives the IOS information of the switch, as well as the uptime and base Ethernet address	4, 9
shutdown	Puts an interface in administratively down mode	4
switchport access vlan *vlan#*	Sets a port on a 2950 to a specific VLAN membership	8
switchport mode trunk	Sets a port on a 2950 to trunking mode	8
Tab	Finishes typing a command for you	4
telnet	Connects, views, and runs programs on a remote device	4, 9
terminal history size	Changes your history size from the default of 10 up to 256	4
tftp-server flash:*ios-name*	Creates a TFTP-server host for a router system image that is run in flash memory.	9
trace	Tests a connection to a remote device and shows the path it took through the internetwork to find the remote device	4
traceroute	Tests IP connectivity	4
traffic-share balanced	Tells the IGRP routing protocol to share links inversely proportional to the metrics	5
traffic-share min	Tells the IGRP routing process to use routes that have only minimum costs	5
trunk on	Sets a port on a 1900 to trunking mode	8
username *name* password *password*	Creates usernames and passwords for authentication on a Cisco router	11
variance	Controls the load balancing between the best metric and the worst acceptable metric	5
vlan 2 name *name*	Creates and names a VLAN	8
vlan database	Puts you into the VLAN database on a 2950 switch	8
vlan-membership static *vlan#*	Sets a port on a 1900 to a specific VLAN membership	8
vtp client	Sets the VTP mode on the switch to client	8

Command	Description	Chapter
vtp domain name	Sets the VTP domain on a switch to the specified name	8
vtp password *password*	Sets the VTP password. All switches that want to participate in the domain must have the same password.	8
vtp server	Sets the VTP mode on the switch to server	8
vtp transparent	Sets the VTP mode on the switch to transparent	8

Glossary

10BaseT   Part of the original IEEE 802.3 standard, 10BaseT is the Ethernet specification of 10Mbps baseband that uses two pairs of twisted-pair, Category 3, 4, or 5 cabling—using one pair to send data and the other to receive. 10BaseT has a distance limit of about 100 meters per segment. *See also: Ethernet* and *IEEE 802.3.*

100BaseT   Based on the IEEE 802.3u standard, 100BaseT is the Fast Ethernet specification of 100Mbps baseband that uses UTP wiring. 100BaseT sends link pulses (containing more information than those used in 10BaseT) over the network when no traffic is present. *See also: 10BaseT, Fast Ethernet,* and *IEEE 802.3.*

100BaseTX   Based on the IEEE 802.3u standard, 100BaseTX is the 100Mbps baseband Fast Ethernet specification that uses two pairs of UTP or STP wiring. The first pair of wires receives data; the second pair sends data. To ensure correct signal timing, a 100BaseTX segment cannot be longer than 100 meters.

A&B bit signaling   Used in T1 transmission facilities and sometimes called "24th channel signaling." Each of the 24 T1 subchannels in this procedure uses one bit of every sixth frame to send supervisory signaling information.

AAA   Authentication, Authorization, and Accounting: A system developed by Cisco to provide network security. *See also: authentication, authorization,* and *accounting.*

AAL   ATM Adaptation Layer: A service-dependent sublayer of the Data Link layer, which accepts data from other applications and brings it to the ATM layer in 48-byte ATM payload segments. CS and SAR are the two sublayers that form AALs. Currently, the four types of AAL recommended by the ITU-T are AAL1, AAL2, AAL3/4, and AAL5. AALs are differentiated by the source-destination timing they use, whether they are CBR or VBR, and whether they are used for connection-oriented or connectionless mode data transmission. *See also: AAL1, AAL2, AAL3/4, AAL5, ATM,* and *ATM layer.*

AAL1   ATM Adaptation Layer 1: One of four AALs recommended by the ITU-T, it is used for connection-oriented, time-sensitive services that need constant bit rates, such as isochronous traffic and uncompressed video. *See also: AAL.*

AAL2   ATM Adaptation Layer 2: One of four AALs recommended by the ITU-T, it is used for connection-oriented services that support a variable bit rate, such as compressed voice traffic. *See also: AAL.*

AAL3/4   ATM Adaptation Layer 3/4: One of four AALs (a product of two initially distinct layers) recommended by the ITU-T, supporting both connectionless and connection-oriented links. Its primary use is in sending SMDS packets over ATM networks. *See also: AAL.*

AAL5   ATM Adaptation Layer 5: One of four AALs recommended by the ITU-T, it is used to support connection-oriented VBR services primarily to transfer classical IP over ATM and LANE traffic. This least complex of the AAL recommendations uses SEAL, offering lower bandwidth costs and simpler processing requirements but also providing reduced bandwidth and error-recovery capacities. *See also: AAL.*

AARP AppleTalk Address Resolution Protocol: The protocol in an AppleTalk stack that maps data-link addresses to network addresses.

AARP probe packets Packets sent by the AARP to determine whether a given node ID is being used by another node in a nonextended AppleTalk network. If the node ID is not in use, the sending node appropriates that node's ID. If the node ID is in use, the sending node will select a different ID and then send out more AARP probe packets. *See also: AARP.*

ABM Asynchronous Balanced Mode: When two stations can initiate a transmission, ABM is an HDLC (or one of its derived protocols) communication technology that supports peer-oriented, point-to-point communications between both stations.

ABR Area Border Router: An OSPF router that is located on the border of one or more OSPF areas. ABRs are used to connect OSPF areas to the OSPF backbone area.

access layer One of the layers in Cisco's three-layer hierarchical model. The access layer provides users with access to the internetwork.

access link A link used with switches that is part of only one virtual LAN (VLAN). Trunk links carry information from multiple VLANs.

access list A set of test conditions kept by routers that determines "interesting traffic" to and from the router for various services on the network.

access method The manner in which network devices approach gaining access to the network itself.

access rate Defines the bandwidth rate of the circuit. For example, the access rate of a T1 circuit is 1.544Mbps. In Frame Relay and other technologies, there may be a fractional T1 connection—256Kbps, for example—however, the access rate and clock rate are still 1.544Mbps.

access server Also known as a "network access server," it is a communications process connecting asynchronous devices to a LAN or WAN through network and terminal emulation software, providing synchronous or asynchronous routing of supported protocols.

accounting One of the three components in AAA. Accounting provides auditing and logging functionalities to the security model.

acknowledgment Verification sent from one network device to another signifying that an event has occurred. May be abbreviated as ACK. *Contrast with: NAK.*

ACR allowed cell rate: A designation defined by the ATM Forum for managing ATM traffic. Dynamically controlled using congestion control measures, the ACR varies between the minimum cell rate (MCR) and the peak cell rate (PCR). *See also: MCR and PCR.*

active monitor The mechanism used to manage a token ring. The network node with the highest MAC address on the ring becomes the active monitor and is responsible for management tasks such as preventing loops and ensuring that tokens are not lost.

active state   In regards to an EIGRP routing table, a route will be in Active state when a router is undergoing a route convergence.

address learning   Used with transparent bridges to learn the hardware addresses of all devices on a network. The switch then filters the network with the known hardware (MAC) addresses.

address mapping   By translating network addresses from one format to another, this methodology permits different protocols to operate interchangeably.

address mask   A bit combination descriptor identifying which portion of an address refers to the network or subnet and which part refers to the host. Sometimes simply called the mask. *See also: subnet mask.*

address resolution   The process used for resolving differences between computer addressing schemes. Address resolution typically defines a method for tracing Network layer (layer 3) addresses to Data Link layer (layer 2) addresses. *See also: address mapping.*

adjacency   The relationship made between defined neighboring routers and end nodes, using a common media segment, to exchange routing information.

administrative distance (AD)   A number between 0 and 255 that expresses the level of trustworthiness of a routing information source. The lower the number, the higher the integrity rating.

administrative weight   A value designated by a network administrator to rate the preference given to a network link. It is one of four link metrics exchanged by PTSPs to test ATM network resource availability.

ADSU   ATM Data Service Unit: The terminal adapter used to connect to an ATM network through an HSSI-compatible mechanism. *See also: DSU.*

advertising   The process whereby routing or service updates are transmitted at given intervals, allowing other routers on the network to maintain a record of viable routes.

AEP   AppleTalk Echo Protocol: A test for connectivity between two AppleTalk nodes where one node sends a packet to another and receives an echo, or copy, in response.

AFI   Authority and Format Identifier: The part of an NSAP ATM address that delineates the type and format of the IDI section of an ATM address.

AFP   AppleTalk Filing Protocol: A Presentation layer protocol, supporting AppleShare and Mac OS File Sharing, that permits users to share files and applications on a server.

AIP   ATM Interface Processor: Supporting AAL3/4 and AAL5, this interface for Cisco 7000 series routers minimizes performance bottlenecks at the UNI. *See also: AAL3/4 and AAL5.*

algorithm   A set of rules or processes used to solve a problem. In networking, algorithms are typically used for finding the best route for traffic from a source to its destination.

alignment error   An error occurring in Ethernet networks, in which a received frame has extra bits—that is, a number not divisible by eight. Alignment errors are generally the result of frame damage caused by collisions.

all-routes explorer packet An explorer packet that can move across an entire SRB network, tracing all possible paths to a given destination. Also known as an all-rings explorer packet. *See also: explorer packet, local explorer packet,* and *spanning explorer packet.*

AM Amplitude modulation: A modulation method that represents information by varying the amplitude of the carrier signal. *See also: modulation.*

AMI Alternate Mark Inversion: A line-code type on T1 and E1 circuits that shows zeros as "01" during each bit cell, and ones as "11" or "00," alternately, during each bit cell. The sending device must maintain ones density in AMI but not independently of the data stream. Also known as binary-coded, alternate mark inversion. *Contrast with: B8ZS. See also: ones density.*

amplitude An analog or digital waveform's highest value.

analog transmission Signal messaging whereby information is represented by various combinations of signal amplitude, frequency, and phase.

ANSI American National Standards Institute: The organization of corporate, government, and other volunteer members that coordinates standards-related activities, approves U.S. national standards, and develops U.S. positions in international standards organizations. ANSI assists in the creation of international and U.S. standards in disciplines such as communications, networking, and a variety of technical fields. It publishes over 13,000 standards, for engineered products and technologies ranging from screw threads to networking protocols. ANSI is a member of the International Electrotechnical Commission (IEC) and International Organization for Standardization (ISO).

anycast An ATM address that can be shared by more than one end system, allowing requests to be routed to a node that provides a particular service.

AppleTalk Currently in two versions, the group of communication protocols designed by Apple Computer for use in Macintosh environments. The earlier Phase 1 protocols support one physical network with only one network number that resides in one zone. The later Phase 2 protocols support more than one logical network on a single physical network, allowing networks to exist in more than one zone. *See also: zone.*

Application layer Layer 7 of the OSI reference network model, supplying services to application procedures (such as electronic mail or file transfer) that are outside the OSI model. This layer chooses and determines the availability of communicating partners along with the resources necessary to make the connection, coordinates partnering applications, and forms a consensus on procedures for controlling data integrity and error recovery. *See also: Data Link layer, Network layer, Physical layer, Presentation layer, Session layer,* and *Transport layer.*

ARA AppleTalk Remote Access: A protocol for Macintosh users establishing their access to resources and data from a remote AppleTalk location.

area A logical, rather than physical, set of segments (based on either CLNS, DECnet, or OSPF) along with their attached devices. Areas are commonly connected to others using routers to create a single autonomous system. *See also: autonomous system.*

ARM   Asynchronous Response Mode: An HDLC communication mode using one primary station and at least one additional station, in which transmission can be initiated from either the primary or one of the secondary units.

ARP   Address Resolution Protocol: Defined in RFC 826, the protocol that traces IP addresses to MAC addresses. *See also: RARP.*

AS   autonomous system: A group of networks under mutual administration that share the same routing methodology. Autonomous systems are subdivided by areas and must be assigned an individual 16-bit number by the IANA. *See also: area.*

AS path prepending   The use of route maps in BGP to lengthen the autonomous system path by adding false ASNs.

ASBR   Autonomous System Boundary Router: An area border router placed between an OSPF autonomous system and a non-OSPF network that operates both OSPF and an additional routing protocol, such as RIP. ASBRs must be located in a non-stub OSPF area. *See also: ABR, non-stub area,* and *OSPF.*

ASCII   American Standard Code for Information Interchange: An 8-bit code for representing characters, consisting of 7 data bits plus 1 parity bit.

ASICs   application-specific integrated circuits: Used in layer 2 switches to make filtering decisions. The ASIC looks in the filter table of MAC addresses and determines which port the destination hardware address of a received hardware address is destined for. The frame will be allowed to traverse only that one segment. If the hardware address is unknown, the frame is forwarded out all ports.

ASN.1   Abstract Syntax Notation One: An OSI language used to describe types of data that are independent of computer structures and depicting methods. Described by ISO International Standard 8824.

ASP   AppleTalk Session Protocol: A protocol employing ATP to establish, maintain, and tear down sessions, as well as sequence requests. *See also: ATP.*

AST   Automatic Spanning Tree: A function that supplies one path for spanning explorer frames traveling from one node in the network to another, supporting the automatic resolution of spanning trees in SRB networks. AST is based on the IEEE 802.1d standard. *See also: IEEE 802.1* and *SRB.*

asynchronous transmission   Digital signals sent without precise timing, usually with different frequencies and phase relationships. Asynchronous transmissions generally enclose individual characters in control bits (called start and stop bits) that show the beginning and end of each character. *Contrast with: isochronous transmission* and *synchronous transmission.*

ATCP   AppleTalk Control Program: The protocol for establishing and configuring AppleTalk over PPP, defined in RFC 1378. *See also: PPP.*

ATDM   Asynchronous Time-Division Multiplexing: A technique for sending information, it differs from normal TDM in that the time slots are assigned when necessary rather than preassigned to certain transmitters. *Contrast with: FDM, statistical multiplexing,* and *TDM.*

ATG   Address Translation Gateway: The mechanism within Cisco DECnet routing software that enables routers to route multiple, independent DECnet networks and to establish a user-designated address translation for chosen nodes between networks.

ATM   Asynchronous Transfer Mode: The international standard, identified by fixed-length 53-byte cells, for transmitting cells in multiple service systems, such as voice, video, or data. Transit delays are reduced because the fixed-length cells permit processing to occur in the hardware. ATM is designed to maximize the benefits of high-speed transmission media, such as SONET, E3, and T3.

ATM ARP server   A device that supplies logical subnets running classical IP over ATM with address-resolution services.

ATM endpoint   The initiating or terminating connection in an ATM network. ATM endpoints include servers, workstations, ATM-to-LAN switches, and ATM routers.

ATM Forum   The international organization founded jointly by Northern Telecom, Sprint, Cisco Systems, and NET/ADAPTIVE in 1991 to develop and promote standards-based implementation agreements for ATM technology. The ATM Forum broadens official standards developed by ANSI and ITU-T and creates implementation agreements before official standards are published.

ATM layer   A sublayer of the Data Link layer in an ATM network that is service-independent. To create standard 53-byte ATM cells, the ATM layer receives 48-byte segments from the AAL and attaches a 5-byte header to each. These cells are then sent to the physical layer for transmission across the physical medium. *See also: AAL.*

ATMM   ATM Management: A procedure that runs on ATM switches, managing rate enforcement and VCI translation. *See also: ATM.*

ATM user-user connection   A connection made by the ATM layer to supply communication between at least two ATM service users, such as ATMM processes. These communications can be uni- or bidirectional, using one or two VCs, respectively. *See also: ATM layer* and *ATMM.*

ATP   AppleTalk Transaction Protocol: A transport-level protocol that enables reliable transactions between two sockets, where one requests the other to perform a given task and to report the results. ATP fastens the request and response together, assuring a loss-free exchange of request-response pairs.

attenuation   In communication, weakening or loss of signal energy, typically caused by distance.

AURP   AppleTalk Update-based Routing Protocol: A technique for encapsulating AppleTalk traffic in the header of a foreign protocol that allows the connection of at least two noncontiguous AppleTalk internetworks through a foreign network (such as TCP/IP) to create an AppleTalk WAN. The connection made is called an AURP tunnel. By exchanging routing information between exterior routers, the AURP maintains routing tables for the complete AppleTalk WAN. *See also: AURP tunnel.*

AURP tunnel   A connection made in an AURP WAN that acts as a single, virtual link between AppleTalk internetworks separated physically by a foreign network such as a TCP/IP network. *See also: AURP.*

authentication   The first component in the AAA model. Users are typically authenticated via a username and password, which are used to uniquely identify them.

authority zone   A portion of the domain-name tree associated with DNS for which one name server is the authority. *See also: DNS.*

authorization   The act of permitting access to a resource based on authentication information in the AAA model.

auto-detect mechanism   Used in Ethernet switch, hub, and interface cards to determine the duplex and speed that can be used.

auto duplex   A setting on layer 1 and layer 2 devices that sets the duplex of a switch or hub port automatically.

automatic call reconnect   A function that enables automatic call rerouting away from a failed trunk line.

autonomous confederation   A collection of self-governed systems that depend more on their own network accessibility and routing information than on information received from other systems or groups.

autonomous switching   The ability of Cisco routers to process packets more quickly by using the ciscoBus to switch packets independently of the system processor.

autonomous system   *See: AS.*

autoreconfiguration   A procedure executed by nodes within the failure domain of a token ring, wherein nodes automatically perform diagnostics, trying to reconfigure the network around failed areas.

auxiliary port   The console port on the back of Cisco routers that allows you to connect a modem and dial the router and make console configuration settings.

B8ZS   Binary 8-Zero Substitution: A line-code type, interpreted at the remote end of the connection, that uses a special code substitution whenever eight consecutive zeros are transmitted over the link on T1 and E1 circuits. This technique assures ones density independent of the data stream. Also known as bipolar 8-zero substitution. *Contrast with: AMI. See also: ones density.*

backbone   The basic portion of the network that provides the primary path for traffic sent to and initiated from other networks.

back end   A node or software program supplying services to a front end. *See also: server.*

bandwidth The gap between the highest and lowest frequencies employed by network signals. More commonly, it refers to the rated throughput capacity of a network protocol or medium.

bandwidth on demand (BoD) This function allows an additional B channel to be used to increase the amount of bandwidth available for a particular connection.

baseband A feature of a network technology that uses only one carrier frequency. Ethernet is an example. Also named "narrowband." *Compare with: broadband.*

baseline Baseline information includes historical data about the network and routine utilization information. This information can be used to determine whether there were recent changes made to the network that may contribute to the problem at hand.

Basic Management Setup Used with Cisco routers when in setup mode. Only provides enough management and configuration to get the router working so someone can telnet into the router and configure it.

baud Synonymous with bits per second (bps), if each signal element represents 1 bit. It is a unit of signaling speed equivalent to the number of separate signal elements transmitted per second.

B channel Bearer channel: A full-duplex, 64Kbps channel in ISDN that transmits user data. *Compare with: D channel, E channel,* and *H channel.*

BDR backup designated router: This is used in an OSPF network to backup the designated router in case of failure.

beacon An FDDI frame or Token Ring frame that points to a serious problem with the ring, such as a broken cable. The beacon frame carries the address of the station thought to be down. *See also: failure domain.*

BECN Backward Explicit Congestion Notification: BECN is the bit set by a Frame Relay network in frames moving away from frames headed into a congested path. A DTE that receives frames with the BECN may ask higher-level protocols to take necessary flow control measures. *Compare with: FECN.*

BGP4 BGP version 4: Version 4 of the interdomain routing protocol most commonly used on the Internet. BGP4 supports CIDR and uses route-counting mechanisms to decrease the size of routing tables. *See also: CIDR.*

BGP Identifier This field contains a value that identifies the BGP speaker. This is a random value chosen by the BGP router when sending an OPEN message.

BGP neighbors Two routers running BGP that begin a communication process to exchange dynamic routing information; they use a TCP port at layer 4 of the OSI reference model. Specifically, TCP port 179 is used. Also known as "BGP peers."

BGP peers *See: BGP neighbors.*

BGP speaker A router that advertises its prefixes or routes.

bidirectional shared tree   A method of shared tree multicast forwarding. This method allows group members to receive data from the source or the RP, whichever is closer. *See also: RP (rendezvous point).*

binary   A two-character numbering method that uses ones and zeros. The binary numbering system underlies all digital representation of information.

binding   Configuring a Network layer protocol to use a certain frame type on a LAN.

BIP   Bit Interleaved Parity: A method used in ATM to monitor errors on a link, sending a check bit or word in the link overhead for the previous block or frame. This allows bit errors in transmissions to be found and delivered as maintenance information.

BISDN   Broadband ISDN: ITU-T standards created to manage high-bandwidth technologies such as video. BISDN presently employs ATM technology along SONET-based transmission circuits, supplying data rates typically between 155Mbps and 622Mbps and now even into the gigabyte range (if you have the big bucks). *See also: BRI, ISDN, and PRI.*

bit   One binary digit; either a 1 or a 0. Eight bits make a byte.

bit-oriented protocol   Regardless of frame content, the class of Data Link layer communication protocols that transmits frames. Bit-oriented protocols, as compared with byte-oriented, supply more efficient and trustworthy full-duplex operation. *Compare with: byte-oriented protocol.*

block size   Number of hosts that can be used in a subnet. Block sizes typically can be used in increments of 4, 8, 16, 32, 64, and 128.

Boot ROM   Used in routers to put the router into bootstrap mode. Bootstrap mode then boots the device with an operating system. The ROM can also hold a small Cisco IOS.

boot sequence   Defines how a router boots. The configuration register tells the router where to boot the IOS from as well as how to load the configuration.

bootstrap protocol   A protocol used to dynamically assign IP addresses and gateways to requesting clients.

border gateway   A router that facilitates communication with routers in different autonomous systems.

border peer   The device in charge of a peer group; it exists at the edge of a hierarchical design. When any member of the peer group wants to locate a resource, it sends a single explorer to the border peer. The border peer then forwards this request on behalf of the requesting router, thus eliminating duplicate traffic.

border router   Typically defined within Open Shortest Path First (OSPF) as a router that connected an area to the backbone area. However, a border router can be a router that connects a company to the Internet as well. *See also: OSPF.*

BPDU   Bridge Protocol Data Unit: A Spanning Tree Protocol initializing packet that is sent at definable intervals for the purpose of exchanging information among bridges in networks.

BRI Basic Rate Interface: The ISDN interface that facilitates circuit-switched communication between video, data, and voice; it is made up of two B channels (64Kbps each) and one D channel (16Kbps). *Compare with: PRI. See also: BISDN.*

bridge A device for connecting two segments of a network and transmitting packets between them. Both segments must use identical protocols to communicate. Bridges function at the Data Link layer, layer 2 of the OSI reference model. The purpose of a bridge is to filter, send, or flood any incoming frame, based on the MAC address of that particular frame.

bridge group Used in the router configuration of bridging, bridge groups are defined by a unique number. Network traffic is bridged between all interfaces that are a member of the same bridge group.

bridge identifier Used to elect the root bridge in a layer 2 switched internetwork. The bridge ID is a combination of the bridge priority and base MAC address.

bridge priority Sets the STP priority of the bridge. All bridge priorities are set to 32768 by default.

bridging loop Loops occur in a bridged network if more than one link to a network exists and the STP protocol is not turned on.

broadband A transmission methodology for multiplexing several independent signals onto one cable. In telecommunications, broadband is classified as any channel with bandwidth greater than 4kHz (typical voice grade In LAN terminology, it is classified as a coaxial cable on which analog signaling is employed. Also known as "wideband."

broadcast A data frame or packet that is transmitted to every node on the local network segment (as defined by the broadcast domain). Broadcasts are known by their broadcast address, which is a destination network and host address with all the bits turned on. Also called "local broadcast." *Compare with: directed broadcast.*

broadcast address Used in both logical addressing and hardware addressing. In logical addressing, the host addresses will be all ones. With hardware addressing, the hardware address will be all ones in binary (all Fs in hex).

broadcast domain A group of devices receiving broadcast frames initiating from any device within the group. Because routers do not forward broadcast frames, broadcast domains are not forwarded from one broadcast to another.

Broadcast (multi-access) networks Broadcast (multi-access) networks such as Ethernet allow multiple devices to connect to (or access) the same network, as well as provide a broadcast ability in which a single packet is delivered to all nodes on the network

broadcast storm An undesired event on the network caused by the simultaneous transmission of any number of broadcasts across the network segment. Such an occurrence can overwhelm network bandwidth, resulting in time-outs.

buffer A storage area dedicated to handling data while in transit. Buffers are used to receive/store sporadic deliveries of data bursts, usually received from faster devices, compensating for the variations in processing speed. Incoming information is stored until everything is received prior to sending data on. Also known as an "information buffer."

bursting Some technologies, including ATM and Frame Relay, are considered burstable. This means that user data can exceed the bandwidth normally reserved for the connection; however, this cannot exceed the port speed. An example of this would be a 128Kbps Frame Relay CIR on a T1—depending on the vendor, it may be possible to send more than 128Kbps for a short time.

bus Any common physical path, typically wires or copper, through which a digital signal can be used to send data from one part of a computer to another.

BUS broadcast and unknown servers: In LAN emulation, the hardware or software responsible for resolving all broadcasts and packets with unknown (unregistered) addresses into the point-to-point virtual circuits required by ATM. *See also: LANE, LEC, LECS,* and *LES.*

bus topology A linear LAN architecture in which transmissions from various stations on the network are reproduced over the length of the medium and are accepted by all other stations. *Compare with: ring topology* and *star topology.*

BX.25 AT&T's use of X.25. *See also: X.25.*

bypass mode An FDDI and Token Ring network operation that deletes an interface.

bypass relay A device that enables a particular interface in the token ring to be closed down and effectively taken off the ring.

byte Eight bits. *See also: octet.*

byte-oriented protocol Any type of data-link communication protocol that, in order to mark the boundaries of frames, uses a specific character from the user character set. These protocols have generally been superseded by bit-oriented protocols. *Compare with: bit-oriented protocol.*

cable range In an extended AppleTalk network, the range of numbers allotted for use by existing nodes on the network. The value of the cable range can be anywhere from a single to a sequence of several touching network numbers. Node addresses are determined by their cable range value.

CAC Connection Admission Control: The sequence of actions executed by every ATM switch while connection setup is performed in order to determine if a request for connection is violating the guarantees of QoS for established connections. Also, CAC is used to route a connection request through an ATM network.

call admission control A device for managing traffic in ATM networks, determining the possibility of a path containing adequate bandwidth for a requested VCC.

call establishment Used to reference an ISDN call setup scheme when the call is working.

call priority   In circuit-switched systems, the defining priority given to each originating port; it specifies in which order calls will be reconnected. Additionally, call priority identifies which calls are allowed during a bandwidth reservation.

call setup   Handshaking scheme that defines how a source and destination device will establish a call to each other.

call setup time   The length of time necessary to effect a switched call between DTE devices.

CBR   constant bit rate: An ATM Forum QoS class created for use in ATM networks. CBR is used for connections that rely on precision clocking to guarantee trustworthy delivery. *Compare with: ABR and VBR.*

CD   carrier detect: A signal indicating that an interface is active or that a connection generated by a modem has been established.

CDP   Cisco Discovery Protocol: Cisco's proprietary protocol that is used to tell a neighbor Cisco device about the type of hardware, software version, and active interfaces that the Cisco device is using. It uses a SNAP frame between devices and is not routable.

CDP holdtime   The amount of time a router will hold Cisco Discovery Protocol information received from a neighbor router before discarding it if the information is not updated by the neighbor. This timer is set to 180 seconds by default.

CDP timer   The amount of time between when Cisco Discovery Protocol advertisements are transmitted out of all router interfaces, by default. The CDP timer is 90 seconds, by default.

CDVT   Cell Delay Variation Tolerance: A QoS parameter for traffic management in ATM networks specified when a connection is established. The allowable fluctuation levels for data samples taken by the PCR in CBR transmissions are determined by the CDVT. *See also: CBR and PCR.*

cell   In ATM networking, the basic unit of data for switching and multiplexing. Cells have a defined length of 53 bytes, including a 5-byte header that identifies the cell's data stream and 48 bytes of payload. *See also: cell relay.*

cell payload scrambling   The method by which an ATM switch maintains framing on some medium-speed edge and trunk interfaces (T3 or E3 circuits). Cell payload scrambling rearranges the data portion of a cell to maintain the line synchronization with certain common bit patterns.

cell relay   A technology that uses small packets of fixed size, known as cells. Their fixed length enables cells to be processed and switched in hardware at high speeds, making this technology the foundation for ATM and other high-speed network protocols. *See also: cell.*

Centrex   A local exchange carrier service, providing local switching that resembles that of an on-site PBX. Centrex has no on-site switching capability. Therefore, all customer connections return to the central office (CO). *See also: CO.*

CER   cell error ratio: The ratio in ATM of transmitted cells having errors to the total number of cells transmitted within a certain span of time.

CGMP   Cisco Group Management Protocol: A proprietary protocol developed by Cisco. The router uses CGMP to send multicast membership commands to Catalyst switches.

channelized E1   Operating at 2.048Mpbs, an access link that is sectioned into 29 B-channels and one D-channel, supporting DDR, Frame Relay, and X.25. *Compare with: channelized T1.*

channelized T1   Operating at 1.544Mbps, an access link that is sectioned into 23 B-channels and one D-channel of 64Kbps each, where individual channels or groups of channels connect to various destinations, supporting DDR, Frame Relay, and X.25. *Compare with: channelized E1.*

CHAP   Challenge Handshake Authentication Protocol: Supported on lines using PPP encapsulation, it is a security feature that identifies the remote end, helping keep out unauthorized users. After CHAP is performed, the router oraccess server determines whether a given user is permitted access. It is a newer, more secure protocol than PAP. *Compare with: PAP.*

checksum   A test for ensuring the integrity of sent data. It is a number calculated from a series of values taken through a sequence of mathematical functions, typically placed at the end of the data from which it is calculated, and then recalculated at the receiving end for verification. *Compare with: CRC.*

choke packet   When congestion exists, it is a packet sent to inform a transmitter that it should decrease its sending rate.

CIDR   It allows a group of IP networks to appear to other networks as a unified, larger entity. In CIDR, IP addresses and their subnet masks are written as four dotted octets, followed by a forward slash and the number of masking bits (a form of subnet notation shorthand). *See also: BGP4.*

CIP   Channel Interface Processor: A channel attachment interface for use in Cisco 7000 series routers that connects a host mainframe to a control unit. This device eliminates the need for an FBP to attach channels.

CIR   committed information rate: Averaged over a minimum span of time and measured in bps, a Frame Relay network's agreed-upon minimum rate of transferring information.

circuit switching   Used with dial-up networks such as PPP and ISDN. Passes data, but needs to set up the connection first—just like making a phone call.

Cisco FRAD   Cisco Frame Relay Access Device: A Cisco product that supports Cisco IPS Frame Relay SNA services, connecting SDLC devices to Frame Relay without requiring an existing LAN. May be upgraded to a fully functioning multiprotocol router. Can activate conversion from SDLC to Ethernet and Token Ring, but does not support attached LANs. *See also: FRAD.*

CiscoFusion   Cisco's name for the internetworking architecture under which its Cisco IOS operates. It is designed to "fuse" together the capabilities of its disparate collection of acquired routers and switches.

Cisco IOS   Cisco Internet Operating System software. The kernel of the Cisco line of routers and switches that supplies shared functionality, scalability, and security for all products under its CiscoFusion architecture. *See also: CiscoFusion.*

CiscoView   GUI-based management software for Cisco networking devices, enabling dynamic status, statistics, and comprehensive configuration information. Displays a physical view of the Cisco device chassis and provides device-monitoring functions and fundamental trouble-shooting capabilities. May be integrated with a number of SNMP-based network management platforms.

Class A network   Part of the Internet Protocol hierarchical addressing scheme. Class A networks have only 8 bits for defining networks and 24 bits for defining hosts and subnets on each network.

Class B network   Part of the Internet Protocol hierarchical addressing scheme. Class B networks have 16 bits for defining networks and 16 bits for defining hosts and subnets on each network.

Class C network   Part of the Internet Protocol hierarchical addressing scheme. Class C networks have 24 bits for defining networks and only 8 bits for defining hosts and subnets on each network.

classful routing   Routing protocols that do not send subnet mask information when a route update is sent out.

classical IP over ATM   Defined in RFC 1577, the specification for running IP over ATM that maximizes ATM features. Also known as "CIA."

classless routing   Routing that sends subnet mask information in the routing updates. Classless routing allows Variable-Length Subnet Masking (VLSM) and supernetting. Routing protocols that support classless routing are RIP version 2, EIGRP, and OSPF.

CLI   command-line interface: Allows you to configure Cisco routers and switches with maximum flexibility.

CLP   Cell Loss Priority: The area in the ATM cell header that determines the likelihood of a cell being dropped during network congestion. Cells with CLP = 0 are considered insured traffic and are not apt to be dropped. Cells with CLP = 1 are considered best-effort traffic that may be dropped during congested episodes, delivering more resources to handle insured traffic.

CLR   Cell Loss Ratio: The ratio of discarded cells to successfully delivered cells in ATM. CLR can be designated a QoS parameter when establishing a connection.

CO   central office: The local telephone company office where all loops in a certain area connect and where circuit switching of subscriber lines occurs.

collapsed backbone   A nondistributed backbone where all network segments are connected to each other through an internetworking device. A collapsed backbone can be a virtual network segment at work in a device such as a router, hub, or switch.

collision   The effect of two nodes sending transmissions simultaneously in Ethernet. When they meet on the physical media, the frames from each node collide and are damaged. *See also: collision domain.*

collision domain   The network area in Ethernet over which frames that have collided will be detected. Collisions are propagated by hubs and repeaters, but not by LAN switches, routers, or bridges. *See also: collision.*

composite metric   Used with routing protocols, such as IGRP and EIGRP, that use more than one metric to find the best path to a remote network. IGRP and EIGRP both use bandwidth and delay of the line by default. However, maximum transmission unit (MTU), load, and reliability of a link can be used as well.

compression   A technique to send more data across a link than would be normally permitted by representing repetitious strings of data with a single marker.

configuration register   A 16-bit configurable value stored in hardware or software that determines how Cisco routers function during initialization. In hardware, the bit position is set using a jumper. In software, it is set by specifying specific bit patterns used to set startup options, configured using a hexadecimal value with configuration commands.

congestion   Traffic that exceeds the network's ability to handle it.

congestion avoidance   To minimize delays, the method a network uses to control traffic entering the system. Lower-priority traffic is discarded at the edge of the network when indicators signal it cannot be delivered, thus using resources efficiently.

congestion collapse   The situation that results from the retransmission of packets in ATM networks where little or no traffic successfully arrives at destination points. It usually happens in networks made of switches with ineffective or inadequate buffering capabilities combined with poor packet discard or ABR congestion feedback mechanisms.

connection ID   Identifications given to each Telnet session into a router. The `show sessions` command will give you the connections a local router will have to a remote router. The `show users` command will show the connection IDs of users telnetted into your local router.

Connectionless   Data transfer that occurs without the creating of a virtual circuit. It has low overhead, uses best-effort delivery, and is not reliable. *Contrast with: connection-oriented. See also: virtual circuit.*

Connectionless Network Service (CLNS)   See *Connectionless.*

connection-oriented   Data transfer method that sets up a virtual circuit before any data is transferred. Uses acknowledgments and flow control for reliable data transfer. *Contrast with: connectionless. See also: virtual circuit.*

console port   Typically an RJ-45 (8-pin modular) port on a Cisco router and switch that allows Command-Line Interface capability.

control direct VCC   One of two control connections defined by Phase I LAN emulation; a bidirectional virtual control connection (VCC) established in ATM by an LEC to an LES. *See also: control distribute VCC.*

control distribute VCC   One of two control connections defined by Phase 1 LAN emulation; a unidirectional virtual control connection (VCC) set up in ATM from an LES to an LEC. Usually, the VCC is a point-to-multipoint connection. *See also: control direct VCC.*

convergence The process required for all routers in an internetwork to update their routing tables and create a consistent view of the network, using the best possible paths. No user data is passed during an STP convergence time.

core layer Top layer in the Cisco three-layer hierarchical model, which helps you design, build, and maintain Cisco hierarchical networks. The core layer passes packets quickly to distribution layer devices only. No packet filtering should take place at this layer.

cost Also known as path cost, an arbitrary value, based on hop count, bandwidth, or other calculation, that is typically assigned by a network administrator and used by the routing protocol to compare different routes through an internetwork. Routing protocols use cost values to select the best path to a certain destination: the lowest cost identifies the best path. Also known as "path cost." *See also: routing metric.*

count to infinity A problem occurring in routing algorithms that are slow to converge where routers keep increasing the hop count to particular networks. To avoid this problem, various solutions have been implemented into each of the different routing protocols. Some of those solutions include defining a maximum hop count (defining infinity), route poising, poison reverse, and split horizon.

CPCS Common Part Convergence Sublayer: One of two AAL sublayers that is service-dependent, it is further segmented into the CS and SAR sublayers. The CPCS prepares data for transmission across the ATM network; it creates the 48-byte payload cells that are sent to the ATM layer. *See also: AAL and ATM layer.*

CPE customer premises equipment: Items such as telephones, modems, and terminals installed at customer locations and connected to the service provider network.

crankback In ATM, a correction technique used when a node somewhere on a chosen path cannot accept a connection setup request, blocking the request. The path is rolled back to an intermediate node, which then uses GCAC to attempt to find an alternate path to the final destination.

CRC cyclic redundancy check: A methodology that detects errors, whereby the frame recipient makes a calculation by dividing frame contents with a prime binary divisor and compares the remainder to a value stored in the frame by the sending node. *Contrast with: checksum.*

crossover cable Type of Ethernet cable that connects a switch to switch, host to host, hub to hub, or switch to hub.

CSMA/CD Carrier Sense Multiple Access with Collision Detection: A technology defined by the Ethernet IEEE 802.3 committee. Each device senses the cable for a digital signal before transmitting. Also, CSMA/CD allows all devices on the network to share the same cable, but one at a time. If two devices transmit at the same time, a frame collision will occur and a jamming pattern will be sent; the devices will stop transmitting, wait a predetermined as well as a self-imposed random amount of time, and then try to transmit again.

CSU channel service unit: A digital mechanism that connects end-user equipment to the local digital telephone loop. Frequently referred to along with the data service unit as CSU/DSU. *See also: DSU.*

CSU/DSU channel service unit/data service unit: Physical layer device used in wide area networks to convert the CPE digital signals to what is understood by the provider's switch. A CSU/DSU is typically one device that plugs into a RJ-45 (8-pin modular) jack, known as the demarcation point.

CTD Cell Transfer Delay: For a given connection in ATM, the time period between a cell exit event at the source user-network interface (UNI) and the corresponding cell entry event at the destination. The CTD between these points is the sum of the total inter-ATM transmission delay and the total ATM processing delay.

cumulative interface delay This is a Cisco term for delay of the line. The composite metric in IGRP and EIGRP is calculated by using the bandwidth and delay of the line by default.

cut-through frame switching A frame-switching technique that flows data through a switch so that the leading edge exits the switch at the output port before the packet finishes entering the input port. Frames will be read, processed, and forwarded by devices that use cut-through switching as soon as the destination address of the frame is confirmed and the outgoing port is identified.

data circuit-terminating equipment DCE is used to provide clocking to DTE equipment.

data compression *See: compression*

data direct VCC A bidirectional point-to-point virtual control connection (VCC) set up between two LECs in ATM and one of three data connections defined by Phase 1 LAN emulation. Because data direct VCCs do not guarantee QoS, they are generally reserved for UBR and ABR connections. *Compare with: control distribute VCC and control direct VCC.*

data encapsulation The process in which the information in a protocol is wrapped, or contained, in the data section of another protocol. In the OSI reference model, each layer encapsulates the layer immediately above it as the data flows down the protocol stack.

data frame Protocol Data Unit encapsulation at the Data Link layer of the OSI reference model. Encapsulates packets from the Network layer and prepares the data for transmission on a network medium.

datagram A logical collection of information transmitted as a Network layer unit over a medium without a previously established virtual circuit. IP datagrams have become the primary information unit of the Internet. At various layers of the OSI reference model, the terms *cell, frame, message, packet,* and *segment* also define these logical information groupings.

Data Link Control layer Layer 2 of the SNA architectural model, it is responsible for the transmission of data over a given physical link and compares somewhat to the Data Link layer of the OSI model.

Data Link layer   Layer 2 of the OSI reference model, it ensures the trustworthy transmission of data across a physical link and is primarily concerned with physical addressing, line discipline, network topology, error notification, ordered delivery of frames, and flow control. The IEEE has further segmented this layer into the MAC sublayer and the LLC sublayer. Also known as the link layer. Can be compared somewhat to the data link control layer of the SNA model. *See also: Application layer, LLC, MAC, Network layer, Physical layer, Presentation layer, Session layer,* and *Transport layer.*

data terminal equipment   *See: DTE.*

DCC   Data Country Code: Developed by the ATM Forum, one of two ATM address formats designed for use by private networks. *Compare with: ICD.*

DCE   data communications equipment (as defined by the EIA) or data circuit-terminating equipment (as defined by the ITU-T): The mechanisms and links of a communications network that make up the network portion of the user-to-network interface, such as modems. The DCE supplies the physical connection to the network, forwards traffic, and provides a clocking signal to synchronize data transmission between DTE and DCE devices. *Compare with: DTE.*

D channel   (1) data channel: A full-duplex, 16Kbps (BRI) or 64Kbps (PRI) ISDN channel. *Compare with: B channel, E channel,* and *H channel.* (2) In SNA, anything that provides a connection between the processor and main storage with any peripherals.

DDP   Datagram Delivery Protocol: Used in the AppleTalk suite of protocols as a connectionless protocol that is responsible for sending datagrams through an internetwork.

DDR   dial-on-demand routing: A technique that allows a router to automatically initiate and end a circuit-switched session per the requirements of the sending station. By mimicking keepalives, the router fools the end station into treating the session as active. DDR permits routing over ISDN or telephone lines via a modem or external ISDN terminal adapter.

DE   Discard Eligibility: Used in Frame Relay networks to tell a switch that a frame can be preferentially discarded if the switch is too busy. The DE is a field in the frame that is turned on by transmitting routers if the committed information rate (CIR) is oversubscribed or set to 0.

dedicated line   Point-to-point connection that does not share any bandwidth.

de-encapsulation   The technique used by layered protocols in which a layer removes header information from the Protocol Data Unit (PDU) from the layer below. *See: encapsulation.*

default route   The static routing table entry used to direct frames whose next hop is not otherwise spelled out in the routing table.

delay   The time elapsed between a sender's initiation of a transaction and the first response they receive. Also, the time needed to move a packet from its source to its destination over a path. *See also: latency.*

demarc   The demarcation point between the customer premises equipment (CPE) and the telco's carrier equipment.

demodulation A series of steps that return a modulated signal to its original form. When receiving, a modem demodulates an analog signal to its original digital form (and, conversely, modulates the digital data it sends into an analog signal). *See also: modulation.*

demultiplexing The process of converting a multiplexed signal, comprising more than one input stream, back into separate output streams. *See also: multiplexing.*

designated bridge In the process of forwarding a frame from a segment to the root bridge, the bridge with the lowest root path cost.

designated port Used with the Spanning Tree Protocol (STP) to designate forwarding ports. If there are multiple links to the same network, STP will shut a port down to stop network loops.

designated router (DR) An OSPF router that creates LSAs for a multiaccess network and is required to perform other special tasks in OSPF operations. Multiaccess OSPF networks that maintain a minimum of two attached routers identify one router that is chosen by the OSPF Hello protocol, which makes possible a decrease in the number of adjacencies necessary on a multiaccess network. This in turn reduces the quantity of routing protocol traffic and the physical size of the database.

desktop layer The access layer is sometimes referred to as the desktop layer. The access layer controls user and workgroup access to internetwork resources.

destination address The address for the network device(s) that will receive a packet.

DHCP Dynamic Host Configuration Protocol: DHCP is a superset of the BootP protocol. This means that it uses the same protocol structure as BootP, but it has enhancements added. Both of these protocols use servers that dynamically configure clients when requested. The two major enhancements are address pools and lease times.

dial backup Dial backup connections are typically used to provide redundancy to Frame Relay connections. The backup link is activated over an analog modem or ISDN.

directed broadcast A data frame or packet that is transmitted to a specific group of nodes on a remote network segment. Directed broadcasts are known by their broadcast address, which is a destination subnet address with all the host bits turned on.

discovery mode Also known as dynamic configuration, this technique is used by an AppleTalk interface to gain information from a working node about an attached network. The information is subsequently used by the interface for self-configuration.

distance vector protocols The distance-vector protocols find the best path to a remote network by judging distance. Each time a packet goes through a router, that's called a hop. The route with the least number of hops to the network is determined to be the best route. However, Cisco's IGRP is considered Distance Vector and uses a composite metric of bandwidth and delay of the line to determine the best path to a remote network.

distance-vector routing algorithm In order to find the shortest path, this group of routing algorithms reports on the number of hops in a given route, requiring each router to send its complete routing table with each update, but only to its neighbors. Routing algorithms of this type tend to generate loops, but they are fundamentally simpler than their link-state counterparts. *See also: link-state routing algorithm* and *SPF.*

distribution layer Middle layer of the Cisco three-layer hierarchical model, which helps you design, install, and maintain Cisco hierarchical networks. The distribution layer is the point where Access layer devices connect. Routing is performed at this layer.

DLCI Data-Link Connection Identifier: Used to identify virtual circuits in a Frame Relay network.

DLSw Data Link Switching: IBM developed Data Link Switching (DLSw) in 1992 to provide support for SNA (Systems Network Architecture) and NetBIOS protocols in router-based networks. SNA and NetBIOS are nonroutable protocols that do not contain any logical layer 3 network information. DLSw encapsulates these protocols into TCP/IP messages that can be routed and is an alternative to Remote Source-Route Bridging (RSRB).

DLSw+ Cisco's implementation of DLSw. In addition to support for the RFC standards, Cisco added enhancements intended to increase scalability and to improve performance and availability.

DNS Domain Name System: Used to resolve host names to IP addresses.

DSAP Destination Service Access Point: The service access point of a network node, specified in the destination field of a packet. *See also: SSAP* and *SAP.*

DSR Data Set Ready: When a DCE is powered up and ready to run, this EIA/TIA-232 interface circuit is also engaged.

DSU data service unit: This device is used to adapt the physical interface on a data terminal equipment (DTE) mechanism to a transmission facility such as T1 or E1 and is also responsible for signal timing. It is commonly grouped with the channel service unit and referred to as the CSU/DSU. *See also: CSU.*

DTE data terminal equipment: Any device located at the user end of a user-network interface serving as a destination, a source, or both. DTE includes devices such as multiplexers, routers, protocol translators, and computers. The connection to a data network is made through data communication equipment (DCE) such as a modem, using the clocking signals generated by that device. *See also: DCE.*

DTR Data Terminal Ready: An activated EIA/TIA-232 circuit communicating to the DCE the state of preparedness of the DTE to transmit or receive data.

DUAL Diffusing Update Algorithm: Used in Enhanced IGRP, this convergence algorithm provides loop-free operation throughout an entire route's computation. DUAL grants routers involved in a topology revision the ability to synchronize simultaneously, while routers unaffected by this change are not involved. *See also: Enhanced IGRP.*

DVMRP Distance Vector Multicast Routing Protocol: Based primarily on the Routing Information Protocol (RIP), this Internet gateway protocol implements a common, condensed-mode IP multicast scheme, using IGMP to transfer routing datagrams between its neighbors. *See also: IGMP.*

DXI   Data Exchange Interface: DXI defines the effectiveness of a network device such as a router, bridge, or hub to act as an FEP to an ATM network by using a special DSU that accomplishes packet encapsulation.

dynamic entries   Used in layer 2 and layer 3 devices to dynamically create a table of either hardware addresses or logical addresses dynamically.

dynamic routing   Also known as "adaptive routing," this technique automatically adapts to traffic or physical network revisions.

dynamic VLAN   An administrator will create an entry in a special server with the hardware addresses of all devices on the internetwork. The server will then report the associated VLAN to a switch that requests it, based on the new device's hardware address.

E1   Generally used in Europe, a wide-area digital transmission scheme carrying data at 2.048Mbps. E1 transmission lines are available for lease from common carriers for private use.

E.164   (1) Evolved from standard telephone numbering system, the standard recommended by ITU-T for international telecommunication numbering, particularly in ISDN, SMDS, and BISDN. (2) Label of field in an ATM address containing numbers in E.164 format.

eBGP   External Border Gateway Protocol: Used to exchange route information between different autonomous systems.

E channel   Echo channel: A 64Kbps ISDN control channel used for circuit switching. Specific description of this channel can be found in the 1984 ITU-T ISDN specification, but was dropped from the 1988 version. *See also: B channel, D channel,* and *H channel.*

edge device   A device that enables packets to be forwarded between legacy interfaces (such as Ethernet and Token Ring) and ATM interfaces based on information in the Data Link and Network layers. An edge device does not take part in the running of any Network layer routing protocol; it merely uses the route description protocol in order to get the forwarding information required.

EEPROM   electronically erasable programmable read-only memory: Programmed after their manufacture, these nonvolatile memory chips can be erased if necessary using electric power and reprogrammed. *See also: EPROM* and *PROM.*

EFCI   Explicit Forward Congestion Indication: A congestion feedback mode permitted by ABR service in an ATM network. The EFCI may be set by any network element that is in a state of immediate or certain congestion. The destination end-system is able to carry out a protocol that adjusts and lowers the cell rate of the connection based on value of the EFCI. *See also: ABR.*

EIGRP   *See: Enhanced IGRP.*

EIP   Ethernet Interface Processor: A Cisco 7000 series router interface processor card, supplying 10Mbps AUI ports to support Ethernet Version 1 and Ethernet Version 2 or IEEE 802.3 interfaces with a high-speed data path to other interface processors.

ELAN   emulated LAN: An ATM network configured using a client/server model in order to emulate either an Ethernet or Token Ring LAN. Multiple ELANs can exist at the same time on a single ATM network and are made up of a LAN emulation client (LEC), a LAN emulation server (LES), a broadcast and unknown server (BUS), and a LAN emulation configuration server (LECS). ELANs are defined by the LANE specification. *See also: LANE, LEC, LECS,* and *LES.*

ELAP   EtherTalk Link Access Protocol: In an EtherTalk network, the link-access protocol constructed above the standard Ethernet Data Link layer.

encapsulation   The technique used by layered protocols in which a layer adds header information to the Protocol Data Unit (PDU) from the layer above. As an example, in Internet terminology, a packet would contain a header from the Data Link layer, followed by a header from the Network layer (IP), followed by a header from the Transport layer (TCP), followed by the application protocol data.

encryption   The conversion of information into a scrambled form that effectively disguises it to prevent unauthorized access. Every encryption scheme uses some well-defined algorithm, which is reversed at the receiving end by an opposite algorithm in a process known as decryption.

Endpoints   *See: BGP neighbors.*

end-to-end VLANs   VLANs that span the switch-fabric from end to end; all switches in end-to-end VLANs understand about all configured VLANs. End-to-end VLANs are configured to allow membership based on function, project, department, and so on.

Enhanced IGRP (EIGRP)   Enhanced Interior Gateway Routing Protocol: An advanced routing protocol created by Cisco, combining the advantages of link-state and distance-vector protocols. Enhanced IGRP has superior convergence attributes, including high operating efficiency. *See also: IGP, OSPF,* and *RIP.*

enterprise network   A privately owned and operated network that joins most major locations in a large company or organization.

EPROM   erasable programmable read-only memory: Programmed after their manufacture, these nonvolatile memory chips can be erased if necessary using high-power light and reprogrammed. *See also: EEPROM* and *PROM.*

ESF   Extended Superframe: Made up of 24 frames with 192 bits each, with the 193rd bit providing other functions including timing. This is an enhanced version of SF. *See also: SF.*

Ethernet   A baseband LAN specification created by the Xerox Corporation and then improved through joint efforts of Xerox, Digital Equipment Corporation, and Intel. Ethernet is similar to the IEEE 802.3 series standard and, using CSMA/CD, operates over various types of cables at 10Mbps. Also called: DIX (Digital/Intel/Xerox) Ethernet. *See also: 10BaseT, Fast Ethernet,* and *IEEE.*

EtherTalk   A data-link product from Apple Computer that permits AppleTalk networks to be connected by Ethernet.

excess burst size   The amount of traffic by which the user may exceed the committed burst size.

excess rate   In ATM networking, traffic exceeding a connection's insured rate. The excess rate is the maximum rate less the insured rate. Depending on the availability of network resources, excess traffic can be discarded during congestion episodes. *Compare with: maximum rate.*

EXEC session   Cisco term used to describe the command-line interface. The EXEC session exists in user mode and privileged mode.

expansion   The procedure of directing compressed data through an algorithm, restoring information to its original size.

expedited delivery   An option that can be specified by one protocol layer, communicating either with other layers or with the identical protocol layer in a different network device, requiring that identified data be processed faster.

explorer frame   Used with Source Route Bridging to find the route to the remote bridged network before a frame is transmitted.

explorer packet   An SNA packet transmitted by a source Token Ring device to find the path through a source-route-bridged network.

extended IP access list   IP access list that filters the network by logical address, protocol field in the Network layer header, and even the port field in the Transport layer header.

extended IPX access list   IPX access list that filters the network by logical IPX address, protocol field in the Network layer header, or even socket number in the Transport layer header.

Extended Setup   Used in setup mode to configure the router with more detail than Basic Setup mode. Allows multiple-protocol support and interface configuration.

external EIGRP route   Normally, the administrative distance of an EIGRP route is 90, but this is true only for what is known as an internal EIGRP route. These are routes originated within a specific autonomous system by EIGRP routers that are members of the same autonomous system. The other type of route is called an external EIGRP route and has an administrative distance of 170, which is not so good. These routes appear within EIGRP route tables courtesy of either manual or automatic redistribution, and they represent networks that originated outside of the EIGRP autonomous system.

failure domain   The region in which a failure has occurred in a token ring. When a station gains information that a serious problem, such as a cable break, has occurred with the network, it sends a beacon frame that includes the station reporting the failure, its NAUN and everything between. This defines the failure domain. Beaconing then initiates the procedure known as autoreconfiguration. *See also: autoreconfiguration* and *beacon.*

fallback   In ATM networks, this mechanism is used for scouting a path if it isn't possible to locate one using customary methods. The device relaxes requirements for certain characteristics, such as delay, in an attempt to find a path that meets a certain set of the most important requirements.

Fast Ethernet   Any Ethernet specification with a speed of 100Mbps. Fast Ethernet is ten times faster than 10BaseT, while retaining qualities such as MAC mechanisms, MTU, and frame format. These similarities make it possible for existing 10BaseT applications and management tools to be used on Fast Ethernet networks. Fast Ethernet is based on an extension of IEEE 802.3 specification (IEEE 802.3u). *Compare with: Ethernet. See also: 100BaseT, 100BaseTX,* and *IEEE.*

fast switching   A Cisco feature that uses a route cache to speed packet switching through a router. *Contrast with: process switching.*

fault tolerance   The extent to which a network device or a communication link can fail without communication being interrupted. Fault tolerance can be provided by added secondary routes to a remote network.

FDDI   Fiber Distributed Data Interface: A LAN standard, defined by ANSI X3T9.5 that can run at speeds up to 200Mbps and uses token-passing media access on fiber-optic cable. For redundancy, FDDI can use a dual-ring architecture.

FDM   Frequency-Division Multiplexing: A technique that permits information from several channels to be assigned bandwidth on one wire based on frequency. *See also: TDM, ATDM,* and *statistical multiplexing.*

FECN   Forward Explicit Congestion Notification: A bit set by a Frame Relay network that informs the DTE receptor that congestion was encountered along the path from source to destination. A device receiving frames with the FECN bit set can ask higher-priority protocols to take flow-control action as needed. *See also: BECN.*

FEIP   Fast Ethernet Interface Processor: An interface processor employed on Cisco 7000 series routers, supporting up to two 100Mbps 100BaseT ports.

filtering   Used to provide security on the network with access lists. LAN Switches filter the network by MAC (hardware) address.

firewall   A barrier purposefully erected between any connected public networks and a private network, made up of a router or access server or several routers or access servers, that uses access lists and other methods to ensure the security of the private network.

fixed configuration router   A router that cannot be upgraded with any new interfaces.

flapping   Term used to describe a serial interface that is going up and down.

Flash   electronically erasable programmable read-only memory (EEPROM). Used to hold the Cisco IOS in a router by default.

flash memory   Developed by Intel and licensed to other semiconductor manufacturers, it is nonvolatile storage that can be erased electronically and reprogrammed, physically located on an EEPROM chip. Flash memory permits software images to be stored, booted, and rewritten as needed. Cisco routers and switches use flash memory to hold the IOS by default. *See also: EPROM* and *EEPROM.*

flat network   Network that is one large collision domain and one large broadcast domain.

floating routes   Used with dynamic routing to provide backup routes (static routes) in case of failure.

flooding   When traffic is received on an interface, it is then transmitted to every interface connected to that device except the interface from which the traffic originated. This technique can be used for traffic transfer by bridges and switches throughout the network.

flow control   A methodology used to ensure that receiving units are not overwhelmed with data from sending devices. Pacing, as it is called in IBM networks, means that when buffers at a receiving unit are full, a message is transmitted to the sending unit to temporarily halt transmissions until all the data in the receiving buffer has been processed and the buffer is again ready for action.

forward/filter decisions   When a frame is received on an interface, the switch looks at the destination hardware address and finds the exit interface in the MAC database. The frame is only forwarded out the specified destination port.

FQDN   fully qualified domain name: Used within the DNS domain structure to provide name-to-IP-address resolution on the Internet. An example of an FQDN is bob.acme.com.

FRAD   Frame Relay access device: Any device affording a connection between a LAN and a Frame Relay WAN. *See also: Cisco FRAD and FRAS.*

fragment   Any portion of a larger packet that has been intentionally segmented into smaller pieces. A packet fragment does not necessarily indicate an error and can be intentional. *See also: fragmentation.*

fragmentation   The process of intentionally segmenting a packet into smaller pieces when sending data over an intermediate network medium that cannot support the larger packet size.

FragmentFree   LAN switch type that reads into the data section of a frame to make sure fragmentation did not occur. Sometimes called modified cut-through.

frame   A logical unit of information sent by the Data Link layer over a transmission medium. The term often refers to the header and trailer, employed for synchronization and error control, that surround the data contained in the unit.

frame filtering   Frame filtering is used on a layer 2 switch to provide more bandwidth. A switch reads the destination hardware address of a frame and then looks for this address in the filter table, built by the switch. It then sends the frame out only the port where the hardware address is located, and the other ports do not see the frame.

frame identification (frame tagging)   VLANs can span multiple connected switches, which Cisco calls a switch-fabric. Switches within this switch-fabric must keep track of frames as they are received on the switch ports, and they must keep track of the VLAN they belong to as the frames traverse this switch-fabric. Frame tagging performs this function. Switches can then direct frames to the appropriate port.

Frame Relay A more efficient replacement of the X.25 protocol (an unrelated packet relay technology that guarantees data delivery). Frame Relay is an industry-standard, shared-access, best-effort, switched Data Link layer encapsulation that services multiple virtual circuits and protocols between connected mechanisms.

Frame Relay bridging Defined in RFC 1490, this bridging method uses the identical spanning-tree algorithm as other bridging operations but permits packets to be encapsulated for transmission across a Frame Relay network.

Frame Relay switching Packet switching for Frame Relay packets that is provided by a service provider.

frame tagging *See: frame identification.*

frame types Used in LANs to determine how a packet is put on the local network. Ethernet provides four different frame types. These are not compatible with each other, so for two hosts to communicate, they must use the same frame type.

framing Encapsulation at the Data Link layer of the OSI model. It is called framing because the packet is encapsulated with both a header and a trailer.

FRAS Frame Relay Access Support: A feature of Cisco IOS software that enables SDLC, Ethernet, Token Ring, and Frame Relay-attached IBM devices to be linked with other IBM mechanisms on a Frame Relay network. *See also: FRAD.*

frequency The number of cycles of an alternating current signal per time unit, measured in hertz (cycles per second).

FSIP Fast Serial Interface Processor: The Cisco 7000 routers' default serial interface processor, it provides four or eight high-speed serial ports.

FTP File Transfer Protocol: The TCP/IP protocol used for transmitting files between network nodes, it supports a broad range of file types and is defined in RFC 959. *See also: TFTP.*

full duplex The capacity to transmit information between a sending station and a receiving unit at the same time. *See also: half duplex.*

full mesh A type of network topology where every node has either a physical or a virtual circuit linking it to every other network node. A full mesh supplies a great deal of redundancy but is typically reserved for network backbones because of its expense. *See also: partial mesh.*

global command Cisco term used to define commands that are used to change the router configuration and that affect the whole router. In contrast, an interface command only affects that interface.

GMII Gigabit MII: Media Independent Interface that provides 8 bits at atime of data transfer.

GNS Get Nearest Server: On an IPX network, a request packet sent by a customer for determining the location of the nearest active server of a given type. An IPX network client launches a GNS request to get either a direct answer from a connected server or a response from a router disclosing the location of the service on the internetwork to the GNS. GNS is part of IPX and SAP. *See also: IPX* and *SAP*.

grafting A process that activates an interface that has been deactivated by the pruning process. It is initiated by an IGMP membership report sent to the router.

GRE Generic Routing Encapsulation: A tunneling protocol created by Cisco with the capacity for encapsulating a wide variety of protocol packet types inside IP tunnels, thereby generating a virtual point-to-point connection to Cisco routers across an IP network at remote points. IP tunneling using GRE permits network expansion across a single-protocol backbone environment by linking multiprotocol subnetworks in a single-protocol backbone environment.

guardband The unused frequency area found between two communications channels, furnishing the space necessary to avoid interference between the two.

half duplex The capacity to transfer data in only one direction at a time between a sending unit and receiving unit. *See also: full duplex*.

handshake Any series of transmissions exchanged between two or more devices on a network to ensure synchronized operations.

H channel high-speed channel: A full-duplex, ISDN primary rate channel operating at a speed of 384Kbps. *See also: B channel, D channel,* and *Echannel*.

HDLC High-Level Data Link Control: Using frame characters, including checksums, HDLC designates a method for data encapsulation on synchronous serial links and is the default encapsulation for Cisco routers. HDLC is a bit-oriented synchronous Data Link layer protocol created by ISO and derived from SDLC. However, most HDLC vendor implementations (including Cisco's) are proprietary. *See also: SDLC*.

helper address The unicast address specified, which configures the Cisco router to change the client's local broadcast request for a service into a directed unicast to the server.

hierarchical addressing Any addressing plan employing a logical chain of commands to determine location. IP addresses are made up of a hierarchy of network numbers, subnet numbers, and host numbers to direct packets to the appropriate destination.

hierarchy Term used in defining IP addressing; in hierarchical addressing, some bits are used for networking and some bits for host addressing. Also used in the DNS structure and the Cisco design model.

HIP HSSI Interface Processor: An interface processor used on Cisco 7000 series routers, providing one HSSI port that supports connections to ATM, SMDS, Frame Relay, or private lines at speeds up to T3 or E3.

holddown The state a route is placed in so that routers can neither advertise the route nor accept advertisements about it for a defined time period. Holddowns are used to avoid accepting bad information. The actual information might be good, but it is not trusted. A route is generally placed in holddown when one of its links fails.

hop   The movement of a packet between any two network nodes. *See also: hop count.*

hop count   A routing metric that calculates the distance between a source and a destination, based on the number of routers in the path. RIP employs hop count as its sole metric. *See also: hop* and *RIP.*

host address   Logical address configured by an administrator or server on a device. Logically identifies this device on an internetwork.

Host-to-Host layer   Layer in the Internet Protocol suite that is equal to the Transport layer of the OSI model.

HSCI   High-Speed Communication Interface: Developed by Cisco, a single-port interface that provides full-duplex synchronous serial communications capability at speeds up to 52Mbps.

HSRP   Hot Standby Router Protocol: A protocol that provides high network availability and provides nearly instantaneous hardware fail-over without administrator intervention. It generates a Hot Standby router group, including a lead router that lends its services to any packet being transferred to the Hot Standby address. If the lead router fails, it will be replaced by any of the other routers—the standby routers—that monitor it.

HSSI   High-Speed Serial Interface: A network standard physical connector for high-speed serial linking over a WAN at speeds of up to 52Mbps.

hubs   Physical layer devices that are really just multiple port repeaters. When an electronic digital signal is received on a port, the signal is reamplified or regenerated and forwarded out all segments except the segment from which the signal was received.

hybrid routing protocol   Routing protocol that uses the attributes of both distance-vector and link-state. Enhanced Interior Gateway Routing Protocol (Enhanced IGRP).

ICD   International Code Designator: Adapted from the subnetwork model of addressing, this assigns the mapping of Network layer addresses to ATM addresses. ICD is one of two ATM formats for addressing created by the ATM Forum to be utilized with private networks. *See also: DCC.*

ICMP   Internet Control Message Protocol: Documented in RFC 792, it is a Network layer Internet protocol for the purpose of reporting errors and providing information pertinent to IP packet procedures.

IEEE   Institute of Electrical and Electronics Engineers: A professional organization that, among other activities, defines standards in a number of fields within computing and electronics, including networking and communications. IEEE standards are the predominant LAN standards used today throughout the industry. Many protocols are commonly known by the reference number of the corresponding IEEE standard.

IEEE 802.1   The IEEE committee specification that defines the bridging group. The specification for STP (Spanning Tree Protocol) is IEEE 802.1D. The STP uses STA (spanning-tree algorithm) to find and prevent network loops in bridged networks. The specification for VLAN trunking is IEEE 802.1Q.

IEEE 802.3   The IEEE committee specification that defines the Ethernet group, specifically the original 10Mbps standard. Ethernet is a LAN protocol that specifies physical layer and MAC sublayer media access. IEEE 802.3 uses CSMA/CD to provide access for many devices on the same network. Fast Ethernet is defined as 802.3U, and Gigabit Ethernet is defined as 802.3Q. *See also: CSMA/CD.*

IEEE 802.5   IEEE committee that defines Token Ring media access.

IGMP   Internet Group Management Protocol: Employed by IP hosts, the protocol that reports their multicast group memberships to an adjacent multicast router.

IGP   interior gateway protocol: Any protocol used by an internetwork to exchange routing data within an independent system. Examples include RIP, IGRP, and OSPF.

IGRP   Interior Gateway Routing Protocol: Cisco proprietary distance vector routing algorithm. Upgrade from the RIP protocol.

ILMI   Integrated (or Interim) Local Management Interface. A specification created by the ATM Forum, designated for the incorporation of network-management capability into the ATM UNI. Integrated Local Management Interface cells provide for automatic configuration between ATM systems. In LAN emulation, ILMI can provide sufficient information for the ATM end station to find an LECS. In addition, ILMI provides the ATM NSAP (Network Service Access Point) prefix information to the end station.

in-band management   In-band management is the management of a network device "through" the network. Examples include using Simple Network Management Protocol (SNMP) or Telnet directly via the local LAN. *Compare with: out-of-band management.*

in-band signaling   In-band signaling is the use of the bearer channel to deliver signaling, as call waiting in analog POTS lines. This is as opposed to out-of-band signaling, as in the case of the D-channel being used to present a second active call in an ISDN circuit.

inside network   In NAT terminology, the inside network is the set of networks that are subject to translation. The outside network refers to all other addresses—usually those located on the Internet

insured burst   In an ATM network, it is the largest, temporarily permitted data burst exceeding the insured rate on a PVC and not tagged by the traffic policing function for being dropped if network congestion occurs. This insured burst is designated in bytes or cells.

interarea routing   Routing between two or more logical areas. *Contrast with: intra-area routing. See also: area.*

interface configuration mode   Mode that allows you to configure a Cisco router or switch port with specific information, such as an IP address and mask.

interface processor   Any of several processor modules used with Cisco 7000 series routers. *See also: AIP, CIP, EIP, FEIP, HIP, MIP, and TRIP.*

Intermediate System to Intermediate System (IS-IS) Intermediate System-to-Intermediate System: An OSI link-state hierarchical routing protocol.

internal EIGRP route These are routes originated within a specific autonomous system by EIGRP routers that are members of the same autonomous system.

Internet The global "network of networks," whose popularity has exploded in the last few years. Originally a tool for collaborative academic research, it has become a medium for exchanging and distributing information of all kinds. The Internet's need to link disparate computer platforms and technologies has led to the development of uniform protocols and standards that have also found widespread use within corporate LANs. *See also: TCP/IP and MBONE.*

internet Before the rise of the Internet, this lowercase form was shorthand for "internetwork" in the generic sense. Now rarely used. *See also: internetwork.*

internet layer Layer in the Internet Protocol suite of protocols that provides network addressing and routing through an internetwork.

Internet protocol (IP) Any protocol belonging to the TCP/IP protocol stack. *See also: TCP/IP.*

internetwork Any group of networks interconnected by routers and other mechanisms, typically operating as a single entity.

internetworking Broadly, anything associated with the general task of linking networks to each other. The term encompasses technologies, procedures, and products. When you connect networks to a router, you are creating an internetwork.

intra-area routing Routing that occurs within a logical area. *Contrast with: interarea routing.*

Inverse ARP Inverse Address Resolution Protocol: A technique by which dynamic mappings are constructed in a network, allowing a device such asa router to locate the logical network address and associate it with a permanent virtual circuit (PVC). Commonly used in Frame Relay to determine the far-end node's TCP/IP address by sending the Inverse ARP request across the local DLCI.

IP Internet Protocol: Defined in RFC 791, it is a Network layer protocol that is part of the TCP/IP stack and offers connectionless service. IP furnishes an array of features for addressing, type-of-service specification, fragmentation and reassembly, and security.

IP address Often called an Internet address, this is an address uniquely identifying any device (host) on the Internet (or any TCP/IP network). Each address consists of four octets (32 bits), represented as decimal numbers separated by periods (a format known as "dotted-decimal"). Every address is made up of a network number, an optional subnetwork number, and a host number. The network and subnetwork numbers together are used for routing, while the host number addresses an individual host within the network or subnetwork. The network and subnetwork information is extracted from the IP address using the subnet mask. There are five classes of IP addresses (A–E), in which classes A-C allocate different numbers of bits to the network, subnetwork, and host portions of the address. *See also: CIDR, IP, and subnet mask.*

IPCP   IP Control Program: The protocol used to establish and configure IP over PPP. *See also: IP* and *PPP.*

IP multicast   A technique for routing that enables IP traffic to be reproduced from one source to several endpoints or from multiple sources to many destinations. Instead of transmitting one packet to each individual point of destination, one packet is sent to a multicast group specified by only one IP endpoint address for the group.

IPX   Internetwork Packet eXchange: Network layer protocol (layer 3) used in Novell NetWare networks for transferring information from servers to workstations. Similar to IP and XNS.

IPXCP   IPX Control Protocol: The protocol used to establish and configure IPX over PPP. *See also: IPX* and *PPP.*

IPXWAN   Protocol used for new WAN links to provide and negotiate line options on the link using IPX. After the link is up and the options have been agreed upon by the two end-to-end links, normal IPX transmission begins.

ISDN   Integrated Services Digital Network: Offered as a service by telephone companies, a communication protocol that allows telephone networks to carry data, voice, and other digital traffic. *See also: BISDN, BRI,* and *PRI.*

IS-IS   *See: Intermediate System-to-Intermediate System (IS-IS)*

ISL routing   Inter-Switch Link routing: A Cisco proprietary method of frame tagging in a switched internetwork. Frame tagging is a way to identify the VLAN membership of a frame as it traverses a switched internetwork.

isochronous transmission   Asynchronous data transfer over a synchronous data-link, requiring a constant bit rate for reliable transport. *Compare with: asynchronous transmission* and *synchronous transmission.*

ITU-T   International Telecommunication Union-Telecommunication Standardization Sector: This is a group of engineers that develops worldwide standards for telecommunications technologies.

Kerberos   An authentication and encryption method that can be used by Cisco routers to ensure that data cannot be "sniffed" off of the network. Kerberos was developed at MIT and was designed to provide strong security using the Data Encryption Standard (DES) cryptographic algorithm.

LAN   local area network: Broadly, any network linking two or more computers and related devices within a limited geographical area (up to a few kilometers). LANs are typically high-speed, low-error networks within a company. Cabling and signaling at the Physical and Data Link layers of the OSI are dictated by LAN standards. Ethernet, FDDI, and Token Ring are among the most popular LAN technologies. *Compare with: MAN.*

LANE   LAN emulation: The technology that allows an ATM network to operate as a LAN backbone. To do so, the ATM network is required to provide multicast and broadcast support, address mapping (MAC-to-ATM), and SVC management, in addition to an operable packet format. Additionally, LANE defines Ethernet and Token Ring ELANs. *See also: ELAN.*

LAN switch   A high-speed, multiple-interface transparent bridging mechanism, transmitting packets between segments of data links, usually referred to specifically as an Ethernet switch. LAN switches transfer traffic based on MAC addresses. *See also: multilayer switch* and *store-and-forward packet switching.*

LAPB   Link Accessed Procedure, Balanced: A bit-oriented Data Link layer protocol that is part of the X.25 stack and has its origin in SDLC. *See also: SDLC* and *X.25.*

LAPD   Link Access Procedure on the D channel: The ISDN Data Link layer protocol used specifically for the D channel and defined by ITU-T Recommendations Q.920 and Q.921. LAPD evolved from LAPB and is created to comply with the signaling requirements of ISDN basic access.

latency   Broadly, the time it takes a data packet to get from one location to another. In specific networking contexts, it can mean either (1) the time elapsed (delay) between the execution of a request for access to a network by a device and the time the mechanism actually is permitted transmission, or (2) the time elapsed between when a mechanism receives a frame and the time that frame is forwarded out of the destination port.

layer   Term used in networking to define how the OSI model works to encapsulate data for transmission on the network.

layer 3 switch   *See: multilayer switch.*

layered architecture   Industry standard way of creating applications to work on a network. Layered architecture allows the application developer to make changes in only one layer instead of the whole program.

LCP   Link Control Protocol: The protocol designed to establish, configure, and test data-link connections for use by PPP. *See also: PPP.*

leaky bucket   An analogy for the generic cell rate algorithm (GCRA) used in ATM networks for checking the conformance of cell flows from a user or network. The bucket's "hole" is understood to be the prolonged rate at which cells can be accommodated, and the "depth" is the tolerance for cell bursts over a certain time period.

learning bridge   A bridge that transparently builds a dynamic database of MAC addresses and the interfaces associated with each address. Transparent bridges help to reduce traffic congestion on the network.

LE ARP   LAN Emulation Address Resolution Protocol: The protocol providing the ATM address that corresponds to a MAC address.

leased line   Permanent connection between two points leased from the telephone companies.

LEC   LAN emulation client: Software providing the emulation of the link layer interface that allows the operation and communication of all higher-level protocols and applications to continue. The LEC runs in all ATM devices, which include hosts, servers, bridges, and routers. *See also: ELAN* and *LES.*

LECS   LAN emulation configuration server: An important part of emulated LAN services, providing the configuration data that is furnished upon request from the LES. These services include address registration for Integrated Local Management Interface (ILMI) support, configuration support for the LES addresses and their corresponding emulated LAN identifiers, and an interface to the emulated LAN. *See also: LES and ELAN.*

LES   LAN emulation server: The central LANE component that provides the initial configuration data for each connecting LEC. The LES typically is located on either an ATM-integrated router or a switch. Responsibilities of the LES include configuration and support for the LEC, address registration for the LEC, database storage and response concerning ATM addresses, and interfacing to the emulated LAN. *See also: ELAN, LEC, and LECS.*

link   A link is a network or router interface assigned to any given network. When an interface is added to the OSPF process, it's considered by OSPF to be a link. This link, or interface, will have state information associated with it (up or down) as well as one or more IP addresses.

link state protocols   In link-state protocols, also called shortest-path-first protocols, the routers each create three separate tables. One of these tables keeps track of directly attached neighbors, one determines the topology of the entire internetwork, and one is used as the routing table. Link-state routers know more about the internetwork than any distance-vector routing protocol

link-state routing algorithm   A routing algorithm that allows each router to broadcast or multicast information regarding the cost of reaching all its neighbors to every node in the internetwork. Link-state algorithms provide a consistent view of the network and are therefore not vulnerable to routing loops. However, this loop-free network is achieved at the cost of somewhat greater difficulty in computation and more widespread traffic (compared with distance-vector routing algorithms). *See also: distance-vector routing algorithm.*

LLAP   LocalTalk Link Access Protocol: In a LocalTalk environment, the data link–level protocol that manages node-to-node delivery of data. This protocol provides node addressing and management of bus access, and it also controls data sending and receiving to ensure packet length and integrity.

LLC   Logical Link Control: Defined by the IEEE, the higher of two Data Link layer sublayers. LLC is responsible for error detection (but not correction), flow control, framing, and software-sublayer addressing. The predominant LLC protocol, IEEE 802.2, defines both connectionless and connection-oriented operations. *See also: Data Link layer and MAC.*

LMI   Local Management Interface: An enhancement to the original Frame Relay specification. Among the features it provides are a keepalive mechanism, a multicast mechanism, global addressing, and a status mechanism.

LNNI   LAN Emulation Network-to-Network Interface: In the Phase 2 LANE specification, an interface that supports communication between the server components within one ELAN.

load   Like IGRP, EIGRP uses only bandwidth and delay of the line to determine the best path to a remote network by default. However, EIGRP can use a combination of bandwidth, delay, load and reliability in its quest to find the best path to a remote network. Load refers to the amount of data on the link.

load balancing   The act of balancing packet load over multiple links to the same remote network.

local explorer packet   In a Token Ring SRB network, a packet generated by an end system to find a host linked to the local ring. If no local host can be found, the end system will produce one of two solutions: a spanning explorer packet or an all-routes explorer packet.

local loop   Connection from a demarcation point to the closest switching office.

LocalTalk   Utilizing CSMA/CD, in addition to supporting data transmission at speeds of 230.4Kbps, LocalTalk is Apple Computer's proprietary baseband protocol, operating at the Data Link and Physical layers of the OSI reference model.

logical address   Network layer address that defines how data is sent from one network to another. Examples of logical addresses are IP and IPX.

loop avoidance   If multiple connections between switches are created for redundancy purposes, network loops can occur. Spanning Tree Protocol (STP) is used to stop network loops while still permitting redundancy.

loopback address   The IP address 127.0.0.1 is called the diagnostic or loopback address, and if you get a successful ping to this address, your IP stack is then considered to be initialized. If it fails, then you have an IP stack failure and need to reinstall TCP/IP on the host.

loopback interface   Loopback interfaces are logical interfaces, which means they are not real router interfaces. They can be used for diagnostic purposes as well as OSPF configuration.

LPD   Line Printer Daemon: Used in Unix world to allow printing to an IPaddress.

LSA   Link-State Advertisement: Contained inside of link-state packets (LSPs), these advertisements are usually multicast packets, containing information about neighbors and path costs, that are employed by link-state protocols. Receiving routers use LSAs to maintain their link-state databases and, ultimately, routing tables.

LUNI   LAN Emulation User-to-Network Interface: Defining the interface between the LAN emulation client (LEC) and the LAN emulation server (LES), LUNI is the ATM Forum's standard for LAN emulation on ATM networks. *See also: LES and LECS.*

MAC   Media Access Control: The lower sublayer in the Data Link layer, it is responsible for hardware addressing, media access, and error detection of frames. *See also: Data Link layer and LLC.*

MAC address   A Data Link layer hardware address that every port or device needs in order to connect to a LAN segment. These addresses are used by various devices in the network for accurate location of logical addresses. MAC addresses are defined by the IEEE standard and their length is six characters, typically using the burned-in address (BIA) of the local LAN interface. Variously called hardware address, physical address, burned-in address, or MAC layer address.

MacIP   In AppleTalk, the Network layer protocol encapsulating IP packets in Datagram Delivery Protocol (DDP) packets. MacIP also supplies substitute ARP services.

MAN   metropolitan area network: Any network that encompasses a metropolitan area; that is, an area typically larger than a LAN but smaller than a WAN. *See also: LAN.*

Manchester encoding   A method for digital coding in which a mid-bit-time transition is employed for clocking, and a 1 (one) is denoted by a high voltage level during the first half of the bit time. This scheme is used by Ethernet and IEEE 802.3.

maximum burst   Specified in bytes or cells, the largest burst of information exceeding the insured rate that will be permitted on an ATM permanent virtual connection for a short time and will not be dropped even if it goes over the specified maximum rate. *Compare with: insured burst. See also: maximum rate.*

maximum hop count   Number of routers a packet is allowed to pass before it is terminated. This is created to prevent a packet from circling a network forever.

maximum rate   The maximum permitted data throughput on a particular virtual circuit, equal to the total of insured and uninsured traffic from the traffic source. Should traffic congestion occur, uninsured information may be deleted from the path. Measured in bits or cells per second, the maximum rate represents the highest throughput of data the virtual circuit is ever able to deliver and cannot exceed the media rate. *Compare with: excess rate. See also: maximum burst.*

MBONE   The multicast backbone of the Internet, it is a virtual multicast network made up of multicast LANs, including point-to-point tunnels interconnecting them.

MBS   Maximum Burst Size: In an ATM signaling message, this metric, coded as a number of cells, is used to convey the burst tolerance.

MCDV   Maximum Cell Delay Variation: The maximum two-point CDV objective across a link or node for the identified service category in an ATM network.

MCLR   Maximum Cell Loss Ratio: The maximum ratio of cells in an ATM network that fail to transit a link or node compared with the total number of cells that arrive at the link or node. MCLR is one of four link metrics that are exchanged using PTSPs to verify the available resources of an ATM network. The MCLR applies to cells in VBR and CBR traffic classes whose CLP bit is set to zero. *See also: CBR, CLP,* and *VBR.*

MCR   Minimum cell rate: A parameter determined by the ATM Forum for traffic management of the ATM networks. MCR is specifically defined for ABR transmissions and specifies the minimum value for the allowed cell rate (ACR). *See also: ACR* and *PCR.*

MCTD   Maximum Cell Transfer Delay: In an ATM network, the total of the maximum cell delay variation and the fixed delay across the link or node. MCTD is one of four link metrics that are exchanged using PNNI topology state packets to verify the available resources of an ATM network. There is one MCTD value assigned to each traffic class. *See also: MCDV.*

media translation   A router property that allows two different types of LAN to communicate—for example, Ethernet to Token Ring.

MIB   Management Information Base: Used with SNMP management software to gather information from remote devices. The management station can poll the remote device for information, or the MIB running on the remote station can be programmed to send information on a regular basis.

MII   Media Independent Interface: Used in Fast Ethernet and Gigabit Ethernet to provide faster bit transfer rates of 4 and 8 bits at a time. Contrast to AUI interface, which is 1 bit at a time.

MIP   Multichannel Interface Processor: The resident interface processor on Cisco 7000 series routers, providing up to two channelized T1 or E1 connections by serial cables connected to a CSU. The two controllers are capable of providing 24 T1 or 30 E1 channel groups, with each group being introduced to the system as a serial interface that can be configured individually.

mips   millions of instructions per second: A measure of processor speed.

MLP   Multilink PPP: A technique used to split, recombine, and sequence datagrams across numerous logical data links.

MMP   Multichassis Multilink PPP: A protocol that supplies MLP support across multiple routers and access servers. MMP enables several routers and access servers to work as a single, large dial-up pool with one network address and ISDN access number. MMP successfully supports packet fragmenting and reassembly when the user connection is split between two physical access devices.

modem   modulator-demodulator: A device that converts digital signals to analog and vice-versa so that digital information can be transmitted over analog communication facilities, such as voice-grade telephone lines. This is achieved by converting digital signals at the source to analog for transmission and reconverting the analog signals back into digital form at the destination. *See also: modulation* and *demodulation.*

modem eliminator   A mechanism that makes possible a connection between two DTE devices without modems by simulating the commands and physical signaling required.

modulation   The process of modifying some characteristic of an electrical signal, such as amplitude (AM) or frequency (FM), in order to represent digital or analog information. *See also: AM.*

MOSPF   Multicast OSPF: An extension of the OSPF unicast protocol that enables IP multicast routing within the domain. *See also: OSPF.*

MPOA   Multiprotocol over ATM: An effort by the ATM Forum to standardize how existing and future Network layer protocols such as IP, IPv6, AppleTalk, and IPX run over an ATM network with directly attached hosts, routers, and multilayer LAN switches.

MTU   maximum transmission unit: The largest packet size, measured in bytes, that an interface can handle.

multicast   Broadly, any communication between a single sender and multiple receivers. Unlike broadcast messages, which are sent to all addresses on a network, multicast messages are sent to a defined subset of the network addresses; this subset has a group multicast address, which is specified in the packet's destination address field. *See also: broadcast* and *directed broadcast.*

multicast address   A single address that points to more than one device on the network by specifying a special non-existent MAC address transmitted in that particular multicast protocol. Identical to group address. *See also: multicast.*

multicast group   Multicast works by sending messages or data to IP multicast group addresses. This group is a defined set of users or hosts that are allowed to read or view the data sent via multicast.

multicast send VCC   A two-directional point-to-point virtual control connection (VCC) arranged by an LEC to a BUS, it is one of the three types of informational links specified by phase 1 LANE. *See also: control distribute VCC* and *control direct VCC.*

multilayer switch   A highly specialized, high-speed, hardware-based type of LAN router, the device filters and forwards packets based on their layer 2 MAC addresses and layer 3 network addresses. It's possible that even layer 4 can be read. Sometimes called a layer 3 switch. *See also: LAN switch.*

multilink   Used to combine multiple async or ISDN links to provide combined bandwidth.

multiplexing   The process of converting several logical signals into a single physical signal for transmission across one physical channel. *Contrast with: demultiplexing.*

NAK   negative acknowledgment: A response sent from a receiver, telling the sender that the information was not received or contained errors. *Compare with: acknowledgment.*

named access list   Used in both standard and extended lists to help with administration of access-lists by allowing you to name the lists instead of using numbers. This also allows you to change a single line of an access-list, which isn't possible in regular, numbered access-lists.

NAT   network address translation: An algorithm instrumental in minimizing the requirement for globally unique IP addresses, permitting an organization whose addresses are not all globally unique to connect to the Internet nevertheless, by translating those addresses into globally routable address space.

native VLAN   Cisco switches all have a native VLAN called VLAN 1. This cannot be deleted or changed in any way. All switch ports are in VLAN 1 by default.

NBP   Name Binding Protocol: In AppleTalk, the transport-level protocol that interprets a socket client's name, entered as a character string, into the corresponding DDP address. NBP gives AppleTalk protocols the capacity to discern user-defined zones and names of mechanisms by showing and keeping translation tables that map names to their corresponding socket addresses.

neighbors   EIGRP and OSPF routers become neighbors when each router sees the other's Hello packets.

neighboring routers   Two routers in OSPF that have interfaces to a common network. On networks with multiaccess, these neighboring routers are dynamically discovered using the Hello protocol of OSPF.

neighborship table   In OSPF and EIGRP routing protocols, each router keeps state information about adjacent neighbors. When newly discovered neighbors are learned, the address and interface of the neighbor is recorded. This information is stored in the neighbor data structure and the neighbor table holds these entries. Neighborship table can also be referred to as neighbor table or neighborship database.

NetBEUI   NetBIOS Extended User Interface: An improved version of the NetBIOS protocol used in a number of network operating systems including LAN Manager, Windows NT, LAN Server, and Windows for Workgroups, implementing the OSI LLC2 protocol. NetBEUI formalizes the transport frame not standardized in NetBIOS and adds more functions. *See also: OSI.*

NetBIOS   Network Basic Input/Output System: The API employed by applications residing on an IBM LAN to ask for services, such as session termination or information transfer, from lower-level network processes.

NetView   A mainframe network product from IBM, used for monitoring SNA (Systems Network Architecture) networks. It runs as a VTAM (Virtual Telecommunications Access Method) application.

NetWare   A widely used NOS created by Novell, providing a number of distributed network services and remote file access.

Network Access layer   Bottom layer in the Internet Protocol suite that provides media access to packets.

network address   Used with the logical network addresses to identify the network segment in an internetwork. Logical addresses are hierarchical innature and have at least two parts: network and host. An example of a hierarchical address is 172.16.10.5, where 172.16 is the network and 10.5 is the host address.

network control protocol   A method of establishing and configuring different Network layer protocols. NCP is designed to allow the simultaneous use of multiple Network layer protocols. Some examples of protocols here are IPCP (Internet Protocol Control Protocol) and IPXCP (Internetwork Packet Exchange Control Protocol).

Network layer   In the OSI reference model, it is layer 3—the layer in which routing is implemented, enabling connections and path selection between two end systems. *See also: Application layer, Data Link layer, Physical layer, Presentation layer, Session layer,* and *Transport layer.*

network segmentation   Breaking up a large network into smaller networks. Routers, switches, and bridges are used to create network segmentation.

NFS   Network File System: One of the protocols in Sun Microsystems' widely used file system protocol suite, allowing remote file access across a network. The name is loosely used to refer to the entire Sun protocol suite, which also includes RPC, XDR (External Data Representation), and other protocols.

NHRP Next Hop Resolution Protocol: In a nonbroadcast multiaccess (NBMA) network, the protocol employed by routers in order to dynamically locate MAC addresses of various hosts and routers. It enables systems to communicate directly without requiring an intermediate hop, thus facilitating increased performance in ATM, Frame Relay, X.25, and SMDS systems.

NHS Next Hop Server: Defined by the NHRP protocol, this server maintains the next-hop resolution cache tables, listing IP-to-ATM address maps of related nodes and nodes that can be reached through routers served by the NHS.

nibble Four bits.

NIC Network Interface Card: An electronic circuit board placed in a computer. The NIC provides network communication to a LAN.

NLSP NetWare Link Services Protocol: Novell's link-state routing protocol, based on the IS-IS model.

NMP Network Management Processor: A Catalyst 5000 switch processor module used to control and monitor the switch.

node address Used to identify a specific device in an internetwork. Can be a hardware address, which is burned into the network interface card, or a logical network address, which an administrator or server assigns to the node.

nonbroadcast multi-access (NBMA) networks Nonbroadcast multi-access (NBMA) networks are types such as Frame Relay, X.25, and Asynchronous Transfer Mode (ATM). These networks allow for multi-access, but have no broadcast ability like Ethernet. So, NBMA networks require special OSPF configuration to function properly and neighbor relationships must be defined.

nondesignated port A switch port that will not forward frames in order to prevent a switching loop. Spanning Tree Protocol (STP) is responsible for deciding whether a port is designated (forwarding) or nondesignated (blocking).

non-stub area In OSPF, a resource-consuming area carrying a default route, intra-area routes, interarea routes, static routes, and external routes. Non-stub areas are the only areas that can have virtual links configured across them and exclusively contain an autonomous system border router (ASBR). *Compare with: stub area. See also: ASBR and OSPF.*

NRZ nonreturn to zero: One of several encoding schemes for transmitting digital data. NRZ signals sustain constant levels of voltage with no signal shifting (no return to zero-voltage level) during a bit interval. If there is a series of bits with the same value (1 or 0), there will be no state change. The signal is not self-clocking. *See also: NRZI.*

NRZI nonreturn to zero inverted: One of several encoding schemes for transmitting digital data. A transition in voltage level (either from high to low or vice versa) at the beginning of a bit interval is interpreted as a value of 1; the absence of a transition is interpreted as a 0. Thus, the voltage assigned to each value is continually inverted. NRZI signals are not self-clocking. *See also: NRZ.*

NT network termination: A point in an ISDN network. *See: NT1* and *NT2.*

NT1 NT1 is the device that converts the two-wire "U" interface to the four-wire "S/T."

NT2 NT2 is an ISDN-compliant switching device, like a PBX, that splits the "S/T" bus into two separate, but electrically equivalent, interfaces. The "T" interface connects to the NT1, while the "S" interface connects to TE1 devices.

NVRAM nonvolatile RAM: Random-access memory that keeps its contents intact while power is turned off.

OC Optical Carrier: A series of physical protocols, designated as OC-1, OC-2, OC-3, and so on, for SONET optical signal transmissions. OC signal levels place STS frames on a multimode fiber-optic line at various speeds, of which 51.84Mbps is the lowest (OC-1). Each subsequent protocol runs at a speed divisible by 51.84. *See also: SONET.*

octet Base-8 numbering system used to identify a section of a dotted decimal IP address. Also referred to as a byte.

ones density Also known as pulse density, this is a method of signal clocking. The CSU/DSU retrieves the clocking information from data that passes through it. For this scheme to work, the data needs to be encoded to contain at least one binary 1 for each 8 bits transmitted. *See also: CSU* and *DSU.*

OSI Open Systems Interconnection: International standardization program designed by ISO and ITU-T for the development of data networking standards that make multivendor equipment interoperability a reality.

OSI reference model Open Systems Interconnection reference model: A conceptual model defined by the International Organization for Standardization (ISO), describing how any combination of devices can be connected for the purpose of communication. The OSI model divides the task into seven functional layers, forming a hierarchy with the applications at the top and the physical medium at the bottom, and it defines the functions each layer must provide. *See also: Application layer, Data Link layer, Network layer, Physical layer, Presentation layer, Session layer,* and *Transport layer.*

OSPF Open Shortest Path First: A link-state, hierarchical routing algorithm derived from an earlier version of the IS-IS protocol, whose features include multipath routing, load balancing, and least-cost routing. OSPF is the suggested successor to RIP in the Internet environment. *See also: Enhanced IGRP, IGP,* and *IP.*

OSPF area An OSPF area is a grouping of contiguous networks and routers. All routers in the same area share a common Area ID. Because a router can be a member of more than one area at a time, the Area ID is associated with specific interfaces on the router. This would allow some interfaces to belong to area 1, while the remaining interfaces can belong to area 0. All of the routers within the same area have the same topology table.

OUI organizationally unique identifier: Code assigned by the IEEE to an organization that makes network interface cards. The organization then puts this OUI on each and every card they manufacture. The OUI is 3 bytes (24 bits) long. The manufacturer then adds a 3-byte identifier to uniquely identify the host. The total length of the address is 48 bits (6 bytes) and is called a hardware address or MAC address.

out-of-band management Management "outside" of the network's physical channels—for example, using a console connection not directly interfaced through the local LAN or WAN or a dial-in modem. *Compare to: in-band management.*

out-of-band signaling Within a network, any transmission that uses physical channels or frequencies separate from those ordinarily used for data transfer.

outside network In NAT terminology, the inside network is the set of networks that are subject to translation. The outside network refers to all other addresses—usually those located on the Internet

packet In data communications, the basic logical unit of information transferred. A packet consists of a certain number of data bytes, wrapped or encapsulated in headers and/or trailers that contain information about where the packet came from, where it's going, and so on. The various protocols involved in sending a transmission add their own layers of header information, which the corresponding protocols in receiving devices then interpret.

packet switch A physical device that makes it possible for a communication channel to share several connections; its functions include finding the most efficient transmission path for packets.

packet switching A networking technology based on the transmission of data in packets. Dividing a continuous stream of data into small units—packets—enables data from multiple devices on a network to share the same communication channel simultaneously but also requires the use of precise routing information.

PAP Password Authentication Protocol: In Point-to-Point Protocol (PPP) networks, a method of validating connection requests. The requesting (remote) device must send an authentication request, containing a password and ID, to the local router when attempting to connect. Unlike the more secure CHAP (Challenge Handshake Authentication Protocol), PAP sends the password unencrypted and does not attempt to verify whether the user is authorized to access the requested resource; it merely identifies the remote end. *See also: CHAP.*

parity checking A method of error-checking in data transmissions. An extra bit (the parity bit) is added to each character or data word so that the sum of the bits will be either an odd number (in odd parity) or an even number (even parity).

partial mesh A type of network topology in which some network nodes form a full mesh (where every node has either a physical or a virtual circuit linking it to every other network node), but others are attached to only one or two nodes in the network. A typical use of partial-mesh topology is in peripheral networks linked to a fully meshed backbone. *See also: full mesh.*

passive state   Regarding an EIGRP routing table, a route is considered to be in the Passive state when a router is not performing a route convergence.

PAT   port address translation: This process allows a single IP address to represent multiple resources by altering the source TCP or UDP port number.

PCM   pulse code modulation: Process by which an analog signal is converted into digital information.

PCR   peak cell rate: As defined by the ATM Forum, the parameter specifying, in cells per second, the maximum rate at which a source may transmit.

PDN   public data network: Generally for a fee, a PDN offers the public access to a computer communication network operated by private concerns or government agencies. Small organizations can take advantage of PDNs, aiding them to create WANs without investing in long-distance equipment and circuitry.

PDU   Protocol Data Unit: The processes at each layer of the OSI model. PDUs at the Transport layer are called segments; PDUs at the Network layer are called packets or datagrams; and PDUs at the Data Link layer are called frames. The Physical layer uses bits.

PGP   Pretty Good Privacy: A popular public-key/private-key encryption application offering protected transfer of files and messages.

phantom router   Used in a Hot Standby Routing Protocol (HSRP) network to provide an IP default gateway address to hosts.

Physical layer   The lowest layer—layer 1—in the OSI reference model, it is responsible for converting data frames from the Data Link layer (layer 2) into electrical signals. Physical layer protocols and standards define, for example, the type of cable and connectors to be used, including their pin assignments and the encoding scheme for signaling 0 and 1 values. *See also: Application layer, Data Link layer, Network layer, Presentation layer, Session layer,* and *Transport layer.*

PIM   Protocol Independent Multicast: A multicast protocol that handles the IGMP requests as well as requests for multicast data forwarding.

PIM-DM   Protocol Independent Multicast Dense Mode: PIM-DM utilizes the unicast route table and relies on the source root distribution architecture for multicast data forwarding.

PIM-SM   Protocol Independent Multicast Sparse Mode: PIM-SM utilizes the unicast route table and relies on the shared root distribution architecture for multicast data forwarding.

Ping   Packet Internet Groper: A Unix-based Internet diagnostic tool, consisting of a message sent to test the accessibility of a particular device on the IP network. The term's acronym reflects the underlying metaphor of submarine sonar. Just as the sonar operator sends out a signal and waits to hear it echo ("ping") back from a submerged object, the network user can ping another node on the network and wait to see if it responds.

pinhole congestion   A problem associated with distance-vector routing protocols if more than one connection to a remote network is known, but they are different bandwidths.

plesiochronous Nearly synchronous, except that clocking comes from an outside source instead of being embedded within the signal as in synchronous transmissions.

PLP Packet Level Protocol: Occasionally called X.25 level 3 or X.25 Protocol, a Network layer protocol that is part of the X.25 stack.

PNNI Private Network-Network Interface: An ATM Forum specification for offering topology data used for the calculation of paths through the network, among switches and groups of switches. It is based on well-known link-state routing procedures and allows for automatic configuration in networks whose addressing scheme is determined by the topology.

point-to-multipoint connection In ATM, a communication path going only one way, connecting a single system at the starting point, called the "root node," to systems at multiple points of destination, called "leaves." *See also: point-to-point connection.*

point-to-point connection In ATM, a channel of communication that can be directed either one way or two ways between two ATM end systems. Also refers to a point-to-point WAN serial connection. *See also: point-to-multipoint connection.*

poison reverse updates These update messages are transmitted by a router back to the originator (thus ignoring the split-horizon rule) after route poisoning has occurred. Typically used with DV routing protocols in order to overcome large routing loops and offer explicit information when a subnet or network is not accessible (instead of merely suggesting that the network is unreachable by not including it in updates). *See also: route poisoning.*

polling The procedure of orderly inquiry, used by a primary network mechanism, to determine if secondary devices have data to transmit. A message is sent to each secondary, granting the secondary the right to transmit.

POP (1) point of presence: The physical location where an interexchange carrier has placed equipment to interconnect with a local exchange carrier. (2) Post Office Protocol (currently at version 3): A protocol used by client e-mail applications for recovery of mail from a mail server.

port security Used with layer 2 switches to provide some security. Not typically used in production because it is difficult to manage. Allows only certain frames to traverse administrator-assigned segments.

port numbers Used at the transport layer with TCP and UDP to keep track of host-to-host virtual circuits.

positive acknowledgment with retransmission A connection-oriented session that provides acknowledgment and retransmission of the data if it is not acknowledged by the receiving host within a certain time frame.

POTS plain old telephone service: This refers to the traditional analog phone service that is found in most installations.

PPP Point-to-Point Protocol: The protocol most commonly used for dial-up Internet access, superseding the earlier SLIP. Its features include address notification, authentication via CHAP or PAP, support for multiple protocols, and link monitoring. PPP has two layers: the Link Control Protocol (LCP) establishes, configures, and tests a link; and then any of various Network Control Protocols (NCPs) transport traffic for a specific protocol suite, such as IPX. *See also: CHAP, PAP,* and *SLIP.*

prefix routing   Method of defining how many bits are used in a subnet and how this information is sent in a routing update. For example, RIP version 1 does not send subnet mask information in the route updates. However, RIP version 2 does. This means that RIP v2 updates will send /24, /25, /26, etc., with a route update, which RIP v1 will not.

Presentation layer   Layer 6 of the OSI reference model, it defines how data is formatted, presented, encoded, and converted for use by software at the Application layer. *See also: Application layer, Data Link layer, Network layer, Physical layer, Session layer,* and *Transport layer.*

PRI   Primary Rate Interface: A type of ISDN connection between a PBX and a long-distance carrier, which is made up of a single 64Kbps D channel in addition to 23 (T1) or 30 (E1) B channels. *See also: ISDN.*

priority queuing   A routing function in which frames temporarily placed in an interface output queue are assigned priorities based on traits such as packet size or type of interface.

privileged mode   Command-line EXEC mode used in Cisco routers and switches that provides both viewing and changing of configurations.

Process/Application layer   Upper layer in the Internet Protocol stack. Responsible for network services.

process switching   As a packet arrives on a router to be forwarded, it's copied to the router's process buffer, and the router performs a lookup on the layer 3 address. Using the route table, an exit interface is associated with the destination address. The processor forwards the packet with the added new information to the exit interface, while the router initializes the fast-switching cache. Subsequent packets bound for the same destination address follow the same path as the first packet.

PROM   programmable read-only memory: ROM that is programmable only once, using special equipment. *Compare with: EPROM.*

propagation delay   The time it takes data to traverse a network from its source to its destination.

protocol   In networking, the specification of a set of rules for a particular type of communication. The term is also used to refer to the software that implements a protocol.

protocol-dependent modules   The protocol-dependent modules, used in the EIGRP routing protocol, are responsible for network layer, protocol-specific requirements that allow multiple protocol support for IP, IPX and AppleTalk.

protocol stack   A collection of related protocols.

Proxy Address Resolution Protocol Proxy ARP: Used to allow redundancy in case of a failure with the configured default gateway on a host. Proxy ARP is a variation of the ARP protocol in which an intermediate device, such as a router, sends an ARP response on behalf of an end node to the requesting host.

pruning The act of trimming down the shortest-path tree. This deactivates interfaces that do not have group participants.

PSE packet switching exchange: The X.25 term for a switch.

PSN packet-switched network: Any network that uses packet-switching technology. Also known as packet-switched data network (PSDN). *See also: packet switching.*

PSTN public switched telephone network: Colloquially referred to as "plain old telephone service" (POTS). A term that describes the assortment of telephone networks and services available globally.

PVC permanent virtual circuit: In a Frame Relay or ATM network, a logical connection, defined in software, that is maintained permanently. *Compare with: SVC. See also: virtual circuit.*

PVP permanent virtual path: A virtual path made up of PVCs. *See also: PVC.*

PVP tunneling permanent virtual path tunneling: A technique that links two private ATM networks across a public network using a virtual path, wherein the public network transparently trunks the complete collection of virtual channels in the virtual path between the two private networks.

QoS quality of service: A set of metrics used to measure the quality of transmission and service availability of any given transmission system.

queue Broadly, any list of elements arranged in an orderly fashion and ready for processing, such as a line of people waiting to enter a movie theater. In routing, it refers to a backlog of information packets waiting in line to be transmitted over a router interface.

R reference point Used with ISDN networks to identify the connection between an NT1 and an S/T device. The S/T device converts the four-wire network to the two-wire ISDN standard network.

RADIUS Remote Authentication Dial-In User Service: A protocol that is used to communicate between the remote access device and an authentication server. Sometimes an authentication server running RADIUS will be called a RADIUS server.

RAM random-access memory: Used by all computers to store information. Cisco routers use RAM to store packet buffers and routing tables, along with the hardware addresses cache.

RARP Reverse Address Resolution Protocol: The protocol within the TCP/IP stack that maps MAC addresses to IP addresses. *See also: ARP.*

RARP server A Reverse Address Resolution Protocol server is used to provide an IP address from a known MAC address.

rate queue   A value, assigned to one or more virtual circuits, that specifies the speed at which an individual virtual circuit will transmit data to the remote end. Every rate queue identifies a segment of the total bandwidth available on an ATM link. The sum of all rate queues should not exceed the total available bandwidth.

RCP   Remote Copy Protocol: A protocol for copying files to or from a file system that resides on a remote server on a network, using TCP to guarantee reliable data delivery.

redundancy   In internetworking, the duplication of connections, devices, or services that can be used as a backup in the event that the primary connections, devices, or services fail.

reference model   Used by application developers to create applications that work on any type of network. The most popular reference model is the Open Systems Interconnection (OSI) model.

reliability   Like IGRP, EIGRP uses only bandwidth and delay of the line to determine the best path to a remote network by default. However, EIGRP can use a combination of bandwidth, delay, load and reliability in its quest to find the best path to a remote network. Reliability refers to the reliability of the link to each remote network.

reliable multicast   When EIGRP sends multicast traffic it uses the Class D address 224.0.0.10. As I said, each EIGRP router is aware of who its neighbors are, and for each multicast it sends out, it maintains a list of the neighbors who have replied. If EIGRP doesn't get a reply from a neighbor, it will switch to using unicasts to resend the same data. If it still doesn't get a reply after 16 unicast attempts, the neighbor is declared dead. People often refer to this process as reliable multicast

Reliable Transport Protocol (RTP)   The reliable transport protocol, used in the EIGRP routing protocol, is responsible for guaranteed, ordered delivery of EIGRP packets to all neighbors

reload   An event or command that causes Cisco routers to reboot.

RIF   Routing Information Field: In source-route bridging, a header field that defines the path direction of the frame or token. If the Route Information Indicator (RII) bit is not set, the RIF is read from source to destination (left to right). If the RII bit is set, the RIF is read from the destination back to the source, so the RIF is read right to left. It is defined as part of the token ring frame header for source-routed frames, which contains path information.

ring   Two or more stations connected in a logical circular topology. In this topology, which is the basis for Token Ring, FDDI, and CDDI, information is transferred from station to station in sequence.

ring topology   A network logical topology comprising a series of repeaters that form one closed loop by connecting unidirectional transmission links. Individual stations on the network are connected to the network at a repeater. Physically, ring topologies are generally organized in a closed-loop star. *Compare with: bus topology* and *star topology.*

RIP   Routing Information Protocol: The most commonly used interior gateway protocol in the Internet. RIP employs hop count as a routing metric. *See also: Enhanced IGRP, IGP, OSPF,* and *hop count.*

RJ connector registered jack connector: Used with twisted-pair wiring to connect the copper wire to network interface cards, switches, and hubs.

rolled cable Type of wiring cable that is used to connect a PC's COM port to a router or switch console port.

ROM read-only memory: Chip used in computers to help boot the device. Cisco routers use a ROM chip to load the bootstrap, which runs a power-on self-test, and then find and load the IOS in flash memory by default.

root bridge Used with Spanning Tree Protocol to stop network loops from occurring. The root bridge is elected by having the lowest bridge ID. The bridge ID is determined by the priority (32,768 by default on all bridges and switches) and the main hardware address of the device.

routed protocol Routed protocols (such as IP and IPX) are used to transmit user data through an internetwork. By contrast, routing protocols (such as RIP, IGRP, and OSPF) are used to update routing tables between routers.

route flap A route that is being announced in an up/down fashion.

route poisoning Used by various DV routing protocols in order to overcome large routing loops and offer explicit information about when a subnet or network is not accessible (instead of merely suggesting that the network is unreachable by not including it in updates). Typically, this is accomplished by setting the hop count to one more than maximum. *See also: poison reverse updates.*

route summarization In various routing protocols, such as OSPF, EIGRP, and IS-IS, the consolidation of publicized subnetwork addresses so that a single summary route is advertised to other areas by an area border router.

router A Network layer mechanism, either software or hardware, using one or more metrics to decide on the best path to use for transmission of network traffic. Sending packets between networks by routers is based on the information provided on Network layers. Historically, this device has sometimes been called a gateway.

Router ID (RID) The Router ID (RID) is an IP address used to identify the router. Cisco chooses the Router ID by using the highest IP address of all configured loopback interfaces. If no loopback interfaces are configured with addresses, OSPF will choose the highest IP address of all active physical interfaces.

routing The process of forwarding logically addressed packets from their local subnetwork toward their ultimate destination. In large networks, the numerous intermediary destinations a packet might travel before reaching its destination can make routing very complex.

routing domain Any collection of end systems and intermediate systems that operate under an identical set of administrative rules. Every routing domain contains one or several areas, all individually given a certain area address.

routing metric   Any value that is used by routing algorithms to determine whether one route is superior to another. Metrics include such information as bandwidth, delay, hop count, path cost, load, MTU, reliability, and communication cost. Only the best possible routes are stored in the routing table, while all other information may be stored in link-state or topological databases. *See also: cost.*

routing protocol   Any protocol that defines algorithms to be used for updating routing tables between routers. Examples include IGRP, RIP, and OSPF.

routing table   A table kept in a router or other internetworking mechanism that maintains a record of only the best possible routes to certain network destinations and the metrics associated with those routes.

RP   Route Processor: Also known as a supervisory processor; a module on Cisco 7000 series routers that holds the CPU, system software, and most of the memory components used in the router.

RSP   Route/Switch Processor: A processor module combining the functions of RP and SP used in Cisco 7500 series routers. *See also: RP and SP.*

RTS   Request To Send: An EIA/TIA-232 control signal requesting permission to transmit data on a communication line.

S reference point   ISDN reference point that works with a T reference point to convert a four-wire ISDN network to the two-wire ISDN network needed to communicate with the ISDN switches at the network provider.

sampling rate   The rate at which samples of a specific waveform amplitude are collected within a specified period of time.

SAP   (1) Service Access Point: A field specified by IEEE 802.2 that is part of an address specification. (2) Service Advertising Protocol: The Novell NetWare protocol that supplies a way to inform network clients of resources and services availability on network, using routers and servers. *See also: IPX.*

SCR   sustainable cell rate: An ATM Forum parameter used for traffic management, it is the long-term average cell rate for VBR connections that can be transmitted.

SDH   Synchronous Digital Hierarchy: One of the standards developed for Fiber Optics Transmission Systems (FOTS).

SDLC   Synchronous Data Link Control: A protocol used in SNA Data Link layer communications. SDLC is a bit-oriented, full-duplex serial protocol that is the basis for several similar protocols, including HDLC and LAPB. *See also: HDLC and LAPB.*

seed router   In an AppleTalk network, the router that is equipped with the network number or cable range in its port descriptor. The seed router specifies the network number or cable range for other routers in that network section and answers to configuration requests from non-seed routers on its connected AppleTalk network, permitting those routers to affirm or modify their configurations accordingly. Every AppleTalk network needs at least one seed router physically connected to each network segment.

sequencing   Used in virtual circuits and segmentation to number segments so they can be put back together again in the correct order.

serial transmission   WAN serial connectors use serial transmission, which takes place one bit at a time, over a single channel.

server   Hardware and software that provide network services to clients.

Session layer   Layer 5 of the OSI reference model, responsible for creating, managing, and terminating sessions between applications and overseeing dataexchange between presentation layer entities. *See also: Application layer, Data Link layer, Network layer, Physical layer, Presentation layer,* and *Transport layer.*

set-based   Set-based routers and switches use the `set` command to configure devices. Cisco is moving away from set-based commands and is using the command-line interface (CLI) on all new devices.

setup mode   Mode that a router will enter if no configuration is found in nonvolatile RAM when the router boots. Allows the administrator to configure a router step-by-step. Not as robust or flexible as the command-line interface.

SF   A super frame (also called a D4 frame) consists of 12 frames with 192 bits each, and the 193rd bit providing other functions including error checking. SF is frequently used on T1 circuits. A newer version of the technology is Extended Super Frame (ESF), which uses 24 frames. *See also: ESF.*

shared tree   A method of multicast data forwarding. Shared trees use an architecture in which multiple sources share a common rendezvous point.

Shortest Path First (SPF)   A type of routing algorithm. The only true SPF protocol is Open Shortest Path First (OSPF).

signaling packet   An informational packet created by an ATM-connected mechanism that wants to establish connection with another such mechanism. The packet contains the QoS parameters needed for connection and the ATM NSAP address of the endpoint. The endpoint responds with a message of acceptance if it is able to support the desired QoS, and the connection is established. *See also: QoS.*

silicon switching   A type of high-speed switching used in Cisco 7000 series routers, based on the use of a separate processor (the Silicon Switch Processor, or SSP). *See also: SSE.*

simplex   A mode at which data or a digital signal is transmitted. Simplex is a way of transmitting in only one direction. Half duplex transmits in two directions but only one direction at a time. Full duplex transmits both directions simultaneously.

sliding window   The method of flow control used by TCP, as well as several Data Link layer protocols. This method places a buffer between the receiving application and the network data flow. The "window" available for accepting data is the size of the buffer minus the amount of data already there. This window increases in size as the application reads data from it and decreases as new data is sent. The receiver sends the transmitter announcements of the current window size, and it may stop accepting data until the window increases above a certain threshold.

SLIP   Serial Line Internet Protocol: An industry standard serial encapsulation for point-to-point connections that supports only a single routed protocol, TCP/IP. SLIP is the predecessor to PPP. *See also: PPP.*

SMDS   Switched Multimegabit Data Service: A packet-switched, datagram-based WAN networking technology offered by telephone companies that provides high speed.

SMTP   Simple Mail Transfer Protocol: A protocol used on the Internet to provide electronic mail services.

SNA   System Network Architecture: A complex, feature-rich, network architecture similar to the OSI reference model but with several variations; created by IBM in the 1970s and essentially composed of seven layers.

SNAP   Subnetwork Access Protocol: SNAP is a frame used in Ethernet, Token Ring, and FDDI LANs. Data transfer, connection management, and QoS selection are three primary functions executed by the SNAP frame.

snapshot routing   Snapshot routing takes a point-in-time capture of a dynamic routing table and maintains it even when the remote connection goes down. This allows the use of a dynamic routing protocol without requiring the link to remain active, which might incur per-minute usage charges.

SNMP   Simple Network Management Protocol: This protocol polls SNMP agents or devices for statistical and environmental data. This data can include device temperature, name, performance statistics, and much more. SNMP works with MIB objects that are present on the SNMP agent. This information is queried, then sent to the SNMP server.

socket   (1) A software structure that operates within a network device as a destination point for communications. (2) In AppleTalk networks, an entity at a specific location within a node; AppleTalk sockets are conceptually similar to TCP/IP ports.

software address   Also called a logical address. This is typically an IP address, but can also be an IPX address.

SOHO   small office/home office: A contemporary term for remote users.

SONET   Synchronous Optical Network: The ANSI standard for synchronous transmission on fiber-optic media, developed at Bell Labs. It specifies a base signal rate of 51.84Mbps and a set of multiples of that rate, known as Optical Carrier levels, up to 2.5Gbps.

source tree A method of multicast data forwarding. Source trees use the architecture of the source of the multicast traffic as the root of the tree.

SP Switch Processor: Also known as a ciscoBus controller, it is a Cisco 7000 series processor module acting as governing agent for all CxBus activities.

span A full-duplex digital transmission line connecting two facilities.

SPAN Switched Port Analyzer: A feature of the Catalyst 5000 switch, offering freedom to manipulate within a switched Ethernet environment by extending the monitoring ability of the existing network analyzers into the environment. At one switched segment, the SPAN mirrors traffic onto a predetermined SPAN port, while a network analyzer connected to the SPAN port is able to monitor traffic from any other Catalyst switched port.

spanning explorer packet Sometimes called limited-route or single-route explorer packet, it pursues a statically configured spanning tree when searching for paths in a source-route bridging network. *See also: all-routes explorer packet, explorer packet, and local explorer packet.*

spanning tree A subset of a network topology, within which no loops exist. When bridges are interconnected into a loop, the bridge, or switch, cannot identify a frame that has been forwarded previously, so there is no mechanism for removing a frame as it passes the interface numerous times. Without a method of removing these frames, the bridges continuously forward them—consuming bandwidth and adding overhead to the network. Spanning trees prune the network to provide only one path for any packet. *See also: Spanning Tree Protocol* and *spanning-tree algorithm.*

spanning-tree algorithm (STA) An algorithm that creates a spanning tree using the Spanning Tree Protocol (STP). *See also: spanning tree* and *Spanning Tree Protocol.*

Spanning Tree Protocol (STP) The bridge protocol (IEEE 802.1D) that enables a learning bridge to dynamically avoid loops in the network topology by creating a spanning tree using the spanning-tree algorithm. Spanning-tree frames called Bridge Protocol Data Units (BPDUs) are sent and received by all switches in the network at regular intervals. The switches participating in the spanning tree don't forward the frames; instead, they're processed to determine the spanning-tree topology itself. Cisco Catalyst series switches use STP 802.1D to perform this function. *See also: BPDU, learning bridge, MAC address, spanning tree,* and *spanning-tree algorithm.*

SPF Shortest Path First algorithm: A routing algorithm used to decide on the shortest-path. Sometimes called Dijkstra's algorithm and frequently used in link-state routing algorithms. *See also: link-state routing algorithm.*

SPID Service Profile Identifier: A number assigned by service providers or local telephone companies and configured by administrators to a BRI port. SPIDs are used to determine subscription services of a device connected via ISDN. ISDN devices use SPID when accessing the telephone company switch that initializes the link to a service provider.

split horizon Useful for preventing routing loops, a type of distance-vector routing rule where information about routes is prevented from leaving the router interface through which that information was received.

spoofing   (1) In dial-on-demand routing (DDR), where a circuit-switched link is taken down to save toll charges when there is no traffic to be sent, spoofing is a scheme used by routers that causes a host to treat an interface as if it were functioning and supporting a session. The router pretends to send "spoof" replies to keepalive messages from the host in an effort to convince the host that the session is up and running. *See also: DDR.* (2) The illegal act of sending a packet labeled with a false address, in order to deceive network security mechanisms such as filters and access lists.

spooler   A management application that processes requests submitted to it for execution in a sequential fashion from a queue. A good example is a print spooler.

SPX   Sequenced Packet Exchange: A Novell NetWare transport protocol that augments the datagram service provided by Network layer (layer 3) protocols, it was derived from the Switch-to-Switch Protocol of the XNS protocol suite.

SQE   Signal Quality Error: In an Ethernet network, a message sent from a transceiver to an attached machine that the collision-detection circuitry is working.

SRB   Source-Route Bridging: Created by IBM, the bridging method used in Token Ring networks. The source determines the entire route to a destination before sending the data and includes that information in routing information fields (RIF) within each packet. *Contrast with: transparent bridging.*

SRT   Source-Route Transparent bridging: A bridging scheme developed by IBM, merging source-route and transparent bridging. SRT takes advantage of both technologies in one device, fulfilling the needs of all end nodes. Translation between bridging protocols is not necessary. *Compare with: SR/TLB.*

SR/TLB   Source-Route Translational Bridging: A bridging method that allows source-route stations to communicate with transparent bridge stations aided by an intermediate bridge that translates between the two bridge protocols. Used for bridging between Token Ring and Ethernet. *Compare with: SRT.*

SSAP   Source Service Access Point: The SAP of the network node identified in the Source field of the packet identifying the Network layer protocol. *See also: DSAP and SAP.*

SSE   Silicon Switching Engine: The software component of Cisco's silicon switching technology, hard-coded into the Silicon Switch Processor (SSP). Silicon switching is available only on the Cisco 7000 with an SSP. Silicon-switched packets are compared to the silicon-switching cache on the SSE. The SSP is a dedicated switch processor that offloads the switching process from the route processor, providing a fast-switching solution, but packets must still traverse the backplane of the router to get to the SSP and then back to the exit interface.

standard IP access list   IP access list that uses only the source IP addresses to filter a network.

standard IPX access list   IPX access list that uses only the source and destination IPX address to filter a network.

star topology   A LAN physical topology with endpoints on the network converging at a common central device (known as a hub) using point-to-point links. A logical ring topology can be configured as a physical star topology using a unidirectional closed-loop star rather than point-to-point links. That is, connections within the hub are arranged in an internal ring. *See also: bus topology* and *ring topology.*

startup range   If an AppleTalk node does not have a number saved from the last time it was booted, then the node selects from the range of values from 65,280 to 65,534.

state transitions   Digital signaling scheme that reads the "state" of the digital signal in the middle of the bit cell. If it is five volts, the cell is read as a one. If the state of the digital signal is zero volts, the bit cell is read as a zero.

static route   A route whose information is purposefully entered into the routing table by an administrator and takes priority over those chosen by dynamic routing protocols.

static VLAN   A VLAN that is manually configured port-by-port. This is the method typically used in production networks.

statistical multiplexing   Multiplexing in general is a technique that allows data from multiple logical channels to be sent across a single physical channel. Statistical multiplexing dynamically assigns bandwidth only to input channels that are active, optimizing available bandwidth so that more devices can be connected than with other multiplexing techniques. Also known as statistical time-division multiplexing or stat mux.

STM-1   Synchronous Transport Module Level 1. In the European SDH standard, one of many formats identifying the frame structure for the 155.52Mbps lines that are used to carry ATM cells.

store-and-forward packet switching   A technique in which the switch first copies each packet into its buffer and performs a cyclic redundancy check (CRC). If the packet is error-free, the switch then looks up the destination address in its filter table, determines the appropriate exit port, and sends the packet.

STP   (1) shielded twisted-pair: A wiring scheme, used in many network implementations, that has a layer of shielded insulation to reduce EMI. (2) Spanning Tree Protocol.

straight-through cable   Type of Ethernet cable that connects a host to a switch, host to a hub, or router to a switch or hub.

stub area   An OSPF area carrying a default route, intra-area routes, and interarea routes, but no external routes. Configuration of virtual links cannot be achieved across a stub area, and stub areas are not allowed to contain an ASBR. *See also: non-stub area, ASBR,* and *OSPF.*

stub network   A network having only one connection to a router.

STUN   Serial Tunnel: A technology used to connect an HDLC link to an SDLC link over a serial link.

subarea   A portion of an SNA network made up of a subarea node and its attached links and peripheral nodes.

subarea node   An SNA communications host or controller that handles entire network addresses.

subchannel   A frequency-based subdivision that creates a separate broadband communications channel.

subinterface   One of many virtual interfaces available on a single physical interface.

subnet   *See: subnetwork.*

subnet address   The portion of an IP address that is specifically identified by the subnet mask as the subnetwork. *See also: IP address, subnetwork,* and *subnet mask.*

subnet mask   Also simply known as mask, a 32-bit address mask used in IP to identify the bits of an IP address that are used for the subnet address. Using a mask, the router does not need to examine all 32 bits, only those indicated by the mask. *See also: address mask* and *IP address.*

subnetting   Used in IP networks to break up larger networks into smaller subnetworks.

subnetwork   (1) Any network that is part of a larger IP network and is identified by a subnet address. A network administrator segments a network into subnetworks in order to provide a hierarchical, multilevel routing structure, and at the same time protect the subnetwork from the addressing complexity of networks that are attached. Also known as a subnet. *See also: IP address, subnet mask,* and *subnet address.* (2) In OSI networks, the term specifically refers to a collection of ESs and ISs controlled by only one administrative domain, using a solitary network connection protocol.

summarization   Term used to describe the process of summarizing multiple routing table entries into one entry.

supernetting   *See: summarization.*

SVC   switched virtual circuit: A dynamically established virtual circuit, created on demand and dissolved as soon as transmission is over and the circuit is no longer needed. In ATM terminology, it is referred to as a switched virtual connection. *See also: PVC.*

switch   (1) In networking, a device responsible for multiple functions such as filtering, flooding, and sending frames. It works using the destination address of individual frames. Switches operate at the Data Link layer of the OSI model. (2) Broadly, any electronic/mechanical device allowing connections to be established as needed and terminated if no longer necessary.

switch block   A combination of layer 2 switches and layer 3 routers. The layer 2 switches connect users in the wiring closet into the access layer and provide 10 or 100Mbps dedicated connections. 1900/2820 and 2900 Catalyst switches can be used in the switch block.

switch fabric   Term used to identify a layer 2 switched internetwork with many switches. More commonly, it is a term used to identify the inner workings of a switch itself. Thus, it is the matrix of pathways that any frame or cell might be able to traverse as it is switched from input port to output port.

switched LAN   Any LAN implemented using LAN switches. *See also: LAN switch.*

synchronous transmission   Signals transmitted digitally with precision clocking. These signals have identical frequencies and contain individual characters encapsulated in control bits (called start/stop bits) that designate the beginning and ending of each character. *See also: asynchronous transmission* and *isochronous transmission.*

syslog   A protocol used to monitor system log messages by a remote device.

T reference point   Used with an S reference point to change a 4-wire ISDN network to a two-wire ISDN network.

T1   Digital WAN that uses 24 DS0s at 64Kbps each to create a bandwidth of 1.536Mbps, minus clocking overhead, providing 1.544Mbps of usable bandwidth.

T3   Digital WAN that can provide bandwidth of 44.763Mbps.

TACACS+   Terminal Access Controller Access Control System Plus: An enhanced version of TACACS, this protocol is similar to RADIUS. *See also: RADIUS.*

tagged traffic   ATM cells with their cell loss priority (CLP) bit set to 1. Also referred to as Discard Eligible (DE) traffic in Frame Relay networks. Tagged traffic can be eliminated in order to ensure trouble-free delivery of higher priority traffic, if the network is congested. *See also: CLP.*

TCP   Transmission Control Protocol: A connection-oriented protocol that is defined at the transport layer of the OSI reference model. Provides reliable delivery of data.

TCP/IP   Transmission Control Protocol/Internet Protocol. The suite of protocols underlying the Internet. TCP and IP are the most widely known protocols in that suite. *See also: IP* and *TCP.*

TDM   Time Division Multiplexing: A technique for assigning bandwidth on a single wire, based on preassigned time slots, to data from several channels. Bandwidth is allotted to each channel regardless of a station's intent to send data. *See also: ATDM, FDM,* and *multiplexing.*

TE   terminal equipment: Any peripheral device that is ISDN-compatible and attached to a network, such as a telephone or computer. TE1s are devices that are ISDN-ready and understand ISDN signaling techniques. TE2s are devices that are not ISDN-ready and do not understand ISDN signaling techniques. A terminal adapter must be used with a TE2.

TE1   Terminal Equipment Type 1. A device with a four-wire, twisted-pair digital interface is referred to as terminal equipment type 1. Most modern ISDN devices are of this type.

TE2   Terminal Equipment Type 2. Devices known as terminal equipment type 2 do not understand ISDN signaling techniques, and a terminal adapter must be used to convert the signaling.

telco   A common abbreviation for the telephone company.

Telnet   The standard terminal emulation protocol within the TCP/IP protocol stack. Method of remote terminal connection, enabling users to log in on remote networks and use those resources as if they were locally connected. Telnet is defined in RFC 854.

terminal adapter (TA)   A hardware interface between a computer without a native ISDN interface and an ISDN line. In effect, a device to connect a standard async interface to a non-native ISDN device, emulating a modem.

terminal emulation   The use of software, installed on a PC or LAN server, that allows the PC to function as if it were a "dumb" terminal directly attached to a particular type of mainframe.

TFTP   Trivial File Transfer Protocol: Conceptually, a stripped-down version of FTP; it's the protocol of choice if you know exactly what you want and where it's to be found. TFTP doesn't provide the abundance of functions that FTP does. In particular, it has no directory browsing abilities; it can do nothing but send and receive files.

TFTP host/server   Trivial File Transfer Protocol is used to send files using IP at the Network layer and UDP at the Transport layer, which makes it unreliable.

thicknet   Also called 10Base5. Bus network that uses a thick coaxial cable and runs Ethernet up to 500 meters.

thinnet   Also called 10Base2. Bus network that uses a thin coax cable and runs Ethernet media access up to 185 meters.

three-way handshake   Term used in a TCP session to define how a virtual circuit is set up. It is called a "three-way" handshake because it uses three data segments.

token   A frame containing only control information. Possessing this control information gives a network device permission to transmit data onto the network. *See also: token passing.*

token bus   LAN architecture that is the basis for the IEEE 802.4 LAN specification and employs token-passing access over a bus topology. *See also: IEEE.*

token passing   A method used by network devices to access the physical medium in a systematic way based on possession of a small frame called a token. *See also: token.*

Token Ring   IBM's token-passing LAN technology. It runs at 4Mbps or 16Mbps over a ring topology. Defined formally by IEEE 802.5. *See also: ring topology* and *token passing.*

toll network   WAN network that uses the public switched telephone network (PSTN) to send packets.

topology database   A topology database (also called a topology table) contains all destinations advertised by neighboring routers. Associated with each entry is the destination address and a list of neighbors that have advertised the destination.

Traceroute   also Trace; IP command used to trace the path a packet takes through an internetwork.

transparent bridging   The bridging scheme used in Ethernet and IEEE 802.3 networks, it passes frames along one hop at a time, using bridging information stored in tables that associate end-node MAC addresses with bridge ports. This type of bridging is considered transparent because the source node does not know it has been bridged, because the destination frames are addressed directly to the end node. *Contrast with: SRB.*

Transport layer   Layer 4 of the OSI reference model, used for reliable communication between end nodes over the network. The transport layer provides mechanisms used for establishing, maintaining, and terminating virtual circuits, transport fault detection and recovery, and controlling the flow of information. *See also: Application layer, Data Link layer, Network layer, Physical layer, Presentation layer,* and *Session layer.*

trap   Used to send SNMP messages to SNMP managers.

TRIP   Token Ring Interface Processor: A high-speed interface processor used on Cisco 7000 series routers. The TRIP provides two or four ports for interconnection with IEEE 802.5 and IBM media with ports set to speeds of either 4Mbps or 16Mbps set independently of each other.

trunk link   Link used between switches and from some servers to the switches. Trunk links carry traffic for many VLANs. Access links are used to connect host devices to a switch and carry only VLAN information that the device is a member of.

TTL   time to live: A field in an IP header, indicating the length of time a packet is valid.

TUD   Trunk Up-Down: A protocol used in ATM networks for the monitoring of trunks. Should a trunk miss a given number of test messages being sent by ATM switches to ensure trunk line quality, TUD declares the trunk down. When a trunk reverses state and comes back up, TUD recognizes that the trunk is up and returns the trunk to service.

tunneling   A method of avoiding protocol restrictions by wrapping packets from one protocol in another protocol's frame and transmitting this encapsulated packet over a network that supports the wrapper protocol. *See also: encapsulation.*

U reference point   Reference point between a TE1 and an ISDN network. The U reference point understands ISDN signaling techniques and uses a 2-wire connection.

UDP   User Datagram Protocol: A connectionless transport layer protocol in the TCP/IP protocol stack that simply allows datagrams to be exchanged without acknowledgments or delivery guarantees, requiring other protocols to handle error processing and retransmission. UDP is defined in RFC 768.

unicast   Used for direct host-to-host communication. Communication is directed to only one destination and is originated only from one source.

unidirectional shared tree   A method of shared tree multicast forwarding. This method allows only multicast data to be forwarded from the RP.

unnumbered frames   HDLC frames used for control-management purposes, such as link startup and shutdown or mode specification.

user mode   Cisco IOS EXEC mode that allows an administrator to perform very few commands. You can only verify statistics in user mode; you cannot see or change the router or switch configuration.

UTP   unshielded twisted-pair: Copper wiring used in small-to-large networks to connect host devices to hubs and switches. Also used to connect switch to switch or hub to hub.

VBR   variable bit rate: A QoS class, as defined by the ATM Forum, for use in ATM networks that is subdivided into real time (RT) class and non–real time (NRT) class. RT is employed when connections have a fixed-time relationship between samples. Conversely, NRT is employed when connections do not have a fixed-time relationship between samples, but still need an assured QoS.

VCC   virtual channel connection: A logical circuit that is created by VCLs (virtual channel links). VCCs carry data between two endpoints in an ATM network. Sometimes called a virtual circuit connection.

VIP   (1) Versatile Interface Processor: An interface card for Cisco 7000 and 7500 series routers, providing multilayer switching and running the Cisco IOS software. The most recent version of VIP is VIP2. (2) Virtual IP: A function making it possible for logically separated switched IP workgroups to run Virtual Networking Services across the switch port.

virtual circuit (VC)   A logical circuit devised to assure reliable communication between two devices on a network. Defined by a virtual path identifier/virtual channel (really the only time "channel" is used) identifier (VPI/VCI) pair, a virtual circuit can be permanent (PVC) or switched (SVC). Virtual circuits are used in Frame Relay and X.25. Known as virtual channel in ATM. *See also: PVC and SVC.*

virtual ring   In an SRB network, a logical connection between physical rings, either local or remote.

VLAN   virtual LAN: A group of devices on one or more logically segmented LANs (configured by use of management software), enabling devices to communicate as if attached to the same physical medium, when they are actually located on numerous different LAN segments. VLANs are based on logical instead of physical connections and thus are tremendously flexible.

VLAN ID   Sometimes referred to as VLAN color, the VLAN ID is tagged onto a frame to tell a receiving switch which VLAN the frame is a member of.

VLSM   variable-length subnet mask: Helps optimize available address space and specify a different subnet mask for the same network number on various subnets. Also commonly referred to as "subnetting a subnet."

VMPS   VLAN Management Policy Server: Used to dynamically assign VLANs to a switch port.

VPN   virtual private network: A method of encrypting point-to-point logical connections across a public network, such as the Internet. This allows secure communications across a public network.

VTP   VLAN Trunking Protocol: Used to update switches in a switch fabric about VLANs configured on a VTP server. VTP devices can be a VTP server, client, or transparent device. Servers update clients. Transparent devices are only local devices and do not share information with VTP clients. VTP devices send VLAN information down trunked links only.

VTP transparent mode   Switch mode that receives VLAN Trunking Protocol VLAN information and passes it on, but doesn't read the information.

WAN   wide area network: Is a designation used to connect LANs together across a DCE (data communications equipment) network. Typically, a WAN is a leased line or dial-up connection across a PSTN network. Examples of WAN protocols include Frame Relay, PPP, ISDN, and HDLC.

wildcard   Used with access-lists and OSPF configurations. Wildcards are designations used to identify a range of subnets.

windowing   Flow-control method used with TCP at the Transport layer of the OSI model.

WINS   Windows Internet Name Service: Name resolution database for NetBIOS names to TCP/IP address.

WinSock   Windows Socket Interface: A software interface that makes it possible for an assortment of applications to use and share an Internet connection. The WinSock software consists of a dynamic link library (DLL) with supporting programs such as a dialer program that initiates the connection.

workgroup layer   The distribution layer is sometimes referred to as the workgroup layer and is the communication point between the access layer and the core. The primary functions of the distribution layer are to provide routing, filtering, and WAN access and to determine how packets can access the core, if needed.

workgroup switching   A switching method that supplies high-speed (100Mbps) transparent bridging between Ethernet networks as well as high-speed translational bridging between Ethernet and CDDI or FDDI.

X Window   A distributed multitasking windowing and graphics system originally developed by MIT for communication between X terminals and Unix workstations.

X.25   An ITU-T packet-relay standard that defines communication between DTE and DCE network devices. X.25 uses a reliable Data Link layer protocol called LAPB. X.25 also uses PLP at the Network layer. X.25 has mostly been replaced by Frame Relay.

ZIP   Zone Information Protocol: A Session layer protocol used by AppleTalk to map network numbers to zone names. NBP uses ZIP in the determination of networks containing nodes that belong to a zone. *See also: ZIP storm* and *zone.*

ZIP storm   A broadcast storm occurring when a router running AppleTalk reproduces or transmits a route for which there is no corresponding zone name at the time of execution. The route is then forwarded by other routers downstream, thus causing a ZIP storm. *See also: broadcast storm* and *ZIP.*

zone   A logical grouping of network devices in AppleTalk. Also used in DNS. *See also: ZIP.*

Index

Note to the Reader: Page numbers in **bold** indicate the principle discussion of a topic or the definition of a term. Page numbers in *italic* indicate illustrations.

D

M

W

X

The Complete CCNA™ Study Solution from SYBEX®

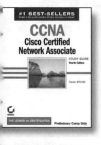 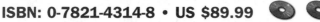
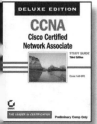

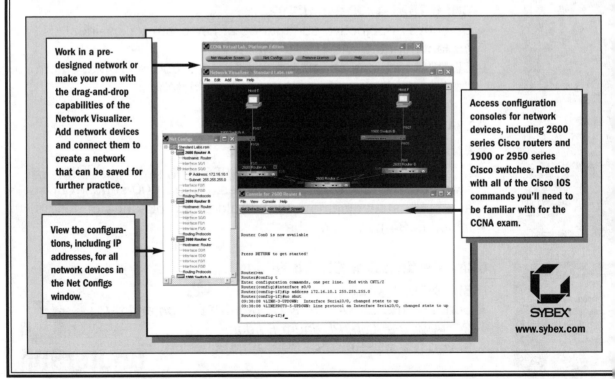

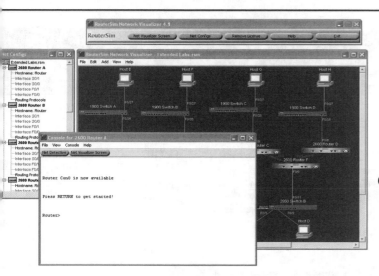

TELL US WHAT YOU THINK!

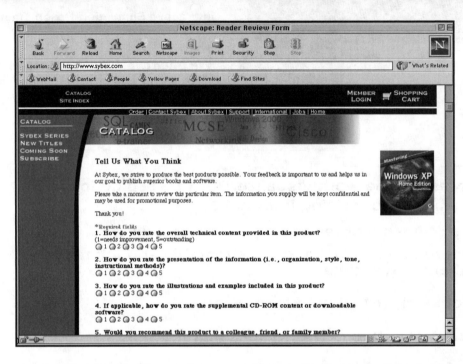

Your feedback is critical to our efforts to provide you with the best books and software on the market. Tell us what you think about the products you've purchased. It's simple:

1. Go to the Sybex website.
2. Find your book by typing the ISBN or title into the Search field.
3. Click on the book title when it appears.
4. Click **Submit a Review.**
5. Fill out the questionnaire and comments.
6. Click **Submit.**

With your feedback, we can continue to publish the highest quality computer books and software products that today's busy IT professionals deserve.

www.sybex.com

SYBEX Inc. • 1151 Marina Village Parkway, Alameda, CA 94501 • 510-523-8233

SYBEX®